## PRAISE FOR *HACKS, LEAKS, AND REVELA*

"For more than a decade, Micah Lee has been on the cutting edge of protecting journalists and their sources from surveillance. It's a gift to all of us that he has downloaded his wisdom into this highly readable and vitally important guide."

—JULIA ANGWIN, PULITZER PRIZE–WINNING
INVESTIGATIVE JOURNALIST AND OPINION
WRITER AT THE *NEW YORK TIMES*

"A fantastic and friendly introduction for journalists, activists, and anyone else who is interested in learning to analyze large datasets but has been too intimidated by the technical details."

—EVA GALPERIN, DIRECTOR OF
CYBERSECURITY AT THE ELECTRONIC
FRONTIER FOUNDATION

"Thanks to whistleblowing leaks, gold mines of valuable digital data now exist. There is no better account than Micah Lee's lively and readable how-to guide for arming journalists and researchers with the tools necessary to find, excavate, and make sense of this rich data."

—GABRIELLA COLEMAN, HARVARD
PROFESSOR, FOUNDER OF HACK_CURIO,
AND TOR PROJECT BOARD MEMBER

"Micah has written a class—not a textbook—for anyone with a computer, an internet connection, and a desire to look into leaks."

—EMMA BEST, INVESTIGATIVE REPORTER
AND CO-FOUNDER OF DISTRIBUTED
DENIAL OF SECRETS

"It's rare to find a book that is instructional, information-rich, and historically important all at once. Lee's guide not only introduces practitioners to data science in a meaningful way but also helps us understand why we do the work we do."

—HARLO HOLMES, CISO AND DIRECTOR
OF DIGITAL SECURITY AT FREEDOM
OF THE PRESS FOUNDATION

"The world is awash in hacked and leaked data, and any investigator or journalist hoping to handle it safely and find the newsworthy threads needs to buy this book."

—A.J. VICENS, REPORTER AT CYBERSCOOP

# HACKS, LEAKS, AND REVELATIONS

## The Art of Analyzing Hacked and Leaked Data

by Micah Lee

no starch
press®

San Francisco

Printed in the United States of America

First printing

27 26 25 24 23    1 2 3 4 5

ISBN-13: 978-1-7185-0312-0 (print)
ISBN-13: 978-1-7185-0313-7 (ebook)

 Published by No Starch Press®, Inc.
245 8th Street, San Francisco, CA 94103
phone: +1.415.863.9900
www.nostarch.com; info@nostarch.com

Publisher: William Pollock
Managing Editor: Jill Franklin
Production Manager: Sabrina Plomitallo-González
Production Editor: Jennifer Kepler
Developmental Editor: Abigail Schott-Rosenfield
Cover Illustrator: Glenn Sorentino
Interior Design: Octopod Studios
Technical Reviewer: Jennifer Helsby
Copyeditor: Rachel Monaghan
Proofreader: Elizabeth Littrell

Library of Congress Control Number: 2023024888

[S]

This book is dedicated to my niblings: Rosie, Sapphire, Zander, and Gabriel. I hope it will meaningfully contribute to a future world for them with more democracy, transparency, and science—and less corruption, authoritarianism, and fascism.

## About the Author

Micah Lee is an investigative journalist, computer security engineer, and open source software developer who is known for helping secure Edward Snowden's communications while Snowden leaked secret NSA documents. Lee is the director of information security at The Intercept and an adviser to the transparency collective Distributed Denial of Secrets. He's a former staff technologist for the Electronic Frontier Foundation and a co-founder of the Freedom of the Press Foundation. Lee is also a Tor Project core contributor, and he develops open source security and privacy tools like OnionShare and Dangerzone.

## About the Technical Reviewer

Jennifer Helsby is a core engineer at Penumbra Labs, where she works on applied cryptography. Previously, she was the lead developer for the SecureDrop project, which enables private and anonymous communications between journalists and their sources, and a postdoctoral researcher at the Center for Data Science and Public Policy at the University of Chicago. She received a PhD in astrophysics at the University of Chicago in 2015.

# BRIEF CONTENTS

# CONTENTS IN DETAIL

# PART III: PYTHON PROGRAMMING       167

# PART IV: STRUCTURED DATA

# 235

## 9
## BLUELEAKS, BLACK LIVES MATTER, AND THE
## CSV FILE FORMAT

### 237

# PART V: CASE STUDIES                                                    387

## 13
## PANDEMIC PROFITEERS AND COVID-19 DISINFORMATION          389

## 14
## NEO-NAZIS AND THEIR CHATROOMS                            427

# ACKNOWLEDGMENTS

I'd like to express my sincere thanks to the following people:

To Abigail Schott-Rosenfield, my editor at No Starch Press, who did an amazing job helping me revise each chapter and encouraging me to slow down when I would have otherwise lost readers with too much technical detail too quickly. Did you know that it takes a lot of work to write a book? I'd also like to thank everyone else at No Starch Press who helped make this book a reality.

To Jen Helsby, my amazingly talented technical reviewer, who double-checked all of my work and suggested many improvements. Thanks to Jen (who also happens to be my Dungeon Master!), I feel incredibly confident in the technical accuracy of this book.

To my Signal group of beta readers, who gave me excellent early feedback: Akil Harris, Kushal Das, Mara Hvistendahl, and Yael Grauer. I'd also like to thank the Aleph developers and the fine journalists at Unicorn Riot for giving feedback on specific chapters.

To my wife, Crystal, for supporting me throughout writing this book, even though it cost us quite a few nights and weekends. Thank you also for encouraging me to publish it under a Creative Commons license in order to remove barriers to access for everyone who needs the skills it teaches, no matter their income or what country they live in.

# INTRODUCTION

Unlike any other point in history, hackers, whistle-blowers, and archivists now routinely make off with terabytes of data from governments, corporations, and extremist groups. These datasets often contain gold mines of revelations in the public interest, and in many cases are freely available for anyone to download. Yet these digital tomes can prove extremely difficult to analyze or interpret, and few people today have the skills to do so.

I wrote this book for journalists, researchers, hacktivists, and anyone else who wants to learn the technologies and coding skills required to investigate these troves of hacked or leaked data. I don't assume any prior knowledge. Along with lessons on programming and technical tools, I've incorporated many anecdotes and firsthand tips from the trenches of investigative journalism. In a series of hands-on projects, you'll work with real datasets, including those from police departments, fascist groups, militias, a Russian ransomware gang, and social networks. Throughout, you'll engage head-on with the dumpster fire that is 21st-century current events: the rise of neofascism and the rejection of objective reality, the extreme partisan divide, and an internet overflowing with misinformation.

By the end of the book, you'll have gained the skills to download and analyze your own datasets, extracting the revelations they contain and transforming previously unintelligible information into your own ground-breaking reports.

## Why I Wrote This Book

I've worked as an investigative journalist for The Intercept since 2013, reporting on a large variety of leaked datasets. The first dataset I cut my teeth on was the Snowden Archive: a collection of top-secret documents from National Security Agency whistleblower Edward Snowden revealing that the NSA spies on pretty much everyone in the world who uses a phone or the internet. I wrote a dozen articles and helped publish over 2,000 secret documents from that dataset, helping bring the issues of privacy and government surveillance to the forefront of public consciousness and leading to the widespread adoption of privacy-protecting technologies.

Huge data leaks like these used to be rare, but today they're increasingly common. In my work at The Intercept, I encounter datasets so frequently I feel like I'm drowning in data, and I simply ignore most of them because it's impossible for me to investigate them all. Unfortunately, this often means that no one will report on them, and their secrets will remain hidden forever. I hope this book helps to change that.

Revelations based on leaked datasets can change the course of history. In 1971, Daniel Ellsberg's leak of military documents known as the Pentagon Papers led to the end of the Vietnam War. The same year, an underground activist group called the Citizens' Commission to Investigate the FBI broke into a Federal Bureau of Investigation field office, stole secret documents, and leaked them to the media. This dataset mentioned COINTELPRO. NBC reporter Carl Stern used Freedom of Information Act requests to publicly reveal that COINTELPRO was a secret FBI operation devoted to surveilling, infiltrating, and discrediting left-wing political groups. This stolen FBI dataset also led to the creation of the Church Committee, a Senate committee that investigated these abuses and reined them in. More recently, Chelsea Manning's 2010 leaks of Iraq and Afghanistan documents helped spark the Arab Spring, and documents and emails stolen by Russian military hackers helped elect Donald Trump as US president in 2016.

As you make your way through this book, you'll download a variety of real hacked and leaked datasets for yourself, learning how they're structured and how to extract their secrets—and perhaps, someday, you'll change history yourself. You'll read stories from many more datasets as well, some of which are private and not available for the public to download.

# What You'll Learn

This book is split into five parts, with each building on the previous part. You'll begin with security and privacy considerations, including how to verify that datasets are authentic and how to safely communicate with sources. You'll then work with datasets in your computer's terminal and on remote servers in the cloud and learn how to make various kinds of datasets searchable, including how to scour email dumps for information. You'll get a crash course in Python programming, with a focus on writing code to automate investigative tasks. These coding skills will allow you to analyze datasets that contain millions of files, which is impossible to do manually. Finally, I'll discuss two exciting real-world case studies from some of my own investigations.

The following outline describes each chapter in greater detail.

### Part I: Sources and Datasets

Part I discusses issues you should resolve before you start analyzing datasets: how to protect your sources, how to keep your datasets and your research secure, and how to acquire datasets safely.

In Chapter 1, you'll learn about how to protect your sources from retaliation. This includes how to safely communicate with sources, how to store sensitive datasets, and how to decide what information to redact. It also covers the critical step of how to authenticate datasets, using the example of chat logs from WikiLeaks and patient records from a far-right anti-vaccine group. You'll learn how to secure your own digital life and, by extension, how to secure the data-driven investigations you're working on. This includes using a password manager, encrypting hard disks and USB disks, sanitizing potentially malicious documents using the Dangerzone application, and more.

In Chapter 2, you'll learn how to acquire copies of hacked and leaked datasets. I'll introduce Distributed Denial of Secrets (DDoSecrets), a transparency collective I'm involved with that hosts copies of all of the datasets you'll work with in this book, and you'll learn how to download datasets from DDoSecrets using BitTorrent. I'll explain several ways to acquire datasets directly from sources and introduce security and anonymity tools like Signal, Tor Browser, OnionShare, and SecureDrop. As an example, I'll explain how I communicated with a source who leaked data from the conservative activist group Tea Party Patriots.

You'll also download a copy of the BlueLeaks dataset, one of the primary datasets you'll work with in this book. BlueLeaks is a collection of 270GB of data hacked from hundreds of US law enforcement websites in the summer of 2020, in the midst of the Black Lives Matter uprising. As you'll see, it's full of evidence of police misconduct. BlueLeaks has been widely covered in the press, but most of it hasn't been reported on yet. By the end of this book, you'll have the tools you need to conduct your own BlueLeaks investigations.

## Part II: Tools of the Trade

In Part II, you'll practice using the command line interface (CLI) to quickly assess leaked datasets and to use tools that don't have graphical interfaces, developing skills you'll apply extensively throughout the rest of the book.

In Chapter 3, you'll learn the basics of controlling your computer through CLI commands, as well as various tips and tricks for quickly measuring and searching datasets like BlueLeaks from the command line. You'll also write your first shell script, a file containing a series of CLI commands.

In Chapter 4, you'll expand your basic command line skills, learning new commands and setting up a server in the cloud to remotely analyze hacked and leaked datasets. As an example, you'll work with the Oath Keepers dataset, which contains emails from the far-right militia that participated in a seditious conspiracy to keep Trump in power after he lost the 2020 election.

In Chapter 5, you'll learn to use Docker, a technology that lets you run a variety of complex software crucial for analyzing datasets. You'll then use Docker to run Aleph, software that can analyze large datasets, find connections for you, and search the data for keywords.

Chapter 6 focuses on tools and techniques for investigating email dumps. You'll read emails from the Nauru Police Force about Australia's offshore detention centers, including many messages about refugees seeking Australian asylum, and from the president of Nauru himself. You'll also investigate emails from a conservative think tank called the Heritage Foundation, which include homophobic arguments against gay marriage. Using the skills you learn, you'll be able to research any email dumps you acquire in the future.

## Part III: Python Programming

In Part III, you'll get a crash course in writing code in the Python programming language, focusing on the skills required to analyze the hacked and leaked datasets covered in future chapters.

Chapter 7 introduces you to basic programming concepts: you'll learn to write and execute Python scripts and commands in the interactive Python interpreter, doing math, defining variables, working with strings and Boolean logic, looping through lists of items, and using functions.

Chapter 8 builds on the Python fundamentals covered previously. You'll learn to traverse filesystems and work with dictionaries and lists. Finally, you'll put theory into practice by writing several Python scripts to help you investigate BlueLeaks and explore leaked chat logs from the Russian ransomware gang Conti.

## Part IV: Structured Data

In Part IV, you'll learn to work with some of the most common file formats in hacked and leaked datasets.

In Chapter 9, you'll learn the structure of the CSV (comma-separated value) file format, viewing CSV files in both graphical spreadsheet software and text editors. You'll then write Python scripts to loop through the rows of a CSV file and to save CSV files of your own, allowing you to further investigate the CSV spreadsheets in the BlueLeaks dataset.

Chapter 10 introduces a custom application called BlueLeaks Explorer that I developed and released along with this book, outlining how I built the app and showing you how to use it. You can use this app to investigate the many parts of BlueLeaks that haven't yet been analyzed, hunting for new revelations about police intelligence agencies across the United States. If you ever need to develop an app to investigate a specific dataset, you can also use this chapter as inspiration.

Chapter 11 focuses on the JSON file format and the Parler dataset of over a million videos uploaded to the far-right social networking site Parler, including thousands of videos of the January 6, 2021, insurrection at the US Capitol. This dataset includes metadata for each video in JSON format, including information like when the video was filmed and in what location. Some of these videos were used as evidence during Donald Trump's second impeachment inquiry. You'll write Python scripts to filter through these videos and plot the GPS coordinates of Parler videos on a map, so you can work with similar location data in future investigations.

In Chapter 12, you'll learn to extract revelations from SQL databases by working with the Epik dataset. Epik is a Christian nationalist company that provides domain name and web hosting services to the far right, including sites known for hosting the manifestos of mass shooters. The Epik dataset contains huge databases full of hacked customer data, along with the true ownership information for domain names for extremist websites—information that's supposed to be hidden behind a domain name privacy service. You'll use your new skills to discover domain names owned by one of the people behind QAnon and the far-right image board 8kun. If you're interested in extremism research, the Epik dataset might be useful for future investigations.

**Part V: Case Studies**

Part V covers two in-depth case studies from my own career, describing how I conducted major investigations using the skills you've learned so far. In both, I explain my investigative process: how I obtained my datasets, how I analyzed them using techniques described in this book, what Python code I wrote to aid this analysis, what revelations I discovered, and what social impact my journalism had.

In Chapter 13, I discuss my investigation into America's Frontline Doctors (AFLDS), a right-wing anti-vaccine group founded during the COVID-19 pandemic to oppose public health measures. I'll explain how I turned a collection of hacked CSV and JSON files into a major news report, revealing that a network of shady telehealth companies swindled tens of millions of dollars out of vaccine skeptics. My report led to a congressional investigation of AFLDS.

In Chapter 14, I describe how I analyzed and reported on massive datasets of leaked neo-Nazi chat logs. I also discuss my role in developing a public investigation tool for such datasets, called DiscordLeaks. This tool aided in a successful lawsuit against the organizers of the deadly Unite the Right rally in 2017, resulting in a settlement of over $25 million in damages against the leaders of the American fascist movement.

**Appendixes**

Appendix A includes tips for Windows users completing the exercises in this book to help your code run more smoothly. Appendix B teaches you *web scraping*, or how to write code that accesses websites for you so that you can automate your investigative work or build your own datasets from public websites.

## What You'll Need

This book is an interactive tutorial: every chapter other than the case studies in Part V includes exercises. Many later exercises require you to have completed earlier ones, so I recommend reading this book sequentially. For example, in Chapter 1, you'll encrypt a USB disk to which you'll download a copy of the BlueLeaks dataset in Chapter 2.

Read this book with your computer open next to you, completing the exercises and trying out technologies and software as you learn about them. The source code for every exercise, as well as the code used in case studies and appendixes, is available in an online repository organized by chapter at *https://github.com/micahflee/hacks-leaks-and-revelations*.

To make this book as accessible as possible, I've tried to keep the requirements simple and affordable. You will need the following:

- **A computer that's running Windows, macOS, or Linux.** Windows is very different from macOS and Linux, but I'll explain all the extra steps Windows users will need to take to set up their computers appropriately. If you're a Linux user, I assume that you're using Ubuntu; if you're using a different version of Linux, you may need to slightly modify the commands.

- **A USB hard disk with at least 1TB of disk space.** You'll use this to store the large datasets you'll work with.

- **An internet connection that can download roughly 280GB of datasets and several more gigabytes of software.** If you live in a country with decent internet service, your home internet should work fine, though it may take hours or days to download the largest datasets in the book. Alternatively, you might find more powerful internet connections at local libraries, coffee shops, or university campuses.

- For the two exercises in which you'll work with datasets from servers in the cloud, you'll also need **a few US dollars (or the equivalent) and a credit card** to pay a cloud hosting provider.

Now grab your laptop, your USB hard disk, and perhaps a coffee or tea, and get ready to start hunting for revelations.

# PART I

## SOURCES AND DATASETS

# 1

## PROTECTING SOURCES AND YOURSELF

Most of us aren't very aware of it, but we're all under surveillance. Telecom companies and tech giants have access to a massive amount of private data about everyone who uses phones and the internet, from our exact physical locations at any given time to the content of our text messages and email, and they can share this data with leak investigators.

Even when our private data doesn't get sent directly to tech companies, our devices still record our every move locally. Can you name every single web page you visited last month? Your web browser probably can, and so can web trackers that follow your activity across the internet.

In addition to the constant background surveillance that everyone faces, workers with access to sensitive datasets are often under even stricter corporate or government surveillance. Their work computers and phones come preinstalled with spyware that monitors everything they do. Database systems keep track of exactly who searches for which search terms and when, and which documents they open, download, or print.

It's in this environment that ordinary people find themselves becoming sources. Through the course of their work, they witness something unethical or disturbing. They might make a folder with incriminating documents, or take screenshots of the company chat, or do some searches on internal databases to learn more and make sure their suspicions are correct. They might email themselves some documents or copy files to a USB stick that they plug into their work computer. They might text their friends or family for advice while thinking about what to do next. Most sources aren't aware of the massive digital trail that they've already left by the time they reach out to a journalist or regulator.

In this chapter, you'll learn about protecting sources and securing the datasets you obtain from them. I'll go over the editorial and ethical considerations involved in redacting documents and deciding what information to publish, as well as where you should store datasets based on how sensitive they are. I'll show you how to verify that datasets are authentic, describing how I've done so in the past for hacked data from COVID-19 pandemic profiteers and chat logs from WikiLeaks. Verifying the authenticity of datasets is not only important to writing accurate stories but also critical to protecting your reputation as a journalist. Finally, you'll learn how to use password managers, encrypt disks, and protect yourself from malicious documents.

## Safely Communicating with Sources

Because everything we do leaves a data trail, protecting sources is complicated and difficult. After you publish a blockbuster report based on information you've obtained from an anonymous whistleblower, you should expect the target of your investigation to launch an investigation of their own into your source's identity. The balance of power between a confidential source and the investigators on their trail is extremely asymmetric. If you're a journalist or researcher trying to protect your source, even doing all the right things perfectly isn't always enough. Because so much of source protection is beyond your control, it's important to focus on the handful of things that aren't.

As a journalist or researcher, verifying that data you've obtained is authentic is one of your core responsibilities. The simplest way to authenticate documents is to ask the company or government that produced them if they're real, but this is fraught with risk to your source. In some cases, you don't want to give up any details that might reveal your source's identity. I'll discuss this further in the "Authenticating Datasets" section later in this chapter. You also might not want to reveal that specific documents have been leaked, a topic you'll learn more about in this chapter's "Redaction" section.

In this section, I'll describe which sources face risks and which don't, as well as strategies for reducing those risks. I'll also discuss the differences between working with confidential sources who have legitimate access to inside information and hackers who break the law to obtain it. It's important to carefully consider how your own choices as an investigator could impact your source, preferably before you even begin speaking with one.

## Working with Public Data

Some datasets don't pose any risk to the source at all. When the government publishes a set of documents in response to a public records request or when documents are made public as part of a lawsuit, you can include as much of the data as you like in your report. This data might contain revelations that powerful people don't want anyone to know, but sharing those won't put anyone at risk of retaliation, since the data is already public.

Similarly, you don't need to worry about source protection for datasets that may contain sensitive data but are public and widely available, such as the BlueLeaks dataset you'll download in Chapter 2. Any information you discover from that dataset has already been scoured by the FBI investigators trying to determine who the hacker was. In these cases, it doesn't matter how many people had access to the documents. There's no chance of accidentally burning your source by providing too many details to a government or corporate media office when you ask if the data is real and if they have a statement. Since the dataset is already public, any damage to the source has already been done.

## Protecting Sensitive Information

If you're dealing with a dataset from a *confidential* source, revealing their identity could cause your source to be fired, arrested, or even murdered. The most basic step you should take to protect your source is to simply not talk about them with anyone that isn't closely collaborating with you on your investigation. Don't post to social media any details about your source that you're not planning on making public, don't talk about them to your friends at parties, and don't even talk about them to colleagues who aren't involved in the investigation.

If you're interviewing a company or government agency about a leaked dataset you've obtained, don't give them any details about your confidential source, even if they directly ask. If you get arrested and the police are demanding to know who your source is, you have the right to remain silent, and you should exercise it: don't give the police any information they don't already have. The only time that you're obligated to reveal information about your source is if a judge orders you to—and even then, you can resist it.

## Minimizing the Digital Trail

Be sure to leave the smallest digital trail possible when communicating with your source. As much as you can, avoid communication by email, SMS messages, phone calls, direct messages in social media apps, and so on. Don't follow your confidential source on social media, and make sure they don't follow you.

If you must send messages or make calls, use an encrypted messaging app like Signal, which I'll cover in Chapter 2, and make sure your source deletes any records of their chats with you. You'll often need to record what your source told you in order to report on it, but take steps to protect those records, such as removing them from messaging apps on your phone and keeping them locally on your computer rather than in a cloud service. If you no longer need your own records of conversations after you've published your report—for potential follow-up stories, for example—then delete them.

Make sure your source knows not to search the internet for you or for the reports you've published in a way that could be associated with them. Google search history has been used as evidence against sources in the past. For example, in 2018, Treasury Department whistleblower Natalie Mayflower Sours Edwards was indicted for allegedly providing a secret dataset to BuzzFeed journalist Jason Leopold. The documents she was accused of leaking detailed suspicious financial transactions involving Republican Party operatives, senior members of Donald Trump's 2020 election campaign, and a Kremlin-connected Russian agent and Russian oligarchs. During the leak investigation, the FBI obtained a search warrant to access her internet search history, and her indictment accused her of searching for multiple articles based on the contents of her alleged leaks shortly after they were published.

### Working with Hackers and Whistleblowers

The steps you must take to protect your source vary greatly depending on the person's technical sophistication. Not all sources are *whistleblowers*, people with inside access to datasets or documents who leak evidence of wrongdoing for ethical reasons. Sometimes your source may be a *hacktivist* who wants to bring down companies or government agencies that they find unjust.

Unlike most whistleblowers, hackers tend to understand that they're under surveillance and that everything they do leaves a digital trail, so they usually take countermeasures to hide their tracks. It's common for whistleblowers to reveal their identities to journalists for verification reasons, even if they aren't publicly named, but hackers typically remain fully anonymous. However, hackers can often provide technical information you can use to independently authenticate a dataset using open source intelligence. As with any source, you can't necessarily trust what hackers tell you, but their expertise can help you independently verify that the data they sent you is authentic. For these reasons, there's often less risk to your source when you publish documents from hackers rather than from whistleblowers.

When communicating with a hacker source, it's important that you stick to your role as a journalist or researcher. In the US, you're not breaking any laws just by speaking with a source who's a hacker, but *your source is almost certainly breaking laws* by hacking into companies or governments and stealing data. Don't do anything that could be construed as conspiring with them. For example, don't ask them to get specific data for you; let them give you whatever data they choose. If you're a journalist working with an established newsroom, you might fare better against legal threats than a freelancer would. While everyone should be protected equally under the law, newsrooms often have resources like lawyers and defense funds. When you're not sure whether something you're doing could get you in trouble, consult a lawyer.

Sometimes sources pretend to be hacktivists or whistleblowers but are actually state-sponsored hackers. For instance, Russian military hackers posed as hacktivists when they compromised the Democratic Party and Hillary Clinton's presidential campaign in 2016, interfering with the US election by sending hacked datasets to WikiLeaks. This sort of dataset might be authentic and newsworthy, but you don't want to end up being a pawn in someone else's information warfare. If you're unsure about your source's credibility or believe that they might have ulterior motives—or if you're confident that they're being dishonest with you—it's important to mention your skepticism about your source, and why you have doubts, in your reporting. WikiLeaks did the opposite: it insisted its source wasn't Russian intelligence when it knew otherwise, and it even spread the conspiracy theory that Seth Rich, a Democratic Party employee who was murdered, was the group's real source, leading to years of harassment against Rich's family members.

## Secure Storage for Datasets

As you prepare to receive a dataset from a source, first assess how sensitive you think that dataset is, since this will inform how you should go about protecting it, as well as how you'll continue protecting your source. As mentioned, some datasets are completely public, while others are highly classified national security secrets, and others are somewhere in between. You might encounter a dataset with unique challenges that doesn't fit into one of these categories, but in general, there are three different levels of sensitivity: low, medium, and high.

### Low-Sensitivity Datasets

A dataset might be low sensitivity if it meets one of the following criteria:

- It's already completely public, such as documents in response to a public records request or public datasets that anyone can download from a transparency collective like Distributed Denial of Secrets. (You'll learn more about DDoSecrets in Chapter 2.)

- Law enforcement or an adversarial corporation has already gained access to the dataset, meaning how you store it won't lead to retaliation against your source.

- It doesn't contain *personal identifiable information*, or *PII*, which I describe in detail in the "Redaction" section on page 14.

Basically, if you can't think of any harm that would result if a given dataset is shared more widely than you intended, including with law enforcement or leak investigators, it's probably low sensitivity.

It's safe to work with low-sensitivity datasets in *the cloud*, by which I mean storage services like Google Drive, iCloud, and Dropbox; hosting services like Amazon Web Services (AWS); and any other service where anyone besides you and the people you're working with will have access to the data. Cloud services are all vulnerable to legal requests, however, so if you're investigating governments or corporations with powerful lawyers, they can send subpoenas to cloud providers to get data associated with your account. Additionally, the data you store in the cloud is only as safe as your account itself. Make sure you have a strong password and turn on features like two-factor authentication to make your account significantly more difficult to hack.

## Medium-Sensitivity Datasets

Most datasets that aren't low sensitivity are medium sensitivity; that is, they're not already public, but securing them doesn't require you to go to extreme measures. For example, a dataset I describe later in this chapter that includes medical records of hundreds of thousands of patients is medium sensitivity. These datasets should be stored on disks that are *encrypted*, or locked in such a way that only the owner should be able to unlock them to access the data. This way, if your laptop is stolen, lost, or seized in a police raid, no one can access your files. If you haven't already encrypted your disk, you'll do so in Exercises 1-1 and 1-2.

Medium-sensitivity data should also stay on your computer's hard disk or a removable disk. Avoid storing it in cloud services unless you have a good reason to do so or you're able to encrypt it in way that the cloud service can't decrypt it. Storing datasets on local encrypted disks greatly reduces the risk of anyone else gaining unauthorized access to them.

You can work with medium-sensitivity data on your typical work computer, as long as you secure your machine. Here's how:

- Make sure your computer's hard disk is encrypted.
- Take steps to protect your computer physically. Make sure the screen locks automatically after a short amount of inactivity and requires a password to unlock.
- Install software updates promptly, and be wary of what programs you install and what documents you open on your computer. If you accidentally run malicious software or open a malicious document, someone could hack your computer and gain access to your datasets.
- Store the dataset on an external USB disk, which allows you to store more data than will fit on your computer and means you can travel with your laptop without worrying about protecting the datasets stored on it. Make sure your external disk is encrypted as well (see the "Disk Encryption" section on page 21 for instructions).
- Don't store files in parts of your computer that are automatically uploaded to the cloud. For example, many Mac users configure their computers to upload their *Documents* folder to iCloud, Apple's cloud

storage service. If your computer is set up this way, don't put files related to these investigations in that folder.

In general, work with medium-security data *locally*, meaning as files stored on your hard disk that aren't exposed to any online services. In some cases it's reasonable to work with medium-security datasets remotely. If you're working with other people, you may need to use an encrypted file-sharing solution so that the service you're using can't decrypt the files, but you and your colleagues can. One simple option is to send files back and forth using the Signal messenger app. And if you or your organization is hosting a secure tool for searching datasets, such as Aleph (covered in Chapter 5), it's also reasonable to copy the data into that tool.

All of the datasets you'll be working with in this book are low sensitivity, since they're already public. The techniques you'll learn throughout the book will apply for medium-sensitivity datasets as well, however, as you'll work with the data locally on your computer. While it's fine to work with these particular datasets in the cloud, learning to work with them locally will give you the practice you need for handling more sensitive datasets.

## High-Sensitivity Datasets

High-sensitivity datasets are by far the most difficult to work with, for good reason. The Snowden Archive, for example, is high sensitivity. I spent years reporting on this massive trove of secret government documents from National Security Agency (NSA) whistleblower Edward Snowden, who exposed the fact that US and allied spy agencies were conducting warrantless surveillance and privacy invasions on an unimaginable scale. We didn't want the FBI or NSA to gain access to it, which made cloud services out of the question, but more important, we didn't want foreign intelligence services to access it either. We assumed that nation-state attackers had the capability to remotely hack pretty much any computer we used unless we took steps to make sure it never connected to any remote network.

Going into detail on how to conduct high-sensitivity investigations is beyond the scope of this book, and you won't need such skills to work through later chapters. However, for future reference, this section outlines how you should proceed if you find yourself working with a cache of top-secret documents.

If a dataset is high sensitivity, until you are close to publishing your report, store it or access it only using *air-gapped* computers—those that never connect to the internet. Move files off the air-gapped computer only when they're already redacted and necessary for publishing. In short, buy a new computer, never connect it to the internet, and use that. Or, if you have an old computer that would work, you can format its disk, reinstall the operating system, and use that computer while never connecting it to the internet. These steps will help you ensure that you're starting from a clean system free of existing trackers or malware. To make it even more secure, unscrew the computer's case and physically remove the wireless hardware.

You'll run into all sorts of challenges related to moving data between your air-gapped computer and your normal work computer—for example, installing or updating software on your air-gapped computer requires downloading it on another computer, carefully verifying that it's legitimate software, and then transferring it to your air-gapped computer to install it. The extra steps are worth it, though, when a breach might have severe consequences.

It's also important that the disk in your air-gapped computer and any USB disks that you use with it are encrypted with strong passphrases. Also consider the physical security of where you store your air-gapped computer and USB disks. If possible, keep them in a safe or vault with a good lock. If that's not possible, at least keep them in a locked room to which few people have keys. Always power off your air-gapped computer when you're not using it to make it harder for attacks against the disk encryption to work.

When working on air-gapped computers, be mindful of nearby internet-connected electronic devices with microphones or cameras. Avoid having conversations related to highly sensitive documents within earshot of microphones, and consider whether any nearby cameras (including smartphones) could capture photographs of your screen.

## Authenticating Datasets

You can't believe everything you read on the internet, and juicy documents or datasets that anonymous people send you are no exception. Disinformation is prevalent. It's important to explain in your published report, at least briefly, what makes you confident in the data. If you can't authenticate it but still want to publish your report in case it's real—or in case others *can* authenticate it—make that clear. When in doubt, err on the side of transparency.

How you go about verifying that a dataset is authentic completely depends on what the data is. You have to approach the problem on a case-by-case basis. The best way to verify a dataset is to use *open source intelligence (OSINT)*, or publicly available information that anyone with enough skill can find. This might mean scouring social media accounts, consulting the Internet Archive's Wayback Machine (*https://web.archive.org*), inspecting metadata of public images or documents, paying services for historical domain name registration data, or viewing other types of public records. If your dataset includes a database taken from a website, for instance, you might be able to compare information in that database with publicly available information on the website itself to confirm that they match.

This book's discussion of OSINT focuses on how I've used it in my own investigations. If you want to learn more, see Michael Bazzell's *OSINT Techniques: Resources for Uncovering Online Information*, along with the companion tools listed at *https://inteltechniques.com/tools*. Bazzell describes a large number of tools and techniques for discovering details that might help you verify datasets using OSINT.

In this section, I'll share two examples of authenticating data from my own experience: one about a dataset from the anti-vaccine group America's Frontline Doctors, and another about leaked chat logs from a WikiLeaks Twitter group.

*In 2023, Twitter rebranded itself as X. In this book, I will continue to refer to accounts and posts that existed before this rebranding as "Twitter accounts" and "tweets."*

## The AFLDS Dataset

In late 2021, in the midst of the COVID-19 pandemic, an anonymous hacker sent me hundreds of thousands of patient and prescription records from telehealth companies working with America's Frontline Doctors (AFLDS). AFLDS is a far-right anti-vaccine group that misleads people about COVID-19 vaccine safety and tricks patients into paying millions of dollars for drugs like ivermectin and hydroxychloroquine, which are ineffective at preventing or treating the virus. The group was initially formed to help Donald Trump's 2020 reelection campaign, and the group's leader, Simone Gold, was arrested for storming the US Capitol on January 6, 2021. In 2022, she served two months in prison for her role in the attack.

My source told me that they got the data by writing a program that made thousands of web requests to a website run by one of the telehealth companies, Cadence Health. Each request returned data about a different patient. To see whether that was true, I made an account on the Cadence Health website myself. Everything looked legitimate to me. The information I had about each of the 255,000 patients was the exact information I was asked to provide when I created my account on the service, and various category names and IDs in the dataset matched what I could see on the website. But how could I be confident that the patient data itself was real, that these people weren't just made up?

I wrote a simple Python script to loop through the 72,000 patients (those who had paid for fake health care) and put each of their email addresses in a text file. I then cross-referenced these email addresses with a totally separate dataset containing PII from members of Gab, a social network popular among fascists, anti-democracy activists, and anti-vaxxers. In early 2021, a hacktivist who went by the name "JaXpArO and My Little Anonymous Revival Project" had hacked Gab and made off with 65GB of data, including about 38,000 Gab users' email addresses. Thinking there might be overlap between AFLDS and Gab users, I wrote another simple Python program that compared the email addresses from each group and showed me all of the addresses that were in both lists. There were several.

Armed with this information, I started scouring the public Gab timelines of users whose email addresses had appeared in both datasets, looking for posts about AFLDS. Using this technique, I found multiple AFLDS patients who posted about their experience on Gab, leading me to believe that the data was authentic. For example, according to consultation notes from the hacked dataset, one patient created an account on the telehealth site and four days later had a telehealth consultation. About a month after that, they posted to Gab saying, "Front line doctors finally came through with HCQ/Zinc delivery" (HCQ is an abbreviation for hydroxychloroquine).

Chapter 13 focuses entirely on my AFLDS investigation and describes the technical details of my Python script in greater depth. By the time you've worked through the intervening chapters, you'll have the Python knowledge to understand how that script worked.

## The WikiLeaks Twitter Group Chat

In late 2017, journalist Julia Ioffe published a revelation in the *Atlantic*: WikiLeaks had slid into Donald Trump Jr.'s Twitter direct messages (DMs). Among other things, before the 2016 election, WikiLeaks suggested to Trump Jr. that even if his father lost the election, he shouldn't concede. "Hi Don," the verified @WikiLeaks Twitter account wrote, "if your father 'loses' we think it is much more interesting if he DOES NOT conceed [*sic*] and spends time CHALLENGING the media and other types of rigging that occurred—as he has implied that he might do."

A long-term WikiLeaks volunteer who went by the pseudonym Hazelpress started a private Twitter group with WikiLeaks and its biggest supporters in mid-2015. After watching the group become more right-wing, conspiratorial, and unethical, and specifically after learning about WikiLeaks' secret DMs with Trump Jr., Hazelpress decided to blow the whistle on the whistleblowing group itself. She has since publicly come forward as Mary-Emma Holly, an artist who spent years as a volunteer legal researcher for WikiLeaks.

To carry out the WikiLeaks leak, Holly logged in to her Twitter account, made it private, unfollowed everyone, and deleted all of her tweets. She also deleted all of her DMs except for the private WikiLeaks Twitter group and changed her Twitter username. Using the Firefox web browser, she then went to the DM conversation—which contained 11,000 messages and had been going on for two and a half years—and saw the latest messages in the group. She scrolled up, waited for Twitter to load more messages, scrolled up again, and kept doing this for *four hours*, until she reached the very first message in the group. She then used Firefox's Save Page As function to save an HTML version of the web page, as well as a folder full of resources like images that were posted in the group.

Now that she had a local, offline copy of all the messages in the DM group, Holly leaked it to the media. In early 2018, she sent a Signal message to the phone number listed on The Intercept's tips page. At that time, I happened to be the one checking Signal for incoming tips. Using OnionShare—software that I developed for this purpose, which I describe in detail in Chapter 2—she sent me an encrypted and compressed file, along with the password to decrypt it. After extracting it, I found a 37MB HTML file—so big that it made my web browser unresponsive when I tried opening it, and which I later split into separate files to make it easier to work with—and a folder with 82MB of resources.

How could I verify the authenticity of such a huge HTML file? If I could somehow access the same data directly from Twitter's servers, that would do it; only an insider at Twitter would be in a position to create fake DMs that show up on Twitter's website, and even that would be extremely challenging. When I explained this to Holly (who, at the time, I still knew only as Hazelpress), she gave me her Twitter username and password. She had already deleted all the other information from that account. With her consent, I logged in to Twitter with her credentials, went to her DMs, and found the Twitter group in question. It immediately looked like it contained the same messages as the HTML file, and I confirmed that the verified account @WikiLeaks frequently posted to the group.

Following these steps made me extremely confident in the authenticity of the dataset, but I decided to take verification one step further. Could I download a separate copy of the Twitter group myself in order to compare it with the version Holly had sent me? I searched around and found DMArchiver, a Python program that could do just that. Using this program, along with Holly's username and password, I downloaded a text version of all of the DMs in the Twitter group. It took only a few minutes to run this tool, rather than four hours of scrolling up in a web browser.

**NOTE** *After this investigation, the DMArchiver program stopped working due to changes on Twitter's end, and today the project is abandoned. However, if you're faced with a similar challenge in a future investigation, search for a tool that might work for you. You could also consider developing your own, using programming skills that you'll learn in Chapters 7 and 8.*

The output from DMArchiver, a 1.7MB text file, was much easier to work with compared to the enormous HTML file, and it also included exact timestamps. Here's a snippet of the text version:

```
[2015-11-19 13:46:39] <WikiLeaks> We believe it would be much better for GOP
to win.
[2015-11-19 13:47:28] <WikiLeaks> Dems+Media+liberals woudl then form a block
to reign in their worst qualities.
[2015-11-19 13:48:22] <WikiLeaks> With Hillary in charge, GOP will be pushing
for her worst qualities., dems+media+neoliberals will be mute.
[2015-11-19 13:50:18] <WikiLeaks> She's a bright, well connected, sadistic
sociopath.
```

I could view the HTML version in a web browser to see it exactly as it had originally looked on Twitter, which was also useful for taking screenshots to include in our final report, as shown in Figure 1-1.

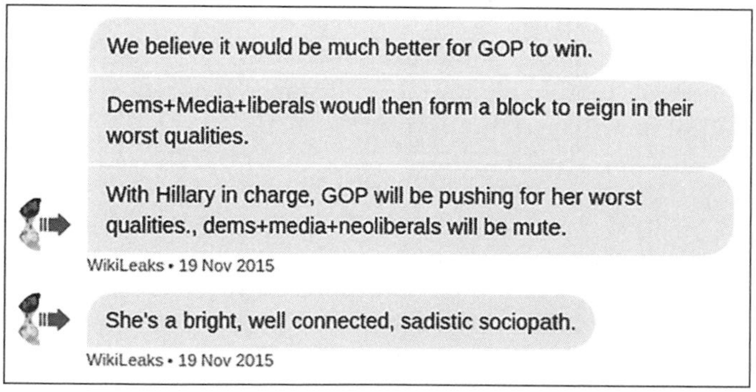

We believe it would be much better for GOP to win.

Dems+Media+liberals woudl then form a block to reign in their worst qualities.

With Hillary in charge, GOP will be pushing for her worst qualities., dems+media+neoliberals will be mute.
WikiLeaks • 19 Nov 2015

She's a bright, well connected, sadistic sociopath.
WikiLeaks • 19 Nov 2015

*Figure 1-1: A screenshot of the leaked HTML file*

Along with the talented reporter Cora Currier, I started the long process of reading all 11,000 chat messages, paying closest attention to the 10 percent of them from the @WikiLeaks account—which was presumably controlled by Julian Assange, WikiLeaks' editor—and picking out everything in the public interest. We discovered the following details:

- Assange expressed a desire for Republicans to win the 2016 presidential election.

- Assange and his supporters were intensely focused on discrediting two Swedish women who had accused him of rape and molestation, as well as discrediting their lawyers. Assange and his defenders spent weeks discussing ways to sabotage articles about his rape case that feminist journalists were writing.

- Assange tried to discredit filmmaker Laura Poitras because of how she portrayed him in *Risk*, the 2016 documentary about WikiLeaks. The film includes a scene in which Assange tells his lawyer that his accusers were part of a "thoroughly tawdry radical feminist political positioning thing," and in another scene he says, "Part of the problem in this case is there's two women, and the public just can't even keep them separate. If there was one, you could go, 'She's a bad woman.' I think that would have happened by now."

- Assange used transphobic and misogynistic language when talking about Chelsea Manning, his source from 2010, and her friends. I discuss Manning's relationship with WikiLeaks further in Chapter 2.

- After Associated Press journalist Raphael Satter wrote a story about harm caused when WikiLeaks publishes personal identifiable information, Assange called him a "rat" and said that, "he's Jewish and engaged in the ((())) issue," referring to an antisemitic neo-Nazi meme. He then told his supporters to "Bog him down. Get him to show his bias."

You can read our reporting on this dataset at *https://theintercept.com/2018/02/14/julian-assange-wikileaks-election-clinton-trump/*. After The Intercept published this article, Assange and his supporters also targeted me personally with antisemitic abuse, and Russia Today, the state-run TV station, ran a segment about me. I discuss WikiLeaks and its history in greater depth in Chapter 2.

The techniques you can use to authenticate datasets vary greatly depending on the situation. Sometimes you can rely on OSINT, sometimes you can rely on help from your source, and sometimes you'll need to come up with an entirely different method.

## Redaction

Once you've authenticated your dataset, you must consider whether or how you want to redact—that is, hide or delete—sensitive information before publishing the results of your investigation. In some cases it might be safe to publish original documents without any redaction, and in others you might choose not to publish any documents at all. In this section I'll discuss how to make these decisions and the reasons you might choose to redact, or not redact, information.

## What Data to Publish

When deciding how much data to publish, consider whether your method of reporting the revelations will enable leak investigators to uncover your source. For example, if a company's human resources department sends an email to all of its 10,000 employees and one of them leaks the message to you, it will be very hard for the company to find the culprit. But if only 10 people have access to a document—or database logs show a list of 10 people who recently accessed it—the company has a real suspect list to work from.

How many people had access to the data you've obtained, how sensitive it is, what your source is risking, and what they're comfortable with are all factors that will determine the different types or quantities of data you publish. The following list provides options to consider, ordered from the most risk to your source to the least:

- Publish unaltered documents or datasets.
- Publish documents after you've redacted them and stripped them of metadata.
- Publish documents after re-creating them from scratch by typing them by hand into new separate documents and publishing those instead. When you re-create documents, you remove any hidden trackers and make it impossible to tell from the documents themselves whether your source obtained them by photographing their screen, copying them to a USB stick, uploading them to a website, or using some other method.
- Don't publish the documents at all; only describe and quote from them.
- Don't even quote from the documents, just describe the revelations they contain. If leak investigators don't know what documents were compromised, only that an accurate news story somehow reveals confidential information, they'll have a harder time making progress in their investigation.

Publishing documents is more transparent to your readers, and providing direct evidence makes your work more credible, but doing so has to be weighed against protecting your source. You'll make these decisions on a case-by-case basis, but always keep in mind the risks that your source faces.

## What to Redact

If you've carefully considered the risks to your source and decided to publish documents rather than just describing them, the next step is to decide what, if any, information in those documents to redact before publishing. There are three reasons for redaction: to continue protecting your source, to protect the privacy of others involved, or to protect government or corporate information that should justifiably remain secret.

## Protecting Your Source

If your dataset includes archives of a private website or databases that your source was logged in to, you'll want to redact their username or any other identifying information before publishing. In addition, make sure you don't accidentally publish metadata that could reveal your source. This book won't describe the many ways that could happen, but here are two common examples: Word documents often include the name of the author, and photos often include GPS coordinates and the type of camera that was used.

In 2012, John McAfee, the controversial millionaire software executive, was on the run. Police raided his home in Belize, and he fled the country. In a blog post, he wrote, "I am currently safe and in the company of two intrepid journalist [*sic*] from Vice Magazine . . . We are not in Belize, but not quite out of the woods yet." That day, *Vice* published its article about McAfee, which included a photograph. According to the photo's metadata, it was taken on an iPhone 4S and included GPS coordinates to a specific house in Guatemala. By not stripping the photo of metadata, *Vice* accidentally published his exact location. If *Vice* had simply taken a screenshot of the image and published that instead, the magazine would have erased the metadata and kept the location secret.

In 2017, when President Donald Trump constantly called the accusations that Russia interfered in the US elections "fake news," NSA whistleblower Reality Winner anonymously mailed a top-secret document to The Intercept with evidence that the NSA had, in fact, witnessed a Russian cyberattack against local election officials. The Intercept published the document, and a short time later Reality Winner was arrested. The published document included a type of metadata called *printer dots*, nearly invisible yellow dots that printers add to paper that include the serial number of the printer and the timestamp of when it was printed. While there's no evidence that leak investigators even noticed them until after Reality Winner was arrested (she was one of six people who had printed this document, and the only one who had written an email to The Intercept), the printer dots could have outed her as well. The Intercept could have mitigated this by re-creating the document (retyping it and re-creating the artwork) and publishing that instead of a scanned version of the original.

## Protecting Personal Information in Datasets

Many datasets include names, email addresses, usernames, phone numbers, home addresses, passwords, and other similar personal identifiable information of people who aren't public figures. Many government and corporate documents include PII for random employees that won't add anything to your story but could make these people targets of harassment. Even when dealing with public figures, in most cases it's still responsible to redact their PII unless publishing it adds value to your report. For example, if the focus of your investigation is a lavish mansion owned by a billionaire, it might be reasonable to publish the address of that mansion. If you're writing an unrelated story about that billionaire, however, there's no reason to include their home address.

Even if you believe the targets of your investigation are jerks, it's better to redact their PII if including it doesn't add to your report. Even jerks have privacy rights, and needlessly publishing PII could be used to discredit your report regardless of the revelations it contains.

The exception to this rule is if publicly outing someone is an important part of your story and could keep other people safe. For example, it's ethical to name someone who is abusive in a workplace or industry or to out someone as a member of a hate group. Even when you're publicly outing someone, though, don't publish unnecessary PII about them, like their home address. If you do, you might be accused of harassment, which could distract the conversation from the wrongdoing you're trying to expose.

### Protecting Legitimate Secrets

Occasionally, governments and companies do in fact have legitimate reasons to keep secrets. In my experience, this is rare—the US government has a severe overclassification problem. This is one reason it's important to ask related parties for comment before you publish your story, though: a government agency or company may give you context that could make you decide not to publicize the data. For example, I was once part of a decision to redact details from a top-secret US government document related to another country's nuclear weapons program.

## Making Requests for Comment

Always give the people or companies on which you're reporting a chance to tell their side of the story. Even if you're confident that they won't respond truthfully or at all, you should still attempt to contact them, explain what you're going to publish, and give them a chance to defend themselves. If they do respond, quote their response in your published report (and if you know they aren't telling the truth, explain that alongside their quote). If they don't respond or they decline to comment, include that in your report as well.

For example, in 2017, I reported on leaked chat logs from neo-Nazis, which I cover in Chapter 14. In my article, I named a member of the pro-slavery hate group League of the South who was arrested during the deadly Charlottesville, Virginia, Unite the Right protest for carrying a concealed handgun. He had posted messages in a chatroom saying that he had "scores to settle" with local antifascists because they had gotten him fired from his job. Using public records, I tracked down his phone number. I set up a new virtual phone number using Google Voice and called him with that, since I didn't want to give him my private number. I left messages, but he never responded.

If your investigation is adversarial—that is, the people you're looking into aren't going to be happy about it—wait until shortly before you publish your report to contact them and tip your hand. It's polite to give them at least 24 hours to respond, while giving them less time to sabotage your story. They might leak your story to a friendly publication to publish first with a positive spin, announce to their followers that a hit piece is coming, or attempt to use legal means to stop you from publishing. I've been involved in investigations where all of those scenarios have happened.

Chances are, you're not an expert in all aspects of what you're reporting on, so it's often a good idea to consult outside experts (university professors, authors, scientists, and so on) and include quotes from them in your published reports. In my own reporting, I've interviewed cryptography professors, disinformation researchers, medical doctors, and civil rights advocates who work for nonprofits. Even if you're an expert on the topic of your investigation, providing outside voices often adds to your story, helping you make stronger arguments.

As long as you trust the experts you're talking with, it's fine to contact them early in the reporting process. It's also common to share confidential documents with them, so long as they agree to keep them secret until you publish. In the case of highly sensitive documents, you might need to arrange for outside experts to visit you in person and view the files on your air-gapped computer. Sometimes these experts can point you in research directions that you wouldn't think to go yourself.

Now that you've seen how to protect your sources and authenticate the information they give you, let's go over some ways to secure your computer and online accounts to keep your datasets and other sensitive records safe.

## Password Managers

Most people's passwords aren't unique, meaning they're reused in multiple places. This is a very bad idea, since any duplicate password is only as secure as the least secure place you've used it. Go to *https://haveibeenpwned.com*, search for your email address or phone number, and you'll see a list of data breaches that you're included in. If your LinkedIn password was exposed in a data breach a few years ago but it's the same password you use for your Gmail account, to log in to your laptop, or to unlock your encrypted USB disk full of sensitive datasets, you may be in trouble.

The solution is to make all your passwords unique as well as strong, which really just means long and random enough that they're impossible to predict. Unfortunately, strong passwords are hard to memorize, and it's impossible for humans to memorize hundreds of passwords that are both strong and unique. Yet we're required to use hundreds of passwords in our daily lives.

Fortunately, we can have computers memorize most of our passwords for us. Password managers are programs that keep track of an encrypted database of passwords that you unlock using a master password, the only one you have to memorize. Password managers often allow you to sync your password database to the cloud, which is fine so long as you're using a strong master password. If a hacker steals your encrypted password database or if your password manager company hands it to the FBI or other authorities, they won't be able to unlock it without your master password. An encrypted password database is completely inaccessible to anyone without the master password. If your master password is strong, it will be literally impossible for them to guess it, and your other passwords will be safe. Encryption is cool like that.

---

### DONALD TRUMP'S TWITTER PASSWORD

I learned from an episode of the excellent podcast *Darknet Diaries*, hosted by Jack Rhysider, that Donald Trump's LinkedIn password was exposed in a 2012 data breach. His password, yourefired, was his signature phrase from *The Apprentice*, the reality TV show he hosted. While he was running for president in 2016, three Dutch hackers, Victor, Edwin, and Matt, who are part of a group called the Guild of the Grumpy Old Hackers, discovered his LinkedIn password in the dataset from that breach. They tried it on Trump's @realDonaldTrump Twitter account and . . . it worked.

---

You might be thinking, "Isn't using a password manager just putting all my eggs in one basket? If it gets hacked, doesn't that give the hacker access to *everything*?" This is true—it's very important to secure your password manager—but not using one at all is like trying to hold hundreds of eggs with just your hands, without using a basket, and without breaking any of them. If you try that, you're bound to drop a lot of your eggs eventually. You also always have the option of using multiple password managers (multiple baskets) for different projects so that if one gets hacked, the others remain secure.

There are several good password managers available, and if you already know of one you like, by all means use it. Here are three that I recommend:

**Bitwarden**    This manager is free and open source, and it syncs passwords between your computers and phone. It has browser extensions to fill in passwords automatically when you log in to websites. It's a good choice for a day-to-day password manager. Download it at *https://bitwarden.com*.

**1Password**    Like Bitwarden, 1Password syncs passwords between your computer and phone and has a browser extension. It's also a good choice for a day-to-day password manager. It costs money, but 1Password gives free licenses to journalists. Download it at *https://1password.com*, or see *https://1password.com/for-journalism/* for more information about the free license program.

**KeePassXC**    This software is great for high-security situations. Unlike Bitwarden and 1Password, KeePassXC doesn't sync your encrypted password database to the cloud, which makes it less convenient but potentially more secure. It works well on air-gapped computers. Download it at *https://keepassxc.org.*

If you'd like to use Bitwarden, 1Password, or a similar password manager that syncs between devices, follow the installation instructions on its website to install the program on your computer, on your phone, and as an extension in your web browser. If you're using a local-only password manager like KeePassXC, just install it on your computer.

When you first set up your password manager, it's extremely important that you not forget your master password. Unlike most website passwords, a master password can't be reset. If you forget it, you're locked out of your password manager forever and you lose all your passwords. Write the master password on a piece of paper until you've memorized it, and then destroy the paper.

The best master passwords are *passphrases*, a sequence of words picked at random from a dictionary. They're also easier to remember than completely random passwords. An example of a good passphrase is *movie-flanked -census6-casino-change.* It has no meaning at all, but with practice it's not too hard to memorize.

Once you've set up your password manager account, add your other passwords to the manager. Start by adding the passwords you use the most: perhaps your email password or passwords to social media accounts. If you've ever reused these passwords, take this opportunity to *change them* and make them better. Whenever you create a new password, use your password manager's password generator, a tool included to help you create strong passwords. Typically, password generators have settings that let you choose whether it should generate a password or a passphrase, whether it should contain numbers or special characters, how long it should be, and so on.

Bitwarden, for example, can create both passwords or passphrases. Figure 1-2 shows Bitwarden's password generator, which is configured to create a passphrase with five words, separated by dashes, capitalized, and including a number.

Bitwarden can also make strong passwords, such as *Frz6ioX4o@cCY.* All of your passwords should either be strong passphrases or passwords like this.

The password generators included in 1Password, KeePassXC, and other password managers all include similar features. While Bitwarden allows you to open the password generator tool independently, some password managers require you to add a new item in your password database or edit an existing one to access the generator.

When you need to come up with a new password, it doesn't matter if you choose to use a password or a passphrase so long as it's strong and unique. However, passphrases tend to be easier to memorize and to enter. For this reason, I tend to use passwords to log in to websites (my password manager fills them in for me) and passphrases for anything that I might need to memorize or enter, such as a disk encryption passphrase or the passphrase to log in to my computer.

Every time you create a new account or log in to an existing one, add the password to your password manager.

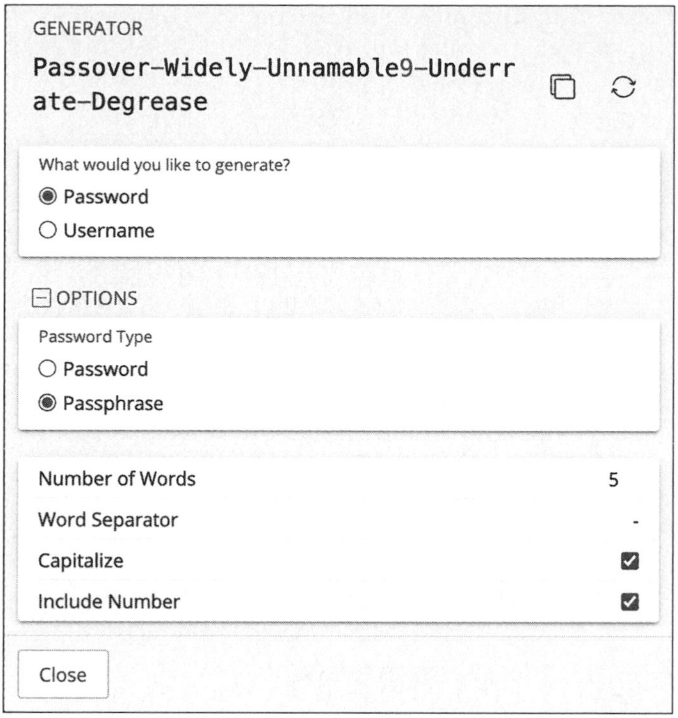

GENERATOR

**Passover-Widely-Unnamable9-Underr ate-Degrease**

What would you like to generate?
- ⦿ Password
- ○ Username

⊟ OPTIONS

Password Type
- ○ Password
- ⦿ Passphrase

| | |
|---|---|
| Number of Words | 5 |
| Word Separator | - |
| Capitalize | ☑ |
| Include Number | ☑ |

Close

*Figure 1-2: Bitwarden's password generator*

## Disk Encryption

Disk encryption allows you to protect your data from people who have physical access to your phone, laptop, or USB disk. It prevents anyone from accessing data on a device if you lose it, someone steals it, it gets confiscated at a border crossing or checkpoint, or your home or office is raided. For example, when the internal disk in your laptop isn't encrypted, anyone with physical access to it can unscrew your laptop's case, remove the disk, and plug it into their own computer, accessing all of the data without needing to know any of your passwords. But when your disk is encrypted, all of this data is completely inaccessible to anyone who doesn't have the right key. If disk encryption is enabled, they'll need to first unlock the disk, typically using a password, a PIN, or biometrics like a fingerprint or face scan. You'll learn how to encrypt your internal disk and your 1TB USB disk in this chapter's exercises.

Although disk encryption is an important part of protecting your data, it doesn't protect against remote attacks. For example, if your laptop is encrypted but someone tricks you into opening a malicious Word document that attacks your computer, disk encryption won't stop them from accessing your files. Disk encryption also won't help much if the attackers get access to your device while it's unlocked—for example, if you step away from your laptop at a coffee shop without locking your screen or if attackers can easily unlock your phone by forcing you to use biometrics. For instance, after arresting you, a cop might wave your phone in front of your face to unlock it with a face scan.

You, of course, won't be relying on disk encryption to commit crimes, but the story of Ross Ulbricht, the creator of the darknet market website Silk Road, is a good illustration of how it can fail you. In 2013, Ulbricht was using his encrypted laptop at the San Francisco Public Library when two undercover FBI agents distracted him by pretending to be lovers in a fight. Making sure his screen was unlocked, they quickly arrested him, then copied important files off of his computer. If his screen had been locked and he'd had a strong password, the disk encryption might have prevented them from accessing his data at all. Ulbricht was charged with money laundering, hacking, drug trafficking, and other crimes.

Encrypting your laptop's internal disk is a basic security measure that everyone should take. It's quick and easy to set up, doesn't require you to do any extra work on a regular basis, and protects your privacy if you lose your device. You can think of it like wearing a seatbelt: there's really no good reason not to do it. Encrypting your laptop's internal disk is especially important if you're going to be working with sensitive data.

## Exercise 1-1: Encrypt Your Internal Disk

This exercise shows you how to encrypt the internal disk in your computer, whether you have a Windows, Mac, or Linux machine. Skip to the appropriate section for your operating system.

### Windows

Different Windows versions and PC models have support for different types of disk encryption. Pro editions of Windows include BitLocker, Microsoft's disk encryption technology, and Home editions include device encryption, which is basically BitLocker with limited features. These features work only if your PC is new enough, though. If your computer came with at least Windows 10 when it was new, it should support disk encryption, but if it came with an earlier version of Windows, it might not. I go over options for how to proceed in this case at the end of this section.

#### BitLocker

To find out whether your computer includes BitLocker, click **Start** (the Windows icon in the bottom left of your computer), search for **bitlocker**, and open **Manage BitLocker**. If your version of Windows supports it, the window should show whether BitLocker is enabled on your *C:* system drive, and you should have the option to enable it. If so, do that now.

When you enable BitLocker, it makes you save a recovery key to either your Microsoft account, a file on a nonencrypted USB disk, or a printed document. Saving your recovery key to your Microsoft account is the simplest option, but it does mean that Microsoft or anyone with access to your Microsoft account can access the key needed to unlock your disk. If you'd prefer to not give Microsoft this access, print the recovery key. You should also save your key in your password manager. If your computer breaks, you'll need your recovery key to access any of the data on your encrypted disk.

### Device Encryption

If your version of Windows doesn't include BitLocker, try device encryption. Click **Start**, then navigate to **Settings ▸ Update & Security** (or **Privacy & Security**, depending on your Windows version). Then go to the Device encryption tab to check whether it's enabled; if not, enable it.

If you see no Device encryption tab, your PC doesn't support device encryption, unfortunately. You have a few options. The easiest option is to upgrade to the Pro version of Windows, which typically costs about $100, and then use BitLocker. Alternatively, use VeraCrypt.

### VeraCrypt

VeraCrypt is free and open source disk encryption software. To begin, download VeraCrypt from *https://veracrypt.fr*, install it on your computer, and open it.

Click **Create Volume** to open the VeraCrypt Volume Creation Wizard. VeraCrypt lets you choose from three types of encrypted volumes. Select **Encrypt the System Partition or Entire System Drive** and click **Next**.

On the Type of System Encryption page, choose **Normal** and click **Next**. On the Area to Encrypt page, choose **Encrypt the Windows System Partition** and click **Next**. On the Number of Operating Systems page, choose **Single-Boot** and click **Next** (unless you have multiple operating systems on your computer, in which case choose **Multi-boot**). On the Encryption Options page, use the default settings and click **Next**.

The next page is the Password page. You'll need to come up with a strong passphrase that you'll have to enter each time you boot up Windows. If that passphrase is weak, your disk encryption will be weak. I recommend generating a strong passphrase and saving it in your password manager—this way, if you forget it the next time you reboot your computer, you can look it up in your password manager on your phone. Enter the passphrase twice and click **Next**.

The next page is called Collecting Random Data. VeraCrypt includes a feature where you move your mouse around the window randomly so that it can collect information from your mouse movements to make the encryption more secure. Move your mouse around until the bar at the bottom of the screen is green, and then click **Next**. Click **Next** again on the Keys Generated page.

The Rescue Disk page prompts you to create a VeraCrypt Rescue Disk, which you can use in the event that your disk gets damaged and you have issues booting Windows. Creating a rescue disk is outside the scope of this book, so check **Skip Rescue Disk Verification** and click **Next**. On the Rescue Disk Created page, click **Next** again.

On the Wipe Mode page, select **None (Fastest)** as the Wipe mode and click **Next**. On the System Encryption Pretest page, click **Test** to test that disk encryption will work properly on your computer—this will reboot your computer, and you'll need to enter your VeraCrypt passphrase to boot up.

When you reboot your computer, it should boot up to the VeraCrypt bootloader, and you'll need to enter the VeraCrypt passphrase to proceed. Under PIM, just press ENTER. If all goes well, it will succeed, Windows will boot up, and VeraCrypt will open on the Pretest Completed page again after you log in. Click **Encrypt** to begin encrypting your internal disk with VeraCrypt. From now on, you'll need to enter your VeraCrypt passphrase each time you boot your computer, but all of your data will also be protected with this passphrase.

### macOS

Apple's disk encryption technology is called FileVault. If you're using macOS Ventura or newer, open the System Settings app, click **Privacy & Security** on the left, and scroll down to the FileVault section. (If you're using a version of macOS older than Ventura, open the System Preferences app, click **Security & Privacy**, and make sure you're on the FileVault tab.) If FileVault is turned off, turn it on.

The password that unlocks your Mac's disk is the password you use to log in to your account. Make sure your Mac password is strong; if it's weak, your disk encryption is weak.

When you enable FileVault, it makes you save a recovery key. Save that key in your password manager. If you forget your Mac password, you'll need the recovery key to access any of your data. If you're using a local password manager that doesn't sync to the cloud, like KeePassXC, store a copy of your recovery key somewhere else as well, such as on a piece of paper kept in a secure location.

### Linux

Linux uses technology called LUKS for disk encryption. You can check the Disks program (in most versions of Linux, to open this program, press the Windows key, type **disks**, and press ENTER) to see whether your internal disk is encrypted. The program shows you all of the disks attached to your computer and allows you to format them (see Figure 1-3). If your internal disk has an unlocked partition with LUKS encryption, disk encryption is enabled.

In this case, my internal disk is the 500GB Samsung SSD listed on the left in Figure 1-3. My disk is partitioned into four parts, and the last part (Partition 4) is 499GB and is encrypted with LUKS. Your disk might look different from mine, but you'll know it's encrypted if the main partition says LUKS.

Unfortunately, you can't just turn LUKS on or off. If your disk isn't encrypted, the only way to encrypt it is to reinstall Linux, this time making sure to encrypt the disk. When you're installing Linux, one of the first steps in the installation process will be to partition your disk; make sure to enable encryption during that step. If you're going to reinstall Linux, always back up your data first. After choosing your encryption passphrase, save a copy of it in your password manager; you'll need it every time you boot up your computer.

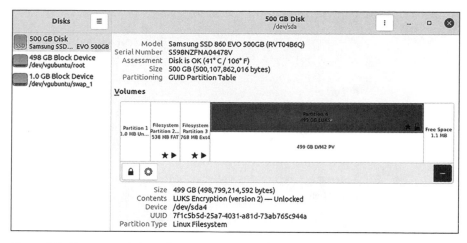

*Figure 1-3: Managing disks and partitions using Disks in Linux*

## Exercise 1-2: Encrypt a USB Disk

Your internal disk alone likely isn't large enough to store all of the datasets you'll need to work with. As mentioned in the book's introduction, in order to complete the exercises in this book and work with the massive datasets, you need a USB disk that's *at least 1TB*. To encrypt that USB disk, you also need to format it, which deletes any data already on it. This exercise shows you how to do that for whichever operating system you're using.

Before you get started, let's go over some background on how mass storage devices (like hard disks, SD cards, and so on) work. Storage devices are typically split into one or more *partitions*, also called *volumes*, with each partition using a format called a *filesystem*. You can think of partitions as cabinets that use different shelving systems (filesystems) to organize data. Different operating systems use different filesystems. Windows often uses a filesystem called NTFS, macOS often uses APFS, and Linux often uses ext4. There are also filesystems that all three operating systems can use, such as ExFAT.

When you erase a storage device, you delete all of the partitions on it so that it contains unallocated space. You can then create a new partition—with USB disks, you'll typically create a single partition that takes up all of the unallocated space—and format it using the filesystem that matches your operating system.

Whether you're working in Windows, macOS, or Linux, begin by plugging your USB disk into your computer. Open your password manager and save a new strong passphrase, created using your password manager's password generator. Name the password something like **datasets USB disk encryption**.

To begin encrypting your disk, skip to the appropriate subsection for your operating system.

## Windows

Windows users with BitLocker should work through the following subsection; if you don't have BitLocker, skip to the VeraCrypt section.

### BitLocker

If you have a Windows computer with BitLocker, use that to encrypt your USB. First, make sure to format the USB disk as NTFS. To do so, click **Start**, search for **disk management**, and open **Create and Format Hard Disk Partitions**. This opens the Windows Disk Management app, as shown in Figure 1-4, which lists all of the disks connected to the PC and lets you format them.

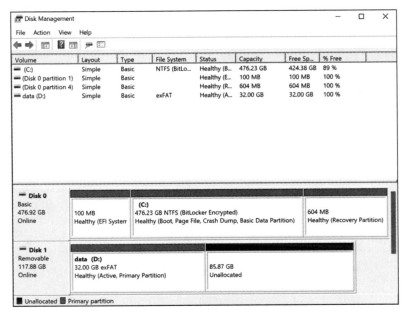

Figure 1-4: The Disk Management app in Windows

The bottom part of the window shows each disk attached to your computer and how they're separated into partitions. Disk 0 is my internal hard disk (as you can see, one of the partitions is *C:*), and Disk 1 is a USB disk (one of those partitions is *D:*). On my computer, Disk 1 has a single 32GB partition, as well as about 86GB of unallocated space.

Find the USB disk you need to format. Right-click on every partition and choose **Delete Volume** until you've deleted all the partitions on the disk. Then right-click on the unallocated space in your disk and choose **New Simple Volume**, which should open a wizard to help you create the volume. Choose the full amount of disk space and format it as NTFS. The wizard will ask you for a *volume label*, which is just a name for your partition; in Figure 1-4, the label for *D:* is *data*. I recommend calling this disk *datasets*.

Once the disk is formatted, click **Start**, search for **bitlocker**, and open **Manage BitLocker**. You should now see your USB disk and have the option to turn on BitLocker. When you enable BitLocker on your USB disk, a window should pop up asking how you would like to unlock this drive. Choose **Use a Password to Unlock the Drive**, then copy and paste your USB disk encryption passphrase from your password manager into the password field. You'll need to paste it into the field to re-enter the password as well. When you enable BitLocker, you'll be required to save a recovery key to a file. Since you're saving the passphrase in a password manager, however, you don't need your recovery key, and you can delete the file.

### VeraCrypt

If you use Windows Home and don't have BitLocker available on your computer, use VeraCrypt to encrypt your USB disk.

If you don't already have VeraCrypt, download it from *https://veracrypt.fr*, install it on your computer, and open it. Click **Create Volume** to open the VeraCrypt Volume Creation Wizard. On the first page of the wizard, VeraCrypt lets you choose from three types of encrypted volumes. Select **Encrypt a Non-system Partition/Drive** and click **Next**.

On the Volume Type page, VeraCrypt asks if you want a standard volume or a hidden one. Select **Standard VeraCrypt Volume** and click **Next**. On the Volume Location page, click **Select Device**, choose the USB disk you want to encrypt, and click **Next**. On the Volume Creation Mode page, select **Create Encrypted Volume and Format It** and click **Next**. On the Encryption Options page, use the default settings and click **Next**. You can't do anything on the Volume Size page, since you're encrypting a whole partition rather than creating an encrypted file container, so just click **Next**.

On the Volume Password page, copy and paste your USB disk encryption passphrase from your password manager into the Password field, and paste it again into the Confirm field. Then click **Next**. On the Large Files page, VeraCrypt asks if you intend to store files larger than 4GB in your VeraCrypt volume. Select **Yes** and click **Next**. On the Volume Format page, under the Filesystem drop-down menu, select **exFAT** and check the box next to **Quick Format**. VeraCrypt also includes a feature where you move your mouse around the window randomly so that it can collect information from your mouse movements to make the encryption more secure. Move your mouse around until the bar at the bottom of the screen is green, and then click **Format**.

A window should pop up, warning you that all of the data on your USB disk will be erased and asking if you're sure you want to proceed. Click **Yes**, and then wait while VeraCrypt creates an encrypted partition on your USB disk. As long as you selected Quick Format on the previous page, this should only take a few seconds. On the Volume Created page, click **Exit** to exit the wizard and get back to the main VeraCrypt window.

After you encrypt a USB disk with VeraCrypt, you need to use VeraCrypt to *mount* it, or make it available on your computer as a drive letter. In the main VeraCrypt window, select an available drive letter (such as *F:*), click **Select Device**, select your VeraCrypt-encrypted USB disk, and click **OK**, then **Mount**. After you provide the encryption passphrase to unlock it, VeraCrypt will mount your encrypted USB disk so you can use it. Now any files that you save to this drive will be stored encrypted on disk.

Before unplugging your USB disk, unmount it by selecting the drive letter in VeraCrypt and clicking **Dismount**.

**NOTE** *VeraCrypt also comes in handy if you need to access the same encrypted disk across operating systems—for example, if you need to use it on both a Windows PC and a Mac. However, for the purposes of this book, only Windows users who don't have BitLocker should use VeraCrypt. In general, you'll have fewer headaches if you stick with the disk encryption software built into your operating system.*

### macOS

Open the Disk Utility app, which you can find in the *Applications/Utilities* folder. This app lists all of the disks attached to your computer and lets you format them.

In Disk Utility, select the USB disk you plugged in and click the **Erase** button. Name the disk *datasets* and choose **APFS (Encrypted)** for format. You will then be prompted for the password to unlock the encrypted disk. Copy and paste the USB disk encryption passphrase that you created at the beginning of this exercise from your password manager into Disk Utility. Disk Utility will also prompt you for a password hint, but because you're saving this passphrase in your password manager and not bothering to memorize it anyway, you can leave the password hint blank.

### Linux

Open the Disks app as you did in Exercise 1-1. Select your USB disk in the list of disks on the left, then click the menu button and choose **Format Disk**. This will delete all of the data on the USB.

Click the + button to add a new partition and set the partition size to the largest option. Name your disk *datasets*, choose **Internal Disk for Use with Linux Systems Only**, and check the box **Password Protect Volume (LUKS)**. It will prompt you to enter a password. Copy and paste the USB disk encryption passphrase that you created at the beginning of this exercise from your password manager into Disks.

## Protecting Yourself from Malicious Documents

Before you start working with any datasets on your encrypted USB disk, you should know how to protect yourself from any potentially malicious documents they may contain.

Have you ever been told to avoid opening email attachments from unknown senders? This is solid computer security advice, but unfortunately for researchers, journalists, activists, and many other people, it's impossible to follow. In these lines of work, it's often your *job* to open documents from strangers, including leaked or hacked datasets.

Opening documents you don't trust is dangerous because it may allow others to hack your computer. PDFs and Microsoft Office or LibreOffice documents are incredibly complex. They can be made to automatically load an image from a remote server, tracking when a document is opened and from what IP address. They can contain JavaScript or macros that, depending on how your software is configured, could automatically execute code when opened, potentially taking over your computer. And like all software, the programs you use to open documents, like Microsoft Office and Adobe Reader, have bugs, which can sometimes be exploited to take over your computer.

This is exactly what Russian military intelligence did during the 2016 US election, for example. First, the Main Directorate of the General Staff of the Armed Forces of the Russian Federation (GRU) hacked a US election vendor known as VR Systems and got its client list of election workers in swing states. It then sent 122 email messages to VR Systems' clients from the email address *vrelections@gmail.com*, with the attachment *New EViD User Guides.docm*. If any of the election workers who got this email opened the attachment using a vulnerable version of Microsoft Word in Windows, the malware would have created a backdoor into their computer for the Russian hackers. (We don't know for sure whether any of the targets opened the malicious attachment.)

Sending malicious email to specific targets in this way as part of a hacking operation is called *spearphishing*. Figure 1-5 shows a spearphishing email message targeting an election worker in North Carolina, which The Intercept obtained using a public records request.

In 2017, Reality Winner leaked a classified document describing this spearphishing attack to The Intercept. Thanks to her whistleblowing, the public knows considerably more about Russia's attacks on the US election in 2016 than it otherwise would. In fact, US states like North Carolina learned that they were under attack by Russian hackers only by *reading The Intercept*. In 2022, two former election officials told *60 Minutes* that Reality Winner's disclosure helped secure the 2018 midterm elections against similar hacking attempts.

To make it safer to open untrusted documents, I developed an open source app called Dangerzone. When you open an untrusted document in Dangerzone, the app converts it into a *known-safe* PDF—one that you can be confident is safe. Using technology called *Linux containers*—which are like quick, small, self-contained Linux computers running inside your normal computer—it converts the original document into a PDF if it's not already one, splits the PDF into different pages, and converts each page into raw pixel data. Then, in another Linux container, it converts the pixel data back into a PDF. You can also ask Dangerzone to use *optical character recognition (OCR)* technology—software that looks at an image of text and figures out what the characters are—to add a text layer back to the PDF so you can still search the text.

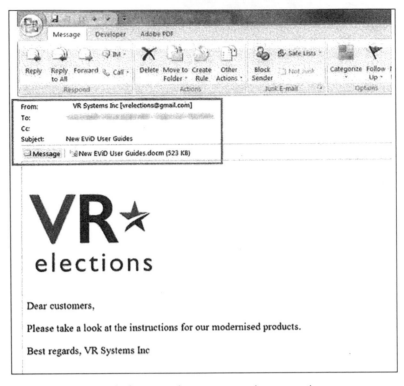

Figure 1-5: A spearphishing email targeting an election worker

Dangerzone is essentially the digital equivalent of printing out a document and rescanning it, stripping anything malicious from it, and removing the original document's digital metadata. If you opened the malicious *New EViD User Guides.docm* document using Dangerzone, it would create a new document called *New EViD User Guides-safe.pdf*. You could then safely open this PDF without risk. As an added benefit, you don't need internet access to use Dangerzone, so it works well on air-gapped computers.

You'll learn more about Dangerzone and Linux containers in Chapter 5, which covers how to make datasets searchable. In the meantime, Exercise 1-3 will show you how to get started with it.

## Exercise 1-3: Install and Use Dangerzone

In this exercise, you'll install Dangerzone and use it to convert documents into known-safe versions. Figure 1-6 shows a screenshot of Dangerzone in action—in this case, converting the untrusted document *D&D 5e - Players Handbook.pdf* to a known-safe version called *D&D 5e - Players Handbook-safe .pdf*, which is also OCR'd and searchable.

Figure 1-6: Dangerzone in action

Download and install Dangerzone from *https://dangerzone.rocks*. The app relies on Linux containers. If you're working on a Windows or macOS machine, the easiest way to get containers running is to use software called Docker Desktop, which you'll be prompted to install the first time you open Dangerzone. (You don't need to do anything with Docker Desktop for now; simply install and open it. You'll learn more about Docker in Chapter 5.)

Now that Dangerzone is installed, try it out. Open any PDF, Microsoft Office document, LibreOffice document, or image on your computer in Dangerzone and convert it to a safe PDF. If someone attaches a document to an email and you don't trust it, download a copy of it first, open Dangerzone, and click **Select Suspicious Documents**. Then browse for the document you downloaded and use Dangerzone to convert it into a known-safe version.

---

### VIRTUAL MACHINES

Another option, which is a bit more complicated, is setting up a *virtual machine (VM)*. VMs are like a stronger version of Linux containers. They isolate the software running inside the VM more than Linux containers can, and they can run on any operating system. If you choose this option, make sure to disable internet access in your VM before opening documents. This way, if the document is malicious, it won't let any attackers know the document was opened.

Giving detailed instructions on using VMs is outside the scope of this book. However, if you want to try them on your own, the easiest way to get started is to use the free and open source virtualization software VirtualBox (*https://www.virtualbox.org*). VirtualBox works for Intel-based Macs, Linux, and Windows computers. At the time of writing, there's a beta version of VirtualBox that supports Apple Silicon Macs, but it has issues. If you have an Apple Silicon Mac,

*(continued)*

> UTM (*https://mac.getutm.app*) is a good choice. It's free and open source, and you can find detailed instructions for installing different operating systems at *https://docs.getutm.app/guides/guides/*. If you'd like something a bit easier, I recommend you try Parallels (*https://www.parallels.com*) or VMware Fusion (*https://www.vmware.com/products/fusion.html*) instead; note, however, that neither is free.

Dangerzone works great with PDFs and Word documents, but not so great with spreadsheets. No matter what type of file you open in Dangerzone, you always end up with a safe PDF, and spreadsheets really aren't meant to be read in that format.

If Dangerzone doesn't do a good enough job with a document you'd like to read, you can open it a few other ways while containing the damage. If you don't believe the document is sensitive, upload it to Google Drive and open it there, using Google's web interface. This way, technically Google is opening the malicious document on its computers instead of you opening it on yours.

## Summary

In this chapter, you've learned how to think about source protection in today's world of widespread digital surveillance. You've also learned about securely storing datasets, depending on their sensitivity; verifying that your datasets are authentic; and redacting information from documents before you publish your final report. You started using a password manager to keep your passwords safe, and you encrypted your internal disk and set up your encrypted *datasets* USB disk. Finally, you practiced turning potentially malicious documents into ones you know are safe to open using Dangerzone.

In the next chapter, you'll put your *datasets* disk to good use by downloading your first hacked dataset.

# 2

## ACQUIRING DATASETS

In early January 2010, 22-year-old Chelsea Manning sat at a Windows computer in a temporary Sensitive Compartmented Information Facility (SCIF)—an enclosed area or room suitable for working with secret documents—in eastern Baghdad. She was downloading half a million secret "significant activity" reports from the military network SIPRNet, a Department of Defense computer network used for transmitting classified information.

As an intelligence analyst working for the US Army, Manning needed regular access to these databases, so she downloaded them for work purposes. Having a local copy would be useful in a war zone where network access can be unreliable. It wasn't until later that month that she decided to leak them to the public, after realizing they documented American war crimes in Iraq and Afghanistan. They would soon become some of the most significant public datasets of the 21st century. "I believe that if the general public, especially the American public, had access to the information contained within the [Iraq War Logs and Afghan War Logs], this could spark a domestic debate on the role of the military and our foreign policy in general," she later said at her court martial hearing.

At the SCIF computer, Manning compressed the files using a program called WinRAR, burned them to a rewritable CD, and left them in the SCIF for easy reference. A few weeks later, at the end of her shift on a Friday night, she slipped the CD into her cargo pocket and headed to her dorm, where she copied the data to her laptop. Eventually, she copied it to the SD card in her digital camera, and on January 23 she flew into the Reagan National Airport just outside of Washington, DC, with the SD card in hand.

In 2010, massive leaks like this were unprecedented. Today, they happen all the time. Back then, WikiLeaks was the only place for sources to go—traditional newsrooms weren't prepared to handle leaks like this. Now, however, there are lots of options: sources can send documents to a transparency collective like Distributed Denial of Secrets (DDoSecrets), they can contact journalists directly using tools like Signal and OnionShare, or they can get in touch with a newsroom by following instructions on its public tips page.

In this chapter, you'll learn best practices for safely acquiring public and private datasets. You'll learn more about the history of WikiLeaks and DDoSecrets, then use a technology called BitTorrent to obtain your own copy of the BlueLeaks dataset from DDoSecrets. You'll download the Signal instant messaging app to securely communicate with sources and learn about PGP encryption, an alternative method of securing messages. You'll practice sending data anonymously with Tor and OnionShare, then read the story of how I communicated with a source using several of these tools. Finally, I'll outline several more ways to securely receive data from sources, including techniques appropriate for professional newsrooms rather than individual reporters.

## The End of WikiLeaks

After deciding she wanted to leak the War Logs, Manning first called a reporter at the *Washington Post*, but she didn't feel like they took her seriously. She tried the *New York Times* but managed only to leave a voicemail, and the paper never returned her call. Finally, she settled on WikiLeaks, a leak site founded in 2006 by Australian information activist Julian Assange. This turned out to be a great choice at the time. In addition to publishing the documents, WikiLeaks worked in partnership with newspapers across the world, including the *New York Times*, the *Guardian*, and *Der Spiegel*, to break major stories about US imperialism. Along with the dataset of 250,000 State Department cables known as Cablegate, the two datasets that Manning leaked were a catalyst for the Arab Spring, the 2011 pro-democracy movement that led to the toppling of governments in the Middle East and North Africa, including the authoritarian regimes in Egypt and Tunisia.

Back then, WikiLeaks was revolutionary, initiating the document-based transparency movement by making massive datasets accessible to the public. The documents that Manning leaked were its first major releases with international consequences, making WikiLeaks a proof-of-concept for sites that allow anyone to anonymously submit leaked documents. Today, nearly every major newsroom in the US and many throughout the world have this capability using open source software like SecureDrop, though news organizations rarely publish raw datasets like WikiLeaks did.

Manning sent these datasets to WikiLeaks several years before the transparency group and its editor, Assange, shifted from a journalism outfit based on the premise that "information wants to be free" to an ethically dubious political organization working to get Donald Trump elected president in 2016. During that US election, WikiLeaks and Assange went off the rails. The group published a dataset full of hacked Democratic National Committee (DNC) and Clinton campaign email messages just in time to distract the news cycle from the infamous *Access Hollywood* audio clip of Trump bragging about committing sexual assault. Assange lied to the public about his source for this data (it was Russian military intelligence), boosting the conspiracy theory that Seth Rich, an unrelated Democratic Party staffer who was murdered in Washington, DC, was his real source. WikiLeaks also promoted the Pizzagate conspiracy theory claiming that high-ranking Democratic Party officials were involved in a child sex-trafficking ring run out of a pizza shop in DC.

Today, WikiLeaks is little more than an X (formerly Twitter) account. Its document submission systems have stopped working, and its website is no longer maintained. The loss of WikiLeaks to the online fever swamp was tragic for investigative journalism around the world, but a new and better organization has grown to take its place: DDoSecrets.

## Distributed Denial of Secrets

Distributed Denial of Secrets, or DDoSecrets, is a nonprofit transparency collective in the US founded by Emma Best in 2018. It's similar to WikiLeaks, but without the toxic ego of Julian Assange and with considerably more transparency around the group's decision-making, and it's largely run by queer people.

DDoSecrets hosts data previously published by WikiLeaks, like the DNC Emails dataset, as well as those WikiLeaks declined to publish, like the Dark Side of the Kremlin dataset, which contains over 100GB of documents and emails from Russian oligarchs and politicians. Notably, it also hosts a great deal of data leaked in the months following Russia's invasion of Ukraine in February 2022. At that time, hackers—mostly claiming to be hacktivists, many identifying with the Anonymous hacktivist movement—bombarded Russia with cyberattacks. They hacked dozens of Russian organizations, including government agencies, oil and gas companies, and finance institutions, and submitted tens of terabytes of data to DDoSecrets to distribute to the public and to journalists.

**NOTE** *I work closely with DDoSecrets as an adviser and sometimes volunteer.*

Anyone can download the following datasets from DDoSecrets:

### BlueLeaks

BlueLeaks is a collection of 270GB of documents from hundreds of US law enforcement and police fusion center websites, released during the height of 2020's Black Lives Matter uprising. You'll know this dataset well by the end of this book, and you'll download a copy of it in this chapter's first exercise.

### Parler

The Parler dataset contains 32TB (yes, terabytes) of video scraped from the right-wing social network Parler, including many from the January 6, 2021, anti-democracy riot at the US Capitol. Many of these videos were used as evidence in Donald Trump's second impeachment inquiry. You'll learn more about this dataset in Chapter 11.

### Epik Fail

The Epik Fail dataset includes 10 years of domain name registrar data from Epik, a company that's notorious for hosting domain names and websites for neo-Nazis and other extremist groups. You'll explore this dataset in Chapter 12.

In addition to public datasets like these, DDoSecrets hosts many private datasets available only to journalists and researchers who request access. Datasets containing large quantities of PII, like names, email addresses, birth dates, or passwords, are often kept private. For example, the Oath Keepers dataset includes gigabytes of data from the American far-right paramilitary organization, including spreadsheets full of the group's member and donor records. That part of the release is limited only to journalists and researchers who request access, but another part, 5GB of email and chat logs, is available to the public. You'll download part of this release in Chapter 4 and work with it in Chapter 6.

DDoSecrets publishes many more datasets than these, and it continues to release new ones all the time. For an inventory of all of those available, as well as instructions on how to request access to the limited-distribution datasets, visit *https://ddosecrets.com*.

**NOTE** *You won't be able to share that DDoSecrets link on X. Shortly after DDoSecrets released BlueLeaks, Twitter permanently suspended the @DDoSecrets account and censored all links to* https://ddosecrets.com, *citing its selectively enforced policy against posting hacked data. Twitter, now X, prevents tweets or even DMs including DDoSecrets links from going through, though WikiLeaks has faced no such censorship.*

DDoSecrets distributes public datasets using a protocol called BitTorrent. To download datasets, you'll need to learn how to use it.

## Downloading Datasets with BitTorrent

At the turn of the 21st century, long before services like Netflix and Spotify made online entertainment cheap and accessible to the public, peer-to-peer file-sharing services like Napster, LimeWire, and Kazaa enjoyed immense popularity because they made downloading pirated media and software so easy. The copyright industry quickly shut down these centralized services with lawsuits, but decentralized technologies rose from their ashes. The most popular of these is BitTorrent. In addition to piracy, BitTorrent is also frequently used to legally distribute large files like Linux operating systems, as well as massive datasets.

BitTorrent works well for sharing controversial data like BlueLeaks, because no one—not the US government, police departments, tech companies, internet service providers, or anyone else—can easily censor it. Traditionally, one computer on the internet hosts data (on a website, for example), and all other computers connect to that host to download it. If someone wants to censor that data, they only have to bring down that single host. With BitTorrent, however, data is hosted in *swarms*, a collection of computers currently sharing a specific set of files. If you want to download some data, you join the swarm by opening a link to the data, called a *torrent*, in your BitTorrent software and become a *peer*. Your BitTorrent software downloads pieces of the data that you need from other peers in the swarm, and in return, you upload pieces of data you already have to peers who need it. Once you have all of the data you need, you can remain in the swarm and continue sharing with peers as long as you keep your BitTorrent software open, making you a *seed*. If you have the internet bandwidth and are allowed to share the files, it's generally good practice to keep seeding, especially if there are few other seeds.

Every BitTorrent swarm needs to have at least one seed in order to enable the peers to finish downloading all the data. The more popular the data, the bigger the swarm, the faster the downloads—and the more difficult censorship becomes. It's hard to block access to every peer in a swarm (swarms can grow to have tens of thousands of peers), and nothing stops more peers from joining. There's no single entity to sue or pressure financially. Swarms often consist of computers distributed around the world, so national laws also can't achieve the censorship they might otherwise aim for.

There is nothing illegal about using BitTorrent to share files that you're legally allowed to share. Blizzard Entertainment has even adopted the technology itself to distribute large video games like *World of Warcraft* to its users, and the Internet Archive, the nonprofit digital library at *https://archive.org*, uses BitTorrent to distribute large files like radio and TV shows. The structure of BitTorrent hosting makes for faster downloads, and bandwidth costs are shared throughout the swarm.

Most publicly available DDoSecrets datasets are distributed through BitTorrent. In order to download something with BitTorrent, you'll need the following:

- A program installed in your computer called a *BitTorrent client*. You can use whatever client you prefer, including a command line version, but I like one called Transmission. It's free and open source and works great in Windows, macOS, and Linux.

- Either a *.torrent* file that you can open in your BitTorrent client or a *magnet link*, a type of URL that starts with *magnet:* and tells your BitTorrent client where to find the full *.torrent* file.

- Roughly 1TB of storage space, at least if you want to download the datasets used in this book. I recommend downloading to the encrypted *datasets* USB disk that you set up in Exercise 1-2.

In a moment, you'll use BitTorrent to download a copy of the BlueLeaks dataset, but first let's take a look at where that data originated.

## The Origins of BlueLeaks

The disparate surveillance systems of local, state, and federal law enforcement agencies in the United States collected enough intelligence to learn critical clues about the September 11, 2001, terrorist attack before it happened. However, each agency kept this information to itself, failing to prevent the attack. Afterward, the US government decided these agencies needed to improve how they share information with each other. Congress directed the newly formed Department of Homeland Security (DHS) to create *fusion centers* across the country, collaborations between federal agencies like the DHS and FBI with state and local police departments, to share intelligence and prevent future terrorist attacks. These fusion centers are the source of much of the BlueLeaks data.

According to a 2012 Senate report, these fusion centers have "not produced useful intelligence to support Federal counterterrorism efforts," and the intelligence reports they produced were "oftentimes shoddy, rarely timely, sometimes endangering citizens' civil liberties and Privacy Act protections, occasionally taken from already-published public sources, and more often than not unrelated to terrorism." Fusion centers had also been caught infiltrating and spying on anti-war activists, and in 2008, the American Civil Liberties Union published a report about fusion center abuses, including spying on religious groups in violation of the First Amendment.

In June 2020, a hacktivist self-identifying with the Anonymous movement hacked 251 law enforcement websites, most of them fusion centers and related organizations. The hacked data, known as BlueLeaks, includes thousands of police documents and spreadsheets with over 16 million rows of data. The data spans from 2007 to June 14, 2020, when the Black Lives Matter uprising triggered by the police murder of George Floyd was in full swing.

While the hacktivist from Anonymous violated the law when they broke into these police websites and stole all this data, in the US it's legal for you to download BlueLeaks, investigate it, and publish your findings.

## Exercise 2-1: Download the BlueLeaks Dataset

In this exercise, you'll download a local copy of the BlueLeaks dataset onto the 1TB USB disk you encrypted in the previous chapter. You'll be investigating the contents of this dataset later in the book.

Download Transmission (*https://transmissionbt.com*) or any BitTorrent client of your choice and install it on your computer following the instructions for your operating system. Load the BlueLeaks page on the DDoSecrets website at *https://ddosecrets.com/wiki/BlueLeaks*. From there, find the magnet link for the BlueLeaks torrent and copy that to your clipboard.

Next, open Transmission. Click **File ▸ Open Torrent Address**, paste the magnet link, and click **Open** to start downloading the data. When you first add this torrent to your client, it will ask where you want to save it. Save it to your *datasets* USB disk, then sit back and watch BitTorrent do its thing. It should connect you to the swarm, start downloading chunks of BlueLeaks from other peers (while possibly uploading chunks to other peers as well), and alert you when it's done downloading. When the download completes, you'll be seeding the BlueLeaks torrent and letting others download from you, until you remove the torrent from Transmission.

The 269GB download might take several hours, or even days if you have a slow internet connection. While you're waiting, read on.

## Communicating with Encrypted Messaging Apps

Most ways you communicate online aren't very secure, even when you send messages that are ostensibly private. This is fine if you're discussing non-sensitive information over Slack, SMS messages, or DMs on social media. However, when communicating with a confidential source who might face retaliation for talking with you, you should always use an encrypted messaging app.

Among encrypted messaging apps like WhatsApp and iMessage, Signal stands out as the best choice for source communications. Unlike other apps, Signal can't be forced to share most information about its users with law enforcement or leak investigators, because it can't access that user data in the first place. The only information the company can retrieve is the date that a user created their Signal account and the date that account most recently connected to Signal. Not even those who might typically be able to spy on your communications, like the messaging app's employees, cloud hosting provider, or internet monitoring agencies, can access your Signal messages. Signal is the primary app I use for sensitive work communication, as well as for personal messaging. If I start out chatting with people on other platforms—SMS, DMs on social media, or anything else—I tend to move the conversation to Signal as soon as possible.

In more detail, here's how Signal ensures that it has as little information about its users as possible:

- Since messages and calls are *end-to-end encrypted*, the Signal service can't access their contents. This means if you type a Signal message to me on your phone (your end) and hit send, the Signal app will encrypt it for me, or in other words, create a totally scrambled version of the message so that it's impossible for anyone but me to unscramble it. The encrypted message then goes to Signal's servers, which forward it to my phone (my end). Once it's on my phone, the Signal app can then decrypt it so I can read the original message. Signal's servers themselves never have access to the original message, only the encrypted version, and they never have the ability to decrypt it—only message recipients do.

- Signal servers don't store metadata, the records of when you send messages and to whom. They also can't access your list of contacts or even the name and avatar associated with your own phone number.

- Signal invented a technology called *sealed sender* that uses cryptography to prevent anyone besides you and the recipient of your message from knowing whom you're communicating with. Even if Signal secretly wanted to store your metadata (or if someone hacked Signal's servers to monitor for metadata), they still wouldn't have access to it.

- Signal doesn't know which phone numbers are part of which Signal groups, or any metadata about the group, such as its name or avatar.

Signal's code is open source, which lets experts inspect it for flaws and backdoors, and its encryption protocol has been peer reviewed by cryptography experts.

Signal's security protocols stand in stark contrast to those of other encrypted messaging apps. WhatsApp, for example, routinely shares metadata with law enforcement, like exactly which phone numbers a surveillance target communicates with and when the target has used them. WhatsApp can even share this data in real time, allowing it to be used as evidence against whistleblowers like Treasury Department employee Natalie Mayflower Sours Edwards, mentioned in Chapter 1. When she was indicted in 2018 and accused of sharing a secret dataset to BuzzFeed journalist Jason Leopold, the evidence against her included real-time metadata from an encrypted messaging app. The metadata showed Edwards and Leopold exchanging hundreds of messages right as Leopold published multiple articles based on this dataset. Edwards and Leopold would have been better off if they had used Signal.

**NOTE**  *The web page* https://signal.org/bigbrother/ *lists the handful of times that Signal has been ordered to share data with law enforcement and how they responded. In all cases, Signal either didn't share any data (because, as the organization says, "It's impossible to turn over data that we never had access to in the first place") or shared only the date that the target Signal account was created and the date that it most recently connected to the service.*

For additional security, you can compare Signal *safety numbers* with another Signal user, allowing you to verify that the end-to-end encryption with that person is secure and isn't being actively tampered with by the Signal service, your internet service provider, or anyone else. From a Signal conversation, you can tap on the name of the person you're talking to at the top, then tap **View Safety Number**. This should show you your safety number, both as a number and as a QR code. If your safety number is the same as the other person's, you can be sure that the end-to-end encryption is secure. If you're physically in the same room, you can both use the safety number screen to scan each other's QR codes to confirm. To confirm remotely, you can copy the safety number and paste it into a different messaging app (not Signal), then send it to the same person. If you confirm that your safety number matches, tap **Mark as Verified**. Once you've verified your safety number with a contact, Signal will make it clear that it's verified and warn you if it ever changes—this could mean the encryption is under attack, but more likely it just means the person you're talking to got a new phone, and you'll have to verify them again.

Once Signal messages are on your device, they're only as safe as your phone itself. Leak investigators searching your phone or your source's phone will have access to all the messages on each device. To protect against device searches, always use Signal's disappearing messages feature, which automatically deletes messages a set amount of time after you view them, unless you have a good reason to retain messages for a specific conversation. You can choose to delete messages anywhere between 30 seconds and 4 weeks after viewing, or set a custom time. I typically set disappearing messages to 4 weeks, change it to an hour or so if I'm sending secret information like a password, and then change it back to 4 weeks. In your Signal privacy settings, I recommend choosing to make all new conversations start with disappearing messages. You should also take steps to lock down your phone itself, like using a strong random passcode so that no one but you can easily unlock your device.

Signal is not only very secure but also very easy to use. Any two people with the app installed can send each other encrypted text messages, share encrypted files, and make encrypted voice and video calls or group chats for multiple users.

## Exercise 2-2: Install and Practice Using Signal

In this exercise, you'll install Signal on your phone and computer and practice using it.

Start with your phone: open the iPhone App Store or the Android Play Store and download the Signal Private Messenger app. After you open the app, you'll need to verify your phone number and set a PIN (save this PIN in your password manager). Signal will also request some permissions. In my opinion, it's perfectly safe to grant all of them. Signal uses the Contacts permission to discover which of your contacts also use the app, but in such a way that it can't access your contact list itself. (If you grant access to your contacts, the app will notify you when one of them creates a Signal account.)

Next, download Signal on your computer from *https://signal.org.* After installing it, you'll need to scan a QR code from your phone to set up your computer as a linked device. Keep in mind that your Signal messages will now be copied to both devices, so make sure to keep them both secure.

To practice sending encrypted messages, get some friends to install Signal too. Send them messages, play with disappearing messages, and try out encrypted voice calls and video calls. If you have enough friends on Signal, start a Signal group.

## Encrypting Messages with PGP

In addition to communicating via secure messaging apps, you can also encrypt messages with PGP ("pretty good privacy") encryption. This encryption method was first developed in 1991 to encrypt email. It has historically been very important in securely communicating with sources and other journalists; I used it extensively while reporting on the Snowden Archive. Compared to modern encrypted messaging apps like Signal, PGP is complicated and error-prone, so I recommend that you avoid it if you can and choose one of the better alternatives instead. However, you may find it useful in future investigations if one of your sources uses it.

PGP works like this: a user creates a file on their computer called a *PGP key*, which can be split into two parts, a *public key* and a *secret key*. If you have a copy of this user's public key, you can use it to encrypt a message so that it can be decrypted only with that secret key. You can then email this scrambled message to the PGP user with the secret key. If anyone else gets access to that email, the message is scrambled and they can't read it. When the person with the secret key checks it, though, they can decrypt it and read the original message.

People sometimes still send me PGP-encrypted email, and I use PGP to respond to them securely. You can find my PGP public key on my personal website, *https://micahflee.com.* I keep my PGP secret key on a USB device called a YubiKey, which looks kind of like a USB stick with a button on it. YubiKeys (and other security keys) are mainly used to lock down online accounts. Even if a hacker knows the username and password to my Google account, for example, they won't be able to log in without first physically stealing my YubiKey, plugging it into their computer, and pressing its button while they try to log in. YubiKeys can also be used to securely store PGP secret keys.

## Staying Anonymous Online with Tor and OnionShare

Tor and OnionShare are both important tools for working with sources who want to send you data anonymously and for conducting investigations where you need to remain anonymous yourself.

Tor is a decentralized network of volunteer servers called *nodes*. It keeps you anonymous online by bouncing your internet connection through a series of these nodes. Tor Browser is a web browser that sends all web traffic through the Tor network. Using Tor Browser works much like using Chrome or Firefox. Let's say you want to anonymously visit the Organized Crime and Corruption Reporting Project's (OCCRP) website at *https://www.occrp .org*. You simply open Tor Browser (which you can download from *https:// www.torproject.org*), wait for it to connect to the Tor network, type **occrp.org** in the address bar, and hit ENTER, and the page will load.

NOTE    *I've been a volunteer in the Tor community for a long time, attending the nonprofit's physical gatherings around the world, sometimes running Tor nodes to contribute to the network, and developing software related to Tor.*

Tor Browser operates more slowly than a normal browser, because it bounces your web traffic between three random Tor nodes around the world before sending it to the OCCRP website. No single node knows both your real IP address, which would reveal your location, and what website you're visiting. This means you don't need to trust the nodes to use them. Even if a Tor node is run by criminals or spies, they won't be able to de-anonymize you, at least not without exploiting a vulnerability in the Tor network itself. When you close Tor Browser, everything about your browsing session gets deleted without leaving a trace on your local computer.

Since Tor allows users to be anonymous online, people routinely use it for hacking websites, creating accounts to spam or phish people, or engaging in similar activities. For this reason, plenty of websites (including Google) are often extremely suspicious of Tor traffic and make Tor users jump through additional hurdles like filling out CAPTCHAs or even blocking them altogether. Unfortunately, this is the price of online anonymity.

In addition to allowing internet users to remain anonymous, Tor can keep servers themselves anonymous. These servers are called Tor *onion services* (sometimes referred to as the *dark web*) and have domain names ending in *.onion*. You can load onion services only by using Tor. Like Tor Browser, onion services also pick three random Tor nodes to route their traffic through. When a user loads an onion site in Tor Browser, it actually requires six hops through the Tor network: three on the Tor Browser side and three on the onion service side.

NOTE    *The .onion domain name is derived from a cryptographic fingerprint of the public key that belongs to the onion service. The Tor protocol ensures that no one else can use that same name without knowing that onion service's secret key.*

OnionShare, which I first developed in 2014 and have been adding features to ever since, is software that makes it easy for anyone to run onion services, allowing them to anonymously and securely send and receive files. It runs a web server directly on your computer, makes that server accessible to others as an onion service, and shows you a *.onion* address to send to someone else. When you start an OnionShare service, you can choose between Share mode, which allows others to download specific files from your computer, or Receive mode, which allows others to upload files to your computer.

OnionShare also supports other modes. With Chat mode, for instance, you can spin up an anonymous chatroom. It doesn't have as many features as a Signal group, but it keeps you significantly more anonymous. With Website mode, you can quickly host a *static website*—a simple website made up of HTML files and resources like images and JavaScript, but without any databases or code running on the server—as an onion service. If someone loads that address in Tor Browser, their connection bounces through the Tor network until it reaches your computer, then loads the website hosted by OnionShare.

Figure 2-1 shows the OnionShare software configured as an anonymous dropbox, allowing my URL recipient (such as a source) to anonymously and securely upload files directly to my computer.

*Figure 2-1: OnionShare in Receive mode*

For example, to use OnionShare to let a source send me data, I'd open OnionShare on my computer, connect to the Tor network, click **Receive Files**, and then click **Start Receive Mode**. The service would give me a URL like *http://ic2kaoao3fspynexwxlajxhb3zwcwrjuf57ykfuq7tsrhzlveeamkrid.onion*. I would send that URL to my source and wait. My source would then open Tor Browser; load that URL, which would load a website hosted directly on my computer; and then upload their files. Because OnionShare uses Tor, I'd have no way of learning my source's IP address, and my source would have no way of learning mine.

Figure 2-2 shows what that web page would look like for my source.

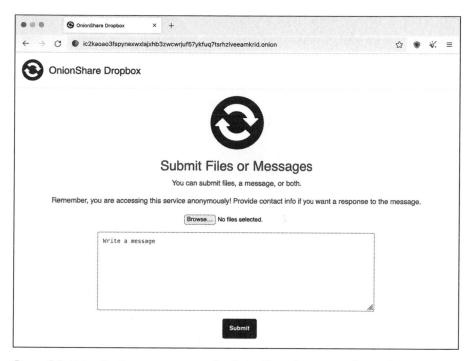

*Figure 2-2: Using Tor Browser to access the OnionShare Receive mode site shown in Figure 2-1*

The URL I sent to my source starts with *http://* and not *https://*. HTTPS encrypts traffic between the web browser and the web server; normally, with just plain HTTP, anyone monitoring the network can spy on exactly what you're doing, what files your uploading, and what passwords you're submitting into forms. Onion services are an exception to this rule, though, since the connection between Tor Browser and an onion service is already end-to-end encrypted. It's possible to add HTTPS to an onion service, but doing so would be redundant and unnecessary. Also notice that the domain name part of the URL in Figure 2-2 is 56 random-looking letters and numbers followed by *.onion*. Unlike with normal domain names, you don't get to choose onion service names. They all look like this.

OnionShare runs a web server directly on your computer. This means third-party companies don't have access to any of the files that are shared in it, but also that you have to time things right. If I sent that OnionShare link and then closed my laptop so it went to sleep, my source wouldn't be able to load the website until I woke my computer up again. OnionShare works best when you're working with people in real time. However, because it uses the Tor network, it's really slow. It might take many hours or even days to transfer gigabytes of data. To transfer especially large datasets, consider using a non-Tor method like those described later in this chapter.

**NOTE** *For more information, read the detailed documentation for OnionShare at* https://docs.onionshare.org.

If you're using OnionShare to send sensitive data, I recommend that you share OnionShare URLs only using encrypted messaging apps like Signal and avoid sending them over insecure communication channels like email or social media DMs. This will prevent anyone who has access to those insecure channels from loading the OnionShare URL first or modifying the OnionShare URL to trick your source into uploading documents to them, for example.

## Exercise 2-3: Play with Tor and OnionShare

In this exercise, you'll install Tor Browser and OnionShare on your computer and practice using them. Download OnionShare from *https://onionshare.org* and Tor Browser from *https://www.torproject.org*, and follow the instructions for your operating system.

Open Tor Browser, search for anything you like, and visit various websites to see how the online experience differs. The default Tor Browser search engine is DuckDuckGo, which works great over Tor. However, you'll find that it's frustrating to use Google, because it constantly forces you to prove you're not a robot by filling out CAPTCHAs. Several websites have both *clearnet* versions (those accessible using normal web browsers) and *.onion* versions. If you're using Tor Browser and visit a website that supports both, like *https://freedom.press*, you'll see the .onion available button in the top right of the address bar. Clicking it should bring you to the onion version of that site.

Figure 2-3 shows the Freedom of the Press Foundation's website in Tor Browser with the .onion available button.

*Figure 2-3: The Freedom of the Press Foundation home page*

Next, try using OnionShare. Open a Share Files tab, browse for some files on your computer, and start the service. Then open Tor Browser, load the OnionShare URL, and download those files. Test out small files, large files, and different settings. Then try setting up an anonymous dropbox to receive files: open OnionShare, open a Receive Files tab, and start the service. In Tor Browser, load the OnionShare URL and upload files to your computer. Again, test out small files, large files, and different settings.

## Communicating with My Tea Party Patriots Source

This section describes a real-world example of how I gathered data from an anonymous source using several tools you've seen so far: Twitter DMs, a PGP-encrypted message, communicating via Signal, and receiving a dataset through OnionShare.

In the summer of 2021, a journalist sent me a DM on Twitter, passing along a note from someone else. The journalist had no idea what the note said, because it was PGP-encrypted. The note looked something like this:

```
-----BEGIN PGP MESSAGE-----

[lots of scrambled letters and numbers]
-----END PGP MESSAGE-----
```

I plugged in my YubiKey and used it to decrypt the PGP message. It simply said:

> interested in data?
> signal: *[redacted phone number]*

At the time, I didn't publish my phone number directly on my social media bios or on my staff profile page on The Intercept's website. If I had, this source could have just contacted me directly on Signal, which would have been much simpler. Nevertheless, using PGP ensured that all communication between us was end-to-end encrypted, and even though Twitter DMs were involved, Twitter didn't have any communication metadata between my source and me.

I opened Signal Desktop on my computer, typed in the phone number I'd found in the PGP-encrypted message, and turned on disappearing messages for the conversation. I said hello and that I was interested in data. At this point I had a secure communication channel with my new source.

The source told me that they had hacked the Tea Party Patriots, a major US conservative organization that bills itself as one of the largest grassroots groups on the right. They wanted to send me a dataset that included membership lists, donation history, and petition data and asked how they should send it. I sent them an OnionShare link to upload the dataset directly to my computer.

I later learned from this dataset that the Tea Party Patriots organization isn't nearly as grassroots as it claims: three ultra-wealthy donors—two of them billionaires—provided the bulk of the group's donations. I also learned that the group's claim of being a network of "over 3 million patriots" was wildly exaggerated: only 144,000 members were marked "active" in the hacked database. (Read my analysis of this dataset at *https://theintercept.com/2021/08/05/tea-party-patriots-hacked-billionaire-donors/.*)

## Other Options for Acquiring Datasets from Sources

In this section, you'll learn a couple more ways to communicate with sources when the skills you've learned so far don't fit your needs.

## Encrypted USB Drives

Some of your future sources may want to send you more data than is feasible to transfer over Tor. In that case, you can consider sending an encrypted USB drive through postal mail.

First, your source encrypts a USB hard drive or a small USB stick using a strong passphrase, via the technologies covered in Chapter 1, and then copies the dataset to the drive. Then they physically mail the USB drive to you. To remain anonymous, they can write your address on the package or envelope but leave the return address blank (at least in the US), attach the right amount of postage, and drop it in a public mailbox. Using an encrypted messaging app like Signal, your source can send you the encryption passphrase. When you receive the drive in the mail, you can use the passphrase to unlock the drive and access the dataset.

If the drive gets intercepted in the mail, the data is encrypted and impossible to access without the passphrase. However, the postal service will know exactly which public mailbox it was mailed from, and if your source isn't careful, they might leave handwriting, fingerprints, DNA, or other clues to their identity in the package.

Keep in mind that sending an encrypted drive costs money, since you need to buy a hard drive and pay for postage, and the package might take a long time to arrive, so this isn't the best option for time-sensitive data.

---

### SENDING ENCRYPTED DATA VIA PUBLIC FILE-SHARING SERVICES

Rather than using an encrypted USB, your source can encrypt their data and upload it to a public file-sharing service like Mega or WeTransfer, if they have the technical skill to do so. The exact process is outside the scope of this book, but here's the gist:

First, your source would need to encrypt the dataset, using one of the following methods:

- Compress the dataset in a password-protected ZIP file, using a strong passphrase. This protects only the file contents, not the filenames themselves, meaning your source may not want to use this method if the filenames in the dataset are sensitive.

- Use software like VeraCrypt (discussed in Chapter 1) to create an encrypted container that's locked with a strong passphrase.

- Use some other disk encryption software that you and the source agree upon. For example, if you both use Macs, you can create an encrypted DMG file using macOS's built-in Disk Utility instead of VeraCrypt.

Once they've encrypted the dataset, the source uploads it to a public file-sharing service. Depending on which service they use, they may need to create an account. If they want to remain anonymous to that service, they might create a temporary email address just for this task and take steps to protect their IP address with a VPN service or Tor Browser. (Uploading a huge dataset to a file-sharing service over Tor is still faster than uploading it to an onion service, because the data takes fewer hops over the Tor network.) Once the encrypted dataset is uploaded, the source sends you a link to it, along with the dataset's passphrase. After you download the dataset, use the passphrase to decrypt it.

If anyone else gets access to the data stored on the file-sharing service— such as an employee of the service, or law enforcement after sending a subpoena demanding that the service hand over data—it will be impossible for them to decrypt the dataset without knowing the passphrase.

## Virtual Private Servers

A *virtual private server (VPS)* is a virtual computer on the internet, hosted by a company like Amazon Web Services (AWS) or DigitalOcean and normally running the Linux operating system, that your source can use to share their data. You'll learn the details of how to set up and work with a VPS in Chapter 4, but here we'll discuss when they might be appropriate for a given investigation.

The VPS option has a few downsides: it works only if your source has the necessary technical skills, it costs a small amount of money, and it's easy for your source to make mistakes if they're trying to remain anonymous. On the upside, a VPS allows your source to use extremely reliable tools to transfer large amounts of data. These tools also support resuming the transfer if it fails midway, and you can even use a VPS anonymously over Tor.

It costs just a few dollars a month to rent a VPS—if you need to use it for only a day or two, it's even cheaper—and you can specify how big its hard disk needs to be depending on how much data your source wants to send you. You can then enable your source to upload data to the server remotely using a technology called *SSH*, which stands for *Secure Shell*. Your source could encrypt the dataset before uploading it if they feel it's sensitive.

Throughout this chapter, you've learned ways individual journalists can receive data from their sources. In the next section, I'll introduce additional tools and techniques appropriate for established newsrooms.

# Whistleblower Submission Systems

As mentioned earlier, when Chelsea Manning tried to contact the *Washington Post* and the *New York Times* to leak the War Logs to the public, neither paper was receptive or even really prepared to accept leaked datasets. Today that's no longer the case. Dozens of major newsrooms now run their own whistleblower submission systems, making it simple to securely and anonymously submit leaked datasets or other tips.

Go to your favorite news site and see if you can find its tips page, which explains to potential sources and whistleblowers how to contact the newsroom securely. Here are a few examples:

- The Intercept: *https://theintercept.com/source/*
- *Washington Post*: *https://www.washingtonpost.com/anonymous-news-tips/*
- *New York Times*: *https://www.nytimes.com/tips*
- ProPublica: *https://www.propublica.org/tips/*
- CNN: *https://www.cnn.com/tips/*
- *Guardian*: *https://www.theguardian.com/securedrop*
- *Globe and Mail*: *https://sec.theglobeandmail.com/securedrop/*

The guidelines on these tips pages are all similar, instructing sources to securely contact the newsroom by either sending a message to a dedicated Signal phone number, physically mailing their documents using the postal service, or reaching out over the open source whistleblower submission software called *SecureDrop*.

The late information activist Aaron Swartz, along with journalist Kevin Poulsen, developed a platform in 2013 called DeadDrop for sources to securely communicate with and send documents to journalists. After Swartz's death, Poulsen handed the project over to the Freedom of the Press Foundation, which renamed it to SecureDrop. At the time, I was the chief technology officer for the Freedom of the Press Foundation and contributed a significant amount of code to the project.

Like OnionShare, SecureDrop turns computers into anonymous dropboxes (also powered by Tor onion services) to enable file sharing. However, it's designed for professional newsrooms. It runs on a dedicated server that's always online and available for sources to use, and it forces more secure and paranoid behavior than OnionShare does—for example, it's designed so that you can open documents sent through SecureDrop only in an airgapped environment.

SecureDrop's increased security protects sources who are potentially risking their lives, but that security comes at a cost. The platform requires a significant amount of work to set up and maintain, including the ongoing daily work of checking it for new submissions. I spent years checking SecureDrop for The Intercept, and I know that it can be frustrating jumping through security hoops when the vast majority of submissions are nonsense or could have been sent in an email. But the effort is worth it if it protects just one genuine whistleblower.

If you work with a newsroom or an organization that wants to accept datasets from sources or whistleblowers, create a tips page on your website and look into SecureDrop. You can learn more about the SecureDrop project at *https://securedrop.org* and read detailed documentation at *https://docs .securedrop.org*.

## Summary

In this chapter, you learned about the demise of WikiLeaks and the genesis of DDoSecrets, and you downloaded a copy of the BlueLeaks dataset using BitTorrent. You've seen some common tools for securely communicating with sources, like Signal, Tor, and OnionShare. You've also learned about a few other techniques for securely and anonymously transferring large amounts of data, as well as about tips pages and SecureDrop.

The next chapter marks the beginning of Part II, where you'll learn how to use the command line interface, a powerful text-based method of controlling your computer. This will prove essential for digging into datasets like BlueLeaks.

# PART II

## TOOLS OF THE TRADE

# 3

# THE COMMAND LINE INTERFACE

*Back in the days of the command-line interface, users were all Morlocks who had to convert
their thoughts into alphanumeric symbols and type them in, a grindingly tedious process
that stripped away all ambiguity, laid bare all hidden assumptions, and cruelly
punished laziness and imprecision.*
—Neal Stephenson, *In the Beginning . . . Was the Command Line*

If you're like most people, you interface with your computer primarily via its graphical desktop environment: you move the pointer with your mouse or trackpad and click icons to run programs and open documents. Programs open in windows that you can resize, maximize, minimize, and drag around the screen. You can run various programs at once in separate windows and switch between them. However, there's an alternative, incredibly powerful interface you can use to communicate with your computer and give it instructions: the *command line interface (CLI).*

Command line interfaces are text-based, rather than graphical, interfaces to interact with your computer. Instead of clicking on icons, you enter commands to run programs in a *terminal emulator* (normally referred to just as a *terminal*). After running a command, you'll typically see text-based output displayed in the terminal.

In this chapter, you'll learn the basic command line skills you need to follow along with the rest of this book. Whether you're using Windows, macOS, or Linux, you'll learn how to install and uninstall software via the command line, how filepaths work, how to navigate around the folders on your computer, and how to use text editors. You'll also write your first *shell script*, a file containing a series of commands.

# Introducing the Command Line

To prepare you to start working on the command line, this section explains some fundamentals: what shells are, how users and paths work in different operating systems, and the concept of privilege escalation.

## The Shell

The *shell* is the program that lets you run text-based commands, while the terminal is the graphical program that runs your shell. When you open a terminal and see a blinking text cursor waiting for commands, you're using a shell. When hackers try to break into a computer, their initial goal is to "pop a shell," or access the text-based interface that allows them to run whatever commands they want.

All operating systems, even mobile ones like Android and iOS, have shells. This book focuses on Unix shells, the kind that come with macOS and Linux (but Windows users can also use them). Most versions of Linux use a shell called bash, and macOS uses one called zsh. These shells are very similar, and for the purposes of this book you can think of them as interchangeable.

Windows, on the other hand, comes with two shells: an older one called Command Prompt (or *cmd.exe*) and a newer one called PowerShell. The *syntax*—rules that define what different commands mean—used by Windows shells is very different from that used by Unix shells. If you're a Windows user, you'll primarily work in a Unix shell for the examples in this book. Setting up your computer to run Linux directly in Windows will be this chapter's first exercise.

To make your shell do something, such as run a program, you carefully enter the desired command and then press ENTER (or RETURN on Mac keyboards). To quit the shell, enter **exit** and press ENTER. Shells are finicky: you need to enter commands using the correct capitalization, punctuation, and spacing, or they won't work. Typos usually result in nothing more serious than error messages, however, and it's easy to go back and fix a mistake in a command. I'll explain how to do so in the "Editing Commands" section on page 68.

## Users and Paths

Although operating systems like Windows, macOS, and Linux are different in some ways, they all share basic building blocks, including users and paths.

All operating systems have *users*, separate accounts that different people use to log in to the same computer. Users generally have home folders, also known as home directories, where their files live. Figure 3-1 shows my terminal in Ubuntu, a popular Linux distribution.

Figure 3-1: My Ubuntu terminal

My username is *micah* and the name of my Ubuntu computer is *rogue*. Your terminal will look different depending on your operating system, username, and computer name.

All operating systems also have filesystems, the collection of files and folders available on the computer (you got a brief introduction to filesystems in Chapter 1 while encrypting your USB disk). In a filesystem, each file and folder has a *path*, which you can think of like the location, or address, of that file. For example, if your username is *alice*, the path of your home folder in different operating systems would look as follows:

- Windows: *C:\Users\alice*
- macOS: */Users/alice*
- Linux: */home/alice*

Windows filesystems operate differently from macOS or Linux filesystems in a few key ways. First, in Windows, disks are labeled with letters. The main disk, where Windows itself is installed, is the *C: drive*. Other disks, like USB disks, are assigned other letters. In Windows, folders in a path are separated with a backslash (\), while other operating systems use forward slashes (/). In Linux, paths are case sensitive, but not in Windows and macOS (by default). For example, in Linux you can store one file called *Document.pdf* and another called *document.pdf* in the same folder. If you try to do the same in Windows, saving the second file overwrites the first.

Let's look at some example paths. If your username is *alice* and you download a file called *Meeting Notes.docx* into the *Downloads* folder, here's what that path would look like:

- Windows: *C:\Users\alice\Downloads\Meeting Notes.docx*
- macOS: */Users/alice/Downloads/Meeting Notes.docx*
- Linux: */home/alice/Downloads/Meeting Notes.docx*

When you plug in a USB disk, it's mounted to different paths for different operating systems. If your disk is labeled *datasets*, the path representing the location of that disk might look as follows:

- Windows: *D:* (or whatever drive letter Windows decides to mount the disk to)
- macOS: */Volumes/datasets*
- Linux: */media/alice/datasets*

It's important to understand how to read paths, since you'll need to include the location of your dataset or files it contains in the commands you run.

## User Privileges

Most users have limited privileges in an operating system. However, the *root user* in Linux and macOS and the *administrator user* in Windows have absolute power. While *alice* may not be able to save files into *bob*'s home folder, for example, the root user has permissions to save files anywhere on the computer. When a Mac asks you to enter your user password to change system preferences or install software, or when a Windows machine asks if you want to allow a program to make changes to your computer, the operating system is asking for your consent before switching from your unprivileged user account to the root or administrator user account.

Most of the time when you're working in a terminal, you run commands as an unprivileged user. To run a command that requires root (or administrative) privileges in Linux and macOS, such as to install a new program, just put sudo in front of it and press ENTER, and you'll be prompted to enter the password for your regular user account.

As an example, the whoami command tells you which user just ran a command. On my computer, if I enter whoami without sudo, the output is micah. However, if I enter sudo whoami, which requires me to type my password, the output is root:

```
micah@rogue:~$ whoami
micah
micah@rogue:~$ sudo whoami
[sudo] password for micah:
root
```

If you recently ran sudo, you can run it again for a few minutes without having to re-enter your password.

**WARNING** *Be very careful when running commands as root, since running the wrong commands as the root user can accidentally delete all of your data or break your operating system. Before using sudo, make sure you have a clear understanding of what you're about to do.*

You can use sudo to gain root access only if your current user has administrator access. If you're the only user on your computer, you're probably an administrator. To find out, try using sudo and see whether you get a "permission denied" error.

Figure 3-2 shows a comic by Randall Munroe from his XKCD website that succinctly demonstrates the power of sudo.

Figure 3-2: Demanding a sandwich with sudo

Before learning more command line code, Windows users must install Ubuntu (see Exercise 3-1). Mac or Linux users can skip to the "Basic Command Line Usage" section on page 62.

## Exercise 3-1: Install Ubuntu in Windows

To work with Ubuntu on a Windows machine, you could install both Windows and Linux or use a virtual machine within Windows, as mentioned in Chapter 1. However, for this book's purposes, it's simplest to use the *Windows Subsystem for Linux (WSL)*, a Microsoft technology that lets you run Linux programs directly in Windows. Opening an Ubuntu window in WSL will, in turn, open a bash shell and let you install and run Ubuntu software. (Technically, WSL does use a VM, but it's fast, managed by Windows, and unobtrusive, running entirely behind the scenes.)

To install WSL, open a PowerShell window as an administrator: click **Start**, search for **powershell**, right-click **Windows PowerShell**, choose **Run as Administrator**, and click **Yes**. Figure 3-3 shows this process, which may look slightly different depending on your version of Windows.

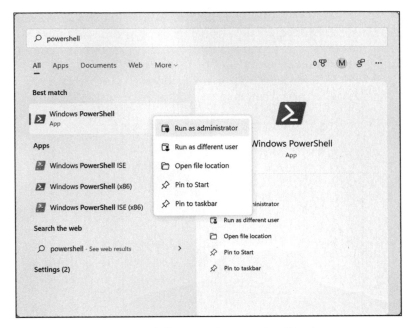

Figure 3-3: Running PowerShell as an administrator in Windows

In your administrator PowerShell window, enter the following command and press ENTER:

```
wsl --install -d Ubuntu
```

This installs the Windows Subsystem for Linux, then downloads and installs Ubuntu Linux on your computer.

Your screen should now look something like this:

```
PS C :\Windows\system32> wsl --install -d Ubuntu
Installing: Windows Subsystem for Linux
Windows Subsystem for Linux has been installed.
Downloading: WSL Kernel
Installing: WSL Kernel
WSL Kernel has been installed.
Downloading: GUI App Support
Installing: GUI App Support
GUI App Support has been installed.
Downloading: Ubuntu
The requested operation is succession. Changes will not be effective until the
system is rebooted.
PS C:\Windows\system32>
```

The final line of this output tells you to reboot your computer. Enter **exit** and press ENTER (or just close the window) to quit PowerShell, then reboot. After you log in to Windows again, you should see an Ubuntu window informing you that the installation may take a few more minutes to complete. Then the window should present you with a prompt asking you to create a new user:

```
Please create a default UNIX user account. The username does not need to match
your Windows username.
For more information visit: https://aka.ms/wslusers
Enter new UNIX username:
```

Ubuntu needs to keep track of its own users rather than the existing users on your Windows computer.

With the Ubuntu terminal window in focus, enter a username and press ENTER. The terminal should then prompt you to create a password:

```
New password:
```

Either use the same password you use to log in to your Windows account or create a new one and save it in your password manager. Enter your password and press ENTER. While you're typing, nothing will appear in the Ubuntu terminal.

The terminal should now prompt you to re-enter your new password; do so and press ENTER, which should drop you into an Ubuntu shell with a prompt and a blinking cursor. My prompt says micah@cloak:~$ because my username is *micah* and the name of my Windows computer is *cloak*:

```
New password:
Retype new password:
passwd: password updated successfully
Installation successful!
--snip--
micah@cloak:~$
```

You can now open Ubuntu in your Windows computer. From this point on, when instructed to open a terminal or run some command line code, use an Ubuntu terminal window unless I specify otherwise.

From within your Ubuntu shell, you can access your Windows disks in the */mnt* folder. For example, you can access the *C:* drive in */mnt/c* and the *D:* drive in */mnt/d*. Suppose I download a document using my web browser and want to access it from Ubuntu. The path to my *Downloads* folder in Windows is */mnt/c/Users/micah/Downloads*, so the document would be in that folder. If I want to access the BlueLeaks data that I downloaded to my USB disk from Ubuntu, then assuming that *D:* is the USB disk's drive, the path would be */mnt/d/BlueLeaks*.

For more details on using Windows and WSL, including information on common problems related to using USB disks in WSL, as well as disk performance issues and various ways to deal with them, check out Appendix A. Wait until you've worked through at least Chapter 4 to start implementing these solutions, since the instructions involve more advanced command line concepts introduced in that chapter.

# Basic Command Line Usage

In this section, you'll learn to use the command line to explore files and folders on your computer. This is a prerequisite to working with datasets, which are just folders full of files and other folders. You'll learn how to open a terminal, list files in any folder, distinguish between relative and absolute paths, switch to different folders in your shell, and look up documentation on commands from within your terminal.

**NOTE** *When learning command line skills, you can always look things up if you run into problems—I still do this every day. You're likely not the first person to encounter any given command line issue, so with a few well-worded internet searches, you can find someone else's solution.*

## Opening a Terminal

To get started, skip to the subsection for your operating system to learn how to open a terminal. Throughout this chapter, keep a terminal open while you're reading to test all the commands.

### The Windows Terminal

Open the Ubuntu app by clicking **Start** in the bottom-left corner of the screen, searching for **ubuntu**, and clicking **Ubuntu**.

You'll use Ubuntu most often for this book, but you may need to open the native Windows terminals occasionally as well. You can likewise open PowerShell and Command Prompt by clicking **Start** and searching for them. Check out the Microsoft program Windows Terminal (*https://aka.ms/terminal*), which lets you open different terminals in different tabs, choosing between PowerShell, Command Prompt, Ubuntu, and others. If you choose to install it, you can open it the same way.

Pin the Ubuntu app or Windows Terminal app to your taskbar so you can quickly open it in the future: right-click its icon and select **Pin to Taskbar**.

### The macOS Terminal

Open the Terminal app by opening Finder, going to the *Applications* folder, double-clicking the *Utilities* folder, and double-clicking **Terminal**. Figure 3-4 shows my macOS terminal running zsh, the default macOS shell. My username is *micah*, and the name of my Mac is *trapdoor*.

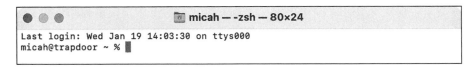

```
● ● ●                    🗇 micah — -zsh — 80×24
Last login: Wed Jan 19 14:03:30 on ttys000
micah@trapdoor ~ % ▉
```

*Figure 3-4: My macOS terminal*

Pin the Terminal app to your dock so you can quickly open it in the future. To do so, after you open Terminal, press CTRL and click the Terminal icon on your dock, then choose **Options ▶ Keep in Dock**.

**The Linux Terminal**

In most Linux distributions, open the Terminal app by pressing the Windows key, typing **terminal**, and pressing ENTER. If you're running Ubuntu (or any other Linux distribution that uses the GNOME graphical environment), pin the Terminal app to your dock so you can quickly open it in the future. To do so, right-click the Terminal icon and select **Add to Favorites**.

## Clearing Your Screen and Exiting the Shell

As you practice using the terminal in the following sections, you'll sometimes want to start fresh, without having to see all the previous commands you ran or their output or error messages. Run this simple command to declutter your terminal:

```
clear
```

This clears everything off the screen, leaving you with nothing but a blank command prompt. Make sure to do this only if you no longer need to see the output of your previous commands. (In the Windows Command Prompt and PowerShell, use cls instead of clear.)

When you're done using the CLI, exit your shell by running this command:

```
exit
```

You can also close the terminal window to exit. If you're running a program when you close the terminal, that program will quit as well.

## Exploring Files and Directories

When you open a terminal, your shell starts out in your user's home folder, represented as a tilde (~). The folder you're currently in is your *current working directory*, or just *working directory*. If you ever forget what directory you're in, run the pwd command (short for "print working directory") to find out.

Running the ls command in your terminal lists all of the files in your working directory. You can use this command to check the contents of folders you're working with. If there are no files or only hidden files, ls won't list anything. To check for hidden files, modify the ls command using -a (short for --all):

```
ls -a
```

When you add anything to the end of a command, like -a, you're using a *command line argument*. Think of arguments as settings that change how the program you're running will act—in this case, by showing hidden files instead of hiding them.

By default, the ls command displays files in a format intended to take up as few lines in your terminal as possible. However, you may want to display one file per line for easier reading and to get more information about each file, such as its size, when it was last modified, permissions, and whether it's a folder. Using the -l argument (short for --format=long) formats the output as a list.

You can use both -a and -l at the same time like so:

```
ls -al
```

Running this command on my Mac gives me the following output:

```
total 8
drwxr-x---+ 13 micah  staff   416 Nov 25 11:34 .
drwxr-xr-x   6 root   admin   192 Nov  9 15:51 ..
-rw-------   1 micah  staff     3 Nov  6 15:30 .CFUserTextEncoding
-rw-------   1 micah  staff  2773 Nov 25 11:33 .zsh_history
drwx------   5 micah  staff   160 Nov  6 15:31 .zsh_sessions
drwx------+  3 micah  staff    96 Nov  6 15:30 Desktop
drwx------+  3 micah  staff    96 Nov  6 15:30 Documents
drwx------+  3 micah  staff    96 Nov  6 15:30 Downloads
drwx------+ 31 micah  staff   992 Nov  6 15:31 Library
drwx------   3 micah  staff    96 Nov  6 15:30 Movies
drwx------+  3 micah  staff    96 Nov  6 15:30 Music
drwx------+  3 micah  staff    96 Nov  6 15:30 Pictures
drwxr-xr-x+  4 micah  staff   128 Nov  6 15:30 Public
```

The first column of this output describes the type of file—whether it's a *directory* (another name for a folder) or an ordinary file—as well as the file's permissions. Directories start with d, and ordinary files start with a hyphen (-). The second column represents the number of links in the file, which isn't relevant for the purposes of this book.

The third and fourth columns represent the user and the *group* that owns the file. In addition to users, operating systems have groups of users that can have their own permissions. For example, in Linux, all users allowed to use sudo are in the *sudo* group. If you create or download a file, its user and group are normally your username. The fifth column is the file size in bytes. For example, in the file called *.zsh_history*, my output is 2,773 bytes.

The next three columns of the output represent the time and date when the file was last modified, and the final column shows the filename.

To see a listing of files in a folder other than the working directory, add the path to that folder to the end of the ls command. For example, this is how I'd create a listing of files in my *code/hacks-leaks-and-revelations* folder, which contains the files released with this book:

```
ls -la code/hacks-leaks-and-revelations
```

I'd get the following output:

```
total 96
drwxr-xr-x  22 micah  staff   704 Jul 27 09:28 .
drwxr-xr-x  12 micah  staff   384 Jul 27 09:28 ..
drwxr-xr-x  12 micah  staff   384 Jul 27 09:28 .git
```

```
drwxr-xr-x   3 micah  staff      96 Jul 27 09:28 .github
-rw-r--r--   1 micah  staff      30 Jul 27 09:28 .gitignore
-rw-r--r--   1 micah  staff   35149 Jul 27 09:28 LICENSE
-rw-r--r--   1 micah  staff    6997 Jul 27 09:28 README.md
drwxr-xr-x   6 micah  staff     192 Jul 27 09:28 appendix-b
drwxr-xr-x   5 micah  staff     160 Jul 27 09:28 chapter-1
drwxr-xr-x   6 micah  staff     192 Jul 27 09:28 chapter-10
drwxr-xr-x  11 micah  staff     352 Jul 27 09:28 chapter-11
drwxr-xr-x  13 micah  staff     416 Jul 27 09:28 chapter-12
drwxr-xr-x   8 micah  staff     256 Jul 27 09:28 chapter-13
drwxr-xr-x   3 micah  staff      96 Jul 27 09:28 chapter-14
drwxr-xr-x   5 micah  staff     160 Jul 27 09:28 chapter-2
drwxr-xr-x  10 micah  staff     320 Jul 27 09:28 chapter-3
drwxr-xr-x  13 micah  staff     416 Jul 27 09:28 chapter-4
drwxr-xr-x  13 micah  staff     416 Jul 27 09:28 chapter-5
drwxr-xr-x  10 micah  staff     320 Jul 27 09:28 chapter-6
drwxr-xr-x  12 micah  staff     384 Jul 27 09:28 chapter-7
drwxr-xr-x  20 micah  staff     640 Jul 27 09:28 chapter-8
drwxr-xr-x  14 micah  staff     448 Jul 27 09:28 chapter-9
```

You'll download your own copy of these files in Exercise 3-7.

## Navigating Relative and Absolute Paths

Programs often require you to provide paths to files or folders, usually when you run a program that works with specific files on your computer. The path that I passed into ls in the previous section, *code/hacks-leaks-and-revelations*, is a *relative* path, meaning it's relative to the current working directory, my home folder. Relative paths can change. For example, if I change my working directory from my home folder (*/Users/micah*) to just */Users*, the relative path to that folder changes to *micah/code/hacks-leaks-and-revelations*.

The *absolute* path to the *code/hacks-leaks-and-revelations* folder is */Users/micah/code/hacks-leaks-and-revelations*, which always provides the location of that folder regardless of my working directory. Absolute paths start with a forward slash (/), which is also known as the root path.

You can use two keywords to access relative paths to specific folders: . (dot), which represents a relative path to the current folder, and .. (dot dot), which represents a relative path to the *parent folder* (the folder that contains the current folder).

## Changing Directories

The cd command (which stands for "change directory") allows you to change to a different folder. To change your working directory to the folder, run:

```
cd path
```

For *path*, substitute the path to the folder to which you'd like to move. You can use either a relative or an absolute path.

Suppose I'm using macOS and have downloaded BlueLeaks to a *datasets* USB disk plugged into my machine. After opening a terminal, I can run the following command to change my working directory to the *BlueLeaks* folder, using the absolute path to the folder:

```
cd /Volumes/datasets/BlueLeaks
```

Alternatively, I can use a relative path to the folder, running the following command from my home folder:

```
cd ../../Volumes/datasets/BlueLeaks
```

Why does the relative path start with ../.. in this example? When I open the terminal, the working directory is my home folder, which in macOS is */Users/micah*. The relative path .. would be its parent folder, */Users*; the relative path ../.. would be */*; the relative path ../../Volumes would be */Volumes*; and so on.

As noted earlier, the tilde symbol (~) represents your home folder. No matter what your working directory is, you can run the following to go back to your home folder:

```
cd ~
```

Use the following syntax to move to a folder inside your home folder:

```
cd ~/folder_name
```

For example, the following command would move you to your *Documents* folder:

```
cd ~/Documents
```

If you run ls again after a cd command, the output should show you the files in the folder to which you just moved.

### Using the help Argument

Most commands let you use the argument -h, or --help, which displays detailed instructions explaining what the command does and how to use it. For example, try running the following:

```
unzip --help
```

This command should show instructions on all of the different arguments that are available to you when using the unzip command, which is used to extract compressed ZIP files.

Here's the output I got when I ran that command on my Mac:

```
UnZip 6.00 of 20 April 2009, by Info-ZIP.  Maintained by C. Spieler.  Send
bug reports using http://www.info-zip.org/zip-bug.html; see README for details.
--snip--
```

```
-p  extract files to pipe, no messages    -l  list files (short format)
-f  freshen existing files, create none   -t  test compressed archive data
-u  update files, create if necessary     -z  display archive comment only
-v  list verbosely/show version info      -T  timestamp archive to latest
-x  exclude files that follow (in xlist)  -d  extract files into exdir
--snip--
```

This output briefly describes what each argument for the `unzip` command does. For example, if you use the `-l` argument, the command shows a list of all of the files and folders inside the ZIP file without actually unzipping it.

### Accessing Man Pages

Many commands also have manuals, otherwise known as *man pages*, which give more detail about how to use those commands. Run the following to access a command's man page:

```
man command_name
```

For example, to read the manual for the `unzip` command, run:

```
man unzip
```

The output should display a longer explanation of how to use the `unzip` command and its arguments.

Use the up and down arrows and the page up and page down keys to scroll through the man pages, or press / and enter a term to search. For example, to learn more details about how the `unzip` command's `-l` argument works, press / and enter **-l**, then press ENTER. This should bring you to the first time -l appears on the man page. Press N to move on to the next occurrence of your search term.

When you're finished, press Q to quit the man page.

## Tips for Navigating the Terminal

This section introduces ways to make working on the command line more convenient and efficient, along with tips for avoiding and fixing errors. It also shows how to handle problematic filenames, such as those with spaces, quotes, or other special characters. A basic understanding of these concepts will save you a lot of time in the future.

### Entering Commands with Tab Completion

Shells have a feature called *tab completion* that saves time and prevents errors: enter the first few letters of a command or a path, then press TAB. Your shell will fill in the rest if possible.

For example, both macOS and Ubuntu come with a program called hex-dump. In a terminal, enter **hexd** and press TAB. This should automatically fill in the rest of the hexdump command. Tab completion also works for paths. For example, Unix-like operating systems use the */tmp* folder to store temporary files. Enter `ls /tm` and press TAB. Your shell should add the p to finish typing out the full command.

If you enter only the first couple letters of a command or a path, there may be more than one way for your shell to complete your line of code. Assuming that you have both *Downloads* and *Documents* folders in your home folder, type `ls ~/Do` and press TAB. You'll hear a quiet beep, meaning that the shell doesn't know how to proceed. Press TAB one more time, and it should display the options, like this:

```
Documents/  Downloads/
```

If you enter a c so that your command so far is `ls ~/Doc` and press TAB, the command should complete to `ls ~/Documents/`. If you enter a w so that your command so far is `ls ~/Dow` and press TAB, it should complete to `ls ~/Downloads/`.

If you've already typed out the path of a folder, you can also press TAB to list files in that folder, or to automatically complete the filename if there's only one file in the folder. For example, say I have my *datasets* USB disk, on which I've downloaded BlueLeaks, plugged into my Ubuntu computer. If I want to change to my *BlueLeaks* folder, I can enter the following and press TAB:

```
cd /Vo
```

This completes the command as follows:

```
cd /Volumes/
```

I press TAB again, and my computer beeps and lists the folders in */Volumes*, which in my case are *Macintosh HD* and *datasets*. I enter **d**, so my command is `cd /Volumes/d`, and press TAB, and the shell completes the command as follows:

```
cd /Volumes/datasets/
```

I press TAB again. My computer beeps again and lists all of the files and folders in my *datasets* USB disk. I enter **B** (the first letter of BlueLeaks) and press TAB, which gives me:

```
cd /Volumes/datasets/BlueLeaks/
```

Finally, I press ENTER to change to that folder.

### Editing Commands

You can also edit commands. When you start typing a command, you can press the left and right arrow keys to move the cursor, allowing you to edit the command before running it. You can also press HOME and END—or, if you're using a Mac keyboard, CONTROL-A and CONTROL-E—to go to the beginning and end of a line, respectively. You can also cycle between commands you've already run using the up and down arrows. If you just ran a command and want to run it again, or to modify it and then run it, press the up arrow to return to it. Once you find the command you're looking for, use the arrow keys to move your cursor to the correct position, edit it, and then press ENTER to run it again.

For example, I frequently get "permission denied" errors when I accidentally run commands as my unprivileged user when I should have run them as root. When this happens, I press the up arrow, then CONTROL-A to go to the beginning of the line, add sudo, and press ENTER to successfully run the command.

## Dealing with Spaces in Filenames

Sometimes filenames contain multiple words separated by spaces. If you don't explicitly tell your shell that a space is part of a filename, the shell assumes that the space is there to separate parts of your command. For example, this command lists the files in the *Documents* folder:

```
ls -lh ~/Documents
```

Under the hood, your shell takes this string of characters and splits it into a list of parts that are separated by spaces: ls, -lh, and ~/Documents. The first part, ls, is the command to run. The rest of the parts are the command's arguments. The -lh argument tells the program to display the output as a list and make the file sizes human-readable. That is, it will convert the file sizes into units that are easier to read, like kilobytes, megabytes, and gigabytes, rather than a large number of bytes. The ~/Documents argument means you want to list the files in that folder.

Suppose you want to use the same command to list the files in a folder with a space in its name, like *~/My Documents*. You'll run into problems if you enter this command:

```
ls -lh ~/My Documents
```

When your shell tries to separate this command into parts, it will come up with ls, -lh, ~/My, and Documents; that is, it sees *~/My Documents* as two separate arguments, ~/My and Documents. It will try to list the files in the folder *~/My* (which doesn't exist), then also list files in the folder *Documents*, which isn't what you intended.

To solve this problem, put the name of the folder in quotes:

```
ls -lh "~/My Documents"
```

The shell sees anything within quotes as a single entity. In this case, ls is the command and its arguments are -lh followed by ~/My Documents.

Alternatively, you can use a backslash (\) to *escape* the space:

```
ls -lh ~/My\ Documents
```

In the Unix family of operating systems, the backslash is called the *escape character*. When the shell parses that string of characters, it treats an *escaped space* (\ followed by a space) as a part of the name. Again, the shell reads ls as the command and -lh and ~/My Documents as its arguments.

### Using Single Quotes Around Double Quotes

You can use the escape character to escape more than spaces. Suppose you want to delete a filename that has a space *and* quotes in it, like *Say "Hello".txt*. You can use the rm command to delete files, but the following syntax won't work:

```
rm Say "Hello".txt
```

Your shell will split this command into the words rm, Say, and Hello.txt. You might think you could solve this by simply adding more quotes

```
rm "Say "Hello".txt"
```

but that won't work either, since you're quoting something that contains quotes already. Instead, surround the argument with single quotes ('), like this:

```
rm 'Say "Hello".txt'
```

Your shell will read this command as rm and the argument as Say "Hello" .txt, exactly as you intended.

Avoid putting spaces, quotes, or other troublesome characters in filenames whenever possible. Sometimes you can't avoid them, especially when working with datasets full of someone else's files. Tab completion helps in those cases, allowing you to enter just enough of the filename so that when you press TAB, your shell will fill out the rest for you. To delete a file in your working directory called *Say "Hello".txt*, for example, entering rm Sa, then pressing TAB, completes the command to rm Say\ \"Hello\".txt with the correct escape characters included, so you don't have to provide the proper syntax yourself.

## Installing and Uninstalling Software with Package Managers

Of the many powerful command line tools that let you quickly work with datasets, only some come preinstalled; you'll need to install the rest yourself. While you're likely used to installing software by downloading an installer from a website and then running it, the command line uses *package managers*, programs that let you install, uninstall, and update software. Nearly all CLI software is free and open source, so Linux operating systems come with large collections of software that you can easily install or uninstall with a single command. Package management projects are also available for macOS (Homebrew) and Windows (Chocolately).

If you're using Linux, you likely use a package manager called apt. This is what the popular Linux operating systems like Ubuntu and Debian use, as well as all of the Linux distributions based on them (including Ubuntu in WSL). If your Linux distribution doesn't use apt, you'll need to look up the package manager documentation for your operating system.

---

**PACKAGE MANAGEMENT FOR NON-UBUNTU LINUX USERS**

You should be able to follow along with this book no matter what version of Linux you're using. Several other Debian-based Linux distributions also rely on apt, like Linux Mint, Pop! OS, and others. If you're using one of these, the apt commands in this book should work, though the names of software packages may be slightly different. If you encounter that issue, run apt search *software_name* to find the name of the package that you should be installing for your operating system.

If you're using a version of Linux that doesn't use apt as its package manager, you'll need to slightly modify this book's commands to use your Linux distribution's package manager. For example, if you're running Fedora, Red Hat, CentOS, or other similar Linux distributions, you'll use a package manager called DNF (for older versions of these distributions, the package manager is called yum). See Fedora's documentation at *https://docs.fedoraproject.org/en-US/quick-docs/dnf/* for more details on using DNF. Arch Linux uses a package manager called pacman (*https://wiki.archlinux.org/title/Pacman*).

If you're using a Linux distribution not mentioned here, read your operating system's package management documentation and learn how to search for, install, uninstall, and update software from the terminal. When you come across an apt command in this book, use your operating system's package manager software instead. Other Linux commands covered in this book should be the same regardless of your distribution.

---

If you're using a Mac, start with Exercise 3-2 to learn how to use Homebrew. If you're using Linux or Windows with WSL, skip to Exercise 3-3 to learn how to use apt. This book mostly uses Unix shells and doesn't cover Chocolately, which installs Windows software instead of Linux software.

## Exercise 3-2: Manage Packages with Homebrew on macOS

To install Homebrew, macOS's package manager, open a browser and go to Homebrew's website at *https://brew.sh*, where you should find the command to install the tool. Copy and paste the installation command into your terminal and press RETURN:

```
/bin/bash -c "$(curl -fsSL https://raw.githubusercontent.com/Homebrew/install/HEAD/install.sh)"
```

This command uses a program called cURL, which I'll discuss later in this chapter, to download a shell script from GitHub. It then runs that script using the bash shell. The script itself uses sudo, meaning that if you enter your password, it will run commands as root on your computer.

This is what the output looks like on my Mac:

```
==> Checking for 'sudo' access (which may request your password)...
Password:
```

Enter the password you use to log in to your Mac and press RETURN to change your status from unprivileged user to root. No characters will appear in the terminal while you're typing.

After you enter your password, Homebrew should show you a list of paths for files that it will install. The output should end with the following message:

```
Press RETURN to continue or any other key to abort:
```

Press RETURN and wait for Homebrew to finish installing. If any problems arise, Homebrew will fail and show you an error message.

**WARNING** *Copying and pasting commands into your terminal can be dangerous: if a hacker tricks you into running the wrong shell script, they could hack your computer. Copy and paste commands in your terminal only from sources you trust.*

Now that you've installed Homebrew, you have access to the brew command, which you can use to install more software. To check whether Homebrew has a certain program available to install, run:

```
brew search program_name
```

For example, Neofetch is a CLI program that displays information about your computer. To see if it's available in Homebrew, run:

```
brew search neofetch
```

The output should list the packages that have *neofetch* in their names or descriptions; in this case, Neofetch should be listed. Similarly combine brew search with other program names to check whether they're available to install.

When you find a package you want to install, run:

```
brew install program_name
```

For example, to install Neofetch, run:

```
brew install neofetch
```

This should download and install the neofetch tool. Try running it:

```
neofetch
```

Figure 3-5 shows Neofetch running on my Mac. The figure is black-and-white in print, but if you run the command on your computer, you should see a rainbow of colors.

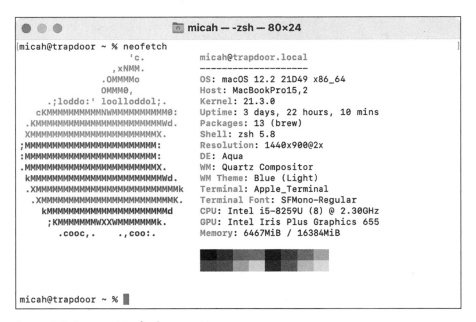

Figure 3-5: Running Neofetch on my Mac

Uninstall programs with the brew uninstall command. For example, run the following to uninstall Neofetch:

```
brew uninstall neofetch
```

To update all programs you've installed with Homebrew to their latest versions, run:

```
brew upgrade --greedy
```

Run **brew help** to see some examples of how to use this command.

Now that you have a package manager installed, you'll practice using the command line in Exercise 3-4.

## Exercise 3-3: Manage Packages with apt on Windows or Linux

You must run most apt commands as root. Before installing or updating software, make sure your operating system has an up-to-date list of available software by opening a terminal and running the following:

```
sudo apt update
```

When I run that command on my Linux computer, I get this output:

```
Hit:1 http://us.archive.ubuntu.com/ubuntu jammy InRelease
Hit:2 http://security.ubuntu.com/ubuntu jammy-security InRelease
Hit:3 http://us.archive.ubuntu.com/ubuntu jammy-updates InRelease
Hit:4 http://us.archive.ubuntu.com/ubuntu jammy-backports InRelease
Reading package lists... Done
Building dependency tree... Done
Reading state information... Done
178 packages can be upgraded. Run 'apt list --upgradable' to see them.
```

This tells me I have 178 packages that can be upgraded. Run the following to upgrade your own software:

```
sudo apt upgrade
```

Here's the output when I run that command:

```
Reading package lists... Done
Building dependency tree... Done
Reading state information... Done
Calculating upgrade... Done
The following packages will be upgraded:
--snip--
178 upgraded, 0 newly installed, 0 to remove and 0 not upgraded.
64 standard security updates
Need to get 365 MB of archives.
After this operation, 2,455 kB of additional disk space will be used.
Do you want to continue? [Y/n]
```

Type Y and press ENTER to install the updates.

You're now ready to install new software. To check whether the package manager has a certain program available to install, run:

```
apt search program_name
```

You don't need to use sudo with this search command because it's not installing or uninstalling anything. However, once you find a package you want to install, run:

```
sudo apt install program_name
```

For example, Neofetch is a CLI program that displays information about your computer. To see if Neofetch is available in your package manager, run:

```
apt search neofetch
```

The output should show a list of packages that have *neofetch* in their names or descriptions; in this case, Neofetch should be listed.

To install the Neofetch tool, run:

```
sudo apt install neofetch
```

You should see a list of packages that you must install in order to use Neofetch. Press Y and then ENTER to download and install them all.

Once installation is complete, try running Neofetch:

```
neofetch
```

Figure 3-6 shows Neofetch running on my Ubuntu computer. The figure is black-and-white in print, but if you run the command on your computer, the output should appear in several different colors.

*Figure 3-6: Running Neofetch on my Ubuntu computer*

Uninstall packages with the `sudo apt remove` command. For example, to uninstall Neofetch, run:

```
sudo apt remove neofetch
```

Now that you have a package manager installed, you'll practice using the command line in Exercise 3-4.

## Exercise 3-4: Practice Using the Command Line with cURL

In this exercise, you'll learn how to determine whether you have a command installed, download web pages, save the output from a file using redirection, and view the contents of files directly from the terminal.

The cURL program is a common way to load web pages from the command line. To load all of the HTML code for the website *https://www.torproject.org*, for example, run the following command:

```
curl https://www.torproject.org
```

To see if cURL is installed, use the `which` command:

```
which curl
```

If cURL is installed, the output should show you the path where the program is installed on your computer (something like */usr/bin/curl*). If not, the output should return you to the shell prompt.

If you don't have cURL, use your package manager to install it. Enter **sudo apt install curl** for Windows with WSL and Linux machines or **brew install curl** for Macs. Then run **which curl** again, and you should see the path to the cURL program.

### Download a Web Page with cURL

When you load a web page, your web browser renders a human-readable version of its content based on the page's HTML, CSS, and JavaScript code. To see the raw HTML content from the web page hosted at *https://example .com*, run the following command in your terminal:

```
curl example.com
```

If you load that site in a browser and then view the HTML source by pressing CTRL-U in Windows or Linux, or ⌘-U in macOS, you should see the same HTML code that this command displays in your terminal.

Some websites are designed to show you text that's easy to read in a terminal when you access them through cURL, as opposed to showing you HTML. For example, *https://ifconfig.co* will tell you your IP address, geolocate it, and tell you what country and city it thinks you're in. Try running the following command:

```
curl https://ifconfig.co
```

This should display your IP address. Next, run the following:

```
curl https://ifconfig.co/country
```

When I run this command, my output is United States. You can try connecting to a VPN server in another country and then run it again; it should detect your web traffic as coming from that other country.

### Save a Web Page to a File

Run the following commands to load *https://example.com* and save it to a file:

```
cd /tmp
curl https://example.com > example.html
```

The first line of code changes your working directory to */tmp*, a temporary folder where files you store get deleted automatically. The second line loads *https://example.com*, but instead of displaying the site's contents for you in the terminal, it redirects them into the file *example.html* and doesn't display anything in the terminal.

The > character takes the output of the command to its left and saves it into the filename to its right. This is called *redirection*. Since you changed to the */tmp* folder before running the curl command and the filename you provided was a relative path, it saved to the file */tmp/example.html*.

Run a directory listing to make sure you've stored the file correctly:

```
ls -lh
```

This should list all the files in */tmp*, which should include a file called *example.html*. Try displaying the contents of that file in your terminal using the cat command:

```
cat /tmp/example.html
```

The terminal isn't always a good place to view a file's contents. For example, long lines will wrap, which may make them difficult to comprehend. In the following section, you'll learn more about the different types of files and how to work with them more easily in the command line.

## Text Files vs. Binary Files

There are many different types of files, but they all fit into one of two categories: *text files* and *binary files*.

Text files are made up of letters, numbers, punctuation, and a few special characters. Source code, like Python scripts (discussed in Chapters 7 and 8); shell scripts; and HTML, CSS, and JavaScript files are all examples of text files. Spreadsheets in CSV (comma-separated value) format and JSON files (discussed in Chapters 9 and 11, respectively) are also text files. These files are relatively simple to work with. You can use the cat command to display text files, as you did in the previous exercise.

Binary files are made up of data that's more than just letters, numbers, and punctuation. They're designed for computer programs, not humans, to understand. If you try to view the contents of a binary file using the cat command, you'll just see gibberish. Instead, you must use specialized programs that understand those binary formats. Office documents like PDFs, Word documents, and Excel spreadsheets are binary files, as are images (like PNG and JPEG files), videos (like MP4 and MOV files), and compressed data like ZIP files.

**NOTE** *The term* binary file *is technically a misnomer, because all files are represented by computers as binary—strings of ones and zeros.*

Text files aren't always easy to understand (if you're not familiar with HTML, viewing it might look like gibberish), but it's at least possible to display them in a terminal. This isn't true for binary files. For example, if you try using cat to display the contents of binary files like PNG images in your terminal, the output will look something like this:

```
?PNG

IHDR?L??
?D??????  Pd@?????Y????????u???+?2???ν???@?!N????  ^?K??E?(??U?N????E??‡??.?Ġ?u_??|?????g?s?‚{?@;?
?sQ
 ?x?)b?hK'?/??L???t?+???eC????+?@????L??????/@c@월7?qӃ?F
                                                      ?L????N??4Ҷ4???!?????
--snip--
```

Your terminal can't display all of the characters that make up PNG images, so those characters just don't get displayed. If you want to see the information stored in a PNG, you need to open it in software that's designed to view images.

To work with the files in datasets or write shell scripts and Python code, you'll need a *text editor*, a program designed to edit text files. You'll install a text editor in Exercise 3-5 to prepare for writing your first shell script.

### Exercise 3-5: Install the VS Code Text Editor

In this exercise, you'll download the free and open source text editor Visual Studio Code (VS Code) and practice using it to view a file. Download VS Code from *https://code.visualstudio.com* and install it. (If you're already familiar with another text editor, feel free to keep using that one instead.)

VS Code comes with a command called code that makes it easy to open files in VS Code directly from your terminal. Once VS Code is finished installing, run the following commands:

```
curl https://example.com > /tmp/example.html
code /tmp/example.html
```

The first line of code saves the HTML from *https://example.com* in the file */tmp/example.html*, just like you did in Exercise 3-4. The second line opens this file in VS Code.

When you open new files and folders in VS Code, it asks whether you trust each file's author, giving you the option to open the file in Restricted Mode. For the exercises in this book, you can open files without using Restricted Mode.

When you open *example.html*, it should look something like this:

```
<!doctype html>
<html>
<head>
    <title>Example Domain</title>

    <meta charset="utf-8" />
    <meta http-equiv="Content-type" content="text/html; charset=utf-8" />
    <meta name="viewport" content="width=device-width, initial-scale=1" />
    <style type="text/css">
    body {
        background-color: #f0f0f2;
        margin: 0;
        padding: 0;
        font-family: -apple-system, system-ui, BlinkMacSystemFont, "Segoe UI", "Open Sans",
"Helvetica Neue", Helvetica, Arial, sans-serif;

    }
--snip--
```

The output shows the same HTML code that you saw in your terminal when you ran cat/tmp/example.html in Exercise 3-4, but this time it should be much easier to read. VS Code and many other text editors have a feature called *syntax highlighting*, where different parts of the file appear in different colors. This makes it far quicker and easier for your brain to interpret source code, and also for you to catch mistakes in syntax.

VS Code is highly customizable and includes a wide variety of extensions that add extra functionality and make the program more pleasant to use. When you open new types of files, for instance, VS Code might ask if you'd like to install extensions to better support those files.

NOTE *To learn more about VS Code's other features, including when to use Restricted Mode, check out the documentation at* https://code.visualstudio.com/docs.

Now that you have some experience running commands in a shell and have set up a text editor, you'll write your first shell script in Exercise 3-6.

## Exercise 3-6: Write Your First Shell Script

As mentioned earlier, a shell script is a text file that contains a list of shell commands. When you tell your shell to run the script, it runs those commands one at a time. Many commands are themselves shell scripts, such as the man command you used earlier in this chapter.

### Navigate to Your USB Disk

Make sure your *datasets* USB disk is plugged in and mounted, and open up a terminal. To change your working directory to the *datasets* disk, skip to the subsection for your operating system.

#### Windows

After mounting your USB disk, open File Explorer by clicking **This PC** on the left. This page will show all of your connected drives and their drive letters. Note your USB disk's drive letter, then change your working directory to the disk by running the following command, substituting *d* for the correct drive letter:

```
cd /mnt/d/
```

Your shell's working directory should now be your *datasets* USB disk. To check, run **ls** to view the files on this disk.

#### macOS

After mounting your *datasets* USB disk, open a terminal and change your working directory to the disk by running the following command:

```
cd /Volumes/datasets
```

Your shell's working directory should now be your *datasets* USB disk. To check, run **ls** to view the files on this disk.

#### Linux

After mounting your *datasets* USB disk, open a terminal and change your working directory to the disk. In Linux, the path to your disk is probably something like */media/<username>/datasets*. For example, my username is *micah*, so I would run this command:

```
cd /media/micah/datasets
```

Your shell's working directory should now be your *datasets* USB disk. To check, run **ls** to view the files on this disk.

## Create an Exercises Folder

The mkdir command creates a new folder. Now that you're in your USB disk drive in your terminal, run the following commands to create a new folder called *exercises*, and then switch to it:

```
mkdir exercises
cd exercises
```

Now make a folder for your Chapter 3 exercises:

```
mkdir chapter-3
```

Next, you'll open the *exercises* folder in VS Code.

## Open a VS Code Workspace

Each VS Code window is called a *workspace*. You can add folders to your workspace, which allows you to easily open any files in that folder or create new ones. To open a VS Code workspace for your *exercises* folder, run the following command:

```
code .
```

If the argument that you pass into code is a folder, like . (the current working directory), VS Code will add that folder to your workspace. If the path is a file, like in Exercise 3-5 when you opened */tmp/example.html*, it will open just that file.

Next, create a new file in the *chapter-3* folder. To do this, right-click the *chapter-3* folder, choose **New File**, name your file *exercise-3-6.sh*, and press ENTER. This should create a new file that you can edit. Since the file extension is *.sh*, VS Code should correctly guess that it's a shell script and use the right type of syntax highlighting.

Figure 3-7 shows a VS Code workspace with the *exercises* folder added and the empty file *exercise-3-6.sh* created.

The VS Code window is split into two main parts. The Explorer panel on the left shows the contents of all of the folders added to your workspace. In this case, it shows *exercises* and everything it contains: a *chapter-3* folder and the *exercise-3-6.sh* file you just created. The right side of the window is the editor, where you'll enter your shell script.

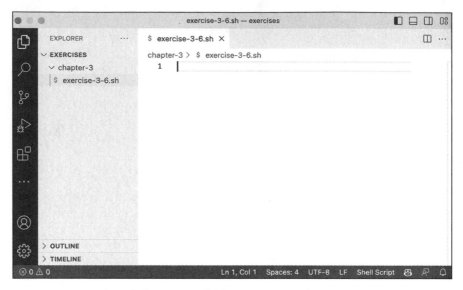

*Figure 3-7: VS Code with the* exercises *folder open in a workspace*

## Write the Shell Script

Enter the following text into *exercise-3-6.sh* in VS Code and save the file:

```bash
#!/bin/bash
echo "Hello world! This is my first shell script."
# Display the current user
echo "The current user is:"
whoami
# Display the current working directory
echo "The current working directory is:"
pwd
```

The first line that starts with #! is called the *shebang*, and it tells the shell which *interpreter*—the program that opens and runs the script—to use. In this case, the shell will use /bin/bash, meaning you're writing a bash script. In this book, you'll add that same shebang to the top of all of your shell scripts. Even if you're working from a shell besides bash, this shebang tells your computer to run the current script using bash.

In shell scripts, lines that start with the hash character (#) are called *comments*, and they don't affect how the code itself works; if you removed the comments from this script, it would run the same way. The first character of the shebang is a hash character, which means that it's technically a comment in bash and zsh.

Comments like # Display the current user work as notes to remind you what your code does when you come back to a script you wrote months or years earlier. Anyone else who works with your code, perhaps trying to fix something or add features, will appreciate your comments for the same reason.

The echo command displays text to the terminal. The whoami command displays the name of the user running the script. The pwd command displays the current working directory.

## Run the Shell Script

Before you can run a script, you need to make it *executable* by giving it permission to run as a program. The chmod command lets you change permissions on files with the following syntax:

```
chmod permissions filename
```

To mark a file as executable, use +x as the *permissions* argument. Run the following command in your terminal (from within your *exercises* folder):

```
chmod +x ./chapter-3/exercise-3-6.sh
```

You can now run the script by entering either its absolute path or its relative path:

```
./chapter-3/exercise-3-6.sh
```

Starting your command with ./ tells your shell that you're entering the relative path to a script.

Here's the output I get when I run this script on my Mac:

```
Hello world! This is my first shell script.
The current user is:
micah
The current working directory is:
/Volumes/datasets/exercises
```

The current user is *micah* and the current working directory is */Volumes/datasets/exercises.*

This script shows you different output depending on your working directory. To demonstrate the differences, here's what happens when I switch to my home folder and then run it again:

```
micah@trapdoor exercises % cd ~
micah@trapdoor ~ % /Volumes/datasets/exercises/chapter-3/exercise-3-6.sh
Hello world! This is my first shell script.
The current user is:
micah
The current working directory is:
/Users/micah
```

This time, the current working directory in the output has changed to */Users/micah.* Try switching to your own home folder with **cd ~** and running the script again.

The script also shows different output depending on which user is running it. So far I've been running it as *micah*, but here's what the output looks like when I run it as root:

```
micah@trapdoor ~ % sudo /Volumes/datasets/exercises/chapter-3/exercise-3-6.sh
Password:
Hello world! This is my first shell script.
The current user is:
root
The current working directory is:
/Users/micah
```

This time, the output lists the current user as root. Try running the script as root on your own computer.

You'll write many more scripts throughout this book. I've included a copy of the code for every exercise in this book's online resources. In Exercise 3-7, you'll download a copy of all of this code.

## Exercise 3-7: Clone the Book's GitHub Repository

Programmers store source code in *git repositories* (or *git repos* for short), which are composed of a collection of files (usually source code) and the history of how they have changed over time. By storing your scripts this way, you can host them on GitHub, a popular website for hosting git repos. Git repos help you share your code with others, and they make it easier for multiple people to write code for the same project. When you *clone* a git repo, you download a copy of it to your computer.

This book comes with a git repo at *https://github.com/micahflee/hacks-leaks -and-revelations* containing the code for every exercise and case study in this book, along with additional instructions and source code related to the book's appendixes. In this exercise, you'll clone this repo and store the copy locally on your computer.

First, check whether the git program is installed on your machine:

```
which git
```

If git is installed, you'll see its path in the output, like */usr/bin/git*. If it's not installed, this command won't display anything in the terminal. In that case, install git by entering the appropriate command for your operating system: **brew install git** for macOS users, or **sudo apt install git** for Linux and WSL users.

Next, in your terminal, change to your USB disk folder. On my macOS computer, I do this with the following command:

```
cd /Volumes/datasets
```

If necessary, replace the path in my command with the appropriate path to your *datasets* USB disk for your operating system.

Once you're in the *datasets* disk, run this command to clone the repo:

```
git clone https://github.com/micahflee/hacks-leaks-and-revelations.git
```

This should create a new folder called *hacks-leaks-and-revelations* containing all of the code from the book's repo.

Finally, add the book's git repo folder to your VS Code workspace. In VS Code, click **File ▸ Add Folder to Workspace**, then browse for the *hacks-leaks-and-revelations* folder on your USB disk. This will add the book's code to your VS Code workspace so you can easily browse through all of the files.

You now have access to solutions for all future exercises! In the following chapters, I'll walk you through the process of writing your own scripts from scratch, but you can also run the complete scripts taken from the git repo or copy and paste their code into your own code.

## Summary

In this chapter, you've learned the basics of command line theory, including how to use the shell in a terminal, run various shell commands, and navigate the shell using features like tab completion. You installed software directly in the terminal using a package manager, and you wrote your first simple shell script.

In the next chapters, you'll put these techniques into practice to explore hundreds of gigabytes of data, make datasets searchable, convert email from a proprietary format to an open format, and write Python code. You'll start in the following chapter by taking a deeper dive into the BlueLeaks dataset.

# 4

## EXPLORING DATASETS IN THE TERMINAL

In this chapter, you'll build on the command line skills you've learned so far and begin investigating real datasets. You'll use for loops to unzip the BlueLeaks files, then search the files to determine which fusion centers have the most data and which documents contain the keywords *antifa* and *Black Lives Matter*. I'll also give an overview of the mysterious encrypted data in the dataset and describe my hypothesis of how the hacker collected the data.

You'll also learn to create Linux cloud servers and connect to them securely for faster internet and extra disk space. As practice, you'll use a remote server to download and briefly examine hacked data from the Oath Keepers militia, a far-right extremist group that participated in the January 6, 2021, US Capitol insurrection.

## Introducing for Loops

The BlueLeaks torrent you downloaded in Exercise 2-1 is 269GB and contains 168 different ZIP files ranging from 49GB to half a kilobyte each. In theory, you could manually unzip these 168 files one at a time to access the data. However, this slow, tedious process becomes impractical with even larger datasets (imagine individually extracting 10,000 ZIP files). In this section, you'll learn to speed up this task by automating it with for loops.

A for loop is a type of command that runs a piece of code once for every item in a list. Each time the code loops, it stores the current item in a *variable*, which you can think of as a placeholder for some value. Code variables are similar to those in math, where the value of $x$ might be different for different problems, but in shell scripting, the values can be text or numbers. Even though each loop runs the same code, the results may be different, because the value of the variable changes with each loop.

For example, the following for loop displays the numbers 1, 2, and 3:

```
for NUMBER in 1 2 3
do
    echo $NUMBER
done
```

This for loop starts with the syntax for *variable_name* in *list_of_items*, followed by do, followed by the commands to run for each item in the list, followed by done. In this case, *variable_name* is NUMBER and *list_of_items* is 1 2 3. The value of the NUMBER variable will be 1 the first time the code loops, 2 during the second loop, and 3 during the third loop.

The echo command displays something, in this case $NUMBER, to the terminal. The dollar sign ($) means the code should display the value of the NUMBER variable, rather than the word NUMBER.

**NOTE** *Using all caps is a common convention for variable names, but it's not required. For example, you could call the variable number instead of NUMBER and display it with echo $number instead of echo $NUMBER. Variable names are case sensitive.*

When you run the previous for loop in your terminal, you should see the following output:

```
1
2
3
```

You can also use a for loop to loop through the output of another shell command, as shown in the following code:

```
for FILENAME in $(ls *.zip)
do
    echo "ZIP filename: $FILENAME"
done
```

The variable name in this code is FILENAME. Next, $(ls *.zip) tells your machine to run the ls *.zip command. This command outputs a list of all of the ZIP files in the current folder, producing a list of filenames. The for loop cycles through that list and runs the code between do and done for each filename. In this case, the echo command prints the filenames to the terminal in ZIP filename: *filename* format.

For example, here's what it looks like when I run this code in the *BlueLeaks* folder in my terminal on macOS:

```
micah@trapdoor BlueLeaks % for FILENAME in $(ls *.zip)
for> do
for>     echo "ZIP filename: $FILENAME"
for> done
ZIP filename: 211sfbay.zip
ZIP filename: Securitypartnership.zip
ZIP filename: acprlea.zip
--snip--
```

Each time the code loops, the value of FILENAME is the name of one of the ZIP files. When the echo command runs, it displays those filenames, one after another.

## Exercise 4-1: Unzip the BlueLeaks Dataset

In this exercise, you'll write a script to unzip all the ZIP files in BlueLeaks so you can work with the data they contain. Once unzipped, the files will take 271GB of additional space on your *datasets* USB.

If you're using macOS or Linux, follow the instructions in "Unzip Files on macOS or Linux" next. If you're using Windows, read that subsection to learn how to write for loops in bash since you'll need that skill later in the book, but you won't need to follow along until "Unzip Files on Windows" on page 92.

### Unzip Files on macOS or Linux

Open a terminal and navigate to your *BlueLeaks* folder by running the following command, replacing *blueleaks_path* with your own folder path:

```
cd blueleaks_path
```

On Linux, I'd use this command (your path will be different):

```
cd /media/micah/datasets/BlueLeaks
```

On macOS, I'd use the following (again, your path will vary):

```
cd /Volumes/datasets/BlueLeaks
```

Run `ls` to see the list of files in this folder and `ls -lh` to see detailed information about these files, like their sizes.

To unzip single files, you use the following syntax:

```
unzip filename
```

For example, run this command to unzip the first file in BlueLeaks:

```
unzip 211sfbay.zip
```

This should extract the 2.6GB *211sfbay.zip* file into the folder called *211sfbay*. Run `ls` again and you should see the new folder containing all of the hacked data from one of the BlueLeaks sites.

However, you want to unzip *all* of the BlueLeaks files. Delete the *211sfbay* folder:

```
rm -r 211sfbay
```

The `rm` command on its own deletes files; to delete entire folders, you include `-r` (short for `--recursive`). The `-r` option deletes all the files in that folder, and all the files in folders in that folder, and so on, before finally deleting the target folder.

Navigate to your text editor, create a new folder in your *exercises* folder called *chapter-4*, and create a new file in the *chapter-4* folder called *exercise-4-1-unzip.sh*. (Storing your script in a separate folder prevents you from polluting the dataset with your own files.) In your new file, enter the following code:

```
#!/bin/bash
for FILENAME in $(ls *.zip)
do
    echo "Unzipping $FILENAME..."
    unzip -o $FILENAME
done
```

Since *exercise-4-1-unzip.sh* is a shell script, it begins with the same #!/bin/bash shebang as the script in Chapter 3. After you define this for loop, the script starts it with do and ends it with done, running the echo "Unzipping $FILENAME..." and unzip -o $FILENAME commands over and over. The echo command displays the value of the FILENAME variable, which changes to a new filename with each loop, and the unzip command unzips that file. The -o argument tells unzip to *overwrite* files if necessary, meaning that if any file being unzipped already exists, the script will replace it with the newer version.

For example, when you run this code on BlueLeaks, the value of FILENAME during the first loop is 211sfbay.zip. The code that runs in this loop is equivalent to the following commands:

```
echo "Unzipping 211sfbay.zip..."
unzip -o 211sfbay.zip
```

The second time the code loops, it runs the same code with `acprlea.zip` as the FILENAME value, and so on.

Change to your *BlueLeaks* folder. On my Mac, I do this by running the following command:

```
cd /Volumes/datasets/BlueLeaks
```

Next, make this shell script executable and run it as follows:

```
chmod +x ../exercises/chapter-4/exercise-4-1-unzip.sh
../exercises/chapter-4/exercise-4-1-unzip.sh
```

These commands assume that your *exercises* folder is in the same folder as the *BlueLeaks* folder. The relative path to your *exercises* folder is *../exercises*, and the relative path to the shell script you just saved is *../exercises/chapter-4/exercise-4-1-unzip.sh*.

After you run these commands, your script should begin unzipping all 168 BlueLeaks files. Sit back, relax, and perhaps enjoy a beverage while you wait for it to finish, which could take hours.

---

### LOOPING THROUGH FILENAMES WITH SPACES

Looping over the output of `ls` as you've just done works only if the filenames don't contain spaces. If they did, your script would fail due to invalid filenames. For example, if you had a file called *Work Documents.zip* in the folder, the for loop would consider it two files, *Work* and *Documents.zip*, as discussed in Chapter 3.

The output of the `ls` command is a *string*—that is, a list of characters—with each filename separated by a newline character (\n), which represents a line break. If you have two files in a folder, *readme.txt* and *Work Documents.zip*, the `ls` command outputs a string like `readme.txt\nWork Documents.zip`.

The bash shell includes an environment variable called IFS (short for "internal field separator"), which the shell uses to figure out how to split strings in a for loop. By default, strings are split by any whitespace: spaces, tabs, or newlines. This is why, if you loop through the string `1 2 3`, you get three smaller strings—1, 2, and 3—separated with spaces. Likewise, looping through the string `readme.txt\nWork Documents.zip` results in the smaller strings `readme.txt`, `Work`, and `Documents.zip`, separated with a newline character and a space.

To work with filenames with spaces, you change the value of the IFS variable so that it splits strings only on newline characters, but not on spaces or tabs. Then you change it back after the loop. Here's an example:

```
#!/bin/bash
ORIGINAL_IFS=$IFS
IFS=$(echo -n "\n")
```

*(continued)*

---

```
for FILENAME in $(ls)
do
    echo "$FILENAME"
done
IFS=$ORIGINAL_IFS
```

Inside the for loop, the FILENAME variable will contain the full filename, even if it includes spaces. You can use code like this to unzip files (as long as they're all ZIP files) or open them using any other CLI program.

None of the ZIP filenames in the BlueLeaks data have spaces, but you may need to use this script on filenames with spaces for future projects.

If you're not using Windows, skip ahead to the "Organize Your Files" section on page 93. Otherwise, read on.

## Unzip Files on Windows

Unzipping files in WSL from a USB disk formatted for Windows might be *very* slow, due to WSL performance problems. Fortunately, there's a much faster way to unzip all 168 files in BlueLeaks, using PowerShell and a program called 7-Zip.

### Install 7-Zip

The open source Windows archiving program 7-Zip lets you extract various types of compressed files. Download and install 7-Zip from *https://www .7-zip.org*. You'll receive a warning saying that the program is made by an unknown publisher, but it's safe to install as long as you've downloaded it from the official website.

After you install 7-Zip, you can use its *7z.exe* program to extract files directly from PowerShell. By default, *7z.exe* should be located in *C:\Program Files\7-Zip\7z.exe*. However, to run the program from any directory, add *C:\Program Files\7-Zip* to your Path environment variable.

*Environment variables* are variables that already exist when you open your shell, as opposed to ones that you create in a for loop or by other methods. The Path environment variable is a list of folders that contain programs. It contains some folders by default, but you can also add your own. When you run 7z, PowerShell looks in each folder listed in Path and checks for a file called *7z.exe*, then runs that program for you.

To add *7z.exe* to Path, click **Start**, search for **environment variables**, and click **Edit the System Environment Variables**. In the window that opens, click **Environment Variables**, and you should see a window with lists of user variables and system variables. Double-click **Path** in the User Variables box, which should show you all of the folders stored in Path. Click **New**, add *C:\Program Files\7-Zip*, and click **OK** to save. If you have a PowerShell window open, close PowerShell and open it again, forcing the shell to use the new changes to the Path environment variable.

You can now use the 7z command to run 7-Zip.

### Unzip in PowerShell with 7-Zip

In a PowerShell terminal, change to the *BlueLeaks* folder on your *datasets* USB disk. For example, on my computer, I run:

```
cd D:\BlueLeaks
```

Next, run the following PowerShell commands (this is the PowerShell version of the *exercise-4-1-unzip.sh* shell script in the previous subsection):

```
$ZipFiles = Get-ChildItem -Path . -Filter "*.zip"
foreach ($ZipFile in $ZipFiles) {
    7z x $ZipFile.FullName
}
```

The first line sets the PowerShell variable $ZipFiles to the list of ZIP files it finds in the current folder, represented by the dot (.). This is followed by a foreach loop, which loops through this list, setting the variable $ZipFile to the name of each file. The 7z command runs over and over again for each different filename, unzipping each file.

When I run these commands in my PowerShell terminal, I get the following output:

```
Scanning the drive for archives:
1 file, 2579740749 bytes (2461 MiB)

Extracting archive: D:\BlueLeaks\211sfbay.zip
--
Path = D:\BlueLeaks\211sfbay.zip
Type = zip
Physical Size = 2579740749
--snip--
```

Your PowerShell window should likewise begin unzipping all 168 BlueLeaks files.

**NOTE** *Once you're finished with this chapter, read Appendix A and implement one of the solutions it describes for avoiding WSL performance problems to make it easier to work with big datasets like BlueLeaks in Windows going forward. You'll use WSL for the remainder of the book, so you'll need a plan to resolve any issues you encounter.*

## Organize Your Files

Your *BlueLeaks* folder should now be full of both ZIP files and extracted folders. Now you'll make a separate *BlueLeaks-extracted* folder for the extracted data and keep the ZIP files themselves in the *BlueLeaks* folder so that you can continue to seed the torrent with them if you like.

Open a terminal (if you're in Windows, switch to a WSL Ubuntu terminal again), change folders to your *datasets* USB disk, and run the following commands:

```
mv BlueLeaks BlueLeaks-extracted
mkdir BlueLeaks
mv BlueLeaks-extracted/*.zip BlueLeaks
```

The mv command moves or renames files. On the first line, it renames the *BlueLeaks* folder *BlueLeaks-extracted*. The mkdir command, which you used in Chapter 3, creates a new empty folder called *BlueLeaks*. The third command moves all of the ZIP files in the *BlueLeaks-extracted* folder into the newly created *BlueLeaks* folder.

Your *datasets* USB disk should now contain a folder called *BlueLeaks* with 250GB of ZIP files, along with another folder called *BlueLeaks-extracted* with 269GB of extracted hacked police data.

## How the Hacker Obtained the BlueLeaks Data

We don't know how the hacker hacked and leaked the BlueLeaks files, but we can make an educated guess based on clues from the dataset.

Imagine that it's June 6, 2020, less than two weeks after Minneapolis cop Derek Chauvin murdered George Floyd by kneeling on his neck for over nine minutes while Floyd struggled to breathe, triggering the summer's Black Lives Matter uprising against police violence. Millions of people took to the streets to demand police accountability and the end of racist police violence in what was "the largest movement in the country's history," according to the *New York Times*.

Now imagine you're a hacktivist. In addition to confronting police in the streets, you're confronting them on the internet. Using OSINT, you've discovered that hundreds of police websites use the same shoddy web application developed by the Texas web development firm Netsential. All these sites run on Windows, use Microsoft's Internet Information Services (IIS) web server software, and are programmed using Microsoft's web framework ASP.NET. They're also all hosted from IP addresses in the same data center in Texas.

After you spend some time poking around one of these sites, the Arizona High Intensity Drug Trafficking Area (AZHIDTA), you find what you were looking for: a *remote code execution vulnerability*, a type of bug that lets you run commands on a remote server, like the Windows server running the AZHIDTA website. (My guess is that the vulnerability started with SQL injection, a technology beyond the scope of this book.)

**WARNING** *I'm about to tell you about a potential URL for a hacking tool left behind by the hacker, but don't actually try loading it in your browser because it might be illegal. Attempting to access someone else's hacking tools is definitely a legal gray area.*

To open a shell on this web server, you use a *web shell*, a web page that, when you submit a form with a command in it, runs that command on the web server and responds with its output. Using the vulnerability you discovered, you save a web shell into a file called *blug.aspx* on the web server's disk. Loading */blug.aspx* on the *https://www.azhidta.org* website in your browser allows you to run whatever commands you want on the server.

The web shell *blug.aspx* is included in the BlueLeaks dataset. In order to understand how this web shell works, I set up a Windows virtual machine with an IIS server to test it, as shown in Figure 4-1. The left side of the screenshot is the shell (in which I ran the command dir c:\). The right side let me browse the server's filesystem and upload new files.

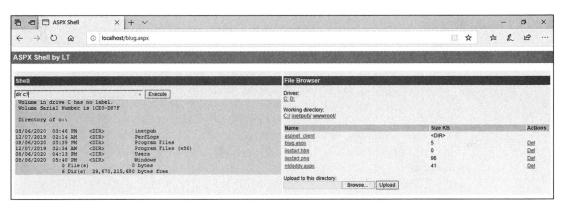

*Figure 4-1: Testing the* blug.aspx *web shell in a Windows VM*

I don't know for sure if this is how the BlueLeaks hack happened, but I think it's very likely. While researching BlueLeaks, I found the following web shell files, all timestamped late on June 6, 2020, making them among the most recently created files in the dataset:

*azhidta/ntdaddy.aspx*    The Classic ASP web shell NTDaddy, developed around 2001 by a hacker named obzerve

*azhidta/blug.aspx*    The ASP.NET web shell called ASPX Shell, developed in 2007 by a hacker named LT

*azhidta/pscp64.exe*    A program that comes with PuTTY, a popular Windows tool for securely copying files to and from remote servers

*icefishx/7z.exe*    A copy of the 7-Zip compression and extraction program

My guess is that the hacktivist first tried to create a *ntdaddy.aspx* web shell, but found that it didn't work because it was developed using an earlier version of ASP called Classic ASP, while the BlueLeaks site used the modern version, ASP.NET. They then created the *blug.aspx* web shell instead, used that shell to upload *pscp64.exe* and *7z.exe*, used *7z.exe* to compress all of the files for a given police website, and uploaded that data to their own server with *pscp64.exe*.

After manually hacking one of the BlueLeaks sites, the hacker likely automated the process for the rest of the BlueLeaks sites. Perhaps they created a shell script that used cURL instead of a web browser to perform the same steps. They could have run that script in a for loop targeting all 251 websites, uploading hundreds of gigabytes of data to themselves, in a single Saturday evening. They then likely forgot to delete the *blug.aspx*, *pscp64.exe*, *7z.exe*, and *ntdaddy.aspx* files before submitting the dataset to DDoSecrets.

## Exercise 4-2: Explore BlueLeaks on the Command Line

In this exercise, you'll start exploring the contents of your unzipped BlueLeaks files, using commands and advanced shell features that let you quickly measure file and folder size and sort and count lines of output.

### Calculate How Much Disk Space Folders Use

The du command (short for "disk usage") is a powerful tool for assessing a new dataset. Linux and macOS come with slightly different versions of du. The Linux version, which is part of a software package called GNU coreutils, is better and more up to date at the time of writing, so you'll use it for this exercise.

Users of Linux and Windows with WSL should already have the correct built-in du tool. If you're using macOS, run **brew install coreutils** in the terminal to install coreutils. After this, the du command will run the macOS version of the tool, while the gdu command will run the coreutils version that you just installed. In the following commands, macOS users should replace du with gdu.

To find out how much space the extracted BlueLeaks dataset takes, open your terminal and run this command, using the path to the *BlueLeaks -extracted* folder on your computer:

```
du -sh --apparent-size /media/micah/datasets/BlueLeaks-extracted
```

The -s argument in this command (short for --summarize) displays the total disk space of a folder rather than how much space each file inside it takes up. The -h argument (short for --human-readable) shows file sizes in units like kilobytes, megabytes, or gigabytes, rather than in terms of system blocks (a unit that changes depending on how your disk is set up). Finally, the --apparent-size argument shows you how big the files actually are, as opposed to how much space they take up on your disk.

The command checks the size of every file in BlueLeaks and adds them all together, so it takes a while to run. When it's done, it should tell you that the *BlueLeaks-extracted* folder takes up 269GB.

**NOTE**    *In addition to using -h to generate human-readable units, you can specify which units you want to use. The -b argument, short for --bytes, shows file sizes in bytes, -k shows them in kilobytes, and -m shows them in megabytes.*

Next, you'll measure the size of an individual folder in BlueLeaks. Change to your *BlueLeaks-extracted* folder; for example, I'd run cd /media/ micah/datasets/BlueLeaks-extracted on my Linux computer. From there, run the following command to measure the size of the *ncric* folder, which contains documents from the Northern California Regional Intelligence Center (NCRIC), the fusion center I've spent the most time researching:

```
du -sh --apparent-size ncric
```

The output should tell you that the *ncric* folder takes 19GB.

To find out the size of each folder in BlueLeaks, you could run the du -sh --apparent-size *path* command for each folder, but it's quicker to use another for loop. Run the following code in the terminal:

```
for FOLDER in $(ls); do du -sh --apparent-size $FOLDER; done
```

As shown here, you can run multiple commands on the same line by separating them with semicolons (;). This one-liner loops through the output of the ls command, which, since you're currently in the *BlueLeaks -extracted* folder, is the name of each BlueLeaks folder. The code stores these names in the FOLDER variable and then, inside each iteration of the loop, runs the du -sh --apparent-size $FOLDER command.

Here are the first few lines of output:

```
2.8G    211sfbay
29M     Securitypartnership
216M    acprlea
65M     acticaz
748M    akorca
--snip--
```

This shows you how much disk space each folder uses.

## Use Pipes and Sort Output

You now know the size of each folder in the BlueLeaks dataset. Next, you'll sort the 168 folders in order of disk space. By determining which folders are the largest, you can quickly tell which fusion centers have the most data and therefore are probably the biggest or most active.

To sort this list of folders by the smallest file size to the largest, use the sort command, which takes a list of text lines and, by default, sorts them *alphanumerically*; that is, text is sorted alphabetically and numbers are sorted by their first numeral. For example, the list file1, file10, file2, . . . , file9 is sorted alphanumerically: since text lines are sorted one character at a time, and since 1 is less than 2, file10 comes before file2.

To sort your BlueLeaks files by file size, modify the command with the -h (--human-numeric-sort) argument. This argument pays attention to the *value* of numbers, not just characters, so it correctly places smaller numerical values before larger ones. It also takes file size units into account, meaning it will place 2MB before 1GB, even though 2 is numerically greater than 1.

In shell scripting, the *pipe* operator (|) lets you take the output of a command to the left of the operator and pipe it into the command on the right. When you pipe input into the sort command, it outputs a sorted version of that input. Run the for loop from the previous subsection, this time piping the output into sort:

```
for FOLDER in $(ls); do du -sh –apparent-size $FOLDER; done | sort -h
```

This line first runs the for loop that measures the space each BlueLeaks folder takes up. The output of this code is a list of lines of text, where each line starts with the human-readable size of a folder. Piping those lines of text as input into the sort -h command sorts those lines numerically while paying attention to the file size units.

Your output should look like this:

```
256      miacxold
256      ncric-history-good
256      ncricSteveBackup
259K     terrorismtip
548K     oaktac
625K     sccpca
--snip--
13G      lacleartraining
14G      jric
19G      ncric
36G      miacx
46G      repo
```

The folders that have the least data should be at the top: *miacxold*, *ncric-history-good*, and *ncricSteveBackup* contain only empty subfolders. The *repo* folder, the largest folder in BlueLeaks, should appear at the bottom of the list, right after *miacx*, the second-largest folder.

## FILE SIZE UNITS AND CONVERSIONS

You're likely familiar with file size units like megabytes and gigabytes, and you might have a mental model of how much information those units can hold: Office documents are often a few megabytes, a two-hour video file might be a gigabyte or two, and a video game might be hundreds of gigabytes. Being able to convert between the different units of disk space is an important skill for working with large datasets.

Units like kilobyte, megabyte, gigabyte, and terabyte sound metric, but they're not. For instance, the *kilo-* prefix denotes a factor of 1,000, but there are 1,024 bytes in a kilobyte. Here's a list of common conversions:

- 1 byte (B): 8 bits, or 8 ones and zeros in binary
- 1 kilobyte (KB): 1,024 bytes
- 1 megabyte (MB): 1,024 kilobytes
- 1 gigabyte (GB): 1,024 megabytes
- 1 terabyte (TB): 1,024 gigabytes
- 1 petabyte (PB): 1,024 terabytes

As an example, the *ncric* folder in BlueLeaks is 20,008,051,852 bytes, which is 19,539,113.1KB, or 19,081.2MB, or 18.6GB—about 160 billion bits.

## Create an Inventory of Filenames in a Dataset

When you're working with an enormous dataset like BlueLeaks, it's helpful to create an inventory of all of the files it contains by listing them in a text file. This way you can easily count the number of files in the dataset or search for filenames without having to go through the much slower process of looping through the dataset itself.

You can create this inventory with the find command, which outputs a list of files and folders in a folder. From within the *BlueLeaks-extracted* folder, run the following command to list all of the files in BlueLeaks:

```
find . -type f
```

The first argument after find is the folder whose contents you want to list. This command uses a dot to find files in the current folder, but you could use any relative or absolute path. The -type f arguments filters the list so it includes only files. (To include only folders, add the -type d arguments.)

When you run this command, the names of the many files in BlueLeaks should start rapidly scrolling across your terminal. To make the output more manageable, run the command again, this time redirecting the output into the file *../BlueLeaks-filenames.txt*:

```
find . -type f > ../BlueLeaks-filenames.txt
```

As discussed in Chapter 3, redirection tells your shell to take the output from the left side of the redirection operator (>) and save it into the file at the path you specify on the right. In this case, the shell sends the list of filenames from the find command to the *BlueLeaks-filenames.txt* file on your *datasets* USB disk, rather than displaying the filenames across your terminal.

To read through these filenames at your leisure, open *BlueLeaks-filenames.txt* in VS Code by running this command:

```
code ../BlueLeaks-filenames.txt
```

It's easier to slowly scroll through these files in your text editor, but there are too many to count with the naked eye.

## Count the Files in a Dataset

The wc command takes some input and tells you how many characters, words, or lines it contains. When used with the -l (or --lines) argument, it counts the number of lines. To count the lines in the *BlueLeaks-filenames.txt* file you created, and by extension count the number of files in BlueLeaks, run the following command:

```
cat ../BlueLeaks-filenames.txt | wc -l
```

The cat command outputs the contents of a file—in this case, *BlueLeaks-filenames.txt*. Instead of displaying it, the command pipes the output into wc to count the number of lines that it contains. It should tell you that there are just over *one million* files in BlueLeaks.

Another way to get the same result is to run the find command from the previous section again, and pipe its output into wc, like this:

```
find . -type f | wc -l
```

That command takes longer to run, though, since it searches through the whole dataset again (press CTRL-C to cancel this command before it finishes).

## Exercise 4-3: Find Revelations in BlueLeaks with grep

In the summer of 2020, while American society was going through a long-due reckoning about the scale of racist police killings, right-wing media (and police) instead focused on the dangers of the protesters themselves. They lumped the modern civil rights movement into two categories: "Black Lives Matter" and "antifa," the latter a label used by antifascist activists since the 1930s. The modern American antifa movement grew in response to the 2016 election of Donald Trump and the mainstreaming of white supremacy in the US.

The grep command will filter input for keywords, letting you search the content of datasets for newsworthy information. In this exercise, you'll use grep to find out what police had to say about antifa during the protests.

### Filter for Documents Mentioning Antifa

You'll start by grepping your list of filenames to find any that include the word *antifa*. From the *BlueLeaks-extracted* folder, search the *BlueLeaks-filenames.txt* file that you created in Exercise 4-2 by running the following command:

```
cat ../BlueLeaks-filenames.txt | grep antifa
```

This command pipes the output of `cat ../BlueLeaks-filenames.txt`, which is a list of a million filenames, into `grep antifa`. This should filter the huge list of filenames to show you only those that include the word *antifa*. However, it returns no results.

Since the `grep` command is case sensitive, try again using the `-i` (or `--ignore-case`) argument:

```
cat ../BlueLeaks-filenames.txt | grep -i antifa
```

When I run this command, I get the following output:

```
./ociac/files/EBAT1/U-FOUO_CFIX__OCIAC_JRA_DVE Use of Social Media_ANTIFA_ANTI-ANTIFA MOVEMENTS
.pdf
./arictexas/files/DDF/ARIC-LES - Situational Awareness - Antifa Activity.pdf
./arictexas/files/DDF/SWTFC-LES - Situational Awareness - ANTIFA Event Notification.pdf
./arictexas/files/DPI/ARIC-LES - Situational Awareness - Antifa Activity.png
./arictexas/files/DPI/SWTFC-LES - Situational Awareness - ANTIFA Event Notification.png
./dediac/files/DDF/ANTIFA - Fighting in the Streets.pdf
./dediac/files/DDF/ANTIFA Sub Groups and Indicators - LES.pdf
./dediac/files/DDF/FBI_PH_SIR_Tactics_and_Targets_Identified_for_4_November_2017_ANTIFA_Rally_in
_Philadelphia_PA-2.pdf
./dediac/files/EBAT1/ANTIFA - Fighting in the Streets.pdf
./dediac/files/EBAT1/ANTIFA Sub Groups and Indicators - LES.pdf
./dediac/files/DPI/ANTIFA - Fighting in the Streets.png
./dediac/files/DPI/FBI_PH_SIR_Tactics_and_Targets_Identified_for_4_November_2017_ANTIFA_Rally_in
_Philadelphia_PA-2.png
```

This command returns 12 results, all files that have the term *antifa* in their filenames. The grep command might highlight your search terms in each line of output by coloring them differently; I've highlighted them here in bold. Open a few of the documents in this list to see what they contain.

**NOTE** *You can run BlueLeaks documents through Dangerzone if you like, but the risks are low with this dataset. These documents are now all public, so if any have tracking technology that lets the original file owner know someone is looking at the document, it doesn't matter much. Given that these are hacked documents from police fusion centers, not attachments on phishing email messages or something similar, they're also unlikely to be malicious.*

I often combine `find` and `grep` to make lists of filenames and filter those lists down, which allows me to locate files on my computer more quickly and precisely than with my operating system's graphical file search tools. For example, suppose you're looking into the *azhidta* folder for the Arizona High Intensity Drug Trafficking Area site. To quickly find any documents that have the word *marijuana* in their filename, you could run `find azhidta | grep -i marijuana`. To count the number of files with *marijuana* in the filenames, you could pipe all of that into the `wc -l` command.

## Filter for Certain Types of Files

In addition to searching for keywords like *antifa* or *marijuana*, grep can help you filter a list of filenames to include only certain file types. Grep for Microsoft Word documents, filenames that end in *.docx*, by running the following command:

```
cat ../BlueLeaks-filenames.txt | grep -i .docx
```

This command uses cat to display the list of filenames in BlueLeaks, then filters it down for those that contain *.docx*. You should see thousands of filenames scroll by. To learn exactly how many, run the command again, this time piping the output into wc -l:

```
cat ../BlueLeaks-filenames.txt | grep -i .docx | wc -l
```

The wc command should tell you that the previous command had 8,861 results.

## Use grep with Regular Expressions

If you scroll through the *.docx* filenames you just found, you'll see that a few of them aren't actually Word documents. For example, the filename *./arictexas/files/DDF/2014 Austin City Limits Festival - APD Threat Overview.docx .pdf* contains *.docx* but is actually a PDF.

When you use grep, you can pass a regular expression (regex for short) into it as an argument. A *regex* is a character or sequence of characters that defines a search pattern. For example, the caret character (^) represents the beginning of a line, and the dollar sign character ($) represents the end of a line. Grepping for something$ will show you only results that end with *something*. Grepping for ^something will show you only results that begin with *something*.

To search just for filenames that end with *.docx*, add a dollar sign ($) to the end of the text you're grepping for. For example, try running the following command:

```
cat ../BlueLeaks-filenames.txt | grep -i .docx$ | wc -l
```

The output should tell you that there are 8,737 results, 124 less than the previous command. That means there are 8,737 Word docs in this dataset.

Run the following command to find out how many Word docs are in the *ncric* folder:

```
cat ../BlueLeaks-filenames.txt | grep ^./ncric/ | grep -i .docx$ | wc -l
```

The cat command outputs the list of filenames in BlueLeaks, which is then piped into the first grep command, which in turn filters your output down to files that begin with *./ncric*, using ^. Next, that output is piped into the second grep command, which further filters the output to files that end with *.docx*, using $. Finally, the remaining output is piped into the wc -1 command, which tells you how many lines are left. The output of the full command should tell you that there are 600 Word docs in the *ncric* folder.

On your own, try using find, grep, and wc to find out how many PDFs (*.pdf*) and Excel documents (*.xlsx*) are in the dataset. You can also experiment with other file types.

## Search Files in Bulk with grep

In addition to piping output from other commands into grep, you can use grep to search directly within text files by using the following syntax:

```
grep search_term filename
```

For example, Linux comes with a file called */etc/passwd*, which includes a list of users on the system. To find just the line about my own user in that file, I can use one of the following commands:

```
grep micah /etc/passwd
cat /etc/passwd | grep micah
```

The grep command opens the */etc/passwd* file and then searches it, while the cat command opens that file and then pipes its contents into grep, which searches it. Both of these commands output the following result:

```
micah:x:1000:1000:,,,:/home/micah:/bin/bash
```

You can use grep to search multiple files, or even folders full of files, for hits all at once. As noted earlier, to search a folder, you use the -r (or --recursive) argument and specify the name of a folder. To specify multiple files at once, use an asterisk (*) as a wildcard character. For example, you can use *.txt as the filename to search all text files in your current folder.

There are CSV spreadsheets in every BlueLeaks folder that contain the contents of the websites' databases. Now that you've grepped for filenames that contain the keyword *antifa*, use the following command to bulk-search the term *Black Lives Matter* in the contents of the files, not just in their filenames:

```
grep -i "black lives matter" */*.csv
```

The -i argument in this command makes the search case insensitive. The black lives matter argument is the search term (in quotation marks, because it has spaces). The */*.csv argument is the path to search, which uses two wildcard characters. These arguments tell grep to open every folder, then each file within those folders that ends in *.csv*, and search for the *black lives matter* keyword.

This command takes some time to run because it's searching all 158,232 CSV files in BlueLeaks. When it's finished, it should show you the lines from CSV files that mention *black lives matter* and tell you in which files it found those lines. For example, here are snippets from a few of the lines of the output from that command:

```
arictexas/IncidentMap.csv:834,"10/26/16 00:00:00",-9.7735716800000006e+01,3.0267881299999999e+0
1,"TX",,"TLO","An APD Police Explorer received a call from a blocked number in which the caller
identified himself as an activist for Black Lives Matter, and identified the recipient by name,
address, and personal descriptors before calling him a racist for having an interest in a LE
career.  No explicit threats were made during the call...
bostonbric/EmailBuilder.csv:<p>
<strong>BRIC SHIELD Alert: </strong>To promote public safety and situational awareness for
events taking place in the City of Boston tonight, the BRIC is sharing the information below
regarding planned activities. </p>... <p><b>Known COB Activities for Tuesday, June 2nd</b></p>
<ul><li>Violence in Boston Inc & Black Lives Matter Rally and Vigil - 4:45 PM at 624 Blue Hill
Avenue. </li><li>Not One More! - 5:00 PM to 8:00 PM. Meeting at Franklin Park Road & Blue Hill
Ave and marching to Franklin Park. </li>...
chicagoheat/Blog.csv:Media sources report that the online activist group Anonymous, or a group
claiming to be Anonymous, has called for a collective 'Day of Rage' to take place in numerous
cities across the United States on Friday, July 15th. The action has been called in solidarity
with the Black Lives Matter movement in light of the recent controversial officer-involved
shootings that resulted in the deaths of Alton Sterling and Philando Castile. The group that
posted the call for action states that acts of violence or rioting are to be condemned.
ncric/Requests.csv:Organizer of a Black Lives Matter Protest for 06/02.  Currently scheduled
1PM meet time at Sears parking lot of Newpark Mall.  They plan to march to City Hall and then
to Fremont PD.  She has repeated she intends for a peaceful protest.  She further claims she
reached out to City and PD to join the march.  Recent graphics encourage non-descript clothing,
heat resistant gloves, turning off Face Id on iPhone etc.
```

The command finds a total of 178 lines in BlueLeaks CSVs that contain the term *black lives matter*. Each is a potential lead for further investigative research.

**NOTE** *The grep command is a great tool for searching the content of text files, but it doesn't work with binary files, like Microsoft Office documents or PDFs. To search those in bulk, you'll need more sophisticated tools, which you'll learn about in Chapter 5.*

On your own, try using grep to filter the list of BlueLeaks filenames for specific words or bulk-search terms within the CSV files. If you find any interesting documents, read them to see if they're newsworthy. Consider narrowing your searches once you find a lead by looking for other related documents. You might focus on a single fusion center or a topic like antifa that spans different centers. Individual documents may contain law enforcement lingo you can use as search terms for related documents. Take detailed notes on what's most revealing in each document, then rely on these notes if you decide to write about your findings.

## Encrypted Data in the BlueLeaks Dataset

As you dig around in the BlueLeaks dataset, you'll notice some patterns. Most folders contain many CSVs, as well as *.aspx* files, the source code of the hacked websites. They also contain *files* subfolders containing the bulk of the files and folders uploaded to each site, including PDFs and Microsoft Office documents.

However, one folder, *repo*, contains just a *config* file and *data*, *index*, *keys*, *locks*, and *snapshots* subfolders. Inside those subfolders are other subfolders and files with apparently random names. There are no documents that can be opened—no spreadsheets or similar files. As you discovered in Exercise 4-2, the *repo* folder is the largest folder in BlueLeaks, at 46GB. Its timestamps are from June 8, 2020, although the latest timestamps for most of the rest of the dataset are from June 6. Without more information, it's not clear what these files mean or how to access them.

When I discover a mystery like this in a dataset, I search the internet. In this case, I searched for the names of the files and folders within the *repo* folder by entering *config data index keys locks snapshots* into a search engine, and found documentation for a CLI program called restic. A restic repository, according to the documentation I found at *https://restic.readthedocs.io/en/latest/100_references.html*, is a folder that holds backup data. Restic repositories contain a *config* file and folders called *data*, *index*, *keys*, *locks*, and *snapshots*, as shown in Figure 4-2.

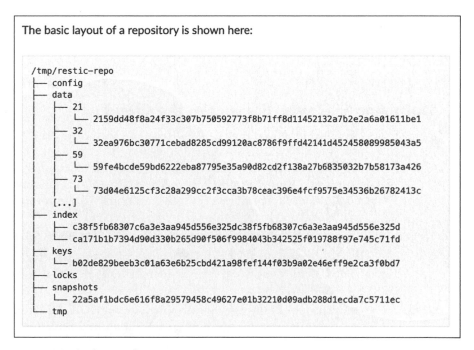

The basic layout of a repository is shown here:

```
/tmp/restic-repo
├── config
├── data
│   ├── 21
│   │   └── 2159dd48f8a24f33c307b750592773f8b71ff8d11452132a7b2e2a6a01611be1
│   ├── 32
│   │   └── 32ea976bc30771cebad8285cd99120ac8786f9ffd42141d4524580899985043a5
│   ├── 59
│   │   └── 59fe4bcde59bd6222eba87795e35a90d82cd2f138a27b6835032b7b58173a426
│   ├── 73
│   │   └── 73d04e6125cf3c28a299cc2f3cca3b78ceac396e4fcf9575e34536b26782413c
│   [...]
├── index
│   ├── c38f5fb68307c6a3e3aa945d556e325dc38f5fb68307c6a3e3aa945d556e325d
│   └── ca171b1b7394d90d330b265d90f506f9984043b342525f019788f97e745c71fd
├── keys
│   └── b02de829beeb3c01a63e6b25cbd421a98fef144f03b9a02e46eff9e2ca3f0bd7
├── locks
├── snapshots
│   └── 22a5af1bdc6e616f8a29579458c49627e01b32210d09adb288d1ecda7c5711ec
└── tmp
```

*Figure 4-2: The layout of a restic respository*

This suggests that the *repo* folder in BlueLeaks contains backup data in restic format. To find out what's inside this backup, I installed the restic package. Users of Linux or Windows with WSL can install restic using apt:

```
sudo apt install restic
```

Mac users can install restic from Homebrew with the following command:

```
brew install restic
```

I ran restic --help and found that I could view the snapshots in a repository with the restic snapshots command, which I then used to try to view the snapshots in the *repo* folder like so:

```
restic snapshots --repo repo/
```

I was then confronted with a password prompt:

```
enter password for repository:
```

This prompt indicates that the backup is encrypted. The only way to proceed is to guess the password, which I haven't been able to do.

While a 46GB folder full of encrypted data in a public leak is rare, it's not uncommon to stumble upon other encrypted files in datasets like Office documents or ZIP files. I can't help but imagine that the most interesting details in any dataset might be the encrypted parts. Password-cracking is outside the scope of this book, but if you can figure out the password for *repo*, please let me know.

## Data Analysis with Servers in the Cloud

So far, you've used the CLI *locally* on your own computer, but you can also use it *remotely* via servers to which you connect through a cloud network. DigitalOcean, AWS, Microsoft Azure, and countless other cloud hosting companies rent virtual private servers (VPSes) to the public, usually for a few dollars a month or a few cents an hour. All the command line skills you've learned so far apply to remote servers, too.

There are many advantages to working with massive datasets in the cloud:

- Instead of dealing with USB hard disks, you can attach virtual hard disks to your virtual servers, increasing their size if you're running low on disk space.
- VPS bandwidth is generally much better than residential or commercial internet service, speeding up large dataset downloads.
- You can also pay for more powerful VPSes for scripts that require significant computational resources, so they no longer take hours or days to finish running.
- Rather than being forced to wait while a script runs on your local machine, you can do whatever you want on your computer, even suspending it or shutting it down, while your remote server is crunching data.
- If your source has the required technical skills, you can ask them to upload data to a VPS with a large hard disk, as discussed in Chapter 2.

They can even do this anonymously using Tor. You can then download the dataset or choose to analyze it remotely on the VPS.

*Avoid working on cloud servers with high- or medium-sensitivity datasets. The cloud hosting provider has total access over your VPS and the data on it and can even give copies of that data to law enforcement or other parties in response to legal requests.*

This section will go into more detail on *SSH (Secure Shell)* software (introduced in Chapter 2), which allows you to securely get a shell on a VPS, as well as two tools that are essential for working remotely on the command line: text-based window managers and CLI text editors. This should prepare you to set up a VPS in the next exercise.

The SSH protocol is a method for securely logging in to another computer remotely. You can connect to a VPS remotely by running the ssh command with a username and the IP address or domain name of the server to which you want to connect. For example, to log in as the root user to the server with the hostname *example.com*, you run:

```
ssh root@example.com
```

You then need to *authenticate* to the server, or prove that you have permission to log in, by typing the user password or using *SSH keys*. Similar to PGP keys (discussed in Chapter 2), generating an SSH key on your computer gives you two files: a public key and a secret key. Once you put your public key on the remote server, only people with your secret key on their computer (hopefully just you) can remotely log in to that server using SSH. If someone spies on your internet, they can't see anything you're doing in your SSH session—they'll just see garbled encrypted data. Every SSH key also has a *fingerprint*, a unique string of characters that identifies that specific key. SSH keys are more secure than passwords, so cloud providers often require that you use them. Once you SSH into a remote server, you'll be dropped into a shell just like the one on your own computer, but running on a computer across the internet.

A *text-based window manager* is software that lets you open and switch between separate shells in the same terminal window, all in the same SSH session. Text-based window managers also allow you to keep programs running in the background even if you disconnect from SSH, by maintaining an active shell session on your VPS. This protects your work if, for example, your laptop dies, you lose internet access, or you close your terminal window by mistake.

For example, say you want to download BlueLeaks on your VPS and then unzip it with a for loop. If you close your terminal window before the loop is done, you'll quit the remote shell, which will close the unzip program, and your remote work will stop. However, if you SSH to your VPS, connect to a window manager session, and then start unzipping BlueLeaks files, you can safely close the terminal window without stopping your work. If you open a new terminal later, SSH back into your server, and open your window manager again, your previous session with all your running programs should reappear. In the upcoming exercise, you'll use the Byobu window manager, which comes with Ubuntu.

When you SSH into a remote server, you don't have easy access to a graphical text editor like VS Code. To edit files—to modify a shell script, for example—you'll need to use a CLI text editor instead. Two popular CLI text editors are nano and vim. The nano text editor is relatively easy to use but doesn't have advanced features, while vim is more powerful but has a steeper learning curve. For simplicity's sake, in the following exercise you'll use nano.

**NOTE**  *Technically, you can use VS Code to edit files remotely over SSH, but there are some limitations. See* https://code.visualstudio.com/docs/remote/ssh *for more information on VS Code's support for editing files over SSH.*

## Exercise 4-4: Set Up a VPS

In this exercise, you'll create an account on a cloud hosting provider, generate an SSH key, create a VPS on your cloud provider, SSH into it, start a Byobu session, and install updates. To follow along you'll need to spend a small amount of money. I provide detailed instructions for using DigitalOcean in this exercise, but use whatever cloud hosting provider you prefer, keeping in mind that the initial steps will likely be slightly different.

Go to *https://www.digitalocean.com* and create an account, providing a credit card number while signing up. Use a strong password, store it in your password manager, and turn on two-factor authentication.

### Generate an SSH Key

To generate an SSH key, open a terminal on your local computer (if you're using Windows, use a WSL terminal) and run:

```
ssh-keygen -t ed25519
```

The ssh-keygen command generates an SSH key, while the options specify the type of encryption key you want to generate—in this case, ed25519, which uses modern elliptic curve encryption and is the most secure option.

After you run this command, the program will ask you a few questions, starting with where you want to save your key. For example, I get the following output on my Mac:

```
Generating public/private ed25519 key pair.
Enter file in which to save the key (/Users/micah/.ssh/id_ed25519):
```

Press ENTER to use the default location for the key, *~/.ssh/id_ed25519*. Next, the program should ask you for a passphrase:

```
Enter passphrase (empty for no passphrase):
```

I recommend generating a random passphrase in your password manager, saving it as *SSH key passphrase*, then copying and pasting the passphrase into your terminal. After pressing ENTER, re-enter your passphrase and press ENTER again.

When you're done, the ssh-keygen command should have created two new files: your SSH secret key in *~/.ssh/id_ed25519* and your SSH public key in *~/.ssh/id_ed25519.pub*.

**NOTE** *If you're using Windows and prefer to SSH from PowerShell, you can install the OpenSSH client directly in Windows. Open a PowerShell window as an administrator and run* **Add-WindowsCapability -Online -Name OpenSSH.Client~~~~0.0.1.0** *to enable using the* ssh *command from PowerShell.*

## Add Your Public Key to the Cloud Provider

Next, add your public key to your new DigitalOcean account. After logging in to the web console, go to the Settings page and switch to the Security tab. Click **Add SSH Key**, then copy and paste your SSH public key into the form.

Back in your terminal, display the content of your public key by running this command:

```
cat ~/.ssh/id_ed25519.pub
```

Here's the output I get:

```
ssh-ed25519 AAAAC3NzaC1lZDI1NTE5AAAAILxYgUq1ePSRSv7LTITG5hecwNBQzs3EZmo4PRzsV4yT micah@trapdoor
.local
```

Your output should look similar, with the last word being your username and the hostname of your own computer. Copy this whole string, starting with ssh-ed25519, and paste it into DigitalOcean, then give it a name, as shown in Figure 4-3.

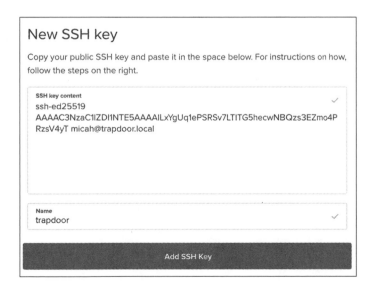

*Figure 4-3: The form for adding a new SSH key to a DigitalOcean account*

Name your SSH keys after the computer on which you generated them, since they're allowing this specific computer to access remote computers. For example, I've called my key *trapdoor*, the name of my Mac.

## Create a VPS

Now that DigitalOcean has your SSH public key, you can create a new VPS. Click **Create** at the top of the DigitalOcean console and follow the instructions to create a new *droplet*, DigitalOcean's term for a VPS. Choose the following settings for your VPS:

1. For Choose an Image, pick **Ubuntu**.

2. For Choose a Plan, pick **Shared CPU ▸ Basic** and choose how much memory, CPU power, hard disk space, and internet bandwidth you want. Less powerful machines are cheaper; more powerful ones are more expensive. For this exercise, choose a relatively cheap option like 1GB of RAM, 1 CPU, 25GB of disk space, and 1TB of bandwidth for $7 per month.

3. For Add Block Storage, you can choose to attach an additional hard disk to your droplet. You don't need to do this now, but in the future, to work with a large dataset like BlueLeaks, you can add more disk space.

4. For Choose a Datacenter Region, choose the host city for your VPS. File transfers between your computer and your server will be fastest if you choose a nearby location, but feel free to create your VPS anywhere you'd like.

5. For Authentication, choose **SSH Keys** and select the SSH key that you just added to your DigitalOcean account.

6. For Select Additional Options, check the box beside Monitoring to see statistics about how much memory and processor power the VPS is using over time from the DigitalOcean console.

7. For Finalize and Create, choose one droplet and give it the hostname *test-vps*.

Click **Create Droplet** and wait a minute or two for DigitalOcean to provision your new VPS, then find its IP address. Figure 4-4 shows the Droplets page of my DigitalOcean account with my new server's IP address, 178.128.22.151.

*Figure 4-4: My test-vps IP address*

Click the IP address to copy it to your clipboard.

## SSH into Your Server

Run the following command to SSH into your server:

```
ssh username@hostname
```

Here, *username* is the user you want to connect to on the remote server, and *hostname* is either the hostname or IP address of the remote server. With DigitalOcean, the username is root and the hostname is the IP address of your server.

Here's what it looks like when I SSH into my server for the first time:

```
micah@trapdoor ~ % ssh root@178.128.22.151
The authenticity of host '178.128.22.151 (178.128.22.151)' can't be established.
ED25519 key fingerprint is SHA256:062oSOXq+G1sGLIzoQdFnQvJE/BU8GLLWnNr5WUOmAs.
This key is not known by any other names
Are you sure you want to continue connecting (yes/no/[fingerprint])?
```

A remote server has its own SSH key, a *server key*. This output shows you the server key's fingerprint and asks whether you want to trust it. If you enter yes, your SSH software will store this fingerprint in the *~/.ssh/known _hosts* file containing all the fingerprints for the SSH servers to which you've connected in the past, so that when you SSH into your server in the future, it shouldn't prompt you again. You can also enter no to cancel, or copy and paste the fingerprint of the server key that you're expecting.

**NOTE**  *If you SSH into a server and the fingerprint isn't what your software expects it to be, SSH will show you a warning message, which could mean that the server key has changed or that your SSH connection is being attacked. This authentication scheme is known as* trust on first use *(TOFU): you trust the first fingerprint you see and deny all other fingerprints for that server in the future.*

Enter **yes** and press ENTER to continue. You should be dropped into a root shell on your remote server:

```
root@test-vps:~#
```

Since you provided DigitalOcean with your SSH public key, you don't need to enter a password to log in. If anyone else tries SSHing to your server, they'll get the Permission denied (publickey) error.

Take a look around your new cloud-based system. Run **ls** to list files, **ls -al** to see hidden files, and **cd** to change to folders.

## Start a Byobu Session

If you used the Ubuntu image to set up your droplet, the Byobu window manager should be installed. Run the **byobu** command to start a Byobu session. (If you're using a different operating system, or if for some reason Byobu isn't installed, you'll get a Command 'byobu' not found error message. Run **apt update**, followed by **apt install byobu**, to install the program.)

The byobu command should drop you into a shell inside of your new session. A line at the bottom of your terminal shows which window you've opened, along with information like the date and time. Each Byobu window is like its own separate shell in the same Byobu session, and you can open as many windows as you want.

To demonstrate how Byobu works, run whoami (which should tell you that you're the root user) and ls -l / (which should show you a list of files in your server's root folder). Now press CTRL-A. Byobu will ask you how you want this keyboard command to operate:

```
Configure Byobu's ctrl-a behavior...

When you press ctrl-a in Byobu, do you want it to operate in:
    (1) Screen mode (GNU Screen's default escape sequence)
    (2) Emacs mode   (go to beginning of line)

Note that:
  - F12 also operates as an escape in Byobu
  - You can press F9 and choose your escape character
  - You can run 'byobu-ctrl-a' at any time to change your selection

Select [1 or 2]:
```

Enter 1 and press ENTER. This allows you to open a new window in Byobu by pressing CTRL-A, followed by C (for "create"). Try that now to open a new empty shell. Press CTRL-A followed by N (for "next") to switch back to your first window. To exit a Byobu window, you run the exit command in that shell.

**NOTE** *See https://www.byobu.org for more complete documentation about this program, including a video tutorial.*

Completely close your terminal window and click through any warnings saying that your active programs will close if you do this. Open a new terminal window and SSH back into your server using the **ssh *username@ hostname*** command. Then run **byobu** again to attach your previous session. Any programs you run inside this Byobu session won't quit when you disconnect from SSH.

## Install Updates

Always install updates when you set up a new server to keep it secure. Run the following commands (you don't need to use sudo, since you're the root user):

```
apt update
apt upgrade
```

Follow the instructions to finish installing updates.

If you ever need to reboot your server (such as after updating the Linux kernel), run the reboot command. You'll get kicked out of your SSH session, but you should be able to SSH back in shortly when the reboot completes. You can also reboot your VPS from DigitalOcean's web console—for example, if the entire server crashed and you can't SSH into it.

## Exercise 4-5: Explore the Oath Keepers Dataset Remotely

In this exercise, you'll use BitTorrent to download the Oath Keepers dataset to your cloud server and explore it using the skills you've gained in this chapter. You'll also learn to copy data from your remote server to your laptop using the rsync command. Finally, you'll delete your VPS to avoid getting charged for time when you're not using it.

The Oath Keepers dataset contains data from the far-right extremist group that participated in the January 6, 2021, US Capitol insurrection. In September 2021, a hacktivist broke into the Oath Keepers servers and made off with the group's email messages, chat logs, membership lists, and other data, and then leaked it to DDoSecrets. You'll continue working with this dataset when you learn to analyze email dumps in Chapter 6.

**NOTE** *This book works only with the publicly available part of the Oath Keepers dataset, which contains email messages and chat logs. To access content like the Oath Keepers' donor and membership lists, which contain PII, contact DDoSecrets.*

Because your home or office internet connection is likely significantly slower than a cloud provider's, it's inefficient to download a dataset to your laptop and then upload it to your remote server. To download the dataset directly to your VPS, you'll use transmission-cli, the command line version of the BitTorrent client you used to download BlueLeaks in Chapter 2. In your VPS, run the following command to install transmission-cli:

```
apt install transmission-cli
```

You can now use the transmission-cli command to download files. You must pass in either the path to a *.torrent* file or a magnet link as an argument. In this exercise, you'll use the torrent file available at *https://ddosecrets .com/wiki/Oath_Keepers*.

Run the following commands:

```
mkdir ~/datasets
cd ~/datasets
```

This creates a new folder called *datasets* on your server, then changes to it. Download the torrent file from the link on the DDoSecrets page and load it into your BitTorrent client with the following commands:

```
wget https://ddosecrets.com/images/0/02/Oath_Keepers.torrent
transmission-cli -w . Oath_Keepers.torrent
```

The wget command downloads files—in this case, *Oath_Keepers.torrent*—and saves them in the current folder. The transmission-cli command downloads the 3.9GB torrent to your server from the BitTorrent swarm and uploads parts of it to other parts of the swarm. The -w . arguments tell transmission-cli to download the torrent into the current working folder. (You could change that to -w ~/Downloads, for example, if you wanted to download it into the *~/Downloads* folder instead.)

**NOTE** *If no torrent file is available for a dataset, you can replace the torrent filename with a magnet link in double quotes as an argument in the* transmission-cli *command.*

When you've finished downloading the torrent, your server will be a seed until you quit the program by pressing CTRL-C. While you're waiting for the dataset to finish downloading, or if you've finished but want to continue seeding the torrent, you can work on your VPS in a separate Byobu shell.

To check how much free space your server has left, run the following command after the download is complete:

```
df -h
```

The df command tells you how much disk space is free on each connected drive, and the -h argument displays these numbers in human-readable units. After downloading the Oath Keepers dataset, I got the following output from these commands on my server:

```
Filesystem      Size  Used Avail Use% Mounted on
tmpfs            98M 1000K   97M   2% /run
/dev/vda1        25G  5.8G   19G  24% /
tmpfs           486M   80K  486M   1% /dev/shm
tmpfs           5.0M     0  5.0M   0% /run/lock
/dev/vda15      105M  5.3M  100M   5% /boot/efi
tmpfs            98M  4.0K   98M   1% /run/user/0
```

As shown in bold, my root partition mounted on / has 25GB of space, has used 5.8GB, and has 19GB free.

Change your working directory to *~/datasets/Oath Keepers*, remembering to put the filepath in quotes or escape the space in the path. For example, you could run this command from the *~/datasets* folder:

```
cd Oath\ Keepers
```

Run the following command to find that the Oath Keepers dataset takes up 3.9GB of space:

```
root@test-vps:~/datasets/Oath Keepers# du -sh --apparent-size .
3.9G    .
```

Next, run the **ls** command to list the files in the *Oath Keepers* folder:

```
root@test-vps:~/datasets/Oath Keepers# ls -lh
total 13M
drwxr-xr-x 2 root root 4.0K Aug  2 23:47 'Oath Keepers.sbd'
-rw-r--r-- 1 root root  12M Aug  2 23:47  messages.json
-rw-r--r-- 1 root root 1.4M Aug  2 23:44  messages_old.json
```

The output shows that this folder contains a folder called *Oath Keepers.sbd*, a 12MB file called *messages.json*, and a 1.4MB file called *messages_old.json*. These JSON files are chat logs.

Switch to the *Oath Keepers.sbd* folder and run **ls** again:

```
root@test-vps:~/datasets/Oath Keepers# cd Oath\ Keepers.sbd/
root@test-vps:~/datasets/Oath Keepers/Oath Keepers.sbd# ls -lh
total 3.9G
-rw-r--r-- 1 root root 2.2M Aug  2 23:45  Archive
-rw-r--r-- 1 root root  23K Aug  2 23:44 'Saved Correspondence'
-rw-r--r-- 1 root root  25K Aug  2 23:44  Systems
-rw-r--r-- 1 root root 2.8M Aug  2 23:44  ak
--snip--
```

The output shows that this folder contains 100 files, each representing a different inbox full of email.

Since you'll use the Oath Keepers dataset later in the book, next you'll copy it from your VPS to your *datasets* USB disk with the rsync program, which synchronizes local folders and remote folders using SSH.

**NOTE**  *The scp command (short for "secure copy") also copies files and folders from your computer to a remote server, or vice versa, over SSH. The BlueLeaks hacker likely used a Windows version of scp, pscp64.exe, to exfiltrate data from the hacked police web servers to a server they controlled. For very large folders, however, rsync is often a better choice than scp, since if it fails halfway through, you can rerun the command and it will start where it left off.*

Open a terminal running locally on your computer (not SSHed to your VPS) and run **which rsync** to check whether rsync is installed. If so, the command returns the path to the program, something like */usr/bin/rsync*. If not, you'll see no output. Windows with WSL and Linux users can install rsync with the following command:

```
sudo apt install rsync
```

macOS users can install it with the following command:

```
brew install rsync
```

To copy a file from a remote server to your local computer, run the following command:

```
rsync -av --progress remote_user@remote_host:remote_path local_path
```

The -av argument is a combination of -a (short for --archive), which preserves the file permissions in the copy you're making, and -v (short for --verbose), which outputs each filename as it copies the files. The --progress argument displays progress bars for each file as it's copying. The rsync command will SSH into the server *remote_host* with the username *remote_user*. If it authenticates successfully, it will download the file or folder at *remote_path* and save it on your computer at *local_path*.

For example, here's how I'd download the Oath Keepers dataset from my VPS to my *datasets* USB disk:

```
rsync -av --progress root@178.128.22.151:"~/datasets/Oath\ Keepers" /Volumes/datasets/
```

In this case, root@178.128.22.151:"~/datasets/Oath\ Keepers" is the *remote_user@remote_host:remote_path* argument, since the *Oath Keepers* folder is in the *datasets* folder in the root user's home folder on my VPS. I put the remote path in quotes and escape the space in the filename, telling my local shell that root@178.128.22.151:"~/datasets/Oath\ Keepers" is a single argument. The *local_path* argument is the /media/micah/datasets/ path to my *datasets* USB disk.

**NOTE** *You can also use rsync to upload files from your computer to a remote server—just put the local_path argument first, as the source, and put the remote_user@remote_host:remote_path argument second, as the destination.*

Here's the output I get when I run this command:

```
receiving incremental file list
Oath Keepers/
Oath Keepers/messages.json
       12,109,624 100%    1.89MB/s    0:00:06 (xfr#1, to-chk=102/104)
Oath Keepers/messages_old.json
        1,393,296 100%    1.65MB/s    0:00:00 (xfr#2, to-chk=101/104)
Oath Keepers/Oath Keepers.sbd/
Oath Keepers/Oath Keepers.sbd/Archive
        2,288,916 100%    1.81MB/s    0:00:01 (xfr#3, to-chk=99/104)
Oath Keepers/Oath Keepers.sbd/Saved Correspondence
           23,192 100%  111.02kB/s    0:00:00 (xfr#4, to-chk=98/104)
Oath Keepers/Oath Keepers.sbd/Systems
           25,382 100%  121.51kB/s    0:00:00 (xfr#5, to-chk=97/104)
Oath Keepers/Oath Keepers.sbd/ak
        2,921,276 100%    4.33MB/s    0:00:00 (xfr#6, to-chk=96/104)
Oath Keepers/Oath Keepers.sbd/al
       41,772,536 100%    6.57MB/s    0:00:06 (xfr#7, to-chk=95/104)
--snip--
```

The rsync command copies every file, one at a time, from the remote folder to the local folder over SSH, displaying a line after each filename that shows the file's download speed and progress. You can press CTRL-C to cancel the command, then rerun that command, and rsync should continue where it left off. This is especially useful when you need to copy gigabytes or terabytes of data spread across millions of files—if the file transfer fails, you can pick up where you left off.

Once rsync finishes running, you'll have downloaded a local copy of the Oath Keepers dataset to your *datasets* USB disk. You'll use this dataset again in Chapter 6, when you learn techniques for researching email dumps.

**WARNING**    *Destroy your VPS from the DigitalOcean web console when you're done with it. Using it for an hour or two should cost you only a few cents, but the bill can get expensive if you don't pay attention.*

## Summary

In this chapter, you've put your command line skills to the test, unzipping the compressed files in BlueLeaks and learning to quickly search and sort datasets. You also worked with servers in the cloud and briefly explored the Oath Keepers dataset.

In the next chapter, you'll continue expanding your command line skills and learn two new tools: Docker, which allows you to run Linux software on any operating system, and Aleph, which allows you to search datasets by keyword.

# 5

## DOCKER, ALEPH, AND MAKING DATASETS SEARCHABLE

When I get my hands on a new dataset, the first thing I do is search it for any juicy, easy-to-find revelations. Depending on the dataset, I might look for politicians, organizations, or the city where I live. In the previous chapter, you learned to search text files like CSV or JSON files using grep, but grep won't work on binary files like PDFs or Office documents. In this chapter, you'll expand your search capabilities with Aleph, an open source investigation tool.

Aleph is developed by the Organized Crime and Corruption Reporting Project, a group of investigative journalists largely based in eastern Europe and central Asia. The tool allows you to *index* datasets, extracting all the text they contain so they're easy to search. You can use Aleph to search for keywords or *entities* (like people, companies, organizations, or addresses) and discover related entities in other datasets. Aleph also performs optical character recognition (OCR), which, as mentioned in Chapter 1, takes flat images like scanned documents or screenshots, uses artificial intelligence to recognize any words, and converts those words into text that you can search or copy and paste.

In the first half of this chapter, you'll learn the ins and outs of using Docker and Docker Compose, the software required for running Aleph. In the second half, you'll use your new Docker skills to run an Aleph server, then index and search part of the BlueLeaks dataset.

## Introducing Docker and Linux Containers

Docker is the most popular software for running *Linux containers*, a type of software package. Linux containers can organize ready-to-go Linux software—complete with all of its dependencies, configuration, and source code—into a single bundle called a *container image* that you can quickly and easily run. The software inside containers is isolated from the rest of your computer; it can't access any of those files unless you allow it to do so.

For example, let's say you want to set up the popular WordPress blogging software in Linux. You use a package manager like apt to install the software WordPress depends on. You then put the WordPress source code in a location on your disk with the right permissions, configure your web server software so it knows where to look for that source code, and configure a database to store the blog's data. You can then save all this work in a Linux container called wordpress and reuse that container to spin up new WordPress sites with a single Docker command.

Because Linux containers are isolated from the rest of your computer, multiple WordPress containers can run at the same time without interfering with each other. If someone hacks the software running in your container, they won't be able to access any of the data located elsewhere on your computer—at least, not without also hacking Docker itself. This is why Dangerzone relies on Linux containers: if a malicious document manages to hack the Dangerzone container you're using, your computer should still be safe. In addition to software like WordPress, you can use Linux containers to run commands in most Linux distributions without having to install those operating systems.

Docker comes with two commands you'll use in this chapter: docker, which runs individual containers, and docker-compose, which lets you run multiple containers at once. You'll practice using the docker command by running Linux containers for the Ubuntu and Kali Linux operating systems, as well as for the data science software Jupyter Notebook. You'll then use docker-compose to run a WordPress server and an Aleph server. Aleph requires a small network of services that communicate with each other, but as with WordPress, you can use a single Docker command to start up all these individual servers in their own containers. This process should prepare you to run Linux containers with Docker for other purposes later in the book.

This chapter covers two applications for running Docker containers: Docker Desktop and Docker Engine. Docker Desktop runs Docker containers on workstation computers in a Linux VM. Docker Engine, on the other hand, runs Docker directly on a Linux computer. Windows and Mac users, turn to Exercise 5-1 to set up Docker Desktop. Linux users, turn to Exercise 5-2 to install Docker Engine.

**NOTE** *It's possible for Linux users to install Docker Desktop, but I don't recommend it for this chapter. Without a VM, Docker will be free to use all of your computer's memory and processors, which will make indexing datasets in Aleph much faster.*

## Exercise 5-1: Initialize Docker Desktop on Windows and macOS

When you installed Dangerzone in Exercise 1-3, Docker Desktop also should have been installed, since Dangerzone requires it. Confirm that Docker Desktop is installed by checking whether your *Applications* folder in macOS or Start menu in Windows has a Docker program; if not, download it from *https://www.docker.com/products/docker-desktop/*.

Open Docker and follow the onscreen instructions to initialize the software. You may need to reboot your computer. Docker Desktop's Linux VM should be up and running before you can use Docker. If you click the Docker icon in your system tray and it tells you that Docker Desktop is running, you're ready to proceed.

If you're using Windows, you can use either PowerShell or Ubuntu with WSL for this chapter, since the docker and docker-desktop commands should run fine in either. Even when you use Docker from PowerShell, it technically relies on WSL under the hood.

If you're using macOS, click the Docker icon in your system tray and choose **Preferences**. Switch to the Resources tab and make sure that the Memory resource is set to at least 6GB—higher if you have more to spare—to be sure Docker's Linux VM has enough memory to handle Aleph. Click **Apply & Restart**.

For either operating system, to test whether Docker is working, open a terminal and run this command:

```
docker run hello-world
```

This command should run a Docker container image called hello-world. If you don't already have the hello-world image on your computer, Docker should download it first. The output should look something like this:

```
Unable to find image 'hello-world:latest' locally
latest: Pulling from library/hello-world
2db29710123e: Pull complete
Digest: sha256:10d7d58d5ebd2a652f4d93fdd86da8f265f5318c6a73cc5b6a9798ff6d2b2e67
Status: Downloaded newer image for hello-world:latest
```

```
Hello from Docker!
This message shows that your installation appears to be working correctly.
--snip--
```

Your computer is ready to run Linux containers. Skip to the "Running Containers with Docker" section on page 123.

## Exercise 5-2: Initialize Docker Engine on Linux

Follow the detailed instructions for Server rather than Desktop at *https:// docs.docker.com/engine/install/* to install Docker Engine for your version of Linux. In Ubuntu, the installation process involves adding a new apt repository to your computer and installing some Docker packages.

Docker Engine on Linux requires root access to run containers. After completing this exercise, if you're using Linux, add sudo to the beginning of all docker or docker-compose commands in this book. To run all your Docker commands as root automatically without using sudo, check the Docker Engine documentation for instructions on adding your Linux user to the docker group; however, keep in mind that doing so decreases your computer's security and isn't recommended.

Once Docker is installed, open a terminal and run:

```
sudo docker run hello-world
```

This command runs a Docker container image called hello-world. If you don't already have the hello-world image on your computer, Docker downloads it first. The output should look something like this:

```
Unable to find image 'hello-world:latest' locally
latest: Pulling from library/hello-world
2db29710123e: Pull complete
Digest: sha256:507ecde44b8eb741278274653120c2bf793b174c06ff4eaa672b713b3263477b
Status: Downloaded newer image for hello-world:latest

Hello from Docker!
This message shows that your installation appears to be working correctly.
--snip--
```

If the hello-world container ran successfully, you can now use the docker command on your computer. Next, run the following command to install the docker-compose package, which will give you access to the docker-compose command:

```
sudo apt install docker-compose
```

Your computer is now ready to run Linux containers.

## Running Containers with Docker

The docker command you've just installed allows you to run Linux containers on your computer. In this section you'll learn how to use this command to open a shell inside containers, force running containers to quit, mount volumes to save persistent data or access certain files, set environment variables, and publish ports so your computer can connect to network services inside your container. This foundational understanding of Docker will prepare you to run Docker containers in Exercise 5-3 and help you troubleshoot any problems you later encounter with Aleph.

**NOTE** *For additional information on Docker commands, run* **docker help** *or check the documentation at* https://docs.docker.com.

### Running an Ubuntu Container

You'll begin by learning how to run a Linux container with the Ubuntu operating system in it. People often base more complicated container images on the Ubuntu container image to access all Ubuntu software that apt can install. An Ubuntu container is also a convenient way to access a shell on a clean Ubuntu system, allowing you to install software or test programs.

Docker commands use the docker *command* syntax. Run the following to start your own Ubuntu container (if you're using Linux, remember to add sudo):

```
docker run -it ubuntu:latest bash
```

This command runs ubuntu:latest, the latest version of the ubuntu image. If that image isn't already on your computer, Docker automatically downloads it from Docker Hub, a library of public container images at *https://hub .docker.com*. Next, the bash command runs, giving you shell access inside that container. Include the -it argument, which is short for -i (or --interactive) and -t (or --tty), after docker run whenever you plan to open a shell in a container, so that any commands you type in the terminal run in the container. Without the -it argument, the bash shell would immediately quit before you could run any commands, as would the container.

This command gives me the following output:

```
micah@trapdoor ~ % docker run -it ubuntu:latest bash
Unable to find image 'ubuntu:latest' locally
latest: Pulling from library/ubuntu
d19f32bd9e41: Pull complete
Digest: sha256:34fea4f31bf187bc915536831fd0afc9d214755bf700b5cdb1336c82516d154e
Status: Downloaded newer image for ubuntu:latest
root@5661828c22a2:/#
```

Since I didn't already have the ubuntu:latest image, the command downloaded that image, started the container, and dropped me into a bash shell. I can now run whatever commands I want inside this container, such as installing software or running programs.

Running the exit command quits the container. If you start a new ubuntu:latest container, it contains none of the old container's data. For example, with the following commands, I create a file called *test.txt* in one container, quit the container, and start a new one:

```
root@5661828c22a2:/# echo "Hacks, Leaks, and Revelations" > test.txt
root@5661828c22a2:/# cat test.txt
Hacks, Leaks, and Revelations
root@5661828c22a2:/# exit
exit
micah@trapdoor ~ % docker run -it ubuntu:latest bash
root@e8888f73a106:/# cat test.txt
cat: test.txt: No such file or directory
root@e8888f73a106:/#
```

The output shows that *test.txt* no longer exists. For data in a container to persist when you rerun the container image, you need to use volumes, as we'll discuss in "Mounting and Removing Volumes" on page 125.

### Listing and Killing Containers

If you've exited your Ubuntu container, run a new one. With that container running in the background, open a second terminal window and run the **docker ps** command. This should show you a list of all containers currently running. Here's the output I get, for example:

| CONTAINER ID | IMAGE | COMMAND | CREATED | STATUS | PORTS | NAMES |
|---|---|---|---|---|---|---|
| 337a795a53b2 | ubuntu:latest | "bash" | 9 minutes ago | Up 9 minutes | | epic_borg |

When you start a container with `docker run`, you can give it a name with the arguments `--name` *your_container_name*. Otherwise, it will be assigned a random name. The container in my `docker ps` output is called `epic_borg`.

To *kill* a container, or force it to quit, you run `docker kill` *container_name*. For example, running the following command in my other terminal window quits my `epic_borg` container:

```
docker kill epic_borg
```

Run this command for your own container. If you switch back to your other terminal window, the container should have quit, and you should be back in your normal shell.

When you exit a container, Docker still keeps track of it, allowing you to restart it if you want. To see all of the containers Docker is tracking, including ones that aren't running anymore, you run **docker ps -a** (short for `--all`). Here's the output I get when I run this command:

```
CONTAINER ID   IMAGE             ...   STATUS                   PORTS     NAMES
337a795a53b2   ubuntu:latest     ...   Exited (0) 43 minutes ago          nostalgic_keldysh
```

It's good practice to run **docker rm** *container_name* to prune your stopped Docker containers when you're done using them. For example, I'd run `docker rm nostalgic_keldysh` to remove my `nostalgic_keldysh` container.

You can run **docker container prune** to remove all stopped containers at once. When I ran this command, I saw the following output:

```
WARNING! This will remove all stopped containers.
Are you sure you want to continue? [y/N]
```

I entered y and got the following output:

```
Deleted Containers:
337a795a53b25e6c28888a44a0ac09fac9bf6aef4ab1c3108844ca447cce4226

Total reclaimed space: 5B
```

This displays the container ID, a long string of random-looking text, for each container that's deleted. In my case, I deleted a single container.

## Mounting and Removing Volumes

Containers support *volumes*, which you can think of as folders in your container designed to store persistent data. You can use volumes to save changes you've made to your container after you quit and remove it.

For example, suppose you start a container without any volumes that runs the PostgreSQL database software. Any data you add to it is saved to the */var/lib/postgresql/data* folder inside your container. When you quit and remove the container, you'll lose all of your data. If you instead *mount* a folder on your host operating system into */var/lib/postgresql/data* on the container, when software in the container accesses that folder, it's actually accessing the folder on your host operating system. You'll still have all of your data when the container closes and is removed, and you can start the container again in the future with the same data.

Docker has two main types of volumes: *bind mounts*, or folders from your host machine mounted into a container, and normal Docker volumes, where Docker keeps track of your persistent folders without your having to provide a path on your host operating system. For example, if you want to store your database container's data in the */Volumes/datasets/volumes/db-data* folder on your host filesystem, you would mount this folder as a bind mount. If you don't need your data to be stored in a specific folder on your host, just use a normal volume, and Docker will keep track of where it's stored.

**NOTE**  *Storing volumes in a Linux VM with Docker Desktop makes them faster than bind mounts, but your VM might run out of disk space if your volumes get too big (if you index large datasets into Aleph, for example). In macOS, you can increase the amount of disk space available to your VM in the Docker Desktop preferences under the Resources tab. In Windows, your VM will use as much space on the C: drive as it needs, but again, this drive could run out of disk space if you're dealing with large amounts of data. Alternatively, you could use bind mounts instead of volumes, storing data on external disks.*

You can also use volumes to access data outside of a container while that container is running. In Exercise 5-5, you'll bind-mount your *datasets* USB disk as a folder in an Aleph container. This way, your container can access the BlueLeaks dataset, allowing you to index it.

Use this command to start a container with a volume:

```
docker run --mount type=volume,src=volume-name,dst=/container/path image
```

Use this command to start a container with a bind mount:

```
docker run --mount type=bind,src=/path/on/host,dst=/container/path image
```

The --mount argument tells Docker that you're going to mount a volume and is followed by comma-separated details about that volume. The type parameter specifies the type of mount: volume for volumes and bind for bind mounts. The src parameter specifies the source of the volume or bind mount. For volumes, its value is the volume name; for bind mounts, its value is the absolute path on your host filesystem to the folder you want to mount. The dst parameter specifies the destination of the volume or bind mount, in both cases the absolute path of the folder inside the container to which you're mounting.

Let's practice these two commands, starting with mounting a volume. Run the following code (your prompt will be different from mine):

```
micah@trapdoor ~ % docker run -it --mount type=volume,src=test-data,dst=/mnt
ubuntu:latest bash
```

```
root@50b8b6f86e4d:/# echo "Hacks, Leaks, and Revelations" > /mnt/test.txt
root@50b8b6f86e4d:/# exit
```

This code starts an Ubuntu container and mounts a volume called test-data into the */mnt* folder in the container. It then saves some data into the */mnt/test.txt* file and exits the container.

Use the following commands to open a separate container, mounting the same volume into it to see whether your data is still there (again, your command prompt will be different):

```
micah@trapdoor ~ % docker run -it --mount type=volume,src=test-data,dst=/mnt
ubuntu:latest bash
root@665f910bb21c:/# cat /mnt/test.txt
Hacks, Leaks, and Revelations
root@665f910bb21c:/# exit
```

This time, because you mounted */mnt* in the test-data volume, the data persisted.

To see a list of the volumes that Docker is managing, run the **docker volume ls** command. You should get the following output:

```
DRIVER     VOLUME NAME
local      test-data
```

You can remove volumes only from containers that have been completely removed from Docker. If you've just stopped a container but Docker is still tracking it, it won't let you remove the volume. Completely remove all stopped containers by running **docker container prune**, which then allows you to remove any volumes attached to those containers. You should get the following output:

```
WARNING! This will remove all stopped containers.
Are you sure you want to continue? [y/N]
```

Enter **y** to continue:

```
Deleted Containers:
665f910bb21ca701be416da94c05ee6a2226117923367d2f7731693062683a402
50b8b6f86e4d0eab9eb0ba9bf006ae0473525d572ea687865f8afca8a92e7087

Total reclaimed space: 82B
```

You can now run **docker volume rm *volume-name*** to remove any volumes attached to those containers, or run **docker volume prune** to delete all volumes that Docker containers aren't currently using. Run **docker volume rm test-data** to remove the test-data volume, then run the **docker volume ls** command again. This time, you shouldn't see any volumes listed in the output.

Next, you'll practice bind mounting by mounting the folder on your host system containing the BlueLeaks dataset into a container running Kali Linux. This Linux distribution is designed for *penetration testing*, in which people hack into systems with permission from the system owners to find and fix security flaws.

If you're a Mac or Linux user, run the following command, replacing the path with the appropriate path on your machine:

```
docker run -it --mount type=bind,src=/Volumes/datasets/BlueLeaks-extracted,dst=/blueleaks
kalilinux/kali-rolling bash
```

This should run a kalilinux/kali-rolling container, mounting your *BlueLeaks-extracted* folder in it at the path */blueleaks*, and drop you into a bash shell.

Windows users might have trouble bind-mounting a folder on the *datasets* USB disk into a container, because Docker Desktop for Windows runs Linux containers using WSL, and WSL doesn't always have access to your USB disks. To avoid this problem, if you plugged in your USB disk after opening a WSL terminal or using Docker, restart WSL by running `wsl --shutdown` in PowerShell. You should see a notification from Docker Desktop asking if you want to restart it. Click **Restart**. After you restart WSL with the USB disk already plugged in, Docker should be able to mount it. (See Appendix A for more information.)

If you're using Windows with PowerShell to work through this chapter, run the following command to mount the folder that contains the BlueLeaks data into */datasets*, replacing `D:/BlueLeaks-extracted` with the appropriate path:

```
docker run -it –mount type-bind,src=D:/BlueLeaks-extracted,dst=/blueleaks kalilinux/
kali-rolling bash
```

If you're using Ubuntu with WSL in Windows, mount the *BlueLeaks* folder by accessing the *D:* drive from */mnt/d* with the following syntax:

```
docker run -it --mount type=bind,src=/mnt/d/BlueLeaks-extracted,dst=/blueleaks kalilinux/
kali-rolling bash
```

From within your Kali container, you can now use the tools that come with Kali on the BlueLeaks dataset. By default, Kali customizes your bash shell to look slightly different than Ubuntu does. The prompt will look something like this:

```
┌──(root㉿6a36e316663c)-[/]
└─#
```

Docker containers are assigned random hostnames. In this case, root is the name of the current user, 6a36e316663c is the hostname of the computer, and / is the current working directory. From here, run **ls /blueleaks/** to list the files in the *BlueLeaks* folder:

```
211sfbay                    iowaintex             pleasantonpolice
Securitypartnership         jerseyvillagepd       prvihidta
acprlea                     jric                  pspddoc
acticaz                     kcpers                publicsafetycadets
--snip--
```

 *You can learn more about volumes and bind mounts at* https://docs.docker.com/
storage/.

## Passing Environment Variables

You can also use environment variables, introduced in Chapter 4, to pass
sensitive information like database credentials into containers. When starting up a container, you pass an environment variable into it using the
-e *variable_name=value* (the -e is short for --env) arguments. Programs in the
container can then access the value of that variable.

For example, run the following command:

```
docker run -it -e DB_USER=root -e DB_PASSWORD=yourefired ubuntu:latest bash
```

This starts an Ubuntu container with the variable DB_USER set to root
and the variable DB_PASSWORD set to yourefired. From inside the container, try
displaying the values of those variables to confirm that you can access this
information there, using the echo $*variable_name* command like so:

```
bash-5.1# echo $DB_USER
root
bash-5.1# echo $DB_PASSWORD
yourefired
```

You'll practice passing environment variables to containers further in
Exercise 5-3.

## Running Server Software

You can also run robust, fully configured software on the operating systems
running in containers. This technique is mostly used to access *server software*,
software to which you can connect over a network using web browsers, database clients, or other similar programs. You'll need this skill for Exercise 5-3
and, eventually, to run Aleph.

Different computers (or VMs, or containers), called *hosts*, are identified
by IP addresses or hostnames. Your own computer's IP address is always
127.0.0.1, and its hostname is always *localhost*. Hosts can listen on different
ports for incoming network connections, meaning the host is available for
other hosts to connect to over a network. A *port* is a number that the computer uses to sort out which network traffic should go to which application.

Different services have different default ports. For example, HTTP and HTTPS services are two types of websites that use port 80 and port 443, respectively. When you load the URL *http://example.com* in your browser, it will try to connect to the host *example.com* on port 80 using HTTP. If you load *https://example.com*, it will try to connect on port 443 using HTTPS.

However, you can change the default ports that services use. If you're running an HTTP service on *localhost* on port 5000, the URL for that service would be *http://localhost:5000*, where *http://* means you're using the HTTP protocol, *localhost* means you're connecting to the *localhost* host, and *:5000* means you're connecting to port 5000 instead of the default HTTP port, 80.

To connect to a network port inside your Docker container, you must *publish* a network port when you run your container, making that port available on the host operating system. To do so, use the arguments -p *host_port*:*container_port* (-p is short for --publish). Once the container starts up, your host operating system will listen on *host_port*. If you connect to that port, your connection will be forwarded to *container_port* inside the container.

Let's look at an example of running server software and publishing a port so that you can connect to it from your host computer. Run the following command:

```
docker run -p 8000:8888 jupyter/scipy-notebook:latest
```

This command should download and run the latest version of the *jupyter/scipy-notebook* container image, which includes the most popular science-related Python libraries. (Jupyter Notebook is a powerful data science tool for creating and sharing computational documents.) Jupyter Notebook starts an HTTP service on port 8888 in the container. The arguments -p 8000:8888 mean that *host_port* is 8000 and *container_port* is 8888. If you connect to *localhost* on port 8000, using either the URL *http://localhost:8000* or *http://127.0.0.1:8000*, you'll now actually connect to port 8888 inside the container.

Here's the output from the previous command:

```
Unable to find image 'jupyter/scipy-notebook:latest' locally
latest: Pulling from jupyter/scipy-notebook
08c01a0ec47e: Pull complete
--snip--
Status: Downloaded newer image for jupyter/scipy-notebook:latest
Entered start.sh with args: jupyter lab
Executing the command: jupyter lab
--snip--

To access the server, open this file in a browser:
    file:///home/jovyan/.local/share/jupyter/runtime/jpserver-7-open.html
Or copy and paste one of these URLs:
    http://cc4a555569e4:8888/lab?token=d570e7d9ecc59bbc77536ea4ade65d02dd575ff3c6713dd4
 or http://127.0.0.1:8888/lab?token=d570e7d9ecc59bbc77536ea4ade65d02dd575ff3c6713dd4
```

The output shows that this command downloaded the latest version of the *jupyter/scipy-notebook* container image from Docker Hub and then ran it. This time, instead of starting a shell in the container, the container runs only the service it was designed for, which is Jupyter Notebook. Each time Jupyter Notebook outputs a log message, the terminal window now displays it.

The end of the output shows three different URLs to access the server. Copy the final URL, paste it in your browser, and change the port number from 8888 to 8000 before you load it. When you connect to your own computer on port 8000 (127.0.0.1:8000), your connection will be forwarded to the container on port 8888. Your browser should load the Jupyter Notebook service running in your container. When this happens, you should see more log messages appear in the terminal.

Figure 5-1 shows a web browser running on my Mac, connected to a Jupyter Notebook server, which is running in my Linux container.

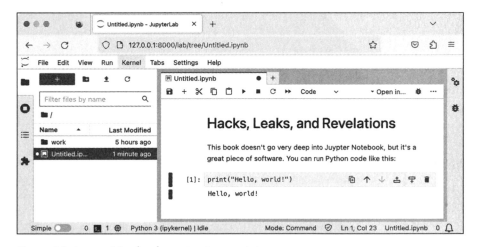

*Figure 5-1: Jupyter Notebook running in a container*

The container keeps running until you press CTRL-C to quit it. If you need to run any other terminal commands while the container is still running, you'll need to open a separate terminal window. For now, press CTRL-C in your terminal to exit the Jupyter Notebook container.

You won't use Jupyter Notebook further in this book, but you'll rely on your new understanding of running server software to run a WordPress website in Exercise 5-3.

**NOTE** *For more information about Jupyter Notebook, visit* https://jupyter.org, *and for thorough documentation on running Jupyter Notebook in Docker, see* https://jupyter-docker-stacks.readthedocs.io.

### Freeing Up Disk Space

Docker images take up a lot of disk space. To free up space quickly, use the following command to delete all of the container images you've downloaded from Docker Hub and other data that Docker stores (besides volumes):

```
docker system prune -a
```

Since this command doesn't delete volumes, it won't delete any of your important data. The next time you use docker run commands, you'll just redownload the container images you need from Docker Hub.

## Exercise 5-3: Run a WordPress Site with Docker Compose

More complicated software like Aleph requires running multiple containers that interact with each other. To do that, you'll need to learn to use Docker Compose, as the docker run command's arguments quickly become hard to keep track of when used to run more complicated containers—those with volumes, environment variables, publishing ports, and so on. It's especially unwieldy to run a single application that requires multiple containers at once.

Docker Compose makes it easier to define and run such Docker applications. The tool allows you to configure your containers (choosing images, volumes, environment variables, published ports, and so on) in a single file, and to start and stop all of your containers with a single command. I often use Docker Compose even for software that requires a single container, because it simplifies keeping track of all of the configuration. You'll need to be proficient in Docker Compose to run an Aleph server.

In this exercise, you'll familiarize yourself with Docker Compose by using it to run WordPress. You won't need WordPress for the remainder of this book, but here it serves as an example to prepare you for using Docker Compose with Aleph.

### Make a docker-compose.yaml File

The YAML file format (*https://yaml.org*) is popular among programmers for storing configuration files because it's relatively human-readable. YAML files have either a *.yml* or *.yaml* file extension. Docker Compose defines containers and their settings in a file called *docker-compose.yaml*.

Open a terminal and change to your *exercises* folder. Make a new folder called *wordpress* for this exercise and then, using your text editor, make a file in that folder called *docker-compose.yaml*. Enter the following code into *that* file (or copy and paste it from *https://github.com/micahflee/hacks-leaks-and -revelations/blob/main/chapter-5/wordpress/docker-compose.yaml*):

```
services:
  wordpress:
    image: wordpress:latest
    volumes:
      - wordpress_data:/var/www/html
    ports:
      - 8000:80
    restart: always
  ❶ environment:
      - WORDPRESS_DB_HOST=db
      - WORDPRESS_DB_USER=wordpress
      - WORDPRESS_DB_PASSWORD=yourefired
      - WORDPRESS_DB_NAME=wordpress
  db:
    image: mariadb:10.9
    volumes:
      - db_data:/var/lib/mysql
    restart: always
  ❷ environment:
      - MYSQL_ROOT_PASSWORD=supersecurepassword
      - MYSQL_USER=wordpress
      - MYSQL_PASSWORD=yourefired
      - MYSQL_DATABASE=wordpress

volumes:
  db_data:
  wordpress_data:
```

YAML files are whitespace sensitive, meaning that indentations affect the meaning of the code. This file defines two containers named wordpress and db. For each container, it defines which container image to use, what volumes to mount, which ports to publish (in the case of the wordpress container), which environment variables to set, and other settings.

The wordpress container uses the wordpress:latest image to create an instance of the WordPress web application. The db container uses the mariadb:10.9 container image to create an instance of a MySQL database server. (MySQL is a popular data management system that you'll learn more about in Chapter 12.)

Because these two containers are defined in the same *docker-compose.yaml* file, by default they're part of the same Docker network so that they can communicate with each other. The wordpress container sets WORDPRESS_DB_HOST to db, the name of the other container, because it connects to that hostname. The wordpress environment variables ❶ also match the db environment variables ❷. If these database credentials aren't the same, WordPress gets a "permission denied" error when trying to connect to the database.

**NOTE** *The WordPress* docker-compose.yaml *file in this example is a slightly modified version of a sample file in the Docker documentation at* https://docs.docker.com/samples/wordpress/. *See the documentation for a more thorough description of how to use Docker Compose.*

## Start Your WordPress Site

In your terminal, change to the folder you created for this exercise and run the following command to start both containers at the same time:

```
docker-compose up
```

The first time you run it, Docker should download the `mariadb:10.9` and `wordpress:latest` container images from Docker Hub. The command should then run a MySQL container and a web server container running WordPress, and you should see logs from both containers scroll by in your terminal. Logs from the `db` container start with `db_1`, while logs from the `wordpress` container start with `wordpress_1`.

The `db` container doesn't need to publish any ports for WordPress to connect to it, since both containers share a Docker network. However, the `wordpress` container publishes ports 8000:80. This means that loading *http://127.0.0.1:8000* in your browser connects to your host operating system on port 8000 and loads the web server in the `wordpress` container running on port 80.

Enter ***http://127.0.0.1:8000*** in your browser, and you're running WordPress! Figure 5-2 shows the WordPress installation process that appears when I load that URL on my Mac after selecting English as my language.

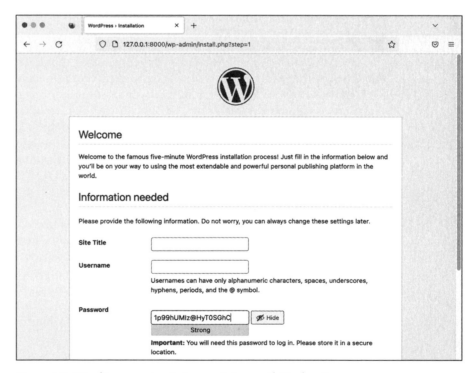

*Figure 5-2: WordPress running in two containers with Docker Compose*

Fill out the form with your WordPress site's title, a username, and a password, and then explore your new WordPress site.

To open a shell and run commands in an active container with Docker Compose, you use the `docker-compose exec` *container_name command* syntax. For example, this is how you'd get a shell in the `wordpress` container:

```
docker-compose exec wordpress bash
```

While `docker-compose run` starts a new container, `docker-compose exec` runs a command in an active container—a little like opening a new terminal window inside a running container.

Exit the shell when you are done. Back in the terminal running `docker -compose up`, press CTRL-C to shut down the containers. Now you're ready to use your new Docker and Docker Compose skills to make your datasets searchable with Aleph.

## Introducing Aleph

> *Truth cannot penetrate a closed mind. If all places in the universe are in the Aleph, then all stars, all lamps, all sources of light are in it, too.*
> —Jorge Luis Borges, "The Aleph"

The Organized Crime and Corruption Reporting Project (OCCRP), founded in 2006, has a history of publishing high-profile investigations into corruption, often leading to criminal investigations, arrests, and seizure of stolen funds. In partnership with dozens of newsrooms around the world, the group relies on large datasets for its investigations. For example, OCCRP, along with the International Consortium of Investigative Journalists (ICIJ), was part of a coalition investigating the Panama Papers, an offshore tax haven dataset that led to over 40 stories about corruption. One of those stories implicated a close friend of Vladimir Putin who had embezzled $230 million from Russian taxpayers. Because OCCRP deals with so much data, it developed Aleph as an investigation tool to make it easier to track white-collar crime, follow the money, and cross-reference various datasets.

OCCRP runs an Aleph server available to the public at *https://data.occrp .org*. This server includes over 250 public datasets with documents from 139 different countries and territories. While there's some overlap with datasets published by DDoSecrets, most public datasets in OCCRP's Aleph server are different. Many of them are regularly updated datasets of public records: registries of company ownership around the world, lists of people and organizations facing international sanctions, and court records. These datasets might not seem exciting on their own, but when your investigation leads you to a specific person or company, they can be crucial for helping you fill in the gaps. OCCRP's Aleph server also contains many more private datasets, which are available to journalists who apply for access.

Take some time to check out OCCRP's Aleph server, explore which public datasets are available, and make some searches. For example, if you search for Rudy Giuliani (Donald Trump's confidant and former lawyer, and the former mayor of New York City) and filter by the US Federal Courts Archive dataset, you'll find a series of court documents that reference Giuliani.

You can upload your own datasets to OCCRP's Aleph server only if OCCRP makes an account for you. Even if you do have an account, you won't be able to upload medium- or high-security datasets without sharing this data with a third party: OCCRP. That's why I help run a private Aleph server for The Intercept. You won't use OCCRP's public Aleph server further in this book. Instead, in Exercise 5-4, you'll run a small Aleph server and bring up Aleph containers on your own laptop.

## Exercise 5-4: Run Aleph Locally in Linux Containers

This exercise prepares you to run your own server directly on your computer with Docker Compose. Instead of accessing Aleph at *https://data.occrp.org*, you'll bring up your Aleph containers and access your private server at *http://127.0.0.1:8080*. You'll use Docker Compose to run the many different services Aleph requires on your computer with a single command.

Make a new folder called *aleph* to use for this exercise and the next. Save a copy of *docker-compose.yml* and *aleph.env.tmpl* from Aleph's git repo, located at *https://github.com/alephdata/aleph*, into the *aleph* folder.

The *docker-compose.yml* file describes the nine containers that Aleph requires and all of their configuration, including the volumes that will save the indexed versions of your datasets. One of these containers, called shell, includes a bind mount that maps your home folder (~) on your host filesystem to */host* in the container:

```
- "~:/host"
```

In your copy of *docker-compose.yml*, delete this line or comment it out by prepending a hash mark (#) to make Aleph run faster and avoid giving the container access to your home folder.

Now rename *aleph.env.tmpl* to *aleph.env*, and open that file in your text editor. This file contains the settings for your Aleph instance on different lines, in the format SETTING_NAME=setting_value, which you'll need to modify in a few ways.

First, run the following command to generate a random value for ALEPH _SECRET_KEY (Windows users, run this in your Ubuntu terminal):

```
openssl rand -hex 24
```

Since you're running Aleph on your computer instead of setting it up on a server for others to use, change ALEPH_SINGLE_USER in *aleph.env* to true instead of false, which allows you to use Aleph without having to create an admin user for yourself. Save the file.

Aleph relies on many different services to run, including three databases: PostgreSQL, Redis, and Elasticsearch. Elasticsearch is designed to search large amounts of data for text strings. For it to operate quickly, it needs to hold lots of data in memory. Linux's default memory management setting `vm.max_map_count` is far too low for Elasticsearch to work properly. If you're using Linux or Windows with WSL, run the following command to increase the value of `vm.max_map_count`:

```
sudo sysctl -w vm.max_map_count=262144
```

If you're using macOS, run `sysctl -w vm.max_map_count=262144` inside of your Linux VM managed by Docker Desktop. To do this, run the following command to start a shell directly in your Linux VM:

```
docker run -it --rm --privileged --pid=host alpine:edge nsenter -t 1 -m -u -n -i sh
```

Once you're in this shell, run this command:

```
sysctl -w vm.max_map_count=262144
```

Run **exit** to exit the Linux VM shell. Each time you restart Docker Desktop, this change is undone, so you'll need to run these commands again to continue using Elasticsearch. (Refer to the "Increasing Elasticsearch Memory in Docker Desktop" box to speed up this process in the future.)

---

### INCREASING ELASTICSEARCH MEMORY IN DOCKER DESKTOP

If you're using macOS, you'll need to change settings before starting the Aleph containers. Instead of referring to this chapter to remember what commands to run, store them as the following shell script (which you can also find at *https:// github.com/micahflee/hacks-leaks-and-revelations/blob/main/chapter-5/aleph/fix -es-memory.sh*):

```
#!/bin/bash
docker run -it --rm --privileged --pid=host alpine:edge \
    nsenter -t 1 -m -u -n -i \
    sysctl -w vm.max_map_count=262144
```

Save a copy of this script in the same folder as your *docker-compose.yml* file for Aleph, and run **chmod +x fix-es-memory.sh** to make sure it's executable. You can now run the script before starting the Aleph containers with just these two commands:

```
./fix-es-memory.sh
docker-compose up
```

You'll need to run this script only once each time you restart Docker Desktop.

---

Finally, for all operating systems, run the following command to start Aleph:

```
docker-compose up
```

The first time you run this command, you'll download a few gigabytes of container images. Text will scroll past in the terminal while Aleph boots up; wait for it to stop.

You also need to run an upgrade command the first time you use Aleph and whenever you upgrade your version of it. Once Aleph finishes booting, open a second terminal, change to the *exercises* folder, and run:

```
docker-compose run --rm shell aleph upgrade
```

This command initializes the databases that Aleph uses by running the command aleph upgrade inside the shell container. Wait for this command to completely finish; you'll know it's done when the program stops displaying output and you end up back at your terminal's command prompt.

**NOTE** *For more detailed documentation for Aleph, see* https://docs.aleph.occrp.org.

## Using Aleph's Web and Command Line Interfaces

Now that you have a local Aleph server, you can explore its two different interfaces: the web interface, which you'll use to investigate datasets, and the CLI interface, which you'll use to index new datasets or administer your Aleph server.

With your Aleph containers up, open *http://127.0.0.1:8080/* in a browser to see the web interface. For example, Figure 5-3 shows Aleph running in Docker containers on my Mac.

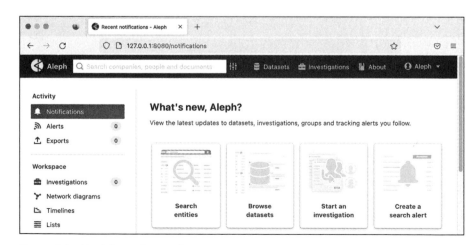

*Figure 5-3: Aleph hosted in Docker containers*

You'll use this interface to search data you upload into Aleph. The search bar at the top allows you to search every dataset you've indexed in your Aleph server at once, and the slider icon just to the right of the search box lets you perform advanced searches.

The Datasets and Investigations buttons at the top show you the datasets in Aleph; for now, both of those pages will be empty. In Aleph, datasets and investigations are both collections of documents, with different user interfaces for exploring each. A dataset should be static, while an investigation is a collection of documents that you might still be adding to.

After performing a search in Aleph, you can optionally save your search query as an alert. This feature is useful only on servers that have multiple users and are configured to send email. In those cases, the server automatically searches any new data indexed into the server for all of a user's saved alerts. If it gets a hit, it sends an email to the user. In the example, you set `ALEPH_SINGLE_USER` to true, so that feature doesn't apply.

In addition to the web-based user interface you just explored, designed for journalists and researchers, Aleph has a command line interface designed for running the Aleph server itself. You must use the command line interface for administrative tasks like creating Aleph users (if you aren't using the `ALEPH_SINGLE_USER` setting in future projects) or indexing folders of data, which you'll do later in this chapter.

To use the command line interface, run `bash` inside the container called `shell` to start an Aleph shell like so:

```
docker-compose run --rm shell bash
```

When you first opened a shell in a container using Docker Compose, you used `docker-compose exec`, which executes a command in an already running container. Here, `docker-compose run` runs a new container in which to execute your command. The `--rm` argument tells Docker to remove the container as soon as your command finishes running. In this case, your command is `bash`, so you can run `exit` in the bash shell to remove this temporary container.

You can now use the `aleph` command. Run `aleph --help` to see a list of all of the commands that Aleph supports. To learn more about a specific command, run `--help` on it. For example, to learn more about the `crawldir` command (which we'll discuss in Exercise 5-5), you'd run `aleph crawldir --help`.

Run `exit` to quit the Aleph shell. Back in your other terminal window, press CTRL-C to shut down all the Aleph containers when you're not using them. When you run `docker-compose up` to start the containers again, all the data in Aleph—including any datasets that you've added to it—will still be there, because that data is stored in Docker volumes, making it persistent.

## Indexing Data in Aleph

Adding data to Aleph is called *indexing*. By loading and processing every file in a dataset, Aleph allows you to extract useful information, which you can browse and search via its web-based user interface.

Indexing works differently for different types of files:

**Office documents and PDFs**   Aleph extracts all of the searchable text from these documents and attempts to find anything that looks like a person's name, a company name, or other types of data that Aleph calls *entities*. It also extracts any metadata it can find.

**Email messages**   Aleph again extracts searchable text and entities. This time, the entities it finds are likely to include both names and email addresses, which it determines by checking the sender and recipient of each email. It also extracts email attachments and indexes those individually.

**Compressed files, such as ZIP files**   Aleph decompresses these files, then indexes each file inside them individually, which can become as recursive as necessary. For example, a ZIP file might contain an email file with an attachment that contains another ZIP file, and so on.

Indexing datasets can take hours, days, or weeks, depending on the size of the dataset and the computational resources available to your Aleph server. In Exercise 5-5, you'll index a single BlueLeaks folder called *icefishx*.

## Exercise 5-5: Index a BlueLeaks Folder in Aleph

The *icefishx* folder contains data from an American police intelligence network called Intelligence Communications Enterprise for Information Sharing and Exchange (ICEFISHX), a partnership between law enforcement in Minnesota, North Dakota, and South Dakota. I've selected this data because it covers the state where Minneapolis cop Derek Chauvin murdered George Floyd, sparking the 2020 Black Lives Matter uprising. Searching this dataset for *George Floyd* might reveal some interesting internal docs about police violence or the protests that it triggered.

### Mount Your Datasets into the Aleph Shell

If you don't already have Aleph running, change to your *aleph* folder and enter the following command:

```
docker-compose up
```

Wait for Aleph to boot up.

In a separate terminal, start an Aleph shell. This time, however, bind-mount your *datasets* USB disk into the container, using the following command, substituting the correct path for your USB disk:

```
docker-compose run --rm -v /Volumes/datasets:/datasets:ro shell bash
```

The arguments in this command are similar to the --mount argument you used earlier to mount a volume with the docker command. The -v argument (short for --volume) is followed by the colon-separated list

*/Volumes/datasets*:`/datasets:ro` containing three parts: the absolute path to the folder on the host operating system (on my computer, this is */Volumes/ datasets*), the absolute path to the folder in the container (*/datasets*), and the `ro` option. Short for "read-only," `ro` gives the container permission to access the files in the bind mount but not to change any of them or create new files.

When you run this command, make sure to use the correct path for your USB disk. In macOS, the path is */Volumes/datasets* or similar; in Linux, it's */media/micah/datasets* or similar; and in Windows with WSL, it's */mnt/d* or similar. If you're using Windows with PowerShell, mount the *D:* drive into the container at the path */datasets* with this command:

```
docker-compose run --rm -v D:/datasets:ro shell bash
```

Altogether, this command runs a new `shell` container and executes the `bash` command inside of it. Your *datasets* folder on your host operating system becomes accessible as the folder */datasets* in the container, and it's mounted in read-only mode, preventing the container from modifying anything on the USB disk.

Now that you have access to your datasets within the Aleph shell, you'll index the *icefishx* data.

### Index the icefishx Folder

To index a dataset, you use the `aleph crawldir` command. Aleph's use of the term *crawl* means to open the folder and index each file in it, then open each subfolder it finds and index each file in that, and so on, until everything in the original folder has been indexed.

Run the following command to start indexing the *icefishx* folder:

```
aleph crawldir -l eng /datasets/BlueLeaks-extracted/icefishx
```

This command tells Aleph to index data in the */datasets/BlueLeaks -extracted/icefishx* folder in the container (which is actually */Volumes/datasets/ BlueLeaks-extracted/icefishx* on my host operating system). The -1 option (short for --language) helps you use OCR on documents. Because different languages use different alphabets and words, using -1 tells the OCR software what language you're dealing with—in this case, English (eng).

Aleph should begin to work its way through each of the 19,992 files in the *icefishx* folder, totaling over 2GB. The output should display the file-name of each file, which is added to a list of files to crawl. Even before the `aleph crawldir` command finishes, Aleph begins to index each file.

Switch to your other terminal window running Docker Compose and watch the output as it indexes and performs OCR on each file.

**NOTE**   *You can use OCR for documents in languages other than English, too. To index a Russian dataset, for example, you'd use -1 rus so that Aleph recognizes Russian words in the Cyrillic alphabet. Under the hood, Aleph uses software called Tesseract to do the OCR; for a list of valid language codes in Tesseract's documentation, see* https://tesseract-ocr.github.io/tessdoc/Data-Files-in-different-versions.html.

The *icefishx* folder took about an hour and a half to index on my Mac. It also used about 17GB worth of Docker volumes. Indexing larger quantities of data could take days and require much more disk space.

## Check Indexing Status

After `aleph crawldir` has finished running, while you're waiting for the indexing to complete, try a few more Aleph commands to query your Aleph server and check the indexing status.

First, run the following command to see a list of all of the datasets and investigations (known together as *collections*) in your Aleph server:

```
root@26430936533f:/aleph# aleph collections
Foreign ID                                           ID  Label
---------------------------------------------------- ---- -----------------
28c82cbe1ba247e6a16e3fb4b7d50a67                     1   Test Investigation
directory:datasets-blueleaks-extracted-icefishx      2   icefishx
```

The Foreign ID field is the unique identifier for each dataset, and the Label field is the human-readable name for the dataset displayed in the Aleph web application. I used the Aleph web interface to create a new investigation called Test Investigation before I started indexing *icefishx*, so I have two collections. When you use the web interface to make investigations, they get assigned completely random foreign IDs. When you use `aleph crawldir` to create them, the Foreign ID is based on the filesystem path that you're indexing; alternatively, you can use the -f *foreign_id* arguments to specify your own if you like.

Next, run the following command while indexing *icefishx* to check the status of the indexing:

```
root@26430936533f:/aleph# aleph status
  Collection Job                               Stage    Pending   Running   Finished
  ---------- ------------------------------    -------  --------- --------- ----------
           2                                             19263     4         3387
           2 a4bb59c4e23b4b96b14d747ff78c69e2  ingest   19239     3         1145
           2 a4bb59c4e23b4b96b14d747ff78c69e2  analyze  24        1         1123
           2 a4bb59c4e23b4b96b14d747ff78c69e2  index    0         0         1119
```

This command displays a table of data that tells you the number of pending, running, and finished tasks for each collection that's indexing, split into analyze, ingest, and index phases. The Collection column shows the ID of the collection—if you look back at the output of `aleph collections`, the ID of the ICEFISHX dataset is 2. When I ran `aleph status`, based on the total pending and finished numbers, indexing was roughly 15 percent complete (though this might be misleading; for example, one of those pending files could be a ZIP file containing another 1,000 files).

If Aleph breaks in the middle of indexing a dataset, you can recover your progress. If you're seeing a lot of error messages in the Docker Compose logs or in the Aleph web interface, the simplest solution is to restart the containers. In your Docker Compose terminal window, you'd press CTRL-C to quit all of the containers and then run docker-compose up to start them again. After a few minutes, your containers should finish booting and the indexing should commence where it left off. If something failed before your aleph crawldir command finished running in the Aleph shell, you can run aleph crawldir again. This will reindex the entire dataset, but it should be quicker the second time around, because it won't redo time-consuming tasks like performing OCR on documents that have already been processed.

You can also check the indexing status via the Aleph web interface. In your browser, navigate to the Investigations page. From there, click the ICEFISHX investigation, and you should see a progress bar showing you how the indexing is doing. Figure 5-4 shows the indexing status from inside the web application.

Figure 5-4: The ICEFISHX dataset in the process of indexing

While you're here, click the gear icon in the top-right corner of the screen and go to **Settings**. From there you can change the label, category, and summary of this dataset. For example, you can change the label from *icefishx* to something more descriptive, like *BlueLeaks: Intelligence Communications Enterprise for Information Sharing and Exchange (ICEFISHX)*. The default category is Investigations. If you change it to anything else, like Leaks, Court Archives, or Other Material, ICEFISHX will appear under Datasets instead of Investigations. For now, stick with the Investigations category.

Sit back and wait for Aleph to finish indexing the ICEFISHX dataset before moving on to the next section, where you'll begin to use Aleph to explore the data.

NOTE    *It's possible to start looking through datasets in Aleph before indexing is complete, but it's best to wait for the full index to finish before digging too deep. If you don't, you'll search only the data that's been indexed to that point, so your searches might miss important documents.*

## Explore BlueLeaks with Aleph

Once you've finished indexing the *icefishx* folder, navigate to the ICEFISHX dataset you've just imported in the Aleph web interface. It should be listed under the Investigations link at the top of the page. The Documents link in the left sidebar lets you manually browse the files in the dataset and open various documents, but where Aleph really shines is its search engine.

When you enter a term in the search field, Aleph searches every dataset you've imported. You can filter your results in a variety of ways, using the left sidebar: for example, you can filter to a specific dataset, a specific date range, or even to documents that mention specific email addresses, phone numbers, or names. Once you've filtered the search results, you can click on documents to preview them.

Figure 5-5 shows some of the 335 search results for the term *George Floyd* in the ICEFISHX dataset.

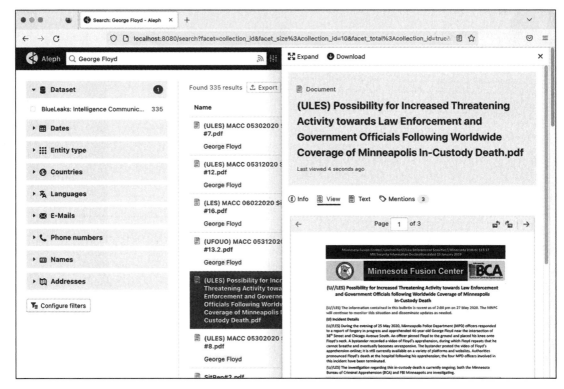

*Figure 5-5: Aleph's search interface with results returned for the term* George Floyd

The document selected in Figure 5-5, classified as U//LES (Unclassified, Law Enforcement Sensitive), was created by the Minnesota Fusion Center on May 27, 2020. It warns of an increase in threatening activity toward law enforcement officers in response to George Floyd's murder in police custody two days earlier. According to the document, two of the four officers involved had been doxed, and people protested outside one of their homes. Thousands of people began marching in the streets, and there were "increased discussions on White Supremacist Extremist (WSE) online forums." The document recommends that police "avoid wearing organizationally-affiliated clothing outside of work settings," "reduce social media footprint and use an alias," and consider "varying travel patterns to avoid surveillance."

Aleph makes it easy to find connections between documents. If you click Expand in the top left of the selected document, you should end up at that document's detail page. This page shows the document's metadata on the left, as well as any names or email addresses it finds that are also mentioned in other documents. If you click on one of those—for example, on someone's name or email—you should be taken to search results that list all of the documents mentioning that person.

When you're done exploring *icefishx*, try indexing additional folders in BlueLeaks or even the entire *BlueLeaks-extracted* folder.

## Additional Aleph Features

There's a lot more to Aleph than what we've covered so far. This section will introduce a few of the other cool things it can do, which you'll find useful in the future as you continue to analyze hacked and leaked datasets. As you've seen, Aleph is great at indexing folders full of a wide variety of documents, but it also supports importing *structured data*—data that follows a consistent and well-defined data model. Entities in Aleph, which I mentioned earlier, are an example of structured data. Specifically, Aleph uses a data model called FollowTheMoney, which contains types of entities like Person, Company, Organization, or Address. Learn more about the FollowTheMoney data model and how to import these entities directly into Aleph at *https://followthemoney.tech*.

When you index a dataset in Aleph, it automatically extracts its best guess at entities—data like the names of people and companies, and phone numbers and addresses—but its guesses are far from perfect. Aleph also allows you to manually create and edit entities in more detail. You can add a list of people to an investigation, for example, providing not just their names but also their contact information and any relationships they have to other entities like their employers. When you're viewing an entity in Aleph's web interface, it shows you all of the data about that entity and links to all of its related entities.

You can also generate entities from data in spreadsheets like CSV or Excel files. For example, the ICEFISHX dataset has a spreadsheet called *Registrations.csv* that lists the name, rank, agency, home address, email address, phone number, supervisor, and other information about all 6,000 people who had accounts on the site. From the detail page of this file in the Aleph web interface, you can click Generate Entities to define exactly how this data should map to entities, and even how these entities should relate to other entities. This could help you build an organization chart of who reports to whom, for example.

In addition to the `aleph crawldir` command you used in Exercise 5-5, there are other ways to index data into Aleph. First, you can use a different CLI program called `alephclient`, which allows you to index data and push it into a remote Aleph server over the internet using Aleph's application programming interface (API), without opening an Aleph shell. APIs are designed to allow software, rather than humans, to communicate. Every user on an Aleph server (or, if it's a server with users disabled, the whole server) has an API secret access key, a credential that allows software to add data to, or otherwise interact with, the Aleph server. You can pass this API key into `alephclient` as an argument to index large datasets on an Aleph server that someone else runs. The command to install `alephclient` is `python3 -m pip install alephclient`.

Alternatively, you can create a new investigation directly in the web interface by clicking Investigations at the top, then New Investigation. You'll be prompted to give your investigation a title and an optional summary and language. You can upload files to your investigation directly from your web browser. This is useful if you want to upload a spreadsheet of names and email address and cross-reference it with the rest of the data in your Aleph server. For uploading big datasets like BlueLeaks, however, using the Aleph shell or `alephclient` is easier and less error-prone.

One of Aleph's most powerful features is its ability to search multiple datasets at once. For example, you could index the BlueLeaks dataset, the Oath Keepers dataset you downloaded in Chapter 4, and several others to search them all for someone's name, email address, or phone number. Since the BlueLeaks dataset is full of PII of law enforcement officers and the Oath Keepers militia is known to recruit retired police, you could check if any Oath Keepers members or donors are mentioned in BlueLeaks. (I recommend waiting to try this until you further explore the Oath Keepers dataset in Chapter 6.)

Aleph can also cross-reference the entities from one dataset with entities in all of the other datasets that have been indexed in a server. Navigating to an investigation and clicking Cross-Reference in the left sidebar allows you to compare each entity in the investigation with entities in every other dataset or investigation. For example, you could upload a spreadsheet of people you're investigating—say, everyone who works at the White House—into an investigation, use the Generate Entities feature to convert it into a detailed list of Person entities, and then cross-reference this list with all of the other datasets you've indexed to see if any White House employees show up in them.

Spend some time experimenting with Aleph and getting to know its features on your own. When DDoSecrets publishes a dataset that you're interested in, try downloading it and indexing it in Aleph. Explore searching multiple datasets at once as well as using the cross-referencing feature. Aleph's documentation is available at *https://docs.aleph.occrp.org*.

# Dedicated Aleph Servers

Running Aleph in containers on your computer works well if you want to search just a few small datasets yourself. However, to index a large amount of data (such as all of BlueLeaks) that will stretch your laptop's computational resources, or to work with others on the same datasets, consider setting up a dedicated Aleph server instead. Full instructions on doing that are outside the scope of this book, but this section provides an introduction.

In Chapter 4, you learned how to create servers in the cloud; earlier in this chapter, you learned how to set up your own Aleph server. By combining those skills, you should be able to set up Aleph running in Docker containers on a cloud server. However, you'll also need to decide how to secure the server and make sure it stays updated. How will you manage its users, and how will you restrict access to the server? How will you know and what will you do if someone hacks it? To run an Aleph server for your organization, I recommend that you bring in a professional system administrator or DevOps engineer to set it up and maintain it over time.

As you set up your server, consider the security levels of the datasets on which you plan to use Aleph. For low- to medium-security datasets, you can host Aleph in a cloud server, which allows you to temporarily give your server more RAM or processing power to index a dataset more quickly. For medium- to high-security datasets, host Aleph on physical hardware, like a server in an office or in a server closet in a data center. Decide whether to require people to come into the office to use Aleph or to configure it so that they can access it over the internet. If you choose the latter, you'll need to secure your Aleph server and the data it contains. For the highest-security datasets, you'll have to download Linux containers on a computer with internet access, export the datasets, and import them on an air-gapped server.

---

### INTELLA AND DATASHARE

You can use software besides Aleph to help you make datasets searchable. As mentioned in Chapter 1, the first leaked dataset I worked on was the Snowden Archive. At that time, Aleph didn't exist. To index and search the Snowden Archive, we used proprietary software called Intella, installed on air-gapped Windows laptops. Intella, developed by Vound Software, is investigation software that was designed for law firms and law enforcement to explore large datasets, like email dumps or the contents of seized computers.

The Intercept used to have a license for Intella Connect, a web-based version of Intella. This software has a few advantages over Aleph: it rarely has technical issues, it comes with tech support, and it allows you to index and search large datasets faster. Like Aleph, Intella Connect supports collaborating with multiple users. After Russia invaded Ukraine in 2022 and hackers started

*(continued)*

dumping terabytes of data from Russian companies online, I began downloading and indexing all of these datasets into Intella Connect. I quickly found that this project was far too complicated for The Intercept alone to handle, especially considering that all of the data was in Russian. I helped spearhead a project to invite outside journalists who spoke Russian or were interested in these datasets to use our Intella service. This project grew into a major international collaboration with OCCRP and dozens of reporters around the world, including both Russian and Ukrainian journalists, to research the Russian datasets. The project's collaborators used both Intella Connect and OCCRP's Aleph server, and we organized our findings on an internal wiki.

The Intercept has now decided to stop paying for Intella Connect and uses Aleph exclusively instead. Intella has some disadvantages: it doesn't have Aleph's ability to cross-reference between datasets and map out relationships between entities, it's quite expensive, and it requires Windows.

Another open source tool for indexing datasets is Datashare, developed by ICIJ, the group that worked in a coalition on the Panama Papers dataset along with OCCRP. Datashare is similar to Aleph but is designed for a single user to run it locally on their computer, rather than on a server. Like Aleph, Datashare runs inside of Docker containers. While it's a very promising project, I ran into issues trying to install it at the time of writing. Because it's open source and actively developed, however, I expect this will improve over time. You can read more about Datashare at *https://datashare.icij.org* and *https://github.com/ICIJ/datashare*.

## Summary

In this chapter, you've learned how to run software in Linux containers using Docker, then applied those skills to run Aleph on your computer and index the *icefishx* folder from BlueLeaks, making it searchable. A search for the keyword *George Floyd* uncovered interesting law enforcement documents about the 2020 racial justice protests that you couldn't have uncovered with just grep. You've also learned about some Aleph features you can explore on your own, the possibility of running a dedicated Aleph server instead of running it on your laptop, and dataset-indexing tools other than Aleph.

You'll revisit Docker in Chapter 10, when you learn to use BlueLeaks Explorer, and in Chapter 12, when you learn about SQL databases. In the following chapter, you'll learn the tools and techniques required to dig through one of the most prevalent forms of data leaks: email dumps.

# 6

## READING OTHER PEOPLE'S EMAIL

After Russia invaded Ukraine in February 2022, hackers started flooding DDoSecrets with stolen data from Russian organizations. The data came in many formats, but the bulk of it—several terabytes' worth—was email. The entire inboxes of government agencies, oil and gas companies, and investment firms were laid bare.

Email leaks are among the most common types of data leaks, and they can have serious consequences. In the 2016 US presidential election between Hillary Clinton and Donald Trump, leaked email messages from the DNC and Clinton campaign chair John Podesta—both hacked by the Russian government—played a major role in Trump's election. The 2020 US presidential election between Trump and Joe Biden also involved email leaks—in this case, stolen from the laptop of Biden's son Hunter.

With so many messages to sort through in email leaks, though, finding a place to start can be overwhelming. Depending on how the email was obtained and what software was running on the hacked server, the leaked data could be in any of several different formats, and it may not be clear how to access the messages it contains.

In this chapter, you'll learn about common formats for leaked email, the benefits and shortcomings of indexing and searching email with Aleph, and how to import email datasets into Thunderbird and Microsoft Outlook. You'll sift through leaked email from the Oath Keepers dataset you downloaded in Chapter 4, in addition to datasets from Australian offshore detention centers and the conservative US think tank the Heritage Foundation. We'll begin by taking a look at the standard composition of an email message.

## The Email Protocol and Message Structure

A *protocol* is a shared language that software developers agree upon to make their code interoperate. The email protocol we use today was first implemented in the early 1980s, got a major revamp in 1995, and hasn't changed much since. Unlike modern centralized messaging systems (Facebook Messenger, for example), this protocol allows anyone to run an email server with their own software. For example, Google runs a server at gmail.com, the Russian search engine Yandex runs one at mail.yandex.com, and the Swiss company Proton runs one at proton.me. These servers are powered by different software but communicate using the same protocol, meaning they can all send messages to one another. *Internet standards*, specifications for how certain types of software should behave, ensure that all email software communicates with a shared protocol and a shared message format.

Because the email message format is an internet standard, all messages have a similar structure. To see what this format looks like, open any email and choose **Show Original** or **View Source**. Each message is a text file with two sections: the headers and body. The headers contain an email's metadata in *Header-Field: Value* format, while the body contains the main text of the message.

The following headers are included in nearly every email message:

```
Subject: What's up?
From: Alice <alice@example.com>
To: Bob <bob@example.com>
```

There are many more headers than these; your email software shows only a few of them. When email servers send, forward, or receive messages, they add headers describing these actions. For example, the common header DKIM-Signature allows you to verify, using cryptography, that an email actually came from the server that it claims sent it. Messages also typically include a Content-Type header, which describes the format of the body text.

After the headers, the email includes a blank line followed by the body. The body is typically in plaintext (text with no formatting), HTML, or Multipurpose Internet Mail Extensions (MIME) format. In MIME email, the most common format, the body is split into parts for text, HTML components, and email attachments.

Though email messages are text files, you can send binary files like PNGs or ZIPs as attachments. Your email client converts the binary file into text using *Base64* encoding and includes that encoded attachment in the message. Just as you can convert any decimal number (that is, one conveyed using 10 digits) into a binary number (conveyed using 2 digits) and back, you can convert any binary data into Base64 data (conveyed using 64 characters). For example, here's how a PNG image containing a 1×1 transparent pixel looks with each of its 86 bytes of data represented as binary digits:

```
10001001 01010000 01001110 01000111 00001101 00001010 00011010 00001010 00000000 00000000
00000000 00001101 01001001 01001000 01000100 01010010 00000000 00000000 00000000 00000001
00000000 00000000 00000000 00000001 00001000 00000110 00000000 00000000 00000000 00011111
00010101 11000100 10001001 00000000 00000000 00000000 00000110 01100010 01001011 01000111
01000100 00000000 11111111 00000000 11111111 00000000 11111111 10100000 10111101 10100111
10010011 00000000 00000000 00000000 00001011 01001001 01000100 01000001 01010100 00001000
11010111 01100011 01100000 00000000 00000010 00000000 00000000 00000101 00000000 00000001
11100010 00100110 00000101 10011011 00000000 00000000 00000000 00000000 01001001 01000101
01001110 01000100 10101110 01000010 01100000 10000010
```

And here's the Base64-encoded version of the same binary file:

```
iVBORw0KGgoAAAANSUhEUgAAAAEAAAABCAYAAAAfFcSJAAAABmJLR0QA/wD/AP+gvaeTAAAAC01E
QVQI12NgAAIAAAUAAeImBZsAAAAASUVORK5CYII=
```

Base64-encoded data looks like a block of seemingly random text that includes capital letters, lowercase letters, numbers, plus signs (+), and forward slashes (/), and sometimes ends with equal signs (=). The Base64-encoded version of some data conveys the same information as the decoded version, but it can be included more compactly in a text file, like an email. When the recipient of the email loads it, their email client will convert it from Base64 text back into a binary file. Sometimes plaintext or HTML email is encoded in Base64 as well (for example, `hello world` is `aGVsbG8gd29ybGQ=` in Base64). Although email messages are text files, you can't rely on `grep` to search them, because much of the content you're hunting for might be Base64-encoded.

Keeping in mind those basics, let's turn now to the specific formats typically encountered in email leaks.

## File Formats for Email Dumps

The most common file formats for email *dumps*, or collections of email messages, are EML files, MBOX files, and PST Outlook data files. You'll download email in each format in the upcoming exercise.

### EML Files

The simplest type of email dump is a folder full of EML files, the standard email message format. An EML file is a text file with the extension *.eml* that contains the raw email message—the headers followed by the body.

When you download an email from your personal account, it will be in EML format. If you have a Gmail account, for example, open a message, click the **More** menu (the three dots icon) in the upper-right corner, and choose **Download Message**. Other email clients should likewise allow you to download individual messages in EML format. You can sometimes read an EML file in a text editor, but you'll frequently be stymied by the Base64-encoded parts, so it's more useful to open it in an email program like Thunderbird, Outlook, or the Mail app on macOS.

You can forward an email inline or as an attachment. Most email systems default to forwarding inline, copying the text of the body of the email you're forwarding into the body of the email you're writing. When you instead forward as an attachment, you attach the raw EML file to the email you're writing. From a Gmail inbox, for example, select the box next to an email message, click the **More** menu, and choose **Forward as Attachment**. Other email clients should allow you to forward email as attachments as well. EML files include information that isn't included in inline forwarded email, such as the original email headers.

EML files don't include information on how the email was organized in the user's inbox, such as the folder where the email was stored. For this reason, people who leak email dumps in EML format often organize the files into folders, with each folder representing a different user's inbox. Sometimes they organize the files from each inbox into subfolders, too.

In Exercise 6-1, you'll download email messages in EML format from the Nauru Police Force dataset.

### MBOX Files

In an MBOX email dump, each file is a collection of many email messages, generally representing a full folder of email. MBOX files often have the file extension *.mbox*, but sometimes they have no file extension at all.

Like EML files, MBOX files are text files that are viewable in a text editor but not very human-readable because of the Base64 encoding. However, you can't just open an MBOX file in an email client to read the email like you can with an EML file. Instead, you'll need to import the file.

The Oath Keepers dataset is a series of MBOX files, one for each hacked inbox. I'll give more detail on the structure of this dataset in Exercise 6-1.

### PST Outlook Data Files

Email dumps may also come in the form of PST files, a proprietary format that represents a Microsoft Outlook inbox with the *.pst* file extension. Microsoft's email server is called Microsoft Exchange. Whenever an

Outlook user wants to create a backup of their email, or when an Exchange server is hacked, the data is downloaded in PST format.

A PST file represents a full email inbox, complete with a hierarchy of folders and their contents. These files can get *big*. For example, in April 2022, hackers made off with 786GB of data from the All-Russia State Television and Broadcasting Company (VGTRK), the largest state-owned media company in Russia, and leaked it to DDoSecrets. This dataset includes 252 PST files, each representing a different email address. One file, *intercoord@vgtrk.ru.pst*, is 48GB alone.

In Exercise 6-1 you'll download a 1GB PST file containing email from the Heritage Foundation.

## Exercise 6-1: Download Email Dumps from Three Datasets

In this exercise, you'll work with three different datasets from the Nauru Police Force, the Oath Keepers, and the Heritage Foundation. You should already have the Oath Keepers dataset from Chapter 4, so you'll download the other two next. You'll also learn more about their contents and structure.

### The Nauru Police Force Dataset

Nauru is a tiny island in the Pacific with a population of about 10,000. While technically it's an independent country, it hosts abuse-ridden offshore detention centers that the Australian government uses to hold immigrants and asylum seekers. The Nauru Police Force dataset (*https://ddosecrets .com/wiki/Nauru_Police_Force*) is a 54GB torrent full of 127 ZIP files, each a copy of all of the email from a specific email address at npf.gov.nr, the domain for the Nauru Police Force. Inside each ZIP file is a collection of folders containing EML files. This dataset contains over 285,000 messages.

For this chapter, you'll be working with the file *iven-notte.zip*, which is about 2.9GB. Download the file directly from *https://data.ddosecrets.com/ Nauru%20Police%20Force/npf.gov.nr/iven-notte.zip*. Once you've done so, save it into a folder called *Nauru Police Force* on your *datasets* USB disk and unzip it. You should end up with a folder called *iven-notte* containing the subfolders *calendar, contacts, deleteditems, drafts, inbox*, and more. Each of these subfolders is full of EML files.

### The Oath Keepers Dataset

The public part of the Oath Keepers dataset is a 3.9GB torrent of MBOX files taken from the server that hosted email for the oathkeepers.org domain. This dataset has a folder called *Oath Keepers.sbd*, containing subfolders called *ak, al, alb, ar, Archive, az*, and many others, each of which is an MBOX file (without the *.mbox* file extension) that contains several email messages. Each US state chapter of the Oath Keepers militia has its own inbox, so, for example, you can find the Arizona chapter's email in the MBOX file *az*. There are a few other MBOX files, including *volunteers* and *stewart.rhodes* (Stewart Rhodes is the founder of the militia and was convicted of seditious conspiracy and sentenced to 18 years in prison for his group's role in the January 6, 2021, attack on the US Capitol). DDoSecrets distributes an additional part of the dataset, which contains donor and membership records, only to journalists and researchers who request access, because it contains so much PII.

If you didn't already download the Oath Keepers dataset in Chapter 4, visit the DDoSecrets page for the Oath Keepers at *https://ddosecrets.com/wiki/ Oath_Keepers*. This page includes a link to the torrent file as well as the magnet link. Add the torrent to your BitTorrent client and download the full dataset, saving it to your *datasets* USB disk.

### The Heritage Foundation Dataset

The Heritage Foundation is a conservative think tank that played a major role in US politics during the Reagan administration. This dataset, a 1GB file called *backup.pst*, is a backup of a personal email account used by an employee on the foundation's major gifts team. His email address was hosted with his residential ISP at the domain embarqmail.com. In 2015, the Twitter user @jfuller290 noticed that the foundation had accidentally put this backup in PST format on a public Amazon S3 bucket—an Amazon cloud service that hosts files—and he tweeted the link to it. (The Heritage Foundation at first claimed that it was hacked, but in fact it had inadvertently made the file public itself.) The email backup was made in 2009, six years before @jfuller290 noticed it.

Visit the DDoSecrets page for the Heritage Foundation at *https:// ddosecrets.com/wiki/Heritage_Foundation*. This page includes links to the torrent as well as a direct download for this dataset. Because the dataset is just a single, relatively small Outlook Data File, directly download it from *https:// data.ddosecrets.com/Heritage%20Foundation/backup.pst* and save it into a folder called *Heritage Foundation* on your *datasets* USB disk.

While you're waiting for these email dumps to finish downloading, read on to learn about the tools you can use to research them.

## Researching Email Dumps with Thunderbird

Before you start reading the email you've downloaded, you'll install and configure *Thunderbird*, an open source email program for Windows, macOS, and Linux that allows you to work with email dumps in different formats. You can use Thunderbird to import folders full of EML or MBOX files and search and read everything inside them. When you open an EML file in Thunderbird, the program will parse the file, Base64-decode everything for you, and let you see HTML email and download attachments.

Thunderbird users typically use the program just to check their personal email, sometimes for multiple email accounts. If you want, you can add your existing email accounts to it and use it to read and write email yourself. For research purposes, though, you'll use Thunderbird to import email into *local folders*, which will allow you to work with the email locally on your computer without connecting to an email server. You don't need internet access when using Thunderbird to research email dumps in this way, which means you can use an air-gapped computer.

Like its sister project, the Firefox web browser, Thunderbird supports third-party extensions that add functionality to the program. The ImportExportTools NG extension is crucial to working with email dumps; it adds support for importing MBOX files and for bulk-importing folders full of EML files, keeping their folder structure intact. However, to import PSTs into Thunderbird, you must first convert them into EMLs using the readpst program. You'll import all three file types into Thunderbird later in the chapter.

After importing email dumps into Thunderbird, you can click through all of the folders and read the email messages as if you were reading your own email. You can also use Thunderbird's built-in search feature to bulk-search all of the email you've imported. However, you can't use Thunderbird to search the content of attachments—for that, you'll need a tool like Aleph, which we'll discuss in "Other Tools for Researching Email Dumps" on page 163.

## Exercise 6-2: Configure Thunderbird for Email Dumps

In this exercise, you'll install Thunderbird and configure it in order to analyze the three email dumps you've downloaded.

Download Thunderbird from *https://www.thunderbird.net* and install it on your computer. When you open the program the first time, it asks if you want to set up an existing email account. While you won't need to use a real email account to research email dumps, adding an account to Thunderbird makes it easier to import these data dumps later on. If you don't want to use Thunderbird to check your real email, I recommend that you create a new email account just for this purpose. Click the **Get a New Email Address** link to create a new free email account directly within Thunderbird on an email provider called Mailfence. Select an email address and generate a random password in your password manager, then provide an existing email address to activate your new account. After creating your account, log in to it with Thunderbird, and you should see the message "Account successfully created."

Next, switch to the main Thunderbird tab. In the Folders sidebar on the left, you should see the email address you added, and beneath it a section called Local Folders. You added an email address just to create the Local Folders section, so if you don't plan on using Thunderbird to check this email account, you can delete it. To do so, click the Thunderbird menu icon in the top-right corner and choose **Account Settings**. Make sure your new email account is selected, click **Account Actions** in the bottom left, and choose **Remove Account**. Select the **Remove Message Data** box and click **Remove**. Now switch back to the main Thunderbird window, and only Local Folders should remain in the left sidebar.

Next, to install the ImportExportTools NG Thunderbird add-on, click the menu icon in the top-right corner and choose **Add-ons and Themes**. Switch to the **Extensions** tab, search for **ImportExportTools NG**, and install the add-on. A lot of this add-on's functionality appears in the Tools menu bar at the top, which appears automatically in macOS. To access it in Windows or Linux, click the menu icon in the top-right corner and choose **View ▸ Toolbars ▸ Menu Bar**. A menu bar should appear at the top of the Thunderbird window. Go to **Tools ▸ ImportExportTools NG** to access the add-on's features.

Finally, click the Thunderbird menu icon and choose **Settings**. Switch to the **Privacy & Security** tab and make sure that Allow Remote Content in Messages is unchecked (it should be unchecked by default). *Remote content* is any content hosted on the internet instead of inside of the email, like images loaded from URLs. When you open an email with remote content, like an HTML email with images, loading those images will leave a trace that the email was opened from a certain IP address.

**NOTE** *Thunderbird will always give you the chance to load remote content on individual email messages if you'd like, but I recommend that you connect to a VPN beforehand so that the VPN's IP address, rather than your IP address, will be tracked (see the "Covering Your Tracks with a VPN Service" box on page 255).*

## Reading Individual EML Files with Thunderbird

During your own investigations, you may find only a few EML files in a dataset, or someone might forward email messages to you as attachments. Thunderbird is a good tool for inspecting these messages individually without needing to import them.

Once your downloads from Exercise 6-1 have finished, try using Thunderbird to view some individual messages. Open your file manager app, like Explorer in Windows or Finder in macOS, and browse to the extracted *iven-notte* folder in the Nauru Police Force dataset. Open the *inbox* folder, right-click one of the EML files, and open it in Thunderbird. Thunderbird should show you the headers, like the date the email was sent, and the From, To, and Subject lines. You can also read the email exactly as it was originally formatted, and if it has attachments, you can open them.

Just as you shouldn't blindly open attachments you receive in your personal email, don't blindly open attachments that you find in email dumps, because they could hack your computer. Refer back to Chapter 1 for tips on how to open such documents safely.

## EXTRACTING ATTACHMENTS FROM EML FILES

A single EML file could contain several file attachments, all Base64-encoded. The munpack program lets you extract these attachments without needing to use an email client. Install munpack with **sudo apt install mpack** in Linux or Windows with WSL, or use **brew install mpack** in Homebrew on macOS. You can then run the command **munpack *filename.eml*** to extract the attachments from an email.

For example, the Nauru Police Force dataset contains an EML file called *68.eml*. When I run munpack 68.eml, it extracts the attachments from that email—in this case, *RegistrationXForm.pdf* and *COPXPassport.pdf*—into the current working folder. You could also use munpack in a script to extract all of the attachments from every email message in an email dump, all from the terminal.

In the following exercises, you'll import each of the email dumps you just downloaded into Thunderbird, starting with the EML files from the Nauru Police Force dataset.

## Exercise 6-3: Import the Nauru Police Force EML Email Dump

To import an email dump with the ImportExportTools NG add-on, select the folder into which you'd like to import it. Always import email dumps into a local folder, rather than a remote folder on an email server. From the Folders sidebar on the main Thunderbird tab, right-click **Local Folders** and choose **New Folder**, as shown in Figure 6-1.

*Figure 6-1: Creating a new local folder in Thunderbird*

Name your folder *Nauru Police Force* and click **Create Folder**. You should now see the *Nauru Police Force* folder in your Local Folders list.

Right-click the *Nauru Police Force* folder you just created and choose **New Subfolder**. Name your subfolder *iven-notte*, the name of the email account whose inbox data you'll be importing, and click **Create Folder**. Right-click the new *iven-notte* subfolder that you just created and choose **ImportExportTools NG ▸ Import EML Messages ▸ All EML Messages from a Directory and Subdirectories**. A dialog will pop up, allowing you to browse for a folder. Select your *iven-notte* subfolder.

This subfolder should immediately start filling up with the 14,964 email messages that you're importing. It will probably take a few minutes to finish (importing all 127 inboxes in this dataset would take considerably longer).

Figure 6-2 shows Thunderbird with the *iven-notte* inbox loaded up. You can see all of the folders and the number of unread messages in each. (If you'd like, you can mark all of these messages as unread to keep track of which messages you have left to read.)

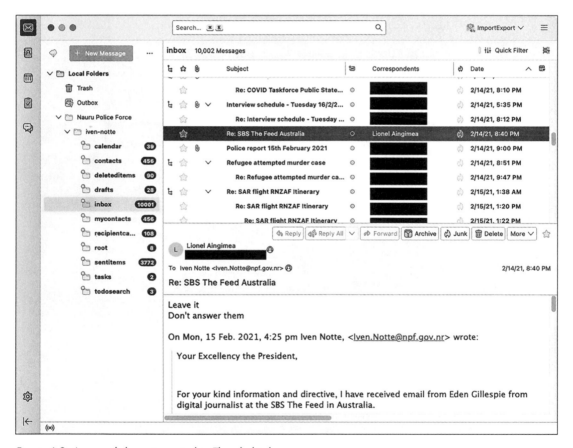

*Figure 6-2: An email dump imported in Thunderbird*

The email selected in Figure 6-2 is in the *inbox* folder and was sent from Lionel Aingimea, the president of Nauru at that time. In the email, he instructs Iven Notte, the Nauru police chief and the inbox owner, to not respond to Australian journalist Eden Gillespie, who had asked about two

Nauru men who had allegedly attacked a refugee worker, possibly run him over, and stolen his motorbike. "Leave it," President Aingimea wrote. "Don't answer them."

Cam Wilson, a reporter for the Australian news site Crikey, dug into the Nauru Police Force dataset and revealed "the appalling disregard for refugees and asylum seekers detained there." You can read Wilson's reporting on Crikey's website, *https://www.crikey.com.au.*

# Searching Email in Thunderbird

Now that you've got Thunderbird configured and loaded with data, you're ready to explore that data. For example, you may want to search the Nauru Police Force dataset for other email from President Aingimea or from Australian politicians. You could also search for email that contains keywords like *refugee* or was written on specific days. This section covers search methods you can use on any email dump you import into Thunderbird.

## Quick Filter Searches

The simplest search option is to filter the email that shows up in the currently selected folder. When viewing a folder, near the top of the Thunderbird window, make sure the Quick Filter button is toggled on so that an extra toolbar appears. This toolbar has buttons to quickly filter out only messages that are unread, contain attachments, or have other properties.

The Quick Filter toolbar also has a search box that you can use to find only messages that include certain text. You can also filter for messages that include the search term in the sender field, recipient field, subject line, or body. This is the most common way I search in Thunderbird. For example, I entered *Aingimea* in the Quick Filter search box to quickly find all of the email related to President Aingimea in the *inbox* folder. I could also put his email address in the search box and filter for messages where he's the sender or the recipient (though he won't be the recipient of any of this email, because this is Iven Notte's inbox, not his).

## The Search Messages Dialog

The Quick Filter search is essentially a more limited version of the Search Messages dialog, which is the most powerful way to search for email in Thunderbird. Open this dialog by clicking the **Edit** menu and choosing **Find ▸ Search Messages**. You can choose which folder to search, or you can elect to search all the email in an account at once. You can then choose more granular search queries. For example, you could find all email messages that mention *asylum* in the body. You can then filter those results by adding further criteria, such as showing only email sent from or to a specific email address or only email with attachments.

There's also a search box in the top right of the Thunderbird window, above the Quick Filter search box, that will quickly search the full email account. I find this feature less useful than the Search Messages dialog. If I can't find what I'm looking for with Quick Filter, I move on to Search Messages, which lets me make my searches as granular as necessary.

## Exercise 6-4: Import the Oath Keepers MBOX Email Dump

In this exercise, you'll import email from the Oath Keepers dataset into Thunderbird. The Oath Keepers dataset contains the files *messages.json* and *messages_old.json*, which are chat logs, and the *Oath Keepers.sbd* folder, which contains 100 files in MBOX format. You'll focus on the latter here. As mentioned previously, you can't open MBOX files in an email client to read the messages like you can with EML files; you must import them into Thunderbird first.

To keep your different datasets separate in Thunderbird, you'll create a new folder for the Oath Keepers data. In the left panel, right-click **Local Folders** and choose **New Folder**. Name your folder *Oath Keepers* and click **Create Folder**. You should now see the *Oath Keepers* folder in your Local Folders list. Right-click the *Oath Keepers* folder you just created and choose **ImportExportTools NG ▶ Import mbox Files ▶ All mbox Files from directory (with sbd structure)**. Browse your filesystem and select the *Oath Keepers.sbd* folder.

Thunderbird might become unresponsive while it imports the 3.9GB of email, not allowing you to click on anything, but be patient. When the import is complete, you should have 100 separate folders full of email.

The Oath Keepers folder with the most email, by far, is *oksupport*, the Oath Keepers support email account. Figure 6-3 shows an email in this folder from a member renouncing his membership shortly after the January 6 attack.

I haven't found many major revelations in this email dump; most of those are contained in the private part of the Oath Keepers database, the membership and donor lists that DDoSecrets distributes only to journalists and researchers. The publicly available email contains many people writing about joining the militia or complaining that they paid their membership dues but haven't had any further communication. There's also a massive amount of spam, including right-wing extremist, conspiratorial, and anti-vaccine bulk email. Look through the various email accounts you imported and try out Thunderbird's search tools to see if you can find anything interesting I missed.

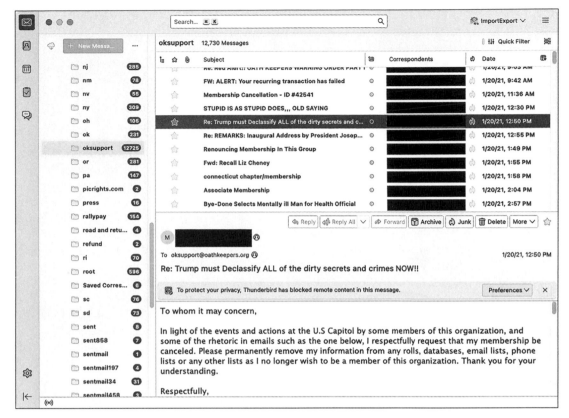

Figure 6-3: An email from the Oath Keepers email dump

## Exercise 6-5: Import the Heritage Foundation PST Email Dump

In this exercise, you'll import the Heritage Foundation email dump, a Microsoft Outlook PST file called *backup.pst*, into Thunderbird. Since the ImportExportTools NG add-on doesn't support PST files, first you'll need to convert the PST into an EML or MBOX file.

The readpst program can convert a PST file into several different formats, including EML and MBOX files. You can access the program by installing the libpst package in macOS or the pst-utils package in Ubuntu. Start by opening a terminal. Mac users, run the following command:

```
brew install libpst
```

Linux and Windows with WSL users, run these commands:

```
sudo apt update
sudo apt install pst-utils
```

Next, change to the folder that contains the *backup.pst* file. For example, on my macOS computer, I run:

```
cd /Volumes/datasets/Heritage\ Foundation
```

To convert a PST file into EML file, you use the following command, where the -e argument tells readpst to output as EML files:

```
readpst -e filename.pst
```

Run that command on the *backup.pst* file like so:

```
readpst -e backup.pst
```

This command creates a folder called *Personal Folders*, which contains additional *Contacts, Heritage, Inbox, Junk E-mail*, and other subfolders (this is how the email in *backup.pst* is organized). Within each folder are several EML files, one for each email message.

**NOTE**    *I've found it easier to import EML files generated by readpst into Thunderbird, but you can also convert PSTs into MBOX files with the readpst -r filename.pst command.*

In the left panel, right-click **Local Folders** and choose **New Folder**, as you did in the previous exercises. Name your folder *Heritage Foundation* and click **Create Folder**. You should now see the *Heritage Foundation* folder in your Local Folders list.

Right-click the *Heritage Foundation* folder, choose **New Subfolder**, and name your new subfolder *backup.pst*. Right-click the *backup.pst* subfolder and choose **ImportExportTools NG ▶ Import EML Messages ▶ All EML Messages from a Directory and Subdirectories**. Browse for the *Personal Folders* folder that you just created using readpst and start the import. This folder should start filling up with over a thousand email messages.

These email messages, all belonging to former Heritage Foundation fundraiser Steve DeBuhr, are meticulously organized into folders. In addition to Heritage Foundation work, this email dump also includes DeBuhr's personal email. This email dump is very old—the latest messages are from 2009—so it's unlikely you'll find very many revelations in here. Since DeBuhr worked with major donors, though, the email in the *Heritage* folder contains many attachments full of financial details. Figure 6-4 shows this email dump in Thunderbird.

Particularly, I noticed as I browsed through this email that the *Social Issues* folder contains homophobic and otherwise bigoted messages that DeBuhr had forwarded from his official heritage.org address account to his personal one.

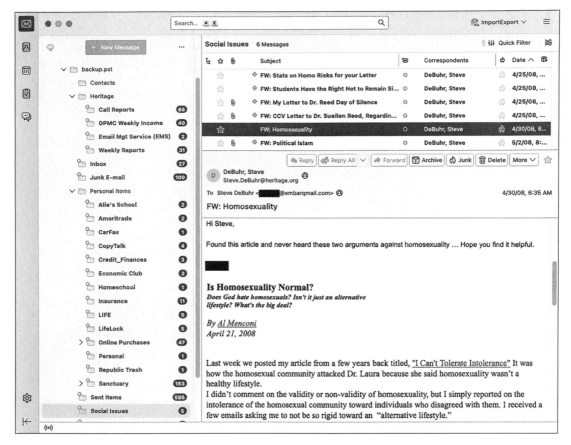

Figure 6-4: A Heritage Foundation email in Thunderbird

## Other Tools for Researching Email Dumps

This chapter has focused on using Thunderbird as a tool for researching email dumps, but in your future work, you might find two alternative tools helpful: Microsoft Outlook and Aleph. In this section I'll go over how you can use each tool to import and search email dumps. You don't need to follow the instructions in this section to work through the rest of the book, but reading along will give you a sense of what the options are and when to use them.

### Microsoft Outlook

Unlike Thunderbird, Microsoft's desktop email program, Outlook, supports importing email dumps directly in PST format. However, Outlook has some downsides. First, it's not free; the cheapest way to get Outlook is to buy a Microsoft 365 license, which, at the time of writing, costs around $7 per month or $70 per year. Second, Outlook is available only for Windows and macOS, not Linux (though Linux users can run Outlook in a Windows VM). Still, you might find Outlook useful if you're familiar with the program and understand its advanced features, or just want to see an email in its original interface.

Let's look at how to import PST files directly into Outlook, using a real example from a hacked Russian email dump. First, set up a Windows VM for Outlook. Do this even if you're a Windows or macOS user who already uses Outlook for email, in order to avoid mixing up your actual email and a leaked email dump. Microsoft publishes free Windows VM images for several different VM programs like VirtualBox, VMWare, and Parallels. Download the VM image at *https://developer.microsoft.com/en-us/windows/downloads/virtual-machines/* and import it into your VM software. You'll also need to install Microsoft Office in your VM. If you have a Microsoft 365 license, download Office from *https://www.office.com* by logging in and clicking the **Install Office** link. If you don't have a license, Microsoft offers a free trial.

When you open Outlook the first time, it prompts you to log in to your Office 365 account to check your license. After that, it prompts you to set up an email account. At the bottom, click the link **Create an Outlook.com Email Address to Get Started** in order to create a new account. Make sure to save your email and password in your password manager. Once you're finished, click **Done**. Outlook should open with the empty inbox of the new email account you just created.

With Outlook set up, add the PST email dumps to it. Click **File ▸ Account Settings ▸ Account Settings**, then click **Data Files ▸ Add** and browse for the PST file you want to add. If you have the disk space to spare, make a copy of the PST file and add the copy instead. All information about this inbox, including details like which messages are marked read, is stored in this file, so working from a copy will prevent you from modifying the original.

The PST file you added should appear in the left sidebar. You can now sift through this inbox as if it were your own. Even the unread email counts you'll see are the actual counts of unread email for each folder at the time the PST file was exported.

As an example, I set up a Windows VM, installed Outlook, logged in to it using my Microsoft 365 account, and added *intercoord@vgtrk.ru.pst* (the 48GB PST file hacked from VGTRK mentioned earlier in this chapter).

Figure 6-5 shows this VGTRK inbox, where I've used Outlook's search feature to search for Такер Карлсон. This is the Cyrillic spelling of Tucker Carlson, the former Fox News host.

The subject line of the selected email in Figure 6-5 translates roughly to "Tucker Carlson sync." The email body contains a translated quote in which Carlson claims that Ukraine is not an independent country, but rather is controlled by the US Democratic Party. The quote also includes the false claim that in 2016, then Vice President Joe Biden fired Ukraine's attorney general for investigating Biden's son Hunter. (In fact, Biden leveraged $1 billion in US aid to persuade Ukraine to oust its top prosecutor, Viktor Shokin, who refused to investigate corruption from powerful Ukrainians. Biden worked in tandem with anti-corruption efforts across Europe: European leaders, as well as civil society groups within Ukraine, urged Shokin to resign for the same reason.) Russian TV likely aired this Tucker Carlson clip, and this email was likely the translation for their Russian dubbed version.

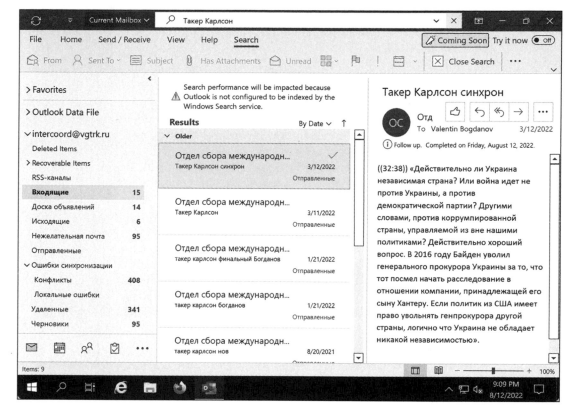

*Figure 6-5: Researching a PST file in Outlook*

**NOTE**  *When working with data dumps in foreign languages that you don't read, you can rely on machine translation tools like DeepL or Google Translate—assuming, of course, that you're comfortable sharing the contents of the leak with a third-party service. I've also found the Google Translate phone app useful: if you hold your phone's camera up to your screen, it will translate text in real time. This works even with scanned documents that aren't OCR'd.*

### Aleph

As you learned in Chapter 5, you can use Aleph to index and browse a wide variety of email, including PST or EML files. When you index a folder containing PSTs, Aleph recognizes the file format and indexes all of the individual messages inside of each PST file, keeping the folder hierarchy intact. Aleph also has the following benefits for working with email dumps:

- Unlike Thunderbird and Outlook, Aleph will also index, make searchable, and even add OCR to email attachments.

- As with any dataset it processes, Aleph will automatically list all of the people and organizations it finds in the dataset, and you can use it to cross-reference that data with other datasets you've indexed.

- If you run an Aleph server for a group of researchers, you can easily enable them to search email dumps; all they need is a web browser and an Aleph account.

Using Aleph for email dumps has a few downsides. First, it requires a lot of technical work to spin up an Aleph server and to index datasets, especially if you plan on putting it on the internet for others to use. In my experience, if you try to import large datasets like email dumps into Aleph, you're likely to run into technical hurdles with your Docker setup. Using Thunderbird is a simpler solution.

Aleph also can't properly index MBOX files; it tries to index them as text files rather than as collections of different email messages. It won't do any Base64-decoding of the data inside MBOX files, so it's not much more useful than grep for this task. If you want an MBOX-formatted email dump indexed in your Aleph server, import it into Thunderbird and then export it again (using ImportExportTools NG) in EML format.

Aleph has other quirks that make working with email dumps more complicated. For example, if there's an email attachment in a format Aleph doesn't understand, it just won't display the attachment at all when you view that email message. If you want to be sure you're seeing everything in the email, download an individual EML file from Aleph and open it in Thunderbird.

In sum, Outlook is a reasonable choice for PST files, and Aleph is a good choice if you're working with groups of people or want to cross-reference an email dump with other datasets. However, Thunderbird is the simplest way to quickly start your email dump investigation, and it supports all email formats.

## Summary

In this chapter, you learned how to import email dumps in the EML, MBOX, and PST formats into Thunderbird to read and search them. You read an email from the president of Nauru, got insights into the type of email the Oath Keepers receive, and explored an old email dump from the Heritage Foundation. You also saw how to use Microsoft Outlook and Aleph as alternatives to Thunderbird. You can use the skills you've learned here in your future email dump investigations.

In the next chapter, you'll level up your technical skills for analyzing datasets by taking a crash course in Python programming.

# PART III

PYTHON PROGRAMMING

# 7

# AN INTRODUCTION TO PYTHON

The skills you've learned in the last few chapters are instrumental for investigating leaked datasets, but having basic programming knowledge is even more powerful. Using Python or other programming languages, you can give your computer precise instructions for performing tasks that existing tools or shell scripts don't allow. For example, you could write a Python script that scours a million pieces of video metadata to determine where the videos were filmed. In my experience, Python is also simpler, easier to understand, and less error-prone than shell scripts.

This chapter provides a crash course on the fundamentals of Python programming. You'll learn to write and execute Python scripts and use the interactive Python interpreter. You'll also use Python to do math, define variables, work with strings and Boolean logic, loop through lists of items, and use functions. Future chapters rely on your understanding of these basic skills.

## Exercise 7-1: Install Python

Some operating systems, including most versions of Linux and macOS, come with Python preinstalled, and it's common to have multiple versions of Python installed at once. This book uses Python 3. After you follow the Python installation instructions for your operating system in this exercise, you should be able to run Python scripts with the python3 (for Linux and Mac) or python (for Windows) command.

### Windows

Download and install the latest version of Python 3 for Windows from *https://www.python.org*. During installation, check the box **Add Python 3.*x* to PATH** (where **3.*x*** is the latest Python 3 version), which allows you to run the python command in PowerShell without using the Python program's absolute path.

Wherever this chapter instructs you to open a terminal, use PowerShell instead of an Ubuntu terminal. You can also learn to use Python in Ubuntu with WSL by following this chapter's Linux instructions, but running Python directly in Windows makes reading and writing data on your Windows-formatted USB disk much faster.

Windows users should replace all instances of python3 with python when running the example code in this chapter.

### Linux

Open a terminal and make sure the python3, python3-pip, and python3-venv packages are installed, using this apt command:

```
sudo apt install python3 python3-pip python3-venv
```

This command either installs the latest version of Python 3 available in the Ubuntu repositories (as well as a few related packages you'll need for this chapter) or does nothing if the packages are already installed.

### macOS

Open a terminal and run the following Homebrew command to make sure python3 is installed:

```
brew install python3
```

This command either installs the latest version of Python 3 available in Homebrew or does nothing if it's already installed.

## Exercise 7-2: Write Your First Python Script

Now that you've downloaded Python, you'll write and run a simple Python script that displays some text in your terminal.

In your text editor, create a new file called *exercise-7-2.py* (all Python scripts end in *.py*). The first time you open a Python script in VS Code, it asks if you want to install the Python extension. I recommend doing so in order to enable VS Code to make suggestions as you're typing. The extension also has various features for highlighting syntax errors and helping you format your code nicely.

Enter the following code (or copy and paste it from *https://github.com/micahflee/hacks-leaks-and-revelations/blob/main/chapter-7/exercise-7-2.py*), then save the file:

```python
print("hacks")
print("leaks")
revelations = "revelations".upper()
print(revelations)
```

As with shell scripts, Python scripts run instructions one line at a time, starting at the top. When you run this code, `print("hacks")` calls a function called `print()` and passes the string hacks into it, displaying hacks in your terminal window. The second line similarly displays leaks. (I'll explain strings in greater detail in the "Python Basics" section on page 172, and functions in the "Functions" section on page 192.)

Next, the script defines a variable called `revelations` and sets its value to the uppercase version of the string revelations. To find the uppercase version of that string, the program calls the `upper()` method, which is a type of function. The final line then displays what's stored in the `revelations` variable: REVELATIONS.

**NOTE**  *I have fond memories of retyping snippets of code from books. When I was a teenager, I taught myself web and video game development by reading programming books and typing the code samples I found into my own editor. I always found that actually retyping the code, rather than copying and pasting it, helped make the concepts stick, so I recommend doing that for the exercises in this book.*

In a terminal, change to your *exercises* folder and run the script you just created with the following command (Windows users, remember to replace `python3` with `python`):

```
micah@trapdoor chapter-7 % python3 exercise-7-2.py
```

The argument in this command is the path to the script that you want to run, *exercise-7-2.py*. You should get the following output:

```
hacks
leaks
REVELATIONS
```

Try making the following changes to your script, running it after each change to see the results:

- Change the text in the print() functions.
- Add new print() functions to display more text.
- Use the string methods lower() and capitalize() instead of upper().

# Python Basics

In this section, you'll learn to write code in the interactive Python interpreter, comment your code, start doing simple math in Python, and use strings and lists. This gentle introduction to Python syntax will let you quickly try out some code on your own, before you dive into more advanced topics.

As you read, don't be shy about searching online for answers to any Python questions you might have beyond what this book covers. I frequently find solutions to Python problems on websites like Stack Overflow, a forum where people can ask technical questions and others can answer them.

## The Interactive Python Interpreter

The *Python interpreter* is a command line program that lets you run Python code in real time, without writing scripts first, allowing you to quickly test commands. To open the Python interpreter, you run the python3 command without any arguments, like so:

```
micah@trapdoor ~ % python3
--snip--
Type "help", "copyright", "credits" or "license" for more information.
>>>
```

The interpreter starts by telling you exactly which version of Python you're using. Similar to a command line interface, it gives you the prompt >>> and waits for you to enter a Python command.

Run the following command:

```
>>> print("Hello World!")
Hello World!
>>>
```

Entering print("Hello World!") and pressing ENTER should immediately run your code, displaying Hello World! on the next line. Exit the interpreter and return to the shell by running **exit()** or pressing CTRL-D.

In the remainder of this book, if my examples include the >>> prompt, that means they're running in the Python interpreter. Run the same code in your own interpreter as you follow along.

## Comments

Writing code can be confusing even to experienced programmers, so it's always a good idea to *comment* your code: add inline notes to yourself or to others who might read your program. If you describe the purpose of a specific portion of code in plain English (or whatever language you speak), whoever looks at this code in the future can understand the gist of what it's doing at a glance.

If a line of code starts with a hash mark (#), the whole line is a comment. You can also add a hash mark after some code, followed by your comment. For example, run the following lines of code:

```
>>> # This is a comment
>>> x = 10 # This sets the variable x to the value 10
>>> print(x)
10
```

This is exactly the same as comments in shell scripting, which you learned about in Chapter 3. Python ignores comments, since they're intended for humans.

## Math with Python

Computers, which are technically complicated calculators, are great at doing math. It might not be immediately apparent, but investigating datasets means constantly dealing with basic math: calculating disk space, counting files, searching for keywords, and sorting lists. Here's how a few basic mathematical operations work in Python:

**Operators**

The arithmetic operators for addition (+), subtraction (−), multiplication (×), and division (/) are mostly the same in Python: +, -, and /, with an asterisk * for multiplication.

**Variables**

In math, a variable is a placeholder, normally a letter like $x$. Variables in math often represent something unknown and it's your job to solve for it, but Python variables are never unknown—they always have a value. Name your Python variables something descriptive like price or number_of_retweets rather than single letters without clear meanings. Variables in Python can represent much more than just numbers, as you'll see later in this chapter.

**Expressions**

An expression is a bit like a sentence made up of numbers, variables, and operators. For example, here are a few expressions:

```
1 + 1
100 / 5
x * 3 + 5
```

Like sentences, expressions need to have the correct syntax. Just like "potato the inside" isn't a valid sentence, 1 1 + isn't a valid expression. Enter the following expressions in the Python interpreter to see how it evaluates them:

```
>>> 1 + 1
2
>>> 100 / 5
20.0
>>> 3.14 * 2
6.28
```

Just like a calculator, Python respects the order of operations. It also supports using parentheses:

```
>>> 100 - 12 * 2
76
>>> (100 - 12) * 2
176
```

As in the rest of math, Python won't allow you to divide by zero:

```
>>> 15 / 0
Traceback (most recent call last):
  File "<stdin>", line 1, in <module>
ZeroDivisionError: division by zero
```

You define a variable in Python by saving a value inside that variable with the equal sign (=). Try defining price and sales_tax variables and then using them in an expression:

```
>>> price = 100
>>> sales_tax = .05
>>> total = price + (price * sales_tax)
>>> print(total)
105.0
```

You can't use variables that you haven't yet defined. For example, if you use an undefined variable x in an expression, you'll get an error:

```
>>> x * 10
Traceback (most recent call last):
  File "<stdin>", line 1, in <module>
NameError: name 'x' is not defined
```

Instead of just setting a variable equal to some value, you'll often want to modify its existing value by a certain amount. For example, if you're keeping track of the total price of items in a shopping cart in the total variable and want to add 10 dollars to that total, you would define the variable like so:

```
total = total + 10
```

Python's += operator performs the same operation:

```
total += 10
```

The += operator adds the number on the right to the variable on the left. The Python operators -=, *=, and /= work the same way. In your Python interpreter, define a variable, then try changing its value using these operators.

## Strings

A *string* is a sequence of characters. Any time you need to load, modify, or display text, you store it in a string. If you load the contents of a text file into a variable in Python (for example, a 5MB EML file that includes attachments), that's a string. But strings are also often very short: in Exercise 7-2, you used the strings "hacks", "leaks", and "revelations".

In Python, strings must be enclosed in either single quotes (') or double quotes ("). Run the following examples, which demonstrate how to use each type of quote. Here is a string with double quotes:

```
>>> "apple"
'apple'
```

Here is the same string with single quotes:

```
>>> 'apple' # The same string with single quotes
'apple'
```

Use double quotes if you have single quotes within the string:

```
>>> "She's finished!"
"She's finished!"
```

Use single quotes if you have double quotes within the string:

```
>>> 'She said, "Hello"'
'She said, "Hello"'
```

Some of the same techniques you learned in Chapter 3 to work with strings in your shell also apply to strings in Python. If your string uses double quotes, you can escape them like so:

```
>>> "She said, \"Hello\""
```

You can similarly escape single quotes in a single-quote string:

```
>>> 'She\'s finished!'
```

Like numbers, strings can be stored in variables. Run the following code to define first_name and last_name variables, replacing my name with yours:

```
>>> first_name = "Micah"
>>> last_name = "Lee"
```

In Python, *f-strings* are strings that can contain variables. To use an f-string, put the letter f before the quotes, then put variable names in braces ({ and }). For example, run the following commands to display the values of the variables you just defined:

```
>>> print(f"{first_name} {last_name}")
Micah Lee
>>> full_name = f"{first_name} {last_name}"
>>> print(f"{first_name}'s full name is {full_name}, but he goes by {first_name}")
Micah's full name is Micah Lee, but he goes by Micah
```

Place expressions inside f-strings in order to evaluate them:

```
>>> print(f"1 + 2 + 3 + 4 + 5 = {1 + 2 + 3 + 4 + 5}")
1 + 2 + 3 + 4 + 5 = 15
```

Python will evaluate the expression for you, in this case 1 + 2 + 3 + 4 + 5, and just print the result, which is 15.

## Exercise 7-3: Write a Python Script with Variables, Math, and Strings

In this exercise, you'll practice the concepts you've learned so far by writing a simple Python script that uses variables and a few basic math expressions and prints some strings. The script calculates how old a person is in months, days, hours, minutes, and seconds, given their name and an age (in years), and then displays this information. In your text editor, create a new file called *exercise-7-3.py* and define these two variables:

```
name = "Micah"
age_years = 38
```

Replace the values of name and age_years with your own name and age.

Next, define some more variables that represent age in different units: months, days, hours, minutes, and seconds. Start with months:

```
age_months = age_years * 12
```

Add a days variable:

```
age_days = age_years * 365
```

Finally, define variables for hour, minutes, and seconds:

```
age_hours = age_days * 24
age_minutes = age_hours * 60
age_seconds = age_minutes * 60
```

Now that you've defined the variables, you can display them to the user. Since the numbers in this exercise are going to get big, you'll include commas to make them easier to read. For example, run this code in the interpreter to display the variable number with commas using an f-string, adding :, after the variable name within the braces:

```
>>> number = 1000000
>>> print(f"the number is: {number}")
the number is: 1000000
>>> print(f"the number is: {number:,}")
the number is: 1,000,000
```

Back in the Python script, add code to display all of the values, like this:

```
print(f"{name} is {age_years:,} years old")
print(f"That would be {age_months:,} months old")
print(f"Which is {age_days:,} days old")
print(f"Which is {age_hours:,} hours old")
print(f"Which is {age_minutes:,} minutes old")
print(f"Which is {age_seconds:,} seconds old")
```

This code uses {name} to display the value of the name variable. That variable is a string, so it doesn't make sense to try to separate it with commas. The rest of the variables are numbers, though, so the code includes :, inside the braces for all of them to include commas in the output. (The age_years values don't need commas, unless you happen to be older than 1,000, but it doesn't hurt to use the :, syntax—it adds a comma only if one is needed.)

Save the file in your text editor. (A complete copy of the script is available at *https://github.com/micahflee/hacks-leaks-and-revelations/blob/main/chapter -7/exercise-7-3.py*.) In a terminal, change to your *exercises* folder for this exercise and run the script. Here's what happens when I do so:

```
micah@trapdoor chapter-7 % python3 exercise-7-3.py
Micah is 38 years old
That would be 456 months old
Which is 13,870 days old
Which is 332,880 hours old
Which is 19,972,800 minutes old
Which is 1,198,368,000 seconds old
```

When you run the script with your name and age, try changing the age and running it again to see how the numbers change.

# Lists and Loops

You'll often need to manage lists when investigating datasets. For example, you might work with lists of filenames or rows in a spreadsheet. In this section, you'll learn how to store lists as variables and loop through those lists in order to run the same code for each list item. You did something similar in Chapter 4 with for loops in the shell, but this time you'll be working in Python.

## Defining and Printing Lists

In Python, lists are defined with brackets ([ and ]), with each item in the list separated by commas (,). You might have a list of numbers:

```
[1, 2, 3]
```

Or of strings:

```
["one", "two", "three"]
```

Or an empty list:

```
[]
```

Just as variables can contain numbers or strings, they can also contain lists. Use this line of code to store a list of letters in the Hebrew alphabet, spelled out using Latin characters, in the hebrew_letters variable:

```
>>> hebrew_letters = ["aleph", "bet", "gimel", "dalet", "he", "vav", "zayin",
"chet", "tet", "yod", "kaf", "lamed", "mem", "nun", "samech", "ayin", "pe",
"tsadi", "qof", "resh", "shin", "tav"]
```

Now use the print() function to display the items in the hebrew_letters variable:

```
>>> print(hebrew_letters)
['aleph', 'bet', 'gimel', 'dalet', 'he', 'vav', 'zayin', 'chet', 'tet', 'yod',
'kaf', 'lamed', 'mem', 'nun', 'samech', 'ayin', 'pe', 'tsadi', 'qof', 'resh',
'shin', 'tav']
```

You can make long lists easier to read by entering each item in the list on its own line, indented, like this:

```
hebrew_letters = [
    "aleph",
--snip--
    "tav"
]
```

Each item in a list has an *index*, a number that represents where in the list that item is located. The index of the first item is 0, the second is 1, the third is 2, and so on. To select a list item, you append brackets with the item's index to the end of the list. For example, to select the first letter in the `hebrew_letters` list, use `hebrew_letters[0]`:

```
>>> print(hebrew_letters[0])
aleph
>>> print(hebrew_letters[1])
bet
```

The first line of code uses the `print()` function to display the item from the `hebrew_letters` list at index 0 (`aleph`), and the second line displays the item at index 1 (`bet`).

Now use negative numbers to select items starting from the end of the list, like so:

```
>>> print(hebrew_letters[-1])
tav
>>> print(hebrew_letters[-2])
shin
```

You can use the `len()` function to count the number of items in a list. For example, run the following code to get the number of items in the `hebrew_letters` list:

```
>>> print(len(hebrew_letters))
22
```

This code uses the `print()` function to display the output of the `len()` function. You could get the same result by storing the output of the `len()` function in a variable:

```
>>> length_of_hebrew_alphabet = len(hebrew_letters)
>>> print(length_of_hebrew_alphabet)
22
```

The first line of code runs `len(hebrew_letters)` and stores the result in the `length_of_hebrew_alphabet` variable. The second line uses the `print()` function to display that result.

You don't have to store a list in a variable to select items from it. For example, run this code to display the second item (at index 1) in the list `[1,2,3]`:

```
>>> print([1,2,3][1])
2
```

The append() method lets you add items to lists. For example, run the following code to add a new color to a list of favorites:

```
>>> favorite_colors = ["red", "green", "blue"]
>>> favorite_colors.append("black")
>>> print(favorite_colors)
['red', 'green', 'blue', 'black']
```

This code defines the variable favorite_colors as a list of strings containing red, green, and blue. It then adds another string, black, to the list by using the append() method, before finally displaying the value of the favorite_colors variable, using the print() function.

When writing code that analyzes datasets, you'll often create an empty list and then append items to that list to make the data easier to work with. For example, you'll learn in Chapter 13 about the code I wrote while investigating America's Frontline Doctors, an anti-vaccine group. To properly analyze a dataset of hundreds of thousands of files containing patient information, I wrote code that created an empty list, opened each file, and appended the pertinent patient data to that list.

## Running for Loops

In Chapter 4, you used a for loop to unzip each BlueLeaks ZIP file. Python also has for loops, and they work the same way they do in shell scripting: by running a snippet of code, called a *block*, on each item in a list. A for loop has the following syntax:

```
for variable_name in list_name:
```

This syntax is followed by a block of indented code. Once you choose a new variable to define in *variable_name*, you can use it in your code block.

For example, run the following code to loop through the hebrew_letters list, store each item in the variable letter, and then display that item:

```
>>> for letter in hebrew_letters:
...     print(letter)
...
```

After you enter the for loop, which ends in a colon (:), the Python interpreter changes the prompt from >>> to ... and waits for you to enter the code block that will run for each item. Indent every line in your block with the same number of spaces, then end your block with a blank line. In this example, the code block that runs is just one line: print(letter).

The code should return the following output:

```
aleph
bet
--snip--
shin
tav
```

In this example, the for loop runs 22 times, once for each item in the list, and stores the item in the variable letter. The first time it loops, the value of letter is aleph. The second time, the value is bet, and so on.

*Indentation tells Python which lines of code are part of your code blocks. If some lines are indented with four spaces, but others with two or three spaces, your Python code won't work. To keep things simple, I recommend always indenting with four spaces. When writing scripts in VS Code, you can indent multiple lines of code by selecting them with your mouse and then pressing TAB (which indents four spaces for you) or unindent by selecting a line and pressing SHIFT-TAB.*

The following, slightly more complicated, example uses the len() function to count not the number of items in a list but characters in a string:

```
>>> for letter in hebrew_letters:
...     count = len(letter)
...     print(f"The letter {letter} has {count} characters")
...
The letter aleph has 4 characters
The letter bet has 3 characters
The letter gimel has 5 characters
--snip--
The letter resh has 4 characters
The letter shin has 4 characters
The letter tav has 3 characters
```

This code tells you how many characters are used to spell the word for each Hebrew letter in the Latin alphabet.

You can use for loops to loop through strings as well, since a string is essentially a list of characters:

```
>>> word = "hola"
>>> for character in word:
...     print(character)
...
h
o
l
a
```

You can run a single for loop as many times as you need for the dataset you're working on. For example, in Chapter 9, you'll write code that can open each of the hundreds of spreadsheets in the BlueLeaks dataset and uses a for loop to run your block of code on each row.

In the next section, you'll learn to make your programs more dynamic and useful by determining which blocks of code should run under which circumstances.

# Control Flow

Python scripts start at the top and run one line of code at a time, but they don't always run these lines consecutively. In for loops, for example, the same block of code might run over and over again before the loop completes and the program continues to the next line. The order in which your lines of code run is your program's *control flow*.

As you start writing code, you'll often alter the control flow by telling your computer to do different things in different situations. If you write a program that loops through a list of files in a dataset, for instance, you may want to run different code when the program reaches a PDF document than when it encounters an MP4 video.

This section teaches you how to run certain blocks of code under certain conditions. To do this, you'll learn how to compare values, use if statements based on these comparisons, and express arbitrarily complicated conditions using Boolean logic, all of which allow you to control the flow of your program. You'll need this sort of logic whenever you write code that searches a dataset for something specific and then responds according to what it finds.

## Comparison Operators

As mentioned earlier in this chapter, expressions that use the arithmetic operators +, -, /, and * generally evaluate to numbers: 1 + 1 evaluates to 2, for example. Expressions in Python also use the following *comparison operators* to compare terms:

&lt;   Less than

&lt;=  Less than or equal to

&gt;   Greater than

&gt;=  Greater than or equal to

==  Equal to (not to be confused with a single equal sign (=), which defines a variable)

!=  Not equal to

A *Boolean* is a type of variable that is either True or False. Expressions that use comparison operators evaluate to Booleans instead of numbers, as in the following examples:

```
>>> 100 > 5
True
>>> 100 < 5
False
>>> 100 > 100
False
>>> 100 >= 100
True
>>> 0.5 < 1
True
>>> 0.999999 == 1
False
```

You can use these same operators to compare strings, too. In Python, saying that one string is less than another means that the former comes before the latter in alphabetical order, as in the following examples:

```
>>> "Alice" == "Bob"
False
>>> "Alice" != "Bob"
True
>>> "Alice" < "Bob"
True
>>> "Alice" > "Bob"
False
```

Strings are case sensitive. If you don't care about capitalization and want to just see whether the strings are made up of the same words, make them both lowercase before you compare them:

```
>>> name1 = "Vladimir Putin"
>>> name2 = "vladimir putin"
>>> name1 == name2
False
>>> name1.lower() == name2.lower()
True
```

This technique allows you to determine whether the data you're evaluating fulfills a given condition. For example, in Chapter 11, you'll write code to analyze the metadata of over a million videos uploaded to the far-right social network Parler. Using comparison operators, you'll determine which videos were filmed on January 6, 2021, in Washington, DC, during the insurrection after Trump lost the 2020 election.

## if Statements

You use if statements to tell your code to do something under certain conditions but not others. The syntax for an if statement is if *expression*: followed by an indented block of code. If the expression evaluates to True, then the code block runs. If the expression evaluates to False, the code doesn't run, and the flow moves on to the next line.

For example, run the following code:

```
>>> password = "letmein"
>>> if password == "letmein":
...     print("ACCESS GRANTED")
...     print("Welcome")
...
ACCESS GRANTED
Welcome
>>>
```

This code sets the value of the password variable to letmein. That means the expression in the if statement (password == "letmein") evaluates to True and the code block runs, so it displays ACCESS GRANTED and Welcome.

Now try including the wrong password in your if statement:

```
>>> password = "yourefired"
>>> if password == "letmein":
...     print("ACCESS GRANTED")
...     print("Welcome")
...
>>>
```

This time, because you set the password to "yourefired", the expression password == "letmein" evaluates to False, and Python doesn't run the if statement's code block.

An if statement can optionally incorporate an else block so that if the condition is true, one code block runs, and if it's false, another block runs:

```
if password == "letmein":
    print("ACCESS GRANTED")
    print("Welcome")
else:
    print("ACCESS DENIED")
```

You can also incorporate elif blocks, short for "else if." These let you make another comparison if the first comparison is false, as shown in Listing 7-1.

```
if password == "letmein":
    print("ACCESS GRANTED")
    print("Welcome")
elif password == "open sesame":
    print("SECRET AREA ACCESS GRANTED")
else:
    print("ACCESS DENIED")
```

*Listing 7-1: Comparing if, elif, and else statements*

In this code, the if statement evaluates the password == "letmein" expression. If it evaluates to True, the code block runs and displays the ACCESS GRANTED and Welcome messages. If the expression evaluates to False, the program moves on to the elif block, which evaluates the password == "open sesame" expression. If that evaluates to True, it runs the block of code that displays SECRET AREA ACCESS GRANTED. If it evaluates to False, the program moves on to the else code block, which displays ACCESS DENIED.

## Nested Code Blocks

You can also accomplish the results of Listing 7-1 with multiple if statements and no elif, using *nested* code blocks, or indented blocks of code inside other indented blocks of code:

```
if password == "letmein":
    print("ACCESS GRANTED")
    print("Welcome.")
else:
    if password == "open sesame":
        print("SECRET AREA ACCESS GRANTED")
    else:
        print("ACCESS DENIED")
```

This code is functionally the same as Listing 7-1.

The more complicated your code, the more nested code blocks may come in handy. You might include for loops inside your if statement code blocks, or if statements inside for loops, or even for loops inside for loops.

You might prefer elif statements to nested if statements purely for readability purposes: it's easier to read and write code with 100 elif statements than code that's indented 100 times because it has 100 nested if statements.

## Searching Lists

The Python in operator, which tells you whether an item appears in a list, is useful for working with lists. For example, to check whether the number 42 appears in a list of numbers, you can use in as follows:

```
favorite_numbers = [7, 13, 42, 101]
if 42 in favorite_numbers:
    print("life, the universe, and everything")
```

To the left of the in operator is a potential item inside a list, and to the right is the list. If the item is in the list, then the expression evaluates to True. If not, it evaluates to False.

You can also use not in to check if an item *isn't* in a list:

```
if 1337 not in favorite_numbers:
    print("mess with the best, die like the rest")
```

Additionally, you can use in to search for smaller strings inside of larger strings:

```
sentence = "What happens in the coming hours will decide how bad the Ukraine
crisis gets for the vulnerable democracy in Russian President Vladimir Putin's
sights but also its potentially huge impact on Americans and an already deeply
unstable world."
if "putin" in sentence.lower():
    print("Putin is mentioned")
```

This code defines the variable sentence, then checks to see if the string putin is inside the lowercase version of that sentence.

## Logical Operators

It's possible to describe any scenario, no matter how complicated, using the *logical operators* and, or, and not. Like comparison operators, logical operators also evaluate to True or False, and they let you combine comparisons.

For example, say you like astronomy and want to know if it's a good time for stargazing. Let's set this up as a logical expression: if ((it's dark out) **and** (it's **not** raining) **and** (it's **not** cloudy)) **or** (you have access to the James Webb Space Telescope), then yes. Otherwise, no. Logical operators let you define this sort of logic in your Python code.

Like other operators, the and and or operators compare an expression on the left with an expression on the right. With and, if both sides are true, the whole expression is true. If either is false, the whole expression is false. For example:

```
True and True == True
True and False == False
False and True == False
False and False == False
```

With or, if either expression is true, the whole expression is true. The whole expression is false only when both expressions are false. For example:

```
True or True == True
True or False == True
False or True == True
False or False == False
```

The not expression differs from the others in that it doesn't use an expression to the left, just to the right. It flips true to false, and false to true. For example:

```
not True == False
not False == True
```

In sum, use and to determine whether two things are both true, use or to determine whether at least one of two things is true, and use not to change a true to a false or vice versa. For example, consider this code:

```
if country == "US" and age >= 21:
    print("You can legally drink alcohol")
else:
    if country != "US":
        print("I don't know about your country")
    else:
        print("You're too young to legally drink alcohol")
```

The first if statement has an expression that compares two other expressions, country == "US" and age >= 21. If country is US and age is greater than or equal to 21, the expression simplifies to True and True. Since both Booleans are true, this evaluates to simply True, and the code block after the if statement runs, printing You can legally drink alcohol to the screen.

The first else block determines what happens if that expression evaluates to False. For example, if country is Italy, but age is 30, the expression simplifies to False and True. Since at least one of the Booleans is false, this evaluates to simply False, so the code block after else runs. Likewise, if country is US but age is 18, then the expression simplifies to True and False. This, too, evaluates to False, so the code block after else runs.

Inside the second else block is a simple if statement without Boolean logic: if country isn't US, the screen displays I don't know about your country. Otherwise (meaning country is US), it displays You're too young to legally drink alcohol.

Just like with math, you can use parentheses in if statements to compare multiple expressions. For example, the drinking age in the US is 21 and the drinking age in Italy is 18. Let's add Italy to this program, this time incorporating an or operator:

```
if (country == "US" and age >= 21) or (country == "Italy" and age >= 18):
    print("You can legally drink alcohol")
else:
    if country not in ["US", "Italy"]:
        print("I don't know about your country")
    else:
        print("You're too young to legally drink alcohol")
```

In plain English, the first if statement tells the program that if your country is the US and you're at least 21 *or* if your country is Italy and you're at least 18, then you can legally drink. In either case, the whole expression in the if statement is true, and the program prints You can legally drink alcohol. If just one of those is true and not the other (for instance, if you're a 19-year-old Italian), the whole statement is still true. That's what or means: if either of the things you're comparing is true, then the whole expression is true.

Use the operator not to turn True values into False or False values into True. For example:

```
if country == "US" and not age >= 21:
    print("Sorry, the drinking age in the US is 21")
```

You could replace not age >= 21 with age < 21 for the same result.

## Exception Handling

Python programs may abruptly quit with an error called an *exception*. This is typically known as "throwing an exception." *Exception handling* ensures that your Python code will run another code block when your code catches an exception, instead of quitting with an error.

You've seen a few examples of exceptions already in this chapter, like when you tried dividing by zero (something you can't do in math) or using a variable that hasn't been defined:

```
>>> 15 / 0
Traceback (most recent call last):
  File "<stdin>", line 1, in <module>
ZeroDivisionError: division by zero
>>> x * 10
Traceback (most recent call last):
  File "<stdin>", line 1, in <module>
NameError: name 'x' is not defined
```

In these cases, Python threw a ZeroDivisionError exception and a NameError exception, respectively.

You can write code that catches exceptions when they're thrown, allowing you to handle them gracefully. For example, let's say you have a list of names called names, and you want display the first name in the list:

```
>>> names = ["Alice", "Bob", "Charlie"]
>>> print(f"The first name is {names[0]}")
The first name is Alice
```

This code displays the value at names[0], or the first item in the names list. This works as expected if there are a few names in the list. But what if names is empty?

```
>>> names = []
>>> print(f"The first name is {names[0]}")
Traceback (most recent call last):
  File "<stdin>", line 1, in <module>
IndexError: list index out of range
```

In this case, since the index 0 doesn't exist because the list is empty, Python throws an IndexError exception.

You can catch this exception using try and except statements, like this:

```
try:
    print(f"The first name is {names[0]}")
except:
    print("The list of names is empty")
```

This code first runs a try statement, followed by a code block. It attempts to run the code in that block, and if it succeeds without hitting an exception, it moves on to the next line of code after the except block. However, if it hits an exception, then it runs the code in the except block before moving on.

Here's what it looks like when there's no exception:

```
>>> names = ["Alice", "Bob", "Charlie"]
>>> try:
...     print(f"The first name is {names[0]}")
... except:
...     print("The list of names is empty")
...
The first name is Alice
```

In this case, the code block after the try statement ran successfully, so the control flow moved on past the except block.

Here's what it looks like when the exception is thrown, but the code catches it and handles it gracefully:

```
>>> names = []
>>> try:
...     print(f"The first name is {names[0]}")
... except:
...     print("The list of names is empty")
...
The list of names is empty
```

The code block after the try statement ran, but Python threw an IndexError exception when it evaluated names[0]. Instead of crashing and displaying an error, this code caught the exception and the except block ran. In this case, the except statement runs if any exception is thrown in the try block, but you can get more granular than that by using different except statements for different types of exceptions. Consider the following example:

```
try:
    --snip--
except ZeroDivisionError:
    # This catches ZeroDivisionError exception
    --snip--
except NameError:
    # This catches NameError exceptions
    --snip--
except IndexError:
    # This catches IndexError exceptions
    --snip--
except:
    # This catches any other exceptions that haven't been caught yet
    --snip--
```

By using except *Exception*:, where you replace *Exception* with a specific exception you're interested in catching, you can write different code to handle different types of exceptions. You'll revisit exception handling in Chapter 10, when you learn how to work with JSON data, and in the Chapter 14 case study on neo-Nazi chat logs.

Now that you know how control flow works in Python, you'll practice some basic Python syntax and make comparisons using if statements and Boolean logic in the next exercise.

## Exercise 7-4: Practice Loops and Control Flow

In social media slang, a common form of mockery is to employ *alternating caps*, or switching from uppercase to lowercase and back to uppercase, when quoting people. For example, here's the text of a viral tweet from the now-suspended Twitter account @BigWangTheoryy:

*failing classes*
Me: "Can I get some extra credit?"
Professor: "cAn i GEt SomE eXtRa creDiT?"

In this exercise, you'll write a Python script that starts with some text and converts it into alternating caps style, using the control flow concepts you learned in the previous section.

In your text editor, create a new file called *exercise-7-4.py*, and start by defining the variable text, like this:

```
text = "One does not simply walk into Mordor"
```

The simplest way to write this script is to start with an empty string, called alternating_caps_text, and then loop through the characters in text, adding characters to alternating_caps_text one at a time and alternating their capitalization as you do so. Add a second line to your script defining that variable, like this:

```
alternating_caps_text = ""
```

Next, you'll define a Boolean variable called should_be_capital. Each time you loop through a character in text, you'll use this Boolean to keep track of whether the current character should be capital or lowercase. For this example, start with a capital letter:

```
should_be_capital = True
```

Beneath that line, add the main part of the script:

```
for character in text:
    if should_be_capital:
        alternating_caps_text += character.upper()
        should_be_capital = False
    else:
        alternating_caps_text += character.lower()
        should_be_capital = True
```

Using a for loop, this code loops through the characters in text, storing each character in the character variable. It then adds these characters to alternating_caps_text, switching between upper- and lowercase.

During each iteration of the for loop, character is another character in text, the variable containing the "One does not simply walk into Mordor" string. The first time the code loops, character is 0. When the code reaches the if statement, should_be_capital evaluates to True for this character, so the code block runs. The += operator adds character.upper() (or the uppercase version of character) to alternating_caps_text. Since the code began by adding a capital letter, you want it to add a lowercase letter next, so you set should_be _capital to False. The code block ends, and the code starts its second loop.

During the second iteration, character is n and should_be_capital evaluates to False. When the code reaches the if statement, the expression evaluates to False, so the else block runs. This is similar to the other block, except that it appends the lowercase version of character, character.lower(), to alternative_caps_text and sets should_be_capital back to True. So far, alternating_caps_text is On.

During the third iteration, character is e and should_be_capital evaluates to True. When the code reaches the if statement, the expression evaluates to True, so that code block runs again, adding a capital E to alternating _caps_text and setting should_be_capital to False again. The code continues in this way for the rest of the characters in text. Note that the uppercase and lowercase versions of the space character, " ".upper() and " ".lower(), are identical. The upper() and lower() methods also don't change punctuation characters like ,, ., !, and so on.

When this for loop is finished, all you have left to do is display the value of alternating_caps_text by adding this line to your script:

```
print(alternating_caps_text)
```

Your Python script is complete (you can also find a complete copy at *https://github.com/micahflee/hacks-leaks-and-revelations/blob/main/chapter-7/ exercise-7-4.py*). Run your script. Here's the output I get:

```
micah@trapdoor chapter-7 % python3 exercise-7-4.py
OnE DoEs nOt sImPlY WaLk iNtO MoRdOr
```

Now change the value of text and run the script again. For example, I changed the value to "There are very fine people on both sides":

```
micah@trapdoor chapter-7 % python3 exercise-7-4.py
ThErE ArE VeRy fInE PeOpLe oN BoTh sIdEs
```

You've gained a beginner's understanding of using lists and loops and controlling the flow of execution. I'll conclude the chapter with one more fundamental programming skill: breaking your code down into simpler chunks using functions.

# Functions

The more complicated your programs get, the more important it is to break the problems you're trying to solve down into smaller chunks and work on them individually. This allows you to focus on the bigger picture, using those smaller chunks of code as building blocks. In this section, you'll learn how to do this using functions.

*Functions*, fundamental building blocks of programming, are reusable chunks of code. They take *arguments*—the variables that you pass into a function—as input and can *return* a value after they finish running. You've already used a few functions that come with Python, like print() and len(), but you can also define your own function and use it as many times as you want without having to rewrite that code. You'll learn how to do that in this section.

## The def Keyword

You can define a new function using the def keyword. For example, this code defines a function called test(), which prints a string to your terminal:

```
>>> def test():
...     print("this is a test function")
...
>>> test()
this is a test function
```

Function definition lines end with a colon and are followed by an indented code block that defines exactly what the function does: in this case, it displays the string this is a test function. This test() function doesn't include any arguments, which means every time you run it, it will do the exact same thing.

Listing 7-2 defines a slightly more complicated function, sum(), that adds two numbers together.

```
def sum(a, b):
    return a + b
```

*Listing 7-2: Defining an example function*

This new function takes a and b as arguments and returns the sum of those two variables. For any function that takes more than one argument, like this one, you separate the arguments with commas (,).

Each variable has a *scope*, which describes which parts of your code can use that variable. The arguments of a function (in this case, a and b), as well as any variables defined inside the function, have a scope that can be accessed only by code in that function's code block. In other words, you can use these a and b variables only inside the sum() function, and they won't be defined outside of that code block.

You can think of defining a function as telling Python, "I'm making a new function with this name, and here's what it does." However, the function itself won't run until you *call* it. Consider the following Python script:

```
def sum(a, b):
    return a + b

red_apples = 10
green_apples = 6
total_apples = sum(red_apples, green_apples)

print(f"There are {total_apples} apples")
```

First, the code defines a function called sum() to be a code block with just a return statement. This function doesn't run yet. The code then defines the red_apples variable, setting its value to 10, and the green_apples variable, setting its value to 6.

The next line starts with total_apples =, but before Python can set the value of that variable, it needs to learn what that value should be. To do that, the code first calls the sum() function, passing in the arguments red_apples and green_apples as a and b. Now that the code is finally calling this function, return a + b runs. In this function call, a is red_apples and b is green_apples. The function returns a + b, which is 16. Now that the sum() function has returned, the code defines a variable called total_apples, setting its value to the return value of the sum() function, 16.

Finally, the code calls the print() function, passing in an f-string as an argument, which displays the total_apples variable. It will display the message There are 16 apples.

## Default Arguments

Function definitions can also have *default arguments*, which means defining their value is optional. If you haven't passed in any values for them when the function is called, the default value is used instead.

For example, consider this function, which, given a number and optionally a number of exclamation marks and question marks, prints a greeting using its arguments:

```
def greet(name, num_exclamations=3, num_questions=2):
    exclamations = "!" * num_exclamations
    questions = "?" * num_questions
    print(f"Hello {name}{exclamations}{questions}")
```

The argument name is a *positional argument*, which means when you call this function, the first argument you pass in always has to be name. However, num_exclamations and num_questions are default arguments, so passing values in for those is optional. The greet() function defines the strings exclamations and questions and sets them to a series of exclamation points and question marks. (In Python, when you multiply a string by a number, you get the original string repeated multiple times; for example, "A" * 3 evaluates to the string AAA.) The code then displays Hello, followed by the value of name, followed by the number of exclamation points and question marks passed into the function.

This function has one positional argument (name) and two default arguments (num_exclamations and num_questions). You can call it just passing in name, without passing values in for the default arguments, and they will automatically be set to 3 and 2, respectively:

```
>>> greet("Alice")
Hello Alice!!!??
```

You can also keep the default value for one of the default arguments, but choose a value for another. When you manually choose a value for a default argument, you're using a *keyword argument*. For example:

```
>>> greet("Bob", num_exclamations=5, num_questions=5)
Hello Bob!!!!!?????
>>> greet("Charlie", num_questions=0)
Hello Charlie!!!
>>> greet("Eve", num_exclamations=0)
Hello Eve??
```

The first function call uses keyword arguments for both num_exclamation and num_questions; the second function call uses a keyword argument only for num_questions and uses the default argument for num_exclamations; and the third function call uses a keyword argument for num_exclamations and uses the default argument for num_questions.

### Return Values

Functions become a lot more useful when they take some input, do some computation, and then return a value, known as the *return value*. The greet() function just described displays output, but it doesn't return a value that I could save in a variable or pass into further functions. However, the len() function you used earlier takes input (a list or a string), does some computation (calculates the length of the list or string), and returns a value (the length).

Here's an example of a function that takes a string s as an argument and returns the number of vowels in the string:

```
def count_vowels(s):
    number_of_vowels = 0
    vowels = "aeiouAEIOU"
    for c in s:
        if c in vowels:
            number_of_vowels += 1

    return number_of_vowels
```

This function brings together many of the concepts covered in this chapter so far: it defines the variable number_of_vowels as 0, then defines the variable vowels as a string containing lowercase and uppercase English vowels. Next, it uses a for loop to loop through each character in s, the string that's passed into the function.

In each loop, the code uses an `if` statement to check whether the character is a vowel (since `vowels` contains both lowercase and uppercase letters, this code considers both a and A to be vowels). If the character is a vowel, the code increases the `number_of_vowels` variable by one. Finally, it returns `number_of_vowels`, which equals however many vowels it counted in `s`.

Here are a few examples of calling this function and passing in different strings:

```
>>> count_vowels("THINK")
1
>>> count_vowels("lizard")
2
>>> count_vowels("zzzzzzz")
0
>>>
```

When you define a variable, you can set its value to the return value of a function just by setting the variable equal to that function call:

```
>>> num_vowels_think = count_vowels("THINK")
>>> num_vowels_lizard = count_vowels("lizard")
```

This code defines the variable `num_vowels_think` and sets its value to the return value of `count_vowels("THINK")`, or the number of vowels in the string THINK. It also defines the variable `num_vowels_lizard` and sets its value to the return value of `count_vowels("lizard")`.

You can then use those variables to define new variables:

```
>>> total_vowels = num_vowels_think + num_vowels_lizard
>>> print(total_vowels)
3
```

This code adds those two variables together, saving their sum in a new variable called `total_vowels`. It then prints the value of `total_vowels` to the terminal.

When a return statement runs, the function immediately ends, so `return` is also useful if you want to stop a function early. For example, the following `is_exciting()` function loops through all the characters in a string `s` to check whether the character is an exclamation point:

```
def is_exciting(s):
    for character in s:
        if character == "!":
            return True

    return False
```

If the function finds an exclamation point, it returns `True`, immediately stopping the function. If it checks each character and finds no exclamation points, it returns `False`. For example, if you call this function and pass in the string !@#$, the function will return True during the first iteration of the loop and immediately end—it will never even get to the second iteration. If you pass in the string hello!, it won't return True until the last iteration of the loop, since it doesn't find the ! until the end of the string. And if you pass in the string goodbye, it will loop through the entire string and not find an exclamation point, so it will return False.

## Docstrings

In *self-documenting* code, documentation is defined as part of the code as docstrings rather than in a separate document. *Docstrings* are strings enclosed by three double quotes (""") or three single quotes (''') on either side, placed as the first line of code after a function definition. When you run the function, the program ignores the docstring, but Python can use it to pull up documentation about the function on request. Docstrings are optional, but they can help other people understand your code.

For example, here's how you'd define the sum() function with a docstring:

```
>>> def sum(a, b):
...     """This function returns the sum of a and b"""
...     return a + b
```

This is exactly the same as the sum() function defined in Listing 7-2, except it includes a docstring.

If you run the help() function, passing in the name of a function (without arguments) as the argument, the Python interpreter will display documentation for that function. For example, running help(sum) gives you the following output:

```
Help on function sum in module __main__:

sum(a, b)
    This function returns the sum of a and b
```

The help() function works for any function, though it's useful only if the programmer who wrote that function included a docstring. In this case, it tells you that it's showing you help for the function called sum() in the __main__ module. You'll learn more about modules in Chapter 8, but they're essentially functions you write yourself. Try running **help(print)** or **help(len)** to view the docstrings for the print() and len() functions.

Press Q to get out of the help interface and back to the Python interpreter.

## Exercise 7-5: Practice Writing Functions

In this exercise, you'll turn the script you wrote in Exercise 7-4 into a function. You can then call this function multiple times, passing text into it so that it returns an alternating caps version of that text each time.

In your text editor, create a new file called *exercise-7-5.py* and create a new function called `alternating_caps()`, which takes in the argument `text`, like this:

```
def alternating_caps(text):
    """Returns an aLtErNaTiNg cApS version of text"""
```

Next, copy the code from Exercise 7-4 and paste it into this function, making sure to indent it so that it aligns with the docstring. Delete the line that defines the text value; instead, define `text` by passing it into the function as an argument. Also change the last line of the Exercise 7-4 code from `print(alternating_caps_text)` to `return alternating_caps_text`. This function shouldn't display the alternating caps version of a string; it should create a variable containing this version of a string and return it.

Your complete function should look like this (you can also find a copy at *https://github.com/micahflee/hacks-leaks-and-revelations/blob/main/chapter-7/exercise-7-5.py*):

```
def alternating_caps(text):
    """Returns an aLtErNaTiNg cApS version of text"""
    alternating_caps_text = ""
    should_be_capital = True

    for character in text:
        if should_be_capital:
            alternating_caps_text += character.upper()
            should_be_capital = False
        else:
            alternating_caps_text += character.lower()
            should_be_capital = True

    return alternating_caps_text
```

Now that you have a function—a reusable chunk of code—you can use it as many times as you want. Call this function a few times, remembering to display its return value using the `print()` function, like this:

```
print("Hacks, Leaks, and Revelations")
print(alternating_caps("This book is amazing"))
print(alternating_caps("I'm learning so much"))
```

You can change the text that you pass in to the `alternating_caps()` function calls to whatever you want.

Here's what it looks like when I run this script:

```
micah@trapdoor chapter-7 % python3 exercise-7-5.py
Hacks, Leaks, and Revelations
ThIs bOoK Is aMaZiNg
I'M LeArNiNg sO MuCh
```

While the output of this script is displayed in a mocking tone, I hope that the sentiment is true for you!

## Summary

This chapter has covered several basic Python programming concepts you'll rely upon in future investigations. You learned to write simple Python scripts that incorporate the major features of the language, including variables, if statements, for loops, and functions. You're ready to continue your Python programming journey in the next chapter, this time writing code to directly investigate datasets.

# 8

## WORKING WITH DATA
## IN PYTHON

The basics of Python are behind you, but there's still a lot to learn. In this chapter, you'll expand your programming skills and start to directly investigate datasets, including BlueLeaks and chat logs leaked from a pro-Putin ransomware gang after Russia invaded Ukraine in 2022.

We'll go over some more advanced Python topics, like how to use modules, how to traverse the filesystem, and how to create your own command line programs in Python. You'll write programs that look through all of the files in a folder, including the hundreds of thousands of files in the BlueLeaks dataset, and learn to add arguments to your programs. You'll also start working with a new type of variable in Python, the dictionary, which will prove handy for working with data that's too complex to store in simple lists. As with the previous chapter, future chapters rely on your understanding of the topics covered here.

# Modules

As you learned in Chapter 7, functions are reusable blocks of code that you can run as many times as you want without having to rewrite any code. Python *modules* are similar, but instead of making a single block of code reusable, they make an entire Python file (or multiple files) reusable. You can think of a module as a separate Python file that you can load into the file you're currently working on.

Python includes a wealth of features, but most of them aren't available to every Python script by default. Instead, they're stored in *built-in* modules, those that come with Python. Once you import a module into your script using an `import` statement, you can access all of the functions, variables, and other Python objects defined in that module using the syntax `module_name` `.item_name`.

For example, the `time` module includes the function `time.sleep()` (pronounced "time dot sleep"), which makes your program wait a given number of seconds before continuing to the next line of code. Run the following commands to import the `time` module and then have it tell Python to wait five seconds:

```
>>> import time
>>> time.sleep(5)
```

Your Python interpreter should wait five seconds before the prompt appears again.

Here are a few of the built-in modules I use the most:

**os**   Includes useful functions for browsing the filesystem, like `os.listdir()` and `os.walk()`. It also includes the submodule `os.path`, which is full of functions to inspect files. For example, it includes `os.path.isfile()` and `os.path.isdir()`, which help determine whether a specific path is a file or a folder.

**csv**   Lets you work with CSV spreadsheet data.

**json**   Lets you work with JSON data.

**datetime**   Includes useful Python features for working with dates and times. For example, it allows you to convert strings like February 24, 2022 5:07:20 UTC+3 (the exact time that Russia invaded Ukraine) into a timestamp that Python can understand and compare with other timestamps, then convert it back into strings of any format you choose.

You'll use the `os` module extensively later in this chapter, the `csv` module in Chapter 9, and the `json` module in Chapter 11. You'll briefly see how `datetime` works later in this chapter when you take a look at chat logs from a ransomware gang, as well as in the Chapter 14 case study, where you'll analyze leaked neo-Nazi chat logs.

As your programs get more complex, you might find it useful to split them up into multiple files, with each file containing a different part of your code. When you do this, you're creating your own modules. The name of the module is the same as its filename. For example, if you define some functions in a file called *helpers.py*, another Python file can access those functions by importing the helpers module. The *helpers.py* file could contain the following code:

```
def get_tax(price, tax_rate):
    return price * tax_rate

def get_net_price(price, tax_rate):
    return price + get_tax(price, tax_rate)
```

This module contains two functions for calculating sales tax, get_tax() and get_net_price(). The following Python script, *price.py*, imports it like so:

```
import helpers
total_price = helpers.get_net_price(50, 0.06)
print(f"A book that costs $50, and has 6% sales tax, costs ${total_price}")
```

The first line, import helpers, makes the functions defined in the helpers module accessible to this script. The second line calls the helpers.get_net _price() function from that module and stores the return value in the variable total_price. The third line displays the value of total_price.

Here's what it looks like when I run this script:

```
micah@trapdoor module % python3 price.py
A book that costs $50, and has 6% sales tax, costs $53.0
```

Running the *price.py* script executes the code defined in the helpers module. Inside that module, the get_net_price() function calls get_tax() and uses its return value to calculate the net price, then returns *that* value back into the *price.py* script.

Before you write your first advanced Python script in Exercise 8-1, let's look at the best way to start new Python scripts.

## Python Script Template

I use the same basic template for all my Python scripts, putting my code into a function called main(), then calling that function at the bottom of the file. This isn't required (you didn't do this for any of the scripts you wrote in Chapter 7, after all), but it's a good way to organize your code. Here's what it looks like:

```
def main():
    pass

if __name__ == "__main__":
    main()
```

The template defines the main() function with a pass statement that tells Python, "Skip this line." I later replace pass with the real body of the script.

Next, the if statement tells Python under which conditions it should run main(). Python automatically defines the __name__ variable, and the definition differs depending on what Python file is being run. If you're running the currently executing Python file directly, then Python sets the value of __name__ to the __main__ string. But if you imported the currently executing Python file from another script, Python sets the value of __name__ to the name of the imported module. Using the example from the previous section, if you run the *helpers.py* script directly, the value of __name__ inside that script will be __main__, but if you run the *price.py* script, then the value of __name__ will be __main__ inside *price.py* and the value of __name__ will be helpers inside *helpers.py*.

In short, if you run your script directly, the main() function will run. But if you import your script as a module into another script or into the Python interpreter, the main() function won't run unless you call it yourself. This way, if you have multiple Python scripts in the same folder, you can have one script import another script to call the functions defined within it without worrying about calling the latter script's main() function.

After I create this template script, I start filling in the main() function with whatever I want the script to do. Putting the main logic of your script inside a function allows you to use the return statement to end main() early, which will quit the script early. You can't use return when you're not in a function.

In the following exercise, you'll put this into practice by writing a script to start investigating BlueLeaks.

## Exercise 8-1: Traverse the Files in BlueLeaks

To efficiently investigate datasets, you need to be able to write code that looks through large collections—sometimes thousands or millions—of files for you. In this exercise, you'll learn various ways to traverse the filesystem in Python using functions in the os module, working with the BlueLeaks dataset. You'll also rely on the foundational skills you learned in Chapter 7, like using variables, for loops, and if statements.

As you read along and run the scripts, feel free to modify the code however you'd like and try running those versions too. You might discover revelations I didn't think to look for.

### List the Filenames in a Folder

Start by using os.listdir() to list the files in the *BlueLeaks-extracted* folder. In your text editor, create a file called *list-files1.py* and enter this short script (or copy and paste it from *https://github.com/micahflee/hacks-leaks-and-revelations/ blob/main/chapter-8/list-files1.py*):

```
import os

def main():
    blueleaks_path = "/Volumes/datasets/BlueLeaks-extracted"
    for filename in os.listdir(blueleaks_path):
        print(filename)

if __name__ == "__main__":
    main()
```

First, the script imports the os module. It then defines the variable blueleaks_path with the path of the *BlueLeaks-extracted* folder (update the script to include the path of this folder on your own computer). The os.listdir() function takes the path to the folder as an argument and returns a list of filenames in that folder. The code uses a for loop to loop through the output of os.listdir(blueleaks_path), displaying each filename.

**NOTE** *Windows paths include the backslash character (\), which Python strings consider an escape character. For example, if your* BlueLeaks-extracted *folder is located at* D:\BlueLeaks-extracted, *Python will misinterpret the string* "D:\BlueLeaks -extracted", *assuming that \B is a special character. To escape your backslashes for any Windows path you store as a string, use \\ instead of \. In this case, set the* blueleaks_path *string to* "D:\\BlueLeaks-extracted".

Run this script. Here's what the output looks like on my computer:

```
micah@trapdoor chapter-8 % python3 list-files1.py
211sfbay
Securitypartnership
acprlea
acticaz
akorca
--snip--
```

Next, you'll try something slightly more advanced. Instead of just listing the filenames in BlueLeaks, you'll check each filename to see whether it's a folder, and if so, you'll open each of those folders and count how many files and subfolders they contain.

## Count the Files and Folders in a Folder

Create a file called *list-files2.py* and enter the following code (or copy and paste it from *https://github.com/micahflee/hacks-leaks-and-revelations/blob/main/chapter-8/list-files2.py*):

```
import os

def main():
    blueleaks_path = "/Volumes/datasets/BlueLeaks-extracted"
❶ for bl_folder in os.listdir(blueleaks_path):
        bl_folder_path = os.path.join(blueleaks_path, bl_folder)
```

```
❷ if not os.path.isdir(bl_folder_path):
       continue

❸ files_count = 0
   folders_count = 0
❹ for filename in os.listdir(bl_folder_path):
       filename_path = os.path.join(bl_folder_path, filename)

     ❺ if os.path.isfile(filename_path):
            files_count += 1

       if os.path.isdir(filename_path):
            folders_count += 1

❻ print(f"{bl_folder} has {files_count} files, {folders_count} folders")

if __name__ == "__main__":
    main()
```

This script counts the number of files and folders it finds within each BlueLeaks folder. It starts like *list-files1.py* does, importing os and defining the blueleaks_path variable (remember to update the variable's value to match the correct path on your computer).

The first for loop cycles through the filenames in your *BlueLeaks-extracted* folder, this time saving each filename in the bl_folder variable, so its value will be something like miacx or ncric ❶. The script then sets the value of the new bl_folder_path variable accordingly. The os.path.join() function connects filenames together to make complete paths. Its first argument is the starting path, and it adds all other arguments to the end of that path. For example, if the value of bl_folder is miacx, then this function will return the string /Volumes/datasets/BlueLeaks-extracted/miacx on my computer (the output will be different if your blueleaks_path is different or if you're using Windows and your filenames use backslashes instead of slashes).

Since you want to look inside bl_folder_path and count the number of files and folders it contains, the script needs to check that it's actually a folder and not a file, using the os.path.isdir() function ❷. If bl_folder_path isn't a folder, the script runs the continue statement. This statement, which can run only inside of loops, tells Python to immediately continue on to the next iteration of the loop. In short, if the script comes across a file instead of a folder, it ignores it and moves on.

The script then prepares to count the number of files and folders within each individual BlueLeaks folder as the code loops by defining the variables files_count and folders_count with a value of 0 ❸.

A second for loop loops through the files in the BlueLeaks folder from the first for loop, saving each filename in the filename variable ❹. Inside this loop, the script defines filename_path as the absolute path for the filename under consideration. For instance, if the value of filename is a string like Directory.csv, then the value of filename_path would be a string like /Volumes/datasets/BlueLeaks-extracted/211sfbay/Directory.csv.

The script then checks to see if this absolute path is a file or a folder, using the os.path.isfile() and os.path.isdir() functions ❺. If the path is a file, the script increments the files_count variable by 1; if it's a folder, the script increments folders_count by 1. When the second for loop finishes running, these two variables should contain the total count of files and folders for the BlueLeaks folder you're currently looping through in the first for loop. Finally, the script displays an f-string that shows these numbers ❻.

Try running the script. The output should show how many files and folders are contained in each BlueLeaks folder, potentially with the list of folders in a different order:

```
micah@trapdoor chapter-8 % python3 list-files2.py
bostonbric has 506 files, 10 folders
terrorismtip has 207 files, 0 folders
ociac has 216 files, 1 folders
usao has 0 files, 84 folders
alertmidsouth has 512 files, 10 folders
chicagoheat has 499 files, 10 folders
--snip--
```

So far, you've combined various functions in the os module to make a list of filenames in your BlueLeaks folder and check whether each name actually refers to a file or to another folder. Now it's time to learn to write code that can also traverse the BlueLeaks folder's nested folders.

## Traverse Folders with os.walk()

Let's say you want to write a program that displays all of the files in a folder and its subfolders, and its subsubfolders, and so on. When you have nested folders but don't actually know how deep the folder structure goes, listing all of the filenames just by using os.listdir(), os.path.isfile(), and os.path.isdir() isn't so simple. Python's os.walk() function solves this problem.

The os.walk() function takes a path to a folder as an argument and returns a list of *tuples*, or multiple values contained in a single value. To define a tuple, you place all of the values, separated by commas, within parentheses. For example, (3, 4) is a tuple, as is ("cinco", "seis", "siete"). Tuples can also contain mixed types like (1, "dos") and can contain any number of values.

The os.walk() function returns a list of tuples where each tuple contains three values:

```
(dirname, subdirnames, filenames)
```

where dirname is a string, subdirnames is a list of strings, and filenames is a list of strings. For example, the following code loops through the return value of os.walk(path):

```
for dirname, subdirnames, filenames in os.walk(path):
    print(f"The folder {dirname} has subfolders: {subdirnames} and files: {filenames}")
```

When you use for loops to loop through lists, you normally assign just a single variable to each item in the list. However, since each item is a tuple, you can assign three variables to it: dirname, subdirnames, and filenames. In each loop, the values for this set of variables will be different: the value of dirname is the path to a folder, the value of subdirnames is a list of subfolders inside that folder, and the value of filenames is a list of files inside that folder.

For example, suppose you have a folder called *example* that contains these subfolders and files:

```
example
├── downloads
│   ├── screenshot.png
│   └── paper.pdf
└── documents
    ├── work
    │   └── finances.xlsx
    └── personal
```

This folder has two subfolders: *downloads* (containing *screenshot.png* and *paper.pdf*) and *documents*. The *documents* folder has its own subfolders: *work* (containing *finances.xlsx*) and *personal*.

The following commands loop through the return value of os.walk ("./example"), where *./example* is the path to this *example* folder, to find the values of dirname, subdirnames, and filenames for each loop:

```
>>> for dirname, subdirnames, filenames in os.walk("./example"):
...     print(f"The folder {dirname} has subfolders: {subdirnames} and files: {filenames}")
...
```

Running this command returns the following output:

```
The folder ./example has subfolders: ['documents', 'downloads'] and files: []
The folder ./example/documents has subfolders: ['personal', 'work'] and files: []
The folder ./example/documents/personal has subfolders: [] and files: []
The folder ./example/documents/work has subfolders: [] and files: ['finances.xlsx']
The folder ./example/downloads has subfolders: [] and files: ['paper.pdf', 'screenshot.png']
```

This code loops once for each folder, including all subfolders, with the path to that folder stored in dirname. The list of subfolders in that folder is stored in subdirnames, and the list of files is stored in filenames. Once you've looped through the folder and all of its subfolders, the for loop ends.

Any time you need to traverse all of the files in a dataset that contains lots of nested folders, you'll want to use os.walk(). With a single for loop, you'll be able to write code that inspects each file in the entire dataset. The os.walk() function has many uses, including figuring out which files are the largest or smallest, as you'll see next.

## Exercise 8-2: Find the Largest Files in BlueLeaks

In this exercise, you'll use os.walk() to write a script that looks through all the files, folders, and subfolders in BlueLeaks; measures the size of each file; and displays the filenames for files over 100MB. This code allows you to loop through all of the files in a folder, no matter how deep the folder structure.

Create a file called *find-big-files.py* and enter the following code (or copy and paste it from *https://github.com/micahflee/hacks-leaks-and-revelations/blob/main/chapter-8/find-big-files.py*):

```python
import os

def main():
    blueleaks_path = "/Volumes/datasets/BlueLeaks-extracted"
    for dirname, subdirnames, filenames in os.walk(blueleaks_path):
        for filename in filenames:
            absolute_filename = os.path.join(dirname, filename)
            size_in_bytes = os.path.getsize(absolute_filename)
            size_in_mb = int(size_in_bytes / 1024 / 1024)
            if size_in_mb >= 100:
                print(f"{absolute_filename} is {size_in_mb}MB")

if __name__ == "__main__":
    main()
```

Inside the main() function, the script first defines the blueleaks_path variable as the path of the *BlueLeaks-extracted* folder and loops through all of the files in the entire BlueLeaks dataset using the os.walk() function. Inside each loop in the first for loop are the dirname, subdirnames, and filenames variables. Each item in the list that os.walk() returns represents a different folder or subfolder in the BlueLeaks dataset, so by the time this loop finishes, the code will have traversed the entire dataset.

To find the biggest files, the next step is to look at each file with another for loop, this time looping through filenames. Inside this second for loop, the script defines absolute_filename to be the absolute path to the filename. Since dirname tells the script which folder it's looking in, and filename tells the script which file it's looking at, the script passes these values into os.path.join() to combine them, creating the absolute path to the filename.

A new function, os.path.getsize(), returns the size, in bytes, of the file under consideration and stores it in the variable size_in_bytes. The script then converts this value from bytes to megabytes (storing that in the variable size_in_mb) and checks if it's greater than or equal to 100MB. If it is, the output displays its filename and file size in megabytes with the print() function.

Try running the script. It will take longer than the previous scripts in this chapter, because this time, you're measuring the size of every single file in BlueLeaks. Here's what the output looks like when I run it (your output may be displayed in a different order):

```
micah@trapdoor chapter-8 % python3 find-big-files.py
/Volumes/datasets/BlueLeaks-extracted/usao/usaoflntraining/files/VVSF00000/001.mp4 is 644MB
```

```
/Volumes/datasets/BlueLeaks-extracted/chicagoheat/html/ZA-CHICAGO HEaT_LR-20160830-034_Final
Files.pdf is 102MB
/Volumes/datasets/BlueLeaks-extracted/nmhidta/files/RFIF300000/722.pdf is 148MB
/Volumes/datasets/BlueLeaks-extracted/nmhidta/files/RFIF200000/543.pdf is 161MB
/Volumes/datasets/BlueLeaks-extracted/nmhidta/files/RFIF100000/723.pdf is 206MB
/Volumes/datasets/BlueLeaks-extracted/fbicahouston/files/VVSF00000/002.mp4 is 145MB
/Volumes/datasets/BlueLeaks-extracted/fbicahouston/files/PSAVF100000/009.mp4 is 146MB
/Volumes/datasets/BlueLeaks-extracted/fbicahouston/files/PSAVF100000/026.mp4 is 105MB
--snip--
```

The script should display the absolute paths of the 101 files in BlueLeaks that are at least 100MB, along with each file's size.

## Third-Party Modules

In addition to built-in modules, Python also supports third-party modules that you can easily incorporate into your own code. Most Python scripts that I write, even simple ones, rely on at least one third-party module (when a Python program depends on third-party modules, they're called *dependencies*). In this section, you'll learn how to install third-party modules and use them in your own scripts.

The Python Package Index (PyPI) contains hundreds of thousands of third-party Python *packages*, or bundles of Python modules, and subpackages. Pip, which stands for Package Installer for Python, is a package manager similar to Ubuntu's apt or macOS's Homebrew used to install packages hosted on PyPI. You can search for packages on PyPI's website (*https://pypi.org*), then install a package by running the `python3 -m pip install package_name` command.

For example, I frequently use a package called Click, which stands for Command Line Interface Creation Kit. The `click` Python module makes it simple to add command line arguments to your scripts. To see what happens when you try importing this module before you've installed it, open a Python interpreter and run `import click`. Assuming you don't already have the package installed, you should see a `ModuleNotFoundError` error message:

```
Traceback (most recent call last):
  File "<stdin>", line 1, in <module>
ModuleNotFoundError: No module named 'click'
>>>
```

Now exit the Python interpreter and install `click` with pip by running the following command:

```
micah@trapdoor ~ % python3 -m pip install click
Collecting click
  Using cached click-8.1.3-py3-none-any.whl (96 kB)
Installing collected packages: click
Successfully installed click-8.1.3
```

Open the Python interpreter again and try importing click once more:

```
>>> import click
>>>
```

If no error messages pop up, you've successfully imported the click module, and its additional features are now available for you to use.

The command to uninstall a package is python3 -m pip uninstall *package_name*. Try uninstalling click:

```
micah@trapdoor ~ % python3 -m pip uninstall click
Found existing installation: click 8.1.3
Uninstalling click-8.1.3:
  Would remove:
    /usr/local/lib/python3.10/site-packages/click-8.1.3.dist-info/*
    /usr/local/lib/python3.10/site-packages/click/*
Proceed (Y/n)? y
  Successfully uninstalled click-8.1.3
```

As you can see, when I ran this command, the output listed the files that pip would need to delete to uninstall the click module, then asked if I wanted to proceed. I entered y and pressed ENTER, and the files were deleted and the module uninstalled.

You can install multiple Python packages at once like so:

```
python3 -m pip install package_name1 package_name2 package_name3
```

The same is true of uninstalling.

It's common to define the Python packages that your script requires inside a file called *requirements.txt*, then install all of them at once with the python3 -m pip install -r requirements.txt command. For example, suppose in addition to using click, you want to use the HTTP client httpx to load web pages inside Python and the sqlalchemy module to work with SQL databases. To include all three in your Python script, first create a *requirements .txt* file with each package name on its own line:

```
click
httpx
sqlalchemy
```

Then run the following command to install them simultaneously:

```
micah@trapdoor chapter-8 % python3 -m pip install -r requirements.txt
Collecting click
  Using cached click-8.1.3-py3-none-any.whl (96 kB)
Collecting httpx
  Using cached httpx-0.23.0-py3-none-any.whl (84 kB)
--snip--
Successfully installed anyio-3.6.1 certifi-2022.9.24 click-8.1.3 h11-0.12.0 httpcore-0.15.0
httpx-0.23.0 idna-3.4 rfc3986-1.5.0 sniffio-1.3.0 sqlalchemy-1.4.41
```

As you can see, this command installs more than just those three Python packages: `rfc3986`, `certifi`, `sniffio`, and so on are also included. That's because `click`, `httpx`, and `sqlachemy` have dependencies of their own. For example, `httpcore` is a dependency of the `httpx` package, so it installs that as well. To summarize, the *requirements.txt* file defines your project's dependencies, each of which might depend on its own list of packages.

**NOTE** *To learn more about how to use `httpx` and other Python modules to automate interacting with websites, check out Appendix B. I recommend waiting until you complete Chapters 7, 8, 9, and 11, however, since the instructions covered in Appendix B rely on the skills you'll pick up in those chapters.*

---

### VIRTUAL ENVIRONMENTS

It's not unusual to have multiple versions of Python and multiple versions of the same dependencies for different projects installed on the same computer. If you routinely install Python packages with pip for various projects, this can get very messy over time. For example, different projects might depend on different versions of the same module to work, but you can't have two versions of a module installed at the same time—at least not without *virtual environments*, which are like stand-alone folders containing your Python dependencies for a specific project. This way, different projects' dependencies won't trip each other up.

To keep things simple, this book doesn't use virtual environments, and it uses only pip to install Python packages. As long as you don't have multiple Python projects requiring specific versions of the few third-party modules this book uses, you should be fine without using a virtual environment.

You can learn more about virtual environments at *https://docs.python.org/ 3/tutorial/venv.html*. For larger Python projects, you might also consider using Python package management programs such as Poetry (*https://python-poetry .org*) or Pipenv (*https://github.com/pypa/pipenv*), which handle the complicated parts of keeping track of Python packages and virtual environments for you.

---

Now that you know how to install third-party modules, you'll practice using Click.

## Exercise 8-3: Practice Command Line Arguments with Click

As you learned in the previous section, the Click package makes it simple to add command line arguments to your scripts. You can use it to define variables to pass into your `main()` function from the terminal, without having to define those variables in your code. In this exercise, you'll learn how to use Click by writing a sample script in preparation for using this module in later exercises.

First, install the Click package with pip again by running `python3 -m pip install click`. Next, open your text editor and enter the following Python script, *exercise-8-3.py* (or copy and paste it from *https://github.com/micahflee/hacks-leaks-and-revelations/blob/main/chapter-8/exercise-8-3.py*):

```python
import click

@click.command()
@click.argument("name")
def main(name):
    """Simple program that greets NAME"""
    print(f"Hello {name}!")

if __name__ == "__main__":
    main()
```

First, the script imports the `click` module. It then runs a few *decorators*, function calls that begin with `@` and add functionality to another function you're about to define—the `main()` function, in this case. The `@click .command()` decorator tells Click that `main()` is a command, and the `@click .argument("name")` decorator tells Click that this command has an argument called `name`.

Next, the script defines the `main()` function, which takes `name` as an argument. This function has a docstring, `Simple program that greets NAME`. Click uses this docstring for its commands when it builds the output for `--help`, as you'll see shortly. The `main()` function simply displays a string with the name you passed in as an argument.

Finally, the script calls the `main()` function. Notice that even though `main()` requires an argument (`name`), the script doesn't explicitly pass that argument in when calling the function. This is where the magic of the Click decorators comes in. When the script calls `main()`, Click will figure out what arguments it needs to pass in, find their values from the CLI arguments, and pass them in for you.

Run the script as follows:

```
micah@trapdoor chapter-8 % python3 exercise-8-3.py
Usage: click-example.py [OPTIONS] NAME
Try 'click-example.py --help' for help.

Error: Missing argument 'NAME'.
```

When you run the program, if you don't pass in the correct CLI arguments, Click tells you what you did wrong. As you can see, you're missing the required `NAME` argument. Click also tells you that you can get help by running the script again with the `--help` argument.

Try running the `--help` command:

```
micah@trapdoor chapter-8 % python3 exercise-8-3.py --help
Usage: click-example.py [OPTIONS] NAME

  Simple program that greets NAME

Options:
  --help  Show this message and exit.
```

This time, the output shows a description of the program based on the docstring. Any CLI program that uses Click will display the docstring for the command when you run it with `--help`.

Try running the command again, this time passing in a name. For example, here's what happens when I pass in `Eve` as the name:

```
micah@trapdoor chapter-8 % python3 exercise-8-3.py Eve
Hello Eve!
```

**NOTE** *You can read more about using Click at* https://click.palletsprojects.com.

## Avoiding Hardcoding with Command Line Arguments

As you've seen in previous chapters, CLI arguments let you run the same program in many different ways, targeting different data. For example, in Chapter 4, you used the `du` command to estimate the disk space of a folder by adding the folder's path as an argument. In `du -sh --apparent-size` *path*, the arguments are `-sh`, `--apparent-size`, and *path*.

The `du` command would be much less useful if it could measure disk space for only a single hardcoded folder. *Hardcoding* means embedding information, like a path, directly into source code. You can avoid hardcoding anything in your CLI programs by having the user provide this information as arguments when running them.

Passing paths into scripts, rather than hardcoding them, makes for a better user experience. In previous exercises in this chapter, you hardcoded the path to your copy of the BlueLeaks dataset into your Python scripts. If you were to pass the appropriate path in as an argument, however, other people could use your script without editing it—they could just pass in *their* path when they ran it.

Using arguments rather than hardcoding can also make your scripts more universally useful. For example, in Exercise 8-2, you wrote a script to find all of the files that are at least 100MB in the BlueLeaks dataset. Using CLI arguments, you could make this script work for any dataset you get your hands on, not just BlueLeaks, and for any minimum file size, allowing you to run it in a variety of situations. You'd just need to pass in the dataset path and the minimum file size as CLI arguments. You'll try this out in the next exercise.

## Exercise 8-4: Find the Largest Files in Any Dataset

In this exercise, you'll modify the script you wrote in Exercise 8-2 to make it work for any dataset, and for any minimum file size, using CLI arguments. In the following chapters, you'll write simple Python scripts that use Click for CLI arguments, so you can provide the paths to the datasets you'll be working with.

Create a new file called *exercise-8-4.py*, and copy and paste the *exercise-8-2 .py* code into it. Next, make the following modifications to the code, highlighted in bold (or find the full modified script at *https://github.com/micahflee/ hacks-leaks-and-revelations/blob/main/chapter-8/exercise-8-4.py*):

```
import os
import click

@click.command()
@click.argument("path")
@click.argument("min_file_size", type=click.INT)
def main(path, min_file_size):
    """Find files in PATH that are at least MIN_FILE_SIZE MB big"""
    for dirname, subdirnames, filenames in os.walk(path):
        for filename in filenames:
            absolute_filename = os.path.join(dirname, filename)
            size_in_bytes = os.path.getsize(absolute_filename)
            size_in_mb = int(size_in_bytes / 1024 / 1024)
            if size_in_mb >= min_file_size:
                print(f"{absolute_filename} is {size_in_mb}MB")

if __name__ == "__main__":
    main()
```

This code imports the click module at the top of the file. Next, it adds Click decorators before the main() function: @click.command() makes the main() function a Click command, and @click.argument() adds path and min_file_size as arguments. The script specifies with type=click.INT that the min_file_size argument should be an *integer*, or a whole number, as opposed to a string. Then it adds path and min_file_size as arguments to the main() function and adds a docstring that describes what this command does.

The new script uses arguments instead of hardcoded values. It deletes the line that defines the blueleaks_path variable, and in the os.walk() function call, it changes blueleaks_path to just path, which is the argument. Finally, it changes 100 in size_in_mb >= 100 to min_file_size.

You can now use this program to find big files in any folder in the BlueLeaks dataset or elsewhere. For example, here's what it looks like when I search for all files that are at least 500MB in */Applications* on my Mac:

```
micah@trapdoor chapter-8 % python3 exercise-8-4.py /Applications 500
/Applications/Dangerzone.app/Contents/Resources/share/container.tar.gz is 668MB
/Applications/Docker.app/Contents/Resources/linuxkit/services.iso is 602MB
```

As you can see, I have only two apps installed that include files this big: Dangerzone and Docker Desktop.

Now that you've seen how to add CLI arguments to your Python scripts using Click, you should be able to avoid hardcoding information like dataset paths in your future programs.

Next, we'll switch gears and explore a new powerful type of Python variable called dictionaries.

# Dictionaries

In the course of your investigations, sometimes you'll need to keep track of data with more structure than a simple list. To do so, you can use Python dictionaries. Instead of a collection of items, a *dictionary* (*dict* for short) is a collection of keys that map to values. *Keys* are labels that you use to save or retrieve information in a dictionary, and *values* are the actual information being saved or retrieved. Nearly every Python script I write that deals with data uses dictionaries. In this section, you'll learn how to define dictionaries, get values from them, add values to them, and update existing values in them.

## Defining Dictionaries

Dictionaries are defined using braces ({ and }), sometimes referred to as curly brackets. Inside the braces is a list of key-value pairs in the format *key*: *value*, where each pair is separated from the next by commas—for example, {"country": "Italy", "drinking_age": 18}. For longer dictionaries, you can make your code more readable by putting each key-value pair on its own line.

Listing 8-1 shows an example dictionary stored in the variable capitals.

```
capitals = {
    "United States": "Washington, DC",
    "India": "New Delhi",
    "South Africa": "Cape Town",
    "Brazil": "Brasília",
    "Germany": "Berlin",
    "Russia": "Moscow",
    "China": "Beijing"
}
```

*Listing 8-1: A dictionary stored in the capitals variable*

In this case, the keys are country names and the values are the capitals of those countries.

Each key in a dictionary can have only one value. If you try to set the same key more than once, Python will save the version you last set. For example, if you define a dictionary and use the name key more than once, the dictionary will overwrite the previous value with the most recent one:

```
>>> test_dict = {"name": "Alice", "name": "Bob", "hobby": "cryptography"}
>>> print(test_dict)
{'name': 'Bob', 'hobby': 'cryptography'}
```

However, you can also use lists, or other dictionaries, as values:

```
>>> test_dict = {"names": ["Alice", "Bob"], "hobby": "cryptography"}
>>> print(test_dict)
{'names': ['Alice', 'Bob'], 'hobby': 'cryptography'}
```

In this case, the value for the key names is `['Alice', 'Bob']`, which itself is a list. You can use a combination of lists and dictionaries to organize pretty much any type of data, no matter how complicated, allowing you to more easily work with it in Python.

## Getting and Setting Values

To retrieve an item you've stored inside a dictionary, add square brackets containing the item's key to the end of the dictionary name. If you try to use a key you haven't defined, your script will crash with a KeyError. For example, here's how to look up the capitals of certain countries in the capitals dictionary:

```
>>> capitals["United States"]
'Washington, DC'
>>> capitals["China"]
'Beijing'
>>> capitals["Kenya"]
Traceback (most recent call last):
  File "<stdin>", line 1, in <module>
KeyError: 'Kenya'
```

When you run capitals["Kenya"], Python throws the error message KeyError: 'Kenya'. This means that Kenya isn't a valid key in the capitals dictionary. You can see that the only keys defined in Listing 8-1 are United States, India, South Africa, Brazil, Germany, Russia, and China. Because Kenya isn't a key in this dictionary, you can't retrieve its value.

You can add new key-value pairs to a dictionary, or update an existing one, like this:

```
>>> capitals["Kenya"] = "Nairobi"
>>> capitals["United States"] = "Mar-a-Lago"
>>> print(capitals)
{'United States': 'Mar-a-Lago', 'India': 'New Delhi', 'South Africa': 'Cape Town', 'Brazil':
'Brasília', 'Germany': 'Berlin', 'Russia': 'Moscow', 'China': 'Beijing', 'Kenya': 'Nairobi'}
```

This code defines a new key, Kenya, with the value Nairobi. It also updates an existing key, United States, to have the value Mar-a-Lago, overwriting its old value, which used to be Washington, DC.

## Navigating Dictionaries and Lists in the Conti Chat Logs

You can combine dictionaries and lists in a single flexible data structure that allows you to represent a wide variety of information. If you're writing Python code to work with datasets, chances are you're going to need both. You might directly load the data in this format, or you might create your own dictionaries and lists to store aspects of the data.

To describe how to use data structures that include a combination of dictionaries and lists, I'll use an example from a real dataset. The day after Russia invaded Ukraine on February 24, 2022, the notorious Russian ransomware gang Conti, known for hacking companies around the world and extorting millions of dollars from them, published a statement on its website throwing its full support behind the Russian government. It threatened any "enemy" who launched cyberattacks against Russia with retaliation against their "critical infrastructure." Three days later, a Ukrainian security researcher anonymously leaked 30GB of internal data from Conti: hacking tools, training documentation, source code, and chat logs. The Conti chat logs originally came in the form of JSON files, which is structured data. When you load JSON files into Python, they'll automatically be loaded as a combination of dictionaries and lists.

In this section, you'll look through some of these chat logs in order to practice working with real leaked data stored in dictionaries and lists. Using Python code, you'll learn how to navigate these structures to access specific pieces of data as well as how to quickly loop through the chat logs and select just the parts you're interested in.

### Exploring Dictionaries and Lists Full of Data in Python

You can download the complete Conti dataset from *https://ddosecrets.com/wiki/Conti_ransomware_chats*. However, for this section, you'll use just one file from the dataset, *2022-02-24-general.json*, which the Ukranian security researcher extracted from a chat system called RocketChat.

Download *2022-02-24-general.json* from *https://github.com/micahflee/hacks-leaks-and-revelations/blob/main/chapter-8/2022-02-24-general.json*. Open a terminal, change to the folder where you stored this file, and open a Python interpreter. Load this file into a dictionary with the following commands:

```
>>> import json
>>> with open("2022-02-24-general.json") as f:
...     data = json.load(f)
...
```

This code uses the json module and loads the data from *2022-02-24-general.json* into the data variable. The chat logs from this file are too long to display in their entirety, but Listing 8-2 shows a snippet of the value of the data dictionary that demonstrates its structure.

```
{
    "messages": [ ❶
        {
--snip--
        },
        {
            "_id": "FmFZbde9ACs3gtw27",
            "rid": "GENERAL",
            "msg": "Некоторые американские сенаторы предлагают помимо соцсетей блокировать в
России ещё и PornHub!",
            "ts": "2022-02-24T22:02:38.276Z",
            "u": {"_id": "NKrXj9edAPWNrYv5r", "username": "thomas", "name": "thomas"},
            "urls": [],
            "mentions": [],
            "channels": [],
            "md": [
                {
                    "type": "PARAGRAPH",
                    "value": [
                        {
                            "type": "PLAIN_TEXT",
                            "value": "Некоторые американские сенаторы предлагают помимо
соцсетей блокировать в России ещё и PornHub!",
                        }
                    ],
                }
            ],
            "_updatedAt": "2022-02-24T22:02:38.293Z",
        },
        {
--snip--
        },
    ],
    "success": True ❷
}
```

*Listing 8-2: Conti chat logs from RocketChat*

The data variable is a dictionary with two keys, messages and success. You access the value of the messages key, which is a list of dictionaries, using the expression data["messages"] ❶. You can tell that the value of data["messages"] is a list because it's enclosed in square brackets ([ and ]), and you can tell that the items inside it are dictionaries because they're enclosed in braces ({ and }). Almost all of the data in this file is stored in this list.

Each dictionary in the data["messages"] list describes a chat message. This snippet of code includes only one of the dictionaries, the ninth chat message in the list (I snipped out the first eight messages, so you can't tell that it's the ninth without looking at the original file). You can access the dictionary that contains that specific chat message using the expression data["messages"][8]. (Remember, in programming we start counting at 0, not 1, so the first item is at index 0, the second item is at index 1, and so on.) If you run the command print(data["messages"][8]) to display the dictionary for the ninth message, the output should match the message in the listing. Notice that just as you place index numbers within brackets to select from lists, you place keys within brackets to select from dictionaries, like ["messages"] or ["success"].

You can also access the value of the success key with data["success"]. Its value is the Boolean True ❷. I'm not entirely sure what this means, but I suspect that the success key was left over from whatever system the Ukrainian researcher used to export these chat messages from RocketChat, confirming that exporting the data was successful and that there were no errors.

The file from which I loaded this code contained 604 different chat messages, each in its own dictionary, that were sent in Conti's #general RocketChat channel on February 24, 2022. I discovered that this list has 604 items by measuring its length with the len() function, like this:

```
>>> len(data["messages"])
604
```

The dictionary for each chat message has many keys: _id, rid, msg, u, urls, and so on.

You can find out what types of data these keys contain using the for *key_variable* in *dictionary* syntax, and you can determine a variable's data type using the type() function. Try this out using the following commands:

```
>>> for key in data["messages"][8]:
...     print(f"{key}: {type(data['messages'][8][key])}")
...
```

This command loops through the data["messages"][8] dictionary and stores each key in the key variable. Then, using the print() function and an f-string, it displays the key (key) and the type of data stored in that key, as shown in the following output:

```
_id: <class 'str'>
rid: <class 'str'>
msg: <class 'str'>
ts: <class 'str'>
u: <class 'dict'>
urls: <class 'list'>
mentions: <class 'list'>
channels: <class 'list'>
md: <class 'list'>
_updatedAt: <class 'str'>
```

In the output, the values at the _id, rid, msg, ts, and _updatedAt keys are all strings. The value at the u key is a dictionary. The value at the urls, mentions, channels, and md keys are lists.

You can get the value of the data at the key using data['messages'][8][key]. Remember that to retrieve the value of a key in a dictionary, you put the key in square brackets. In this case, the key itself is stored in the variable key, so you can get its value by putting key inside the square brackets.

To find out what type of data that is, then, just pass the value into the type() function.

## Selecting Values in Dictionaries and Lists

When working with datasets, you often end up with structures like this: a mess of dictionaries and lists that you need to make sense of. Being able to select the exact values you're looking for is an important skill. To practice navigating through dictionaries and lists, take a closer look at the value of just one of these keys, the md key, by running the following command:

```
>>> print(data["messages"][8]["md"])
```

In the output, you can tell that this value is a list because it's surrounded by square brackets:

```
[{'type': 'PARAGRAPH', 'value': [{'type': 'PLAIN_TEXT', 'value': 'Некоторые американские
сенаторы предлагают помимо соцсетей блокировать в России ещё и PornHub!'}]}]
```

The list's single item is a dictionary, which is surrounded by braces. The dictionary has a type key whose value is PARAGRAPH, as well as a value key. The value of value is another list with one item containing another dictionary; that dictionary itself contains type and value keys, where the value of type is PLAIN_TEXT.

These data structures can have as many sublists and subdictionaries as you'd like. To select specific values, after the data variable keep adding square brackets containing an index (if it's a list) or a key (if it's a dictionary) until you get to the value you're looking for. For example, use the following command to access the value of the value key in the inner dictionary within the inner list, which is in another value key in the outer dictionary in the outer list:

```
>>> print(data["messages"][8]["md"][0]["value"][0]["value"])
```

You already know that data["messages"][8] is a dictionary that represents a chat message. To find the value of the md key in that dictionary, you include["md"] in the command. As you can tell from inspecting the structure in Listing 8-2, this is a list with one item, so adding [0] selects that item. This item is a dictionary, and you select the value of its value key by adding ["value"]. This item is another list with one item, so you again add [0] to select that one item. This is yet another dictionary, so you can select the value of the final inner value key by adding another ["value"].

You should get the following output:

```
Некоторые американские сенаторы предлагают помимо соцсетей блокировать в России ещё и PornHub!
```

In English, the message that you just displayed says, "Some American Senators suggest blocking PornHub in Russia in addition to social networks!" It was posted right after Russia started its invasion of Ukraine, and

US and European leaders immediately began imposing economic sanctions on Russia. After invading Ukraine, the Russian government censored access to Twitter and Facebook from the Russian internet. Rumors spread that PornHub, a popular American porn website, would block access to Russian users (though this didn't happen). This same user followed up their first post with "That's it, we're done," and then "They will take away our last joys!"

## Analyzing Data Stored in Dictionaries and Lists

Whenever I work with any sort of structured data, I find myself looping through a list of dictionaries and selecting specific pieces of data. As long as you understand its structure, you can write your own similar code to quickly pull out the relevant information, no matter what dataset you're working with. For example, you might want to view the chat logs in the format *timestamp username: message* in order to hide the unimportant sections of data so that you can directly copy and paste the relevant parts into machine translation systems like DeepL or Google Translate. Run the following commands to display all of the messages in data["messages"] in that format:

```
>>> for message in data["messages"]:
...     print(f"{message['ts']} {message['u']['username']}: {message['msg']}")
...
```

You should get the following output:

```
--snip--
2022-02-24T22:02:49.448Z thomas: последние радости у нас заберут
2022-02-24T22:02:44.463Z thomas: ну все, приплыли)
2022-02-24T22:02:38.276Z thomas: Некоторые американские сенаторы предлагают помимо соцсетей
блокировать в России ещё и PornHub!
2022-02-24T22:00:00.347Z thomas:
2022-02-24T21:58:56.152Z rags: угу :(
--snip--
```

Since data["messages"] is a list, each time the for loop in this command runs, it updates the value of the message variable to a different item in that list. In this case, each item is a different dictionary. Inside the for loop, the print() function displays three values: the timestamp (message['ts']), the username (message['u']['username']), and the message itself (message['msg']).

You can change this command to display whatever information you'd like from each message. Maybe you're interested is the user's ID rather than their username. In that case, you could display message['u']['_id'].

The previous output shows the same messages about PornHub just discussed, as well as a message posted just before that from another user, rags. If you're interested in seeing only the messages posted by rags, view those by running the following commands:

```
>>> for message in data["messages"]:
...     if message["u"]["username"] == "rags":
...         print(f"{message['ts']} {message['u']['username']}: {message['msg']}")
...
```

This code is similar to the previous example. A for loop loops through each message in data["messages"], and then a print() statement displays specific pieces of information from that message. This time, though, each loop also contains an if statement. Each time the code finds another message, it checks to see if the username is rags and, if so, displays the message. Otherwise, it moves on to the next message. You should get the following output:

```
2022-02-24T22:08:49.684Z rags: давай бро спокойной ночи
2022-02-24T22:03:50.131Z rags: сча посмотрю спасиб =)
2022-02-24T21:58:56.152Z rags: угу :(
--snip--
```

Finally, suppose you want to figure out how many messages each person posted, perhaps to find the most active poster in the #general chatroom on this day. The simplest way to do this is to create a new empty dictionary yourself and then write code to fill it up. Run the following command to create an empty dictionary called user_posts:

```
>>> user_posts = {}
```

The keys in this dictionary will be usernames, and the values will be the number of posts from that user. Fill up the user_posts dictionary with the following code:

```
>>> for message in data["messages"]:
...     username = message["u"]["username"]
...     if username not in user_posts:
...         user_posts[username] = 1
...     else:
...         user_posts[username] += 1
...
>>>
```

Again, this code uses a for loop to loop through the messages. Next, it defines the username variable as message["u"]["username"], the username of the person who posted the message the code is currently looping through. Next, using an if statement, the code checks to see if this username is already a key in the user_posts dictionary. (It's not checking to see if the string username is a key, but rather if the *value* of the username variable, like thomas or rags, is a key.)

If this user doesn't exist in the user_posts dictionary, the program adds a key to this dictionary and sets the value at that key to 1, with the line user_posts[username] = 1. Otherwise, it increases the value by 1, with user_posts[username] += 1. By the time the for loop finishes running, the user_posts dictionary should be complete. The keys should be all of the usernames found in the messages, and the values should be the total number of messages for that user.

Use the following code to display the information inside the user_posts dictionary, viewing the data you just collected:

```
>>> for username in user_posts:
...     print(f"{username} posted {user_posts[username]} times")
...
```

You should get the following output:

```
weldon posted 64 times
patrick posted 62 times
rags posted 38 times
thomas posted 58 times
ryan posted 2 times
kermit posted 151 times
biggie posted 39 times
stanton posted 12 times
angelo posted 102 times
Garfield posted 61 times
jaime posted 2 times
grem posted 5 times
jefferson posted 1 times
elijah posted 6 times
chad posted 1 times
```

These are the users who posted in Conti's #general chatroom, in their RocketChat server, on the day Russia invaded Ukraine in 2022. The user *kermit* posted 151 times, more than any other user.

In these examples, you looped through hundreds of chat messages, but the same concepts would work with millions or billions of messages or with data representing any sort of information.

---

### REVELATIONS IN THE CONTI DATASET

This dataset includes far more chat logs than just a few messages worrying about a porn site getting blocked. The example I used in this section included the chat logs for the #general channel for a single day, but the logs for this RocketChat server span from July 24, 2021, to February 26, 2022. The leak also includes many logs from the chat service known as Jabber, including some where Conti hackers discuss hacking a contributor to the OSINT-based investigative journalism group Bellingcat. The hackers were hoping to find information

---

In this section, you learned how to work with flexible data structures that combine dictionaries and lists, including how to pick out specific elements that you're interested in and how to quickly traverse them by looping through them. These skills will often prove useful when you're writing Python scripts to help you analyze data.

Now that you're familiar with data structures that combine dictionaries and lists, it's time to create your own to map out the CSV files in BlueLeaks.

## Exercise 8-5: Map Out the CSVs in BlueLeaks

Each folder in BlueLeaks includes data from a single hacked law enforcement website in the form of hundreds of CSV files. These files contain some of the most interesting information in all of BlueLeaks, such as the contents of bulk email that fusion centers sent to local cops, or "suspicious activity reports." In this exercise, you'll construct a map of the contents of the dataset.

By manually looking in different BlueLeaks folders, I noticed that each folder seems to have a file called *Company.csv* (each containing different content), but only one folder, *ncric*, has a file called *911Centers.csv*. Clearly, not all of the BlueLeaks sites have the same data. Which CSV files are in every folder in BlueLeaks, which are in some folders, and which are unique to a single folder? Let's write a Python script to find out.

As with most programming problems, there are multiple ways you could write a script that answers this question. If you feel comfortable enough with Python by now that you'd like a challenge, try writing one on your own. Otherwise, follow along with this exercise. Either way, the program must meet the following requirements:

- Make the script accept an argument called `blueleaks_path` using Click.
- Create an empty dictionary called `csv_to_folders`. Your script should fill this dictionary with data. The keys should be CSV filenames,

and the values should be lists of BlueLeaks folders that contain this CSV.

- Loop through all of the files and folders in blueleaks_path. For each folder, loop through all of the files it contains. For each CSV file, add data to the csv_to_folders dictionary.
- Display the contents of the csv_to_folders dictionary.

In each step that follows, I'll quote a snippet of code, explain how it works, and give you a chance to run it as is. You'll then add more features to that code and run it again. It's good practice to write code in small batches, pausing frequently to test that it works as you expect. This will help you catch bugs early, making the process of debugging much simpler.

### Accept a Command Line Argument

Create an *exercise-8-5.py* file and enter the Python template:

```
def main():
    pass


if __name__ == "__main__":
    main()
```

Next, instead of hardcoding the path to the BlueLeaks data like you did in Exercise 8-2, let's use Click to pass in the path as a command line argument, blueleaks_path. To do so, make the following modifications to your code (the added syntax is highlighted in bold):

```
import click


@click.command()
@click.argument("blueleaks_path")
def main(blueleaks_path):
    """Map out the CSVs in BlueLeaks"""
    print(f"blueleaks_path is: {blueleaks_path}")


if __name__ == "__main__":
    main()
```

This code modifies the template to import the click module, adds the correct decorators before the main() function, adds the blueleaks_path argument to the main() function, and adds a simple docstring to the main() function so that running this script with --help will be more useful. Finally, it includes a line to display the value of blueleaks_path, so that you can confirm the code is working when you run it.

Try running your script with --help to see if the help text works, and with a value for blueleaks_path to see if the argument is successfully sent to the main() function:

```
micah@trapdoor chapter-8 % python3 exercise-8-5.py --help
Usage: exercise-8-4.py [OPTIONS] BLUELEAKS_PATH

  Map out the CSVs in BlueLeaks

Options:
  --help  Show this message and exit.
micah@trapdoor chapter-8 % python3 exercise-8-5.py test-path
blueleaks_path is: test-path
```

If your output looks like this, everything is working correctly so far.

## Loop Through the BlueLeaks Folders

Now that you can use the blueleaks_path CLI argument, make the following modifications to your code to have it loop through all of the folders it finds in that path:

```python
import click
import os

@click.command()
@click.argument("blueleaks_path")
def main(blueleaks_path):
    """Map out the CSVs in BlueLeaks"""
    for folder in os.listdir(blueleaks_path):
        blueleaks_folder_path = os.path.join(blueleaks_path, folder)

        if os.path.isdir(blueleaks_folder_path):
            print(f"folder: {folder}, path: {blueleaks_folder_path}")

if __name__ == "__main__":
    main()
```

First, you import the os module in order to be able to list all of the files in the *BlueLeaks-extracted* folder using the os.listdir() function. Inside the main() function, a for loop loops through the return value of os.listdir (blueleaks_path), the list of filenames inside the folder at blueleaks_path.

Inside the loop, the code defines blueleaks_folder_path as the path of the specific BlueLeaks folder for the current loop. For example, if the value of blueleaks_path is */Volumes/datasets/BlueLeaks-extracted*, and at this point in the for loop, the value of folder is *icefishx*, then the value of blueleaks_folder_path will be */Volumes/datasets/BlueLeaks-extracted/icefishx*.

You want to look inside subfolders in the *BlueLeaks-extracted* folder, not inside files. If there are any files in that folder, you want to skip them. To meet these requirements, the code includes an if statement that checks whether blueleaks_folder_path is actually a folder. Finally, the code displays the current value of folder and blueleaks_folder_path.

Run your script again. This time, pass in the real path to your *BlueLeaks -extracted* folder:

```
micah@trapdoor chapter-8 % python3 exercise-8-5.py /Volumes/datasets/BlueLeaks-extracted
folder: bostonbric, path: /Volumes/datasets/BlueLeaks-extracted/bostonbric
folder: terrorismtip, path: /Volumes/datasets/BlueLeaks-extracted/terrorismtip
folder: ociac, path: /Volumes/datasets/BlueLeaks-extracted/ociac
--snip--
```

The output should show that the folder variable holds just the name of the folder, like *bostonbric*, and the blueleaks_folder_path variable includes the full path to that folder, like */Volumes/datasets/BlueLeaks-extracted/bostonbric*. When you run this on your own computer, you may see these values in a different order than what's shown here.

### Fill Up the Dictionary

You now have a script that accepts blueleaks_path as an argument and then loops through every folder in that path. Adding the code in bold creates the csv_to_folders dictionary and starts to fill it up with data:

```
import click
import os

@click.command()
@click.argument("blueleaks_path")
def main(blueleaks_path):
    """Map out the CSVs in BlueLeaks"""
    csv_to_folders = {}

    for folder in os.listdir(blueleaks_path):
        blueleaks_folder_path = os.path.join(blueleaks_path, folder)

        if os.path.isdir(blueleaks_folder_path):
            for filename in os.listdir(blueleaks_folder_path):
                if filename.lower().endswith(".csv"):
                    if filename not in csv_to_folders:
                        csv_to_folders[filename] = []

                    csv_to_folders[filename].append(folder)

if __name__ == "__main__":
    main()
```

Your goal with this script is to map out which CSV files are in which BlueLeaks folders. To store this data, the code creates the empty dictionary csv_to_folders at the top of the main() function. The next step is to fill up that dictionary.

The code loops through all of the filenames in blueleaks_path, checking each to see if it's a folder. Removing the print() statement in the previous iteration of the code, this code instead adds a second for loop that loops through all of the files in that specific BlueLeaks folder.

In this second for loop, an if statement checks whether the filename ends in *.csv*. This if statement calls the lower() method on the filename string, which returns a lowercase-only version of the string. The code then calls the endswith() method on that lowercase string, which returns a Boolean describing whether the string ends with the string that was passed in. If the string filename ends with *.csv*, *.CSV*, or *.cSv*, the lower() method will convert the file extension to *.csv*, and endswith() will return True. If filename ends with anything else, like *.docx*, then endswith() will return False.

Each time the code following this if statement runs, it means the program has found a CSV (called filename) in the current BlueLeaks folder (called folder). You want csv_to_folders to be a dictionary where the keys are CSV filenames and the values are lists of folders. This code checks to see if the key filename has been created in csv_to_folders, and if it hasn't, creates it and set its value to an empty list ([]). Finally, after the code has confirmed that the filename key has been created and is a list, it appends the value of folder to that list.

These last lines are tricky, so let's dig in a little more. The first time the script comes across a CSV filename (like *CatalogRelated.csv*), the script sets the value of that key in csv_to_folders to an empty list. If the same filename exists in another BlueLeaks folder later on, the expression filename not in csv_to_folders will evaluate to False (meaning csv_to_folders["CatalogRelated .csv"] already exists), so the code following the if statement won't run. Finally, the code appends folder, the name of the BlueLeaks folder it's currently looking in, to the list of folders that include that filename.

Pause and try running the script so far:

```
micah@trapdoor chapter-8 % python3 exercise-8-5.py /Volumes/datasets/BlueLeaks-extracted
```

This should take a moment to run but displays nothing, since you're not yet using the print() function anywhere. The code is simply creating the csv_to_folders dictionary and filling it up with data.

### Display the Output

By the time the previous version of the script runs, the csv_to_folders dictionary should contain a complete set of CSV filenames, mapped to the BlueLeaks sites where they were found. The following code should show you what the program found:

```
import click
import os

@click.command()
@click.argument("blueleaks_path")
def main(blueleaks_path):
    """Map out the CSVs in BlueLeaks"""
    csv_to_folders = {}

    for folder in os.listdir(blueleaks_path):
        blueleaks_folder_path = os.path.join(blueleaks_path, folder)
```

```
        if os.path.isdir(blueleaks_folder_path):
            for filename in os.listdir(blueleaks_folder_path):
                if filename.lower().endswith(".csv"):
                    if filename not in csv_to_folders:
                        csv_to_folders[filename] = []

                    csv_to_folders[filename].append(folder)

    for filename in csv_to_folders:
        print(f"{len(csv_to_folders[filename])} folders | {filename}")

if __name__ == "__main__":
    main()
```

The added code in bold loops through all of the keys (each a CSV filename) in csv_to_folders, then displays the number of BlueLeaks folders that contain that file (len(csv_to_folders[filename])) along with the filename itself.

You can find this final script at *https://github.com/micahflee/hacks-leaks-and-revelations/blob/main/chapter-8/exercise-8-5.py*. When you run it, the output should look like this:

```
micah@trapdoor chapter-8 % python3 exercise-8-5.py /Volumes/datasets/BlueLeaks-extracted
161 folders | CatalogRelated.csv
161 folders | Blog.csv
161 folders | EmailBuilderOptions.csv
--snip--
1 folders | HIDTAAgentCategory.csv
1 folders | Lost.csv
1 folders | AgencyContacts.csv
```

Since this script displays the number of folders at the beginning of each line of output, you can pipe the output into sort -n to sort it numerically in ascending order, like so:

```
micah@trapdoor chapter-8 % python3 exercise-8-5.py /Volumes/datasets/BlueLeaks-extracted | sort
-n
1 folders | 1Cadets.csv
1 folders | 1Mentors.csv
1 folders | 1Unit.csv
--snip--
161 folders | VideoDownload.csv
161 folders | VideoHistory.csv
161 folders | VideoOptions.csv
```

Most of the CSV files are in either a single folder or all 161 folders. However, there are a few exceptions: *Donations.csv* should be in 10 folders, *SARs.csv* should be in 25, and so on. This information would have taken you many hours of busywork to find manually.

At this point, you've learned the basics of navigating the filesystem in Python. You've seen how to loop through folders using os.listdir(), loop through entire folder structures using os.walk(), and look up information about the files and folders you find. In the next section, you'll learn how to actually read the contents of a file you find and create new files yourself.

# Reading and Writing Files

To follow the rest of this book, you'll need to know one more major Python concept: how to read and write files. During a data investigation, you'll almost certainly need to read the contents of files, especially CSV and JSON files. You'll also probably want to be able to create new files, by calculating some data of your own and saving it to a spreadsheet, for example. In this section you'll learn how to open files and write or read content to them.

In programming, to work with a file, you first need to open it and specify the *mode*—that is, whether you're planning on *reading* from or *writing* to this file. To open an existing file and access its contents, open it for reading using mode r. To create a new file and put data in it, open it for writing using mode w.

## Opening Files

To prepare to work with a file, whether for writing or reading, you use the built-in Python function open(). To open it for reading, you use the following code:

```
with open("some_file.txt", "r") as f:
    text = f.read()
```

This code uses a with statement, which tells Python that after the open() function is done running, it should set the variable f to that function's return value. The f variable is a *file object*, a type of variable that allows you to read or write data to a file. The first argument to the open() function is a path, and the second argument is the mode, which in this example is "r" for reading.

In the code block after the with statement, you can call methods on f to interact with the file. For example, f.read() will read all of the data in the file and return it—in this case, storing it in the text variable.

To open a file for writing, you set the mode to "w" like so:

```
with open("output.txt", "w") as f:
    f.write("hello world")
```

The open() function returns the file object f. To write data into the file, you can use the f.write() method. Here, this code is opening a file called *output.txt* and writing the string hello world to it.

In the next two sections, you'll learn more about using f.write() to write to files and f.read() and f.readlines() to read from files.

## Writing Lines to a File

Text files are made up of a series of individual characters. Consider a text file with these contents:

```
Hello World
Hola Mundo
```

You could also represent the entire contents of this file as a Python string:

```
"Hello World\nHola Mundo\n"
```

The first character of the string is H, then e, then l, and so on. The 12th character (counting the space), \n, is a special character known as a *newline* that represents a break between lines. As with shell scripting, the backslash is the escape character in Python, so a backslash followed by another character represents a single special character.

Newlines are used to write lines to a file. Try running these commands in your Python interpreter:

```
>>> with open("output.txt", "w") as f:
...     f.write("Hello World\n")
...     f.write("Hola Mundo\n")
...
12
11
```

The 12 and 11 in the output represent the number of bytes written. The first f.write() call wrote 12 bytes, because the string Hello World takes 11 bytes of memory: it has 11 characters, plus 1 for the newline character. The second call wrote 11 bytes, since Hola Mundo takes 10 bytes of memory, plus 1 for the newline character.

In your terminal, use the following command to view the file you just wrote:

```
micah@trapdoor ~ % cat output.txt
Hello World
Hola Mundo
```

If you had written the same code but without the newlines, the output would have been Hello WorldHola Mundo, with no line breaks.

## Reading Lines from a File

Run the following command to read the file you just created:

```
>>> with open("output.txt", "r") as f:
...     text = f.read()
...
```

This code reads all of the data from the file and saves it in the string text. In fact, this might look familiar: earlier in this chapter, in the "Exploring Dictionaries and Lists Full of Data in Python" section, we used similar code to load the leaked Conti chat logs into a Python dictionary.

Since splitting text files into multiple lines is so common, file objects also have a convenient method called `readlines()`. Instead of reading all of the data into a file, it reads only one line at a time, and you can loop over the lines in a `for` loop. Try this out by running the following commands:

```
>>> with open("/tmp/output.txt", "r") as f:
...     for line in f.readlines():
...         print(line)
...
Hello World

Hola Mundo
```

This code opens the file for reading, then loops through each line in the file. Each line is stored in the variable `line`, then displayed with the `print()` function. Because the `line` variable in each loop ends in `\n` (for example, the first line is `Hello World\n`, not `Hello World`), and the `print()` function automatically adds an extra `\n`, the output shows an extra hard return after each line.

If you don't want to display these extra newlines, you can use the `strip()` method to get rid of any whitespace (spaces, tabs, or newlines) from the beginning and end of the string. Run the same code, but this time strip out the newline characters on each line:

```
>>> with open("/tmp/output.txt", "r") as f:
...     for line in f.readlines():
...         line = line.strip()
...         print(line)
...
Hello World
Hola Mundo
```

You'll practice the basics of how to read and write files in Python in the following exercise.

## Exercise 8-6: Practice Reading and Writing Files

In Exercise 7-5, you wrote a function that converts a string to an alternating caps version, like `This book is amazing` to `ThIs bOoK Is aMaZiNg`. To practice your newfound reading and writing files, in this exercise, you'll write a script to create an alternating caps version of all of the text in an entire text file.

If you'd like a challenge, you can try programming your own script to meet the following requirements:

- Accepts two arguments, input_filename and output_filename, using Click
- Opens the file input_filename for reading and loads its contents into the string text
- Opens the file output_filename for writing and saves the alternating caps version of text to that new file

Otherwise, follow along with my explanation of the following code, which implements this iNcReDiBlY uSeFuL command line program.

Start by copying the alternating_caps() function that you wrote in Exercise 7-5 into a new Python script called *exercise-8-6.py*. Next, make the modifications highlighted in bold here (or copy the final script at *https://github.com/micahflee/hacks-leaks-and-revelations/blob/main/chapter-8/exercise-8-6.py*):

```python
import click

def alternating_caps(text):
    """Returns an aLtErNaTiNg cApS version of text"""
    alternating_caps_text = ""
    should_be_capital = True

    for character in text:
        if should_be_capital:
            alternating_caps_text += character.upper()
            should_be_capital = False
        else:
            alternating_caps_text += character.lower()
            should_be_capital = True

    return alternating_caps_text

@click.command()
@click.argument("input_filename")
@click.argument("output_filename")
def main(input_filename, output_filename):
    """Converts a text file to an aLtErNaTiNg cApS version"""
    with open(input_filename, "r") as f:
        text = f.read()

    with open(output_filename, "w") as f:
        f.write(alternating_caps(text))

if __name__ == "__main__":
    main()
```

This code first imports the click module, used for the arguments, and then defines the alternating_caps() function. Again, the main() function is a Click command, but this time it takes two arguments, input_filename and output_filename.

Once the `main()` function runs, the section for reading and writing files runs. The code opens `input_filename` for reading and loads all of the contents of that file into the string `text`. It then opens `output_filename` for writing and saves the alternating caps version of that string into the new file. It does so by running `alternating_caps(text)`, which takes `text` as an argument and returns its alternating caps version, and then passes that return value directly into `f.write()`, writing it to the file.

To demonstrate how this script works, try running it on the famous "To be, or not to be" soliloquy from *Hamlet*. First, save a copy of the soliloquy found at *https://github.com/micahflee/hacks-leaks-and-revelations/blob/main/chapter-8/shakespeare.txt* to a file called *shakespeare.txt*. Here are the original contents of *shakespeare.txt*, displayed using the cat command:

```
micah@trapdoor chapter-8 % cat shakespeare.txt
To be, or not to be, that is the question:
Whether 'tis nobler in the mind to suffer
The slings and arrows of outrageous fortune,
Or to take Arms against a Sea of troubles,
And by opposing end them: to die, to sleep
No more; and by a sleep, to say we end
--snip--
```

Next, pass that filename into your script to create an alternating caps version of that file. Here's what happens when I do it:

```
micah@trapdoor chapter-8 % python3 exercise-8-5.py shakespeare.txt shakespeare-mocking.txt
micah@trapdoor chapter-8 % cat shakespeare-mocking.txt
To bE, oR NoT To bE, tHaT Is tHe qUeStIoN:
wHeThEr 'TiS NoBlEr iN ThE MiNd tO SuFfEr
tHe sLiNgS AnD ArRoWs oF OuTrAgEoUs fOrTuNe,
Or tO TaKe aRmS AgAiNsT A SeA Of tRoUbLeS,
aNd bY OpPoSiNg eNd tHeM: tO DiE, tO SlEeP
No mOrE; aNd bY A SlEeP, tO SaY We eNd
--snip--
```

First, I ran the script, passing in *shakespeare.txt* as `input_filename` and *shakespeare-mocking.txt* as `output_filename`. The script itself displayed no output (it doesn't include any `print()` statements), but it did create a new file. I then used cat to display the contents of that new file, which is indeed an alternating caps version of Hamlet's soliloquy.

## Summary

Congratulations on making it through a crash course in the fundamentals of Python programming! You've learned how to bring extra functionality to your scripts with built-in and third-party Python modules. You've also learned how to make your own CLI programs using Click, how to write code that traverses the filesystem, how to work with structured data using dictionaries and lists, and how to read and write files.

You'll use these skills throughout the following chapters as you dig through various datasets, uncovering revelations you'd never discover otherwise. In the next chapter, you'll write Python programs that loop through rows in the BlueLeaks CSV spreadsheets, transforming the data into a more workable format. You'll get practice writing the content of law enforcement bulk email messages to files, and you'll use Python to create your own CSV spreadsheets.

# PART IV

## STRUCTURED DATA

# 9

## BLUELEAKS, BLACK LIVES MATTER, AND THE CSV FILE FORMAT

The BlueLeaks dataset is full of an overwhelming number of documents, but it's not immediately obvious where to start or how to make sense of the data they contain. Before beginning an investigation, I needed a way to efficiently determine the significance of these documents. After manually digging through many files, I discovered that the context I needed was in the hundreds of CSV spreadsheets in each BlueLeaks folder. In this chapter, you'll learn how to investigate CSV files like these yourself.

You'll view CSVs in both graphical spreadsheet and text editing software, write Python code to loop through the rows of a CSV, and save CSVs of your own. You'll then put this knowledge into practice by digging through the CSVs in the BlueLeaks dataset, focusing on data from the NCRIC fusion center. This is the data I myself have primarily focused on since BlueLeaks was published years ago, but there are over a hundred other folders in the dataset full of newsworthy revelations. By the end of this chapter, you'll have the tools to continue investigating these folders, as well as similar datasets loaded with CSVs.

## Installing Spreadsheet Software

The most user-friendly way to view the contents of a CSV file is to open it using spreadsheet software such as LibreOffice Calc, Microsoft Excel, Apple Numbers, or Google Sheets. Spreadsheet software is a great option to see the data you're dealing with in an organized way, and it can also be a powerful tool to analyze CSVs. However, in many cases, depending on the data you're working with, you'll need to go beyond such software and write custom code to work with CSVs.

If you already have a favorite spreadsheet program, you can use that for the projects in this book. If not, I suggest using LibreOffice Calc since it's free, open source, and available for Windows, macOS, and Linux; it's also what I've used for the examples in this chapter. Installing LibreOffice (*https://www.libreoffice.org*) installs a whole suite of office software, including Calc.

Alternatively, Microsoft Excel is a good option, but it costs money and isn't available for Linux. If you have a Mac, you can also use Apple's free spreadsheet software, Numbers. Finally, you can consider using Google Sheets, the spreadsheet feature of Google Docs. Google Docs is free and works in Windows, macOS, and Linux, since it's web-based. The problem with Google Sheets and any other cloud-based spreadsheet software (like the web-based version of Microsoft Excel) is that you have to upload a copy of your CSV file to a third-party service before you can view it. For public datasets like BlueLeaks, this is okay. However, it's better to use desktop spreadsheet software when you're dealing with more sensitive datasets.

Spreadsheet software, when used with more complicated spreadsheet formats such as Microsoft Excel files (*.xlsx*) or ODF Spreadsheet files (*.ods*), is powerful and feature-rich. It can do math, like summing all of the values in a column, and visualize data, like creating pie charts or line graphs. None of these features are supported in CSV files, though, so I won't discuss them in this book.

Once you have your spreadsheet software installed, you're ready to learn more about the structure of CSV files.

## Introducing the CSV File Format

You can think of spreadsheets as tables of data. The top row normally has headers for each column, and the rest of the rows represent data that matches those headers. CSV is the simplest spreadsheet format. You can open CSV files using software like Microsoft Excel or LibreOffice Calc, or you can view them in a text editor and use CLI tools like grep to search them.

BlueLeaks is full of CSV files, but the original data from the fusion center websites wasn't in that format. The BlueLeaks dataset includes source code for those websites, and by reviewing that, I discovered that each site had actually stored its data in a Microsoft Access database file. The BlueLeaks hacker exported tables from the Access databases and saved that data in CSV format before leaking it to DDoSecrets.

CSV files are simply text files made up of multiple lines representing rows in a table. Each line contains a list of values, usually separated by commas (hence the name *comma-separated values*), with each value representing a *cell* in the spreadsheet. Sometimes a spreadsheet row is referred to as a *record*, with each cell in that row referred to as a *field* in that record. Typically, each row contains the same number of cells.

Here's an example CSV file called *city-populations.csv*:

```
City,Country,Population
Tōkyō,Japan,37400000
Delhi,India,28514000
Shanghai,China,25582000
São Paulo,Brazil,21650000
Mexico City,Mexico,21581000
Cairo,Egypt,20076000
```

You can find a copy of this file in the book's GitHub repository at *https://github.com/micahflee/hacks-leaks-and-revelations/blob/main/chapter-9/city-populations.csv*. I'll use this file as an example CSV later in this chapter, so download it now (or re-enter it) and save it in a folder for this chapter's exercises.

Table 9-1 shows the data from the *city-populations.csv* file organized into rows and columns.

**Table 9-1:** City Populations

| City | Country | Population |
| --- | --- | --- |
| Tōkyō | Japan | 37,400,000 |
| Delhi | India | 28,514,000 |
| Shanghai | China | 25,582,000 |
| São Paulo | Brazil | 21,650,000 |
| Mexico City | Mexico | 21,581,000 |
| Cairo | Egypt | 20,076,000 |

When a value includes commas, it must be surrounded by quotation marks. For example, the values "Hello, World" and "Hola, Mundo" both contain commas. Here's how they look in a CSV file along with fields for their respective languages:

```
Language,Greeting
English,"Hello, World"
Español,"Hola, Mundo"
```

Table 9-2 shows this data organized into rows and columns.

**Table 9-2:** Translations of "Hello, World"

| Language | Greeting |
|----------|----------|
| English | Hello, World |
| Español | Hola, Mundo |

It's common to enclose every value in quotes, regardless of whether it includes commas. Here's another version of the previous spreadsheet, now with every value in quotes:

```
"Language","Greeting"
"English","Hello, World"
"Español","Hola, Mundo"
```

As with shell scripting and Python programming, you can escape quotes in CSVs by using a backslash and double quotes (\"). For example, the value `"Not I,"` said the cow contains both quotes and commas, so to add it to a CSV file you would surround the entire value in quotes and escape the inner quotes, like this:

```
"\"Not I,\" said the cow"
```

Because the CSV file format is so simple, it's one of the most commonly used spreadsheet formats, especially for anyone working with spreadsheets using code. Like CSVs, SQL databases also store *tabular data* (data that can be represented in a table), so CSVs are a convenient format for exporting tables from them. In fact, all of the CSVs in BlueLeaks are exported SQL tables from the databases that power law enforcement and fusion center websites. (You'll learn about SQL databases in Chapter 12; for now, you'll work with the exported CSVs.)

Now that you understand a bit about the CSV file format, let's take a look at some real CSV data from BlueLeaks.

## Exploring CSV Files with Spreadsheet Software and Text Editors

In your graphical file browser (such as Explorer in Windows or Finder in macOS), browse to the *BlueLeaks-extracted* folder on your USB disk. You'll start by examining the *dediac* subfolder, which contains data from the Delaware Information Analysis Center. Scroll through the files in this folder—nearly all of them are CSVs—and open *Documents.csv* in your graphical spreadsheet software.

When you open a file in LibreOffice Calc or other spreadsheet software, you'll likely be presented with a window asking you to confirm the settings for this CSV. Figure 9-1 shows the window that pops up when I open *Documents.csv* in LibreOffice Calc on my Mac.

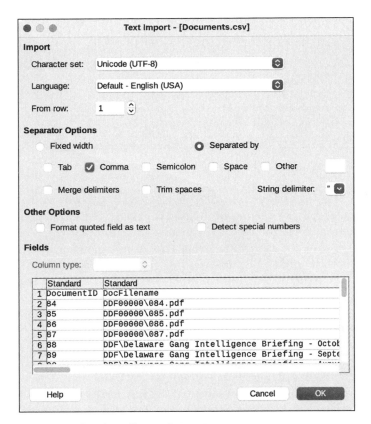

Figure 9-1: The LibreOffice Calc Text Import settings

The most important setting to select is the correct separator character, which is, in this and most cases, a comma (,). Some CSVs separate values with characters other than commas, like semicolons (;) or tabs (\t), though this is rare. In the future if you aren't sure which character your CSV uses, you can open the CSV in a text editor first to check.

Click **OK** to open the spreadsheet. This one should open quickly, but sometimes CSVs are huge—hundreds of mega- or gigabytes—so you may need to wait several seconds, or even minutes, for a large CSV to finish loading.

Figure 9-2 shows part of the *Documents.csv* spreadsheet in LibreOffice Calc.

| | A | B | C | D | E | |
|---|---|---|---|---|---|---|
| 1 | DocumentID | DocFilename | Author | DateEntered | SortOrder | DocTitle |
| 2 | 84 | DDF00000\084.pdf | | 10/21/11 13:40:33 | | Daily Roll-Call Bulletin 102111 |
| 3 | 85 | DDF00000\085.pdf | | 10/24/11 13:40:33 | | Daily Roll-Call Bulletin 102411 |
| 4 | 86 | DDF00000\086.pdf | | 10/25/11 13:40:33 | | Daily Roll-Call Bulletin 102511 |
| 5 | 87 | DDF00000\087.pdf | | 10/26/11 13:40:33 | | Daily Roll-Call Bulletin 102611 |
| 6 | 88 | DDF\Delaware Gang Intelligence Briefing - October 2011.pdf | | 10/14/11 00:00:00 | | Pagans Motorcycle Club - Delaware Gang In |
| 7 | 89 | DDF\Delaware Gang Intelligence Briefing - September 2011.pdf | | 09/08/11 00:00:00 | | Dead Man, Inc. - Delaware Gang Intelligence |
| 8 | 90 | DDF\Delaware Gang Intelligence Briefing - August 2011.pdf | | 08/11/11 00:00:00 | | Crips - Delaware Gang Intelligence Bulletin - |
| 9 | 91 | DDF\Daily Roll-Call Bulletin 102711.pdf | | 10/27/11 15:18:28 | | Daily Roll-Call Bulletin 102711 |
| 10 | 92 | DDF\Threat Assessment Delaware State Fair July 2011.pdf | | 07/05/11 00:00:00 | | Delaware State Fair - 2011 |
| 11 | 93 | DDF\Threat Assessment NASCAR September 2011.pdf | | 09/01/11 00:00:00 | | NASCAR - Sept. 2011 |
| 12 | 94 | DDF\NASCAR May 2011 Threat Assessment.pdf | | 05/16/11 00:00:00 | | NASCAR - May 2011 |
| 13 | 103 | DDF00000\103.pdf | | 10/28/11 11:37:10 | | DHS Daily Infrastructure Bulletin 101911 |
| 14 | 104 | DDF00000\104.pdf | | 10/28/11 11:37:10 | | DHS Daily Infrastructure Bulletin 102011 |

*Figure 9-2: Viewing* Documents.csv *in LibreOffice Calc*

This spreadsheet has 23 columns and 6,934 rows (one of which is the header row). At the top of the file, the dates in the DateEntered column are from 2011. You can find the most recent data in a spreadsheet by *sorting* it, either in ascending (from smaller to bigger) or descending (bigger to smaller) order. I'll show you how to sort this spreadsheet in LibreOffice Calc, but the instructions should be similar for other spreadsheet software and apply to any spreadsheet you want to sort.

First, since you don't want to sort the header row, click **View ▸ Freeze Cells ▸ Freeze First Row**. This should freeze the header row, so now when you scroll up and down, the headers will remain at the top of the file.

Next, you need to pick which column you want to sort by. To see the most recent documents at the top, sort by DateEntered descending. Before sorting this column, you must tell the spreadsheet software that those fields are dates with times and specify how they're formatted (otherwise, the software might assume they're strings and sort them alphabetically). Click column D to select all of the cells in that column and then click **Data ▸ Text to Columns**. This pops up a window that lets you define what type of data is in each column. At the bottom of the window, click the DateEntered column and choose **Date (MDY)** from the Column Type drop-down, because the dates in this data are formatted with month, then date, then year. Click **OK**.

Now that the spreadsheet software knows the correct format for the DateEntered cells, you can sort it by this column. Click the DateEntered header cell to select it (make sure not to select the whole column, just the header cell) and then click **Data ▸ Sort Descending**. This should reorder all of the rows so that the row with the most recent DateEntered is at the top and the one with oldest is at the bottom. In *Documents.csv*, the most recent documents are from June 6, 2020, during the Black Lives Matter protests. Some of the most recent document titles include "Special Bulletin Planned Protests 060620 1800 UPDATE," "ANTIFA Sub Groups and Indicators – LES," and "ANTIFA - Fighting in the Streets."

I often use graphical spreadsheet programs to search CSVs. In LibreOffice, as well as in other spreadsheet programs, you can find specific cells using the Find feature. Press CTRL-F (or, in macOS, ⌘-F), enter your search term, and press ENTER. This should search every cell in the spreadsheet for your term. You can use this method to find a row containing, for example, a specific ID number or email address.

When you close the spreadsheet, don't save your changes. It's good practice to avoid changing original documents in a dataset. If you want to keep a record of your changes, save the file as a copy in either the ODF Spreadsheet (*.ods*) or Excel (*.xlsx*) format.

Now let's look at the same CSV in a text editor instead of spreadsheet software. Here are the first few lines of the *Documents.csv* file, as viewed in a text editor like VS Code:

```
DocumentID,DocFilename,Author,DateEntered,SortOrder,DocTitle,Description,ShortDescription,
PageIdentifier,Keywords,DocumentCategoryID,URLLaunchNewBrowser,URL,Featured,YoutubeLink,
YoutubeVideoName,FrontPageText,YouTubeStartTime,DocFileName2,PreviewImage,ForceSaveAsDialog,
OpenInIframe,DeleteDate
84,"DDF00000\084.pdf",,"10/21/11 13:40:33",,"Daily Roll-Call Bulletin 102111",,,52,,36,0,,0,,,,
,,"DPI00000\084.png",0,0,
85,"DDF00000\085.pdf",,"10/24/11 13:40:33",,"Daily Roll-Call Bulletin 102411",,,79,,36,0,,0,,,,
,,"DPI00000\085.png",0,0,
86,"DDF00000\086.pdf",,"10/25/11 13:40:33",,"Daily Roll-Call Bulletin 102511",,,86,,36,0,,0,,,,
,,"DPI00000\086.png",0,0,
--snip--
```

Because text editors show you only the text when you view a CSV file, without lining up the columns like spreadsheet software does, it's less clear which value matches to which header for each row. There's no simple way to manipulate the data, either—you can't sort it by DateEntered like you can in LibreOffice Calc or Microsoft Excel. However, it's simple to write code that loads the data from CSVs into dictionaries, allowing you to manipulate it in any way you choose, as you'll do later in this chapter.

Now that you're familiar with the structure of CSVs, you're ready to see how I began my investigation into the BlueLeaks dataset.

## My BlueLeaks Investigation

I didn't even realize that my local police intelligence agency, the Northern California Regional Intelligence Center (NCRIC, pronounced "nick-rick"), existed until I discovered it in the BlueLeaks dataset in June 2020. In this section I describe how I went about my investigation into BlueLeaks, what I discovered in the NCRIC portion of the dataset, and a specific revelation I found in one of the NCRIC CSV files.

### Focusing on a Fusion Center

After downloading BlueLeaks, I indexed it in The Intercept's Intella server to make it easier to search. This allowed me and journalists I worked with to quickly search it for keywords and find interesting documents. However, I could tell that searching for keywords would only get me so far. There was so much data that if I only searched terms like *Black Lives Matter*, I was bound to miss a lot of it. Moreover, the searches I did make often led me to CSVs, which would take more work to untangle.

BlueLeaks was split into hundreds of folders, each one belonging to a different law enforcement organization. Since almost all of these organizations were unfamiliar to me, though, I couldn't tell from the names which folder belonged to which organization. I started my own spreadsheet to keep track of this, manually adding rows for each folder as I matched organizations and their websites to it. Eventually, I realized that I could automate this with a Python script.

I also used shell scripting to figure out which folders had the most data, because I guessed they were the largest or most active fusion centers. I quickly discovered that the *ncric* folder, one of the largest in the dataset, held documents for NCRIC, so that's where I decided to focus my digging.

## Introducing NCRIC

NCRIC, based in San Francisco, shares information between federal agencies, local police departments across Northern California, and private industry partners, including tech companies. As I discovered by combing through the CSVs in this dataset, it also provides services to local cops, like monitoring social media or helping break into locked smartphones, and it hosts events and classes for law enforcement officers.

Using a custom tool I developed called BlueLeaks Explorer, which I'll discuss in detail in Chapter 10, I examined everything I could find in the *ncric* folder dated within the 13 days between George Floyd's murder and when NCRIC was hacked. I discovered that twice a day, NCRIC emailed over 14,000 cops an updated list of Black Lives Matter protests. Local police and other partners could also log in to NCRIC's website and submit suspicious activity reports (SARs) to distribute to the fusion center's partners. Local police also requested NCRIC's help with monitoring the social media accounts of protest organizers and, in two instances, with identifying threats against white female teenagers who were facing harassment after making racist statements and using anti-Black slurs.

## Investigating a SAR

By investigating a row from a CSV file, I found a PDF of a scanned letter that turned out to be newsworthy. The letter, written by an unhinged San Francisco–area lawyer to a local district attorney's office, called a polite student from Oregon an "antifa terrorist." In this section, I describe how I found this revelation in BlueLeaks, what it contains, and how the BlueLeaks CSVs reference other documents in the dataset.

When I grepped the CSV files in the *ncric* folder for the word *antifa*, I found that there were only a handful of references in the files *EmailBuilder .csv*, *Requests.csv*, *SARs.csv*, and *Survey.csv*. In particular, this row in *SARs.csv* stood out because it referenced a student protester, allegedly a member of an antifa group, and mentioned "Radicalization/Extremism":

```
micah@trapdoor ncric % grep -ri antifa *.csv
--snip--
SARs.csv:14277,"06/05/20 14:20:09","6/5/2020","Marin","The attached letter was received via US
Postal Service this morning. The letter was passed on from an anonymous party claiming to be a
lawyer who was contacted by [redacted name] who is a University of Oregon student. [Redacted
name] appears to be a member of the Antifa group and is assisting in planning protesting
efforts in the Bay Area despite living in Oregon.","[redacted IP address]",,"NCRICLawEnforceme
ntReporting",,"Unknown",,"[redacted phone number]","f14e1d15-a052-489c-968b-5fd9d38544e1",
"20200596","0820",,"Bay Area",,0,,0,0,0,,0,0,,,0,0,0,0,,,,,"[redacted name]",,,,0,,,,,,,"
[redacted name]","[redacted name]","[redacted name]",,,"Marin County District Attorney's
Office",,,,,"SARF100014\277.pdf",,,,,"- Other -",,,,,,"Letter.pdf",,,,,,,"[redacted]@marincounty
.org","AM","1",,,,,,0,0,"Radicalization/Extremism,Suspicious Incident",,"Emergency
Services,Government Facility",,,"No"
--snip--
```

Looking into the *SARs.csv* file, I found that it lists one month of SARs submitted to NCRIC. The earliest report was May 6, 2020, and the latest was June 6, 2020, so my guess is that NCRIC retains SARs only for a month.

Try opening this file, *ncric/SARs.csv*, in your spreadsheet software, and you'll see that it's difficult to parse. There are 91 different columns, and some of the cells are filled with so much text that even with a large monitor, you can see only part of a row at a time. To make it easier to read, I copied the content of the BriefSummary cell from the spreadsheet and pasted it into my text editor, something that I frequently needed to do with the CSVs in this dataset before I developed BlueLeaks Explorer. Here are the relevant fields from the row that caught my eye:

**SARSid**   14277

**FormTimeStamp**   06/05/20 14:20:09

**IncidentDate**   6/5/2020

**ThreatActivity**   Radicalization/Extremism,Suspicious Incident

**BriefSummary**   The attached letter was received via US Postal Service this morning. The letter was passed on from an anonymous party claiming to be a lawyer who was contacted by *[redacted name]* who is a University of Oregon student. *[Redacted name]* appears to be a member of the Antifa group and is assisting in planning protesting efforts in the Bay Area despite living in Oregon.

**Subjects**   *[redacted name]*

**AgencyOrganizationNameOther**   Marin County District Attorney's Office

**File1**   SARF100014\277.pdf

**File1Name**   Letter.pdf

**EmailAddress**   *[redacted]*@marincounty.org

**PhoneNumber**   *[redacted phone number]*

The SAR listed the full name, email address, and phone number of the person who had submitted it. I looked them up online and discovered that they worked as an investigator for the district attorney's office in Marin County (just north of San Francisco). On June 5 at 2:20 PM (per the FormTimestamp field), the day before NCRIC was hacked, they logged in to the NCRIC website and submitted the SAR form. They included a PDF called *Letter.pdf* (per the File1Name field), though the website saved it in the *SARF100014* folder as *277.pdf* (per the File1 field).

> **NOTE** *The server that hosted NCRIC's website and all of the other BlueLeaks sites was running Windows, which is why folders in paths are separated by backslashes (\ ), like* SARF100014\277.pdf, *instead of forward slashes (/ ).*

Each BlueLeaks folder has a subfolder called *files*, where you can find the files referenced in the CSV. See if you can find the PDF referenced in the File1 field in the *ncric* folder. It should be at the path *ncric/files/ SARF100014/277.pdf* (see Figure 9-3).

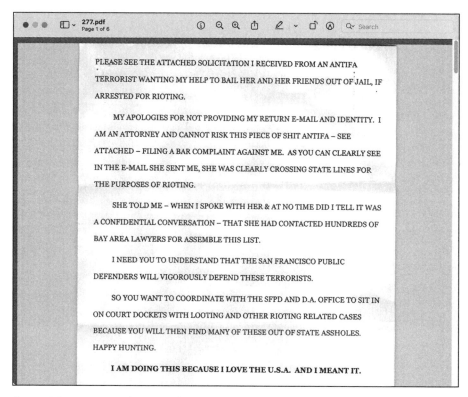

*Figure 9-3: A PDF attachment in the SAR submitted by an investigator from the Marin County DA's office*

The PDF shows a letter in all caps mailed to the Marin County DA's office by a Bay Area attorney: "PLEASE SEE THE ATTACHED SOLICITATION I RECEIVED FROM AN ANTIFA TERRORIST WANTING MY HELP TO BAIL HER AND HER FRIENDS OUT OF JAIL, IF ARRESTED FOR RIOTING." He explained that he was remaining anonymous because he "CANNOT RISK THIS PIECE OF SHIT ANTIFA [. . .] FILING A BAR COMPLAINT AGAINST ME," and warned that "THE SAN FRANCISCO PUBLIC DEFENDERS WILL VIGOROUSLY DEFEND THESE TERRORISTS." He ended his letter, "HAPPY HUNTING."

Further down in the PDF, the attorney included the solicitation from the "antifa terrorist," shown in Figure 9-4.

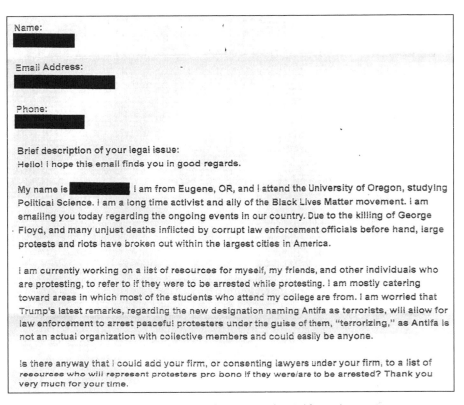

*Figure 9-4: The letter that the Oregon student sent to the California lawyer*

"I am a long time activist and ally of the Black Lives Matter movement," the Oregon student wrote. ". . . Is there anyway [*sic*] that I could add your firm, or consenting lawyers under your firm, to a list of resources who will represent protesters pro bono if they were/are to be arrested? Thank you very much for your time." The Marin County DA investigator apparently believed that this was useful enough intelligence that they logged in to their account on NCRIC's website and submitted it as "suspicious activity" for other law enforcement officers around Northern California to access. Under threat activity, they chose Radicalization/Extremism.

**NOTE** *You can read more about my findings from this SAR in the first article I wrote about BlueLeaks, at* https://theintercept.com/2020/07/15/blueleaks-anonymous -ddos-law-enforcement-hack/. *To learn more about what I discovered while researching NCRIC in general, check out my in-depth article at* https://theintercept .com/2020/08/17/blueleaks-california-ncric-black-lives-matter-protesters/.

In theory, I could have stumbled upon the PDF in Figure 9-3 on its own; I might have just randomly clicked through documents and happened to open *ncric/files/SARF100014/277.pdf*, the path to the PDF in question. I could also have indexed the *ncric* folder in Aleph, OCRing all of the documents, and searched for *antifa*. However, the PDF alone doesn't explain who uploaded it to the NCRIC website, when and why they uploaded it, and how they described the document. Moreover, if you're interested in focusing on activity in the fusion center from a specific time period, it's easier to find which documents are relevant by their timestamps in the CSV files. If you're researching BlueLeaks yourself, you can quickly find all of the documents associated with a time period by sorting the spreadsheets by date, reading all the rows in the CSVs for that time period, and looking at the documents that those rows reference.

Whenever you find an interesting document in BlueLeaks, search the CSVs for its filename to figure out why that document is there to begin with. It could be an attachment in a SAR, part of a bulk-email message the fusion center sent to thousands of local police, or included for other reasons. In the case of *277.pdf*, now you know this document was uploaded as an attachment to a SAR by an investigator in a DA's office. The CSV provides the investigator's summary of the document's contents, along with their contact information, which you can use to reach out to them for comment before publishing your findings.

Now that you've seen the type of data *SARs.csv* contains, you need a way to easily read the long blocks of text in those CSV cells without having to copy and paste them into a text editor. We'll cover that in Exercise 9-1, but first, let's have a quick tutorial on how to write code that works with CSV files.

## Reading and Writing CSV Files in Python

As you learned in Chapter 8, Python modules bring extra functionality into the script that you're writing. It's easy to load CSVs and turn each row into a Python dictionary using Python's built-in csv module. You'll need csv for this chapter's exercises, so import it using the following command:

```
import csv
```

After importing it, you can take advantage of its functionality. The csv features I use the most are csv.DictReader(), which lets you parse rows of a CSV as dictionaries, and csv.DictWriter(), which lets you save your own CSVs from data stored in dictionaries.

The following code loads a CSV file and loops through its rows by using csv.DictReader():

```
with open(csv_path) as f:
    reader = csv.DictReader(f)
    for row in reader:
        print(row)
```

This code assumes the path to the CSV filename is in the `csv_path` variable, which could be a string that you hardcoded or a CLI argument you passed into your program. After opening the CSV file with `open(csv _path)` and storing the file objects as `f`, the code defines a new variable called reader and sets its value to `csv.DictReader(f)`, which prepares you to read rows from this CSV. The `reader` object acts a little like a list of dictionaries, where each dictionary represents a row. Although it's not actually a list, you can use a `for` loop to loop through it as if it were. Inside the `for` loop, `row` is a dictionary that represents the data in a row from the spreadsheet.

The process of saving new CSVs is similar to loading them, except you use `csv.DictWriter()`. For example, the following code uses Python to save the *city-populations.csv* file discussed in the "Introducing the CSV File Format" section earlier in this chapter:

```
headers = ["City", "Country", "Population"]
with open(csv_path, "w") as f:
    writer = csv.DictWriter(f, fieldnames=headers)
    writer.writeheader()
    writer.writerow({"City": "Tōkyō", "Country": "Japan", "Population": 37400000})
    writer.writerow({"City": "Delhi", "Country": "India", "Population": 28514000})
    writer.writerow({"City": "Shanghai", "Country": "China", "Population": 25582000})
    writer.writerow({"City": "São Paulo", "Country": "Brazil", "Population": 21650000})
    writer.writerow({"City": "Mexico City", "Country": "Mexico", "Population": 21581000})
    writer.writerow({"City": "Cairo", "Country": "Egypt", "Population": 20076000})
```

This code first defines the headers of the spreadsheet in the list `headers`, then opens the output file (`csv_path`) for writing. Creating a `csv.DictWriter()` object allows you to save data into the CSV. You must pass the headers in as a keyword argument called `fieldnames`. You must also run `writer .writeheader()`, which saves the header row to the CSV file, before writing any of the data rows.

You can then add rows to the spreadsheet by running `writer.writerow()`, passing in a dictionary whose keys match your headers. For example, the first call of `writer.writerow()` passes in the dictionary `{"City": "Tōkyō", "Country": "Japan", "Population": 37400000}`. The keys for this dictionary are the same as the headers for the CSV: `City`, `Country`, and `Population`.

In the following exercises, you'll use your new CSV programming skills to write scripts that make the data hidden in BlueLeaks CSVs easier to read and understand.

**NOTE** *To learn more about the `csv` module, you can find the full documentation, including plenty of example code, at* https://docs.python.org/3/library/csv.html.

## Exercise 9-1: Make BlueLeaks CSVs More Readable

While it's easier to read *SARs.csv* in a spreadsheet program than in a text editor, it's still quite difficult. As mentioned earlier, there are 91 columns (though most of their values are blank), and some of the text fields, like BriefSummary, contain way too much text to see at one time in a spreadsheet cell. In this exercise, you'll write a script that makes *SARs.csv* (or any CSV with similar content) easier to read by showing you the data a single row at a time.

This exercise is designed not just to show you how to work with the *SARs.csv* file, but to give you practice looping through the rows and fields in a CSV. These skills will come in handy whenever you write code that reads data from CSVs.

For a challenge, you could try programming your own script to meet the following requirements:

- Make this script accept an argument called csv_path using Click, which you first learned to use in Exercise 8-3.

- Import the csv module and loop through all of the rows in the CSV located at csv_path, loading each row as a dictionary, as discussed in the previous section.

- For each row, display all of the *non-empty* values for its columns. If a value is empty, meaning it's an empty string (""), skip it. There's no reason to display all of the columns when so many of them have blank values.

- Display each field on its own line. For example, one line could show SARSid: 14277 and the next line could show FormTimeStamp: 06/05/20 14:20:09.

- Output a separator line like === between each row so that you can tell rows apart.

Alternatively, follow along with the rest of this exercise and I'll walk you through the programming process. Start with the usual Python script template in a file called *exercise-9-1.py*:

```
def main():
    pass

if __name__ == "__main__":
    main()
```

Next, you'll modify your script to accept the csv_path argument.

### Accept the CSV Path as an Argument

Instead of hardcoding the path to a specific CSV, let's use Click to accept the path as an argument. Here's the code that does that (with modifications shown in bold):

```
import click

@click.command()
@click.argument("csv_path")
def main(csv_path):
    """Make BlueLeaks CSVs easier to read"""
    print(f"CSV path: {csv_path}")

if __name__ == "__main__":
    main()
```

Just like in Exercise 8-4, this code imports the click module, adds Click decorators before the main() function to turn it into a command that accepts the csv_path argument, and adds a docstring. For now, it also displays the value of csv_path so you can test if the program works. Run the code to test it as follows:

```
micah@trapdoor chapter-9 % python3 exercise-9-1.py some-csv-path.csv
CSV path: some-csv-path.csv
```

The script just displays the CSV path that was passed in. So far, so good.

## Loop Through the CSV Rows

Next, you'll modify the code to open the CSV in csv_path, and, using the csv module, create a csv.DictReader() object to loop through the rows of that CSV:

```
import click
import csv

@click.command()
@click.argument("csv_path")
def main(csv_path):
    """Make BlueLeaks CSVs easier to read"""
    with open(csv_path, "r") as f:
        reader = csv.DictReader(f)
        for row in reader:
            print(row)

if __name__ == "__main__":
    main()
```

This code now imports the csv module at the top. When the main() function runs, the code opens the file at csv_path for reading, creating a file object variable called f. As noted in "Reading and Writing CSV Files in Python," you can use csv.DictReader() to loop through a CSV file, getting access to each row as a dictionary. The code does this next, creating a variable called reader and setting it equal to csv.DictReader(f). Using reader, the code then loops through each row and displays the dictionary containing its data.

Test the code again, this time passing in the path to *SARs.csv* as the CLI argument. Make sure you use the correct path for your copy of the BlueLeaks dataset:

```
micah@trapdoor chapter-9 % python3 exercise-9-1.py /Volumes/datasets/BlueLeaks-extracted/ncric/
SARs.csv
{'SARSid': '14166', 'FormTimeStamp': '05/14/20 19:15:03', 'IncidentDate': '2020-05-11',
'County': 'Santa Clara', 'BriefSummary': '*INFO ONLY- no action required* \n\nThe San Francisco
PD was contacted by the CIA Threat Management Unit regarding a suspicious write-in to the
CIA\'s public website apparently by a subject [redacted name] (DOB: [redacted birthdate]). See
details below.\n\n-------- Original message --------\nFrom: ADAMCP4 \nDate: 5/13/20 12:17
(GMT-08:00)\nTo: "[redacted name] (POL)" \nSubject: CIA Passing Potential Threat Information\
nThis message is from outside the City email system. Do not open links or attachments from
untrusted sources.\nGood afternoon,\nPer our conversation, Mr. [redacted name] wrote in to
CIA's public website with the following two messages.  A CLEAR report showed Mr. [redacted
name]'s address to be in Dixon, CA.  Dixon, CA police made contact with the Subject's mother
who reported she has not had contact with him in quite some time and last knew him to be in the
Bay area, likely off his medication.  She reported he suffers from bi-polar disorder.
--snip--
```

The output shows that during each loop, the row variable is a dictionary containing the values for that row. So far, the code is simply displaying this whole dictionary. This is a good start, but it still doesn't make the text much easier to read. To do that, you'll display each field on its own row.

### Display CSV Fields on Separate Lines

The following modified code displays each row separately:

```
import click
import csv

@click.command()
@click.argument("csv_path")
def main(csv_path):
    """Make BlueLeaks CSVs easier to read"""
    with open(csv_path, "r") as f:
        reader = csv.DictReader(f)
        for row in reader:
            for key in row:
                if row[key] != "":
                    print(f"{key}: {row[key]}")

            print("===")

if __name__ == "__main__":
    main()
```

Rather than just displaying the row dictionary, this code loops through all of its keys, storing each in the variable key. Since key is the key to the dictionary row, you can look up its value by using row[key]. You only want to display fields that aren't blank, so after making sure that this key doesn't have a blank value, the code displays both it and the value. Finally, after it has finished looping through all of the keys in each row, the code displays the separator === between the rows.

You can find a copy of the complete script at *https://github.com/micahflee/ hacks-leaks-and-revelations/blob/main/chapter-9/exercise-9-1.py*. Run the final script like so:

```
micah@trapdoor chapter-9 % python3 exercise-9-1.py /Volumes/datasets/BlueLeaks-extracted/
ncric/SARs.csv
SARSid: 14166
FormTimeStamp: 05/14/20 19:15:03
IncidentDate: 2020-05-11
County: Santa Clara
BriefSummary: *INFO ONLY- no action required*

The San Francisco PD was contacted by the CIA Threat Management Unit regarding a suspicious
write-in to the CIA's public website apparently by a subject [redacted name] (DOB: [redacted
birthdate]). See details below.

-------- Original message --------
From: ADAMCP4
Date: 5/13/20 12:17 (GMT-08:00)
To: "[redacted name] (POL)"
Subject: CIA Passing Potential Threat Information
This message is from outside the City email system. Do not open links or attachments from
untrusted sources.
Good afternoon,
Per our conversation, Mr. [redacted name] wrote in to CIA's public website with the following
two messages.  A CLEAR report showed Mr. [redacted name]'s address to be in Dixon, CA.  Dixon,
CA police made contact with the Subject's mother who reported she has not had contact with him
in quite some time and last knew him to be in the Bay area, likely off his medication.  She
reported he suffers from bi-polar disorder.
--snip--
ThreatActivityOther: Suspicious write-in received by the CIA
ImpactedEntity: Government Facility
===
SARSid: 14167
FormTimeStamp: 05/15/20 10:46:00
IncidentDate: 5/14/2020
County: Sonoma
BriefSummary: Handheld radio went missing. Radio was in the dozer tender or in the office of
the Santa Rosa shop at station 41. The dozer tender was parked outside of the shop. There has
been unknown individuals seen passing on the compound near the shop. Dozer tender did not
appear to have been broken into. Dozer tender is usually locked but could have been missed
while the operator was off duty. Unsure of when exactly the radio went missing. Could of been
anytime within the last month.
--snip--
```

This time, the output should display === between the rows and display each field of a row on its own line. If there are any blank fields, the program skips them.

Using the command line skills you learned in Chapters 3 and 4, redirect the output into a file with the following command:

```
python3 exercise-9-1.py /Volumes/datasets/BlueLeaks-extracted/ncric/SARs.csv > SARs.txt
```

This should run your script again, this time saving the output into *SARs.txt* instead of displaying it in your terminal. Now you can easily scroll through the saved output in a text editor like VS Code and search it for keywords to learn about the "suspicious activity" that occurred in Northern California from May 6 to June 6, 2020.

Next we'll move on from SARs to explore another important spreadsheet in NCRIC: *EmailBuilder.csv*.

## How to Read Bulk Email from Fusion Centers

The primary purpose of fusion centers is to share information between local, state, and federal law enforcement agencies. They do this, essentially, by sending bulk email to a large list of local police officers. You can find the content of this email for all sites in BlueLeaks, including NCRIC, in the *EmailBuilder.csv* file located in each site's folder. These files include the content of all of the bulk-email messages each fusion center sent until June 6, 2020, when it was hacked.

Some of these messages are security bulletins from federal agencies like the FBI or the Department of Homeland Security (DHS). Others contain content directly created by the fusion center—for example, NCRIC and other fusion centers around the US generated detailed daily lists of protests against police brutality during the summer of 2020. For the 13 days of NCRIC data that I looked at in detail, over half of the bulk email contained information about largely peaceful protests.

The SARs spreadsheet contains plaintext data, so it's easy to read in a text editor. But the bulk-email spreadsheet contains data in HyperText Markup Language (HTML) format, making it difficult to read unless you use a web browser. In this section, you'll learn to more easily read the HTML content of NCRIC's bulk email, find the recipients of each email, and find the documents attached to the email messages. Open *ncric/EmailBuilder.csv* in your spreadsheet software to follow along.

### Lists of Black Lives Matter Demonstrations

Most of the intelligence on Black Lives Matter protests flowed through NCRIC's Terrorism Liaison Officer (TLO) program, whose purpose is to keep the intelligence center's members "engaged & knowledgeable about current terrorist tactics, techniques & trends, regional crime trends & threats, and Officer safety information," according to the TLO page on NCRIC's website. During the summer of 2020, this counterterrorism program didn't focus on terrorism so much as upcoming racial justice protests.

This section describes the twice-daily lists of upcoming protests that TLO sent to thousands of local cops. Not only is this incredibly newsworthy—a counterterrorism program abused to monitor racial justice protests—but these were the most common bulk-email messages that NCRIC sent during the 13-day period I examined.

For example, here are the most interesting fields from the most recent row in *ncric/EmailBuilder.csv* (this CSV has 81 columns in total, most of which didn't contain any relevant information):

**EmailBuilderID**   6170

**EmailFrom**   NCRIC <info@ncric.net>

**EmailSubject**   NCRIC TLO Bulletin LES

**EmailBody**   <base href="https://ncric.ca.gov/"> <font face="Calibri, Times"> UNCLASSIFIED//<font color="#ee0000">LAW ENFORCEMENT SENSITIVE</font></font> [. . .]

**Attachment1**   EBAT1\Events_060620_1800.pdf

**DateSent**   06/06/20 20:25:06

**EmailTable**   Registrations

**SentEmailList**   EBSE00006\170.csv

This row tells us that on the evening of June 6, 2020, NCRIC sent an email with the subject line "NCRIC TLO Bulletin LES" to the list of people described in *EBSE00006\170.csv* (LES stands for Law Enforcement Sensitive). The email included the PDF attachment located at *EBAT1\ Events_060620_1800.pdf*.

The body of the email is the HTML in the EmailBody column. HTML is the markup language that describes web pages, so it can be hard to make sense of when you're not viewing it in a web browser. To read this email body, in your text editor, create a new file called *EmailBuilder -6170.html* (since 6170 is the EmailBuilderID). Copy the content of the EmailBody field from your spreadsheet software for this row, paste it into this file, and save it. You can now open this file in a web browser to view it, but before you do that, you may want to read the "Covering Your Tracks with a VPN Service" box to consider mitigating what information you might leak by opening it.

---

### COVERING YOUR TRACKS WITH A VPN SERVICE

The BlueLeaks CSV files are full of HTML code, such as the EmailBody field in the *EmailBuilder.csv* files. Many of these blocks of HTML include embedded images. If you read through the HTML code in the EmailBody cell in the preceding example, you'll see that it loads an image hosted on NCRIC's server at the

*(continued)*

URL *https://ncric.org/html/Picture2.jpg?135653*. Viewing HTML from BlueLeaks in a web browser makes it much easier to read and understand compared to trying to read the HTML code directly, but it will also cause your computer to make an internet request to the law enforcement servers themselves. These servers will most likely log your IP address, leaving clues that you're investigating them.

For the BlueLeaks dataset, it doesn't matter much if the fusion center servers track your IP address. It's not illegal to load images off of law enforcement websites. For more sensitive datasets, however, it's prudent to hide your IP address from organizations you're investigating. You can load these images while hiding your real IP address by connecting to a *virtual private network (VPN)* service, which reroutes your internet traffic through its own server, then forwards your traffic to those websites. This leaves the VPN server's IP address, rather than your own, in the websites' web logs.

For example, say you load the *EmailBuilder-6170.html* file in your web browser from your home in San Francisco. If you load images hosted on *https://ncric.org*, a San Francisco IP address from a residential neighborhood will show up in the website's logs. The site might be able to determine that this IP address belongs to you by sending a data request to your internet service provider, for example. If you first connect to a VPN, however—one in New York, let's say—then they'll see a New York IP address from a data center in their logs instead. They'll still know that someone loaded the image, but it won't be immediately obvious that *you* loaded the image. Everyone using that VPN service shares its IP address, making it harder to track down individual users.

While VPNs may make you anonymous from the websites you're visiting, they don't make you anonymous from the VPN provider itself. Use a trustworthy VPN provider that you believe isn't logging your traffic and selling it. Additionally, contrary to popular opinion, commercial VPN services don't prevent websites from tracking your browsing habits; that's mostly done using a technology called cookies. In other words, VPNs don't stop the Googles and Facebooks of the world from following you around the web.

*Consumer Reports* publishes in-depth reviews of different VPN services, comparing them on overall privacy and security, whether they've had public security audits, whether they're open source, and whether they include misleading marketing. VPN services normally cost a few dollars a month. For the most part, I recommend avoiding free VPNs; they're nearly all scams set up to spy on their users and sell their data, or even to inject advertisements into web pages users visit. The only exception I know of are VPNs powered by the open source software Bitmask, like the one run by the Seattle-based tech collective Riseup. You can learn more about Bitmask from *https://bitmask.net*, and you can learn about Riseup's free VPN service at *https://riseup.net/en/vpn*.

Whether or not you've connected to a VPN service (the choice is yours), open *EmailBuilder-6170.html* using a web browser by double-clicking on it in your file manager. Figure 9-5 shows what it looks like in a web browser.

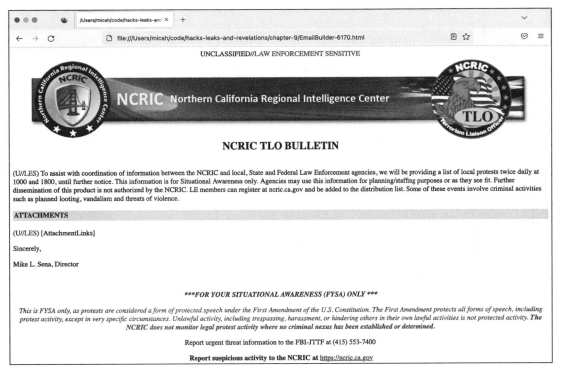

*Figure 9-5: HTML from the EmailBody field in a row of EmailBuilder.csv, viewed in a web browser*

As you can see from the screenshot, this email body is a template, not the email itself. The HTML files stored inside CSVs for BlueLeaks sites are all templates. When sending the email, the NCRIC site would replace [AttachmentLinks] with the actual links to the email attachments as well as replacing other placeholders in the template. The attachments themselves are listed as fields in the CSV.

This email contained one attachment, as noted in the Attachment1 field of the most recent row in *EmailBuilder.csv*: the PDF file *EBAT1\ Events_060620_1800.pdf*. Figure 9-6 shows the first page of that document.

The NCRIC Terrorism Liaison Officer program distributed this list to local police across Northern California. The events included Novato Peaceful Car Caravan, Taking a Knee for Change, and the Noe Valley Police Violence Protest with Social Distancing (the protests took place during the COVID-19 pandemic, after all).

| UNCLASSIFIED//LAW ENFORCEMENT SENSITIVE |
|---|

**\*\*\*FOR YOUR SITUATIONAL AWARENESS (FYSA) ONLY \*\*\***

This is FYSA only, as protests are considered a form of protected speech under the First Amendment of the U.S. Constitution. The First Amendment protects all forms of speech, including protest activity, except in very specific circumstances. Unlawful activity, including trespassing, harassment, or hindering others in their own lawful activities is not protected activity. The NCRIC does not monitor legal protest activity where no criminal nexus has been established or determined.

CAUTION: This document contains raw information currently being evaluated and is for Informational Purposes Only.

### Timeline of Events

| | (This timeline is continually updated and not complete) | | | | Last Date/Time of Update: | | 6/6/2020 17:54 |
|---|---|---|---|---|---|---|---|
| Date | TOPIC | Event Title | Start Time | End Time | Address | City | County |
| 6/6/2020 | Black Lives Matter | Pleasant Hill Black Lives Matter Peaceful Protest | 900 | 1100 | Pleasant Hill PD, 330 Civic Dr | Pleasant Hill | Contra Costa |
| 6/6/2020 | Black Lives Matter | Rally For Justice | 930 | 1030 | Saratoga City Hall, 13777 Fruitvale Ave | Saratoga | Santa Clara |
| 6/6/2020 | Car Caravan | Novato Peaceful Car Caravan | 900 | | Rowland Blvd behind Costco - To S Novato blvd to Downtown Novato | | |
| 6/6/2020 | Family Friendly March | Coastside March to Fight Racism | 1000 | | Pacifica Community Center, 540 Crespi Drive | Pacifica | San Mateo |
| 6/6/2020 | March | Taking a Knee for Change | 1000 | 1200 | Candlestick Park | San Francisco | San Francisco |
| 6/6/2020 | March | African Community March | 1100 | | 901 E Santa Clara St | San Jose | Santa Clara |
| 6/6/2020 | | Noe Valley Police Violence Protest with Social Distancing | 1100 | | Noe Valley | San Francisco | San Francisco |
| 6/6/2020 | clean up | Bay Area Clean Up Rally | 1100 | | | Oakland | Oakland |
| 6/6/2020 | peace and wellness run | peace and wellness run | 1130 | | lake merritt 2300 lakeshore avenue | oakland | Alameda |
| 6/6/2020 | Black Lives Matter | Across the Golden Gate Bridge (Valid Permit) | 1200 | 1400 | Starting on SF side | SF/Marin | SF/Marin |
| 6/6/2020 | | Nationwide Protest | | | 24th & Mission; and DC | San Francisco | San Francisco |
| 6/6/2020 | | walking in unity | 1200 | | ogawa plaza to lake merrit ampitheater | Oakland | Alameda |
| 6/6/2020 | March to PD | Mobilization for Organization | 1200 | | 450 Civic Center Plaza | Richmond | Contra Costa |
| 6/6/2020 | | Palo Alto Peaceful Protest | 1200 | 1330 | Palo Alto City Hall, 250 Hamilton Ave | Palo Alto | Santa Clara |
| 6/6/2020 | Community Youth | Equality Is The Soul Of Liberty | 1200 | 1500 | Palo Alto PD, 250 Hamilton Ave | Palo Alto | Santa Clara |
| 6/6/2020 | Protest | Mill Valley Protest Against Racism/Police Violence | 1200 | | Downtown at the Depot, Down Miller to Safeway | Mill Valley | Marin |

*Figure 9-6: A list of upcoming Black Lives Matter protests in the file* Events_060620_1800.pdf

You can use the SentEmailList and EmailTable values to discover how many, and exactly which, local police officers received these daily bulletins. The value of SentEmailList is the path to a CSV file itself: *EBSE00006\170 .csv*. When you open that CSV file (it's in *ncric/files*), you can see that it has 14,459 rows (one of which is the header) and looks like this:

```
IDs,Registrations
63861
63862
63929
63930
--snip--
```

In short, this CSV contains a huge list of ID numbers. The value of EmailTable in the *EmailBuilder.csv* row is Registrations, which is a good hint. Since I knew that these IDs must match up to rows in some other table, I decided to check the file *Registrations.csv*.

Open that spreadsheet yourself at *ncric/Registrations.csv*. It has 185 columns and over 29,000 rows, apparently listing everyone who had an account on NCRIC's website. It includes each user's full name; the agency they work for and whether it's local, state, federal, or military; their email address, physical address, and cell phone number; their supervisor's name and contact information; their password hash; and other details.

The first column of *Registrations.csv* is called RegistrationsID. Each ID in the *EBSE00006\170.csv* file can be cross-referenced with one of these registrations. For example, the person in *Registrations.csv* with the RegistrationsID 63861 works at the Santa Clara County Sheriff's Office, lives in San Jose, has an email address at the domain pro.sccgov.org, and has a phone number with a 408 area code. In other words, NCRIC sent the email to this list of 14,458 contacts, whose contact details can be found in the *Registrations.csv* file. The BlueLeaks dataset includes this information about everyone who received bulk email through any of the websites. In Exercise 9-3, when you read through bulk email found in BlueLeaks, you'll be able to look up exactly who received these email messages.

## *"Intelligence" Memos from the FBI and DHS*

As mentioned earlier, in addition to detailed lists of upcoming protests, NCRIC also frequently forwarded memos from its federal partners— agencies like the FBI and DHS—to its list of over 14,000 local cops. These memos largely contained internet rumors, hoaxes that had already been debunked but that federal agencies apparently fell for, and warnings about violence from protesters that didn't materialize.

For example, in the row in *EmailBuilder.csv* with the EmailBuilderID of 6169, the email body says, "The NCRIC is disseminating this (U//LES) Update on behalf of the FBI." The Attachment1 value in that row is *EBAT1\SITREP-6-JUN-1300_OPE.pdf*, an unclassified FBI document dated June 6, 2020. The document is full of cherry-picked quotes from social media posts threatening violence, but without any context. There was no way of knowing how many followers an account had, how much engagement their post had, or even if they were parodies.

The "Social Media Exploitation (SOMEX)" section of this FBI document describes people using Facebook, Snapchat, and Instagram to post "flyers seeking to hire 'professional anarchists.'" This appears to reference an internet hoax from late May 2020. In fact, I found multiple articles debunking this hoax on fact-checking sites, including Snopes, PolitiFact, and *Reuters*, dated a week before the FBI distributed this memo. The fake recruitment flyer offers to compensate "professional anarchists" with $200 per direct action, and includes the text "Funded by George Soros." (Antisemitic right-wing Americans frequently and falsely claim that Soros, a Jewish billionaire, funds left-wing protesters.) The flyer also included the phone number for a local branch of the Democratic Party. Both this local Democratic Party branch and Soros's Open Society Foundations confirmed that the flyer was a fake, but this didn't stop the FBI from distributing it to NCRIC, which disseminated it to 14,458 local police across Northern California.

The DHS also sent several memos to NCRIC to distribute to the center's list. For example, take a look at the row in *EmailBuilder.csv* with the EmailBuilderID of 6144. The email body says, "The NCRIC is disseminating the Intelligence Note '(U//FOUO) Some Violent Opportunists Probably Engaging in Organized Activities' on behalf of DHS," and the attached document is *EBAT1\(U—FOUO) IN - Some Violent Opportunists Probably Engaging in Organized Activities 06012020.pdf.*

The attached PDF declares, "As the protests persist, we assess that the organized violent opportunists—including suspected anarchist extremists—could increasingly perpetrate nationwide targeting of law enforcement and critical infrastructure." (This didn't happen.) The memo goes on to say that an NYPD official "had strong evidence that suspected anarchist groups had planned to incite violence at protests, including by using encrypted communications." Incidentally, if you completed Exercise 2-2 and installed Signal, you too are now a user of encrypted communications.

As noted in Chapter 1, it's important to reach out to the people you're investigating to get their side of the story. Mike Sena, NCRIC's executive director, told me that his intelligence agency was monitoring Black Lives Matters protests in order to make sure that they remained safe. "We weren't keeping track of the protests themselves, but we were identifying where we were gonna have gatherings of people," he said. "That's our concern; we want to make sure the events are safe—and if there are any threats that come up that may be associated with any of those events that we're able to get that threat data to whatever agency may have protection responsibilities."

It's also good practice to contact outside experts—those who know more about the subject matter than you do—for comment. Vasudha Talla, a senior staff attorney with the American Civil Liberties Union of Northern California, told me, "Really what we have here is overbroad collection and dissemination of people's protected First Amendment activity, and it's untethered to any basis in the law."

As you can see, there are a lot of newsworthy details in *EmailBuilder.csv*. However, it's still somewhat difficult to work with, especially because of the HTML email bodies. Soon you'll write some code to make all of the bulk email easier to read. To do that, first you will need to learn the basics of HTML.

## A Brief HTML Primer

In the following exercise, you'll write some Python code that in turn writes some HTML code. This section covers just enough HTML syntax to get you through this chapter.

HTML is made up of components called *tags*. For example, consider the following HTML:

```
<p>Hello world</p>
```

This code opens a `<p>` tag (which represents a paragraph), includes some content (the text `Hello world`), and then closes the `<p>` tag with `</p>`. You open a tag with `<tag-name>` and close it with `</tag-name>`.

HTML typically includes tags inside of tags inside of tags. It's common to indent HTML code for legibility, but unlike in Python, indenting is completely optional. Here's an example of a simple web page in HTML, indented to make it easier to read:

```
<html>
    <head>
        <title>My Super Cool Web Page</title>
    </head>
    <body>
        <h1>Under Construction</h1>
        <p>This web page is under construction!</p>
    </body>
</html>
```

The whole page is wrapped in the `<html>` tag. Inside that, there's a `<head>` tag, which includes metadata about the web page, and then a `<body>` tag, which includes the content of the web page. The `<title>` tag is a metadata tag that describes the title of the web page, which is what's displayed in the browser tab itself. Inside the `<body>`, the biggest heading is `<h1>`, followed by a `<p>` paragraph.

There are plenty of other tags in HTML, but in the following exercise, you'll use just two more: `<ul>` and `<li>`. The `<ul>` tag stands for "unordered list," and it's how you make bulleted lists in HTML. Inside the `<ul>` tag are `<li>` tags, which stand for "list item." For example, here's some HTML for a simple bulleted list:

```
<ul>
    <li>Bash</li>
    <li>Python</li>
    <li>HTML</li>
</ul>
```

When displayed in a web browser, that HTML code would look like this:

- Bash
- Python
- HTML

The less-than and greater-than characters (< and >) are used to open and close tags in HTML. If you want to display literal less-than or greater-than characters in HTML, you have to *HTML escape* them. This is similar to escaping in shell scripts and Python code, but the syntax is different. Escape < by replacing it with &lt; and escape > by replacing it with &gt;. For example, here's some HTML code that displays the text I <3 you in a paragraph:

```
<p>I &lt;3 you</p>
```

There are a few other special characters in HTML that are each escaped in their own way. For example, you'd use &amp; to escape an ampersand (&).

In the next exercise, you'll make the email messages in *EmailBuilder.csv* easier to read by writing a script that automatically saves an HTML file for each one. This will also make it much simpler for you to find the newsworthy ones.

## Exercise 9-2: Make Bulk Email Readable

For this exercise, you'll write a script similar to the one you wrote in Exercise 9-1, but instead of displaying text output to the screen, you'll save HTML output to files. This allows you to look through a folder full of HTML files, each one a different bulk email, open these files in a web browser, and read them in a more legible format. While this particular exercise is designed specifically for the *EmailBuilder.csv* files in BlueLeaks, it's common to find HTML in datasets, so being able to write a similar script could help you in the future.

For a challenge, you can try programming your own script to meet the following requirements:

- Make this script accept two arguments called `emailbuilder_csv_path` and `output_folder_path` using Click. The `emailbuilder_csv_path` argument should be the path to an *EmailBuilder.csv* file, and the `output_folder_path` argument should be the path to a folder in which to save the HTML files.

- Make sure the folder at `output_folder_path` exists by importing the os module and running `os.makedirs(output_folder_path, exist_ok=True)`.

- Import the `csv` module and loop through all of the rows in the CSV located at `emailbuilder_csv_path`, loading each row as a dictionary.

- For each row, save a new HTML file. This file should include information from the bulk-email fields most relevant for your purposes: EmailBuilderID, EmailFrom, EmailSubject, DateSent, Attachment1, and SentEmailList. It should also include the HTML body of the email itself, EmailBody.

Otherwise, follow along with the rest of this exercise and I'll walk you through the programming process. Start with the usual Python script template in a file called *exercise-9-2.py*:

```
def main():
    pass


if __name__ == "__main__":
    main()
```

Next, you'll modify your script to make the script accept command line arguments using Click.

### Accept the Command Line Arguments

The following code has been modified to import the `click` module and accept some command line arguments:

```
import click

@click.command()
@click.argument("emailbuilder_csv_path")
@click.argument("output_folder_path")
def main(emailbuilder_csv_path, output_folder_path):
    """Make bulk email in BlueLeaks easier to read"""
    print(f"Path to EmailBuilder.csv: {emailbuilder_csv_path}")
    print(f"Output folder path: {output_folder_path}")

if __name__ == "__main__":
    main()
```

First, the code imports the click module, and then it uses Click decorators to make the main() function a Click command that accepts two arguments, emailbuilder_csv_path and output_folder_path. The code also has two print() statements that display the values of the two arguments. The emailbuilder_csv_path argument should point to the path of a BlueLeaks *EmailBuilder.csv*, which you'll load and loop through, and the output_folder_path argument should be the path to a folder in which you'll store the HTML files for the bulk-email messages.

Test your code and make sure it's working as expected so far, replacing the path to *EmailBuilder.csv* with the appropriate path for your computer:

```
micah@trapdoor chapter-9 % python3 exercise-9-2.py /Volumes/datasets/BlueLeaks-extracted/
ncric/EmailBuilder.csv output
Path to EmailBuilder.csv: /media/micah/datasets/BlueLeaks-extracted/ncric/EmailBuilder.csv
Output folder path: output
```

As expected, the script displays the values of the two arguments.

### Create the Output Folder

Next, use Python to create the folder in output_folder_path where you'll save the HTML files:

```
import click
import os

@click.command()
@click.argument("emailbuilder_csv_path")
@click.argument("output_folder_path")
def main(emailbuilder_csv_path, output_folder_path):
    """Make bulk emails in BlueLeaks easier to read"""
    os.makedirs(output_folder_path, exist_ok=True)

if __name__ == "__main__":
    main()
```

To be able to use the os.makedirs() function, first the script imports the os module. Then it uses the os.makedirs() function to create a new folder in Python, passing in the path to the folder to create, output_folder_path.

The exists_ok=True keyword argument tells this function that it's fine if that folder already exists; otherwise, if the folder already existed, the script would crash with an error message. This way, the first time you run this script with a specific output folder, it will create that folder and use it to store the HTML files. If you run the script again in the future with that same output folder, it will use the folder that's already there.

When you run the complete script at the end of this exercise, you'll be able to browse the files in this folder to read through the bulk-email messages sent by a fusion center.

### Define the Filename for Each Row

The goal of this script is to save an HTML file for each row in the spreadsheet. To do this, you'll need to load the CSV, loop through its rows, and figure out the filename for each HTML file that you're going to save. Next, define the filename variable, naming each HTML file based on data that you found in that row. To do so, make the following modifications:

```
import click
import os
import csv

@click.command()
@click.argument("emailbuilder_csv_path")
@click.argument("output_folder_path")
def main(emailbuilder_csv_path, output_folder_path):
    """Make bulk emails in BlueLeaks easier to read"""
    os.makedirs(output_folder_path, exist_ok=True)

    with open(emailbuilder_csv_path) as f:
        reader = csv.DictReader(f)
        for row in reader:
            filename = (
                f"{row['EmailBuilderID']}_{row['DateSent']}_{row['EmailSubject']}.html"
            )
            filename = filename.replace("/", "-")
            filename = os.path.join(output_folder_path, filename)
            print(filename)


if __name__ == "__main__":
    main()
```

The script starts by importing the csv module. As in the previous exercise, the code then opens the CSV file and creates a CSV reader using csv.DictReader(). Using a for loop, the code loops through each row in the CSV.

Rather than just displaying information, you ultimately want to save each row as an HTML file. To prepare to write the code that actually generates those files in the next section, this code defines a filename variable with the name of the unique HTML file to be generated for each row. In order to make it unique, the code defines filename using the current row's EmailBuilderID, DateSent, and EmailSubject fields, and ends it with the .html file extension. For example, according to this format, the filename for the bulk email described in the previous section would be *6170_06/06/20 20:25:06_NCRIC TLO Bulletin LES.html*.

The code defines filename as an f-string surrounded in double quotes ("). The variables inside it, like row["EmailSubject"], have quotes of their own, but you can't use the double-quote character inside a double-quoted f-string without Python mistakenly thinking you're closing the f-string. Instead, this code uses single quotes (') for the variables within the f-string: row['EmailSubject'].

The slash characters (/) contained in the DateSent column are invalid characters for filenames because slashes separate folders in a path. To address this, the line filename = filename.replace("/", "-") replaces any slashes it finds in the filename with dash characters (-). This generates the valid filename *6170_06-06-20 20:25:06_NCRIC TLO Bulletin LES.html*.

Finally, this code uses os.path.join(), discussed in Chapter 8, to append filename to the end of output_folder_path, giving you the complete path to the file you're going to write. You'll ultimately save the HTML file in this path. For example, if the filename output_folder_path is output and filename is 6170_06-06-20 20:25:06_NCRIC TLO Bulletin LES.html, os.path.join() updates filename to be output/6170_06-06-20 20:25:06_NCRIC TLO Bulletin LES.html.

To make sure everything is working so far, the code displays this final filename. Pause and test your code, using the correct filepath for your operating system:

```
micah@trapdoor chapter-9 % python3 exercise-9-2.py /Volumes/datasets/BlueLeaks-extracted/
ncric/EmailBuilder.csv output
output/4867_09-04-18 09:13:49_2018 CNOA Training Institute.html
output/4868_09-04-18 14:33:27_SMS Important.html
output/4869_09-04-18 14:47:52_Brian SMS from Netsential.html
output/4870_09-05-18 12:57:23_(U--LES) Officer Safety-Welfare Check Bulletin - Wesley Drake
GRIFFIN.html
--snip--
```

The output should show a unique filename for each row in the *EmailBuilder.csv* spreadsheet. All you need to do now is actually write those HTML files.

### Write the HTML Version of Each Bulk Email

The purpose of saving each row of *EmailBuilder.csv* as an HTML file is to more easily read these bulk-email messages by loading the HTML in a web browser. You'll obviously want to see the email body, but it would also be helpful to display some basic metadata about the email: the date it was sent, the subject, and so on. The following code writes the HTML files, automatically filling in both the metadata and the email body with data from the CSV:

```
import click
import os
import csv
import html

@click.command()
@click.argument("emailbuilder_csv_path")
@click.argument("output_folder_path")
def main(emailbuilder_csv_path, output_folder_path):
    """Make bulk emails in BlueLeaks easier to read"""
    os.makedirs(output_folder_path, exist_ok=True)

    important_keys = [
        "EmailBuilderID",
        "EmailFrom",
        "EmailSubject",
        "DateSent",
        "Attachment1",
        "SentEmailList",
    ]

    with open(emailbuilder_csv_path) as f:
        reader = csv.DictReader(f)
        for row in reader:
            filename = f"{row['EmailBuilderID']}_{row['DateSent']}_{row['EmailSubject']}.html"
            filename = filename.replace("/", "-")
            filename = os.path.join(output_folder_path, filename)

            with open(filename, "w") as html_f:
                html_f.write("<html><body>\n")
                html_f.write("<ul>\n")
                for key in important_keys:
                    html_f.write(f"<li>{key}: {html.escape(row[key])}</li>\n")
                html_f.write("</ul>\n")
                html_f.write(f"{row['EmailBody']}\n")
                html_f.write("</body></html>\n")
                print(f"Saved file: {filename}")

if __name__ == "__main__":
    main()
```

First, the code imports the html module, which will be used later on to escape HTML code. The code starts by defining a list, called important_keys, of all of the important keys to include in the final HTML file. This code is positioned near the top of the main() function, before the for loop, so that this variable will be available inside each loop, and therefore every HTML file will include these same fields.

Inside the for loop, the code stores each row of the spreadsheet in the dictionary row, so you can access its fields using keys. Then, the code opens the HTML file for writing with the command with open(filename, "w") as html_f: (as you saw in "Reading and Writing Files" in Chapter 8). The file object for the HTML file is the html_f variable. Inside this with statement, the code then starts writing the HTML file by calling html_f.write() and passing in a string containing HTML, first for <html> and <body> tags and then for a <ul> tag to represent a bulleted list.

Next, the code fills in the bulleted list with the important metadata. Using a for loop, it loops through the keys in important_keys, writing each piece of metadata to the HTML file in its own <li> tag, in the format

---

`<li><strong>`*metadata_item:*`</strong>` *metadata_value*`</li>`

---

where *metadata_item* is the name of an important piece of metadata in key, and *metadata_value* is the value of that piece of metadata in row[key]. For example, *metadata_item* might be EmailBuilderID, and *metadata_value* might be 6170, as in the example CSV row in the "Lists of Black Lives Matter Demonstrations" section.

Instead of displaying the value with row[key], though, this line of code uses html.escape(row[key]). This is necessary because some of the fields you want to include use angle brackets (< and >), which indicate tags in HTML. For example, if the value of the FromEmail field is NCRIC <info@ncric.net>, your web browser will interpret <info@ncric.net> as an HTML tag called info@ncric.net, which isn't a real tag, so nothing will display. In Python, the html.escape() function lets you HTML escape a string. For example, html.escape("NCRIC <info@ncric.net>") returns the string NCRIC &lt;info@ncric .net&gt; and that's what gets saved to the HTML file, so that when you later view that file, the string displays correctly as NCRIC <info@ncric.net>.

When the for loop finishes running, all of the important metadata will have been written to the HTML file. The code then writes </ul> to close the bulleted list tag. After displaying the bulleted list of important fields, the code displays the EmailBody field in a <div> tag. This time, it doesn't HTML escape this field, because you want to load the email's HTML in a browser. Finally, the <body> and <html> tags are closed with </body></html>.

You can find the complete script at *https://github.com/micahflee/hacks-leaks -and-revelations/blob/main/chapter-9/exercise-9-2.py*. This is the most complicated Python script you've written so far in this book, but it's about to pay off. Run it on the NCRIC data, using the filepath appropriate for your operating system:

---

```
micah@trapdoor chapter-9 % python3 exercise-9-2.py /Volumes/datasets/BlueLeaks-extracted/
ncric/EmailBuilder.csv output
Saved file: output/4867_09-04-18 09:13:49_2018 CNOA Training Institute.html
Saved file: output/4868_09-04-18 14:33:27_SMS Important.html
Saved file: output/4869_09-04-18 14:47:52_Brian SMS from Netsential.html
Saved file: output/4870_09-05-18 12:57:23_(U--LES) Officer Safety-Welfare Check Bulletin -
Wesley Drake GRIFFIN.html
--snip--
```

---

This output looks similar to the last time you ran the script, except now it also creates a folder full of 5,213 new HTML files—one for every row of NCRIC's *EmailBuilder.csv* file—in the output folder you specified. The information now included in the filenames allows you to browse through the files in your file manager, exploring those that look most interesting.

Figure 9-7 shows the list of files generated when I ran this script.

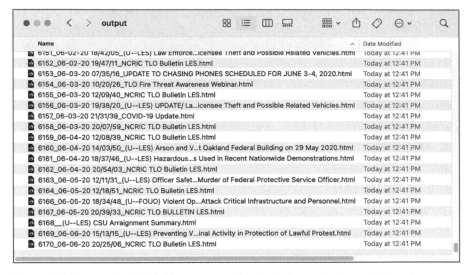

*Figure 9-7: Viewing the HTML files generated by the Python script in macOS Finder*

This folder contains the thousands of HTML files that your Python script just created. The first part of the filename is the EmailBuilderID, followed by DateSent, followed by EmailSubject. To read one of these bulk emails, just double-click the HTML file to open it in a web browser. If you want more information about a specific bulk email, you can always look it up by EmailBuilderID in the original spreadsheet.

To see what the final HTML output looks like, open one of these files in your text editor. For example, here's the final HTML output from the *6098_05-18-20 12/45/12_Chasing Cell Phones presented via Zoom Webinar.html* file:

```
<html><body>
<ul>
<li><strong>EmailBuilderID:</strong> 6098</li>
<li><strong>EmailFrom:</strong> NCRIC &lt;info@ncric.net&gt;</li>
<li><strong>EmailSubject:</strong> Chasing Cell Phones presented via Zoom Webinar</li>
<li><strong>DateSent:</strong> 05/18/20 12:45:12</li>
<li><strong>Attachment1:</strong> </li>
<li><strong>SentEmailList:</strong> EBSE00006\098.csv</li>
</ul>
<div><base href="https://ncric.org/">
<a style="font: bold 15px Arial" target="_blank" href="https://ncric.org/EBForms.aspx?EBID=5499
&EBType=R">- Click Here To Register -</a><br><br><div><div style="font-weight: bold">Chasing
Cell Phones</div>
--snip--
</div>
</body></html>
```

All of the bolded parts have been filled in automatically by the Python code. In the bulleted list at the top, `EmailBuilderID`, `EmailFrom`, and so on are keys from the `important_keys` list, and 6098, NCRIC `&lt;info@ncric.net&gt;`, and so on are HTML-escaped values from the `row` dictionary. Below the bulleted list, inside the `<div>` tag, is the email body—the value of `row["EmailBody"]`.

Figure 9-8 shows what these bulk email messages look like in a web browser. In this case, I opened a bulk email sent out on May 18, 2020, advertising a course called Chasing Cell Phones hosted by the Northern California High Intensity Drug Tracking Area. The class was designed to teach police how to get valuable evidence directly off of suspects' cell phones or from third-party sources like cell phone providers.

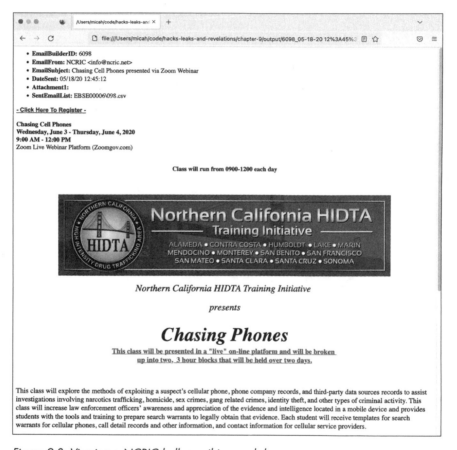

*Figure 9-8: Viewing a NCRIC bulk email in a web browser*

You can use the script from this exercise to make the bulk email from any BlueLeaks folder more readable; just run the script on the appropriate *EmailBuilder.csv* file.

The BlueLeaks folder names alone don't immediately make clear which folders belong to which organizations. Let's fix that by creating a spreadsheet that associates each BlueLeaks folder with its organization name, website title, and URL.

## Discovering the Names and URLs of BlueLeaks Sites

It's obvious what organization some BlueLeaks folders belong to based on the folder name. You can reasonably guess that the *alabamafusioncenter* folder has data from the Alabama Fusion Center. But most aren't so clear. Can you guess what *ciacco* is? How about *nvhidta* or *snorca*?

After manually looking through the CSV files in various BlueLeaks folders, I discovered that the file *Company.csv* contains, hidden among its 108 columns, the name and URL of each site. Some BlueLeaks folders, it turns out, host more than one site. For example, in Table 9-3, which shows these columns from NCRIC's *Company.csv* file, you can see that the *ncric* folder hosts 18 different sites at different URLs.

**Table 9-3:** Data from *ncric/Company.csv*

| CompanyID | CompanyName | WebsiteTitle | URL |
|---|---|---|---|
| 1 | NCRIC.net | Northern California Regional Intelligence Center - NCRIC | ncric.net |
| 2 | NCRIC New | Northern California Regional Intelligence Center - NCRIC | upinsmoke.ncric.net |
| 3 | NCRIC | Northern California Regional Intelligence Center - NCRIC | ncric.org |
| 4 | NCHIDTA | Northern California Regional Intelligence Center - NCRIC | nchidta.org |
| 7 | NCHIDTA.net | Northern California Regional Intelligence Center - NCRIC | nchidta.net |
| 8 | NCRTTAC.org | Northern California Regional Intelligence Center - NCRIC | ncrttac.org |
| 10 | NCRTTAC.org | Northern California Regional Intelligence Center - NCRIC | www.ncrttac.org |
| 11 | Northern California Most Wanted | Northern California Most Wanted - Serving The Bay Area and Surrounding Counties | northerncaliforniamostwanted.org |
| 12 | Northern California Most Wanted | Northern California Most Wanted | northerncaliforniamostwanted.com |
| 14 | Northern California Most Wanted | Northern California Most Wanted | ncmostwanted.org |
| 15 | NCRIC Private Sector Mobile Registration | Northern California Regional Intelligence Center - NCRIC | psp.ncric.net |
| 16 | NCHIDTA.com | Northern California Regional Intelligence Center - NCRIC | nchidta.com |
| 17 | NCRIC | NCRIC Mobile | |
| 19 | NCRIC | Northern California Regional Intelligence Center - NCRIC | passwordreset.ncric.ca.gov |
| 20 | NCHIDTA | NCHIDTA Mobile | |

| CompanyID | CompanyName | WebsiteTitle | URL |
| --- | --- | --- | --- |
| 21 | NCHIDTA (New) | Northern California Regional Intelligence Center - NCRIC | new.nchidta.org |
| 22 | NCRIC | Northern California Regional Intelligence Center - NCRIC | ncric.ca.gov |
| 23 | NCRIC NEW | Northern California Regional Intelligence Center - NCRIC | new.ncric.ca.gov |

As you can see here, the *ncric* folder hosts not only the NCRIC site but also the sites for the Northern California High Intensity Drug Trafficking Area (NCHIDTA); the Northern California Most Wanted, which lists wanted fugitives; and others. However, all these websites share the same code and databases.

Since almost every BlueLeaks folder contains a *Company.csv* file listing all of the sites associated with that folder, we can write a script to automatically extract this information and format it as a CSV file. This will open the door for you to pick which fusion center you want to research—perhaps there's one in a city near you.

## Exercise 9-3: Make a CSV of BlueLeaks Sites

The script you write in this exercise will loop through each BlueLeaks folder, open its *Company.csv* file, and save information about the organizations whose websites are hosted in that folder into a CSV file that you create. For a challenge, you can try programming your own script to do the following:

- Accept two arguments: `blueleaks_path`, the path to your extracted BlueLeaks data, and `output_csv_path`, the path to the new CSV file that the script will create.

- Include these headers: `BlueLeaksFolder` (the BlueLeaks folder name), `CompanyID`, `CompanyName`, `WebsiteTitle`, and `URL` (you'll find these latter fields in the various *Company.csv* files).

- Open `output_csv_path` for writing and create a `csv.DictWriter()` object (see "Reading and Writing CSV Files in Python" on page 248), passing in the file object and the headers.

- Loop through each folder in BlueLeaks. You can get a list of all the file-names with `os.listdir(blueleaks_path)`.

- Inside each BlueLeaks folder, open the *Company.csv* file if it exists, and loop through all of the rows in that CSV. For each row, select the information you want to save and then write it to your CSV.

- Map out exactly what websites each BlueLeaks folder hosts in your output CSV.

Otherwise, the rest of this exercise will walk you through the programming process. Start with the usual Python script template in a file called *exercise-9-3.py*:

```
def main():
    pass

if __name__ == "__main__":
    main()
```

Next, modify your script to accept the blueleaks_path and output_csv_path command line arguments:

```
import click

@click.command()
@click.argument("blueleaks_path")
@click.argument("output_csv_path")
def main(blueleaks_path, output_csv_path):
    """Make a CSV that describes all the BlueLeaks folders"""

if __name__ == "__main__":
    main()
```

You've done this enough times at this point that you can safely assume the arguments are working properly without testing the script.

## Open a CSV for Writing

The simplest way to program this script is to first open a CSV file for writing and then loop through each folder in BlueLeaks, adding rows to this CSV. Start by just opening the CSV file for writing, using the following code:

```
import click
import csv

@click.command()
@click.argument("blueleaks_path")
@click.argument("output_csv_path")
def main(blueleaks_path, output_csv_path):
    """Make a CSV that describes all the BlueLeaks folders"""
    headers = ["BlueLeaksFolder", "CompanyID", "CompanyName", "WebsiteTitle", "URL"]
    with open(output_csv_path, "w") as output_f:
        writer = csv.DictWriter(output_f, fieldnames=headers)
        writer.writeheader()

if __name__ == "__main__":
    main()
```

First, the code imports the csv module. It then defines what the headers of the output CSV will be in the variable headers. As noted in "Reading and

Writing CSV Files in Python," in order to create a `csv.DictWriter()` object, you'll need to pass in this list of headers for your CSV file.

Next, the code opens the output CSV file for writing, this time calling it `output_f`, and creates the `csv.DictWriter()` object, saving it in the `writer` variable. Finally, the program writes the header row to the CSV. To write the remaining rows, you'll need to run `writer.writerow()`, passing in a dictionary that represents the row.

Try running the script so far:

```
micah@trapdoor chapter-9 % python3 exercise-9-3.py /Volumes/datasets/BlueLeaks-extracted sites
.csv
```

The script itself shouldn't display any output; it should just create an output CSV file, *sites.csv*. Try displaying its contents using cat:

```
micah@trapdoor chapter-9 % cat sites.csv
BlueLeaksFolder,CompanyID,CompanyName,WebsiteTitle,URL
```

You should see that the file currently contains only header rows.

### Find All the Company.csv Files

Now that you can write rows to your CSV, the next step is to loop through the BlueLeaks sites, looking for *Company.csv* files, using the following code:

```python
import click
import csv
import os

@click.command()
@click.argument("blueleaks_path")
@click.argument("output_csv_path")
def main(blueleaks_path, output_csv_path):
    """Make a CSV that describes all the BlueLeaks folders"""
    headers = ["BlueLeaksFolder", "CompanyID", "CompanyName", "WebsiteTitle", "URL"]
    with open(output_csv_path, "w") as output_f:
        writer = csv.DictWriter(output_f, fieldnames=headers)
        writer.writeheader()

        for folder_name in os.listdir(blueleaks_path):
            company_csv_path = os.path.join(blueleaks_path, folder_name, "Company.csv")
            if os.path.exists(company_csv_path):
                print(company_csv_path)

if __name__ == "__main__":
    main()
```

This code imports the os module. After creating the CSV writer, it loops through the return value of the `os.listdir()` function, which returns a list of all the files inside the BlueLeaks folder. It then defines a new company_csv _path variable as the path to the *Company.csv* file inside that BlueLeaks folder. Finally, the os.path.exists() function makes sure that this specific *Company.csv* file actually exists, and if so, the code displays its path. Try running the code so far:

```
micah@trapdoor chapter-9 % python3 exercise-9-3.py /Volumes/datasets/BlueLeaks-extracted sites
.csv
/media/micah/datasets/BlueLeaks-extracted/vlnsn/Company.csv
/media/micah/datasets/BlueLeaks-extracted/njuasi/Company.csv
/media/micah/datasets/BlueLeaks-extracted/stopwesttexasgangs/Company.csv
--snip--
```

As you can see, the script displays paths for all of the *Company.csv* files in BlueLeaks. (Yours might display them in a different order than mine.)

### Add BlueLeaks Sites to the CSV

The final step is to open all the *Company.csv* files whose paths you've just listed, loop through their rows, and add new rows to your output CSV file based on them:

```python
import click
import csv
import os


@click.command()
@click.argument("blueleaks_path")
@click.argument("output_csv_path")
def main(blueleaks_path, output_csv_path):
    """Make a CSV that describes all the BlueLeaks folders"""
    headers = ["BlueLeaksFolder", "CompanyID", "CompanyName", "WebsiteTitle", "URL"]
    with open(output_csv_path, "w") as output_f:
        writer = csv.DictWriter(output_f, fieldnames=headers)
        writer.writeheader()

        for folder_name in os.listdir(blueleaks_path):
            company_csv_path = os.path.join(blueleaks_path, folder_name, "Company.csv")
            if os.path.exists(company_csv_path):
                with open(company_csv_path, "r") as input_f:
                    reader = csv.DictReader(input_f)
                    for row in reader:
                        output_row = {
                            "BlueLeaksFolder": folder_name,
                            "CompanyID": row["CompanyID"],
                            "CompanyName": row["CompanyName"],
                            "WebsiteTitle": row["WebsiteTitle"],
                            "URL": row["URL"],
                        }
                        writer.writerow(output_row)

                print(f"Finished: {folder_name}")


if __name__ == "__main__":
    main()
```

The added code opens the company_csv_path, this time for reading instead of writing, and now calling the file object input_f. It then creates a csv.DictReader() object to read the data from this CSV and loops through its rows.

For each row, the code creates a new dictionary called output_row that contains the name of the BlueLeaks folder you're currently working in, as well as CompanyID, CompanyName, WebsiteTitle, and URL from *Company.csv*. It then uses the CSV writer you created in the previous section to save that row to your output CSV file. When the code finishes looping through all of the rows in a *Company.csv* file, it displays a message to show it's done with that folder.

You can find the complete script at *https://github.com/micahflee/hacks-leaks-and-revelations/blob/main/chapter-9/exercise-9-3.py*. Run your final script like so:

```
micah@trapdoor chapter-9 % python3 exercise-9-3.py /Volumes/datasets/BlueLeaks-extracted sites
.csv
Finished: vlnsn
Finished: njuasi
Finished: stopwesttexasgangs
--snip--
```

When you run this script, the output displays a line for each BlueLeaks folder showing that it has finished running. But more importantly, it creates the file *sites.csv*. Figure 9-9 shows what that file looks like in LibreOffice Calc.

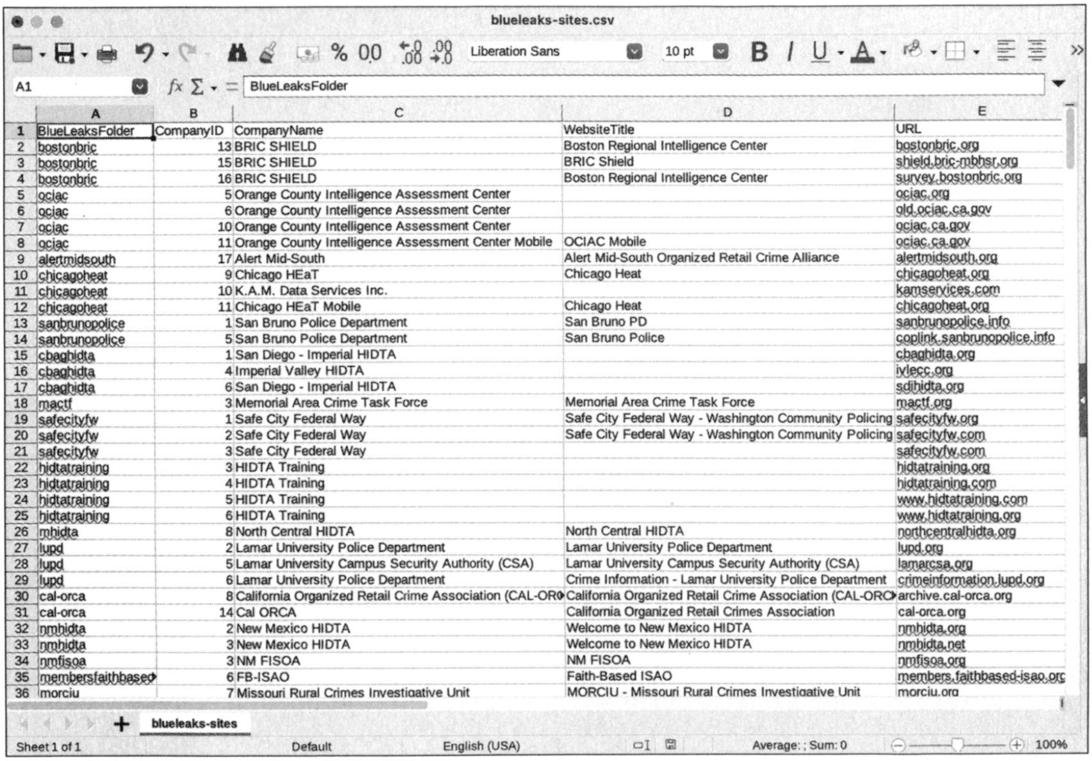

| | A | B | C | D | E |
|---|---|---|---|---|---|
| 1 | BlueLeaksFolder | CompanyID | CompanyName | WebsiteTitle | URL |
| 2 | bostonbric | 13 | BRIC SHIELD | Boston Regional Intelligence Center | bostonbric.org |
| 3 | bostonbric | 15 | BRIC SHIELD | BRIC Shield | shield.bric-mbhsr.org |
| 4 | bostonbric | 16 | BRIC SHIELD | Boston Regional Intelligence Center | survey.bostonbric.org |
| 5 | ociac | 5 | Orange County Intelligence Assessment Center | | ociac.org |
| 6 | ociac | 6 | Orange County Intelligence Assessment Center | | old.ociac.ca.gov |
| 7 | ociac | 10 | Orange County Intelligence Assessment Center | | ociac.ca.gov |
| 8 | ociac | 11 | Orange County Intelligence Assessment Center Mobile | OCIAC Mobile | ociac.ca.gov |
| 9 | alertmidsouth | 17 | Alert Mid-South | Alert Mid-South Organized Retail Crime Alliance | alertmidsouth.org |
| 10 | chicagoheat | 9 | Chicago HEaT | Chicago Heat | chicagoheat.org |
| 11 | chicagoheat | 10 | K.A.M. Data Services Inc. | | kamservices.com |
| 12 | chicagoheat | 11 | Chicago HEaT Mobile | Chicago Heat | chicagoheat.org |
| 13 | sanbrunopolice | 1 | San Bruno Police Department | San Bruno PD | sanbrunopolice.info |
| 14 | sanbrunopolice | 5 | San Bruno Police Department | San Bruno Police | coplink.sanbrunopolice.info |
| 15 | cbaghidta | 1 | San Diego - Imperial HIDTA | | cbaghidta.org |
| 16 | cbaghidta | 4 | Imperial Valley HIDTA | | ivlecc.org |
| 17 | cbaghidta | 6 | San Diego - Imperial HIDTA | | sdihidta.org |
| 18 | mactf | 3 | Memorial Area Crime Task Force | Memorial Area Crime Task Force | mactf.org |
| 19 | safecityfw | 1 | Safe City Federal Way | Safe City Federal Way - Washington Community Policing | safecityfw.org |
| 20 | safecityfw | 2 | Safe City Federal Way | Safe City Federal Way - Washington Community Policing | safecityfw.com |
| 21 | safecityfw | 3 | Safe City Federal Way | | safecityfw.com |
| 22 | hidtatraining | 3 | HIDTA Training | | hidtatraining.org |
| 23 | hidtatraining | 4 | HIDTA Training | | hidtatraining.com |
| 24 | hidtatraining | 5 | HIDTA Training | | www.hidtatraining.com |
| 25 | hidtatraining | 6 | HIDTA Training | | www.hidtatraining.org |
| 26 | mhidta | 8 | North Central HIDTA | North Central HIDTA | northcentralhidta.org |
| 27 | lupd | 2 | Lamar University Police Department | Lamar University Police Department | lupd.org |
| 28 | lupd | 5 | Lamar University Campus Security Authority (CSA) | Lamar University Campus Security Authority (CSA) | lamarcsa.org |
| 29 | lupd | 6 | Lamar University Police Department | Crime Information - Lamar University Police Department | crimeinformation.lupd.org |
| 30 | cal-orca | 8 | California Organized Retail Crime Association (CAL-OR | California Organized Retail Crime Association (CAL-ORC | archive.cal-orca.org |
| 31 | cal-orca | 14 | Cal ORCA | California Organized Retail Crimes Association | cal-orca.org |
| 32 | nmhidta | 2 | New Mexico HIDTA | Welcome to New Mexico HIDTA | nmhidta.org |
| 33 | nmhidta | 3 | New Mexico HIDTA | Welcome to New Mexico HIDTA | nmhidta.net |
| 34 | nmfisoa | 3 | NM FISOA | NM FISOA | nmfisoa.org |
| 35 | membersfaithbase | 6 | FB-ISAO | Faith-Based ISAO | members.faithbased-isao.org |
| 36 | morciu | 7 | Missouri Rural Crimes Investigative Unit | MORCIU - Missouri Rural Crimes Investigative Unit | morciu.org |

*Figure 9-9: The CSV output created by the final Exercise 9-3 script*

Once you've created the CSV, you can use your graphical spreadsheet software to freeze the header row at the top and sort the columns however you'd like. If you live in the US, try finding the fusion center that covers your region; that might be a good place to start digging. You can use the skills you've learned in this chapter and the Python scripts you've written to make the files for your chosen fusion center easier to work with.

Before you get too deep into your BlueLeaks investigations, though, I recommend reading Chapter 10, where I'll introduce you to software that might save you time and allow you to uncover more interesting revelations.

## Summary

In this chapter, you started investigating CSV spreadsheets. You've learned how to open and examine them using spreadsheet software, as well as how to read and write them using Python code, sharpening your programming skills along the way. You've also learned more about the BlueLeaks dataset structure and how to find hidden details, such as who posted which SARs and what documents were sent out as part of which bulk email messages, in the spreadsheets.

You've explored just a few CSVs in BlueLeaks so far, including *SARs.csv* and *EmailBuilder.csv* in NCRIC and *Company.csv* in all of the folders, but there's still much more to investigate. In the next chapter, you'll learn how to research the BlueLeaks dataset in depth using my custom-built software, BlueLeaks Explorer.

# 10

## BLUELEAKS EXPLORER

In some ways, I spent the summer of 2020 like many other Americans. I mostly stayed at home, avoiding COVID-19 like the plague it is; I spent far too many hours doom-scrolling through social media feeds; and occasionally I put on an N95 mask, grabbed some hand sanitizer, and hit the streets to protest the police killings of George Floyd, Breonna Taylor, and countless other Black Americans. But I also spent much of that summer writing code that would make it easier for me and other journalists at The Intercept to make sense of the sprawling BlueLeaks dataset.

My efforts culminated in a piece of open source software, which I released as part of this book, called BlueLeaks Explorer. BlueLeaks Explorer is a web application that allows you to examine the BlueLeaks data almost as if you could log in as an admin on the actual websites that were hacked. BlueLeaks Explorer is a little like a large Python script that makes all of the CSVs in BlueLeaks easier to work with, like the scripts you wrote in Chapter 9.

In this chapter, you'll continue to investigate the BlueLeaks dataset, this time using BlueLeaks Explorer. I'll give you a thorough overview of the software, including how to set it up on your own computer and how to start researching BlueLeaks with it. I'll conclude the chapter by explaining the technology behind the app and pointing you to its Python source code on GitHub. If you ever need to develop an app to investigate a specific dataset, you can use this chapter as inspiration.

## Undiscovered Revelations in BlueLeaks

As discussed in the previous chapter, my BlueLeaks investigation focused on the data from the *ncric* folder. Even within that folder, I concentrated on the final two weeks of data, focusing on police surveillance of the Black Lives Matter movement. Other journalists dug into different parts of the dataset, investigating fusion centers in places like Maine and Texas.

Notably, journalist Nathan Bernard broke several stories for the local news-and-arts magazine *Mainer* based on BlueLeaks documents from the Maine Information and Analysis Center (MIAC), Maine's fusion center. These included stories about MIAC disseminating unverified rumors, sometimes based on satirical social media posts, that were first spread by far-right activists on social media and then included in FBI and DHS intelligence reports, similar to the FBI warning discussed in Chapter 9 about a George Soros–funded group hiring "professional anarchists." "This bogus intel gives cops a dangerously distorted sense of what to expect during demonstrations by portraying peaceful protesters as highly trained, paid and organized criminal actors intent on causing mayhem," Bernard wrote in one article.

Additionally, John Anderson and Brant Bingamon wrote a series of articles for the *Austin Chronicle*, a local paper in Austin, Texas, based on BlueLeaks documents from the Austin Regional Intelligence Center (ARIC), Austin's fusion center. Anderson wrote about ARIC's practice of monitoring for and distributing lists of local Black Lives Matter protests (just like NCRIC did during the summer of 2020) and about several SARs posted to ARIC, including one where the "suspicious activity" was someone mailing a package of toys to Lebanon. Bingamon wrote stories revealing that ARIC had monitored local leftist groups in Austin, and that some ARIC courses for law enforcement teach junk science—including a technique for detecting deception called Scientific Content Analysis (SCAN), which a 2016 study concluded has "no empirical support" (*https://www.ncbi .nlm.nih.gov/pmc/articles/PMC4766305/*).

MIAC, ARIC, and NCRIC are some of the BlueLeaks sites that have received the most interest, but many more haven't gotten any attention at all. By the end of this chapter, you'll have all the tools you need to do a deep dive on any BlueLeaks folder you choose and search for newsworthy revelations. To start, you'll install BlueLeaks Explorer in Exercise 10-1.

## Exercise 10-1: Install BlueLeaks Explorer

You can find BlueLeaks Explorer's source code at *https://github.com/micahflee/blueleaks-explorer*. That GitHub page includes instructions on how to get it up and running locally on your computer, but I'll explain all the steps in this exercise as well.

The BlueLeaks Explorer app is packaged as a Docker image and published to Docker Hub at *https://hub.docker.com/r/micahflee/blueleaks-explorer*. You'll run it locally on your computer using Docker and point it at your BlueLeaks folder. Before you begin, make sure you've completed the exercises in Chapter 5 so that you understand how to use Docker and Docker Compose.

### Create the Docker Compose Configuration File

Start by creating a new folder called *blueleaks-explorer*. This folder will require about 5GB of disk space. Create a new file in that folder called *docker-compose.yaml* and open it in your text editor.

**NOTE** *If you're using Windows, I recommend that you follow this chapter in Ubuntu with WSL rather than PowerShell (see Appendix A for information about performance issues you might encounter when using Docker in Windows). You can open an Ubuntu terminal, create the* blueleaks-explorer *folder in your Linux filesystem using* **mkdir blueleaks-explorer***, and edit the* docker-compose.yaml *file in VS Code by running* **code docker-compose.yaml***, all from Ubuntu.*

Here's how I created the folder and made the *docker-compose.yaml* file on my Mac. You can do the same in Linux or Windows with WSL:

```
micah@trapdoor ~ % mkdir blueleaks-explorer
micah@trapdoor ~ % cd ~/blueleaks-explorer
micah@trapdoor blueleaks-explorer % code docker-compose.yaml
```

Add the following code to your *docker-compose.yaml* file, replacing */Volumes/datasets/BlueLeaks-extracted* with the path that maps to */data /blueleaks* in your own *BlueLeaks-extracted* folder:

```
version: "3.9"
services:
  app:
    image: micahflee/blueleaks-explorer:latest
    ports:
      - "8000:80"
    volumes:
      - /Volumes/datasets/BlueLeaks-extracted:/data/blueleaks
      - ./databases:/data/databases
      - ./structures:/data/structures
```

This file describes the settings for the BlueLeaks Explorer Docker container. The container is called app and is set to use the latest version of the micahflee/blueleaks-explorer Docker container image, which you'll download from Docker Hub. The ports section maps port 8000 on your computer to port 80 inside the container. This means that once the BlueLeaks Explorer app is running, you can load it on your browser at *http://localhost:8000*. The volumes section maps folders on your machine to folders inside the container.

Save the *docker-compose.yaml* file.

## Bring Up the Containers

In a terminal window, change to the *blueleaks-explorer* folder that you just made, then run this command to download the BlueLeaks Explorer Docker image and start the server:

```
docker-compose up
```

The first time you run the command, the output should end with something like this:

```
blueleaks-explorer-app-1  | * Serving Flask app 'app'
blueleaks-explorer-app-1  | * Debug mode: off
blueleaks-explorer-app-1  |   WARNING: This is a development server. Do not use
                                it in a production deployment. Use a production
                                WSGI server instead.
blueleaks-explorer-app-1  | * Running on all addresses (0.0.0.0)
blueleaks-explorer-app-1  | * Running on http://127.0.0.1:80
blueleaks-explorer-app-1  | * Running on http://172.19.0.2:80
blueleaks-explorer-app-1  |   Press CTRL+C to quit
```

At this point, BlueLeaks Explorer is running on your computer, but it hasn't been initialized. If you load *http://localhost:8000* in your browser, you should get an error telling you as much.

## Initialize the Databases

The first time you use BlueLeaks Explorer, you must run a script to convert the many CSV files in BlueLeaks into SQLite databases. SQLite is lightweight SQL database software that can store a whole database in a single file (you'll learn more about SQL databases in Chapter 12). All of the CSVs in BlueLeaks were originally formatted as SQL tables, which the hacker exported into CSV format. Converting these CSV files back into database tables makes it easier for the Python code that runs BlueLeaks Explorer to query for and access items within those tables, then display them in the web app. For example, when searching for SARs that contain a specific string, BlueLeaks Explorer might search all the BriefSummary fields in the SARs table, trying to find reports that mention that string.

To initialize BlueLeaks Explorer, open a separate terminal window, change to your *blueleaks-explorer* folder, and run this command:

```
docker-compose exec app poetry run python ./initialize.py
```

This will run `poetry run python ./initialize.py` in your already running app container. The *initialize.py* Python script will take a while to finish running, since it's transforming thousands of CSV files into hundreds of SQLite databases; it took my computer about 50 minutes.

**NOTE** *If you're curious about the details of what the initialization script is doing, take a look at the source code. BlueLeaks Explorer is open source, meaning you can check out the* initialize.py *file in the project's git repository at* https://github.com/micahflee/ blueleaks-explorer/blob/main/src/initialize.py.

When *initialize.py* finishes running, refresh *http://localhost:8000* in your web browser to pull up BlueLeaks Explorer, as shown in Figure 10-1.

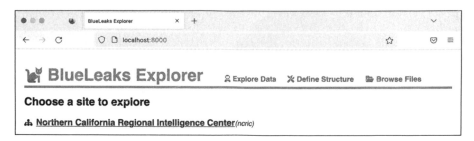

*Figure 10-1: The freshly installed BlueLeaks Explorer app*

Each fusion center is unique: it's run by different people, has different priorities and goals, and keeps track of different data. To make the best use of BlueLeaks Explorer, you need to spend some time understanding how the data in your target fusion center is laid out. I call this layout the *structure* of a BlueLeaks site. This refers to which tables contain useful information (some tables are empty or contain irrelevant data about the website layout), which columns in those tables are useful, and how the various tables are related.

The top of every page in BlueLeaks Explorer includes three links, as shown in Figure 10-1: Explore Data, Define Structure, and Browse Files. It would be difficult to automatically figure out the structure of a BlueLeaks site, in part because it's subjective—individual users determine what information is interesting or useless for their purposes. Therefore, the Define Structure page brings you to an editor where you can define your own structures for BlueLeaks sites. Under Explore Data, you can find structures you've already created for individual BlueLeaks sites. Since you're running BlueLeaks Explorer locally on your own computer, you'll have access only to structures you've made yourself or that are included in the BlueLeaks Explorer Docker image. Finally, Browse Files lists all of the files in BlueLeaks, enabling you to link to specific documents or embed images; it's simply a web interface to the raw BlueLeaks data, as if you were looking at it in a file browser.

*If you set up a VPN to hide your IP address from fusion center websites as described in "Covering Your Tracks with a VPN Service" in Chapter 9, you may want to use a VPN for this chapter as well. Though BlueLeaks Explorer is hosted on your own computer, viewing content within it might load images from fusion center sites, and clicking links could bring you to those sites.*

In the following section, you'll begin by exploring the data for the NCRIC site using a structure that I've already created.

## The Structure of NCRIC

BlueLeaks Explorer allows you to browse and search all of the tables in any BlueLeaks site that you have a structure for. To demonstrate the features of the app—including listing the tables in a BlueLeaks site, viewing and searching the data in those tables, viewing data from related tables, and viewing images and documents associated with rows of data—you'll start by exploring the NCRIC data. This will help you understand how structures are constructed before you make your own.

### Exploring Tables and Relationships

As directed in Exercise 10-1, make sure your BlueLeaks Explorer Docker container is running and load *http://localhost:8000* in your browser. From the Explore Data section, click **Northern California Regional Intelligence Center**. Figure 10-2 shows this page.

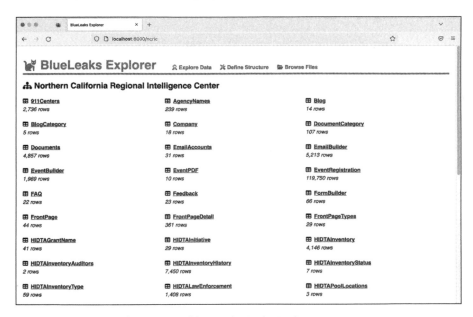

*Figure 10-2: Viewing the NCRIC tables in BlueLeaks Explorer*

Here, you can see a list of tables in the *ncric* folder, as well as the number of rows of data in each table. The EmailBuilder table has 5,213 rows, for example. I've hidden all of the tables that are empty or contain information I considered irrelevant so that they don't show up here.

When I first defined the NCRIC structure, I started by exploring the data in each table, one at a time (I'll explain how you can do this for other parts of BlueLeaks later in the chapter). I found that the following tables contained the most interesting and potentially newsworthy data:

**EmailBuilder**   Contains all of the bulk email NCRIC sends out to its large list of local police and private industry partners

**EventBuilder**   Describes events that NCRIC put on, complete with their descriptions, PDF flyers, and lists of who attended

**FormBuilder**   Contains a list of forms on NCRIC's website for a variety of purposes, like submitting SARs, requesting technical help, or even registering for an account with the fusion center

**Requests**   Includes requests from local police for the fusion center's assistance with tasks like monitoring social media and breaking into locked phones

**SARs**   Contains suspicious activity reports, which, as you learned in the previous chapter, are files submitted to NCRIC in which people report behavior that they believe could be criminal or otherwise suspicious

**SurveyForm**   Includes surveys that NCRIC requests from attendees of events it has hosted

Different tables within BlueLeaks relate to each other in various ways. For example, as you know from the previous chapter, many of the BlueLeaks sites include the tables Documents and DocumentCategory. Both of these tables contain a field called DocumentCategoryID. One row in the Documents table in the *ncric* folder, for instance, describes a document titled *FBI NSIR Tradecraft Alert Voter Suppression*. The DocFilename field contains the path of a PDF. The DocumentCategoryID is 167. Looking at the row with that DocumentCategoryID in the DocumentCategory table, you can see that the CategoryName is Elections. Now you know that NCRIC put this document in the Elections category. In database-speak, two tables that are connected via a shared field have a *relationship*. The SurveyForm table, which lists surveys for attendees of NCRIC-hosted events to fill out, is also related to the Survey table, which includes the actual survey feedback.

BlueLeaks Explorer makes it easy to quickly find related information within a BlueLeaks site. Click the Documents table from the list of tables shown in Figure 10-2. You should see a list of documents, each on its own row in the Documents table. In the Search field, enter **Voter Suppression** to bring up the FBI NSIR Tradecraft Alert Voter Suppression document, shown in Figure 10-3.

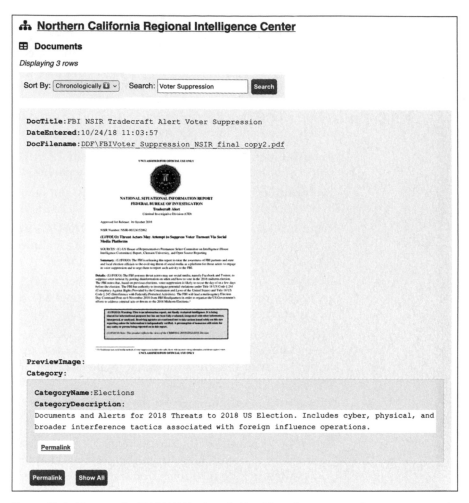

*Figure 10-3: Viewing the FBI NSIR Tradecraft Alert Voter Suppression document in BlueLeaks Explorer*

When you view a document row using the NCRIC structure I defined, BlueLeaks Explorer will show you a link to the file itself—in this case, a PDF. It also shows a preview of the file if it's available (the path to the preview image is listed in the PreviewImage field), along with the document category—in this case, Elections.

If you click the filename link, the PDF will open. Dated October 16, 2018, the document warns, "The FBI assesses threat actors may use social media, namely Facebook and Twitter, to suppress voter turnout by posting disinformation on when and how to vote in the 2018 midterm election." It points out examples of voter suppression tactics on social media from the 2016 election, such as a Spanish-language meme claiming that you can vote for Hillary Clinton by texting "Hillary" to a specific phone number—tricking voters into falsely believing they voted for Clinton.

Next, click **Permalink** under the Elections category to get to the category itself. Your URL should now be *http://localhost:8000/ncric/DocumentCategory/167,* and from here you should see all 11 documents categorized in Elections. You can click Permalink under any of those documents to view it. You can easily flip between documents and their categories in this way because I defined a relationship in the NCRIC structure between the Document and DocumentCategory tables. The permalink brings you to a unique URL just for that row. During an investigation, you can keep track of any interesting items in the dataset using their permalinks so you can easily refer back to them later on. The Show All link will show all of the hidden fields for this row. I've configured the Documents table to show only a handful of fields: DocTitle, DateEntered, DocFilename, URL, PreviewImage, and the DocumentCategory relationship. Clicking Show All will show you the remaining hidden fields as well.

## Searching for Keywords

For a concrete example of how BlueLeaks Explorer makes it easier to investigate the BlueLeaks documents, let's revisit the SAR described in "Investigating a SAR" in Chapter 9, in which a lawyer reported a student protester. This time, instead of manually grepping CSV files and copying and pasting big blocks of text from fields in spreadsheets for easier reading, you'll do it all in BlueLeaks Explorer.

Go back to the NCRIC list of tables, click **SARs**, and search for **antifa** to find that specific row. Figure 10-4 shows the record. The File1 row should display a clickable link to the PDF originally attached to the SAR, allowing you to quickly open the document. If you click it, you'll immediately be able to read the PDF in another browser tab.

Figure 10-4: Viewing a SAR in BlueLeaks Explorer

Now that you have an idea of how to navigate BlueLeaks Explorer, it's your turn to explore other parts of the BlueLeaks dataset beyond NCRIC.

## Building Your Own BlueLeaks Structure

In this section, you'll learn how to define your own structure for another BlueLeaks site, the Los Angeles Joint Regional Intelligence Center (JRIC). By the end of this section, you'll have the tools you need to create structures for all of the BlueLeaks sites.

Building out a BlueLeaks Explorer site structure takes work, but it also helps you gain a much clearer understanding of the data. Once you've started cleaning up a few of the tables, you can spend time reading them, looking for newsworthy revelations. As you read, you'll probably end up tweaking the structure to help you in your research, and you'll also likely start cleaning up new tables as you discover relationships to them.

### Defining the JRIC Structure

Some structures, like the one I constructed for NCRIC, are already included with BlueLeaks Explorer. To either edit existing structures or define new ones, load BlueLeaks Explorer in your browser and click **Define Structure** at the top of the screen. Figure 10-5 shows the page that should pop up.

On the Define Structure page, every structure that is already defined is listed under Edit Structures. In Figure 10-5, this is just a single structure, NCRIC. To edit a structure, simply click its name. The BlueLeaks sites that don't yet have a structure are listed by their folder name under Define a New Structure, along with a button to create that new structure. Scroll down until you see the listing for *jric*, and click **Create**.

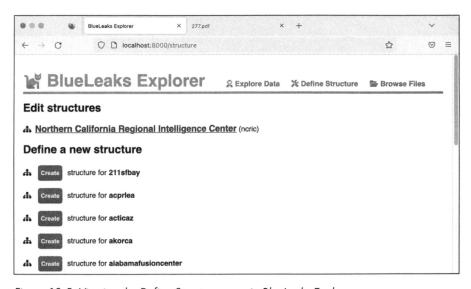

*Figure 10-5: Viewing the Define Structure page in BlueLeaks Explorer*

In the page that opens, you can configure exactly how BlueLeaks Explorer should work when you investigate the JRIC data, as shown in Figure 10-6. The top of the page displays the name of the site, which defaults to the BlueLeaks folder name, *jric*.

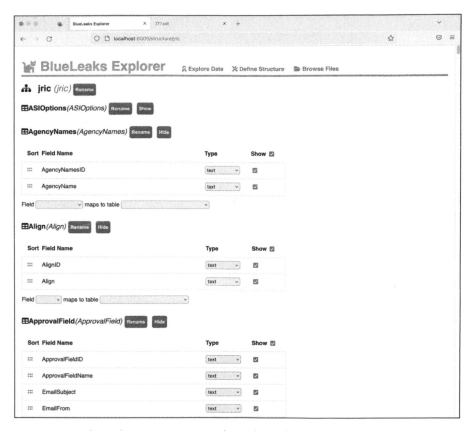

Figure 10-6: Editing the JRIC structure in BlueLeaks Explorer

Click **Rename** next to the site name and enter **Los Angeles Joint Regional Intelligence Center**. Every time you make a change like this, you should see the message "You have unsaved changes," with a Save button, in the bottom-right corner. Click **Save**.

Below the site name, the Edit Structure page lists all of the tables in this BlueLeaks site. Next to each table name is the Rename button, as well as buttons to show or hide the table. BlueLeaks Explorer automatically detects tables that don't have any rows and hides them by default; this is why the ASIOptions table starts out hidden. You can also manually hide tables that you don't care about to reduce clutter when you're actually investigating this site later on.

Now that you've created the JRIC structure, open the **Explore Data** link at the top in a separate browser tab. You should see that the Los Angeles

Joint Regional Intelligence Center site has been added to the list of sites to explore. Figure 10-7 shows the new Explore Data page.

*Figure 10-7: The Explore Data page after you've created the JRIC structure*

Any additional structures you create for other BlueLeaks sites will also appear on this page.

Click the JRIC link to pull up all the tables in this site. As you work through the rest of the section, and when building a structure in BlueLeaks Explorer in general, keep two tabs open: the Explore Data and Define Structure pages. This way, when you save changes in the Define Structure tab, you can refresh the Explore Data tab to see them implemented.

### Showing Useful Fields

In Exercise 9-3, you wrote a Python script to automatically create a spreadsheet mapping the names of BlueLeaks folders to their associated organizations. You found this information in *Company.csv*, a spreadsheet with 108 different columns. Only a few fields in this spreadsheet proved to be relevant, which makes this a good table for practicing showing only useful fields.

In your Explore Data tab, click the Company table. You should see the page shown in Figure 10-8. There are 7 rows displayed, each containing all 108 different fields, some of which include lots of HTML. Because each row has so many fields, this figure shows only the fields at the beginning of the first row of data.

The text in these fields isn't very readable yet, but that's easy to fix. Back in your Define Structure tab, scroll down until you find the Company table. For each field, you can choose the type from a drop-down menu and toggle a checkbox to set whether or not you want it to appear in the Explore Data page. For example, you probably don't care about the value of BannerAdHeight, so you'd want to hide that field.

You can also click the checkbox next to Show at the top of the table to toggle all the checkboxes at once. Click it now to uncheck—that is, hide—all of the fields in the Company table. From here, you can scroll through and select only the most useful fields to display.

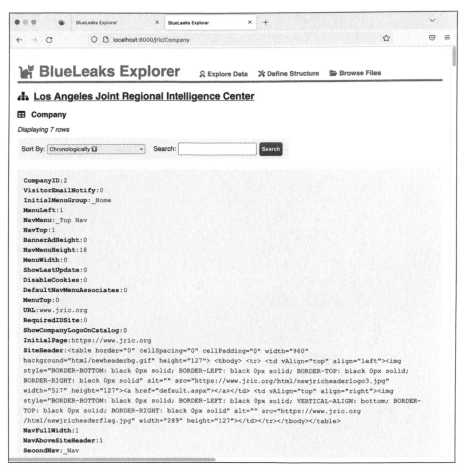

Figure 10-8: Exploring data in JRIC's Company table before editing the structure

By reading through the Explore Data page, I can guess that the most useful fields include URL, InitialPage, SiteHeader, and CompanyName. Back on the Define Structure page, check the boxes next to these fields to show them and then click **Save**. Refresh the Explore Data page. It should now look like Figure 10-9.

The Explore Data page still lists all seven rows in the Company table, but this time it shows only the four specific fields you selected, which makes it much easier to read through. As you can see from the second row of data, the Explore Data page also hides empty fields—the leads.jric.org row doesn't have anything in its SiteHeader field, so BlueLeaks Explorer skips that field.

You can still see all of the hidden fields for any row by clicking the Show All button below it. In the course of an investigation, you might discover that a field you chose to hide is actually useful, in which case you can edit the structure again to display it.

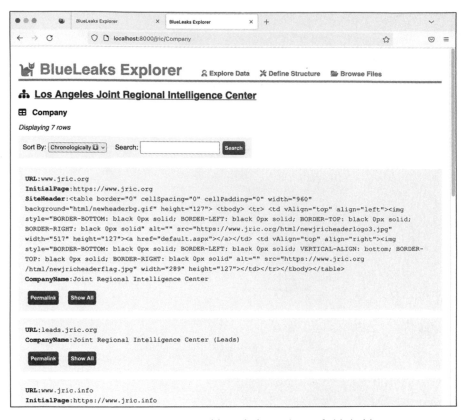

*Figure 10-9: Viewing JRIC's Company table with the irrelevant fields hidden*

## Changing Field Types

The Explore Data page is much more readable now, but it's still not perfect. The SiteHeader field is hard to read because it's a block of HTML. It would also be nice if CompanyName appeared at the top of the list of fields. Let's make one more change to fix that.

Every field in BlueLeaks Explorer starts out as text, and it's up to you to change the type if you think there's a better way to display that field. Here are all of the types that are available:

**text**  Displays the value as text; this is the default for all fields

**html**  Renders the value as an HTML web page

**pre**  Displays the field's value as text in a fixed-width font and preserves all of the original spacing (see the BriefSummary field in Figure 10-4 for an example)

**image**  Loads an image from a path directly in your browser; choose this type only if the field contains a path to an image (see the PreviewImage field in Figure 10-3 for an example)

**attachment** Displays a filepath as a text link directly to the file; choose this type only if the field contains a path to a non-image file (see the DocFilename field in Figure 10-3 for an example)

**survey** Recognizes the format of SurveyData fields, which appear only in Survey tables and contain feedback from attendees of events hosted by fusion centers—and makes the results easier to read

Back in the Edit Structure tab, find the SiteHeader field. This field has a Type drop-down menu that's currently set to text; switch it to **html**. Now scroll down until you find the CompanyName field. Click the grip icon to the left of it and drag it to the top of the list of fields. Click **Save** again and refresh the Explore Data tab. Your Company table should now look like Figure 10-10.

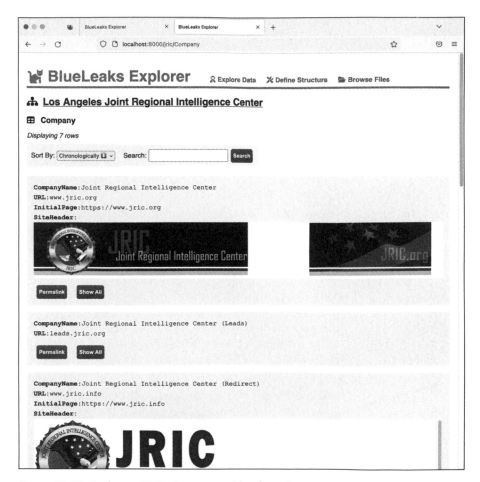

Figure 10-10: Exploring JRIC's Company table after editing its structure

Because you changed the SiteHeader field type from text to HTML, BlueLeaks Explorer renders it as HTML and loads the JRIC header image hosted from JRIC's web server. Figure 10-10 also shows that the CompanyName field is now listed first for each row.

### Adding JRIC's Leads Table

In your Explore Data tab, go back to the JRIC table listing. This time, click the Leads table. If you read through its rows, you'll see that this table is full of SARs. It's similar to NCRIC's SARs table, except that its leads are submitted by both the fusion center's partners and members of the public, and it appears to retain data forever, whereas the NCRIC SARs table includes only one month's worth of SARs. To get more practice using BlueLeaks Explorer, including setting up a relationship between two tables, you'll define the structure for the Leads table next.

In your Define Structure tab, find the Leads table, hide all of its columns, and repeat the steps you followed with the Company table to show only the useful fields, selecting the most appropriate type for each. After reading through the first several rows of Leads data in the Explore Data tab, I decided to show FormTimeStamp, County, PhoneNum, EmailAddress, ActivityDate, ActivityTime, ActivityDetails, full-name, Information, NSFormName, FUpload, and FUploadName. Feel free to show or hide different fields yourself.

After saving the structure and refreshing the Explore Data page, I get these fields from the first row in the Leads table:

**FormTimeStamp**    06/07/20 00:39:09

**County**   Los Angeles

**PhoneNum**   *[redacted]*

**EmailAddress**   *[redacted]*@torrenceca.gov

**ActivityDate**   06/06/20 00:00:00

**ActivityTime**   1345

**ActivityDetails**   On the above date and time officers were dispatched to a call of a suspicious package. Upon, arrival [*sic*] officers noticed that the package had bottles with a cloth items [*sic*] sticking out of the top of the bottle resembling a Molotov Cocktail. This package was in the general area of a BLM protest that was going on. (see attached report and photos)

**NSFormName**   PublicCountyLeadSheet

**FUpload**   LFU00010\984.docx

**FUploadName**   200020437.docx

The FUpload and FUploadName fields both contain filenames. Notice that FUpload seems to be the path to a file inside the BlueLeaks dataset. Back in the Define Structure page, change the type of FUpload from text to attachment, save your changes, and refresh the Explore Data page. The FUpload field should now link to *http://localhost:8000/blueleaks-data/jric/files/ LFU00010/984.docx*, which loads the document from your local copy of the data. You can click this link to read it if you're curious. The filename is *984.docx*, but it appears that the person who submitted this lead originally uploaded the file as *2000020437.docx*.

Looking through other rows in this Leads table, I also notice that values in the NSFormName field are different for different leads. My guess is that this field describes which form was filled out to add this lead to JRIC's database. Most of the values for NSFormName appear to be PublicCountyLeadSheet or LeadSheetPrivateSectorAndPublic. Is the Leads table related to some other table that describes forms? Let's find out.

## Building a Relationship

Go back to the page listing all of the tables in JRIC and click the table named FormBuilder. This table doesn't have a field called NSFormName, but it does have one called FormName. If you search the table for PublicCountyLeadSheet and LeadSheetPrivateSectorAndPublic, you will see that the row with ID 1 has a FormName value of PublicCounty LeadSheet, and the row with ID 2 has a FormName value of LeadSheet PrivateSectorAndPublic. (From the FormBuilder table page, you could sort it by FormBuilderID ascending to see these first two rows in that table as well.) Because the NSFormName field on the Leads table maps to the FormName field on the FormBuilder table, there's a relationship between these two tables. Let's create that relation in BlueLeaks Explorer.

Back in the Define Structure page, scroll down to the bottom of the Leads table. After the list of fields, there's another section that says Field Maps to Table. Both Field and Table are drop-down menus. Click the Field drop-down menu to list all of the fields in this table and select **NSFormName**. Click the Table drop-down menu, which lists all of the other tables in this BlueLeaks site, and choose **FormBuilder**. Once you select the table, you should see a third drop-down menu that lets you choose the field in that table. Choose **FormName** and click **Create Relationship**. A prompt should pop up, asking, "What is the name of this relationship?" Enter **Form** and click **OK**, then save your changes.

Back in the Explore Data tab, navigate back to the Leads table. For each lead, you should now see all of the fields from the form that was used to submit the lead. However, as Figure 10-11 shows, it's difficult to read.

As you can see, the related form is displayed, but, like the Company table you worked with previously, far too many fields are shown, including blocks of HTML that are difficult to make sense of. To fix this, you'll edit the structure of the FormBuilder table as you did with the Company and Leads tables. As you build structures, I recommend finishing one table so that it displays nicely, then moving on to related ones.

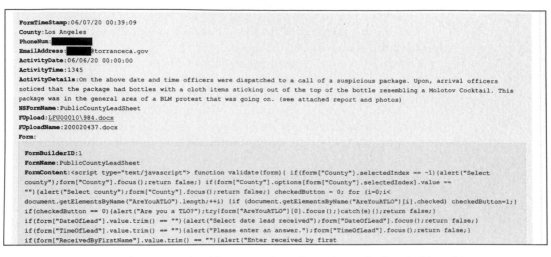

```
FormTimeStamp:06/07/20 00:39:09
County:Los Angeles
PhoneNum:█████████
EmailAddress:█████████@torranceca.gov
ActivityDate:06/06/20 00:00:00
ActivityTime:1345
ActivityDetails:On the above date and time officers were dispatched to a call of a suspicious package. Upon, arrival officers
noticed that the package had bottles with a cloth items sticking out of the top of the bottle resembling a Molotov Cocktail. This
package was in the general area of a BLM protest that was going on. (see attached report and photos)
NSFormName:PublicCountyLeadSheet
FUpload:LFU00010\984.docx
FUploadName:200020437.docx
Form:

  FormBuilderID:1
  FormName:PublicCountyLeadSheet
  FormContent:<script type="text/javascript"> function validate(form){ if(form["County"].selectedIndex == -1){alert("Select
  county");form["County"].focus();return false;} if(form["County"].options[form["County"].selectedIndex].value ==
  ""){alert("Select county");form["County"].focus();return false;} checkedButton = 0; for (i=0;i<
  document.getElementsByName("AreYouATLO").length;++i) {if (document.getElementsByName("AreYouATLO")[i].checked) checkedButton=1;}
  if(checkedButton == 0){alert("Are you a TLO?");try{form["AreYouATLO"][0].focus();}catch(e){};return false;}
  if(form["DateOfLead"].value.trim() == ""){alert("Select date lead received");form["DateOfLead"].focus();return false;}
  if(form["TimeOfLead"].value.trim() == ""){alert("Please enter an answer.");form["TimeOfLead"].focus();return false;}
  if(form["ReceivedByFirstName"].value.trim() == ""){alert("Enter received by first
```

Figure 10-11: An item in the JRIC Leads table, now with a relationship to the FormBuilder table

Go back to the Define Structure tab, find the FormBuilder table, and hide all of its fields. Check the boxes to show FormName and FormContent, and change FormContent's type from text to **html**. You already added a relationship to the Leads table that links it to the FormBuilder table, so while you're here, create a relationship in the other direction as well. Scroll down to the bottom of the FormBuilder table and add a new relationship: map the FormName field to the Leads table's NSFormName field. This time, when you create the relationship, name it *Submissions*. Save your changes in the Define Structure tab.

In your Explore Data tab, navigate to the Leads page again to see what it looks like. Now as you scroll through each lead, you can see which form was filled out to submit it. Figure 10-12 shows a different example from the Leads table.

In this case, a member of the public rather than a fusion center member filled out this form, using a fake name and email address (John Doe and *idont@thinkso.org*). They wrote a message, in all caps, about a fireworks store in Pahrump, Nevada, just over the border from California:

> ON SATURDAYS, ALL 3 STORES ARE PACKED AND OVER
> 90% OF THE TRAFFIC IS FROM CA. THEY ARE ALSO
> ALMOST ALL BLACK OR MEXICAN. NO DISRESPECT
> TO RACE, BUT DOESNT THAT SORT OF MEET YOUR
> PROFILE OF PROBLEMS LATELY? I DONT REALLY CARE
> ABOUT THE CAUSES EITHER WAY, BUT THE UNREST IS
> HURTING TRUMP. I WOULD BET YOU HAVE A FEW ANTIFA
> PEOPLE BUYING FIREWORKS TO CAUSE TROUBLE. JUST
> THOUGHT I WOULD MENTION IT.

```
FormTimeStamp:06/06/20 16:31:22
County:LosAngeles
EmailAddress:IDONT@THINKSO.ORG
fullname:JOHN DOE
Information:JUST WONDERING IF YOU GUYS HAVE TROUBLE MAKERS USING FIREWORKS. IF SO, YOU MAY WANT TO LOOK AT THE
FIREWORKS STORES IN PAHRUMP NEVADA. ON SATURDAYS, ALL 3 STORES ARE PACKED AND OVER 90% OF THE TRAFFIC IS FROM
CA. THEY ARE ALSO ALMOST ALL BLACK OR MEXICAN. NO DISRESPECT TO RACE, BUT DOESNT THAT SORT OF MEET YOUR PROFILE
OF PROBLEMS LATELY? I DONT REALLY CARE ABOUT THE CAUSES EITHER WAY, BUT THE UNREST IS HURTING TRUMP. I WOULD
BET YOU HAVE A FEW ANTIFA PEOPLE BUYING FIREWORKS TO CAUSE TROUBLE. JUST THOUGHT I WOULD MENTION IT.
NSFormName:LeadSheetPrivateSectorAndPublic
Form:

  FormName:LeadSheetPrivateSectorAndPublic
  FormContent:

  Lead Sheet: Private Sector and General Public
  Important: If this is an emergency - Call 911.
  For Non-Emergency Traffic Related Issues:
  Call CHP: 1-800-TELL-CHP (1-800-835-5247)
  This site is not for traffic reporting!
  Please complete the form below and click "Submit". If you experience any technical difficulties
  please fax the lead sheet to (562) 345-1766 and/or call (888) 705-5742.

  Your First Name:*
  Your Last Name:*
  Your Phone Number (Include Area Code):
  Your Email:*
  Your Business or Agency Name:
  InfraGard Member:                    - Select - v
  Your Address:
  Your City:
  Your State:
  Your Zip Code:
  Your County:*                        - Select -       v
  Please describe your information:



  Upload Attachments (if available):   Browse   No file selected
Permalink
```

Figure 10-12: An item in the JRIC Leads table, with a cleaned-up relationship to the FormBuilder table

BlueLeaks Explorer shows you LeadSheetPrivateSectorAndPublic, the form that was filled out to submit this lead. Scroll to the bottom of the form and click **Permalink** to go to a page that shows just the LeadSheetPrivateSectorAndPublic form in the FormBuilder table. Because of the Submissions relationship you created, this page should show you everything that was submitted to JRIC using this form—all 1,949 leads submitted by the public.

## Verifying BlueLeaks Data

Whenever you're looking at leaked or hacked data, you should always do additional research outside of the dataset itself to help verify that the data is authentic and put it into context. By looking at the Company table in the previous section, you learned that the JRIC site is hosted at *https://www.jric.org*.

Load that link in Tor Browser (covered in Chapter 2) or while connected to a VPN, and check out the JRIC website.

At the time of writing, I could tell from the website that this fusion center focuses on the Los Angeles area. Some of the BlueLeaks sites went offline after the hack in 2020, but many, like JRIC, remained online. Figure 10-13 shows JRIC's website, loaded anonymously in Tor Browser.

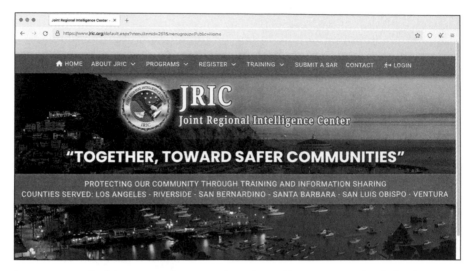

Figure 10-13: The home page of JRIC's website, https://www.jric.org, loaded in Tor Browser

It wasn't clear to me that JRIC was a fusion center focused on Los Angeles, or what its mission was, until I viewed its website. If you click around the JRIC site to get a better understanding of the types of information it collects, you can then use BlueLeaks Explorer to view that information. For example, if you click the Submit a SAR link at the top of the home page, you can find the forms that add SARs to the Leads table.

You've only explored a small amount of content in the JRIC data so far. Now it's time to finish building the structure so you can explore the rest.

## Exercise 10-2: Finish Building the Structure for JRIC

In the previous sections, you started building the structure for the JRIC data. You cleaned up the Company, Leads, and FormBuilder tables and created a relationship between the latter two tables, allowing you to see which form was submitted to create each lead and which leads were created from each form. In this exercise, you'll use your newfound knowledge to finish defining the structure for the other tables in JRIC. This will give you a clearer understanding of exactly what data was stored there, making it much easier to continue your investigation. It will also give you practice creating structures for the rest of the BlueLeaks sites.

You can play with BlueLeaks Explorer however you wish to customize the JRIC structure to suit your preferences. However, if you're not sure where to start, I recommend beginning with the first table (AgencyNames), then the second (Align), and so on, finishing with the last table (VideoOptions). If you run into a table that has a relationship to another table, work on the related table first before you continue down the list.

For example, here's how I'd start the AgencyNames table. In the Explore Data tab, in the list of JRIC tables, click **AgencyNames**. This table has 1,396 rows, and each row has just two fields: AgencyNamesID and AgencyName. The names appear to be various military agencies, police departments, school districts, and other organizations—my guess is these are all of JRIC's partners. This data is pretty easy to read and search by itself, so I'd consider this table done already.

Still in the Explore Data tab, I'd move on to the Align table. This has just three rows, with the Align field as Left, Right, or Center. This table is completely useless for the purposes of an investigation. In the Define Structure tab, find the Align table, click the **Hide** button, then click **Save**. Back in the Explore Data tab, refresh the page, and you'll see that the Align table has disappeared.

I find that when building a BlueLeaks Explorer structure, it helps to read some raw data to begin with, just to try to understand what it is and how it should be formatted. If you see any fields that are obviously HTML, for example, change their type from text to **html**. Once you have an understanding of what the important fields are, you can hide the rest. And once you're done deciding what fields to show and what their types should be, you can add any relationships as appropriate.

Once you've structured the JRIC data to more easily explore it, do some investigating. The JRIC data includes an entire series of training videos for the Terrorism Liaison Office, split into different modules. Check out the Video and VideoCategory tables; at the time of writing, no one has reported on this information.

Now that you know how to define structures in BlueLeaks Explorer, you can do the same for any other sites in the BlueLeaks dataset to investigate them in greater depth. BlueLeaks Explorer is most useful when paired with a tool like Aleph, described in Chapter 5, that indexes the data so you can search it for keywords. If you index all of the data in BlueLeaks, you can search it all at once to find documents in various BlueLeaks sites. Then, once you discover the sites you're interested in, you can do a deep dive on them using BlueLeaks Explorer.

## The Technology Behind BlueLeaks Explorer

Sometimes a dataset is so complicated—and so newsworthy—that it's worth writing a custom application just to help you make sense of it. BlueLeaks Explorer is one such application. The information covered in this book, especially in Chapters 7 and 8, provides a solid foundation for the additional independent research required to build an app like this yourself.

There are many different ways to go about writing custom apps for investigating datasets. In this section, I describe the technologies and libraries I used to develop BlueLeaks Explorer: first those I used to build the *backend* (the web server), then those I used for the *frontend* (the user interface that runs in a web browser). I personally like this *tech stack*, or combination of technologies an app uses, but this is by no means an exhaustive list of possibilities. Most of the technologies described here are outside the scope of this book; this section provides just a brief introduction to inspire future research.

If you feel confident in your programming skills and are inclined to do so, you can make improvements to my BlueLeaks Explorer code in the git repo and submit them back into the project, since it's open source.

## The Backend

I developed the backend of BlueLeaks Explorer in Python, relying on a third-party Python package called Flask, a simple framework for building web apps. You can learn more about using Flask at *https://flask.palletsprojects.com*. You can also check out the source code for BlueLeaks Explorer, specifically *app.py* at *https://github.com/micahflee/blueleaks-explorer/blob/main/src/app.py*, to see exactly how I used Flask for this project.

The backend also makes use of built-in Python modules, primarily json (which you'll learn about in the next chapter) and sqlite3, which lets you run SQL queries on the SQLite databases that represent BlueLeaks sites. When a web browser loads the web server powered by Flask, the web server responds with HTML that loads some JavaScript code. This is the frontend, described in the following section.

The backend also implements an API, which allows the frontend to communicate with it. For example, when the frontend wants to know the list of sites that already have structures, it can load */api/sites* on the backend, which returns this data in JSON format. If it wants to retrieve data in JSON format from a specific table on a specific site, it can load */api/<site>/<table>*. In this case, the Python code uses the sqlite3 module to look up this data in the SQLite3 database for that BlueLeaks site, and then returns what it finds to the frontend.

## The Frontend

To develop web applications, you'll have to program not in Python but in JavaScript, since this is the programming language that web browsers understand. I developed the frontend of BlueLeaks Explorer using a JavaScript framework called Vue.js (*https://vuejs.org*). If you're like me and find that you really enjoy writing code, I recommend that you try learning JavaScript so that you can make web applications. You can find the frontend source code at *https://github.com/micahflee/blueleaks-explorer/tree/main/src/frontend/src*.

Using Vue.js, the BlueLeaks Explorer frontend includes a series of pages designed to display data it retrieves by making HTTP requests to the backend. When you save a structure that you're working on in BlueLeaks Explorer, the frontend also sends data to the backend, which then saves the structure as a JSON file.

## Summary

In this chapter, you got BlueLeaks Explorer up and running locally on your computer using Docker. You've learned how to define structures for each BlueLeaks site, make the data in the tables easier to read, and create relationships between tables. Now that you have the skills required to investigate anything in the sprawling BlueLeaks dataset, let me know if you find any revelations!

In the next chapter, you'll learn more about the JSON file format. You'll work with a dataset containing a million JSON files related to the January 6, 2021, attack on the US Capitol and continue to hone your Python skills by writing code to find the most important files within it.

# 11

## PARLER, THE JANUARY 6 INSURRECTION, AND THE JSON FILE FORMAT

On the morning of January 6, 2021, two months after Donald Trump lost the 2020 election to Joe Biden by about 6 million votes, thousands of Trump's supporters prepared to storm the US Capitol in Washington, DC, hoping to subvert democracy. "We will never give up. We will never concede," Trump told the crowd from the National Mall, just south of the White House. "We fight like hell, and if you don't fight like hell, you're not going to have a country anymore."

Smartphones in hand, the pro-Trump, anti-democracy activists recorded the entire event. They posted their photos and videos online, many to the far-right social media site Parler. In this chapter, you'll learn to work with the massive trove of video evidence collected from that day's insurrection in a popular file format called JavaScript Object Notation (JSON). You'll learn how JSON data is structured and write Python code to scour a million JSON files full of Parler video metadata to find specific videos. You'll also learn about working with Global Positioning System (GPS) coordinates, including how to plot points on a map, since many of the videos include GPS coordinates in their metadata. All of these skills could serve you well in your future investigations.

Let's start with a brief history of how the Parler dataset became available to the public.

## The Origins of the Parler Dataset

The protesters at the US Capitol insurrection filmed themselves marching with Don't Tread on Me, Fuck Biden, and Trump flags; tearing down fences; fighting with riot cops; smoking weed; smashing windows and then storming the Capitol building through them; throwing chairs at police; and threatening the lives of members of Congress and Vice President Mike Pence. They uploaded these videos to Parler in real time as they filmed them.

During the attack on the Capitol, pro-Trump rioters attacked police officers with baseball bats, flag poles, and pipes, injuring at least 138 of them. One officer, Brian Sicknick, was hospitalized and died the next day. In the weeks and months following the attack, four more officers who responded that day died by suicide. A Capitol Police officer shot and killed Ashli Babbitt, a rioter who attempted to breach the doors to the US Senate chamber where senators were sheltering. Three more Trump supporters died during the riot: one from being crushed to death in the crowd, one from a stroke, and one from a heart attack.

Days after the attack, citing Parler's unwillingness to moderate content that encourages and incites violence, Apple and Google banned the Parler app from their app stores. Amazon Web Services (AWS), the major cloud hosting service that Parler had relied on, kicked the company off its service. It took Parler a month and a half to bring its site back up. Before it went down, though, a quick-thinking archivist downloaded over a million videos from the site. In this section, I'll describe how she downloaded the videos and how they were used in Trump's second impeachment trial.

### How the Parler Videos Were Archived

On the Saturday after the January 6 attack, John Paczkowski and Ryan Mac published an email in BuzzFeed News from the Amazon AWS Trust & Safety Team to Parler. Amazon informed Parler that it "cannot provide services to a customer that is unable to effectively identify and remove content that encourages or incites violence against others," and that "we plan to suspend Parler's account effective Sunday, January 10th." Less than 48 hours before Parler went dark, a hacker named @donk_enby, with the help of other archivists, raced to download a copy of all of the videos and images uploaded to the social network.

Parler, it turns out, lacked security measures that prevent automatic scraping of the site's data. *Web scraping* is a method of automated data collection where you use code to load web pages, rather than manually loading them in a browser, and extract their data. This chapter won't cover how to scrape the web like @donk_enby did, but if you're curious, you can learn how in Appendix B.

Parler's website didn't have any *rate limiting*, a security feature that prevents users from accessing the site too frequently, so nothing stopped a single computer from making millions of web requests. The URLs of Parler posts appeared to have random IDs, but @donk_enby discovered that they also had hidden incremental IDs (1, 2, 3, and so on), so a script could easily loop through every ID, make a web request to download every post, and then find the URLs for every video and image to download. While Parler did strip metadata from videos uploaded by its users, they also left original copies of videos that contained this metadata at predictable URLs. @donk_enby downloaded versions of the videos that contained a wealth of hidden information, including, in many cases, the GPS coordinates of where the video was filmed.

When @donk_enby archived this data, she saved it to an AWS S3 bucket, an AWS service for hosting files that never runs out of disk space. (It's ironic that, in response to AWS kicking Parler off its service, she saved copies of the videos to a different part of AWS.)

Because there's no widely agreed-upon definition of hacking, whether or not Parler was "hacked" is a matter of perspective. Technically, @donk_enby scraped public content from a public website, which isn't illegal and doesn't require bypassing security—had Parler even had any that would have prevented this. The same thing is often true of illegal hacking, though; people break into systems that are barely protected or accidentally left open to the public.

By Sunday night, @donk_enby had managed to archive at least 32TB of videos. "I hope that it can be used to hold people accountable and to prevent more death," she told *Vice*. She worked with DDoSecrets to make a copy of the data available to the public—the copy you'll work with in this chapter.

## The Dataset's Impact on Trump's Second Impeachment

On January 13, a week after the deadly riot at the Capitol and a week before Joe Biden's inauguration as the new president, the US House of Representatives impeached Trump for "incitement of insurrection," making Trump the first president in US history to be impeached twice.

During the impeachment trial in the US Senate, which took place in February at the beginning of Biden's administration, the impeachment managers showed many videos of violent Trump supporters that @donk_enby had archived from Parler as evidence to support their case. "I had an efficient way to download it all. I knew what was there, but it seemed that nobody else could see the value," she told CNN at the time. "I hope it inspires more people with similar skills to mine to use those skills for good."

Ultimately, 57 percent of the Senate, including seven members of the Republican Party, found Trump guilty, while 43 percent—all of whom were Republicans—found him not guilty. The US Constitution requires a two-thirds majority of the Senate to convict, so Trump was acquitted. However, over 1,000 people were charged in connection to the January 6 insurrection. Two members of the far-right Oath Keepers militia, including its leader, Stewart Rhodes, and four members of the Proud Boys hate group, including its former leader, Enrique Tarrio, were convicted of seditious conspiracy. Several other members of these groups were also convicted of lesser crimes. Rhodes was sentenced to 18 years in prison in May 2023, and Tarrio was sentenced to 22 years in prison in September 2023.

Further investigating this dataset is obviously in the public interest. Let's get started in Exercise 11-1.

## Exercise 11-1: Download and Extract Parler Video Metadata

The Parler data is so large that it's not practical, for the purposes of this chapter, to download it all. Instead, you'll start with just the video metadata DDoSecrets has made available separately. The metadata contains useful information about each video, like its file format, when it was filmed, what type of phone or camera was used to film it, and in some cases the GPS coordinates describing where it was filmed. In this exercise, you'll learn how to use the metadata to select and download individual videos to view.

**NOTE**    *If you're using Windows, I recommend that you follow along with this chapter using your Ubuntu terminal instead of PowerShell and that you save this data in your WSL Linux filesystem (for example, in ~/datasets), instead of in your Windows-formatted USB disk (/mnt/c or /mnt/d). Because of disk performance issues with WSL, I found that working with this data in Linux rather than directly in Windows was significantly faster. If you've only used Python in Windows so far, install Python in Ubuntu with the command* `sudo apt install python3 python3-pip`, *then install the* click *Python module by running* `python3 -m pip install click`. *You'll need the* click *module for the exercises in this chapter. Refer to Appendix A to learn more about solving performance issues in WSL if you run into any problems.*

### Download the Metadata

Since the Parler dataset takes up so much disk space, DDoSecrets couldn't publish it using BitTorrent like it does with most of its other public releases. To seed that torrent, you would need a single server with 32TB of data, and no one would be able to connect to the swarm to download it because no one has 32TB of disk space lying around. Instead, DDoSecrets hosts the Parler data on its public data web server. If you know the filename of a Parler video, you can download it from *https://data.ddosecrets.com/Parler/Videos/<filename>*.

You can also download a full list of filenames, *ddosecrets-parler-listing.txt.gz*, and metadata for all of the video files, *metadata.tar.gz*. Files ending in *.gz* are compressed using a format called GZIP, so you can tell from the filename that *ddosecrets-parler-listing.txt.gz* is a compressed text file. Files ending in *.tar*, called *tarballs*, also combine multiple files and folders together into a single file. Tar files aren't compressed, though—they take up as much disk space as all of the files they contain—so it's common to compress them with GZIP, resulting in *.tar.gz* files. The *metadata.tar.gz* file is a GZIP-compressed tarball.

Start by downloading *ddosecrets-parler-listing.txt.gz* and *metadata.tar.gz* using the `wget` command. This command is similar to `curl`, but it downloads a file and saves it to disk by default instead of displaying it in your terminal. Check if you already have `wget` installed by running **which wget**. If you don't, install it on macOS with **brew install wget**, or on Linux or Windows with WSL with **sudo apt install wget**.

Open a terminal. Create a new folder for the Parler data you'll download, and change to that folder. (If you're using Windows with WSL, make sure you create it in your WSL Linux filesystem, such as at *~/datasets/Parler*.) For example, here's how I did it on my Mac, creating the folder on my *datasets* USB disk:

```
micah@trapdoor ~ % cd /Volumes/datasets
micah@trapdoor datasets % mkdir Parler
micah@trapdoor datasets % cd Parler
micah@trapdoor Parler %
```

Now use `wget` to download the list of filenames by running the following command:

```
micah@trapdoor Parler % wget https://data.ddosecrets.com/Parler/Videos/ddosecrets-parler
-listing.txt.gz
--snip--
Resolving data.ddosecrets.com (data.ddosecrets.com)... 172.67.75.15, 104.26.3.199,
104.26.2.199
Connecting to data.ddosecrets.com (data.ddosecrets.com)|172.67.75.15|:443... connected.
HTTP request sent, awaiting response... 200 OK
Length: 17790173 (17M) [application/octet-stream]
Saving to: 'ddosecrets-parler-listing.txt.gz'

ddosecrets-parler-listin 100%[===================================>]  16.97M  29.1MB/s    in 0.6s

... (29.1 MB/s) - 'ddosecrets-parler-listing.txt.gz' saved [17790173/17790173]
```

The output should show that you've downloaded the 17MB *ddosecrets -parler-listing.txt.gz* file. The `wget` program shows you a progress bar of your download in your terminal.

Next, download the video metadata by running the following command:

```
wget https://data.ddosecrets.com/Parler/Videos/metadata.tar.gz
```

Check to make sure you've successfully downloaded the files by running **ls -lh**. You should get the following output:

```
-rw-r--r-- 1 micah  staff    17M Mar 28  2021 ddosecrets-parler-listing.txt.gz
-rw-r--r-- 1 micah  staff   203M Mar 15  2021 metadata.tar.gz
```

The file containing the list of filenames should be 17MB, and the metadata file should be 203MB.

## Uncompress and Download Individual Parler Videos

To uncompress GZIP files, you'll use the gunzip command with the following syntax: gunzip *filename.gz*. Running gunzip on a gzipped file deletes the original file and leaves you with the uncompressed version without the *.gz* file extension.

Uncompress the *ddosecrets-parler-listing.txt.gz* file by running the following command:

```
gunzip ddosecrets-parler-listing.txt.gz
```

Your original 17MB file, *ddosecrets-parler-listing.txt.gz*, should be replaced with a 43MB text file called *ddosecrets-parler-listing.txt*, which contains over one million lines, one for each video that @donk_enby archived.

To make sure it worked, run **ls -lh** again. Your output should look something like this:

```
-rw-r--r--  1 user  staff   43M Mar 28  2021 ddosecrets-parler-listing.txt
-rw-r--r--  1 user  staff  203M Mar 15  2021 metadata.tar.gz
```

Count the number of files in *ddosecrets-parler-listing.txt* with the following command:

```
cat ddosecrets-parler-listing.txt | wc -l
```

As you learned in Chapter 4, the cat command displays the content of a file, and piping that command's output into **wc -l** counts the number of lines in that file. The output should be 1031509, meaning there are 1,031,509 lines in *ddosecrets-parler-listing.txt*.

If you load the file in a text editor, it should look like this:

```
2021-01-12  18:31:54  77632730  0002bz1GNsUP
2021-01-12  18:37:33  14586730  00031x5cSwSB
2021-01-12  18:37:33  822706    0004D2lOBGpr
2021-01-12  18:37:33  17354739  000EyiYpWZqg
2021-01-12  18:37:33  2318606   000SbGUM7vD4
2021-01-12  18:37:33  5894269   000oDvV6Bcfd
2021-01-12  18:37:36  20806361  0012uTuxv9qQ
2021-01-12  18:37:34  45821231  0015NlYOyUB5
--snip--
```

The first and second columns of text show the date and time that @donk_enby first uploaded each file to the S3 bucket, just after scraping it. The third column is the size of the file, in bytes, and the final column is the filename. All of the video files in the Parler dataset have similar random-looking names. These are the original IDs that Parler used for each video, and they don't have file extensions.

Now that you know the filenames of each Parler video, you can download individual files from *https://data.ddosecrets.com/Parler/Videos/<filename>*. Let's try downloading one of the first videos listed in *ddosecrets-parler-listing .txt*. First, use the following commands to create a *videos* folder and switch to that folder:

```
micah@trapdoor Parler % mkdir videos
micah@trapdoor Parler % cd videos
```

Next, run the following command to download the Parler file *0003lx5cSwSB*:

```
wget https://data.ddosecrets.com/Parler/Videos/0003lx5cSwSB
```

You can normally tell the format of a file based on its file extension, but since these Parler video filenames don't have extensions, use the following file command to determine the format of *0003lx5cSwSB*:

```
file 0003lx5cSwSB
```

The output, `0003lx5cSwSB: ISO Media, MP4 v2 [ISO 14496-14]`, shows that the file is an MP4 video. To make it easier to open in video-playing software, you'll need to add the *.mp4* extension to the filename. You can rename files using the command `mv source_path dest_path`, which moves a file from a source path to a destination path. To rename *0003lx5cSwSB* to *0003lx5cSwSB.mp4*, run the following command:

```
mv 0003lx5cSwSB 0003lx5cSwSB.mp4
```

You can now watch *0003lx5cSwSB.mp4* in software like VLC Media Player. Figure 11-1 shows a screenshot from this video, which features Trump battling the "fake news" media and calls him the "Savior of the Universe."

Figure 11-1: A screenshot from a pro-Trump Parler video showing an altered image of Trump riding a motorcycle

In your terminal, run **cd ..** to change out of the *videos* folder you just created and back to the Parler dataset folder.

There are over a million videos in this dataset, and most likely, only a small fraction contain anything newsworthy. If you randomly pick individual videos to download and watch, chances are you'll be wasting a lot of time. To more efficiently find interesting videos, let's take a closer look at the metadata.

### Extract Parler Metadata

To view the Parler metadata, you'll need to extract the *metadata.tar.gz* tarball. In your terminal, uncompress and extract *metadata.tar.gz* using the tar command:

```
tar -xvf metadata.tar.gz
```

Because it's so common to gzip tar archives, the tar command will automatically detect if it's gzipped and uncompress it for you, so you don't need to manually do the gunzip step yourself. In the -xvf argument, x tells tar to extract the files from *metadata.tar*, v (meaning verbose) tells tar to display each filename it extracts in the terminal, and f means that the next argument is a filename for the tarball on which this command will run.

Your output should look like this:

```
x metadata/
x metadata/.aws/
x metadata/meta-00CnBY5xCdca.json
x metadata/meta-0003lx5cSwSB.json
x metadata/meta-0070HNolzi3z.json
x metadata/meta-00BIFOMnOyi1.json
x metadata/meta-0002bz1GNsUP.json
--snip--
```

The command might take 10 minutes or so to extract the over one million JSON files in *metadata.tar.gz* into a new folder called *metadata*, depending on the speed of your hard disk. (If you're using Windows with WSL and this step is going very slowly, consult Appendix A for performance tips.)

Feel free to run ls on the *metadata* folder or view it in a file browser, but beware that there are so many files that those simple tasks will take a long time (it took over five minutes for the ls command to finish running on my computer). Figure 11-2 shows the files in the *metadata* folder in Finder on macOS.

The files in this folder are all named *meta-<ID>.json*, where *ID* is the original video ID from Parler. For example, you can find the metadata for the file *0003lx5cSwSB*, the video you downloaded in the previous section, at *metadata/meta-0003lx5cSwSB.json*. All of these metadata files are in the JSON file format, so let's take a closer look at that now.

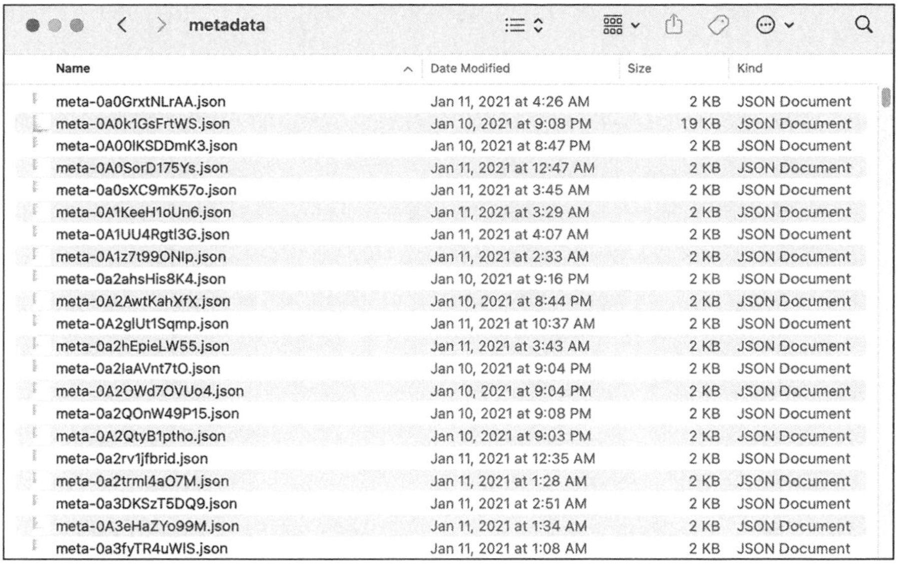

Figure 11-2: Some of the extracted Parler metadata files

## The JSON File Format

JSON is a format used to store information in text strings. One of its main benefits is that it's human-readable. Some file formats are designed for computers rather than humans to understand. If you run cat on a PDF file, for example, you'll see random-looking output in your terminal. You need to open the PDF in a program like Adobe Reader to understand the information it contains. However, humans can easily read the JSON text format just by viewing it in a text editor or by using the cat command.

JSON is one of the most widely used data formats, and the one most APIs communicate with. Whenever you visit a website that does anything interactive, chances are your web browser and the website's server are passing JSON data back and forth. This is one reason why hacked data, as well as data scraped from APIs, is often full of JSON files. Most of the data from the America's Frontline Doctors dataset, covered in detail in Chapter 13, is in JSON format, as is much of the data hacked from Gab, the right-wing social network discussed in Appendix B.

In this section, you'll learn more about JSON syntax and how to load JSON data into Python scripts.

### Understanding JSON Syntax

JSON has JavaScript in its name because it was first derived from that programming language, but it's a *language-independent* data format: you can work with JSON data in JavaScript, Python, or any other programming language. Using their own JSON libraries, programming languages can convert JSON text strings into structured data (such as Python's dictionaries and lists) and also convert that structured data back into JSON text strings that can be loaded by code in any other programming language.

To get an idea of the structure of a JSON file, run the following command in your terminal to display the metadata for the Parler video with the filename *0003lx5cSwSB*:

```
cat metadata/meta-0003lx5cSwSB.json
```

The output should look like Listing 11-1.

```
[{
  "SourceFile": "-",
  "ExifToolVersion": 12.00,
  "FileType": "MP4",
  "FileTypeExtension": "mp4",
  "MIMEType": "video/mp4",
  "MajorBrand": "MP4 v2 [ISO 14496-14]",
  "MinorVersion": "0.0.0",
  "CompatibleBrands": ["mp42","mp41","iso4"],
  "MovieHeaderVersion": 0,
  "CreateDate": "2020:10:15 09:35:29",
  "ModifyDate": "2020:10:15 09:35:29",
  "TimeScale": 48000,
  "Duration": "0:01:59",
--snip--
```

*Listing 11-1: Video metadata for the file 0003lx5cSwSB*

As you can see, FileType is MP4. The CreateDate is 2020:10:15 09:35:29, meaning that this video was filmed on October 15, 2020, at 9:35 AM, and the Duration is 0:01:59, or 1 minute and 59 seconds.

JSON syntax is extremely similar to Python syntax but uses different terminology to describe types of information:

**Object**

A set of key-value pairs. An object is essentially equivalent to a dictionary in Python and even uses the same syntax. In JSON, however, keys *must* be strings. Objects are defined between braces ({ and }), and keys and values are separated with colons—for example, {"first_name": "Frederick", "last_name": "Douglass"}. The JSON output for Listing 11-1 also includes a JSON object.

**Array**

An ordered list of items. An array is essentially equivalent to a list in Python and uses the same syntax. Arrays are defined between brackets ([ and ]), and items are separated by commas. The JSON output in Listing 11-1 has a few arrays, such as ["mp42","mp41","iso4"].

**Boolean**

A value of either true or false. These work the same as True and False in Python, but they're lowercase in JSON.

**Number**

Any whole number or number with decimals in it, such as 2600 or 3.14. These are similar to numbers in Python, though while Python makes a distinction between integers (whole numbers) and floating points (numbers with decimals), JSON does not.

**String**

A sequence of text characters—for example, "videos have metadata?". This is exactly the same as a string in Python, except that JSON strings *must* be enclosed double quotes ("), whereas Python also allows you to use single quotes (').

**null**

A keyword representing an empty value. This is very similar to Python's None keyword.

All JSON data is made up of combinations of these types, so it's important to understand their exact syntax. If you use any invalid syntax, such as surrounding a string with single quotes instead of double quotes or using the Boolean True instead of true, the JSON data won't load properly.

Unlike in Python code, whitespace isn't important in JSON data. For example, consider this JSON string:

```
{"abolitionists":[{"first_name":"Frederick","last_name":"Douglass"},{"first_name":"John","last
_name":"Brown"},{"first_name":"Harriet","last_name":"Tubman"}]}
```

To write the same JSON string in a more human-readable format, you can split it into multiple lines and add indentation:

```
{
    "abolitionists": [
        {
            "first_name": "Frederick",
            "last_name": "Douglass"
        },
        {
            "first_name": "John",
            "last_name": "Brown"
        },
        {
            "first_name": "Harriet",
            "last_name": "Tubman"
        }
    ]
}
```

You might encounter JSON files in datasets that are formatted either way. I often open JSON files in VS Code and use the text editor's built-in format feature to reformat the JSON for legibility. To format a document in VS Code, click **View ▶ Command Palette ▶ Format Document** and press ENTER.

## Parsing JSON with Python

You can turn JSON data into Python dictionaries and lists using Python's built-in json module. First, open a Python interpreter and import the module:

```
>>> import json
```

The function in this module that I use the most is json.loads(). This takes a string with JSON data as an argument, parses the string into a Python object like a dictionary or a list, and returns that object. For example, define a string called json_data and set its value to a JSON string with the following command:

```
>>> json_data = '{"first_name": "Frederick", "last_name": "Douglass"}'
```

The value you set json_data to looks similar to a dictionary, but since it's surrounded by single quotes, it's actually a string. In Python, the type() function tells you the type of a variable. You can confirm that json_data is a string with the following command:

```
>>> type(json_data)
<class 'str'>
```

This output shows that json_data is a class of type str (Chapter 14 will touch on classes), meaning it's a string. Now define a variable called obj and set its value to the return value of the json.loads() function:

```
>>> obj = json.loads(json_data)
```

Here, json.loads() takes a string as input and, if the string contains valid JSON, converts it into structured data—in this case, storing the resulting object in obj. Use the type() function on obj now to see what type of variable it is:

```
>>> type(obj)
<class 'dict'>
```

The output shows that you've parsed this JSON data into a Python dictionary (a dict), which you can now use like any other dictionary. For example, to put the value at the last_name key of this dictionary in an f-string and then display it, use the following command:

```
>>> print(f"Hello, Mr. {obj['last_name']}.")
Hello, Mr. Douglass.
```

To practice accessing structured data, in your terminal, change to your Parler dataset folder, and then open a Python interpreter. Run the following commands to load the metadata from a Parler video as structured data. I've chosen the file *metadata/meta-HS34fpbzqg2b.json*, but feel free to load whichever file you'd like:

```
>>> import json
>>> with open("metadata/meta-HS34fpbzqg2b.json") as f:
...     json_data = f.read()
...
>>> obj = json.loads(json_data)
```

You now have the video metadata in the variable obj. The simplest way to start inspecting it is to display it to the screen with the print() function:

```
>>> print(obj)
[{'SourceFile': '-', 'ExifToolVersion': 12.0, 'FileType': 'MOV', 'FileTypeExtension': 'mov',
'MIMEType': 'video/quicktime', 'MajorBrand': 'Apple QuickTime (.MOV/QT)', 'MinorVersion':
'0.0.0', 'CompatibleBrands': ['qt '], 'MediaDataSize': 139501464, 'MediaDataOffset': 36,
--snip--
```

This output looks a little like JSON, but it's a Python object—in this case, a list with a nested dictionary. Use the len() function you learned about in Chapter 8 to count how many items are in this list:

```
>>> len(obj)
1
```

Since any given Parler video metadata file contains the metadata only for one video, there's only one item in this list. In order to access that metadata, you need to select the first item in the list. To do that, use obj[0] (remember, 0 is the first index for any list) as follows:

```
>>> print(obj[0])
{'SourceFile': '-', 'ExifToolVersion': 12.0, 'FileType': 'MOV', 'FileTypeExtension': 'mov',
'MIMEType': 'video/quicktime', 'MajorBrand': 'Apple QuickTime (.MOV/QT)', 'MinorVersion':
'0.0.0', 'CompatibleBrands': ['qt '], 'MediaDataSize': 139501464, 'MediaDataOffset': 36,
--snip--
```

This time, the output starts with a brace, meaning the item is a dictionary. Now use a for loop to view all of the keys in this dictionary:

```
>>> for key in obj[0]:
...     print(key)
...
SourceFile
ExifToolVersion
FileType
--snip--
GPSLatitude
GPSLongitude
Rotation
GPSPosition
```

Each key listed in this output represents a different piece of video metadata from the JSON file. You can also select values from this dictionary using their keys. For example, try printing the values for the GPSLatitude and GPSLongitude keys:

```
>>> print(obj[0]["GPSLatitude"])
38 deg 53' 26.52" N
>>> print(obj[0]["GPSLongitude"])
77 deg 0' 28.44" W
```

These values represent the GPS coordinates for the location where this video was filmed.

Since JSON makes it easy to convert structured data into strings and back, when creating BlueLeaks Explorer I used JSON files to store the structure of BlueLeaks sites, as described in the section "The Technology Behind BlueLeaks Explorer" in Chapter 10. When you create a structure for a BlueLeaks site, BlueLeaks Explorer stores all of the configuration for that site in a dictionary, then saves that information to a JSON file. If you quit BlueLeaks Explorer and then run it again later, it loads that JSON file back into a dictionary. Since the Parler metadata comes in JSON format, you can also write Python code that loads these JSON files to easily access that metadata, as you'll do later in this chapter.

To learn more about the json module, you can find the documentation and plenty of example code at *https://docs.python.org/3/library/json.html*.

## Handling Exceptions with JSON

The json.loads() function will throw an exception if you pass an invalid JSON string into it, like this:

```
>>> json.loads("this isn't valid json")
Traceback (most recent call last):
  File "<stdin>", line 1, in <module>
  File "/Library/Frameworks/Python.framework/Versions/3.10/lib/python3.10/json/__init__.py",
line 346, in loads
    return _default_decoder.decode(s)
```

```
  File "/Library/Frameworks/Python.framework/Versions/3.10/lib/python3.10/json/decoder.py",
line 337, in decode
    obj, end = self.raw_decode(s, idx=_w(s, 0).end())
  File "/Library/Frameworks/Python.framework/Versions/3.10/lib/python3.10/json/decoder.py",
line 355, in raw_decode
    raise JSONDecodeError("Expecting value", s, err.value) from None
json.decoder.JSONDecodeError: Expecting value: line 1 column 1 (char 0)
```

A json.decoder.JSONDecodeError exception means that the string you passed in doesn't contain valid JSON data. In this case, it's telling you the error in the JSON string is at line 1, column 1, and character 0, meaning the error is located at the first character of the string. If you have a longer JSON string that's mostly valid but just has a little syntax issue, this error message can help you determine which piece of your syntax is wrong.

Validating JSON data is a common use for Python exception handling, which you learned about in "Exception Handling" in Chapter 7. For example, let's say you have a string called json_data. The following code will catch exceptions in case this string contains invalid JSON data:

```
try:
    obj = json.loads(json_data)
    print("The JSON is valid")
    print(obj)
except json.decoder.JSONDecodeError:
    print("Invalid JSON")
```

This code uses try and except statements to catch the json.decoder.JSON DecodeError exception if it gets thrown. If json_data is a valid JSON string, it will display The JSON is valid, followed by the information in obj. If the JSON string is invalid, the script will display Invalid JSON and then continue running without crashing.

To load a JSON file in Python functions such as main(), you must first load the content of the file into a string like so

```
with open("filename.json") as f:
    json_data = f.read()
```

replacing *filename.json* with whatever file you're loading, such as metadata/ meta-HS34fpbzqg2b.json to load the metadata for the *HS34fpbzqg2b* video file. As you learned in "Reading and Writing Files" in Chapter 8, this code opens the file as a file object f and then stores its content into a string called json_data.

Next, you'd run that string through json.loads() to convert it from a string into structured data, like this:

```
try:
    obj = json.loads(json_data)
except json.decoder.JSONDecodeError:
    print("Invalid JSON")
    return
```

When this code finishes running, if the JSON string was valid, `obj` will contain the JSON data. Otherwise, it will display `Invalid JSON` and then return early from the function. The remaining code in the function can access the data in `obj`.

To prepare for using this module to write Python scripts that parse the Parler metadata files, next we'll look at how to access values like GPS coordinates from JSON files with several command line programs.

## Tools for Exploring JSON Data

While we've been focusing primarily on working with JSON files using Python, sometimes writing a Python script is overkill if you just want to quickly search a large block of JSON text. In this section, you'll learn to use our old friend grep, as well as a more powerful tool called jq, to search JSON files.

### Counting Videos with GPS Coordinates Using grep

As you know from Chapter 4, the command line programs grep and wc are incredibly powerful tools to quickly assess datasets. In a single command, and without needing to write a Python script, you can use grep to efficiently search inside JSON files.

For example, let's say you want to figure out how many Parler video metadata files include GPS coordinates. Open a terminal, switch to your Parler dataset folder, and run the following command to grep for the string `GPSCoordinates`:

```
micah@trapdoor Parler % grep -r GPSCoordinates metadata
```

The first argument, -r (short for --recursive), tells grep to look inside every file in the given folder. The next argument, `GPSCoordinates`, is the string to search for. The final argument, `metadata`, is the name of the folder to search.

When you run this command, your terminal should quickly fill with GPS coordinates:

```
metadata/meta-31VC1ufihFpa.json: "GPSCoordinates": "22 deg 8' 0.60\" S, 51 deg 22' 4.80\" W",
metadata/meta-ImUNiSXcoGKh.json: "GPSCoordinates": "0 deg 0' 0.00\" N, 0 deg 0' 0.00\" E",
metadata/meta-70Tv9tAQUKyL.json: "GPSCoordinates": "36 deg 10' 49.08\" N, 115 deg 26' 45.60\"
W, 1922.566 m Above Sea Level",
metadata/meta-P2w4Q0gv5n9U.json: "GPSCoordinates": "26 deg 14' 46.32\" N, 80 deg 5' 38.76\" W,
3.424 m Above Sea Level",
--snip--
```

However, you're trying to find how many of these videos have GPS coordinates, not necessarily what those coordinates are. If coordinates are still loading in your terminal, press CTRL-C to cancel the command, then pipe the output of grep into `wc -l` to count how many lines get displayed:

```
micah@trapdoor Parler % grep -r GPSCoordinates metadata | wc -l
64088
```

Of the slightly more than one million videos, about 64,000 have GPS coordinates.

Programs like grep and wc can only take you so far in your attempts to efficiently search large quantities of data. For example, if the JSON files you're searching are formatted on a single line, rather than split into multiple lines like the Parler files, grep will search the entire block of JSON data for your string rather than a line at a time. You can't use grep to extract specific fields of data from JSON, either. For that, the best tool for the job is a program called jq.

## Formatting and Searching Data with the jq Command

The jq program allows you to take JSON data as input and select key information from it. In this section, you'll learn how to use it to extract specific information from the Parler files.

First, you'll need to install jq. Mac users can do so by running the **brew install jq** command. Linux or Windows with WSL users, run the **sudo apt install jq** command.

You can use the jq command to indent JSON data and show syntax highlighting in your terminal, making the data easier to read. For example, try running this command in your terminal:

```
cat metadata/meta-HS34fpbzqg2b.json | jq
```

The first part of the command, `cat metadata/meta-HS34fpbzqg2b.json`, outputs the content of that JSON file, which contains the metadata for a single Parler video. The second part, `| jq`, pipes that output as input into jq.

The output should look like this:

```
[
  {
    "SourceFile": "-",
    "ExifToolVersion": 12,
    "FileType": "MOV",
    "FileTypeExtension": "mov",
    "MIMEType": "video/quicktime",
    "MajorBrand": "Apple QuickTime (.MOV/QT)",
    "MinorVersion": "0.0.0",
    "CompatibleBrands": [
      "qt  "
    ],
--snip--
    "GPSLatitude": "38 deg 53' 26.52\" N",
    "GPSLongitude": "77 deg 0' 28.44\" W",
```

```
      "Rotation": 180,
      "GPSPosition": "38 deg 53' 26.52\" N, 77 deg 0' 28.44\" W"
   }
]
```

This version includes syntax highlighting (as in VS Code) and formats the JSON data so that the items in every array and object are listed on separate lines and indented.

You can also use jq to filter for details from inside the JSON data. For example, suppose you just want to know the GPS coordinates from this JSON file. In the preceding code, you can tell from the bracket character at the beginning that this JSON data is an array. The first value of the array is an object, since it starts with a brace character, and one of the keys of the object is GPSPosition. To filter for GPSPosition, pass ".[0].GPSPosition" as an argument into the jq command, as follows:

```
micah@trapdoor Parler % cat metadata/meta-HS34fpbzqg2b.json | jq ".[0].GPSPosition"
"38 deg 53' 26.52\" N, 77 deg 0' 28.44\" W"
```

In this command, .[0] selects the first item of the list in the file named *metaHS34fpbzqg2b.json*, and .GPSPosition selects the value with the key GPSPosition from the object. The output shows the value of the GPSPosition field, "38 deg 53' 26.52\" N, 77 deg 0' 28.44\" W".

If you're interested in learning more about how to use jq, check out its website at *https://stedolan.github.io/jq*. You'll also revisit it in Chapter 14, where I explain how I used it to understand the structure of leaked neo-Nazi chat logs.

Now that you have a foundational understanding of JSON, you'll try your hand at writing Python code that works with it in Exercise 11-2.

## Exercise 11-2: Write a Script to Filter for Videos with GPS from January 6, 2021

In this exercise, you'll write a Python script that filters the Parler videos down to just those filmed on January 6, 2021, whose metadata includes GPS coordinates. You'll do this by looping through all the JSON files in the dataset, converting them into Python objects, and inspecting their metadata to show you just the ones you're looking for.

For a challenge, you can try programming your own script to meet the following requirements:

- Make this script accept an argument, parler_metadata_path, using Click. This will be the path to the *metadata* folder full of JSON files.

- Define a new variable called count that keeps track of the number of Parler videos that include GPS coordinates in their metadata, and set it to 0.

- Loop through all of the JSON files in the *metadata* folder. For each loop, your program should run the content of each JSON file through the json.loads() function to turn it into a Python object. As described in the "Parsing JSON with Python" section, each object is technically a list containing one element, a dictionary full of all of the video's metadata.

- Check to see if that video's metadata dictionary includes the key GPSCoordinates and if the date stored in the key CreateDate is January 6, 2021. If both of these are true, the script should display a message that this file includes GPS coordinates and is from January 6, 2021, and increment the count variable by 1.

- Have the program display a message after looping through all the metadata files that tells the user the total number of videos with GPS coordinates from January 6, 2021 (which should be stored in the count variable, now that you're done counting).

Alternatively, follow along with the rest of this exercise and I'll walk you through the programming process.

### Accept the Parler Metadata Path as an Argument

Start with the usual Python script template:

```
def main():
    pass

if __name__ == "__main__":
    main()
```

Next, make the following modifications to your script so that it accepts the parler_metadata_path CLI argument. This way, when you run the script, you can pass in the path to the *metadata* folder as an argument, which the code will use to open all of the JSON files inside that folder. The modifications are shown in bold:

```
import click

@click.command()
@click.argument("parler_metadata_path")
def main(parler_metadata_path):
    """Filter Parler videos with GPS that were filmed Jan 6, 2021"""
    print(f"Parler metadata path: {parler_metadata_path}")

if __name__ == "__main__":
    main()
```

This code first imports the click module, then uses it to make the main() function accept the argument parler_metadata_path. It also adds a docstring to show what the script does when you run it with the --help argument. Finally, the print() function will print the value of parler_metadata_path to the screen.

Test your code to make sure it works so far, replacing the argument with the path to your own *metadata* folder:

```
micah@trapdoor chapter-11 % python3 exercise-11-2.py /Volumes/datasets/Parler/metadata
Parler metadata path: /Volumes/datasets/Parler/metadata
```

Sure enough, the code should display the same string, stored in parler_metadata_path, that you passed in as an argument.

### Loop Through Parler Metadata Files

Next, add some code that will loop through all of the JSON files in the *metadata* folder and run json.loads() on their contents to convert them into structured data in Python. Modify your code as follows:

```python
import click
import os
import json

@click.command()
@click.argument("parler_metadata_path")
def main(parler_metadata_path):
    """Filter Parler videos with GPS that were filmed Jan 6, 2021"""
    for filename in os.listdir(parler_metadata_path):
        abs_filename = os.path.join(parler_metadata_path, filename)
        if os.path.isfile(abs_filename) and abs_filename.endswith(".json"):
            with open(abs_filename) as f:
                json_data = f.read()

            try:
                metadata = json.loads(json_data)
                print(f"Successfully loaded JSON: {filename}")
            except json.decoder.JSONDecodeError:
                print(f"Invalid JSON: {filename}")
                continue

if __name__ == "__main__":
    main()
```

The code imports the os and json modules at the top of the file so it can use the functions they contain later on. The program then loops through the return value of the os.listdir() function, which returns the list of files in the *metadata* folder, storing each filename in the variable filename.

Inside the for loop, the code defines a new variable called abs_filename to be the absolute path of the JSON file the code is working with each time it loops. It creates the absolute path by concatenating parler_metadata_path with filename using the os.path.join() function. Now that the code knows the full filename, it checks to make sure that this is actually a file, not a folder, and that it ends with *.json*.

If the code confirms the file is JSON, it loads all of the data from this file into the variable json_data and then converts that string into structured data, saved in the variable metadata, using try and except statements, as described in the "Handling Exceptions with JSON" section. If there are no syntax errors in an individual JSON file, the code displays a message to the screen saying that the file loaded successfully. Otherwise, it displays an error and moves on to the next file using the continue statement. In a for loop, continue statements immediately end the current loop and move on to the next loop.

To summarize, at this point the code is looping through every file in the *metadata* folder, and for each JSON file it comes across, opening it and loading its content as a text string. It then converts this string into a Python object using the json.loads() function, storing the object in the metadata variable, and displays a message that it successfully loaded. If the file didn't successfully load, the message says that the JSON was invalid, and the code continues on to the next JSON file.

Run the program again, replacing the argument with the path to your own *metadata* folder:

```
micah@trapdoor chapter-11 % python3 exercise-11-2.py /Volumes/datasets/Parler/metadata
Successfully loaded JSON: meta-gzK2iNatgLLr.json
Successfully loaded JSON: meta-31VC1ufihFpa.json
Successfully loaded JSON: meta-ZsZRse5JGx8j.json
--snip--
```

If your output shows many messages saying different JSON files loaded successfully, your code is working. Once you've determined that your output looks correct, you can press CTRL-C to cancel the script before it finishes running.

### Filter for Videos with GPS Coordinates

Your code currently loops through all of the Parler metadata files, loads each file, and converts it into a Python object so you can work with it. Next, you need to filter out the videos that include GPS coordinates and to count those videos. To do so, make the following modifications:

```
import click
import os
import json

@click.command()
@click.argument("parler_metadata_path")
def main(parler_metadata_path):
    """Filter Parler videos with GPS that were filmed Jan 6, 2021"""
    count = 0

    for filename in os.listdir(parler_metadata_path):
        abs_filename = os.path.join(parler_metadata_path, filename)
```

```
        if os.path.isfile(abs_filename) and abs_filename.endswith(".json"):
            with open(abs_filename) as f:
                json_data = f.read()

            try:
                metadata = json.loads(json_data)
            except json.decoder.JSONDecodeError:
                print(f"Invalid JSON: {filename}")
                continue

            if "GPSCoordinates" in metadata[0]:
                print(f"Found GPS coordinates: {filename}")
                count += 1

    print(f"Total videos with GPS coordinates: {count:,}")

if __name__ == "__main__":
    main()
```

This code defines a new variable called count and starts its value out as
0. This will keep track of the number of videos with GPS coordinates. After
each JSON file is loaded into the metadata variable, an if statement checks
if the key GPSCoordinates exists inside this metadata dictionary. Remember
from the previous section that metadata is a list with one item, making
metadata[0] the actual dictionary your code is checking. If this video metadata does have the GPSCoordinates field, the control flow moves to the code
block after the if statement. Otherwise, it moves on to the next loop.

When the Python script comes across metadata that includes GPS coordinates, it displays the name of the file with print() and increments count
by 1. This way, by the time this for loop is finished, count will contain the
total number of videos that have GPS coordinates in their metadata. Finally,
after the for loop completes, the code displays that total count with a second call to the print() function. As you learned in Chapter 8, the :, in the
f-string will display larger numbers with comma separators.

Run your program again:

```
micah@trapdoor chapter-11 % python3 exercise-11-2.py /Volumes/datasets/Parler/metadata
Found GPS coordinates: meta-31VC1ufihFpa.json
Found GPS coordinates: meta-ImUNiSXcoGKh.json
Found GPS coordinates: meta-70Tv9tAQUKyL.json
--snip--
Found GPS coordinates: meta-1FMyKoVq53TV.json
Found GPS coordinates: meta-YOjO2wy1Z7RO.json
Found GPS coordinates: meta-aZlkDfPojhxW.json
Total videos with GPS coordinates: 63,983
```

Because this script loads the JSON data from over a million files, it
might take a few minutes to finish running. In the end, your script should
find 63,983 videos with GPS coordinates. There should also be 63,984 lines
of output: one with the name of each metadata file that has GPS coordinates, and one at the end that lists the total.

### Filter for Videos from January 6, 2021

Now you'll whittle down that list of roughly 64,000 videos even further to find out which were filmed on January 6, 2021.

You can tell the date on which a video was filmed from the CreateDate field in its metadata, as shown earlier in Listing 11-1. The value of this field looks something like this:

```
"CreateDate": "2020:12:28 17:25:47",
```

To use the CreateDate field to filter the results further, make the following modifications to your code:

```python
import click
import os
import json

@click.command()
@click.argument("parler_metadata_path")
def main(parler_metadata_path):
    """Filter Parler videos with GPS that were filmed Jan 6, 2021"""
    count = 0

    for filename in os.listdir(parler_metadata_path):
        abs_filename = os.path.join(parler_metadata_path, filename)
        if os.path.isfile(abs_filename) and abs_filename.endswith(".json"):
            with open(abs_filename, "rb") as f:
                json_data = f.read()

            try:
                metadata = json.loads(json_data)
            except json.decoder.JSONDecodeError:
                print(f"Invalid JSON: {filename}")
                continue

            if (
                "GPSCoordinates" in metadata[0]
                and "CreateDate" in metadata[0]
                and metadata[0]["CreateDate"].startswith("2021:01:06")
            ):
                print(f"GPS + Jan 6: {filename}")
                count += 1

    print(f"Total videos with GPS coordinates, filmed Jan 6: {count:,}")

if __name__ == "__main__":
    main()
```

Rather than just checking for videos with GPS coordinates, now the code also checks for those that have a CreateDate that starts with 2021:01:06. Once the code determines that the metadata in the current loop has GPS coordinates and was created on January 6, 2021, it displays the filename with print(f"GPS + Jan 6: {filename}"). When the for loop is finished, it displays the total count.

The expression in this code's if statement is surrounded by parentheses, and the three conditions inside those parentheses are indented. This is purely cosmetic; the code would work exactly the same if it were all on one line, but this formatting makes it slightly easier to read.

You can find the final script in the book's GitHub repo at *https://github .com/micahflee/hacks-leaks-and-revelations/blob/main/chapter-11/exercise-11-2.py*. Run the completed script like so:

```
micah@trapdoor chapter-11 % python3 exercise-11-2.py /Volumes/datasets/Parler/metadata
GPS + Jan 6: meta-xHkUeMHMFx3F.json
GPS + Jan 6: meta-eGqmDWzzOoSh.json
GPS + Jan 6: meta-WhQeLMyPWIrG.json
--snip--
GPS + Jan 6: meta-fhqU4rQ4ZFzO.json
GPS + Jan 6: meta-pTbZXLmXGyyn.json
GPS + Jan 6: meta-hL6OMjItBhOW.json
Total videos with GPS coordinates, filmed Jan 6: 1,958
```

The script might still take a few minutes to run, but this time, there should be fewer results. Only 1,958 Parler videos have GPS coordinates and were filmed on January 6, 2021; this is about 3 percent of the videos with GPS coordinates, and less than 0.2 percent of all of the videos.

Watching almost 2,000 videos, while perhaps unpleasant, is at least feasible. We can still do better, though. In all likelihood, some of those January 6 videos weren't actually filmed at the insurrection itself, but just happened to be uploaded the same day from other locations. To prepare for filtering this list further in order to find videos filmed at the insurrection, you'll need some background on working with GPS coordinates.

## Working with GPS Coordinates

In this section, you'll learn how latitude and longitude coordinates work and how to look them up on online map services like Google Maps. You'll also learn how to convert between different GPS formats and measure the rough distance between two locations. I'll introduce a few new Python features, including the split() and replace() methods for modifying strings and the float() function for converting a string into a decimal number.

### Searching by Latitude and Longitude

You can define any location on Earth using two coordinates: latitude and longitude. These coordinates are measured in degrees, with each degree split into 60 minutes and each minute split into 60 seconds. Latitude goes from 90 degrees North, which is the North Pole, to 0 degrees at the equator, to 90 degrees South, which is the South Pole. Longitude goes from 180 degrees West, which is in the middle of the Pacific Ocean, to 0 degrees, which cuts through England, to 180 degrees East, back to that same location in the middle of the Pacific.

For example, if you look up the metadata for the Parler video with filename *HS34fpbzqg2b* (which shows Trump supporters removing barricades around the Capitol building while police officers stand by and watch), you'd find the following GPS coordinates:

Latitude: 38 deg 53′ 26.52″ N

Longitude: 77 deg 0′ 28.44″ W

That means this video was filmed at the latitude of 38 degrees, 53 minutes, 26.52 seconds North and the longitude of 77 degrees, 0 minutes, 28.44 seconds West.

You can use various online map services, like Google Maps, to search by GPS coordinates and see exactly where on Earth they point to. To search the coordinates contained in the Parler metadata, you'll need to slightly modify them so that Google Maps will recognize them, loading *https://www .google.com/maps* and entering these coordinates as the string 38°53′26.52″, −77°0′28.44. Try searching for those coordinates in Google Maps now. Figure 11-3 shows the exact location this video was filmed: just outside the US Capitol building, where police had set up barricades.

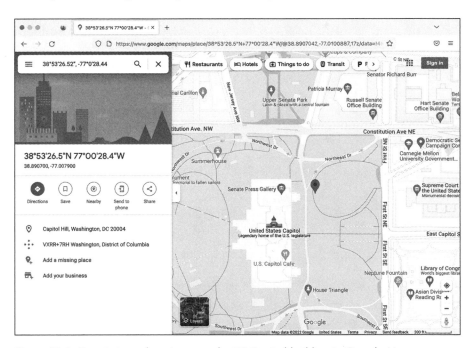

*Figure 11-3: Pinpointing a location near the US Capitol building in Google Maps*

You can also use Google Maps to discover the GPS coordinates of any given point. If you right-click anywhere on the map, a context menu should pop up showing you the GPS coordinates of that point. However, when you do this, the coordinates it shows you will look slightly different because they'll be in decimal format.

In the next section, you'll learn to convert from decimals to degrees, minutes, and seconds.

## Converting Between GPS Coordinate Formats

GPS coordinates in decimal format show the number of degrees on the left side of the decimal point, and converted minutes and seconds values on the right side. For example, consider the GPS coordinates from the *HS34fpbzqg2b* video:

- The latitude is 38 degrees, 53 minutes, 26.52 seconds North, which is 38.8907 in decimal.

- The longitude is 77 degrees, 0 minutes, 28.44 seconds West, which is −77.0079 in decimal.

One degree is 60 minutes and one minute is 60 seconds, meaning there are 3,600 seconds in a degree. The formula to convert from degrees, minutes, and seconds to decimal format is *degrees* + (*minutes* / 60) + (*seconds* / 3,600). Latitudes are negative in the Southern Hemisphere but positive in the Northern Hemisphere, while longitudes are negative in the Western Hemisphere but positive in the Eastern Hemisphere. The latitude for the *HS34fpbzqg2b* video is positive, while the longitude is negative.

Decimal numbers are simpler to work with in code. Since the GPS coordinates in the Parler metadata are formatted as degrees, minutes, and seconds, let's use some Python code to convert them to decimal format. The gps_degrees_to_decimal() function in Listing 11-2 takes a GPS coordinate from the Parler metadata as an argument and returns the decimal version.

```
def gps_degrees_to_decimal(gps_coordinate):
    parts = gps_coordinate.split()
    degrees = float(parts[0])
    minutes = float(parts[2].replace("'", ""))
    seconds = float(parts[3].replace('"', ""))
    hemisphere = parts[4]
    gps_decimal = degrees + (minutes / 60) + (seconds / 3600)
    if hemisphere == "W" or hemisphere == "S":
        gps_decimal *= -1
    return gps_decimal
```

*Listing 11-2: The gps_degrees_to_decimal() function*

This function introduces some new Python features. First, the split() string method splits a string into a list of parts based on whitespace. For example, this method would convert the string '77 deg 0\' 28.44" W' into the list of strings ['77', 'deg', "0'", '28.44"', 'W']. The line parts = gps _coordinate.split() stores the return value of gps_coordinate.split() into the parts variable. If you passed that string into this function as gps_coordinate, this would mean the following:

- parts[0] is the string 77.
- parts[1] is the string deg.
- parts[2] is the string 0' (0 followed by a single quote).
- parts[3] is the string 28.44" (28.44 followed by a double quote).
- parts[4] is the string W.

Before you can do math with strings in Python, you must convert them into *floating-point numbers*—which are just numbers that can contain decimals—using the float() function. Listing 11-2 uses float() to set the value of degrees to the floating-point version of parts[0]. In this case, it converts the value of the string 77 in gps_coordinate to the floating-point number 77.0.

The next line of code similarly uses the replace() string method to convert the minutes value to a floating-point number. This method searches the string for the first argument and replaces it with the second argument. For example, "GPS is fun".replace("fun", "hard") returns the string GPS is hard. When you run parts[2].replace("'", ""), you're replacing the single quote character (') with an empty string, in order to delete that character. This would convert the string 0' from gps_coordinate to 0 and then convert 0 to the floating-point number 0.0.

The next line uses replace() to delete the double quote character ("), converting the string 28.44" from gps_coordinates to 28.44, then converting that into the floating-point number 28.44 and saving it as seconds.

The rest of the function is more straightforward. It defines the variable gps_decimal as the decimal version of the GPS coordinates that are passed in an argument, using the formula to convert the coordinates to decimal format using the numbers in degrees, minutes, and seconds. If the coordinates are in the Western or Southern Hemisphere, the code gps_decimal *= -1 makes gps_decimal a negative number. Finally, the function returns gps _decimal, the decimal version of the GPS coordinates.

Since the GPS coordinates in the Parler data come in strings of degrees, minutes, and seconds, you'll use the gps_degrees_to_decimal() function in the next exercise to convert them to decimal format. First, though, you'll need to know how to calculate distances between two GPS coordinates.

## Calculating GPS Distance in Python

To determine which Parler videos were filmed in Washington, DC, based on their GPS coordinates, you can begin by finding the coordinates for the center point of the city and then imagine a circle around that point. You can consider a video to have been filmed in the city if its metadata has both a longitude and latitude within that circle. This won't tell you if the video was exactly filmed within the Washington, DC, city limits, but it's close enough. In this section, I'll review the simple math required to do this calculation.

The Earth isn't flat, but for the purposes of this chapter, pretend that Washington, DC, is a flat plane. You can think of GPS coordinates as a 2D point on a Cartesian coordinate system, where longitude represents the $x$ axis (East and West) and latitude represents the $y$ axis (North and South). Since you can look up the coordinates of the center of Washington, DC, and you know the coordinates for where each video was filmed, you can use the distance formula to determine if it's inside the circle.

The distance formula, as you might recall from geometry class, is used to calculate the distance between two points. It states that the distance between two points equals the square root of $((x_2 - x_1)^2 + (y_2 - y_1)^2)$, where $(x_1, y_1)$ is one point and $(x_2, y_2)$ is another point. As an example, Figure 11-4 shows the distance between the White House and the US Capitol, with the White House at point $(x_1, y_1)$ and the US Capitol at point $(x_2, y_2)$.

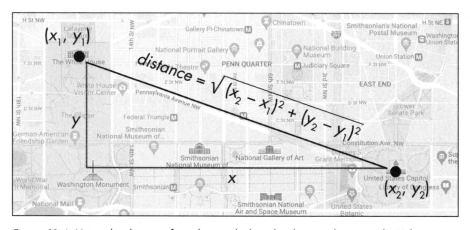

Figure 11-4: Using the distance formula to calculate the distance between the White House and the US Capitol

To determine if a given Parler video was filmed in Washington, DC, you'll compare the city center with the GPS coordinates of a Parler video. The center point of DC is constant, and when you loop through the JSON files of Parler metadata, you can find all the relevant GPS coordinates. If you plug these points into the distance formula, you can determine whether the distance is close enough to the center to be considered inside the city.

**NOTE** *Since the Earth isn't actually flat, using the distance formula will only be relatively accurate for short distances, like 20 kilometers. It's possible to calculate much more accurate distances between GPS coordinates using spherical geometry, but that requires using trigonometry functions like sine, cosine, and arctangent. Using the distance formula is much simpler and accurate enough for our purposes.*

Listing 11-3 shows a Python distance() function that implements the distance formula.

```
import math

def distance(x1, y1, x2, y2):
    return math.sqrt((x2 - x1) ** 2 + (y2 - y1) ** 2)
```

*Listing 11-3: The distance() function*

The distance formula requires you to calculate a square root, which you can do using Python's math.sqrt() function. To access this function, first you import the math module at the top of the file. The distance() function takes the x1, x2, y1, and y2 arguments, then calculates the distance formula, returning the distance between the two points. (In Python, ** is the power operator, so we write $x^2$ as x**2.) If you call distance() and pass any two points into it as arguments, it will return the distance between them.

## Finding the Center of Washington, DC

Now you'll find the coordinates of the center of Washington, DC, so that you can use the distance formula to compare them against those from a Parler video. Load *https://www.google.com/maps* in your browser and search for **Washington DC**. Right-click the US Capitol building, which is approximately at the center of the city. Google Maps should show you the GPS coordinates of that point (see Figure 11-5); click them to copy them. Your GPS coordinates might be slightly different, depending on where exactly you clicked.

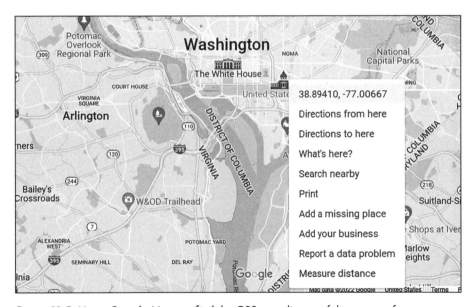

*Figure 11-5: Using Google Maps to find the GPS coordinates of the center of Washington, DC*

If the radius of the imaginary circle around Washington, DC, is about 20 kilometers, you can consider any videos filmed within 0.25 degrees to be inside the city. I decided on 0.25 degrees by checking the GPS coordinates on the outskirts of DC and comparing them to the coordinates in the city center.

Armed with the gps_degrees_to_decimal() and distance() Python functions and the GPS coordinates for the center of Washington, DC, you're ready to finish filtering the Parler videos to find the insurrection videos in Exercise 11-3.

## Exercise 11-3: Update the Script to Filter for Insurrection Videos

In this exercise, you'll filter the results of the Exercise 11-2 script even further, searching just for videos filmed in Washington, DC. First, make a copy of *exercise-11-2.py* and rename it *exercise-11-3.py*. Now modify *exercise-11-3.py* to match the following code:

```
import click
import os
import json
import math

def gps_degrees_to_decimal(gps_coordinate):
    parts = gps_coordinate.split()
    degrees = float(parts[0])
    minutes = float(parts[2].replace("'", ""))
    seconds = float(parts[3].replace('"', ""))
    hemisphere = parts[4]
    gps_decimal = degrees + (minutes / 60) + (seconds / 3600)
    if hemisphere == "W" or hemisphere == "S":
        gps_decimal *= -1
    return gps_decimal

def distance(x1, y1, x2, y2):
    return math.sqrt((x2 - x1) ** 2 + (y2 - y1) ** 2)

def was_video_filmed_in_dc(metadata):
    dc_x = -77.0066
    dc_y = 38.8941
    x = gps_degrees_to_decimal(metadata[0]["GPSLongitude"])
    y = gps_degrees_to_decimal(metadata[0]["GPSLatitude"])
    return distance(dc_x, dc_y, x, y) <= 0.25

@click.command()
@click.argument("parler_metadata_path")
def main(parler_metadata_path):
    """Filter Parler videos that were filmed in Washington DC and on Jan 6, 2021"""
    count = 0

    for filename in os.listdir(parler_metadata_path):
        abs_filename = os.path.join(parler_metadata_path, filename)
```

```
        if os.path.isfile(abs_filename) and abs_filename.endswith(".json"):
            with open(abs_filename, "rb") as f:
                json_data = f.read()

            try:
                metadata = json.loads(json_data)
            except json.decoder.JSONDecodeError:
                print(f"Invalid JSON: {filename}")
                continue

            if (
                "GPSLongitude" in metadata[0]
                and "GPSLatitude" in metadata[0]
                and "CreateDate" in metadata[0]
                and metadata[0]["CreateDate"].startswith("2021:01:06")
                and was_video_filmed_in_dc(metadata)
            ):
                print(f"Found an insurrection video: {filename}")
                count += 1

    print(f"Total videos filmed in Washington DC on January 6: {count:,}")

if __name__ == "__main__":
    main()
```

This code first defines the gps_degrees_to_decimal() function from Listing 11-2 and the distance() function from Listing 11-3, importing the required math module at the top of the file. It will later use gps_degrees_to _decimal() to convert GPS coordinates from the Parler video metadata into decimal format and distance() to calculate the distance between that GPS coordinate and the center of Washington, DC.

Next, the code defines the was_video_filmed_in_dc() function. This function takes a single argument, metadata, which contains the Parler video metadata loaded from its JSON file. It returns True if the GPS coordinates in that metadata are located inside Washington, DC, but otherwise returns False.

The was_video_filmed_in_dc() function first defines the *x* and *y* coordinates you found for the city center in the variables dc_x and dc_y. Next, it defines the *x* and *y* coordinates of the Parler video, storing those values in the variables x and y. Since the GPS coordinates in the GPSLongitude and GPSLatitude metadata fields aren't in decimal format, it first passes those strings into the gps_degrees_to_decimal() function to convert them from degrees, minutes, and seconds into decimals and then saves the return values into x and y.

Finally, was_video_filmed_in_dc() calls the distance() function to determine the distance between these two points. The return value is this expression:

```
distance(dc_x, dc_y, x, y) <= 0.25
```

The `distance()` function returns a number representing the distance between the center of Washington, DC, and the location where the video was filmed. If that number is less than or equal to 0.25 (roughly 20 kilometers), the expression evaluates to `True`; otherwise, it evaluates to `False`. Thus, the `was_video_filmed_in_dc()` function returns a Boolean.

With these functions defined at the top of the file, the remaining changes to the script are minimal. The code updates the docstring, since our script's purpose has changed. It also updates the `if` statement that checks whether or not an insurrection video was found. The version of this script from Exercise 11-2 just checked if the metadata included a `GPSCoordinates` field, but now it checks for the fields `GPSLongitude` and `GPSLatitude` as well. The videos with GPS coordinates contain all three of these fields. `GPSCoordinates` is just a single field that contains both longitude and latitude. However, since you need separate values for longitude and latitude, it's simpler to use the metadata fields that are already separated. Finally, the `if` statement confirms that the video was filmed in Washington, DC, by calling `was_video_filmed_in_dc(metadata)`.

If all of these conditions are true—the metadata contains `GPSLongitude` and `GPSLatitude`; the metadata contains `CreateDate` with a value matching January 6, 2021; and the GPS coordinates in the metadata show that the video was filmed in Washington, DC—then the code displays a message saying it found an insurrection video and increments `count`. Finally, after the script has finished looping through all of the Parler metadata files, it displays the total number of insurrection videos found.

You can find the final script in the book's GitHub repo at *https://github .com/micahflee/hacks-leaks-and-revelations/blob/main/chapter-11/exercise-11-3.py*. Run your complete script now, making sure to pass in the correct path to your Parler *metadata* folder:

```
micah@trapdoor chapter-11 % python3 exercise-11-3.py /Volumes/datasets/Parler/metadata
Found an insurrection video: meta-QPsyYtwu4zJb.json
Found an insurrection video: meta-Hcv3lzEsnWaa.json
Found an insurrection video: meta-6dDTCsYzK3k3.json
--snip--
Found an insurrection video: meta-eLSgf3w5r4PI.json
Found an insurrection video: meta-goLOHLdYn3Pb.json
Found an insurrection video: meta-a7DW37R386K3.json
Total videos filmed in Washington DC on January 6: 1,202
```

The script should find 1,202 insurrection videos. This means that out of the 1,958 videos uploaded to Parler on January 6 that included GPS coordinates, at least 61 percent were videos of the insurrection itself. (It's possible that more videos uploaded to Parler were also from the insurrection that day but just didn't include GPS coordinates in their metadata.) Manually watching 1,202 Parler videos is still unpleasant, but at least it's not as bad as watching 1,958.

You now know which of the Parler videos were from the January 6 insur-rection, but you can draw even more interesting conclusions from this data-set (and others that contain similar location data) when you visualize the data on a map.

## Plotting GPS Coordinates on a Map with simplekml

Rather than just displaying a list of insurrection video filenames, you could plot the locations of those videos on a map, allowing you to easily choose which videos you'd like to watch first. You could also map all Parler videos that contain GPS coordinates around the world, in case there are other newsworthy videos in this dataset that don't relate to the January 6 insur-rection. In this section, you'll learn to write Python code to create a file of Parler location data that you can then upload to an online map service to visualize it.

Google Earth (*https://earth.google.com*) allows you to upload a file in Keyhole Markup Language (KML), a file format designed to describe geo-graphical features such as points on a map. KML was created in 2004 spe-cifically for use with Google Earth, and it became a standard file format for describing geographic data in 2008.

Listing 11-4 shows an example KML file.

```
<?xml version="1.0" ?>
<kml xmlns="http://www.opengis.net/kml/2.2"
xmlns:gx="http://www.google.com/kml/ext/2.2">
    <Document id="1">
        <Placemark id="3">
            <name>New York City</name>
            <description>The Big Apple</description>
            <Point id="2">
```

```
          <coordinates>-74.006393,40.714172,0.0</coordinates>
        </Point>
      </Placemark>
    </Document>
</kml>
```

*Listing 11-4: A file written in KML, example.kml*

As you can see, the KML format is similar to HTML. Both formats are extensions of XML, or Extensible Markup Language, so they share the same rules. The first line, starting with <?xml, is called the XML prolog, and it defines some metadata about this file. The entire contents of the KML file are wrapped in a <kml> tag. Inside this is a <Document> tag, and inside this are one or more <Placemark> tags. Each <Placemark> represents a point on a map: its name, description, and GPS coordinates in decimal format. This example file describes a single point for New York City.

To plot GPS coordinates on Google Earth, you must generate a KML file that contains these coordinates and then upload it to the service. The simplest way to create KML files is by using the simplekml Python module. You can use this module to create a new KML object, create a new point on it for each Parler video with GPS coordinates, and then save that KML object to a *.kml* file.

Install the simplekml module by running the following command:

```
python3 -m pip install simplekml
```

Now use the module in the Python interpreter to generate the *example .kml* file from Listing 11-4:

```
>>> import simplekml
>>> kml = simplekml.Kml()
>>> kml.newpoint(name="New York City", description="The Big Apple", coords=[(-74.006393,
40.714172)])
<simplekml.featgeom.Point object at 0x101241cc0>
>>> kml.save("example.kml")
```

After importing the simplekml module, this code defines the value of the kml variable as the output of simplekml.Kml(), which returns a KML object. It then uses the kml.newpoint() method to add GPS points to the KML file it's creating. While this example just adds one point for New York City, with the description "The Big Apple," you can add as many points as you want. Note that the value of the coords argument must be a list of tuples, with each tuple containing longitude and latitude coordinates in decimal format. Finally, after adding points, the code saves the KML file by running kml.save() and passes an output filename.

You can find further documentation for the simplekml Python module at *https://simplekml.readthedocs.io.*

There are many different ways to plot GPS points, including alternative online services like MapBox (*https://www.mapbox.com*), which allows you to upload a CSV of GPS coordinates to generate points on a map and even embed that map into articles on your website.

In future projects, you may need to visualize sensitive geographic data without sharing it with a third-party service like Google Earth or MapBox. The free and open source desktop software QGIS (*https://qgis.org*) allows you to create maps locally on your computer, though it's pretty complicated to use. You can also write Python code that pulls data from OpenStreetMap (*https://www.openstreetmap.org*), a vast and completely free and open source mapping resource that allows you to create geographic images with GPS points on them. These options aren't as simple as using online tools, and explaining how they work is beyond the scope of this book.

You don't necessarily need GPS coordinates in your dataset to visualize location data on a map. If you have addresses, or even just city names or postal codes, you could convert that information to GPS coordinates and then plot those on a map. You could do the same with IP addresses, converting them to their rough GPS locations.

You now know how to create KML files full of location data that can be mapped in Google Earth. As your final exercise in this chapter, you'll generate KML files based on GPS coordinates in the Parler dataset.

## Exercise 11-4: Create KML Files to Visualize Location Data

So far, we've focused on finding Parler videos filmed in Washington, DC, during the January 6 insurrection. While this is undoubtedly the most newsworthy part of this dataset, there could be other things we're missing. Parler is a global far-right social network. What other far-right videos did people post to it? Does it contain any interesting data from other countries, such as Russia? In this exercise, you'll write a script that creates two KML files full of GPS coordinates from the Parler dataset to visualize in Google Earth:

- A *parler-videos-all.kml* file containing all videos with GPS coordinates
- A *parler-videos-january6.kml* file containing videos with GPS coordinates filmed on January 6, 2021

This exercise will give you experience creating KML files and using Google Earth to visualize location data, a skill that will likely come in handy for any future dataset you come across that includes location data.

You'll base your script for this exercise off the script you wrote in Exercise 11-3. For a challenge, you can try programming your own script to meet the following requirements:

- Make this script accept an argument, `parler_metadata_path`, using Click. This will be the path to the *metadata* folder full of JSON files.

- Import the `simplekml` module and create two KML objects (one for each KML file you'll be creating). Loop through the Parler video metadata JSON files, and add different points to the appropriate KML objects depending on the metadata. Points for all videos should be added to *parler-videos-all.kml*, and points only for videos with the `CreateDate` of January 6, 2021, should be added to *parler-videos-january6.kml*.

- Give every point you add to a KML object a name, a description, and GPS coordinates in decimal format. The name should be the Parler video ID (for example, `HS34fpbzqg2b`), and the description should be a string containing the video's download link (for example, `https://data .ddosecrets.com/Parler/Videos/HS34fpbzqg2b`) as well as important metadata fields such as `CreateDate`, `FileTypeExtension`, or others you're interested in.

- Make your script loop through all of the metadata JSON files and filter them for videos that contain GPS coordinates.

Alternatively, follow along with the instructions in the rest of this exercise.

### Create a KML File for All Videos with GPS Coordinates

You'll begin by writing a script to loop through all of the Parler metadata JSON files and add any GPS coordinates it finds to a single KML file, *parler -videos-all.kml*, including only the video URL in the description, not any metadata. Make a copy of the *exercise-11-3.py* script and name it *exercise-11-4.py*, then make the following modifications:

```
import click
import os
import json
import simplekml

def json_filename_to_parler_id(json_filename):
    return json_filename.split("-")[1].split(".")[0]

def gps_degrees_to_decimal(gps_coordinate):
    parts = gps_coordinate.split()
    degrees = float(parts[0])
    minutes = float(parts[2].replace("'", ""))
    seconds = float(parts[3].replace('"', ""))
    hemisphere = parts[4]
    gps_decimal = degrees + (minutes / 60) + (seconds / 3600)
    if hemisphere == "W" or hemisphere == "S":
        gps_decimal *= -1
    return gps_decimal
```

```python
@click.command()
@click.argument("parler_metadata_path")
def main(parler_metadata_path):
    """Create KML files of GPS coordinates from Parler metadata"""
    kml_all = simplekml.Kml()

    for filename in os.listdir(parler_metadata_path):
        abs_filename = os.path.join(parler_metadata_path, filename)
        if os.path.isfile(abs_filename) and abs_filename.endswith(".json"):
            with open(abs_filename) as f:
                json_data = f.read()

            try:
                metadata = json.loads(json_data)
            except json.decoder.JSONDecodeError:
                print(f"Invalid JSON: {filename}")
                continue

            if (
                "GPSLongitude" in metadata[0]
                and "GPSLatitude" in metadata[0]
                and metadata[0]["GPSLongitude"] != ""
                and metadata[0]["GPSLatitude"] != ""
            ):
                name = json_filename_to_parler_id(filename)
                description = f"URL: https://data.ddosecrets.com/Parler/Videos/{name}"
                lon = gps_degrees_to_decimal(metadata[0]["GPSLongitude"])
                lat = gps_degrees_to_decimal(metadata[0]["GPSLatitude"])

                print(f"Found a video with GPS coordinates: {filename}")
                kml_all.newpoint(name=name, description=description, coords=[(lon, lat)])

    kml_all.save("parler-videos-all.kml")

if __name__ == "__main__":
    main()
```

Since you're going to be mapping this data, you don't need the code that detects if a video is in Washington, DC—you'll be able to tell by zooming into Washington, DC. Therefore, this code deletes the distance() and was_video_filmed_in_dc() functions from the previous script, as well as the math import. The new code imports the simplekml module at the top of the file so that you can use it later in the script.

Next, the code defines the function json_filename_to_parler_id(). This function is only a single, complex line of code that takes the filename of a Parler metadata JSON file as an argument, then returns the Parler ID associated with that file. For example, say the value of json_filename is meta-31VC1ufihFpa.json. In this case, the expression json_filename.split("-") will evaluate to the list ['meta', '31VC1ufihFpa.json']. Since Python starts counting at zero, the code selects the second item in that list (the string 31VC1ufihFpa.json) by adding [1] to that expression, making it json_filename.split("-")[1]. Next, it splits *that* string on the period character with the expression `json_filename.split("-")[1].split(".")`, which returns the list `['31VC1ufihFpa', 'json']`. It then selects the first item in that list (the string `31VC1ufihFpa`) by adding `[0]` to that expression, making it `json_filename .split("-")[1].split(".")[0]`. The `json_filename_to_parler_id()` function just returns the result of that expression, which is the Parler ID.

In the `main()` function, the code defines a new KML object called `kml_all` to contain all the GPS points found in the Parler metadata. The rest of this code should be familiar to you from Exercises 11-2 and 11-3. It loops through the Parler *metadata* folder looking for JSON files, loading the JSON data for each file it finds into the `metadata` variable. This time, the `if` statement ensures that the metadata dictionary contains the keys `GPSLongitude` and `GPSLatitude` and that those values aren't blank.

When the code finds a Parler video that contains non-empty GPS fields, it sets up variables with the data it needs to add the point to the KML files: `name`, `description`, `lon`, and `lat`. It defines `name` as the return value of the `json_filename _to_parler_id()` function, meaning the name of the point will be the video's Parler ID. It defines `description` as the video's download URL. Using the `gps_degrees_to_decimal()` function, it defines `lon` and `lat` as the longitude and latitude, in decimal format, of the GPS coordinates found in the metadata.

After defining these variables, the code runs `kml_all.newpoint()` to add the GPS point to the KML object. It sets the point's name to `name`, its description to `description`, and its coordinates to a list of points; in this case, the list has only one point, a tuple containing `lon` and `lat`. Finally, when the for loop is complete, the code calls the `kml_all.save()` function to save all of these GPS points into the file *parler-videos-all.kml*.

Run the final script, changing the path in the argument to the path to your Parler *metadata* folder:

```
micah@trapdoor chapter-11 % python3 exercise-11-4.py /Volumes/datasets/Parler/metadata
Adding point 2XpiJFsho2do to kml_all: -117.6683, 33.490500000000004
Adding point bcHZhpDOFnXd to kml_all: -1.3391, 52.04648888888889
--snip--
```

Since the Parler dataset contains about 64,000 videos with GPS coordinates, the script should return about 64,000 lines of output, each including a video's Parler ID, longitude, and latitude. When the script finishes running, it should also create a 20MB KML file called *parler-videos-all.kml* in the same folder as the script.

Open *parler-videos-all.kml* in a text editor. The file's contents should look like this:

```
<?xml version="1.0" ?>
<kml xmlns="http://www.opengis.net/kml/2.2" xmlns:gx="http://www.google.com/kml/ext/2.2">
    <Document id="1">
        <Placemark id="3">
            <name>2XpiJFsho2do</name>
            <description>URL:https://data.ddosecrets.com/Parler/Videos/2XpiJFsho2do</description>
            <Point id="2">
                <coordinates>-117.6683,33.490500000000004,0.0</coordinates>
```

```
            </Point>
        </Placemark>
        <Placemark id="5">
            <name>bcHZhpDOFnXd</name>
            <description>URL:https://data.ddosecrets.com/Parler/Videos/bcHZhpDOFnXd</description>
            <Point id="4">
                <coordinates>-1.3391,52.04648888888889,0.0</coordinates>
            </Point>
        </Placemark>
--snip--
```

This file should contains 64,000 `<Placemark>` tags, each representing a different Parler video with GPS coordinates.

Now that you've created a KML file that contains *all* of the Parler location data, you'll modify your script further to create a KML file with just the videos from January 6, 2021.

## Create KML Files for Videos from January 6, 2021

Your script so far has a KML object called kml_all, and the code adds all of the GPS points in the Parler metadata to it. Make the following changes to your code to create another KML object, kml_january6, and just add GPS points from videos filmed on January 6, 2021, to it. Since this script is getting long, I'll quote just the main() function, the only part that is modified:

```python
@click.command()
@click.argument("parler_metadata_path")
def main(parler_metadata_path):
    """Create KML files of GPS coordinates from Parler metadata"""
    kml_all = simplekml.Kml()
    kml_january6 = simplekml.Kml()

    for filename in os.listdir(parler_metadata_path):
        abs_filename = os.path.join(parler_metadata_path, filename)
        if os.path.isfile(abs_filename) and abs_filename.endswith(".json"):
            with open(abs_filename, "rb") as f:
                json_data = f.read()

            try:
                metadata = json.loads(json_data)
            except json.decoder.JSONDecodeError:
                print(f"Invalid JSON: {filename}")
                continue

            if (
                "GPSLongitude" in metadata[0]
                and "GPSLatitude" in metadata[0]
                and metadata[0]["GPSLongitude"] != ""
                and metadata[0]["GPSLatitude"] != ""
            ):
                name = json_filename_to_parler_id(filename)
                description = f"URL: https://data.ddosecrets.com/Parler/Videos/{name}<br>"
                for key in [
```

```
            "CreateDate",
            "FileTypeExtension",
            "Duration",
            "Make",
            "Model",
            "Software",
        ]:
            if key in metadata[0]:
                description += f"{key}: {metadata[0][key]}<br>"
        lon = gps_degrees_to_decimal(metadata[0]["GPSLongitude"])
        lat = gps_degrees_to_decimal(metadata[0]["GPSLatitude"])

        print(f"Adding point {name} to kml_all: {lon}, {lat}")
        kml_all.newpoint(name=name, description=url, coords=[(lon, lat)])

        if "CreateDate" in metadata[0] and metadata[0]["CreateDate"].startswith(
            "2021:01:06"
        ):
            print(f"Adding point {name} to kml_january6: {lon}, {lat}")
            kml_january6.newpoint(
                name=name, description=url, coords=[(lon, lat)]
            )

    kml_all.save("parler-videos-all.kml")
    kml_january6.save("parler-videos-january6.kml")
```

At the top of the main() function, this script adds another KML object called kml_january6. The code will add points to this file only from January 6, 2021. Next, the for loop will loop through each Parler metadata file, parse the JSON, and determine whether or not it has GPS coordinates. If so, the code will prepare variables so it can add the point to the KML objects. But this time, instead of the description variable containing just the video's download URL, it will also include metadata.

When defining description, the code adds <br> at the end, which is the HTML tag for a line break. This way, when you visualize this KML file, the description will show the URL on the first line, and the metadata will start on the next line. The code then loops through a list of metadata keys to add to the description, including CreateDate, FileTypeExtension, Duration, Make, Model, and Software. If there are any other pieces of metadata you'd like to include, feel free to add them to your script.

In each loop, the code checks to see if the metadata for the current video includes that key, and if so, adds its value to description, inserting a line break after each piece of metadata. For example, if the code is looking at the JSON file *meta-g09yZZCplavI.json*, description will appear as follows:

```
URL: https://data.ddosecrets.com/Parler/Videos/g09yZZCplavI
CreateDate: 2021:01:06 20:08:25
FileTypeExtension: mov
Duration: 25.24 s
Make: Apple
Model: iPhone XS Max
Software: 14.3
```

(The actual value of the `description` string will contain <br> for the line breaks, but this is how the description will look in Google Earth.)

Next, the code uses another `if` statement to see if that video was created on January 6, 2021, and if so, adds that point to `kml_january6`. It does this by checking that the file has a `CreateDate` metadata field and that the date in that field is from January 6, 2021, just as you did in Exercise 11-2. Finally, when the script finishes looping through all of the Parler videos, after saving the points in `kml_all` to *parler-videos-all.kml*, it also saves the points in `kml_january6` to *parler-videos-january6.kml*.

You can find the final script in the book's GitHub repo at *https://github.com/micahflee/hacks-leaks-and-revelations/blob/main/chapter-11/exercise-11-4.py*. Run your complete script like so:

```
micah@trapdoor chapter-11 % python3 exercise-11-4.py /Volumes/datasets/Parler/metadata
Adding point 2XpiJFsho2do to kml_all: -117.6683, 33.490500000000004
Adding point bcHZhpDOFnXd to kml_all: -1.3391, 52.04648888888889
--snip--
Adding point VNYtKrEURiZs to kml_all: -97.0244, 33.1528
Adding point VNYtKrEURiZs to kml_january6: -97.0244, 33.1528
Adding point KptnQksS5Xr8 to kml_all: -77.0142, 38.8901
--snip--
```

When the script is finished running, it should have created two KML files: a 31MB file called *parler-videos-all.kml* (the file is bigger this time because the descriptions are longer) and a 929KB file called *parler-videos-january6.kml*.

Now that you've put in the hard work of generating KML files full of GPS coordinates, you can move on to the fun part: visualizing this data using Google Earth. This will allow you to scroll around the globe picking which videos you'd like to watch.

## Visualizing Location Data with Google Earth

In this section, you'll learn how to visualize location data in the KML files that you just created using Google Earth, marking each Parler video with a pin on a map. Not only will this let you visualize exactly where all of the videos with GPS coordinates were filmed, but this will also make it considerably simpler to download these videos to watch.

When you created those KML files, you set the description for each Parler video to include its download URL. Once you load a KML file into Google Earth and turn it into pins on a map, you can click on a video's pin to see its description and then click the link in the description to download the video. In a web browser, load Google Earth at *https://earth.google.com*. (You don't have to log in to a Google account, though doing so enables you to save your work and revisit it later.) In the menu bar on the left, choose **Projects ▸ Open ▸ Import KML File from Computer**. Browse for the *parler-videos-all.kml* file you created in the previous exercise and open it. When it's done loading, click the pencil icon to edit the title of this project, name it

*All Parler Videos*, and press ENTER. This should create a pin on the map for each Parler video in the entire dataset, labeled by its ID.

Repeat this process for *parler-videos-january6.kml*, and name this one **Parler Videos from January 6, 2021**. In the Projects panel on the left of the screen, you should see your two projects.

By clicking the eye icon, you can show and hide Google Earth projects to choose which KML files you want displayed. With the pins you want displayed, you can rotate the Earth and zoom in on whatever you'd like. You can double-click on the map, click the plus (+) button to zoom in, and click the minus (−) button to zoom out.

For example, to investigate just the insurrection videos, show that project and hide the others. Figure 11-6 shows Google Earth zoomed in on the US Capitol building in Washington, DC, with just the videos from the January 6 insurrection showing. The pins in the figure are all videos of the January 6 insurrection, and the pins located over the Capitol building itself are videos filmed by Trump supporters who were actively trespassing inside the US Capitol that day.

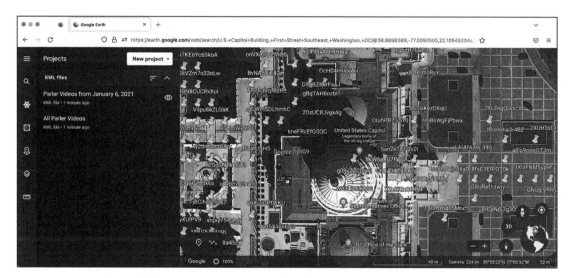

*Figure 11-6: Google Earth, focused on the US Capitol building, with pins at the GPS points in* parler-videos-january6.kml

When you find a video you're interested in, click its pin to view its description. You should see the URL to download the video, and you can watch it using software like VLC Media Player.

You can also use Google Earth to search for a location so you can see the individual pins there. For example, you could hide the Parler Videos from January 6, 2021, project and instead show pins for the All Parler Videos project, then search for *Moscow*. Figure 11-7 shows Google Earth zoomed in on the city of Moscow, Russia. As the figure indicates, only a handful of videos whose metadata included GPS coordinates were filmed there and uploaded to Parler.

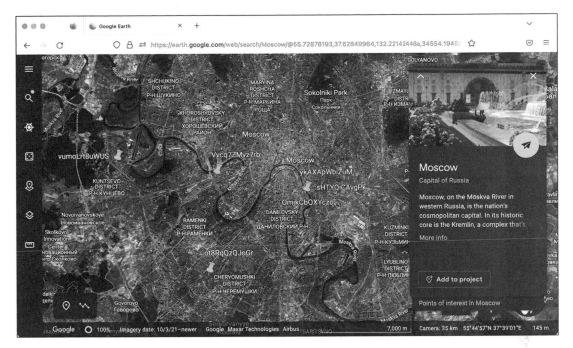

Figure 11-7: Parler videos filmed in Moscow

Click the pin for the video labeled *ykAXApWbiZuM*. You should see the following description:

```
URL: https://data.ddosecrets.com/Parler/Videos/ykAXApWbiZuM
CreateDate: 2020:06:28 21:56:41
FileTypeExtension: mov
Duration: 0:06:51
Make: Apple
Model: iPhone 7 Plus
Software: 13.5.1
```

As you can see, this video was filmed on June 28, 2020 (during the Black Lives Matter uprising), with an iPhone 7 Plus running iOS 13.5.1. Right-click the link to see the option to download the video. This way, your web browser won't try opening it directly in a new tab, where it might not display properly.

If you're interested, you can open the video file using VLC Media Player to watch it. In the recording, a tattooed American white supremacist who runs a Confederate-themed barber shop in Moscow goes on a racist and homophobic rant, in part explaining why he moved to Russia. "I voted Trump in office in 2016," he said. "But the fact is, nothing's gonna change. The fact is, all these Trump supporters in America all the time can't see the real problem. Your real problem is fucking Jews in America." Figure 11-8 shows a screenshot from the video where he's telling Parler users that he's a real white supremacist and not a liberal troll, as people were accusing him of being.

*Figure 11-8: A screenshot from a Parler video filmed by an American white supremacist in Moscow*

He goes on to fantasize about mass shooting Black Lives Matter protesters. "I watch the news in America. I see all these fucking [N-word]s, antifa fucking scum. Ripping down the monuments. It angers me more than anything. What I don't understand is where's the fucking police to stop any of this?" he asks. "How come nobody's shooting these motherfuckers? If I was in Los Angeles still, seeing all this rioting and looting going on, I'd be up on a motherfucking building with my AK-47 just spraying the fucking crowd."

If you're curious about the complete metadata from this video, you can check the original file at *meta-ykAXApWbiZuM.json*. If you wanted to see more videos posted by this Parler user, you could modify your script to filter videos that were filmed on the exact device by checking for the same `Make`, `Model`, and `Software` fields. You might find some other users' videos, but chances are you'll also find more videos from this poster as well.

The media spent the bulk of its time focusing on Parler videos they knew were taken in Washington, DC, on the day of the insurrection. If you're interested in further exploring this dataset, you might try to find videos from other far-right protests, or events with far-right counterprotesters. For example, you could create a KML file that includes the date ranges of the specific 2020 Black Lives Matters protests and explore those videos. You might find video evidence of other crimes.

## Viewing Metadata with ExifTool

When @donk_enby downloaded the Parler videos and extracted metadata from them in JSON format, she used a command line program called `exiftool`. This program is one of the investigation tools I use most frequently, and this section explains how to use it.

If you run `exiftool` followed by a filepath, it will attempt to find metadata stored in that file and show it to you. It works on a variety of file formats, including Microsoft Office documents, PDFs, images, and videos. You can use it to find hidden information in the metadata of those documents, such as the author of a Word document, which type of phone or camera was used to take a photo, and much more.

You don't need to run exiftool on the Parler videos since @donk_enby did it for you, but most of the time, you won't be so lucky. If you want to search for hidden information in BlueLeaks documents, for example, you'd need to run exiftool on them yourself. In this subsection, to learn how exiftool works, you'll use it to view the metadata on one of the Parler videos in JSON format.

Mac users, install exiftool by running the **brew install exiftool** command; users of Linux or Windows with WSL, install it with the **sudo apt install libimage-exiftool-perl** command. In your terminal, change to the *videos* folder in your Parler dataset folder and use wget to download the Parler video with the ID *HS34fpbzqg2b*:

```
wget https://data.ddosecrets.com/Parler/Videos/HS34fpbzqg2b
```

You can use exiftool to look at the metadata of a file by running exiftool *filename*. Run it on the *HS34fpbzqg2b* file that you just downloaded with the following command:

```
exiftool HS34fpbzqg2b
```

The output should show all the metadata for this video file:

```
--snip--
File Type Extension           : mov
--snip--
Model                         : iPhone XR
Software                      : 14.2
Creation Date                 : 2021:01:06 13:57:49-05:00
--snip--
GPS Position                  : 38 deg 53' 26.52" N, 77 deg 0' 28.44" W
```

Along with other information, the metadata shows that this video's file extension is *.mov*, it was recorded using an iPhone XR running iOS 14.2 on January 6, 2021, at 1:57 PM, and it was filmed at the GPS coordinates 38 deg 53′ 26.52″ N, 77 deg 0′ 28.44″ W.

Since the file extension for this video is *.mov*, rename it by running **mv HS34fpbzqg2b HS34fpbzqg2b.mov**. You can open *HS34fpbzqg2b.mov* in a program like VLC Media Player just to see what it contains: police officers stepping out of the way while Trump supporters remove barricades surrounding the Capitol building.

When @donk_enby used exiftool to extract the metadata from the Parler videos, she used the -json argument to extract it in JSON format. Here's how you do that for *HS34fpbzqg2b*:

```
micah@trapdoor videos % exiftool HS34fpbzqg2b -json
[{
  "SourceFile": "HS34fpbzqg2b",
  "ExifToolVersion": 12.42,
```

```
  "FileName": "HS34fpbzqg2b",
--snip--
  "GPSLatitude": "38 deg 53' 26.52\" N",
  "GPSLongitude": "77 deg 0' 28.44\" W",
  "Rotation": 180,
  "GPSPosition": "38 deg 53' 26.52\" N, 77 deg 0' 28.44\" W"
}]
```

The -json argument makes the output much easier to work with than exiftool's default output.

## Summary

In this chapter, you've learned about the secrets hidden in the metadata of over a million videos uploaded to Parler, many of them by insurrectionists filming themselves during the January 6 riot in Washington, DC. You've learned the syntax of the JSON file format and how to work with JSON data in your own Python scripts. You've written a series of scripts that filtered the list of a million videos down to just the ones that were, according to their metadata, filmed on January 6, 2021, in Washington, DC, during the attack on the US Capitol by supporters of Donald Trump. You now have the skills necessary to write code that analyzes JSON in your own investigations. Finally, you've seen how you can convert GPS coordinates from degrees to decimal and plot them on a map, an invaluable skill for future investigations that involve location data.

In the next chapter, you'll explore one more technology that's common in hacked and leaked datasets: SQL databases. You'll use the SQL skills you learn to dig into the hacked databases of Epik, a hosting and domain name company that provides service to much of the American fascist movement.

# 12

## EPIK FAIL, EXTREMISM RESEARCH, AND SQL DATABASES

On a Saturday morning in late October 2018 in Pittsburgh, Pennsylvania, Robert Bowers posted a message to the fascist-friendly social network Gab. "[Hebrew Immigrant Aid Society] likes to bring invaders in that kill our people," he wrote. "I can't sit by and watch my people get slaughtered. Screw your optics, I'm going in." He was parroting the "great replacement" conspiracy theory, popularized in the US by former Fox News host Tucker Carlson, which claims that Jews are replacing white people with immigrants of color.

Armed with an AR-15 assault rifle and three Glock semi-automatic pistols, Bowers entered the Tree of Life Synagogue, where three different Jewish congregations were holding Shabbat services that morning, and committed the deadliest antisemitic terrorist attack in US history. He killed 11 people and wounded 6 others, including several Holocaust survivors.

That day, several companies kicked Gab off their platforms. GoDaddy, the registrar that Gab used to buy the domain gab.com, sent Gab a letter saying it had "discovered numerous instances of content on your site that both promotes and encourages violence against people." Gab was down only for a few days, though, thanks in part to the domain name registrar and web hosting company Epik, which soon took over registration for gab.com.

In this chapter, you'll learn about Epik, its extremist customers, and the 2021 data breach that exposed hundreds of gigabytes of customer data. You'll download and learn to work with some of the leaked data, most of which is in the format of structured query language, or SQL (often pronounced "sequel"). SQL is a popular database technology that many websites, online services, and local software use to store data. This chapter focuses on MySQL databases, which use the SQL software that Epik uses. You'll also practice using database software called MariaDB, a community-maintained version of MySQL. Finally, you'll learn to run a SQL server (software that allows you to host SQL databases), import the data, and write your own code to search it, skills that will prepare you for investigating your own SQL datasets in the future.

## The Structure of SQL Databases

I have briefly discussed SQL databases in previous chapters, including Chapter 10, where you converted CSVs into SQLite databases for BlueLeaks Explorer. There are many types of SQL databases, including PostgreSQL, Microsoft SQL Server, Oracle SQL, and the aforementioned MySQL and SQLite. While they're all based on SQL, they have minor differences that mean they're not entirely compatible with each other. SQL databases are popular; therefore, so are SQL data breaches.

Some SQL database software is proprietary. For example, Microsoft SQL Server is the version of SQL that Microsoft products require, and it runs only on Windows. Oracle is another proprietary version of SQL; if you get a leaked Oracle database, you'll need to use Oracle software to access it. PostgreSQL and MySQL are free and open source and run on Linux servers, making them popular and widely used in web development. SQLite is another free and open source version of SQL. It can't handle huge databases, but it's very simple and convenient for small ones—iPhone and Android apps frequently store their settings in a SQLite database, for example.

NOTE    *Some datasets may require you to set up a SQL database server that you're unfamiliar with, or figure out how to convert them into a type of SQL you already know, in order to analyze them. I once contributed to an investigation based on a leaked Chinese police database that revealed the suffocating surveillance of China's Uyghur minority group in the Xinjiang region. It was an Oracle database, but it's unclear whether the Chinese police paid for it or were pirating it. Because Oracle is proprietary and the investigating technologists didn't have an Oracle license or experience with this version of SQL, they decided to convert it into a PostgreSQL database so they could more easily work with the data. Read the full report by Yael Grauer at* https://theintercept.com/2021/01/29/china-uyghur-muslim-surveillance-police/.

Next we'll look at what relational databases are, how SQL servers typically work, and the terminology used to describe SQL databases and the data they contain.

## Relational Databases

SQL databases are made up of tables, which you can think of as spreadsheets comprising a list of rows, with each row containing the same columns, or *fields*. SQL databases are useful because they're *relational*, meaning that data in different tables can relate to each other. You saw this firsthand when working with BlueLeaks Explorer: the BlueLeaks folders had individual spreadsheets like *Documents.csv* and *DocumentCategory.csv*, but once you converted them into SQLite databases, you could rely on the relationship between the Documents and the DocumentCategory tables to browse BlueLeaks documents by category.

Let's look at a simple example: a database that contains two related tables for books and authors. Table 12-1 shows the information stored in the authors table.

**Table 12-1:** The authors Table

| id | name |
|----|------|
| 1 | Micah Lee |
| 2 | Carl Sagan |

Table 12-2 shows the information stored in the books table.

**Table 12-2:** The books Table

| id | title | author_id |
|----|-------|-----------|
| 1 | Hacks, Leaks, and Revelations | 1 |
| 2 | Pale Blue Dot | 2 |
| 3 | Contact: A Novel | 2 |

Each SQL database can contain multiple tables, and each table has a defined set of fields. For example, Table 12-2 has id, title, and author_id fields.

Every table in a SQL database normally has a unique id field that *auto-increments*, meaning that when you add rows of data to the table, the first row is automatically given an id of 1, the second is given an id of 2, and so on, ensuring that no two rows ever have the same id. If Table 12-1 included two authors named Micah Lee, it would be clear in the database that they're not the same person, because the ID for each row would be different.

In general, tables relate to each other using these unique ID numbers. Let's say you're browsing through the books table and come across *Contact: A Novel*. Who wrote it? According to the data in its row, the author_id is 2. To find out who the author is, you'd look at the authors table for the row with the id of 2 to find that it's Carl Sagan.

This example deals with a small amount of data, but SQL databases can become huge and complicated. For example, instead of two authors, you might find a database with 10 million users and all sorts of tables that relate to it using a field called user_id.

## Clients and Servers

Most types of SQL databases are *server* software, meaning you install a SQL server to hold all of the data. Other computers then use a SQL *client* to communicate with that server to search for, add, or update data. This communication is similar to how websites work: a web server has the software that runs the website, while a web browser (the client) connects to the server remotely to load web pages, submit forms, and so on. SQL clients communicate to servers using SQL queries, also known as *statements*. Similarly to English, SQL queries start with a *verb* that describes an action being taken and have *clauses* that further describe that action. All SQL queries end with semicolons (;).

Each SQL server can host multiple databases. For example, you could run 20 different WordPress websites on the same MySQL server by having each website use a different database. The Epik dataset includes data from nine different MySQL databases. If you downloaded them all, you could import all nine into the same MySQL server. Because much of the Epik data is in MySQL format, in Exercise 12-1 you'll run a MySQL server in Docker. Once you have a server running, you'll connect to it later using a client to import the data and begin your analysis.

In this chapter, you'll try out two different MySQL clients: the web-based client Adminer and the mysql command line client, which allows you to interact with the database from the terminal. For MySQL, Adminer is more user-friendly for manually browsing a SQL database, but mysql is especially useful for working on remote servers and creating or restoring database backups. For a simpler introduction to working with clients, you'll use Adminer in the first half of this chapter, then move on to the command line client. All clients interact with servers in the same way, sending SQL queries to the SQL server, which runs them and returns a response. Therefore, the skills you learn using Adminer will also apply to the CLI client.

SQL servers also normally have a system of users and permissions that allow you to grant a given user access to some databases but not others. The root user on MySQL and other databases has total access to every database on the server. When you're researching a leaked database, it's fine to run all of your searches as the root user since you're typically the only person using that server. However, if you're running a database that strangers online might use, such as a website powered by a SQL database, you should use non-root database users with restricted permissions. This way, if one of those strangers hacks your database, they'll have access only to what that specific database user has permissions for.

## Tables, Columns, and Types

You can store only a single type of data in each column in a SQL table. For example, you can store strings, but not numerals, in the title column of Table 12-2 (though you could get around this by storing a string representation of a number, like the string '1' instead of the number 1).

Data types differ slightly depending on the flavor of SQL you're using. However, you'll generally see types representing numbers, times, or strings of text. The following list includes some common SQL types that are all valid in MySQL:

**INT** Integers or whole numbers

**DECIMAL** Numbers with decimal places

**DATE** A specific date

**DATETIME** A specific date, along with the time of day

**VARCHAR** A string of characters of a specified length

**TEXT** Also a string of text

If Table 12-2 were stored in a MySQL database, id would be type INT, title would be type TEXT, and author_id would be type INT. If you tried storing the string "hola" in the author_id field, the SQL server would respond with an error message, because the data isn't an integer.

---

### THE HISTORY OF MARIADB

MySQL was first released in 1995 as open source SQL database software maintained by the Swedish company MySQL AB. For nearly two decades it reigned as the most popular database for web apps, ushering in the early internet's Web 2.0 era. Wildly popular web app software like WordPress, Drupal, Joomla, and MediaWiki (which powers Wikipedia) were all built on MySQL databases and developed in the PHP programming language.

In 2008, Sun Microsystems acquired MySQL AB, and with it the MySQL software. In 2009, Oracle announced that it was acquiring Sun Microsystems. The MySQL community had many concerns about the future of the project in Oracle's hands, including that it would cease to be open source. In response, the database's original creator, Michael "Monty" Widenius, forked MySQL into a new version, MariaDB, that would remain open forever. (*Forking* an open source project means starting a whole new open source project that's based on the code of an existing project.) Many of the original MySQL developers stopped working on MySQL and moved to the MariaDB project.

MariaDB is completely compatible with MySQL, and you can seamlessly switch between the two database servers and clients. The command line client that comes with MySQL will connect to a MariaDB server, and the command line client that comes with MariaDB will connect to a MySQL server. I've found that it's easier to get MariaDB up and running than the original

*(continued)*

MySQL software, so you'll use a MariaDB server for the exercises in this chapter. However, since MariaDB is completely compatible with MySQL, it's common to use the terms interchangeably. I'll refer to both as MySQL for the remainder of the chapter, except when referring to specific MariaDB software packages.

When Widenius originally created MySQL, he named it after his daughter, My. When he forked MySQL into MariaDB in 2009, he named the new project after his youngest daughter, Maria.

The simplest way to run a MariaDB server on your computer is by using Docker containers, like you did in Exercise 5-3 when you set up a local WordPress website as practice using Docker Compose. In the following exercises, you'll get a MySQL server up and running, connect to your new server using MySQL clients, and practice using SQL.

## Exercise 12-1: Create and Test a MySQL Server Using Docker and Adminer

With Docker, you can quickly run different types of SQL servers on your computer, no matter what operating system you're running. In this exercise, you'll run a MariaDB server on your computer using Docker Compose. Once you have the server up and running, you'll use the Adminer MySQL client to add the contents of Tables 12-1 and 12-2 to it as a test. You'll move on to working with real leaked data later in the chapter, but you'll start by experimenting with some simple example databases.

### Run the Server

Create a folder for this chapter's exercises and a *docker-compose.yaml* file in that folder. Type the following code into the file (or copy and paste it from *https://github.com/micahflee/hacks-leaks-and-revelations/blob/main/chapter-12/ docker-compose.yaml*):

```
version: '3.9'
services:
  db:
    image: mariadb:10.9
    environment:
      MARIADB_ROOT_PASSWORD: this-is-your-root-password
      MARIADB_ROOT_HOST: "%"
    ports:
      - 3306:3306
    volumes:
      - ./db_data:/var/lib/mysql
```

```
adminer:
  image: adminer
  ports:
    - 8080:8080
```

The *docker-compose.yaml* file in Exercise 5-3 used a db service running MariaDB, and a wordpress service running the WordPress container. In that case, wordpress connected to db to run queries in order to save and load website content. This code uses an adminer service to likewise connect to the db service.

The code provides the version number of the Compose specification with which the file is written (3.9). It then defines the two services and includes the version of the mariadb container image that the db service runs. It sets the database root user's password to this-is-your-root-password (change this to a different password if you like). As noted earlier, you'll work as the database's root user throughout this chapter, since you're the only one accessing this database. It publishes port 3306, meaning that you can connect to the server with a MySQL client on *localhost* at port 3306, and configures a volume to store all of MariaDB's database files in a *db_data* folder. You'll import several gigabytes of data into this database.

The adminer service runs the latest version of the adminer container image. Adminer publishes port 8080, so you can load Adminer in a web browser at *http://localhost:8080*.

Open a terminal, change to the folder for this chapter's exercises, and start the containers with the following command:

```
docker-compose up
```

The first time you start the containers, your computer downloads the container images from Docker Hub, if you don't already have them. After the containers start, you should see that a *db_data* folder containing all of the data stored in the database so far has been added to your *exercises* folder.

### Connect to the Database with Adminer

You just started two containers, one for your MySQL server and the other for your MySQL client, Adminer. Now you'll connect to Adminer and use it to log in to your MySQL server. To access Adminer, open a browser and load *http://localhost:8080*. You should see the Adminer login page shown in Figure 12-1. Here you can choose the type of database to which you're connecting and what credentials you'll use to log in. Keep System as MySQL, keep Server as db, set Username to **root**, and set Password to **this-is-your-root-password** (or whatever you used in your *docker-compose.yaml* file). Leave the Database field blank, since you haven't imported any databases yet.

Once you've logged in, you should see a list of default databases: information_schema, mysql, performance_schema, and sys. MariaDB uses these to store information it needs to run the database server, so in general, you shouldn't touch them. Instead, you'll create new databases and work with them.

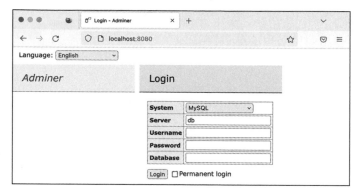

Figure 12-1: The Adminer login page

## Create a Test Database

To test out your new MySQL server, you'll create a brand-new database and enter Tables 12-1 and 12-2. Click the **Create Database** link, enter **books** in the field that pops up, and click **Save**. Once you've created the books database, click the **Create Table** link. Under Table Name, enter **authors**.

To add a column in Adminer, you enter its name under the Column Name header and choose a data type. To enter the first column from Table 12-1, create an **id** column and choose type **int** (short for "integer," as mentioned earlier). Select the **AI** radio button, which sets this column to auto-increment. When you've finished, create the second column, **name**, with type **text**.

Figure 12-2 shows what the form should look like when you've finished.

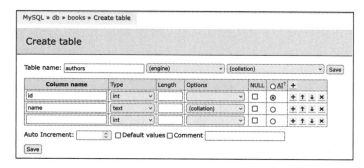

Figure 12-2: Creating the authors table in Adminer

Click **Save** to finish creating the table in the database. Adminer should bring you to the structure page for your new table, showing you the two columns you just created. Your table should start out empty, without any rows.

At the top of the window, you should see page navigation links (for example, MySQL ▸ db ▸ books in Figure 12-2). Click **books** to return to the books database page, then click **Create Table** again to create Table 12-2, giving it the name **books**. Add the following columns:

- An **id** column with type **int** and **AI** checked
- A **title** column with type **text**
- An **author_id** column

*Adminer is smart enough to determine on its own that the author_id column uses the int type and relates to the authors.id column, so it will automatically set the type to authors.*

Figure 12-3 shows what this form should look like once you've added these columns.

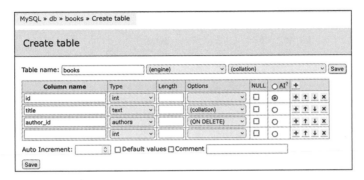

*Figure 12-3: Creating the books table in Adminer*

Click **Save**. You've now created a books database with two tables, authors and books, but there isn't any data in it yet.

Now that you have a MySQL database running on your computer and access to the Adminer MySQL client, you're ready to run your own SQL queries. Your first queries will add the data from Tables 12-1 and 12-2 into their corresponding MySQL tables.

## Exercise 12-2: Query Your SQL Database

In this exercise, you'll learn the syntax of SQL queries. You'll be using MySQL, but the syntax is nearly identical to that of all other types of SQL, so this section should give you a solid foundation for writing SQL queries in general. You'll learn the different verbs and practice running SQL queries to add, update, delete, and most importantly, search the data in SQL databases.

Make sure that your Docker containers from Exercise 12-1 are up, then load Adminer in your web browser at *http://localhost:8080*. Also make sure you've logged in to your MySQL server as the root user, using the same password from the previous exercise. When you're ready, click the **books** database to begin.

## INSERT Statements

So far the books database you created in Exercise 12-1 includes the tables authors and books, but those tables don't have any rows.

To add new rows to your tables, you use the INSERT verb as follows:

```
INSERT INTO table_name (column1, column2, ...) VALUES (value1, value2, ...);
```

In Adminer, click the **SQL Command** link in the left sidebar. In the empty field that pops up, enter the following INSERT queries:

```
INSERT INTO authors (name) VALUES ('Micah Lee');
INSERT INTO authors (name) VALUES ('Carl Sagan');
INSERT INTO books (title, author_id) VALUES ('Hacks, Leaks, and Revelations', 1);
INSERT INTO books (title, author_id) VALUES ('Pale Blue Dot', 2);
INSERT INTO books (title, author_id) VALUES ('Contact: A Novel', 2);
```

These commands insert all of the rows into the two tables in the database, one row at a time. The first two lines insert rows into the authors table, just setting the name field, while the last three lines insert rows into the books table, setting the title and author_id fields. These INSERT statements don't specify id values because the id field for both tables auto-increments, starting with 1.

While you don't need to set the id field when inserting into the books table, you do need to set the author_id field manually, which is how you tell the database who the author of each book is. Since the authors table started out empty, the author row for Micah Lee should have an id of 1 (as it was the first row added to the table), and the row for Carl Sagan should have an id of 2. When the code inserts the Hacks, Leaks, and Revelations title, it sets author_id to 1, and when it inserts the two books by Carl Sagan, it sets author_id to 2.

**NOTE** *In this chapter I write SQL keywords like INSERT and WHERE in all caps, but doing so is just a popular convention. SQL keywords aren't case sensitive, so you can use insert, where, select, and so on if you prefer.*

Figure 12-4 shows the process of inserting data into the authors and books tables by running these five INSERT queries.

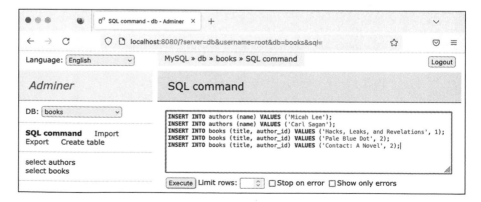

Figure 12-4: Running INSERT queries in Adminer

Once you've entered this series of SQL queries into Adminer, click **Execute** to run them, which should insert all of these rows into your database. Click **select** in the left sidebar to view the new data in the database. Figure 12-5 shows all of the rows in the books tables in Adminer.

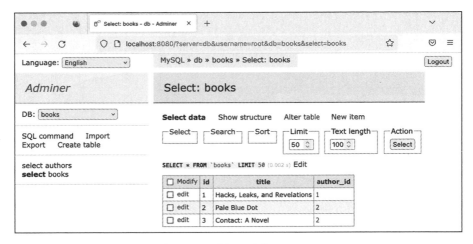

Figure 12-5: Viewing rows in the books table in Adminer

Right above the table of data in Figure 12-5, you can see the line SELECT * from 'books' LIMIT 50 (0.0002 s), which is the SQL statement Adminer executed to retrieve this data from the MySQL database, followed by the amount of time it took for the query to run.

## SELECT Statements

While INSERT statements add information to SQL databases, SELECT statements ask a database for specific information. When investigating leaked SQL databases, you'll likely spend most of your time writing SELECT statements.

You can use a SELECT statement to select all of the books by a certain author or, in the case of Epik data, all of the domain names registered by a specific person. Here's the general syntax:

```
SELECT column1, column2, ... FROM table_name WHERE condition ORDER BY column1,
column2, ...;
```

When your SQL client runs a SELECT statement, the SQL server returns a table of data. To select everything in the books table, click the **SQL Command** link in Adminer's left sidebar and run the following query:

```
SELECT * FROM books;
```

This command uses an asterisk (*) as a wildcard character, which means you'd like the response to include all columns. It also leaves out the

WHERE clause, so it will include all of the rows in the books table without filtering them. Figure 12-6 shows these results in Adminer.

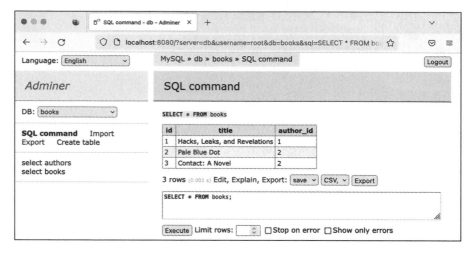

Figure 12-6: Running a SELECT query in Adminer

After running a SELECT query, click Adminer's **Export** link to export the data returned as a CSV spreadsheet. The options in the first drop-down menu are *open*, which allows you to open a CSV directly in your browser; *save*, used to download the CSV; and *gzip*, which lets you download a compressed version of the CSV. The three options in the second drop-down menu allow you to save the file with data separated by commas, semicolons, or tab characters.

You can open spreadsheets created this way in software like Microsoft Excel or LibreOffice Calc and work with the data using that software. This makes it easier to share the data with colleagues or use advanced features like visualizing the data.

### Selecting Individual Fields

You previously ran the SELECT * FROM *table_name* query to select all the columns in a table, but you can also choose only specific columns. Say you want to return only a list of titles in the table. Select the title field alone with this query:

```
SELECT title FROM books;
```

Instead of including all columns, this table includes only the book titles. The SQL server should return the results shown in Table 12-3. (For the remainder of this section, for simplicity's sake, I'll represent the information returned from SQL queries as tables in text rather than Adminer screenshots.)

**Table 12-3:** The title Column in the books Table

| title |
| --- |
| Hacks, Leaks, and Revelations |
| Pale Blue Dot |
| Contact: A Novel |

When you're working with larger databases, select only the columns you need so your queries will finish faster.

## Sorting Results

Use the ORDER BY clause to sort the results of your queries. For example, to select all of the columns in the books table, with the results sorted by the book title, run this query:

```
SELECT * FROM books ORDER BY title;
```

The results of this query will be ordered alphabetically by the title column, as shown in Table 12-4.

**Table 12-4:** All Columns in the books Table, Ordered by the title Column

| id | title | author_id |
| --- | --- | --- |
| 3 | Contact: A Novel | 2 |
| 1 | Hacks, Leaks, and Revelations | 1 |
| 2 | Pale Blue Dot | 2 |

By default, results are sorted in ascending order: text fields are ordered alphabetically; number fields are ordered from smallest to largest; and date fields are ordered from earliest to latest. You can sort the results in descending order by using the DESC keyword. For example, use the following query to select all of the books, ordered by title column in reverse alphabetical order:

```
SELECT * from books ORDER BY title DESC;
```

You can also sort results by more than one column. For example, to first order the books by author_id (so the results will include all books by author 1 first, then by author 2, and so on), and then by title (so that within each author's list of books, the books are sorted by title), run this query:

```
SELECT * from books ORDER BY author_id, title;
```

This should order the results first by author_id, then by title, as shown in Table 12-5.

**Table 12-5:** All Columns in the books Table, Ordered by author_id and title

| id | title | author_id |
|----|-------|-----------|
| 1 | Hacks, Leaks, and Revelations | 1 |
| 3 | Contact: A Novel | 2 |
| 2 | Pale Blue Dot | 2 |

In this case, all of the books by the author with author_id of 1 (Micah Lee) are shown first, and the books by the author with author_id of 2 (Carl Sagan) are shown next. The books for each author are then sorted alphabetically by title.

### Counting Rows in a Table

SQL databases have built-in functions you can run as part of your queries. For example, to find out how many rows are in the books table, use the COUNT() function:

```
SELECT COUNT(*) FROM books;
```

After you run this command, the SQL server should return the results shown in Table 12-6.

**Table 12-6:** Counting the Number of Rows in the books Table

| COUNT(*) |
|----------|
| 3 |

Selecting COUNT(*) from a table is considerably faster than selecting all of the rows in that table and then counting them.

### Filtering SELECT Results with WHERE Clauses

You can also filter the results you get back using the WHERE clause. For instance, to find the titles of books written by Micah Lee, run the following query:

```
SELECT title FROM books WHERE author_id=1;
```

The SQL server should return the results shown in Table 12-7.

**Table 12-7:** The title of books Where author is Micah Lee

| title |
|-------|
| Hacks, Leaks, and Revelations |

Similarly to Python if statements, the WHERE clause also supports parentheses and Boolean logic operators AND and OR, as well as the comparison operators greater than (>), greater than or equal to (>=), less than (<), and less than or equal to (<=). For example, say you want to search for books with an id between 10 and 100, including the number 10 but not the number 100. Try that out with the following query:

```
SELECT * FROM books WHERE id >= 10 AND id < 100;
```

You can use the equals (=) operator to search for exact strings. For example, run the following command to find all of the authors with the name Carl Sagan:

```
SELECT * FROM authors WHERE name='Carl Sagan';
```

This search is case sensitive, so while it would find authors named Carl Sagan, it wouldn't find authors named CARL SAGAN or carl sagan. For a case-insensitive search, use the LIKE operator. Try running the following command:

```
SELECT * FROM authors WHERE name LIKE 'carl sagan';
```

This command finds authors named Carl Sagan, CARL SAGAN, carl sagan, or any other capitalization.

The LIKE operator supports the wildcard character, the percent sign (%), which will match any characters. Querying the authors table where name LIKE '%lee%' will search for rows where name contains any number of characters (%), followed by lee, followed by any number of characters again (%). For example, to find all of the authors with Lee in their names, run:

```
SELECT * FROM authors WHERE name LIKE '%lee%';
```

This query returns the row with the name Micah Lee, but it would also return Stan Lee, Lee Young-ae, and Andrea Leeds.

To search just for people with the last name Lee, run this query:

```
SELECT * FROM authors WHERE name LIKE '% lee';
```

In this case, there's only one wildcard character at the beginning of the string, followed by a space, followed by lee. This query will return Stan Lee, since this name matches any number of characters, followed by a space, followed by lee. However, it won't return Lee Young-ae; this name matches any number of characters but has no space followed by lee, and it contains extra characters after lee.

Using logical operators, you can combine as many conditions as you want. For example, to look for books written by Carl Sagan that have the word *blue* in their titles, run this query:

```
SELECT * FROM books WHERE author_id=2 AND title LIKE '%blue%';
```

You could expand on that query by running the following query to also check for books with *green* or *red* in their titles:

```
SELECT *
FROM books
WHERE
    author_id=2 AND
    (
        title LIKE '%red%' OR
        title LIKE '%green%' OR
        title LIKE '%blue%'
    );
```

This query uses both the logical operators AND and OR, as well as parentheses. When you run it, the SQL server will reject any rows where author_id isn't 2 and where title doesn't contain at least one of the strings red, green, or blue.

This final query has multiple lines, with some of them indented. As your queries get longer, using whitespace like this can make your SQL queries easier to read. In general, I tend to write short queries on a single line and split longer queries into multiple lines. You'll continue indenting your queries in the following sections.

You should now have a basic understanding of how to select data from a table in a SQL database. In the next section, you'll learn to select data from multiple tables at once.

## JOIN Clauses

Because SQL databases are relational, you can select data from and receive results from columns from multiple tables simultaneously using JOIN clauses. You can think of these clauses as the SQL server combining (joining) multiple tables into a single table, then selecting rows from that combined table.

For example, say you want to write a single query that will return a table of book titles and their authors, relying on the title field in the books table and the name field in the authors table. Run the query in Listing 12-1 to select a table of results from columns in those two tables at once.

```
SELECT
    books.title,
    authors.name
FROM books
JOIN authors ON books.author_id = authors.id;
```

*Listing 12-1: Selecting from both the books and the authors tables using the JOIN clause*

Since this query involves more than one table, you must specify the names of the columns you want to select in the format *table_name.column _name*. The SQL query selects the book title with books.title and the author name with authors.name. The FROM clause shows that this query is selecting *from* the books table and joining this table with the authors table. The JOIN clause explains how the two tables are related: the SQL server knows that a books row is related to an authors row if the value of books.author_id matches the value of authors.id.

When you run this query, the SQL database uses the books.author _id = authors.id relationship specified in the JOIN clause to build the combined table shown in Table 12-8, from which it can then select rows.

**Table 12-8:** The books and authors Tables, Combined on books.author_id = authors.id

| books.id | books.author_id | books.title | authors.id | authors.name |
|----------|-----------------|-------------|------------|--------------|
| 1 | 1 | Hacks, Leaks, and Revelations | 1 | Micah Lee |
| 2 | 2 | Pale Blue Dot | 2 | Carl Sagan |
| 3 | 2 | Contact: A Novel | 2 | Carl Sagan |

Each row in this combined table includes all of the columns from both the books and the authors tables. First, notice that the value in each row for books.author_id is the same as the authors.id value. This is because of the books.author_id = authors.id relationship specified in the JOIN clause. In each row, the books fields contain full rows from the books table, and the authors fields contain full rows from the authors table. Since Carl Sagan has two books in this database, his books take up two rows in the combined table.

The SELECT query in Listing 12-1 selects the columns books.title and authors.name from this combined table. This final result of the query should contain the information in Table 12-9.

**Table 12-9:** Results from the Query in Listing 12-1

| title | name |
|-------|------|
| Hacks, Leaks, and Revelations | Micah Lee |
| Pale Blue Dot | Carl Sagan |
| Contact: A Novel | Carl Sagan |

The SQL server responds with a single table of rows that contains fields from both tables, based on the books.author_id = authors.id relationship specified in the JOIN clause.

The type of join described in this section is technically called an INNER JOIN, which is the default type of join in MySQL. In addition to INNER joins, however, you can also use LEFT and RIGHT joins.

### Using LEFT and RIGHT Joins

There are two additional ways to join tables together in SQL: LEFT JOIN and RIGHT JOIN queries. Each time you join two tables, the table from which you're selecting is the "left" table (books, in the previous example). The table with which you're joining is the "right" table (authors, in this case). LEFT JOIN means that the combined table should contain all of the rows from the left table, but not necessarily all of the rows from the right table. As you might guess, RIGHT JOIN means that the combined table should contain all the rows in the right table, but not necessarily those from the left. Finally, as you saw in the previous section, INNER JOIN means that the results should contain only rows where the relationship holds. That is, if there are any rows in the left table that don't match any rows in the right table—and vice versa—based on the join relationship, then those rows won't be included in the results.

To demonstrate how this works, use the following query to add a row to the authors table, replacing *Your Name* with your own name:

```
INSERT INTO authors (name) VALUES ('Your Name');
```

Now run the query in Listing 12-2.

```
SELECT
    books.title,
    authors.name
FROM authors
LEFT JOIN books ON books.author_id = authors.id;
```

*Listing 12-2: Selecting from the authors table and doing a LEFT JOIN to the books table*

This query is similar to the one in Listing 12-1, but this time it selects from the authors table (making it the left table) and joins it with the books table (making that the right table), using a LEFT JOIN instead of an INNER JOIN. The results of that query contain the information in Table 12-10.

**Table 12-10:** Results from a LEFT JOIN Query, with the Left Table Containing More Rows

| title | name |
|---|---|
| Hacks, Leaks, and Revelations | Micah Lee |
| Pale Blue Dot | Carl Sagan |
| Contact: A Novel | Carl Sagan |
| NULL | *Your Name* |

Table 12-10 has an extra row that the output of Listing 12-1 didn't have. In this row, the book title column is NULL, a SQL term meaning "empty," and the author name column is your own name. Because this is a LEFT JOIN, the results include all rows from the left table (authors), even though there aren't any rows from the right table (books) associated with it in the relationship.

If you ran the same query as Listing 12-2 but instead used an INNER JOIN (or just a JOIN, since inner joins are the default join type), the results wouldn't include that last row. Your LEFT JOIN results included all rows from the left table (authors), including the extra author you added (your own name). But when you do an INNER JOIN, the results include only rows from the left and right tables where a relationship holds. Since there aren't any books with the books.author_id set to your own author.id, the relationship doesn't hold, so the results don't include that row.

Which type of JOIN you need to use depends on the type of analysis you're trying to do. INNER JOIN is a reasonable default, but if the SQL results you're getting are missing data that you want, then you'll probably want to use a LEFT JOIN instead.

### Using WHERE Clauses with Joins

As with other SELECT statements, you can use the WHERE clause along with JOIN clauses to filter your results. To find all titles written by Carl Sagan without knowing what his id is in the authors table, run this query:

```
SELECT books.title
FROM books
LEFT JOIN authors ON books.author_id = authors.id
WHERE authors.name = 'Carl Sagan';
```

This query selects the column books.title from the books table and joins it with the authors table using the books.author_id = authors.id relationship. It then filters those results to only show the rows where authors.name is Carl Sagan. This query should return the results shown in Table 12-11.

**Table 12-11:** Selecting from the books Table Based on a Column in the Related authors Table

| title |
| --- |
| Pale Blue Dot |
| Contact: A Novel |

As with the other SELECT statement, you can also sort your results. If you wanted to sort these by title, you'd add ORDER BY books.title to the query.

You've now learned the trickiest parts of searching SQL databases for information. Next, we'll discuss two more simple SQL verbs: UPDATE and DELETE.

## UPDATE Statements

You can update rows in a table using the UPDATE verb, which uses this syntax:

```
UPDATE table_name SET column1=value1, column2=value2, ... WHERE condition;
```

For example, try updating this book's title to include its subtitle by running the follow query:

```
UPDATE books
SET title='Hacks, Leaks, and Revelations: The Art of Analyzing Hacked and Leaked Data'
WHERE id=1;
```

This should have updated the title of the book with the id of 1 from Hacks, Leaks, and Revelations to Hacks, Leaks, and Revelations: The Art of Analyzing Hacked and Leaked Data.

### DELETE Statements

To delete rows in a table, use the DELETE verb, which takes the following syntax:

```
DELETE FROM table_name WHERE condition;
```

For example, you could delete the Hacks, Leaks, and Revelations book from the database by running this query (but don't do this now, as you'll want to keep this row for exercises later in the chapter):

```
DELETE FROM books WHERE id=1;
```

In this case, the condition is id=1, so this query finds any rows with an id of 1 and deletes them. Alternatively, if you wanted to delete all of the books with me as the author, the condition could be author_id=1. Or if you wanted to delete all of the books with *blue* in their titles, the condition could be title LIKE '%blue%'.

## Introducing the MySQL Command Line Client

So far, you've run all of your SQL queries through Adminer for a simpler user experience as you learned the basics of SQL. MySQL clients like Adminer work well for everyday tasks like browsing data in databases, running individual queries, and quickly creating new tables. However, for some tasks, you'll need to use the mysql command line client.

For example, later in this chapter, you'll use the mysql client to import data from a SQL backup file from the Epik dataset into your MySQL server. SQL backup files are simply text files, generally with filenames that end in *.sql*, full of SQL queries—sometimes several gigabytes of SQL queries. To import the backup, the client runs each query in the file, one after the other. Adminer's import feature allows you to upload a *.sql* file, but the Adminer Docker service has an upload limit of 128MB by default. The SQL backup from the Epik dataset you'll work with later in this chapter is 1.2GB compressed, so it would be impossible to import it using Adminer. (Once you import it, however, you can use either client to run queries on the data.)

The MySQL command line client is also useful for working on remote servers, which I'll discuss later in the chapter. After you SSH into a server on the cloud, you can use the mysql command to connect to the MySQL service and then run SQL queries there.

The command line client isn't ideal for all tasks. For example, if your query results include many columns, each line of output might be wider than your terminal window, causing the output to wrap, which makes it very difficult to read. Moreover, the command line client displays all the output in your terminal. If you're running many queries, it might be cumbersome to scroll back through your terminal history to find specific results that you ran previously. For everyday queries, it's easier to use a graphical client like Adminer.

---

**PYTHON AND MYSQL**

You can also consider writing Python code that interacts with MySQL databases, where your Python script acts as the SQL client. For example, you wrote Python scripts in Chapter 9 that loop through every row in a CSV and then run a block of code; you might want to similarly loop through every row returned in response to a SELECT query. To write Python code that connects to a MySQL database and runs queries, you can use a module called PyMySQL. For Python code that runs SQL queries, the table of data often isn't displayed—instead, it's stored in a variable, typically a list of dictionaries that you can loop through. For more information, see the documentation for the PyMySQL module at *https://pymysql.readthedocs.io*.

---

So far, you've seen SQL query results displayed in Adminer as HTML tables. If you run the same queries using the mysql client, the data will be displayed as text in your terminal. You'll test this in Exercise 12-3.

## Exercise 12-3: Install and Test the Command Line MySQL Client

In this exercise, you'll install and practice using the MariaDB command line client mysql, which has the same name and works in the same way as the official MySQL client.

Start by opening a terminal. If you're using a Mac, install it in Homebrew by running this command:

```
brew install mariadb
```

If you're using Linux or Windows with WSL, install it by running this command:

```
sudo apt install mariadb-client
```

You can now use the mysql command to connect to your MySQL database. To do so, run the following command:

```
mysql -h localhost --protocol=tcp -u root -p
```

The -h argument (short for --host) tells the client the IP address or hostname of the MySQL server to which you want to connect. In this case, the hostname is localhost, since the server is running locally on your computer. The --protocol=tcp argument tells the MySQL client to connect to the server over the network, which is required when you're running the server in a Docker container. The -u argument (short for --user) tells the client that you're logging in as the root user, in this case. Finally, -p (short for --password) tells the client that this user is protected with a password.

After you run the mysql command, press ENTER. The MySQL client should prompt you to type the root user's password:

```
Enter password:
```

Once you enter the correct password, you should end up in the MySQL shell:

```
Welcome to the MariaDB monitor.  Commands end with ; or \g.
Your MariaDB connection id is 104
Server version: 10.9.4-MariaDB-1:10.9.4+maria~ubu2204 mariadb.org binary distribution

Copyright (c) 2000, 2018, Oracle, MariaDB Corporation Ab and others.

Type 'help;' or '\h' for help. Type '\c' to clear the current input statement.

MariaDB [(none)]>
```

From here, you can run all the same SQL queries you did in Adminer. However, to work in the command line client, you'll need to know a few additional queries.

## MySQL-Specific Queries

Queries like INSERT and SELECT are typically nearly identical between different versions of SQL, but each version has unique queries for actions like returning a list of databases in the server or a list of tables in a database. To navigate around a MySQL server from the command line client, you'll need to know the following MySQL-specific queries:

**SHOW DATABASES;**   Shows a list of all of the databases on your MySQL server

**USE *database_name;***   Switches you into a specific database, so you can start running queries there

**SHOW TABLES;**   Shows a list of all of the tables in the currently selected database

**DESCRIBE TABLE *table_name;***   Shows you the columns in a table

There are other MySQL-specific queries, but these are all you'll need to know for the purposes of this book.

*Technically, Adminer uses these queries too, but it runs them for you in the background. When you use the command line client, you have to run them yourself. For example, when Adminer showed you a list of databases, it ran* SHOW DATABASES; *for you in order to find the list; when you selected the* books *database, technically it ran* USE books; *for you.*

Let's test these queries. Run the following command to list all of the available databases on your MySQL server:

```
MariaDB [(none)]> SHOW DATABASES;
+--------------------+
| Database           |
+--------------------+
| books              |
| information_schema |
| mysql              |
| performance_schema |
| sys                |
+--------------------+
5 rows in set (0.068 sec)
```

The result of this query lists all of the databases in this MySQL server. In this case, it lists the books database you created in Exercise 12-1 and the four databases that come with MySQL by default.

Switch to the books database:

```
MariaDB [(none)]> USE books;
Reading table information for completion of table and column names
You can turn off this feature to get a quicker startup with -A

Database changed
MariaDB [books]>
```

After you run USE books;, the prompt should change from MariaDB [(none)]> to MariaDB [books]>, letting you know which database is currently selected. When you run normal SQL queries with verbs like SELECT or INSERT, they'll run in the currently selected database.

Now that you've selected a database, list all of its tables with the following command:

```
MariaDB [books]> SHOW TABLES;
+----------------+
| Tables_in_books |
+----------------+
| authors        |
| books          |
+----------------+
2 rows in set (0.025 sec)
```

This database has two tables, authors and books. List all of the columns in the books table:

```
MariaDB [books]> DESCRIBE books;
+-----------+---------+------+-----+---------+----------------+
| Field     | Type    | Null | Key | Default | Extra          |
+-----------+---------+------+-----+---------+----------------+
| id        | int(11) | NO   | PRI | NULL    | auto_increment |
| title     | text    | NO   |     | NULL    |                |
| author_id | int(11) | NO   | MUL | NULL    |                |
+-----------+---------+------+-----+---------+----------------+
3 rows in set (0.023 sec)
```

This displays a table of data with each row representing a different column in the table that you're describing, including all of the attributes of each column. For example, you can see that the id column has the type of int and is set to auto-increment.

The queries you just ran return information about the MySQL server itself—what databases it contains, what tables those databases contain, and what columns are in each table. You can also query for the data stored in the database itself. For example, try running the following query to get a list of all of the books stored in the books table:

```
MariaDB [books]> SELECT * FROM books;
+----+-----------------------------+-----------+
| id | title                       | author_id |
+----+-----------------------------+-----------+
|  1 | Hacks, Leaks, and Revelations |       1 |
|  2 | Pale Blue Dot                 |       2 |
|  3 | Contact: A Novel              |       2 |
+----+-----------------------------+-----------+
3 rows in set (0.012 sec)
```

You can run any of the queries that you ran in Adminer using the CLI client, and the rows will be displayed in your terminal.

At any point, you can run exit to quit:

```
MariaDB [(books)]> exit
Bye
```

This will drop you back into your terminal.

You've made it through the crash course on SQL and are ready to start tackling real data! In the rest of the chapter, you'll learn more about Epik and its massive data breach, then download and analyze a MySQL database backup from the Epik dataset.

## The History of Epik

Epik, a Seattle-area company founded by Rob Monster in 2009, has long provided domain name and web hosting services to neo-Nazi and far-right websites. Its customers have included the notorious neo-Nazi website the Daily Stormer, the conspiracy website InfoWars, the Proud Boys hate group, and the Oath Keepers right-wing militia, which you learned about in Chapter 6. After Gab moved to Epik, Monster baselessly claimed that much of the hate speech on Gab was posted by liberals who wanted to make the service look bad.

As I mentioned in this chapter's introduction, in October 2018, Robert Bowers posted a message to Gab shortly before committing the deadliest antisemitic terrorist attack in US history. GoDaddy deplatformed Gab, so it moved its domain hosting service to Epik. This wasn't the only time that Epik helped save a far-right platform that was getting deplatformed after a mass shooting.

In addition to helping save Gab, Epik started hosting the domain name for the far-right message board then known as 8chan (now rebranded as 8kun) after a similar mass shooting in 2019. Patrick Crusius posted a manifesto to 8chan shortly before killing 23 people and injuring 23 more in a Walmart in El Paso, Texas, the deadliest anti-Latino terrorist attack in recent US history. Crusius's manifesto also spouted the "great replacement" conspiracy theory. After the attack, Cloudflare suspended 8chan's service, but Epik was there to quickly bring the site back online.

Epik also handled domain hosting for Parler, the social media site discussed in the previous chapter, after various platforms banned it in the aftermath of the deadly January 6, 2021, attack on the US Capitol. Epik has since become a popular domain name registrar for far-right and conservative websites worried about getting deplatformed. America's Frontline Doctors, the anti-vaccine disinformation group I discuss in the following chapter, has also registered its domains with Epik, though it's not at risk of being deplatformed.

In this section, you'll learn about the history and motivation behind the Epik hack and the type of information this dataset contains.

### The Epik Hack

On September 1, 2021, less than a year before the US Supreme Court's 2022 decision to overturn the constitutional right to abortion, the state of Texas passed the most restrictive abortion law in the US—more restrictive, at the time, than any law passed since the 1973 Supreme Court decision Roe v. Wade. The Texas Heartbeat Act banned abortions six weeks after pregnancy, before many people even realize they're pregnant. The law is enforced by civil lawsuits: any member of the public who believes in forced birth can sue anyone who performs or facilitates abortions, creating a chilling effect for reproductive health care.

An anti-abortion lobbyist group quickly set up a website by the name ProLifeWhistleblower.com, inviting the public to anonymously submit private details about people they believed were obtaining or facilitating abortions. GoDaddy kicked the group off its platform, citing a violation of its terms of service, so the site switched its domain hosting to Epik. Epik soon caved to public pressure and likewise stopped providing service, but this was enough to catch the attention of hackers.

In September and October of 2021, in a series of hacks dubbed Operation Epik Fail, hackers identifying with Anonymous hacked Epik incredibly thoroughly, releasing hundreds of gigabytes of data on BitTorrent. DDoSecrets downloaded a copy of this data, added it to its leak archive, and also made it accessible to download from its public data server, rather than just using BitTorrent. Most data breaches expose a database, a collection of email, or a cache of documents. This breach included all of these, along with bootable disk images from Epik's servers—essentially, the entire hard disks that powered its servers. You could use bootable disk images to run a snapshot of Epik's complete servers in a virtual machine. With some work, this would allow you to rifle through *everything* hosted on these servers.

The hackers published their leaks in three parts over the course of four weeks. In a press release accompanying the first data leak (see Figure 12-7), they announced that they had released "a decade's worth of data" from Epik. "This dataset is all that's needed to trace the actual ownership and management of the fascist side of the Internet that has eluded researchers, activists, and, well, just about everybody," the press release continued.

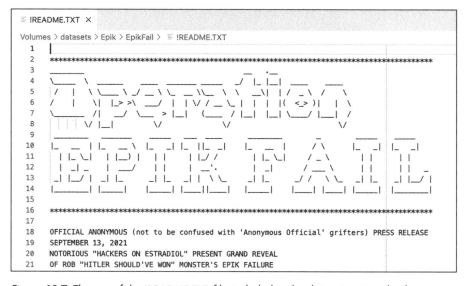

*Figure 12-7: The top of the* !README.TXT *file included in the dataset, written by the Epik hackers*

It's true: the Epik dataset includes 10 years of data from the company, including all of the data from nine MySQL databases. These databases include tables full of customers of various Epik products, like their domain name registrar; their service that protects websites against attacks, called BitMitigate; and their VPN service, called Anonymize. The databases also include information about domain name purchases, email forwarding for these domains, credit card transactions, customers' passwords, and more.

The most important data in the Epik dataset, in my opinion, is the WHOIS privacy data containing information on the owners behind the domain names Epik hosts.

## Epik's WHOIS Data

*WHOIS* (pronounced "who is") data is the public ownership information you're required to provide when buying a domain name. This generally includes contact details like names, email addresses, phone numbers, and physical addresses, along with the domain's registrant contact, administrative contact, and technical contact (in many cases, the same person plays all three roles). Which organization keeps track of WHOIS records depends on the domain name in question, but the records are all public. A quick internet search should turn up plenty of online services that allow you to look up WHOIS data for any given domain. The whois command line tool also lets you look up WHOIS data from a terminal.

Public WHOIS data creates a major privacy issue, since it allows anyone to easily discover not only the owner of a domain but also their PII. To combat this, many domain registrars offer WHOIS privacy services, where they'll put their own information in the WHOIS record or just replace the owner name with something like REDACTED FOR PRIVACY on their customers' behalf.

Epik runs a WHOIS privacy service, hiding the ownership information of many far-right domain names from the public. But the Epik dataset includes that hidden information. As long as a domain name was registered on Epik before September 2021, when the hack occurred, you can use this dataset to look up its true owners.

You can find the WHOIS ownership data associated with any domain name simply by running **whois *domain_name*** in a terminal. This command will look up the public information, meaning that if a domain uses a WHOIS privacy service, you won't get to see who actually owns it. For example, you would run the following command to find the ownership information about the Oath Keepers domain name, oathkeepers.org:

```
whois oathkeepers.org
```

When I ran this command, I got the following output:

```
--snip--
Creation Date: 2009-03-01T21:07:55Z
Registry Expiry Date: 2032-03-01T21:07:55Z
Registrar: Epik Inc.
Registrar IANA ID: 617
Registrar Abuse Contact Email: abuse@epik.com
Registrar Abuse Contact Phone: +1.425366881
Domain Status: ok https://icann.org/epp#ok
Registry Registrant ID: REDACTED FOR PRIVACY
Registrant Street: REDACTED FOR PRIVACY
Registrant City: REDACTED FOR PRIVACY
Registrant State/Province: WA
Registrant Name: REDACTED FOR PRIVACY
```

```
Registrant Organization: Anonymize, Inc.
Registrant Postal Code: REDACTED FOR PRIVACY
Registrant Country: US
Registrant Phone: REDACTED FOR PRIVACY
Registrant Phone Ext: REDACTED FOR PRIVACY
Registrant Fax: REDACTED FOR PRIVACY
Registrant Fax Ext: REDACTED FOR PRIVACY
Registrant Email: Please query the RDDS service of the Registrar of Record
identified in this output for information on how to contact the Registrant,
Admin, or Tech contact of the queried domain name.
--snip--
```

Public WHOIS data told me that oathkeepers.org was first registered on March 1, 2009; it expires in 2032; and its current registrar was Epik. However, all the contact information for the person who registered it was listed as REDACTED FOR PRIVACY, effectively hiding the domain ownership information from the public.

If you search the Epik dataset for this domain name, however, as you'll learn to do later in this chapter, you can find all the redacted site ownership details. When I searched the dataset, I found that the oathkeepers.org registrant organization is Oath Keepers, and the registrant name is Stewart Rhodes. As noted in Chapter 6, Rhodes is the Oath Keepers founder who was convicted of seditious conspiracy for his role in the January 6, 2021, attack and subsequently sentenced to 18 years in prison. The dataset also includes Rhodes' phone number, email address, and a physical address in Granbury, Texas.

Interestingly, the administrator and technical contacts for this domain lists the company eJam Systems LLC, along with the name Edward Durfee, an email address at ejamsystems.com, a phone number, and a home address in Northvale, New Jersey. eJam Systems LLC appears to be a right-wing company, run by Edward Durfee, that did tech work for the Oath Keepers. None of this information was available in the WHOIS records, but now it's all public, thanks to the Epik hack. If you check out the email in the *sentmail648* folder you imported in Chapter 6, you'll find messages from the address *oksupport@oathkeepers.org* all signed by Edward Durfee, IT Support.

**NOTE** *In Chapter 1, I discussed not revealing unnecessary PII. In this case, I believe that publishing Durfee's name, the city he lives in, and the name of his company is in the public interest. Since he's an organizer for the Oath Keepers, a group that attempted to subvert democracy, this makes him a legitimate target of reporting. There's no public interest in publishing his home address, phone number, or email address, though.*

After the Epik hack, reporter Mikael Thalen wrote an article for the Daily Dot based on the leaked WHOIS data and focusing on Ali Alexander, one of the primary organizers on January 6 and a major activist in the Stop the Steal movement. Thalen used the Epik data to show that in the days following the riot, Alexander began turning on WHOIS privacy for over 100 domains he owned, nearly half of them connected to the election lie, such as stopthestealmovement.com and stopthestealnews.com. You can read

Thalen's reporting at *https://www.dailydot.com/debug/ali-alexander-epik-hack -web-domains-capitol-riot/*.

In Exercise 12-4, you'll download part of the Epik dataset and get ready to start exploring it yourself.

## Exercise 12-4: Download and Extract Part of the Epik Dataset

The Epik dataset is split into three folders: *EpikFail, EpikFailTheB:Sides*, and *EpikFailYouLostTheGame*, which you can download either using BitTorrent or from DDoSecrets' public data server at *https://data.ddosecrets.com/Epik/*. Inside the first folder, *EpikFail*, are three subfolders: *emails, filesystems*, and *sql*. The *emails* folder contains email messages from a single email account related to Epik, while the *filesystems* folder contains all of the files taken from one of Epik's Linux servers. The *sql* folder, by far the largest folder in the first part of the Epik dataset, contains backups of MySQL databases. For this exercise, you'll download a single MySQL backup file, *api_system.sql.gz*, which takes only 1.2GB of disk space.

On your *datasets* USB disk, create a new folder called *Epik* for the Epik dataset, and then download *api_system.sql.gz* from *https://data.ddosecrets.com/ Epik/EpikFail/sql/api_system.sql.gz* and save it there. Now, open a terminal (if you're in Windows, use an Ubuntu terminal) and change to the *Epik* folder on your *datasets* USB disk like so:

```
micah@trapdoor ~ % cd /Volumes/datasets/Epik
micah@trapdoor Epik % ls -lh
total 0
-rw-r--r--  1 user  staff  1.2G Sep 17  2021 api_system.sql.gz
```

The file is a compressed backup of a MySQL database with the extension *.sql.gz*, meaning that it was compressed using GZIP discussed in Chapter 11. To extract the *api_system.sql.gz* file, run the following command:

```
gunzip api_system.sql.gz
```

SQL data compresses very well: the original *api_system.sql.gz* file is 1.2GB, but the extracted version, *api_system.sql*, is 20GB, taking up 16 times as much disk space.

Now that you've extracted the file, the next step is to import it into your MySQL database in Exercise 12-5.

## Exercise 12-5: Import Epik Data into MySQL

The Epik dataset includes nine separate MySQL databases. To keep things simple, the exercises in this chapter require you to import and explore data only in the *api_system.sql* database into your MySQL server. Each *.sql* file in the Epik dataset represents a full database containing several tables. In order to import one of these files into MySQL, first you'll need to create a database for it.

## Create a Database for api_system

You'll use the mysql command line client to create a new database called epikfail_api_system. Prefixing your database title with epikfail_ will help you keep it separate from other databases you might import in the future.

Open a terminal and run the following command to connect to your MySQL server as the root user:

```
micah@trapdoor ~ % mysql -h localhost --protocol=tcp -u root -p
Enter password:
Welcome to the MariaDB monitor. Commands end with ; or \g.
--snip--
```

After logging in with the root password, run this command to create the epikfail_api_system database:

```
MariaDB [(none)]> CREATE DATABASE epikfail_api_system;
Query OK, 1 row affected (0.015 sec)
MariaDB [(none)]> exit
Bye
```

Congrats, you've just created a new database!

## Import api_system Data

The simplest way to import a MySQL backup into a MySQL client is to pipe the data into the mysql program, by running the following command:

```
cat filename.sql | mysql -h localhost --protocol=tcp -u root -p database_name
```

The problem is that you'd see no output—no progress bars or any other indication that it's actually working. This is fine for small SQL backups that take a few seconds to import, but it might take hours or days to import large backups. To solve this problem, I use a simple program called pv, which stands for "Pipe Viewer," to display a progress bar. The pv command is similar to the cat command, but it also displays useful output so you can be sure your command is running.

If you're using a Mac, install pv in Homebrew by running the following command:

```
brew install pv
```

If you're using Linux or Windows with WSL, install pv by running the following command:

```
sudo apt install pv
```

Once you've installed pv, make sure you're in the *Epik* folder and run this command:

```
pv api_system.sql | mysql -h localhost --protocol=tcp -u root -p epikfail_api_system
```

Just like cat, pv should load data from *api_system.sql* and pipe it into mysql, but this time it should show you a progress bar like this one, complete with the import speed and the estimated time that it will finish:

```
micah@trapdoor Epik % pv api_system.sql | mysql -h localhost --protocol=tcp -u root -p
epikfail_api_system
Enter password:
2.89GiB 0:33:47 [ 587KiB/s] [=====>                    ] 14% ETA 3:14:56
```

In this example, I had been running the import for 33 minutes and 47 seconds. It had progressed through 2.89GB of the data (14 percent) and estimated it would finish in 3 hours and 15 minutes, at a current speed of 587KB per second (though import speed varies greatly depending on which query is currently running). It took me a total of four hours to import *api_system.sql*.

---

### TROUBLESHOOTING DURING DATABASE IMPORTS

Something can always go wrong while you're in the middle of importing a database. You could accidentally close your terminal window, stopping the import partway through. Your laptop could run out of battery, or you could accidentally unplug your USB disk. You might need to cancel the import midway through (by pressing CTRL-C). If anything like this happens, don't worry. It's fairly simple to delete your database, create a new one, and start the import over again. Unfortunately, though, you can't continue where you left off.

To restart an interrupted import, you can drop the database using the DROP DATABASE *database_name*; statement. This deletes the whole database and all of its tables. Create a new database and import the data again. For example, if your epikfail_api_system import was interrupted, you start over by running these MySQL queries as the root user with the following commands:

```
DROP DATABASE epikfail_api_system;
CREATE DATABASE epikfail_api_system;
```

Then start the import again.

---

Wait for the data from *api_system.sql* to finish importing before you move on to the next section. (It's possible to run queries on the database before it's fully imported, but you'll only get results from the data that's been imported so far.)

## Exploring Epik's SQL Database

Once *api_system.sql* has finished importing, it's time to dive in and take a look at the epikfail_api_system database. With databases like this, a good tactic is to manually view each table and try to determine if it contains data worth exploring further. To begin my investigation, I looked at the first rows in each of the 49 tables in epikfail_api_system, starting with the backorder table and ending with the whoisxmlapi_cache table. I tried to get a sense of what information that table held, if it was related to other tables in the database, and how many rows of data there were.

In this section, I'll guide you through the tables that stood out to me in the epikfail_api_system database. You can use either Adminer or the mysql command line client: they both query the same SQL server and will receive the same tables of data in response. When your interest is piqued, you can try running your own queries as well. It's good practice to refrain from running INSERT, UPDATE, or DELETE queries in leaked databases that you're investigating. However, SELECT queries don't modify anything in the database, so you can run as many as you want at any point, then continue following along when you're done.

### The domain Table

The domain table in the epikfail_api_system database has over 1.6 million rows in it and is clearly a list of domain names in Epik's system. Count the number of rows in this table using the following query:

```
SELECT COUNT(*) FROM domain;
```

Table 12-12 shows the results from that query.

**Table 12-12:** Counting the Rows in the domain Table

| COUNT(*) |
| --- |
| 1688005 |

Columns in the domain table include id, name (the domain name, in all caps), cr_date (presumably the domain name's creation date), and exp_date (presumably the domain name's expiration date).

To look at the 10 most recently created domains in this table, run the following query:

```
SELECT id, name, cr_date, exp_date
FROM domain
ORDER BY cr_date DESC
LIMIT 10;
```

This command uses the `ORDER BY cr_date DESC` clause to sort data returned by the `cr_date` column, in descending order (from most recent to oldest, in this case). The `LIMIT 10` clause in the following line limits the results to only 10 rows; if you left that clause out, the command would return all 1.6 million rows.

Table 12-13 shows the results from this query.

**Table 12-13:** Selecting the Most Recently Created Domains

| id | name | cr_date | exp_date |
|---|---|---|---|
| 17803243 | MAKEAPPLIANCESWORKAGAIN.COM | 2021-03-01 01:41:52 | 2022-03-01 01:41:52 |
| 17803233 | BEREANBAPTISTPORTCHARLOTTE.ORG | 2021-03-01 01:33:26 | 2022-03-01 01:33:26 |
| 17803213 | WECONSIGNGUNS.NET | 2021-03-01 01:32:04 | 2022-03-01 01:32:04 |
| 17803223 | WECONSIGNGUNS.COM | 2021-03-01 01:32:04 | 2022-03-01 01:32:04 |
| 17803183 | MAINEANTIQUEMALL.COM | 2021-03-01 01:29:42 | 2022-03-01 01:29:42 |
| 17803203 | MAINEANTIQUESTORE.COM | 2021-03-01 01:29:42 | 2022-03-01 01:29:42 |
| 17803193 | MAINEANTIQUESHOP.COM | 2021-03-01 01:29:42 | 2022-03-01 01:29:42 |
| 17803173 | WOOGITYBOOGITY.COM | 2021-03-01 01:20:35 | 2022-03-01 01:20:35 |
| 17803163 | NAMECAESAR.COM | 2021-03-01 01:17:52 | 2022-03-01 01:17:52 |
| 17803153 | SCENICBOATTOUR.COM | 2021-03-01 01:17:11 | 2022-03-01 01:17:11 |

To search the list of Epik domains for ones containing specific keywords, use the `LIKE` operator in the `WHERE` clause. For example, try using the following queries to search for domains that mention the word *Trump*, ordered by the most recently created domains:

```
SELECT id, name, cr_date, exp_date
FROM domain
WHERE name LIKE '%trump%'
ORDER BY cr_date DESC;
```

As you learned earlier, using `LIKE` makes the search case insensitive, and % characters are wildcards. Filtering the results by `name LIKE '%trump%'` will display only results that include *trump* (regardless of capitalization) somewhere in their name.

The query returns 413 results total. Table 12-14 shows the first 10 results.

Clearly, many people used Epik to register Trump-related domain names. These results don't include any ownership information for these domains, though. To find that missing information, let's take a look at the privacy table.

**Table 12-14:** Domains That Include the Word *Trump*

| id | name | cr_date | exp_date |
|---|---|---|---|
| 17802593 | TRUMPISM.IO | 2021-02-28 23:45:44 | 2022-02-28 23:45:44 |
| 17750903 | TRUMPWONINALANDSLIDE.COM | 2021-02-23 08:52:33 | 2022-02-23 08:52:33 |
| 17750913 | DONALDTRUMPWONINALANDSLIDE.COM | 2021-02-23 08:52:33 | 2022-02-23 08:52:33 |
| 17676023 | DUMP-TRUMP.NET | 2021-02-22 21:38:40 | 2022-02-22 21:38:40 |
| 17694803 | TRUMPBEEGIRLS.COM | 2021-02-19 00:14:23 | 2026-02-19 00:14:23 |
| 17672243 | TRUMP2020.NET | 2021-02-17 17:43:32 | 2022-02-17 17:43:32 |
| 17661353 | FANTRUMP.COM | 2021-02-16 19:04:43 | 2022-02-16 19:04:43 |
| 17662513 | DONALDTRUMP.TRUTH | 2021-02-16 13:22:16 | 2022-02-16 13:22:16 |
| 17662433 | TRUMP.TRUTH | 2021-02-16 13:22:13 | 2022-02-16 13:22:13 |
| 17615793 | VOTELARATRUMP.COM | 2021-02-14 17:38:12 | 2023-02-14 17:38:12 |

## The privacy Table

The privacy table has 721,731 rows of data. Like the domain table, it has a domain column that lists domain names, but it also includes columns with all of the private WHOIS details. Relevant columns include admin_org, admin _name, admin_email, admin_address, admin_phone, and other similar information. There are also numerous similar columns with tech_, bill_, and reg_ prefixes. The data in this table includes WHOIS data for the administrator contact, the technical contact, the billing contact, and the registrant contact. There's also a date_add column with a timestamp, presumably noting when this domain was added to Epik's system.

I mentioned earlier that, in 2019, Patrick Crusius posted a manifesto to 8chan before killing 23 people and injuring 23 more in El Paso, Texas. In the aftermath of the terrorist attack, 8chan moved its domain name hosting to Epik. With that in mind, search the data for 8chan.co, 8chan's domain name, to see who is behind the site:

```
SELECT * FROM privacy WHERE domain='8CHAN.CO';
```

Table 12-15 shows partial results from this query. The query selects all columns (*), but I included only the admin_ columns here because the tech_, bill_, and reg_ columns all have the exact same data that appears in the admin_ column.

This domain was added to Epik's system the night of August 4, 2019. This was the day after Crusius posted his manifesto to 8chan and then went on his anti-Latino murder spree.

It's public knowledge that Jim Watkins and his son, Ron Watkins, ran 8chan at the time (they are also behind today's rebrand, 8kun). According to the HBO documentary miniseries *Q: Into the Storm*, directed and produced by Cullen Hoback, the pair are also by far the most likely people behind the QAnon conspiracy cult. Jim Watkins, an American, lived in the

Philippines at the time of Crusius's rampage. As you can see from the hidden WHOIS data, the admin address is for a property in the Philippines. This increases confidence that the data is authentic, and also gives key data points about Jim Watkins in case we wanted to research him further: an address and phone number.

**Table 12-15:** Ownership Data for the Domain 8chan.co

| id | 2429814 |
|---|---|
| domain | 8CHAN.CO |
| date_add | 2019-08-04 23:01:11 |
| admin_org | Loki Technology, Incorporated |
| admin_name | Jim Watkins |
| admin_email | domains@nttec.com |
| admin_address | *redacted* |
| admin_city | Pasig |
| admin_state | NCR |
| admin_zip | 1600 |
| admin_country | PH |
| admin_cc | PH |
| admin_phone | +63.*redacted* |

Since Watkins runs a website popular among American terrorists and is likely one of the people behind QAnon, the next logical step is to check if he or his company, Loki Technology, owned any other domain names on Epik. To find out, try running this query in the epikfail_api_system database:

```
SELECT * FROM privacy WHERE admin_email='domains@nttec.com';
```

This query searches for domains that list admin_email as domains@nttec .com, which is the administrator email address on 8chan.co. However, it returns just a single row for that domain. Run the following query, modified with the expression admin_email LIKE '%@nttec.com' to check for domains where admin_email is any email address at the nttec.com domain:

```
SELECT * FROM privacy WHERE admin_email LIKE '%@nttec.com';
```

However, this query has the same results. For your next query, switch tactics and search for domains that list admin_org as anything mentioning Loki Technology, using the admin_org LIKE '%Loki Technology%' expression. The expression includes wildcard characters, just in case Watkins listed his company slightly differently on different domains, like "Loki Technology, Inc." instead of "Loki Technology, Incorporated":

```
SELECT * FROM privacy WHERE admin_org LIKE '%Loki Technology%';
```

This query returns the same result. For a final query, search the domains that list admin_name as Jim Watkins, using LIKE to make the search case insensitive:

```
SELECT * FROM privacy WHERE admin_name LIKE 'Jim Watkins';
```

Unfortunately, all these queries return just one result: the 8chan.co row.

In the next section, you'll learn about how I eventually found more information about domains owned by Jim Watkins in the Epik dataset, just not in the epikfail_api_system database. For now, let's look at some final interesting tables in this database.

### The hosting and hosting_server Tables

The hosting table has 3,934 rows and appears to show websites that Epik actually runs the servers for, not just the domain name registration. Columns include domain, cr_date, username, password (in plaintext, though it's not clear what these usernames and passwords are for), plan (like silver, gold, or platinum), server_id, and others. Run the following query to view the most recent rows:

```
SELECT id, domain, cr_date, plan, server_id
FROM hosting
ORDER BY cr_date DESC
LIMIT 5;
```

Since the query uses the ORDER BY cr_date DESC clause, the results will be sorted from most recent to oldest. The LIMIT 5 clause means the results will include at most five rows. Table 12-16 shows the results from this query.

**Table 12-16:** Recent Rows in the hosting Table

| id | domain | cr_date | plan | server_id |
|-------|---------------------|---------------------|-------------------|-----------|
| 33613 | THELIBERATEDPRESS.COM | 2021-02-28 18:08:06 | bronze | 23 |
| 39573 | REICKERTSPLUMBING.COM | 2021-02-28 17:30:18 | email | 23 |
| 39563 | IANLAZAR.COM | 2021-02-28 16:50:10 | bronze | 23 |
| 39553 | APAYWEEKLY.COM | 2021-02-28 16:16:08 | sitebuilder-basic | 23 |
| 39543 | BOUNCETHEBOX.COM | 2021-02-28 15:24:08 | silver | 23 |

I tried loading several of the domain names in this table in a browser. Some of them are down, while others appear to be websites for random businesses. I quickly noticed that the server_id column implies a relationship with another table. I guessed the related table was most likely the hosting_server table and began to run queries on that.

The `hosting_server` table has only six rows, each a different server that Epik uses to host websites. Run this query to see the data in this table:

```
SELECT id, api_host, login_host, login_port, username, password
FROM hosting_server;
```

Table 12-17 shows the query results.

**Table 12-17:** The hosting_server Table

| id | api_host | login_host | login_port | username | password |
|----|----------|------------|------------|----------|----------|
| 1 | 192.187.99.50 | hosting.epik.com | 2082 | epikhost | *redacted* |
| 2 | 204.12.206.186 | hosting5.epik.com | 2083 | hostinge | *redacted* |
| 3 | 88.214.193.70 | hosting6.epik.com | 2083 | hostinge | *redacted* |
| 13 | 88.214.193.195 | hosting7.epik.com | 2083 | hostinge | *redacted* |
| 14 | 88.214.193.163 | hosting8.epik.com | 2083 | hostinge | *redacted* |
| 23 | 88.214.194.85 | hosting9.epik.com | 2083 | hostinge | *redacted* |

The passwords in this table are all in plaintext. In fact, if you load *https://hosting9.epik.com:2083* in Tor Browser, you'll see the login page for cPanel, software that's used to manage shared web hosting systems like this. The usernames and passwords in the `hosting_server` table are likely the credentials to log in to this cPanel server—but don't actually try this out. As noted earlier, it's fine for you to see the passwords scattered across datasets, but actually attempting to log in to an account with them is illegal. In any case, Epik has probably changed its passwords since the data breach.

All of the recent websites in the `hosting` table have a `server_id` of 23. Check how many websites are hosted on that server by running a query to join it with the `hosting_server` table:

```
SELECT COUNT(*)
FROM hosting
LEFT JOIN hosting_server ON hosting_server.id=hosting.server_id
WHERE hosting.server_id=23;
```

The result is 1,155, so that's the number of websites the server with ID 23 hosts.

What about the rest of the servers? The quickest way to figure out how many websites each server hosts is to use a GROUP BY clause, like this:

```
SELECT
    server_id,
    COUNT(*) AS server_count
FROM hosting
LEFT JOIN hosting_server ON hosting_server.id=hosting.server_id
GROUP BY hosting.server_id;
```

This query groups by hosting.server_id, which means each row of the results will show the number of rows in the hosting table with that server_id. Table 12-18 shows the results of this query.

**Table 12-18:** The Number of Websites Hosted on Each Server

| server_id | server_count |
|-----------|--------------|
| 3         | 762          |
| 13        | 1474         |
| 14        | 543          |
| 23        | 1155         |

While there's always more to learn, you should now have the SQL skills to write powerful queries that can help you quickly find what you're looking for, even in tables with millions of rows.

## Working with Epik Data in the Cloud

The MySQL databases from Epik contain an overwhelming amount of data that's useful for extremism research, and only a fraction of that data is in the *api_system.sql.gz* backup that you've imported for this chapter. Some of the other databases, such as *intrust.sql.gz*, contain even more interesting information. If you're curious, I suggest downloading, importing, and investigating all nine MySQL databases from the Epik dataset.

Some of these databases would likely take your computer days to finish importing and would require a large amount of disk space. It's more convenient to download and work with databases like these on a server in the cloud rather than on your local computer. To do so, follow these steps:

1. Create a new VPS on a cloud service provider (making sure it has plenty of disk space) and SSH into it, like you did in Exercise 4-4.

2. Use wget to download just the compressed database backups, a total of 14GB, from *https://data.ddosecrets.com/Epik/EpikFail/sql/*. Alternatively, using a CLI BitTorrent client, you could download the entire first part of the Epik dataset, which is 35GB of data, similar to what you did in Exercise 4-5.

3. Extract the compressed MySQL database backups as you did in Exercise 12-4. By the time you're done extracting these files, you'll have 145GB of MySQL backup files.

4. Install a MySQL server on your VPS. There are various ways of doing this, but one option is to install Docker on your VPS and run a MySQL server as you did in Exercise 12-3. Since your VPS will be running Linux, just make sure to follow the Linux instructions there.

5. Using the command line MySQL client, create nine databases, one for each backup file. Next, using pv and mysql, import all nine database

backups as you did in Exercise 12-5. This step will likely take your VPS several days to finish, but since the remote server is handling the import, this won't disrupt other work on your computer.

These are essentially the steps I followed when I investigated the Epik dataset at The Intercept. The downside to doing this all in the cloud is that you'll need to pay a monthly bill to your hosting provider for the server that you're using. However, once you have a remote MySQL server full of Epik databases, you can use a MySQL client to connect to it and run queries, which will allow you to analyze hundreds of gigabytes of leaked databases.

The most useful part of the Epik dataset, in my opinion, is the fact that you can use it to peel back the curtain behind Epik's WHOIS privacy service. You did this some in the "Exploring Epik's SQL Database" section, but you looked only in the privacy table of the epikfail_api_system database. But that isn't the only place where you can find WHOIS privacy data.

The nine different MySQL databases in the Epik leak appear to have lots of duplicate data. For example, the epikfail_intrust database has a table called domains_whois with all of the same columns as the privacy table. The domains_whois table has 1.4 million rows of data, roughly twice as many as the privacy table, though many of the rows appear to contain similar data. In the epikfail_whois database, there's a table called data with similar columns and 1.3 million rows of data. All three tables have various duplicates of the same WHOIS data, so you may want to search them all before concluding that a domain name ownership isn't in this dataset.

In the "Exploring Epik's SQL Database" section, you ran some queries in epiktrust_api_system to find domains that Jim Watkins owns other than 8chan.co, but they fell short. If you import additional databases, can you find other domains he owns? When I ran similar queries in the epikfail_intrust database on the domains_whois table, which has more data than the privacy table in the epiktrust_api_system database, I got some hits. If you want to run this query yourself, you'll need to first download and import the *intrust.sql* database into your MySQL server.

Here's the query I ran to search the domains_whois table in the epikfail_intrust database for domains owned by Jim Watkins's company:

```
SELECT * FROM domains_whois WHERE admin_email LIKE '%@nttec.com';
```

Table 12-19 lists the truncated results of this query, showing only some of the columns. As you can see, Jim Watkins owns all of the domains listed in the results.

At the time of writing, the domain 5ch.net loaded a Japanese-language site called 5channel. When I loaded 2ch.net, it failed with a "connection timed out" error from Cloudflare, and when I loaded bbspink.com, I got an "access denied" error from Cloudflare saying that the site blocks connections from the US. I connected to a VPN in Europe and tried again; this time, it redirected to 5ch.net. If you'd like, you can try the same steps yourself.

**Table 12-19:** Other Domains Owned by Jim Watkins from the `epikfail_intrust` Database

| id | domain | date_update | admin_org | admin_name | admin_email |
|---|---|---|---|---|---|
| 8615894 | 8CH.NET | 2019-10-13 01:27:05 | Loki Technology, Incorporated | Jim Watkins | domains@nttec.com |
| 8615904 | 8CHAN.CO | 2019-10-13 01:27:06 | Loki Technology, Incorporated | Jim Watkins | domains@nttec.com |
| 8615944 | 5CH.NET | 2019-10-13 01:27:07 | Loki Technology, Incorporated | Jim Watkins | domains@nttec.com |
| 8615984 | 2CH.NET | 2019-10-13 01:27:08 | Loki Technology, Incorporated | Jim Watkins | domains@nttec.com |
| 8616004 | BBSPINK.COM | 2019-10-13 01:27:09 | Loki Technology, Incorporated | Jim Watkins | domains@nttec.com |

As you explore more databases, you'll discover that writing SQL queries to find what you're looking for takes some trial and error. Sometimes the results from one query will inform what you should search for next—as you've seen, I used the email that Watkins registered 8chan.co with to find his other domains, for example. When you don't find what you're looking for, tweak your queries to make them more broad, or search a different field that might give you similar information.

## Summary

In this chapter, you've learned how to run your own MySQL server on your computer using Docker containers. You took a crash course in SQL, the language used to communicate with SQL servers, and were introduced to Epik, the online service provider for right-wing extremists and American terrorists who have committed mass murder. Finally, you downloaded a MySQL database backup from the 2021 Epik Fail dataset, imported it into your own local MySQL server, and ran SQL queries to begin investigating it yourself.

This marks the conclusion of Part IV, which has given you the foundational tools and techniques to explore almost any dataset you can get your hands on. Part V, the final two chapters of the book, doesn't include any exercises. Instead, it describes real data-driven investigations I've worked on in the past, shows you what code I wrote and why, and explains exactly how I used the skills I've taught you throughout this book to find revelations. I hope you'll use these case studies as inspiration for your own future data-driven investigations.

# PART V

## CASE STUDIES

# 13

## PANDEMIC PROFITEERS AND COVID-19 DISINFORMATION

*About a month ago, there was an article printed in a newspaper I had never heard of
called The Intercept. I discovered that The Intercept is a rag far left of the New York Times.
They printed an article alleging that the telemedicine company to which America's
Frontline Doctors referred people—a third-party telemedicine company—had had patient
data breaches, that it had been hacked. This got the telemedicine company, of course,
very nervous. They thought they had good firewalls up. They spent about $200,000 to prove
that there was no actual hack, that it was all made up. It was all a lie. But it was the
basis for Congressman Clyburn's investigation into me! And I thought to myself,
That sounds very familiar. A fake story in a rag paper.*
—Dr. Simone Gold, founder of America's Frontline Doctors,
speaking at a November 2021 event hosted by the David Horowitz Freedom Center,
an Islamophobic hate group, in Palm Beach, Florida

On September 11, 2021, an anonymous hacker sent me
about 100MB of compressed data from, in the words of
my source, "the horse paste peddlers." My source was
looking into America's Frontline Doctors (AFLDS),
an anti-science propaganda group founded in 2020 to
support President Trump in his opposition to public
health policies during the coronavirus pandemic.

AFLDS, along with a small network of telehealth companies that my source told me were "hilariously easy" to hack, falsely claims to its sizable online audience that COVID-19 vaccines are dangerous and ineffective. It also promotes the drugs hydroxychloroquine (commonly used to treat malaria and lupus) and ivermectin (commonly used as a dewormer in livestock) as miracle cures for the virus. AFLDS creates high-quality anti-vaccine propaganda videos and distributes them to hundreds of thousands of followers across social media platforms.

The hacker sent me two datasets from two separate companies: Cadence Health, which ran the platform AFLDS used to give telehealth consultations to patients, and Ravkoo Pharmacy, which filled prescriptions for these drugs. After investigating over 1GB of JSON and CSV files cumulatively contained in the decompressed datasets, I discovered that AFLDS and its partners duped tens of thousands of people into seeking ineffective treatments and charged them at least $15 million—likely much more—for consultations and prescriptions for these drugs.

The revelations from my investigation led the US House Select Subcommittee on the Coronavirus Crisis, headed by Rep. James Clyburn (D-SC), to open an investigation into AFLDS and SpeakWithAnMD; technically, AFLDS worked directly with SpeakWithAnMD for providing telehealth consultations, and Cadence Health was SpeakWithAnMD's vendor for managing the technology. Clyburn called these groups "predatory actors" that have been "touting misinformation and using it to market disproven and potentially hazardous coronavirus treatments." The committee recommended that the Federal Trade Commission open its own investigation into these companies and later expanded its investigation to also cover Cadence Health.

Also in response to my reporting, other reporting on AFLDS, and pro-science activism in the medical community, the Medical Board of California (MBC) opened an investigation into Dr. Simone Gold, the founder of AFLDS, to determine if she should be stripped of her medical license. (At the time of writing, she is still licensed in California, as well as in Florida, where she has since moved.) AFLDS later accosted MBC president Kristina Lawson in a parking garage with cameras as part of an anti-science propaganda video it was producing.

Because the AFLDS dataset is full of medical records and PII, none of it is public, so you won't be able to work with it yourself. Instead, I'll describe the data, show redacted pieces of it, and show snippets of the Python code I wrote to make sense of it. If a similar dataset ever drops in your lap, the skills you've learned in this book so far and the strategies described in this chapter, along with perhaps some additional independent study, should enable you to investigate it just like I did.

# The Origins of AFLDS

Before we get into the dataset, let's take a look at how AFLDS was founded, including its ties to Trump's 2020 reelection campaign and the conservative advocacy group the Tea Party Patriots, as well as exactly how AFLDS's extremely profitable scheme succeeded in swindling vaccine skeptics into spending millions of dollars on phone consultations and bogus medicine for COVID-19.

On May 11, 2020, a senior staffer in Donald Trump's reelection campaign and the Republican activist group CNP Action held a conference call. An audio recording of this call was leaked to Center for Media and Democracy, a progressive watchdog group, which gave a copy of the recording to the Associated Press (AP), which in turn reported on it. A key topic of discussion was reportedly finding "extremely pro-Trump doctors" to go on TV and defend Trump's plan to rapidly reopen the economy, despite the more cautious safety guidance coming from the Centers for Disease Control and Prevention (CDC). Nancy Schulze, a Republican Party activist married to a former Republican member of Congress, said on the call that she had a list of doctors willing to defend Trump's policies and that "those are the types of guys that we should want to get out on TV and radio to help push out the message."

Dr. Gold was the "extremely pro-Trump doctor" they were looking for. During AP's reporting of this conference call, a public relations firm distributed an open letter to Trump signed by over 400 doctors, calling the pandemic lockdown policies a "mass casualty event." Dr. Gold's signature was at the top of the letter, though she denied coordinating her efforts with the Trump campaign. This open letter was released after AP had sent requests for comment to individuals on the call and to Trump's reelection campaign, but before it had published its article. This letter appears to be, at least in part, an attempt to preempt the article with a positive spin, something that might happen when you reach out for comment while doing adversarial journalism, as discussed in Chapter 1.

In June 2020, weeks after the conference call and the open letter, Gold founded an Arizona nonprofit called the Free Speech Foundation. The enterprise started with a million-dollar annual budget and fiscal sponsorship from the Tea Party Patriots Foundation, the major US conservative organization introduced in Chapter 2. AFLDS launched on July 27, 2020, as a Free Speech Foundation project. Gold, along with other doctors in white lab coats, held a press conference on the steps of the Supreme Court building where they falsely claimed that a cocktail of hydroxychloroquine, azithromycin, and zinc could cure COVID-19. The event was livestreamed on Breitbart. Then-President Trump shared videos of the press conference on Twitter, garnering millions of views before tech companies took them down for violating rules against pandemic misinformation.

## SIMONE GOLD, INSURRECTIONIST

Simone Gold isn't just an anti-vaxxer quack doctor getting rich off of fake cures for COVID-19; she's also one of the insurrectionists who stormed the US Capitol on January 6, 2021. After Gold pleaded guilty to misdemeanor trespassing, she was sentenced to two months in prison, a year of supervised release, and a $9,500 fine.

In response to Gold's arrest, AFLDS went on a fundraising spree, claiming that the charge against her was a politically motivated trampling of her free speech rights. The group raised more than $430,000 by the date of her sentencing, which the judge called "unseemly." He also accused AFLDS of "mischaracterizing" her trial, "telling your supporters that this is a political prosecution of a law-abiding physician that's designed to threaten and intimidate any American who dares to exercise their First Amendment rights."

After Gold reported to prison in July 2022, her California medical license was automatically placed on "inactive" status, meaning she was barred from practicing medicine (though it was reactivated after she was released). While she served her sentence, AFLDS continued to fundraise off of her plight, including sending a newsletter that unironically cited an article from The Intercept about privacy issues in her prison.

John Strand, a former underwear model who hosted some of AFLDS's short medical disinformation videos and who had become romantically involved with Gold as her employee, was also arrested during the Capitol riot. Unlike Gold, he did not plead guilty to misdemeanor trespassing, opting instead to try his luck at trial. He was found guilty of four misdemeanors and one felony (obstructing an official proceeding) and was sentenced in June 2023 to 32 months in prison and fined $10,000.

In early 2021, well into the pandemic, AFLDS set up a system on its website to sell $90 telemedicine consultations so people could get prescriptions for hydroxychloroquine—a drug that, at that point in the pandemic, had already been debunked as a treatment for COVID-19. On January 3, Gold told a packed, maskless church audience in Tampa, Florida, that AFLDS made "hydroxychloroquine available for the entire nation by going to our website. Then you can consult with a telemedicine doctor. And whether you have COVID, or you don't have COVID, or you're just worried about getting COVID, you can get yourself a prescription and they mail it to you." She insisted, "The big fight wasn't the virus, it was the fear."

Figure 13-1 shows the AFLDS website advertising prescriptions for COVID-19 "medication."

If one of AFLDS's hundreds of thousands of followers watched one of the group's anti-vaccine propaganda videos and decided that they needed ivermectin or hydroxychloroquine, first they would click the prominent Contact a Physician button on the AFLDS home page. This brought them to SpeakWithAnMD, the telehealth partner's website. Clicking the button on that site to book a consultation sent the patient to a page to create an account at Cadence Health, a vendor of SpeakWithAnMD. Cadence Health provided the actual telehealth platform that SpeakWithAnMD used.

*Figure 13-1: The home page on AFLDS's website from March 4, 2022*

The patient would then fill out a form answering medical questions; click through the disclaimer "As a potential patient, I acknowledge and understand that the Hydroxychloroquine (HCQ) and Ivermectin have been deemed 'Highly Not Recommended' by the WHO, FDA, CDC, and NIH"; and enter their credit card information to pay $90 for a consultation. In the next few days, the patient would receive a phone call from someone in AFLDS's network of physicians, who would write them a prescription for the unproven drugs. ABC News paid the $90, got a call from someone who wrote them a prescription for ivermectin, and recorded the prescriber saying, "I don't have any medical knowledge as far as the medicine, or even about COVID."

At the time, the prescriptions were almost always processed through the online pharmacy Ravkoo. The patient would call Ravkoo, read their credit card number on the phone, and get the drugs mailed to their door. Sometimes they would be charged as much as $700 for ivermectin; Ravkoo didn't accept health insurance for these sales.

When I started this investigation, I wasn't familiar with any of these companies. It was obvious that AFLDS was in the business of misleading its followers about public health so it could sell ineffective alternatives for preventing and treating COVID-19. But I didn't know how SpeakWithAnMD, Cadence Health, or Ravkoo fit into the scheme. Were they in on the AFLDS scam, or were they legitimate businesses that just happened to work with AFLDS?

Next, I'll show you step-by-step how I unraveled this entire COVID-19 pandemic profiteering scheme, starting with a description of the datasets that my hacker source sent me.

## The Cadence Health and Ravkoo Datasets

The 100MB of compressed data from my source included records for hundreds of thousands of patients, in two separate files. This section describes how I stored and extracted these sensitive documents, revisits some basic command line data analysis (as you learned about in Chapter 4), and describes some of the key types of data I discovered in the dataset.

### Extracting the Data into an Encrypted File Container

Because patient records are more sensitive than other medium-sensitivity data, I took additional precautions to secure this dataset and my work with it. I created an encrypted file container, a 5GB encrypted file that I could unlock with a strong passphrase stored in my password manager. This is where I saved the original dataset, as well as all of my notes, code, and other files related to this investigation, giving me an extra layer of protection in case my computer is ever compromised. Even then, whoever accesses my data won't be able to access the patient records without knowing the passphrase.

I used Linux software called zuluCrypt to manage my encrypted file container, but VeraCrypt, which you learned about in Chapter 1, would also have been a good option and is available on any operating system. ZuluCrypt is similar to VeraCrypt, but it's slightly nicer to use and works only in Linux. I could also have used Disk Utility in macOS to create encrypted DMG files.

My source sent me two tarball files: *hipaa_special.tar.zst* (33MB) and *horse_around_find_out.tar.zst* (74MB). Here's a listing of them:

```
micah@trapdoor data % ls -lh
total 215904
-rwx------  1 micah  staff    32M Sep 14  2021 hipaa_special.tar.zst
-rwx------  1 micah  staff    73M Sep 13  2021 horse_around_find_out.tar.zst
```

In Chapter 11, you worked with a similar file format, *.tar.gz*, where files are compressed using the GZIP algorithm. These *.tar.zst* files were compressed using a different algorithm, Zstandard. Installing the Zstandard package allowed me to uncompress this type of file using the command `tar -xf` *filename*. The `-xf` argument combines `-x`, which tells `tar` to extract the file, and `-f`, which indicates that the following argument is the filename that you're extracting. The `tar` program detects that this is a Zstandard file and uses `zstd` to uncompress it. Finally, because `tar` extracts a file into the current working folder, I created new folders, changed to them, and then extracted the data into that folder. For example, here's how I extracted *hipaa_special.tar.zst*:

```
micah@trapdoor data % mkdir hipaa_special
micah@trapdoor data % cd hipaa_special
micah@trapdoor hipaa_special % tar -xf ../hipaa_special.tar.zst
```

As you learned in Chapter 3, these commands make a new folder called *hipaa_special*, change to that folder, and then extract the *hipaa_special.tar.zst* file from the parent folder.

Likewise, the following commands change to the parent folder, make a new folder called *horse_around_and_find* out, change to that folder, and then extract *horse_around_find_out.tar.zst* into that folder:

```
micah@trapdoor hipaa_special % cd ..
micah@trapdoor data % mkdir horse_around_find_out
micah@trapdoor data % cd horse_around_find_out
micah@trapdoor horse_around_find_out % tar -xf ../horse_around_find_out.tar.zst
```

After extracting these folders, I did what I always do the first time I encounter any new dataset: start measuring it with command line tools.

## Analyzing the Data with Command Line Tools

First, I wanted to know how much disk space these files took up and how many files were in each folder. I used the command line tricks described in Chapter 4 to figure this out:

```
micah@trapdoor data % gdu --apparent-size -sh hipaa_special
493M    hipaa_special
micah@trapdoor data % find hipaa_special -type f | wc -l
  281546
micah@trapdoor data % gdu --apparent-size -sh horse_around_find_out
691M    horse_around_find_out
micah@trapdoor data % find horse_around_find_out -type f | wc -l
    215
```

Because I ran these commands on my Mac, I used the gdu command from the coreutils Homebrew package to estimate disk space (rather than the du command for Linux). The find command created a list of files in the given folder, and that list was piped into the wc -l command, which counted the number of files listed. My output showed that the *hipaa_special* folder took 493MB of space and contained 281,546 files, and the *horse_around _find_out* folder took 691MB of space and contained 215 files. Let's look at one at a time.

### Viewing the hipaa_special Folder

It was clear at this point that *hipaa_special* contained far more files than I could manually read. I ran the following command to view the first few lines of filenames in the *hipaa_special* folder listing, so I could get a feel for what was in there and start opening some of those files next:

```
micah@trapdoor data % ls -lh hipaa_special | head
```

My code piped the output of the ls command into the head command, which by default displays the first 10 lines of input. This way, I didn't need to watch hundreds of thousands of filenames scroll by just to get a sense of the folder's contents.

My output showed that the folder contains small files with numeric file-names and no file extensions:

```
--snip--
-rw-r--r--   1 micah   staff    8.1K Sep 13  2021 100000
-rw-r--r--   1 micah   staff    1.3K Sep 13  2021 100001
-rw-r--r--   1 micah   staff    1.3K Sep 12  2021 100002
-rw-r--r--   1 micah   staff    1.4K Sep 13  2021 100003
-rw-r--r--   1 micah   staff    1.5K Sep 13  2021 100004
-rw-r--r--   1 micah   staff    1.5K Sep 13  2021 100005
-rw-r--r--   1 micah   staff    1.5K Sep 13  2021 100006
-rw-r--r--   1 micah   staff    1.3K Sep 13  2021 100007
-rw-r--r--   1 micah   staff    1.3K Sep 13  2021 100008
```

When I opened one of these files in VS Code, I could quickly see that it was a JSON file. Each of these files, I discovered, was a record for a different user in Cadence Health's system. For example, Listing 13-1 shows a redacted version of the file *244273*.

```
{
    "result": true,
    "provider": {
        "provider_id": null,
        "npi": null,
        "spi": null,
        "partner_id": null,
        "user_id": 244273, ❶
        --snip--
        "fname": "redacted",
        "lname": "redacted",
        "phone": "redacted",
        "work_phone": "",
        "work_phone_ext": "",
        "email": "redacted@hotmail.com",
        "state": "CA",
        "certified_states": [],
        "gender": "F",
        "fax": null,
        "ssn": 999999999,
        "birthdate": "redacted",
        "addressLine1": "redacted",
        "zipcode": "redacted",
        "city": "redacted",
        "avatar": "avatar\/default_avatar.png",
        "id": 78410,
        "partner": ",3,", ❷
        "timezone": "America\/Los_Angeles",
        "role_id": 3,
        --snip--
        "alcohol_type": null,
        "alcohol_amount": null,
        "current_physician": null,
```

```
    "consultationNotes": [ ❸
        {
            "value": 179820,
            "text": "09\/04\/2021 13:47:28", ❹
            "note": "This visit was performed via telemedicine.\nThe patient confirmed
knowledge of the limitations of the use of telemedicine were verbally confirmed by the
provider.\nVerification of patient identity was established.\nVerbal consent was obtained for
medical treatment obtained\n\nThe patient is being interviewed via phone Platform\n\nPatient
has need for covid meds in regards to: ivermectin\nSymptoms onset date: 7 days\n\nOccupation:\
nChronic Medical illnesses: denies heart lung or liver problems\
--snip--
be required.",
            "practice": "covid19_treatment"
        }
    ],
    "internalNotes": []
    }
}
```

*Listing 13-1: An example JSON file from* hipaa_special

I could see that the filename (*244273*) matched the patient's user ID ❶. The record also includes a reference to a partner ❷. This value is in an odd format, but I quickly discovered that it's a comma-separated list of partner IDs with, for some reason, blank values at the beginning and end of the list. I don't know why Cadence Health chose to represent which partners each patient belonged to as a string rather than a JSON array, which would have been cleaner. Once I figured out that they had made this choice, though, it was simple enough to work around. I discovered that the vast majority of the patients have a value of ,3, for partner, which, as you'll see later in this chapter, means they're AFLDS patients.

The record also includes the patient's name, email, address, date of birth, other personal information, and detailed consultation notes. In some of the patient records, the consultationNotes array ❸ is empty, but in this case, it lists details. I assume that patients with empty consultation notes created an account in the Cadence Health system but never paid the $90 and therefore didn't have any telehealth consultations. The patient from this file had their $90 phone consultation on September 4, 2021, at 1:47 PM ❹.

This dataset includes patient records similar to that shown in Listing 13-1 for 281,000 patients.

My source told me that they had created their own account in the Cadence Health system while they were hacking it. As they used the website, they watched exactly which URLs their web browser loaded. When they noticed that the URL that returned their own patient record included their patient ID, they tried loading similar URLs with other IDs. Those URLs returned other users' patient records. Therefore, my source simply wrote a script to download all 281,000 patient records and stored them in individual JSON files. The *hipaa_special.tar.zst* file contains the output of that script.

## Viewing the horse_around_find_out Folder

The *horse_around_find_out* folder is much smaller and easier to deal with. I ran the following command to find out what files it contained (this folder contains a small enough number of files that there was no reason to pipe it into head):

```
micah@trapdoor data % ls -lh horse_around_find_out
```

My output showed that the files in this folder are mostly JSON files from Cadence Health and CSVs from the Ravkoo pharmacy site, as well as a few other files:

```
--snip--
-rw-r--r--    1 micah  staff  387M Sep 12  2021 cadence_allpatients_all.json
-rw-r--r--    1 micah  staff   13K Sep 12  2021 cadence_allpharmacies_all.json
-rw-r--r--    1 micah  staff  317K Sep 12  2021 cadence_allproviders_all.json
-rw-r--r--    1 micah  staff  3.9K Sep 12  2021 cadence_allteams_all.json
-rw-r--r--    1 micah  staff   15K Sep 13  2021 cadence_api.txt
-rw-r--r--    1 micah  staff  103M Sep 12  2021 cadence_contacts_all.json
-rw-r--r--    1 micah  staff  1.0M Sep 12  2021 cadence_getPrescriptionPad_all.json
-rw-r--r--    1 micah  staff  983K Sep 11  2021 cadence_health_partners.json
drwxr-xr-x  202 micah  staff  6.3K Sep 12  2021 cadence_js
-rw-r--r--    1 micah  staff  238K Sep 12  2021 cadence_providers_2.json
-rw-r--r--    1 micah  staff  321K Sep 12  2021 ravkoo_contact.csv
-rw-r--r--    1 micah  staff  1.8M Sep 12  2021 ravkoo_drugs.csv
-rw-r--r--    1 micah  staff   51K Sep 12  2021 ravkoo_insurance.csv
-rw-r--r--    1 micah  staff  149M Sep 13  2021 ravkoo_rxdata.csv
-rw-r--r--    1 micah  staff   60K Sep 12  2021 ravkoo_screenshot.png
-rw-r--r--    1 micah  staff  361B Sep 12  2021 ravkoo_third_parties.csv
```

I started manually opening these files to see what they contain. The *cadence_api.txt* file appears to contain a few hundred lines of JavaScript code that lists URLs within the Cadence Health API, possibly used by the hacker to download the data. The *cadence_js* folder contains several inscrutable JavaScript files, probably the code that powered the Cadence Health website itself.

The folder also contains the file *ravkoo_screenshot.png*, a screenshot from Ravkoo's Super Admin interface, shown in Figure 13-2. I never had access to the interface itself, just this screenshot. It appears that the links on the left represent tables of data from Ravkoo's database, and the information on the right displays all of the data from a selected table.

My source told me that they had discovered a secret URL for this admin interface, though they didn't explain exactly how they found it. Anyone could create an account on Ravkoo's system, and as long as they were logged in, they could go to the URL for this interface. From there, they could click the table names in the list on the left to access all of Ravkoo's data from their web browser. My source built the CSV files they sent me (*ravkoo_contact .csv*, *ravkoo_drugs.csv*, and so on) by scraping the data from the Ravkoo Super Admin interface, just as @donk_enby did to create the Parler dataset. (See Appendix B for more information on web scraping.)

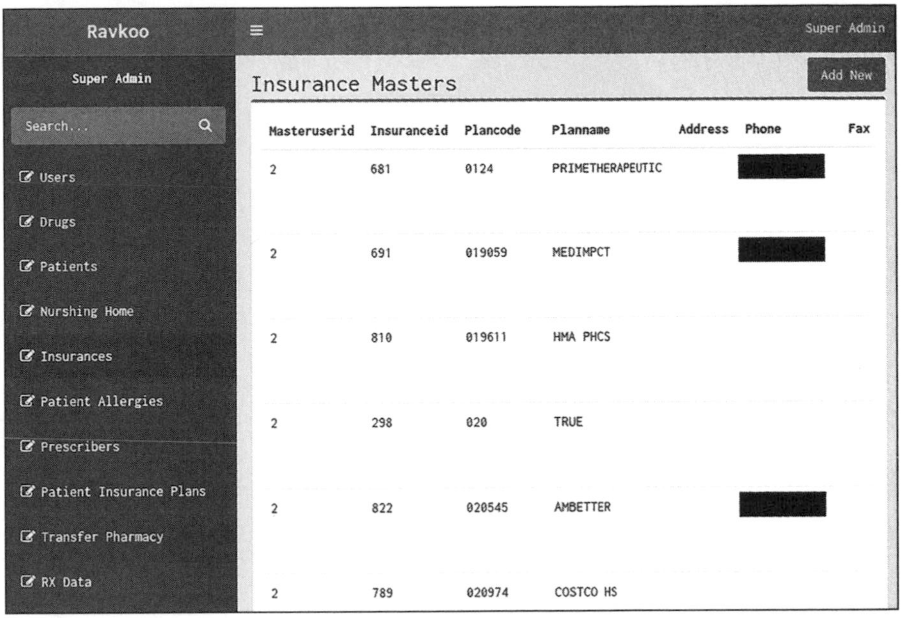

Figure 13-2: A screenshot from the secret Ravkoo Super Admin interface

I could see that the *horse_around_and_find_out* folder contained mostly JSON and CSV files, but I needed to do more research to determine their significance.

### Viewing the cadence_allpatients_all.json File

I started by looking at the largest file in *horse_around_and_find_out*, the 387MB *cadence_allpatients_all.json* file. This enormous JSON object lists information about every Cadence Health patient, including much of the same data listed in the *hipaa_special* patient records. Listing 13-2 shows a redacted section of the data from this file for a single patient.

```
{
    "name": "redacted",
    "id": 168692,
    "fname": "redacted",
    "mname": null,
    "lname": "redacted",
    "email": "redacted@gmail.com",
    "password": "redacted_password_hash",
    "ssn": 999999999,
    "phone": "redacted",
    "fax": null,
    "birthdate": "redacted",
    "gender": "F",
    "maritalStatus": null,
    "addressLine1": "redacted",
    "addressLine2": null,
    "zipcode": "redacted",
```

```
    "city": "redacted",
    "state": "NJ",
    "language": null,
--snip--
    "created_at": "2021-08-18 14:04:58",
    "updated_at": "2021-08-18 14:04:58",
--snip--
```

*Listing 13-2: An example JSON object describing a patient in* cadence_allpatients_all.json

Many of these fields have a value of null, meaning they're empty. The Cadence Health software likely made it optional to collect this information, and AFLDS chose not to do so for its patients. The value of the ssn field (presumably for Social Security number) is 999999999 in this example. All patients in this JSON file have their SSN set either to this number or to null, so it appears that this dataset doesn't include real SSNs. The *cadence _allpatients_all.json* file also included each user's password hash. Someone with all these password hashes could potentially recover the original passwords for users without strong passwords. The value of created_at appears to be the timestamp for when this patient record was created—in other words, when this person created their account.

After reading through several patient records in my text editor, I had a decent understanding of the type of data in this file, so I moved on to examining the smaller files.

### Viewing the cadence_health_partners.json File

The *cadence_health_partners.json* file contains a JSON object with a list of 17 of Cadence's partners, such as America's Frontline Doctors, SpeakWithAnMD, and Dr. Zelenko. Listing 13-3 shows a redacted example of the AFLDS partner from that file.

```
{
    "id": 3,
    "name": "America's Frontline Doctors",
    --snip--
    "practices": "covid19,followupvisit",
    --snip--
    "one_merchant_security_key": "redacted",
    "stripe_publishable_key": "dev+admin@cadencehealth.us",
    "stripe_secret_key": "redacted",
    "virtual_visit_price": {
        "covid19": "90.00",
        "followupvisit": "59.99"
    },
--snip--
```

*Listing 13-3: An example JSON object describing a partner in* cadence_health_partners *.json*

Each partner has unique id and name fields, along with many others that describe the partner's settings. The first lines of this JSON object show that AFLDS's `id` is `3`. The `practices` field is a string containing a comma-separated list of telehealth consultation types that this partner offers (`covid19` and `followupvisit`, in this case). This JSON object includes secret tokens for payment processors in the lines with fields for `one_merchant_security_key` and `stripe_secret_key`, which I've redacted. The `virtual_visit_price` field is a JSON object containing other fields for each type of practice this partner offers and, in this case, shows that AFLDS charges $90 for COVID-19 visits and $59.99 for follow-up visits.

After reviewing *cadence_health_partners.json* and the patient data in the *hipaa_special* folder, I noticed a relationship between the two. Each partner's JSON object has an `id`, and each patient has a `partner` field. Listing 13-3 shows that AFLDS's partner `id` is `3`, indicating that the patient in Listing 13-1 with a `partner` value of `,3,` was an AFLDS patient.

### The ravkoo_rxdata.csv File

Of the six Ravkoo files, I found that *ravkoo_rxdata.csv* was by far the biggest. Figure 13-3 shows a portion of the data in this spreadsheet.

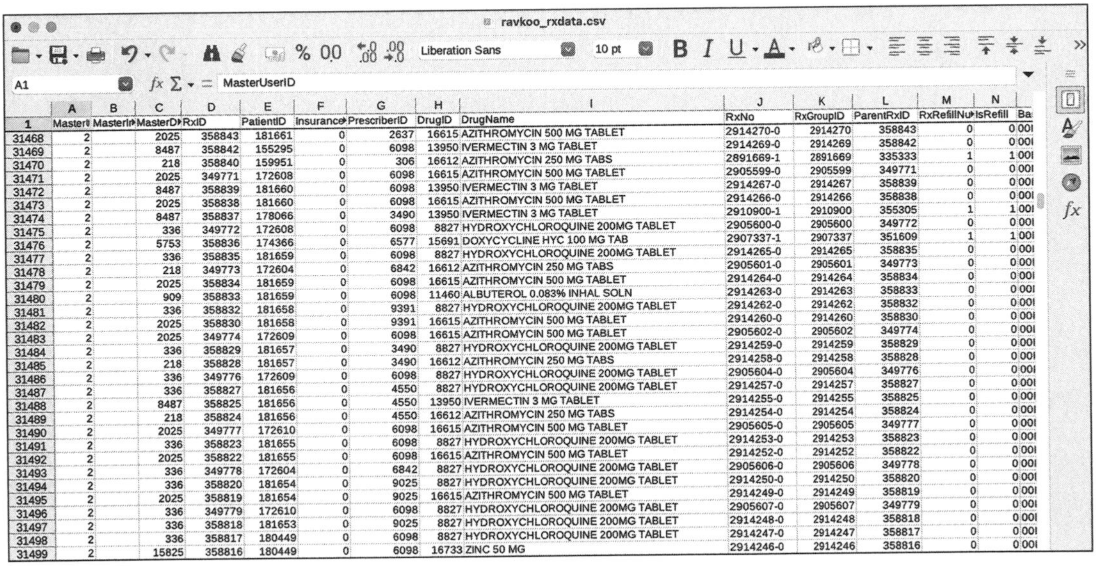

| 1 | MasterI | MasterIn▸ | MasterD▸ | RxID | PatientID | Insurance▸ | PrescriberID | DrugID | DrugName | RxNo | RxGroupID | ParentRxID | RxRefillNu▸ | IsRefill | Ba |
|---|---|---|---|---|---|---|---|---|---|---|---|---|---|---|---|
| 31468 | 2 | | 2025 | 358843 | 181661 | 0 | 2637 | 16615 | AZITHROMYCIN 500 MG TABLET | 2914270-0 | 2914270 | 358843 | 0 | 0 | 00I |
| 31469 | 2 | | 8487 | 358842 | 155295 | 0 | 6098 | 13950 | IVERMECTIN 3 MG TABLET | 2914269-0 | 2914269 | 358842 | 0 | 0 | 00I |
| 31470 | 2 | | 218 | 358840 | 159951 | 0 | 306 | 16612 | AZITHROMYCIN 250 MG TABS | 2891669-1 | 2891669 | 335333 | 1 | 1 | 00I |
| 31471 | 2 | | 2025 | 349771 | 172608 | 0 | 6098 | 16615 | AZITHROMYCIN 500 MG TABLET | 2905599-0 | 2905599 | 349771 | 0 | 0 | 00I |
| 31472 | 2 | | 8487 | 358839 | 181660 | 0 | 6098 | 13950 | IVERMECTIN 3 MG TABLET | 2914267-0 | 2914267 | 358839 | 0 | 0 | 00I |
| 31473 | 2 | | 2025 | 358838 | 181660 | 0 | 6098 | 16615 | AZITHROMYCIN 500 MG TABLET | 2914266-0 | 2914266 | 358838 | 0 | 0 | 00I |
| 31474 | 2 | | 8487 | 358837 | 178066 | 0 | 3490 | 13950 | IVERMECTIN 3 MG TABLET | 2910900-1 | 2910900 | 355305 | 1 | 1 | 00I |
| 31475 | 2 | | 336 | 349772 | 172608 | 0 | 6098 | 8827 | HYDROXYCHLOROQUINE 200MG TABLET | 2905600-0 | 2905600 | 349772 | 0 | 0 | 00I |
| 31476 | 2 | | 5753 | 358836 | 174366 | 0 | 6577 | 15691 | DOXYCYCLINE HYC 100 MG TAB | 2907337-1 | 2907337 | 351609 | 1 | 1 | 00I |
| 31477 | 2 | | 336 | 358835 | 181659 | 0 | 6098 | 8827 | HYDROXYCHLOROQUINE 200MG TABLET | 2914265-0 | 2914265 | 358835 | 0 | 0 | 00I |
| 31478 | 2 | | 218 | 349773 | 172604 | 0 | 6842 | 16612 | AZITHROMYCIN 250 MG TABS | 2905601-0 | 2905601 | 349773 | 0 | 0 | 00I |
| 31479 | 2 | | 2025 | 358834 | 181659 | 0 | 6098 | 16615 | AZITHROMYCIN 500 MG TABLET | 2914264-0 | 2914264 | 358834 | 0 | 0 | 00I |
| 31480 | 2 | | 909 | 358833 | 181659 | 0 | 6098 | 11460 | ALBUTEROL 0.083% INHAL SOLN | 2914263-0 | 2914263 | 358833 | 0 | 0 | 00I |
| 31481 | 2 | | 336 | 358832 | 181658 | 0 | 9391 | 8827 | HYDROXYCHLOROQUINE 200MG TABLET | 2914262-0 | 2914262 | 358832 | 0 | 0 | 00I |
| 31482 | 2 | | 2025 | 358830 | 181658 | 0 | 9391 | 16615 | AZITHROMYCIN 500 MG TABLET | 2914260-0 | 2914260 | 358830 | 0 | 0 | 00I |
| 31483 | 2 | | 2025 | 349774 | 172609 | 0 | 6098 | 16615 | AZITHROMYCIN 500 MG TABLET | 2905602-0 | 2905602 | 349774 | 0 | 0 | 00I |
| 31484 | 2 | | 336 | 358829 | 181657 | 0 | 3490 | 8827 | HYDROXYCHLOROQUINE 200MG TABLET | 2914259-0 | 2914259 | 358829 | 0 | 0 | 00I |
| 31485 | 2 | | 218 | 358828 | 181657 | 0 | 3490 | 16612 | AZITHROMYCIN 250 MG TABS | 2914258-0 | 2914258 | 358828 | 0 | 0 | 00I |
| 31486 | 2 | | 336 | 349776 | 172609 | 0 | 6098 | 8827 | HYDROXYCHLOROQUINE 200MG TABLET | 2905604-0 | 2905604 | 349776 | 0 | 0 | 00I |
| 31487 | 2 | | 336 | 358827 | 181656 | 0 | 4550 | 8827 | HYDROXYCHLOROQUINE 200MG TABLET | 2914257-0 | 2914257 | 358827 | 0 | 0 | 00I |
| 31488 | 2 | | 8487 | 358825 | 181656 | 0 | 4550 | 13950 | IVERMECTIN 3 MG TABLET | 2914255-0 | 2914255 | 358825 | 0 | 0 | 00I |
| 31489 | 2 | | 218 | 358824 | 181656 | 0 | 4550 | 16612 | AZITHROMYCIN 250 MG TABS | 2914254-0 | 2914254 | 358824 | 0 | 0 | 00I |
| 31490 | 2 | | 2025 | 349777 | 172610 | 0 | 6098 | 16615 | AZITHROMYCIN 500 MG TABLET | 2905605-0 | 2905605 | 349777 | 0 | 0 | 00I |
| 31491 | 2 | | 336 | 358823 | 181655 | 0 | 6098 | 8827 | HYDROXYCHLOROQUINE 200MG TABLET | 2914253-0 | 2914253 | 358823 | 0 | 0 | 00I |
| 31492 | 2 | | 2025 | 358822 | 181655 | 0 | 6098 | 16615 | AZITHROMYCIN 500 MG TABLET | 2914252-0 | 2914252 | 358822 | 0 | 0 | 00I |
| 31493 | 2 | | 336 | 349778 | 172604 | 0 | 6842 | 8827 | HYDROXYCHLOROQUINE 200MG TABLET | 2905606-0 | 2905606 | 349778 | 0 | 0 | 00I |
| 31494 | 2 | | 336 | 358820 | 181654 | 0 | 9025 | 8827 | HYDROXYCHLOROQUINE 200MG TABLET | 2914250-0 | 2914250 | 358820 | 0 | 0 | 00I |
| 31495 | 2 | | 2025 | 358819 | 181654 | 0 | 9025 | 16615 | AZITHROMYCIN 500 MG TABLET | 2914249-0 | 2914249 | 358819 | 0 | 0 | 00I |
| 31496 | 2 | | 336 | 349779 | 172610 | 0 | 6098 | 8827 | HYDROXYCHLOROQUINE 200MG TABLET | 2905607-0 | 2905607 | 349779 | 0 | 0 | 00I |
| 31497 | 2 | | 336 | 358818 | 181653 | 0 | 9025 | 8827 | HYDROXYCHLOROQUINE 200MG TABLET | 2914248-0 | 2914248 | 358818 | 0 | 0 | 00I |
| 31498 | 2 | | 336 | 358817 | 180449 | 0 | 6098 | 8827 | HYDROXYCHLOROQUINE 200MG TABLET | 2914247-0 | 2914247 | 358817 | 0 | 0 | 00I |
| 31499 | 2 | | 15825 | 358816 | 180449 | 0 | 6098 | 16733 | ZINC 50 MG | 2914246-0 | 2914246 | 358816 | 0 | 0 | 00I |

*Figure 13-3: Viewing* ravkoo_rxdata.csv *in LibreOffice Calc format*

This 149MB CSV spreadsheet contained 340,000 rows of data, each representing a prescription filled. Each prescription included the name and dosage of the drug, usage instructions, information about refills, the date it was filled, a Remarks column (where many of the rows list `AMERICAS FRONT LINE DOCTORS–ENCORE`), and other information.

After a cursory review of *ravkoo_rxdata.csv*, it was clear that it might contain revelations about how much money AFLDS and the companies it worked with charged for bogus COVID-19 health care. However, its current format would make it difficult to work with. I needed to transform the data in order to more easily make sense of it.

# Creating a Single Spreadsheet of Patients

I wanted to separate the AFLDS patients who had paid $90 for phone consultations from the total list of patients, many of whom had never paid, so I could get a clearer idea of the scale of AFLDS's scam. For each of these paying patients, I wanted to find their name, gender, birth date, the date they created their Cadence Health account, and the number of telehealth consultations they had.

The *cadence_allpatients_all.json* file contained information about all of the patients, including the previously discussed created_at timestamp. However, it didn't include the consultation notes, and I needed those to determine how many consultations the patient actually had. Meanwhile, the 281,000 JSON files in the *hipaa_special* folder had information about all of the patients, including consultation notes, but it didn't have the created_at timestamp.

I decided to write a Python script to comb through the *cadence _allpatients_all.json* file and all the files in the *hipaa_special* folder, pull out the information I was looking for, and save it all in a single CSV. Here's the Python code for my script (you can also find a copy in the book's GitHub repo at *https://github.com/micahflee/hacks-leaks-and-revelations/blob/main/chapter -13/create-aflds-patients-csv.py*):

```python
import json
import csv
import os

# Turn a JSON file into a Python dict or list
def data_from_json(filename):
    with open(filename) as f:
        return json.loads(f.read())

# Export a CSV full of AFLDS patients
def main():
    # Load patient data from cadence_allpatients_all.json
    patients_data = data_from_json(
        "data/horse_around_find_out/cadence_allpatients_all.json"
    )
    # Keep track of the created_at timestamps for each patient's id
    patient_ids_to_created_at = {}
    for patient in patients_data["patients"]:
        patient_ids_to_created_at[patient["id"]] = patient["created_at"]

    # Start the list of AFLDS patients that have had at least one consultation
    patient_rows = []

    # Loop through every file in the hipaa_special folder
    for patient_id in os.listdir("data/hipaa_special"):
        # Load the patient data
        data = data_from_json(os.path.join("data/hipaa_special", patient_id))

        # Some of the patient records are empty. This skips them
        if not data["result"]:
            continue
```

```python
        # Make sure AFLDS (id 3) is in the list of partners
        partner_ids = data["provider"]["partner"].split(",")
        if "3" in partner_ids:
            # Count how many consultations this patient has
            num_consultations = len(data["provider"]["consultationNotes"])

            # If they have had more than one, add them to the list
            if num_consultations > 0:
                patient_rows.append(
                    {
                        "user_id": data["provider"]["user_id"],
                        "created_at": patient_ids_to_created_at[
                            data["provider"]["user_id"]
                        ],
                        "fname": data["provider"]["fname"],
                        "lname": data["provider"]["lname"],
                        "email": data["provider"]["email"],
                        "city": data["provider"]["city"],
                        "state": data["provider"]["state"],
                        "gender": data["provider"]["gender"],
                        "birthdate": data["provider"]["birthdate"],
                        "num_consultations": num_consultations,
                    }
                )

    # Write the CSV file
    csv_filename = "aflds-patients.csv"
    headers = [
        "user_id",
        "created_at",
        "fname",
        "lname",
        "email",
        "city",
        "state",
        "gender",
        "birthdate",
        "num_consultations",
    ]
    with open(csv_filename, "w") as f:
        writer = csv.DictWriter(f, headers)
        writer.writeheader()
        writer.writerows(patient_rows)

if __name__ == "__main__":
    main()
```

You won't be able to run this or any other script in this chapter without a copy of the private dataset, so I'll summarize how it worked.

First, the script loaded *cadence_allpatients_all.json* as a Python object. It then looped through each patient in that object, keeping track of which user_id mapped to which created_at timestamp in a dictionary.

It created an empty list called `aflds_patients` and then looped through every filename in the *hipaa_special* folder, where each file represents a different patient. For each filename, it loaded the corresponding JSON file as a Python object representing a patient. If the `partner` field included the ID 3 (meaning that the record was associated with AFLDS), and if the length of the `consultationNotes` field was greater than 0 (meaning there was at least one consultation), then it added this patient to the `aflds_patients` list, making sure to include the patient's `created_at` timestamp, too.

It opened a new CSV file, *aflds-patients.csv*, for writing, and then wrote the `aflds_patients` list as rows in the CSV file.

After working through the exercises in this book, you should have all the skills you need to write your own similar scripts. This is true for all of the scripts I wrote for this investigation, which you'll see throughout this chapter. For example, in Chapter 8, you learned about dictionaries and lists; in Chapter 9, you learned how to use the `csv` module to create your own CSV spreadsheets; and in Chapter 11, you learned how to load and work with data in JSON format. This script incorporates all these techniques.

Running this script created a 6.4MB CSV file called *aflds-patients.csv* with 72,000 rows. Figure 13-4 shows a redacted view of this spreadsheet. As you can see, this data is significantly easier to make sense of compared to hundreds of thousands of small JSON files, and one enormous one.

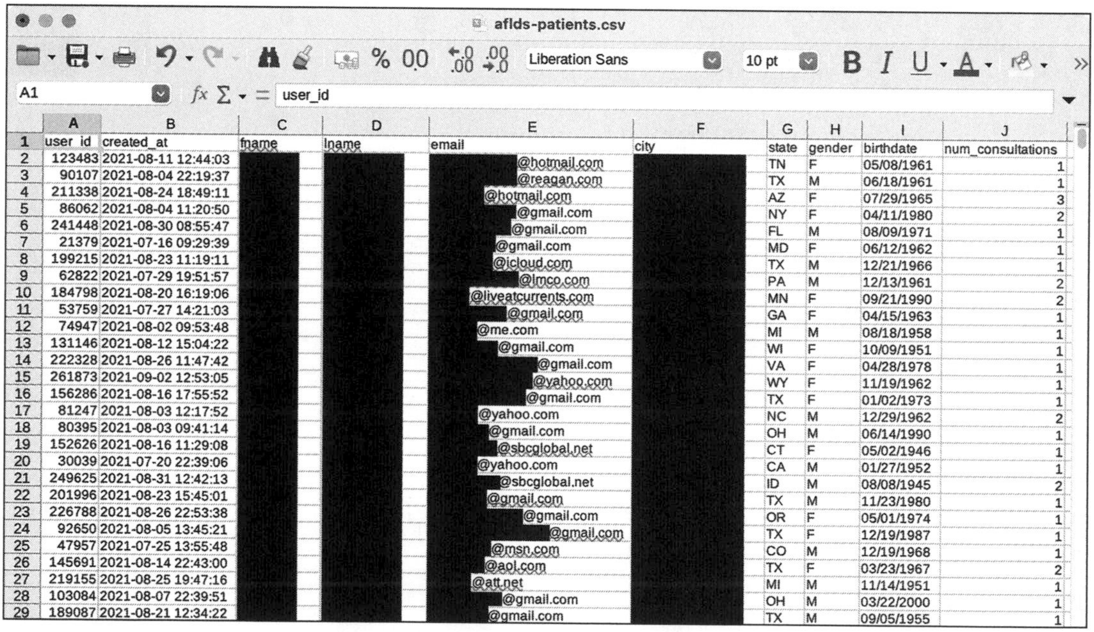

Figure 13-4: A redacted view of aflds-patients.csv

This spreadsheet lists the 72,000 AFLDS patients who were referred to SpeakWithAnMD and actually bought a $90 consultation. If each patient paid $90, these consultations alone would have cost them, collectively, $6.4 million. Many of the patients had multiple consultations, so I estimate patients were charged *$6.7 million* from consultations alone. There's no way of knowing just from this data how the money was distributed, but it was likely split between AFLDS, individual physicians in its network, and SpeakWithAnMD.

My source's dataset included all of the patient data in Cadence Health's database. When I sorted the spreadsheet on the created_at column, which includes the dates each patient created their Cadence account, I could see that the earliest patients made their accounts on July 16, 2021, and the latest patients created theirs on September 12, 2021, when my source hacked Cadence Health. While only 72,000 patients paid for $90 consultations, I had data for an additional 180,000 AFLDS patients who created Cadence accounts but never had a consultation, meaning that 90 percent of the 281,000 patients in the Cadence Health database during this time span were referred by AFLDS.

While AFLDS had been selling $90 consultations since January 2021, Roque Espinal, Cadence Health's CEO, confirmed to me that his service for SpeakWithAnMD launched on July 16. Since this is the date of the earliest patient data I have, this means that my source collected records for *all* of Cadence's patients. My source's data shows that in the two-month period between July and September, AFLDS charged its patients an average of $100,000 a day from $90 consultations alone. If AFLDS brought in that much each day during the first half of the year as well, it would have brought in an additional *$18 million* in revenue. Again, this is just from selling consultations; it doesn't include the cost of the prescription drugs.

At this point in my investigation, it was clear that AFLDS was spreading medical disinformation, and it seemed evident that SpeakWithAnMD and Ravkoo were at least aware of this and were profiting from it as well. However, I wasn't sure if Cadence Health, which provided a service to SpeakWithAnMD, had realized what its service was being used for. But before exploring that further, I decided to switch gears and start looking at Ravkoo's drug prescription data.

## Calculating Revenue from Prescriptions Filled by Ravkoo

The *ravkoo_rxdata.csv* spreadsheet introduced earlier has 340,000 rows, each representing a prescription that was filled. It includes a DrugName column with values like IVERMECTIN 3 MG TABLET, a cost column with the price of that prescription, and a Fill_Date column with the date that the prescription was filled.

By sorting the spreadsheet by Fill_Date, I could see that the Ravkoo pharmacy filled the first prescription on November 27, 2020, and the last ones were filled on August 24, 2021. The SpeakWithAnMD data covers a two-month period, but the Ravkoo data covers a nine-month period. That is, my dataset contained two months' worth of patient records, but nine months' worth of prescription records. In this section I describe the Python code I wrote to gain a better understanding of what drugs Ravkoo sold and how much of them related to quack cures for COVID-19.

## Finding the Price and Quantity of Drugs Sold

To find out how much money Ravkoo charged patients for each specific drug, I wrote another script, shown in Listing 13-4 (you can also find a copy of it at *https://github.com/micahflee/hacks-leaks-and-revelations/blob/main/chapter-13/create-ravkoo-csv.py*).

```python
import csv

# Export a CSV that adds up prescriptions and their costs for each drug
def main():
    # A dictionary that maps drug names to another dictionary containing the
    # prescription count and total cost for that drug
    drugs = {}

    # Add up the number of prescriptions and total cost for all drugs, to display
    # at the end
    prescription_count = 0
    total_cost = 0

    # Loop through ravkoo_rxdata.csv, and count prescriptions and costs
    with open("data/horse_around_find_out/ravkoo_rxdata.csv") as f:
        reader = csv.DictReader(f)
        for row in reader:
            if row["DrugName"] not in drugs:
                drugs[row["DrugName"]] = {"prescription_count": 0, "total_cost": 0}

            # Count prescriptions and cost for this drug
            drugs[row["DrugName"]]["prescription_count"] += 1
            drugs[row["DrugName"]]["total_cost"] += float(row["Cost"])

            # Count prescriptions and cost for _all_ drugs
            prescription_count += 1
            total_cost += float(row["Cost"])

    # Write the CSV file
    headers = [
        "drug_name",
        "prescription_count",
        "total_cost",
    ]
    csv_filename = "ravkoo.csv"
    with open(csv_filename, "w") as f:
        writer = csv.DictWriter(f, headers)
        writer.writeheader()
        for drug_name in drugs:
            writer.writerow(
                {
```

```
            "drug_name": drug_name,
            "prescription_count": drugs[drug_name]["prescription_count"],
            "total_cost": int(drugs[drug_name]["total_cost"]),
        }
    )

    print(f"Number of prescriptions: {prescription_count:,}")
    print(f"Total cost: ${int(total_cost):,}")

if __name__ == "__main__":
    main()
```

*Listing 13-4: The Python script* create-ravkoo-csv.py, *which adds up Ravkoo prescriptions and drug costs and exports a CSV of the results*

First this script created an empty dictionary called drugs, which mapped drug names to another dictionary containing prescription_count and total_cost values. It then loaded *ravkoo_rxdata.csv* and looped through its rows. For each row, if the DrugName wasn't in the drugs dictionary yet, the script added it, then incremented the drug's prescription count by 1 and added the Cost value to that drug's total cost. It saved all of the data in drugs into a CSV called *ravkoo.csv*. Finally, the script counted up the total number of prescriptions and the total cost for *all* drugs sold to all patients and displayed it in the terminal.

Here's the output I got when I ran the script:

```
micah@trapdoor AFLDS % python3 create-ravkoo-csv.py
Number of prescriptions: 340,000
Total cost: $15,119,473
```

My output showed that patients paid over $15 million to Ravkoo for all the prescriptions in the hacked data. However, many of these prescriptions might not have anything to do with AFLDS or bogus COVID-19 cures.

The resulting CSV file, *ravkoo.csv*, contained 1,552 rows, the number of unique DrugName values in the original *ravkoo_rxdata.csv*. Figure 13-5 shows this spreadsheet, sorted descending by total_cost, to show which drugs cost patients the most money.

How much of this revenue was from drugs that AFLDS pushed on its followers? The drug that cumulatively cost patients the most was IVERMECTIN 3 MG TABLET, which was prescribed 63,409 times, at a total cost of $4.6 million. Ivermectin is used primarily to treat parasites in livestock, but it's also occasionally used to treat scabies and lice in humans. I didn't know for sure that all of these ivermectin sales were directly from AFLDS, but it was suspicious that ivermectin was bringing in so much money during the COVID-19 pandemic, when disinformation about its efficacy was rampant.

Another row had the drug_name of IVERMECTIN 3MG PO TAB (the same dose of ivermectin, just with a slightly different name DrugName value from *ravkoo_rxdata.csv*) that cost 883 patients another $98,900. Other drugs like hydroxychloroquine and azithromycin had the same problem: there were different DrugName values that actually represented the same drug. If I wanted to know the total revenue from each individual drug, I would have to combine all of the ivermectin prescriptions into one row and do the same with the other drugs.

| | A | B | C | D |
|---|---|---|---|---|
| 1 | drug_name | prescription_count | total_cost | |
| 2 | IVERMECTIN 3 MG TABLET | 63409 | 4632068 | |
| 3 | AZITHROMYCIN 500 MG TABLET | 22830 | 2136678 | |
| 4 | BUDESONIDE 0.5 MG/2ML SUSP | 103 | 1316185 | |
| 5 | BUDESONIDE 05 MG 2 ML NEBULIZER SUSPENSION | 175 | 1232497 | |
| 6 | HYDROXYCHLOROQUINE 200MG TABLET | 82362 | 991162 | |
| 7 | CICLOPIROX OLAMINE 0.77% TO CREAM | 107 | 336098 | |
| 8 | BUDESONIDE 025 MG2 ML SUS | 92 | 311199 | |
| 9 | AZITHROMYCIN 250 MG TABS | 1983 | 277408 | |
| 10 | HYDROXYCHLOROQUINE 200 MG TABLET | 10261 | 242888 | |
| 11 | BUDESONIDE 0.25 MG/2ML SUSP | 27 | 224380 | |
| 12 | TADALAFIL 20 MG TABS | 67 | 216804 | |
| 13 | ZINC 50 MG | 82277 | 174905 | |
| 14 | VALACYCLOVIR HCL 500 MG TAB | 267 | 168600 | |
| 15 | RESTASIS 0.05% OP LIQ | 257 | 147362 | |
| 16 | PULMICORT FLEXHALER 180MCG | 2506 | 136218 | |
| 17 | IPLEDGE-CLARAVIS 40 MG CAPS | 100 | 119194 | |
| 18 | VALACYCLOVIR HCL 500MG PO T | 171 | 108666 | |
| 19 | BUDESONIDE 1 MG2 ML NEBULIZER SUSPENSION | 27 | 105215 | |
| 20 | IVERMECTIN 3MG PO TAB | 883 | 98821 | |

Figure 13-5: Viewing ravkoo.csv in LibreOffice Calc

## Categorizing Prescription Data by Drug

Because I was investigating AFLDS, I was most interested in the drugs that the group promotes: ivermectin, hydroxychloroquine, and a few others. In addition to ivermectin, AFLDS promotes the *Zelenko protocol*, named after Dr. Vladimir Zelenko, the American doctor who, at the start of the pandemic in March 2020, claimed (without evidence) that he had successfully treated hundreds of COVID-19 patients using a combination of hydroxychloroquine, azithromycin, and zinc sulfate. (The AFLDS website on treatment options also lists vitamin C as part of the Zelenko protocol.) Zelenko also spread other medical disinformation, claiming, for example, that more children die from COVID-19 vaccines than from the virus itself. Then-President Trump publicly lauded Zelenko's work, saying that he himself took hydroxychloroquine to treat COVID-19.

I wanted to see how much of Ravkoo's business consisted of selling these drugs. To do this, I'd have to reorganize the data. I needed to create a similar spreadsheet, but instead of having a column for the DrugName lifted directly from the hacked data, I wanted that column to be a category of prescriptions. Once I had a straightforward spreadsheet that mapped individual drugs to their revenue, I could visualize that data—for example, in a pie chart.

The *ravkoo.csv* spreadsheet showed me the most commonly prescribed drugs. Based on the names of these drugs, I came up with a list of categories: Ivermectin, Hydroxychloroquine, Azithromycin, Zinc, Vitamin C, and

Other. In other words, the most commonly prescribed drugs were exactly what AFLDS was promoting.

I then wrote another script very similar to the one in Listing 13-4, but with one additional step. For every row in the *ravkoo_rxdata.csv* spreadsheet, the script determined which of those categories the drug fit into and added up the number of prescriptions and cost for each category. It then saved all of this data as a CSV called *ravkoo-categories.csv*.

Here's my Python script (you can also find it at *https://github.com/ micahflee/hacks-leaks-and-revelations/blob/main/chapter-13/create-ravkoo -categories-csv.py*):

```python
import csv

# Export a CSV that adds up prescriptions and their costs for each category of drug
def main():
    # A dictionary that maps drug categories to another dictionary containing the
    # prescription count and total cost for that drug category
    drug_categories = {}

    # Loop through ravkoo_rxdata.csv, and count prescriptions and costs
    with open("data/horse_around_find_out/ravkoo_rxdata.csv") as f:
        reader = csv.DictReader(f)
        for row in reader:
            if "ivermectin" in row["DrugName"].lower():
                category = "Ivermectin"
            elif "hydroxychloroquine" in row["DrugName"].lower():
                category = "Hydroxychloroquine"
            elif "azithromycin" in row["DrugName"].lower():
                category = "Azithromycin"
            elif "zinc" in row["DrugName"].lower():
                category = "Zinc"
            elif "vitamin c" in row["DrugName"].lower():
                category = "Vitamin C"
            else:
                category = "Other"

            if category not in drug_categories:
                drug_categories[category] = {"prescription_count": 0, "total_cost": 0}

            # Count prescriptions and cost for this drug category
            drug_categories[category]["prescription_count"] += 1
            drug_categories[category]["total_cost"] += float(row["Cost"])

    # Write the CSV file
    headers = [
        "drug_category",
        "prescription_count",
        "total_cost",
    ]
    csv_filename = "ravkoo-categories.csv"
    with open(csv_filename, "w") as f:
        writer = csv.DictWriter(f, headers)
        writer.writeheader()
```

```
for category in drug_categories:
    writer.writerow(
        {
            "drug_category": category,
            "prescription_count": drug_categories[category][
                "prescription_count"
            ],
            "total_cost": int(drug_categories[category]["total_cost"]),
        }
    )

if __name__ == "__main__":
    main()
```

After running this script, I ended up with a file called *ravkoo-categories.csv*. Table 13-1 shows the data from this spreadsheet, detailing Ravkoo's prescription sales.

**Table 13-1:** Categories of Drugs Sold by Ravkoo

| Drug category | Prescription count | Total cost |
|---|---|---|
| Hydroxychloroquine | 92,646 | $1,234,727 |
| Zinc | 82,608 | $177,336 |
| Ivermectin | 64,300 | $4,734,163 |
| Other | 42,193 | $6,476,213 |
| Vitamin C | 31,281 | $52,712 |
| Azithromycin | 26,972 | $2,444,319 |

This data clearly revealed Ravkoo's role in AFLDS's scam: *87 percent* of all prescriptions sold by Ravkoo are for fake COVID-19 treatments. Over a nine-month period, patients collectively paid *$8.6 million* to Ravkoo for snake oil that they were told would prevent or cure COVID-19. This is in addition to the roughly $6.7 million (and potentially many millions more) that patients paid SpeakWithAnMD for phone consultations. As far as I can tell, Ravkoo's only role in the scheme was as a pharmacy, and it didn't receive any money from the phone consultations. AFLDS also, at various times, worked with different pharmacies.

By the time The Intercept published this investigation into AFLDS, Ravkoo CEO Alpesh Patel told me that his company had already stopped doing business with SpeakWithAnMD. "The volume over there went up crazy, and we didn't feel comfortable," he said. "And we don't have that much capacity to fill that many prescriptions." Using OSINT, which you learned about in Chapter 1, I confirmed that Patel was telling the truth: after scouring the internet about AFLDS, including reading reporting from other journalists and pro-science activists on Twitter who were keeping track of the group, I discovered that AFLDS ran some Telegram channels, including one specifically for its patients. In this Telegram channel,

I discovered that patients had posted messages about Ravkoo no longer working with SpeakWithAnMD or AFLDS.

## A Deeper Look at the Cadence Health Patient Data

At this point, I knew that 72,000 AFLDS patients paid for $90 telehealth consultations and that 87 percent of Ravkoo's prescriptions were for fake COVID-19 cures. I wanted to further understand the patient data, and there was still a lot more to dig into. Who were SpeakWithAnMD's other partners besides AFLDS, and how much of the company's business did they make up? And what could I learn about the AFLDS patients themselves? To answer these questions, I wrote more Python code.

### Finding Cadence's Partners

I wanted to know how much of SpeakWithAnMD's business, and by extension Cadence Health's business, came from AFLDS. The file *cadence_health_partners.json* includes a list of all the partners, so I wrote a Python script that counted the number of patients associated with each one, shown in Listing 13-5 (you can also find a copy at *https://github.com/micahflee/hacks-leaks-and-revelations/blob/main/chapter-13/create-cadence-partners-csv.py*).

```python
import json
import csv

# Turn a JSON file into a Python dict or list
def data_from_json(filename):
    with open(filename) as f:
        return json.loads(f.read())

# Convert the comma-separated list of partners, like ",3,", into a Python list
# of partners, like ["America's Frontline Doctors"]
def get_partners(partner_lookup, patient):
    partners = []
    partner_ids = patient["partner"].split(",")
    for partner_id in partner_ids:
        if partner_id != "":
            partners.append(partner_lookup[int(partner_id)])

    return partners

# Export a CSV that lists Cadence partners
def main():
    partner_rows = []

    # Load the Cadence patient data
    patients_data = data_from_json(
        "data/horse_around_find_out/cadence_allpatients_all.json"
    )
```

```python
    # Load the Cadence partners data
    partners_data = data_from_json(
        "data/horse_around_find_out/cadence_health_partners.json"
    )

    # Create a dictionary that maps a partner ID with its name
    partner_lookup = {}
    for partner in partners_data:
        partner_lookup[partner["id"]] = partner["name"]

    # Loop through all of the partners
    for partner in partners_data:
        # Count how many patients use this partner
        patients = 0
        for patient in patients_data["patients"]:
            patient_partners = get_partners(partner_lookup, patient)
            for patient_partner in patient_partners:
                if patient_partner == partner["name"]:
                    patients += 1

        # Add the partner's row
        partner_rows.append(
            {
                "ID": partner["id"],
                "Name": partner["name"],
                "Domain": partner["domain"],
                "Patients": patients,
            }
        )

    # Write the CSV file
    headers = ["ID", "Name", "Domain", "Patients"]
    csv_filename = "cadence-partners.csv"
    with open(csv_filename, "w") as f:
        writer = csv.DictWriter(f, headers)
        writer.writeheader()
        writer.writerows(partner_rows)

if __name__ == "__main__":
    main()
```

Listing 13-5: The create-cadence-partners-csv.py script returns the number of patients associated with each Cadence Health partner.

First, my script loaded *cadence_allpatients_all.json* and *cadence_health _partners.json* as Python objects. It created an empty list called partner_rows, then looped through each partner. Inside this for loop was a nested for loop which, for each partner, looped through each patient checking to see if that patient used that partner. The script then added this information (the partner's ID, name, and domain, along with the tally of its associated patients) to the partner_rows list. Finally, it saved its findings in a CSV called *cadence-partners.csv*.

Table 13-2 shows the data from this spreadsheet, describing all of Cadence Health's partners and how many patients they have.

**Table 13-2:** Cadence Health Partners

| ID | Name | Domain | Patients |
|----|------|--------|----------|
| 1 | Encore Telemedicine | encore.cadencehealth.us | 7 |
| 2 | SpeakWithAnMD | speakwithanmd.cadencehealth.us | 21,193 |
| 3 | America's Frontline Doctors | aflds.cadencehealth.us | 255,266 |
| 4 | Corstet | corstet.cadencehealth.us | 1,604 |
| 5 | Dr. Zelenko | drzelenko.cadencehealth.us | 55 |
| 6 | Encore Demo | encoredemo.cadencehealth.us | 5 |
| 7 | Kim's Pharmacy | kims.cadencehealth.us | 6 |
| 8 | TelMDFirst | telmdfirst.cadencehealth.us | 2,410 |
| 9 | Dr. Tsifutis | drtsifutis.cadencehealth.us | 301 |
| 10 | Dr. Immanuel | drimmanuel.cadencehealth.us | 3 |
| 11 | Dr. Palumbo | drpalumbo.cadencehealth.us | 29 |
| 12 | Dr. Boz | drboz.cadencehealth.us | 311 |
| 13 | Dr. Parker | drparker.cadencehealth.us | 409 |
| 14 | Dr. Johnson | drajohnson.cadencehealth.us | 3 |
| 15 | DEV | localhost:8080 | 1 |
| 16 | HablaConUnMD.com | hablaconunmd.cadencehealth.us | 0 |
| 17 | VirtuaFirst, PLLC | vf.cadencehealth.us | 0 |

Out of 281,603 patients, AFLDS referred 255,266 to SpeakWithAnMD and, by extension, Cadence Health. That means that 90 percent of the patients in Cadence's database came from AFLDS.

I learned some additional interesting information from the partners list. The first partner listed, Encore Telemedicine, is SpeakForAnMD's parent company. The fourth, Corstet, is owned by Jerome Corsi, who also owns Encore Telemedicine. Corsi is a former host of the conspiracy show *InfoWars*, a proponent of the racist "birtherism" conspiracy theory about former US president Barack Obama's citizenship. He was also caught up in special counsel Robert Mueller's investigation into Russian interference in the 2016 election. The list of partners also includes individual doctors, including Dr. Zelenko of "Zelenko protocol" fame and Dr. Stella Immanuel, one of the AFLDS doctors from the previously mentioned press conference in front of the Supreme Court building. After that event, she quickly earned viral fame for having claimed that the uterine disorder endometriosis is caused by women dreaming of sex with demons and witches.

This spreadsheet confirmed that the bulk of the Cadence data was related to AFLDS patients. I decided to dig even deeper into AFLDS patient data to see what revelations could be hiding there.

## Searching for Patients by City

The *aflds-patients.csv* spreadsheet I created from the original dataset, containing 72,000 rows of patients who were referred by AFLDS and who had at least one consultation, includes columns for city and state. This location data allowed me to write another Python script to count how many patients were from each city and look up GPS coordinates for that city so I could plot them on a map.

In Chapter 11, you worked with GPS coordinates you found directly in Parler video metadata and plotted them on a map using Google Earth. In this case, however, I had only cities and states, so I needed to look up their GPS coordinates myself. I wrote a script to convert the names of the cities in the spreadsheet into GPS coordinates, a process called *geocoding*.

Listing 13-6 shows my Python script (you can also find a copy at *https://github.com/micahflee/hacks-leaks-and-revelations/blob/main/chapter-13/create-cities-csv.py*).

```python
import csv
import json
import time
import httpx

geocode_api_key = "PUT_GEOCODE_API_KEY_HERE"

# Export a CSV that for each city lists its GPS coordinates and the number of patients there
def main():
    # This dictionary maps names of cities (in format "City, State", like "New York, NY")
    # to a dictionary with info about that city (number of patients, GPS coordinates)
    cities = {}

    # Count how many patients are in each city
    with open("aflds-patients.csv") as f:
        reader = csv.DictReader(f)

        for row in reader:
            city = f"{row['city']}, {row['state']}"

            if city not in cities:
                cities[city] = {"count": 0}

            cities[city]["count"] += 1

    print(f"Found patients in {len(cities):,} cities")

    # Look up GPS coordinates for each city
    for city in cities:

        # Give each API request 3 tries, in case a connection fails
        tries = 0
```

```
        success = False
        while not success:
            try:
                print(
                    f"Loading GPS coordinates for: {city} ({cities[city]['count']} patients)"
                )
                r = httpx.get(
                    "https://app.geocodeapi.io/api/v1/search",
                    params={
                        "apikey": geocode_api_key,
                        "text": city,
                        "size": 1,
                        "boundary.country": "US",
                    },
                )
                success = True

            # The connection failed
            except:
                tries += 1
                if tries == 3:
                    print("Failed, skipping")

                print("Sleeping 2s and trying again")
                time.sleep(2)

        try:
            data = json.loads(r.text)
            if "features" in data and len(data["features"]) > 0:
                cities[city]["lon"] = data["features"][0]["geometry"]["coordinates"][0]
                cities[city]["lat"] = data["features"][0]["geometry"]["coordinates"][1]
        except:
            cities[city]["lon"] = None
            cities[city]["lat"] = None

# Write the CSV file
headers = [
    "count",
    "city",
    "lon",
    "lat",
    "label",
]
csv_filename = "cities.csv"
with open(csv_filename, "w") as f:
    writer = csv.DictWriter(f, fieldnames=headers)
    writer.writeheader()
    for city in cities:
        writer.writerow(
            {
                "count": cities[city]["count"],
                "city": city,
                "lon": cities[city]["lat"],
```

```
                "lat": cities[city]["lon"],
                "label": f"{city} ({cities[city]['count']})",
            }
        )


if __name__ == "__main__":
    main()
```

*Listing 13-6: The* create-cities-csv.py *script geocodes city and state names.*

To perform the geocoding, the script used an API. Of the various options, I chose one called Geocodeapi, simply because it seemed easy to use and was free for the number of requests I planned on making. I made an account at *https://geocodeapi.io*, created an API key, and stored it my script in the variable geocode_api_key. In order to make the API calls, the script used the third-party Python module httpx. (For more details on this module, check out Appendix B.)

After defining the API key, my script created an empty dictionary called cities to map city names to information about it—specifically, the number of patients and its GPS coordinates.

The script then loaded *aflds-patients.csv* and looped through each patient. For each, it created a new string called city in the format *City, State* (for example, Atlanta, Georgia). If city didn't exist in the cities dictionary yet, the script set cities[city] = {"count": 0}. Then it added 1 to cities[city] ["count"]. By the time this loop finished running, cities contained a list of every city where there are patients, as well as the number of patients in that city.

The next step was geocoding for each city. Another for loop looped through cities and, using the httpx.get() function, made an HTTP request for each city to the Geocodeapi API, passing along the city name and my API key. When the script got a response with GPS coordinates, it stored the latitude and longitude in cities[city]["lat"] and cities[city]["lon"]. This step takes a few hours since it's making thousands of API requests, so it displayed text in the terminal before each one, allowing me to get a sense of the progress while it was running.

Finally, the script wrote all of the data in the cities dictionary into a CSV called *cities.csv*.

When I ran the script, I got the following output:

```
micah@trapdoor AFLDS % python3 create-cities-csv.py
Found patients in 15,196 cities
Loading GPS coordinates for: roan mountain, TN (1 patients)
Loading GPS coordinates for: El Paso, TX (22 patients)
Loading GPS coordinates for: Paulden, AZ (7 patients)
Loading GPS coordinates for: Athens, NY (5 patients)
Loading GPS coordinates for: Estero, FL (31 patients)
Loading GPS coordinates for: Columbia, MD (16 patients)
Loading GPS coordinates for: Houston, TX (371 patients)
Loading GPS coordinates for: Newtown Square, PA (14 patients)
```

```
Loading GPS coordinates for: Plymouth, MN (32 patients)
Loading GPS coordinates for: Blairsville, GA (20 patients)
Loading GPS coordinates for: shelby twownhsip, MI (1 patients)
Loading GPS coordinates for: Waukesha, WI (13 patients)
--snip--
```

Figure 13-6 shows *cities.csv*, sorted by number of patients per city.

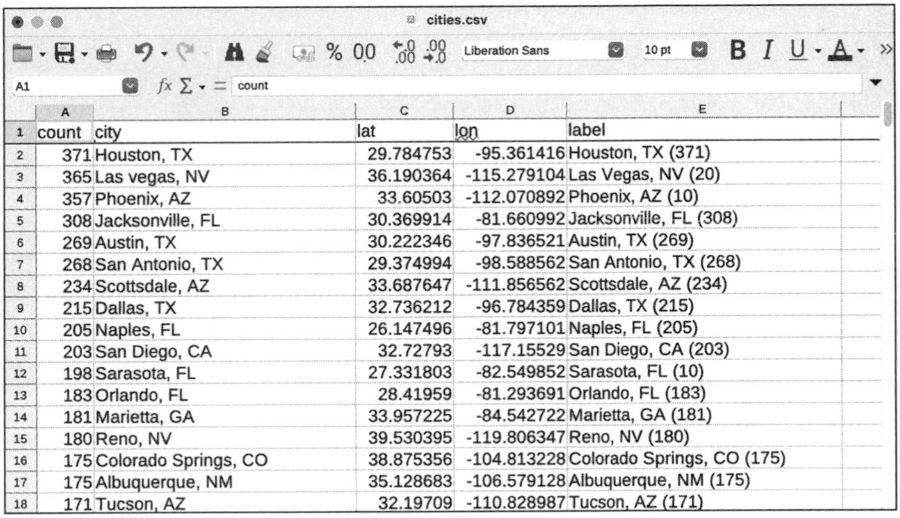

| | A | B | C | D | E | |
|---|---|---|---|---|---|---|
| 1 | count | city | lat | lon | label | |
| 2 | 371 | Houston, TX | 29.784753 | -95.361416 | Houston, TX (371) | |
| 3 | 365 | Las vegas, NV | 36.190364 | -115.279104 | Las Vegas, NV (20) | |
| 4 | 357 | Phoenix, AZ | 33.60503 | -112.070892 | Phoenix, AZ (10) | |
| 5 | 308 | Jacksonville, FL | 30.369914 | -81.660992 | Jacksonville, FL (308) | |
| 6 | 269 | Austin, TX | 30.222346 | -97.836521 | Austin, TX (269) | |
| 7 | 268 | San Antonio, TX | 29.374994 | -98.588562 | San Antonio, TX (268) | |
| 8 | 234 | Scottsdale, AZ | 33.687647 | -111.856562 | Scottsdale, AZ (234) | |
| 9 | 215 | Dallas, TX | 32.736212 | -96.784359 | Dallas, TX (215) | |
| 10 | 205 | Naples, FL | 26.147496 | -81.797101 | Naples, FL (205) | |
| 11 | 203 | San Diego, CA | 32.72793 | -117.15529 | San Diego, CA (203) | |
| 12 | 198 | Sarasota, FL | 27.331803 | -82.549852 | Sarasota, FL (10) | |
| 13 | 183 | Orlando, FL | 28.41959 | -81.293691 | Orlando, FL (183) | |
| 14 | 181 | Marietta, GA | 33.957225 | -84.542722 | Marietta, GA (181) | |
| 15 | 180 | Reno, NV | 39.530395 | -119.806347 | Reno, NV (180) | |
| 16 | 175 | Colorado Springs, CO | 38.875356 | -104.813228 | Colorado Springs, CO (175) | |
| 17 | 175 | Albuquerque, NM | 35.128683 | -106.579128 | Albuquerque, NM (175) | |
| 18 | 171 | Tucson, AZ | 32.19709 | -110.828987 | Tucson, AZ (171) | |

*Figure 13-6: Results from* cities.csv

Armed with GPS coordinates, I could now plot the patient data on a map. I used an online service called MapBox (*https://www.mapbox.com*), mentioned in Chapter 11, to display circles on a map for each of the 15,196 cities—the more patients from that city, the bigger the circle. MapBox has a user interface that makes it simple to upload a CSV file with GPS coordinates and indicate how you want the data to be visualized on a map. MapBox also allows you to embed maps directly into web pages. When I published my article, I embedded this map into it so readers could interact with it themselves. Figure 13-7 shows that map, zoomed in on the United States.

People in every state in the country, as well as Washington, DC, paid $90 for telehealth consultations, including 8,600 people in California, 8,000 in Florida, and 7,400 in Texas. The dots on the map show only cities with at least 10 AFLDS patients.

In addition to the cities patients lived in, the data also included their birth dates, making it simple to calculate their ages. Since age is a major risk factor for COVID-19, I explored this data next.

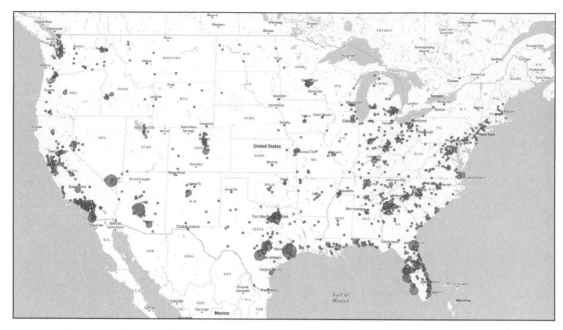

Figure 13-7: A map of cities in the US with AFLDS patients as of September 11, 2021

### Searching for Patients by Age

Your age plays a major role in how likely you are to get seriously sick or die from COVID-19. During the pandemic, the CDC published statistics that described individual risk for COVID-19 infection, hospitalization, and death based on your age. Up until May 2023, the CDC continually updated these statistics as new data came in and as the pandemic changed. When I published my findings in September 2021, people who were 50 to 64 years old were 4 times more likely to be hospitalized and 30 times more likely to die from COVID-19 than 18- to 29-year-olds. People who were 65 to 74 were 5 times more likely to be hospitalized and 90 times more likely to die.

While I was writing my report, there were no COVID-19 treatments that worked well (except for monoclonal antibodies, which were difficult to administer and not widely available). The only way for older people to greatly reduce their risk of death or serious illness was to get vaccinated. AFLDS spent a lot of resources convincing people that COVID-19 vaccines are dangerous and that wearing masks to prevent the spread of COVID-19 is a violation of personal freedom.

When patients created an account on the Cadence Health website, they were asked to enter their date of birth. I wrote a script to calculate their age and organize them into the same age groups that the CDC used so that I could see their likelihood of getting hospitalized or dying. Listing 13-7 shows the Python code for that script (you can also find it at *https://github.com/ micahflee/hacks-leaks-and-revelations/blob/main/chapter-13/create-ages-csv.py*).

```python
import csv
from datetime import datetime, timedelta

# Export a CSV that shows how many patients are part of each age group
def main():
    # Age groups, the same ones used in CDC data
    age_groups = {
        "<0": 0,
        "0-4": 0,
        "5-17": 0,
        "18-29": 0,
        "30-39": 0,
        "40-49": 0,
        "50-64": 0,
        "65-74": 0,
        "75-84": 0,
        "85+": 0,
        ">100": 0,
    }

    sept2021 = datetime(2021, 9, 11)

    with open("aflds-patients.csv") as f:
        reader = csv.DictReader(f)

        for row in reader:
            birthdate = datetime.strptime(row["birthdate"], "%m/%d/%Y")
            age = sept2021 - birthdate

            if age < timedelta(0):
                age_groups["<0"] += 1
            elif age < timedelta(365 * 5):
                age_groups["0-4"] += 1
            elif age < timedelta(365 * 18):
                age_groups["5-17"] += 1
            elif age < timedelta(365 * 30):
                age_groups["18-29"] += 1
            elif age < timedelta(365 * 40):
                age_groups["30-39"] += 1
            elif age < timedelta(365 * 50):
                age_groups["40-49"] += 1
            elif age < timedelta(365 * 65):
                age_groups["50-64"] += 1
            elif age < timedelta(365 * 75):
                age_groups["65-74"] += 1
            elif age < timedelta(365 * 85):
                age_groups["75-84"] += 1
            elif age < timedelta(365 * 100):
                age_groups["85+"] += 1
            else:
                age_groups[">100"] += 1

    # Write the CSV file
    headers = [
        "age_group",
```

```
        "patients",
    ]
    csv_filename = "ages.csv"
    with open(csv_filename, "w") as f:
        writer = csv.DictWriter(f, headers)
        writer.writeheader()
        for age_group in age_groups:
            writer.writerow(
                {
                    "age_group": age_group,
                    "patients": age_groups[age_group],
                }
            )

if __name__ == "__main__":
    main()
```

*Listing 13-7: The* create-ages-csv.py *script calculates patients' ages and groups them by age.*

My script first defined a dictionary called age_groups, with keys for each of the CDC's age groups and values set to 0. I also added two other age groups: people less than 0 years old and people older than 100, because (as I discovered while writing the script) some patients had put birth dates in the future or in the far past.

The script then loaded *aflds-patients.csv* and looped through each patient, calculating the patient's age as of September 2021 (when I was doing this investigation). Based on their age, the script determined which age group the patient belonged to and incremented age_groups by 1. By the time the loop finished, the age_groups dictionary contained a count of the number of patients in each group.

Finally, the script saved the information from age_groups into a CSV spreadsheet called *ages.csv*. Table 13-3 shows the results.

**Table 13-3:** AFLDS Patients by Age Group

| Age group | Patients |
| --- | --- |
| Less than 0 | 702 |
| 0 to 4 | 48 |
| 5 to 17 | 159 |
| 18 to 29 | 3,047 |
| 30 to 39 | 8,190 |
| 40 to 49 | 14,698 |
| 50 to 64 | 31,007 |
| 65 to 74 | 11,441 |
| 75 to 84 | 2,079 |
| 85+ | 317 |
| Greater than 100 | 338 |

After running the script and reviewing the data it created, I could see that some people clearly lied about their birth date: 702 people entered birth dates in the future, which would make them younger than 0 years old, and another 338 people entered dates that would make them older than 100 or even 1,000. The other 71,000 people entered birth dates that are likely correct.

I then combined this data with the CDC's statistics about COVID-19 risks based on age, ignoring the obviously fake birth dates. Table 13-4 shows how many AFLDS patients belong to each age group, along with how likely people in that age group were to get infected with COVID-19 and, if infected, how likely they were to be hospitalized or die. (All rates are relative to people in the 18-to-29 age group, because this group has had the most infections.)

**Table 13-4:** AFLDS Patients by Age Group and Risk

| Age group | AFLDS patients | Risk of infection | Risk of hospitalization | Risk of death |
| --- | --- | --- | --- | --- |
| 0 to 4 | 48 | <1x | <1x | <1x |
| 5 to 17 | 159 | 1x | <1x | <1x |
| 18 to 29 | 3,047 | Reference group | Reference group | Reference group |
| 30 to 39 | 8,190 | 1x | 2x | 4x |
| 40 to 49 | 14,698 | 1x | 2x | 10x |
| 50 to 64 | 31,007 | 1x | 4x | 30x |
| 65 to 74 | 11,441 | 1x | 5x | 90x |
| 75 to 84 | 2,079 | 1x | 9x | 220x |
| 85+ | 317 | 1x | 15x | 570x |

My script showed that 44 percent of AFLDS patients are between 50 and 64, making them 30 times more likely to die from COVID-19 than younger people. Another 16 percent of AFLDS patients are between 65 and 74, making them 90 times more likely to die. In just the two-month period covered by the Cadence patient data, *nearly 45,000 people* older than 50 rejected science and instead put their trust in AFLDS during the COVID-19 pandemic. I wonder how many deaths AFLDS is responsible for.

## Authenticating the Data

While in the midst of analyzing the data, I knew I also needed to verify that this data was authentic before I could publish my findings. The data my source gave to me certainly appeared to be authentic, but I wanted to be more confident.

I started by creating an account on Cadence Health's website. Sure enough, the fields I was asked to fill out with account information were the same fields present in the Cadence patient data. I also used Firefox's developer tools to look at the web requests my browser was making and saw that it matched the data I had; for example, the partner ID associated with my account was 3, the partner ID for AFLDS. (I discuss the developer tools built into web browsers like Firefox and Chrome in more detail in Appendix B.)

The data looked legitimate, but I wanted to check that these patients were real people. To do that, I decided to cross-reference this data with another dataset. Gab, the social network popular among fascists, anti-democracy activists, and anti-vaxxers that I first discussed in Chapter 1, was hacked in early 2021, with 65GB of data leaked to DDoSecrets. This data included about 38,000 email addresses for Gab users.

**NOTE** *Due to PII, DDoSecrets distributes its Gab data only to journalists and researchers. You can learn more about this dataset at* https://ddosecrets.com/wiki/GabLeaks.

I made a list of 72,000 AFLDS patient email addresses, along with a separate list of 38,000 Gab user email addresses. I then wrote a Python script to load both lists and see if there were any email addresses in common. The script found several matches. I started looking through the Gab timeline of each match to see if I could find references to AFLDS, specifically to receiving medication, and found the verification I was looking for.

One 56-year-old patient created their Cadence Health account on July 26, 2021. Their patient record included consultation notes from July 30, the date of their phone consultation. On September 4, they posted a link to Gab for a tractor supply store that sells ivermectin paste for livestock, asking, "Should I pick some up?" Two days later they posted an update: "All sold out!" The day after that, they posted a comment saying, "Front line doctors finally came through with HCQ/Zinc delivery." HCQ is short for hydroxychloroquine.

Figure 13-8 shows a screenshot from this Gab thread. (Every post includes eight usernames; I've redacted all of them.)

The Ravkoo data didn't include patient email addresses, so I couldn't think of an obvious way to authenticate it with OSINT like I did for the Cadence Health data. Instead, I found the phone number for Ravkoo CEO Alpesh Patel and gave him a call. After I informed him that I was a journalist, that Ravkoo had been breached, and that I had all its prescription records, his immediate response was, "That can't be right. Our platform is secure." After I emailed him the screenshot of Ravkoo's Super Admin interface, though, I could hear the panic in his voice. "That's a breach in HIPAA, so I have to report that first," he said, referring to the US health care privacy law. "That's an even more serious issue than your journalism."

He wanted me to tell him the name of the hacker and said he would report all of this to the FBI. I didn't tell him my source's name, of course. Unless you're actively being compelled by a judge, you're never obligated to tell anyone anything about your sources. In any case, I never learned my source's name, which helps keep it secret.

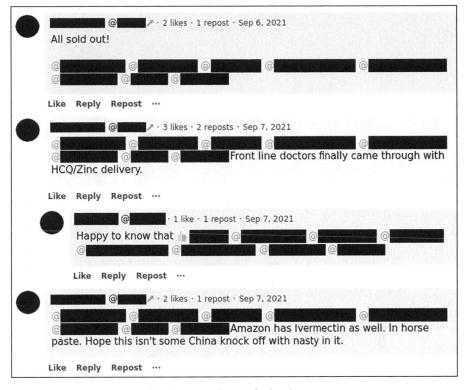

Figure 13-8: A Gab screenshot that I used to verify the data

Patel then said, "I have to call my CTO," and hung up. Ravkoo had in fact been breached. We gave Patel ample opportunity to refute any of the information we planned on publishing, but it was all accurate.

You can read my full investigative report at *https://theintercept.com/2021/ 09/28/covid-telehealth-hydroxychloroquine-ivermectin-hacked/*.

## The Aftermath

After completing this in-depth data-driven investigation, the day before The Intercept was ready to publish our findings, I reached out to everyone involved to explain the revelations that we had discovered and give them a chance to comment.

Roque Espinal, Cadence Health's CEO, said that he had no idea that his platform was being used by AFLDS. "I'm totally flabbergasted. I had to look up exactly who these people were," he said. "I'm fully vaccinated. My children are fully vaccinated. I'm trying to make heads and tails of this right now." After I spoke with him, Espinal told me he immediately cut off service from SpeakWithAnMD. "I don't want to be associated with any crap like that. None of that quackery that's going on."

Espinal said that he was invited to a Zoom meeting with representatives from AFLDS, SpeakWithAnMD, and "16 different attorneys." He told me that he said, "I'm ending my contract with you guys immediately," and disconnected from the meeting. SpeakWithAnMD's telehealth system went down that day, and AFLDS patients couldn't pay for $90 consultations for a full week (saving them an estimated $700,000 on bogus consultations during that time).

Espinal also claimed that Cadence Health didn't collect credit card payments from patients at all—that this was all SpeakWithAnMD's work. He said that Cadence was paid a total of $17,500 for providing service to SpeakWithAnMD (he showed me the invoices he'd sent). The latter company went on to rake in millions of dollars with the help of the services Cadence provided.

## HIPAA's Breach Notification Rule

Espinal told me that Cadence Health didn't directly host AFLDS's patient database; instead, he said, SpeakWithAnMD hosted it in an AWS account. But Jim Flinn, a public relations agent working for SpeakWithAnMD, insisted the opposite: that the hacked database was hosted in Cadence Health's AWS account, not in SpeakWithAnMD's.

Both sides refuse to admit that health care data was breached from their servers. And while Ravkoo Pharmacy began notifying patients of their data breach—something that HIPAA required it to do within two months of discovering it—neither SpeakWithAnMD nor Cadence Health has followed this rule, and at the time of writing, patients haven't been notified of the breach. One of these companies is in violation of HIPAA's breach notification rule.

## Congressional Investigation

In October 2021, the US House of Representative's Select Subcommittee on the Coronavirus Crisis launched an investigation into AFLDS and SpeakWithAnMD based on my reporting, as well as reporting on AFLDS by Vera Bergengruen for *Time* magazine. The committee's chair, Rep. James Clyburn, wrote letters to AFLDS founder Simone Gold and to Jerome Corsi, owner of SpeakWithAnMD's parent company, demanding detailed records from both companies. These included documents related to ownership, organizational structure, and staffing; details about the doctors' training and qualifications; numbers of patients and what they were prescribed; and descriptions of the companies' total revenue and net income for each quarter.

"Attempts to monetize coronavirus misinformation have eroded public confidence in proven treatments and prevention measures and hindered efforts to control the pandemic," Clyburn wrote in his letter to AFLDS. "Some Americans who have been influenced by misinformation have chosen not to get vaccinated, delayed receiving evidence-based treatment, and ingested unapproved substances in harmful quantities." Clyburn also wrote a letter to the Federal Trade Commission requesting that the agency investigate whether these companies are in violation of federal laws.

In January 2022, the House committee announced that "despite repeated assurances of compliance, SpeakWithAnMD has failed to produce any documents responsive to the Select Subcommittee's requests." Then in February, after being stonewalled by SpeakWithAnMD, Clyburn expanded the committee's investigation to include Cadence Health as well. Unfortunately, nothing more resulted from Congress's investigation into AFLDS, SpeakWithAnMD, and Cadence Health.

## Simone Gold's New Business Venture

With a federal investigation into AFLDS underway, the group apparently decided it was time to leave the snake oil business and stick to disinformation and anti-vax litigation. At the time of writing, SpeakWithAnMD's website is still online, but patients are no longer able to book a telehealth consultation. Cadence Health's website is down—Espinal told me he fired his company's only customer, SpeakWithAnMD.

Simone Gold herself wasn't done pushing evidence-free health care. In June 2022, AFLDS sent a newsletter to its supporters announcing her new venture, GoldCare: a telemedicine "health care" service that early adopters could subscribe to for $83 a month, designed to entirely replace evidence-based health care. "If you are reading this email, you are aware that there is overwhelming evidence that the government did its best to kill people during Covid," Gold wrote. "If you prefer not to pay money every month just to play Russian Roulette, you will stop feeding the beast and join us. [. . .] Our system is ethical, of the highest quality, and will ultimately cost less than conventional insurance."

## Scandal and Infighting at AFLDS

Under pressure from California investigators, Gold moved to Naples, Florida. As she prepared to serve two months in prison for storming the Capitol on January 6, 2021, she resigned from her position on the AFLDS board, staying on as a well-paid consultant. While she was behind bars, leaders at AFLDS conducted an audit of her use of the group's charity funds. AFLDS had received at least $10 million in donations, *in addition* to all of the money it had scammed out of patients. While more than a million Americans were dying from COVID-19 during the pandemic, what was Gold doing with all that money?

Joey Gilbert, a Nevada lawyer and former professional boxer, took over from Gold as chair of the AFLDS board while she was in prison. According to a lawsuit filed in November 2022 against Gold by Gilbert and other AFLDS board members, Gold lived rent-free with John Strand, her boyfriend who had stormed the Capitol with her, in a $3.6 million mansion purchased using AFLDS charity funds. The lawsuit also alleged that she was spending $12,000 a month on a bodyguard, $5,600 a month for a housekeeper, and $50,000 a month on credit card expenses—all AFLDS's money. Furthermore, it accused her of purchasing three cars, including a Mercedes-Benz, and taking unauthorized private jet flights, including a single trip that cost $100,000, with AFLDS money.

Finally, the lawsuit accused Gold of hijacking AFLDS resources for her own business. Gilbert claimed that Gold used the Naples mansion to house GoldCare employees and that she enlisted AFLDS employees to work for GoldCare while on the AFLDS payroll. For her part, Gold accused the AFLDS leaders of destroying her nonprofit, demanding that they resign. "Just as the mother lioness will not let her baby lion be murdered, neither will I," Gold wrote in an email to them, according to an affidavit in the lawsuit.

After Gold was released from prison, she regained control of AFLDS. She locked the employees out of their email, pressured an employee to hand over the password to the group's Telegram account with hundreds of thousands of followers, and took control over the AFLDS website. There, she posted press releases claiming that, while she had discussed resigning from her position, those discussions "were never legally actualized" and asserting that she's the legitimate leader of AFLDS. Gold wrote in an email to AFLDS supporters that "the allegations are cetegorically [*sic*] false," and that "under my leadership, AFLDS will never tolerate corruption, no matter the personal price." At the time of publication, the ultimate fate of AFLDS is still unknown, but Gold appears to control the reins.

## Summary

In this chapter, you've seen how I turned 100MB of compressed files from an anonymous hacker into a groundbreaking report on AFLDS. That report resulted in a congressional investigation and contributed to the demise of a corrupt network of telehealth companies that profited off the COVID-19 pandemic. I explained exactly how I went about investigating the Cadence Health and Ravkoo datasets, all in JSON and CSV format. You also read through the Python code I wrote to answer specific questions about the data and to convert it into formats that I could visualize—all skills that you can use in your own data-heavy investigations. I explained how I used OSINT to authenticate the data, as well as the story of AFLDS fracturing and descending into chaos in the aftermath.

The next and final chapter of this book describes another case study in which I developed a custom tool to research chat logs from neo-Nazi Discord servers, contributing to the victory of a lawsuit against the organizers of the deadly 2017 Unite the Right rally.

# 14

## NEO-NAZIS AND THEIR CHATROOMS

In early August 2017, hundreds of white supremacists assembled in the city of Charlottesville, Virginia, for the Unite the Right rally. The protesters—hailing from groups like Vanguard America, Identity Evropa, League of the South, and the Ku Klux Klan—flew Nazi and Confederate battle flags, wore red "Make America Great Again" hats, and chanted slogans like "Jews will not replace us!"

On August 12, James Alex Fields Jr., described by his high school history teacher as "deeply into Adolf Hitler and white supremacy," drove a car into a group of counterprotesters, murdering 32-year-old Heather Heyer and injuring 19 other people. Earlier in the event, Fields was seen marching with a Vanguard America shield. That same day, a group of six white men followed 20-year-old Black special ed assistant teacher DeAndre Harris into a parking garage and beat him with poles and metal pipes, an attack that was caught on film and posted to the internet. In response to the racist violence, Trump famously said that there were "very fine people on both sides."

The Unite the Right rally, like much of the American fascist movement's activism during the 2017–2021 Trump presidency, was largely organized online using Discord, a group chat platform designed for gamers. In Discord, users join *servers*, a group of chatrooms, or a *channel*, a single chatroom. Each channel covers different topics. Fascists created Discord servers for their regional hate groups, as well as for projects like organizing Unite the Right.

An antifascist infiltrator gained access to the server used to organize Unite the Right, called Charlottesville 2.0, as well as many other servers used by fascists at the time. They then leaked the chat logs to Chris Schiano and Dan Feidt, journalists working with the independent nonprofit news collective Unicorn Riot. The leak took the form of screenshots from the Discord app, large JSON files containing thousands of messages, and audio recordings from voice meetings.

In this chapter, I describe how the JSON chat log files were structured and how I went about analyzing them, using techniques covered in Chapter 11. I'll describe the custom app that I wrote to investigate this dataset and explain how I used it to investigate a Discord server called Pony Power, whose members doxed their political enemies. You'll also learn the inside story of DiscordLeaks, Unicorn Riot's public searchable archive based on my app, which contains millions of chat messages from far-right Discord servers. Finally, I discuss a major hack of the American neo-Nazi organization Patriot Front that took place four and a half years after the Charlottesville rally. This hack included chat logs from RocketChat, a self-hosted system that Unicorn Riot also hosts in DiscordLeaks.

Like my reporting on the AFLDS dataset, this case study is an example of journalism with real-world impact. My work, along with that of Unicorn Riot, antifascist infiltrators, and other anonymous developers, helped lead to a court settlement against the most notorious American white supremacist leaders and organizations, resulting in over $25 million worth of damages. I hope that this case study will inspire your own work on datasets of structured chat logs, should you obtain them in the future. With the rise of remote work and the increasing popularity of chat platforms like Discord, Slack, and RocketChat, this type of leak is only getting more common.

I'll start with a brief description of how these chat logs were leaked.

## How Antifascists Infiltrated Neo-Nazi Discord Servers

Unicorn Riot reporters covered the Unite the Right gathering on the ground in Charlottesville. In the following days, the collective announced that it had received anonymously leaked chat logs from the far-right groups that took part in the rally, and particularly from the Charlottesville 2.0 Discord server. It began publishing articles based on these leaks, showing evidence of premeditated plans for violence, memes about hitting protesters with cars, and posts made after the event celebrating Heather Heyer's murder. It also published ZIP files containing thousands of screenshots from the infiltrated Discord servers. Researchers, both amateur and professional, immediately began correlating breadcrumbs from these chat logs with photos and videos of the event that were posted to social media to identify specific fascist activists.

Alongside Charlottesville 2.0, other leaked fascist Discord servers had names like Vibrant Diversity, Ethnoserver, Safe Space 3, and 4th Reich. Some servers only had a few dozen users, while others had over a thousand. The most active server at the time, Vibrant Diversity, included a channel called #problematic_oven, where users shared racist memes. The 4th Reich server included a #rare_hitlers channel, where users shared vintage propaganda from Nazi Germany.

Once the reporting of Unicorn Riot and others had made it clear to Discord that Nazis were relying on its service, the chat platform shut down many far-right chat servers and accounts. "Discord's mission is to bring people together around gaming. We're about positivity and inclusivity. Not hate. Not violence," the company said in a statement. "We will continue to take action against white supremacy, nazi ideology, and all forms of hate." Shutting down individual servers and accounts didn't work, though; fascists simply created new accounts and set up new chat servers. Just as quickly, antifascists infiltrated those new servers and continued to leak chat logs to Unicorn Riot.

Fascists started spreading conspiracy theories that there were no infiltrators but that Discord itself was selling their chat logs to the Southern Poverty Law Center, a nonprofit that monitors hate groups. "The Charlottesville planning server was leaked, even though it was highly secure and no one could figure out who could have leaked it," Andrew Anglin, founder of the notorious neo-Nazi website the Daily Stormer, wrote in an April 2018 blog post. "Since then, servers have been repeatedly leaked. People have been doxed without being able to figure out how they were doxed. Repeatedly and consistently, I have been given reason to believe that these are not Discord 'leaks,' but data being bought by our enemies." This wasn't true, of course. Anglin provided no evidence for the claim, Discord's privacy policy promises that it doesn't sell user data, and we know exactly how the data was leaked: antifascists were invited into the group by pretending to be racists.

A few weeks after Unite the Right, I got a hold of some of these chat logs myself and began to analyze them.

## Analyzing Leaked Chat Logs

In late August of 2017, after Unicorn Riot had started publishing articles based on leaked chats, someone from the collective asked me if I'd like to cover the fascist chat logs for The Intercept. While journalism can be competitive, with each newsroom racing to publish breaking news first without getting scooped, the opposite is often true when it comes to complicated datasets. When it's clear that there's no way that a single newsroom has the resources to discover all of the revelations in a dataset, it only makes sense to bring in other newsrooms and share access to the data. This sort of collaboration helps everyone because different newsrooms have different audiences, and it makes real-world impact from the reporting more likely.

My Unicorn Riot contact sent me a ZIP file full of JSON files and screenshots of Discord chats that covered several Discord servers. The JSON files contained more complete logs of everything posted to these chatrooms, while the screenshots captured only specific conversations. While screenshots are initially simpler to use because you don't need to write any code or use special tools to read them, having the chat logs in a structured data format like JSON is much more useful in the long run. The best way to peruse screenshots of chats is to open individual images, read them one at a time, take note of the filenames that contain interesting content, and refer back to them as needed. This quickly becomes unwieldy when you're dealing with thousands of screenshots.

I started digging into the JSON files to see what I was dealing with. Specifically, I used the handy command line tool jq to figure out exactly how this data was structured in order to find the lists of users and channels and read the messages in each channel.

**NOTE** *Besides manually reading screenshots and taking notes, another option would have been to index the screenshots in software like Aleph, which you used in Chapter 5. Aleph would then perform OCR on the images, extracting their text and enabling me to search them for keywords. This might be helpful in locating specific messages, but in the end, it's still not as useful as structured data. If I were dealing with this data today and only had screenshots without access to JSON data, I would definitely rely on Aleph.*

### Making JSON Files Readable

Each JSON file within the ZIP file sent by my source contained the entire archive of chat logs from a given Discord server. For example, one 29MB JSON file was called *VibrantDiversityComplete-Sept5at327PM*. For the purposes of this book, I've renamed it *VibrantDiversity.json* to make the following examples easier to read.

When I opened this file in a text editor, its contents looked like this:

```
{"meta":{"users":{"231148326249037824":{"name":"D'Marcus Liebowitz"},"232213403974893569":{"nam
e":"northern_confederate"},"279620004641767424":{"name":"‹Unlimited Power‹"},"23338059623405977
6":{"name":"OrwellHuxley"},"289851780521787392":{"name":"badtanman"},"337421867700715524":{"nam
e":"spadegunner"},"315936522656546818":{"name":"erz1871"},"122932975724789761":{"name":"Archer"
},"201547638129164290":{"name":"SLUG2_"},"288899711929286667":{"name":"million plus"},"25019824
--snip--
```

This block of data is not very human-readable. As you learned in Chapter 11, it's much easier to read JSON data that's been reformatted using line breaks, indentation, and syntax highlighting. Using the jq command, I formatted it and added syntax highlighting in my terminal like so:

```
micah@trapdoor Discord-JSON-Scrapes % cat VibrantDiversity.json | jq
{
  "meta": {
    "users": {
      "231148326249037824": {
        "name": "D'Marcus Liebowitz"
      },
      "232213403974893569": {
        "name": "northern_confederate"
      },
      "279620004641767424": {
        "name": "<Unlimited Power<"
      },
--snip--
```

Running this command added formatting and syntax highlighting to the file's contents, but still resulted in 29MB of text madly scrolling through my terminal. To understand the data better, I needed to run more specific commands that would reveal its overall structure.

## Exploring Objects, Keys, and Values with jq

I could tell by looking at the beginning of the JSON data that the whole file was one large JSON object, and one of that object's keys was meta. I ran the following jq command to see what other keys there were:

```
cat VibrantDiversity.json | jq 'keys'
```

The output told me that the data for each Discord server includes two parts, data and meta:

```
[
  "data",
  "meta"
]
```

Guessing that meta included the metadata for the server, I ran the following command to determine the keys of the meta object:

```
cat VibrantDiversity.json | jq '.meta | keys'
```

This command piped the output of cat VibrantDiversity.json as input into the jq '.meta | keys' command. It looks like there's a second pipe there, but there's not. The string '.meta | keys' is actually just a single argument into jq. The pipe character is how you chain multiple jq filters together so that the output of one gets piped into the output of the next; in this case, .meta outputs the value of the meta key and pipes it into keys, which outputs the keys from that value.

The output showed me that the metadata included information about channels, servers, and users:

```
[
  "channels",
  "servers",
  "userindex",
  "users"
]
```

So far, I had only looked at the keys of JSON objects. It was time to look at some of the content, starting with the servers. By running jq '.meta .servers', I could look at the value of the servers key inside the meta object:

```
cat VibrantDiversity.json | jq '.meta.servers'
```

The output in Listing 14-1 showed that *VibrantDiversity.json* lists a single server in the metadata sections, Vibrant Diversity, just as I expected.

```
[
  {
    "name": "Vibrant Diversity",
    "type": "SERVER"
  }
]
```

Listing 14-1: The list of servers in VibrantDiversity.json

I could tell that this output was an array, since it was a list of items surrounded by brackets ([ and ]).

Next, I wanted to see what channels this server had, so I ran the following command to view the value of the channels key in the meta object:

```
cat VibrantDiversity.json | jq '.meta.channels'
```

Listing 14-2 shows the output of this command.

```
{
  "274024266435919872": {
    "server": 0,
    "name": "rules"
  },
  "274262571367006208": {
    "server": 0,
    "name": "general"
  },
  "292812979555139589": {
    "server": 0,
    "name": "effortposting"
  },
  "288508006990348299": {
    "server": 0,
    "name": "problematic_oven"
```

```
  },
  "274055625988898816": {
    "server": 0,
    "name": "music"
  },
  "3439799742241550337": {
    "server": 0,
    "name": "gun-posting-goes-here"
  },
  "328841016352440320": {
    "server": 0,
    "name": "food-posting"
  },
  "274025126641795074": {
    "server": 0,
    "name": "share_contact_info"
  },
  "288901961313550336": {
    "server": 0,
    "name": "recruiting"
  }
}
```

*Listing 14-2: The list of channels in the Vibrant Diversity server*

Whereas the output in Listing 14-1 was an array, the output for `.meta.channels` was a JSON object, as indicated by the braces ({ and }) surrounding it.

The keys for this object are long numbers, presumably the ID of the channel, and their values are objects that contain the server and name keys. For example, the channel with key 288508006990348299 has the value {"server": 0, "name": "problematic_oven"}. The server value for all of these channels is 0. I guessed that this was the index of the servers array from Listing 14-1. Since there was only one server in this JSON file, the index for all of the channels is the first item in the list, 0. The name value was problematic_oven. When I later read the chats in this channel, it was full of antisemitic posts and Nazi memes, and the word *oven* was clearly a reference to the Holocaust. This was definitely a neo-Nazi chat server.

I wanted to see a list of this server's users, so I ran the following command to view the value of the users key in the meta object:

```
cat VibrantDiversity.json | jq '.meta.users'
```

Listing 14-3 shows my output.

```
{
  "231148326249037824": {
    "name": "D'Marcus Liebowitz"
  },
  "232213403974893569": {
    "name": "northern_confederate"
  },
  "279620004641767424": {
```

```
    "name": "<Unlimited Power<"
  },
--snip--
```

*Listing 14-3: The list of users in the Vibrant Diversity server*

Just like the list of channels in Listing 14-2, the output for .meta.users in Listing 14-3 is a JSON object. The keys are long numbers, presumably the ID of the user, and the values are objects with just a single key, the user's name.

So far, I had explored the metadata keys channels, servers, and users, but there was one left: the userindex key. I ran the following command to view the userindex key's value:

```
cat VibrantDiversity.json | jq '.meta.userindex'
```

Listing 14-4 shows my output.

```
[
  "231148326249037824",
  "232213403974893569",
  "279620004641767424",
--snip--
```

*Listing 14-4: The list of user IDs for each user in the Vibrant Diversity server*

The output for the .meta.userlist command was a JSON array rather than an object, and each item in the array was a string that looks like a Discord ID. Sure enough, the first item, 231148326249037824, turned out to be the ID of the first user from Listing 14-3, D'Marcus Liebowitz. At this point I didn't fully understand the purpose of userlist, but it soon became clear, as you'll see later in this section.

Armed with a basic understanding of the server's metadata, I ran the following command to find the keys for the data object:

```
cat VibrantDiversity.json | jq '.data | keys'
```

Listing 14-5 shows my output.

```
[
  "274024266435919872",
  "274025126641795074",
  "274055625988898816",
  "274262571367006208",
  "288508006990348299",
  "288901961313550336",
  "292812979555139589",
  "328841016352440320",
  "343979974241550337"
]
```

*Listing 14-5: The keys to the data object in the Vibrant Diversity server*

These keys are the same channel IDs from Listing 14-2, so I guessed that the values of each key contained the actual messages in those chat channels. Because I needed to start somewhere, I decided to view the chat messages from the #problematic_oven channel, so I ran the following command:

```
cat VibrantDiversity.json | jq '.data."288508006990348299"'
```

The full argument for this jq command is surrounded by single quotes. The .data part of the filter looks in the key data, and the ."288508006990348299" part of the filter looks in the key 288508006990348299, which is the ID of the #problematic_oven channel. I put the ID in quotes so that jq would know that this key was a string and not a number.

As with the first time I used jq to read this JSON file, the output of this command scrolled through a large block of text, though considerably less than before. In this case, the output showed chat messages from only a single channel, rather than showing all of the data in the JSON file. Listing 14-6 shows just a few chat messages from the middle of the output.

```
micah@trapdoor Discord-JSON-Scrapes % cat VibrantDiversity.json | jq '.data
."288508006990348299"'
{
--snip--
  "352992491282366485": {
    "u": 4,
    "t": 1504230368205,
    "m": "we need more white girls with nice asses"
  },
  "352992512752746496": {
    "u": 4,
    "t": 1504230373324,
    "m": "no more gay jew shit"
  },
  "352992579949690890": {
    "u": 1,
    "t": 1504230389345,
    "m": "you're not allowed to oogle anyone whiter than med"
  },
  "352992652687441920": {
    "u": 1,
    "t": 1504230406687,
    "m": "if i catch you looking at anglo/celtic/nordic girls you're banned"
  },
--snip--
```

Listing 14-6: Chat messages from the #problematic_oven channel in the Vibrant Diversity server

Just like the channels in Listing 14-2, this output is a JSON object with keys that contain long numbers. In this case, these keys appeared to be message IDs, and the values appeared to be details about that specific chat message. In each message, the u field represented the user and the m field contained the message content. The t field was a Unix timestamp, the number of seconds or sometimes milliseconds since January 1, 1970, a common way to represent specific dates and times in computer science. These particular timestamps were in milliseconds.

At this point, I knew that I was looking at a conversation between two neo-Nazis. The top two messages in Listing 14-6 are from a user with the ID of 4, and the bottom two messages are from a user with the ID of 1. Because the value of t gets bigger with each message, these appear to be displayed in chronological order. I decided to take a closer look at the message 352992512752746496, from user 4, with the timestamp 1504230373324.

### Converting Timestamps

Unix timestamps are a useful way for computers to store an entire date—the year, month, day, and time of day—in a single number. I needed to convert the timestamp associated with that message into human-readable format to find out the date and time when the message was posted.

I used the following lines of code in the Python interpreter to convert the 1504230373324 timestamp into a more human-readable Python datetime object:

```
>>> from datetime import datetime
>>> timestamp = datetime.fromtimestamp(1504230373324 / 1000)
>>> print(timestamp)
```

The syntax in this code is similar to the code you used to import modules in Chapter 8. Rather than import *module*, this code takes the syntax from *module* import *resource_name*, loading a single datetime resource from the datetime module. Next, the code defines a variable called timestamp and sets its value to the return value of the datetime.fromtimestamp() function. This function takes the number of seconds since January 1, 1970, as an argument. Because the Discord logs are in milliseconds rather than seconds, this code first divides the Discord timestamp by 1,000 to convert it to seconds before passing it into the function. The function returns a Python datetime object.

When I displayed the datetime object with print(timestamp), I could see that this chat message was posted on August 31, 2017, at 6:46 PM:

```
2017-08-31 18:46:13.324000
```

I now had an idea of the timeframe in which this chat exchange took place. Next, I wanted to see which users were involved.

### Finding Usernames

I wanted to find the username for person who'd posted the 352992512752746496 message in Listing 14-6. The u value for this message was 4, so I checked to see if 4 was a valid user ID from the output in Listing 14-3 but found that it wasn't there; all of the user IDs in that JSON object are 18 digits long. I turned to the output in Listing 14-4 that shows the value of userindex in the meta object. The value of userindex is an array of strings, each an 18-digit user ID.

As described in Chapter 11, JSON arrays are lists of items in a specific order. Objects, on the other hand, don't have any order. You select values from arrays using their numerical indices, starting from index 0 for the first item. Because objects don't have numerical indices, there's no concept of the first, second, or third item in the object; you could edit a JSON file to rearrange the object's items, and it would still be the same object. For this reason, I guessed that the u value was actually an index of the userindex array.

To determine which user ID corresponded to the user whose u value was 4, I looked for the value of userindex at index 4 by running the following command:

```
cat VibrantDiversity.json | jq '.meta.userindex[4]'
```

This command is similar to the one in Listing 14-4, but because it uses .meta.userindex[4], it selects the value at index 4 of the .meta.userindex array and just displays that result. My output showed that this value was the string 289851780521787392, an 18-digit user ID:

```
"289851780521787392"
```

Now that I had a user ID, I used it in the following command to find the matching username:

```
cat VibrantDiversity.json | jq '.meta.users."289851780521787392"'
```

Like the previous command, this command selects just one value to output. In this case, it selects the meta key, then the users key, then the 289851780521787392 key. The result is an object that includes a name key:

```
{
  "name": "badtanman"
}
```

The name *badtanman* was the username I was looking for.

In the chat logs quoted in Listing 14-6, the user *badtanman* is talking to someone with the u value of 1. To find that person's username, I ran the same commands, substituting the appropriate ID numbers:

```
micah@trapdoor Discord-JSON-Scrapes % cat VibrantDiversity.json | jq '.meta.userindex[1]'
"232213403974893569"
micah@trapdoor Discord-JSON-Scrapes % cat VibrantDiversity.json | jq '.meta.users."232213403974
893569"'
{
  "name": "northern_confederate"
}
```

I'd found that the snippet of chat messages in Listing 14-6 was a conversation between *badtanman* and *northern_confederate* on the night of August 31, 2017.

Running all of these jq commands, along with running code in the Python interpreter to convert timestamps, is tedious. If confronted with a large volume of chat logs, you don't want to research every group of messages this way. But when you're exploring an unfamiliar dataset for the first time, you need to manually explore it like this until you better understand how the data is structured. After doing this preliminary analysis, I could use my new understanding of the chat logs to write Python scripts or even a full custom app (like I ended up developing for this dataset) to aid my research.

Before I actually started writing Python code to more easily parse these chat logs, though, I noticed a file that I'd missed before in the Unicorn Riot ZIP file that might make researching this dataset a lot easier.

## The Discord History Tracker

The ZIP file from my Unicorn Riot contact had dozens of files in it, most of them JSON files and PNG screenshots, along with a few folders containing other JSON files. I'd immediately zeroed in on the JSON files to analyze their data structure, but until now I hadn't noticed the file *logviewer.html*. This was an HTML and JavaScript file that, when opened in a web browser, would allow me to load JSON chat log files and read through them.

After talking with my Unicorn Riot contact, I learned that this local HTML file is part of a piece of open source software called Discord History Tracker. This software, not affiliated with Discord, lets users save an offline copy of everything they have access to in a given Discord server in JSON format. Antifascist activists used this software to exfiltrate chat logs from Vibrant Diversity, Charlottesville 2.0, and other fascist-run Discord servers.

Discord History Tracker included two components. The main component was in charge of actually creating a backup of a Discord server. The user would load the Discord server in their web browser, open their developer tools, and copy and paste the Discord History Tracker JavaScript code into their browser's console. This would then scrape all of the data in the Discord server and save a backup file in JSON format. The second component of Discord History Tracker was the *logviewer.html* file, which contained offline HTML software for viewing those backup files.

Figure 14-1 shows *logviewer.html* loaded in a web browser. In the screenshot, I've scrolled to the aforementioned messages between *badtanman* and *northern_confederate* from the #problematic_oven channel.

**NOTE** *The screenshot in Figure 14-1 shows software from 2017. The Discord History Tracker interface has changed considerably since then. Among other changes, it now saves the data in SQLite databases, rather than as JSON files, and you can view the logs in a desktop app instead of using the* logviewer.html *file. You can learn more about the software at* https://dht.chylex.com.

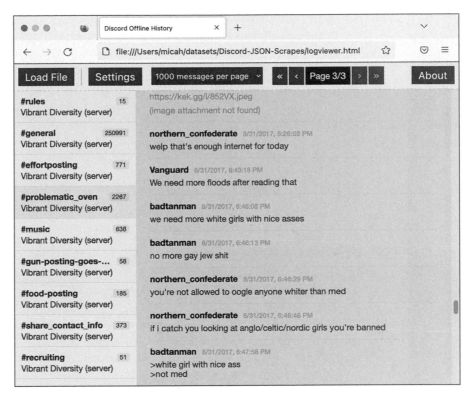

Figure 14-1: The August 31, 2017, chat between badtanman and northern_confederate,
viewed in the Discord Offline History web app

This offline HTML viewer software made it considerably easier to
navigate and read the contents of the JSON files. I could click through
the channels on the left, and then read through a page of chats at a time.
However, it also lacked some features that would be important for my ongoing
investigation:

- There was no simple way to search for individual messages. For example, suppose I wanted to search for mentions of Berkeley, the city I lived
  in at the time. I would have to click a channel like #general, use my web
  browser's search feature to search for *Berkeley*, and then find which messages appeared in the #general channel. I would also need to change
  the settings to display all messages per page so I could search them all
  at once, rather than displaying just 1,000 messages at a time, as shown
  in Figure 14-1. I would then have to replicate this search for every other
  channel in the server, and if I wanted to search other Discord servers as
  well, I'd have to replicate it for each channel in each server.

- The offline viewer only supported looking at one server at a time, but
  I wanted to be able to search multiple servers at once and also track a
  single user's messages across different servers.

- There was no way to generate hyperlinks leading to individual messages. When you're taking notes for a story based on chat logs like this, it's helpful to track the messages of interest. Without links, you'll regularly have to go back and search for specific messages all over again.

I decided to build my own web application to add these missing features. I already had all of the chat logs in a structured format, which is by far the biggest requirement to build a custom app, as you learned in Chapter 10's discussion of BlueLeaks Explorer. If I'd had only screenshots of the Discord servers, a custom app with these features wouldn't have been possible. Screenshots aren't structured data, and there's no easy way to write software that allows you to browse the chat messages they contain.

## A Script to Search the JSON Files

As you've learned throughout this book, understanding how the data is structured is a prerequisite to writing code that works with it. Therefore, I decided to use the knowledge I'd gained from manually investigating the JSON files with jq to build a simple Python script that let me search one of the JSON files for keywords. Initially I thought I might be able to use this script to do all of the analysis I needed, but that turned out to be wrong; I ended up writing a complete custom app to investigate this dataset as well. Even so, this first (considerably simpler) script allowed me to use Python code to express the structure of the dataset that I'd already gleaned, which simplified the process of programming the full web app. In this section I go over exactly how my initial Discord JSON search script worked.

For example, I knew my script needed to be able to display chat messages based on what I searched for. Let's say I wanted my code to display the following chat message from Listing 14-6:

```
"352992491282366485": {
  "u": 4,
  "t": 1504230368205,
  "m": "we need more white girls with nice asses"
}
```

The value of the u key is 4, but now I knew how to find the actual username of the person who posted this message. First, my code needed to look in the JSON's meta object and select the fourth item in the userindex array, which is the user ID 289851780521787392. My code then would look again in the JSON's meta object, this time for the users key, and use that user ID as the key to get this user object:

```
{
  "name": "badtanman"
}
```

My code would select the name string from that object to get the user-name of the message poster, badtanman, and then replicate the whole process to display the correct username for every message.

I opened my text editor and started writing a Python script, *discord-json -search.py*, to search one of the JSON files for keywords. Here's my completed source code (you can also find it at *https://github.com/micahflee/hacks-leaks-and -revelations/blob/main/chapter-14/discord-analysis/discord-json-search.py*):

```
#!/usr/bin/python3
import sys
import json
import click
from datetime import datetime

def highlight(message, query): ❶
    new_message = ""
    index = 0
    while True:
        new_index = message.lower().find(query.lower(), index)
        if new_index > 0:
            # Found
            new_message += message[index:new_index]
            new_message += click.style(
                message[new_index : new_index + len(query)], underline=True
            )
            index = new_index + len(query)
        else:
            # Not found
            new_message += message[index:]
            break

    return new_message

def display(channel_name, server_name, user_name, timestamp, message, query): ❷
    click.echo(
        "{} {}".format(
            click.style("#{}".format(channel_name), fg="bright_magenta"),
            click.style("[server: {}]".format(server_name), fg="bright_black"),
        )
    )
    click.echo(
        "{} {}".format(
            click.style(user_name, bold=True),
            click.style(timestamp.strftime("%c"), fg="bright_black"),
        )
    )
    click.echo(highlight(message, query))
    click.echo("")

def search(data, query): ❸
    # Loop through each channel
    for channel_id in data["data"]: ❹
        # Get the channel name and server name
        channel_name = data["meta"]["channels"][channel_id]["name"] ❺
```

```
        server_name = data["meta"]["servers"][
            data["meta"]["channels"][channel_id]["server"]
        ]["name"]

        for message_id in data["data"][channel_id]: ❻
            # Pull the user data, timestamp, and message body from the message
            user_index = data["data"][channel_id][message_id]["u"]
            user_id = data["meta"]["userindex"][user_index]
            user_name = data["meta"]["users"][user_id]["name"]
            timestamp = datetime.fromtimestamp(
                data["data"][channel_id][message_id]["t"] / 1000
            )
            message = data["data"][channel_id][message_id]["m"]

            # Is the query in the message?
            if query.lower() in message.lower(): ❼
                display(channel_name, server_name, user_name, timestamp, message, query)

@click.command()
@click.argument("filename", type=click.Path(exists=True))
@click.argument("query")
def main(filename, query): ❽
    # Load the JSON file
    try:
        with open(filename) as f:
            data = json.loads(f.read())
    except:
        print("Failed to load JSON file")
        sys.exit()

    # Search
    search(data, query)


if __name__ == "__main__":
    main()
```

It's simplest to explain how this script worked from bottom to top, since that's how it executed and also how I programmed it. The main() function ❽ is a Click command that takes two arguments: the filename for a JSON file with Discord chat logs called filename, and a search term called query. The code opened the filename that was passed in and parsed it using json.loads() to turn it into a JSON object. Then it called the search() function, passing in the data from the JSON file and the search query.

The search() function ❸ is where all the magic happened. I knew from my previous analysis that these Discord JSON objects had two keys: the data key, which contained the messages in each channel, and the meta key, which contained metadata about these messages. My script started by looping through every channel in data['data'] ❹, then using its channel_id to look up that channel's name and server in the metadata ❺. It then looped through every message in that channel ❻ and stored the message's username, time-stamp, and the message itself in variables.

The code then checked to see if the search query that was passed into the script as a CLI argument (stored in query) existed in the message (stored in message) ❼. As described in Chapter 7, it converted both strings to lowercase using the lower() method to make the search case insensitive. If the lowercase version of the message contained the lowercase version of the search term, the script then passed all of the relevant variables into the display() function to display the message in the terminal.

The display() function ❷ took arguments for metadata about a message, the message text itself, and the search term and used those to display the message. This code used click.echo() instead of print() to display text to the terminal, and it used click.style() to apply different colors and formatting. (You could do all of this just with the print() function, but the click module makes it simpler to style terminal output.) After displaying two lines of metadata for the message, the script then displayed the output of the highlight() function, which returned the message itself in color with the search term underlined.

The highlight() function ❶ created an empty string called new_message and then made it a copy of message, the original message it displayed, except with all instances of the search term underlined using click.style(). It then returned new_message and displayed it to the terminal in the display() function.

For example, if I wanted to search *VibrantDiversity.json* for the term *berkeley*, I could run:

```
python3 discord-json-search.py ~/datasets/Discord-JSON-Scrapes/VibrantDiversity.json "berkeley"
```

The output listed over a hundred chat messages that mentioned Berkeley. Each message showed the name of the channel, the name of the Discord server, the user who posted it and when, and the content of the message. Here's the first snippet of output, which highlighted the search term in the message with an underline:

```
#general [server: Vibrant Diversity]
Hector Sun Sep  3 20:19:11 2017
Look at how many antifa were at Boston and Berkeley.  We need numbers.  We can't
have rallies with less than a thousand people now.  Even that's a low number.
--snip--
```

The first message that mentioned Berkeley was a post from the user *Hector* in the #general channel on September 3, 2017. This user was complaining about the relatively small number of fascists that showed up to their rallies in Boston and Berkeley, compared to the "antifa" counterprotesters.

This script allowed me to search a full Discord server for keywords, but it still lacked several of the features that I wanted: it could work with only one Discord leak at a time, and there was no easy way to browse through and read the data sequentially or to save links to specific interesting messages. I started building out a web application to help me perform these missing tasks.

## My Discord Analysis Code

I've found that after obtaining a large dataset full of structured data, building a custom web application to explore it, as I did with BlueLeaks Explorer, makes it much easier to find its hidden revelations. After writing *discord-json -search.py*, I spent about a week creating Discord Analysis, a custom web app to analyze leaked Discord chat logs.

Since I wanted to be able to search multiple Discord servers at once, I decided that the best solution would be to convert all of the data from JSON files into a SQL database. I used a Python tech stack that I was already familiar with, Flask (discussed briefly in Chapter 10), for the web app and SQLAlchemy for communicating with the SQL database.

SQLAlchemy is an *Object Relational Mapping (ORM)* Python module that's useful for making code that works with SQL databases simpler to write and more secure. ORMs allow you to work with SQL databases in such a way that you don't have to directly write any SQL code yourself, which means your projects won't be vulnerable to SQL injection. This web app used Flask-SQLAlchemy, a Flask extension that adds SQLAlchemy support to Flask apps.

While developing my Discord Analysis web app, I was actively using it to research the leaked neo-Nazi chat logs. If I had new questions about the data (like what other messages a user posted) or found that I needed new features (like limiting my search to a single server), I would program them in as I went along. This is typically how I build research tools: I start using them long before they're complete, and I let the direction of my research guide which features I add next.

In this section, I explain how I went about developing the different components of the app: designing a SQL database, importing chat logs from the Discord JSON files into that database, and building the web interface to research the chat logs. You'll learn how I used SQLAlchemy to define database tables, insert rows into them, and select rows from them. You'll also learn how I used Flask to build this web app, including how to make Jinja templates and how to define routes—skills you'll need if you build your own Flask web apps in the future.

NOTE    *Fully explaining how to build a Flask and SQLAlchemy web app is outside the scope of this book. Instead, I go over how I went about building this app in broad strokes, which should still be useful if you ever decide to build a similar one yourself. The best way to learn how to make your own Flask app is by exploring Flask's excellent documentation at* https://flask.palletsprojects.com; *that's how I learned. The Flask documentation includes a tutorial that walks you through every step of developing a simple web app. The Python skills you've learned from Chapters 7 and 8 are more than enough for you to follow along with the tutorial. You can also find docs for SQLAlchemy at* https://www.sqlalchemy.org *and for Flask's SQLAlchemy extension at* https://flask-sqlalchemy.palletsprojects.com.

The code for Discord Analysis, which has quietly been public on my GitHub account for years, hasn't been updated much since 2017, with the exception of some small changes I made when preparing it for this book. I don't plan on maintaining it. Still, you should be able to get it running locally if you'd like to explore it further, and you can use it as inspiration for your own future projects that use a similar tech stack. Read through this section to see how it works, and then if you're curious, try getting it running locally yourself.

As I explain the app, I'll quote sections of the source code. It's too long to include all of it here, but you can find the full code online in the book's GitHub repository at *https://github.com/micahflee/hacks-leaks-and-revelations/ tree/main/chapter-14/discord-analysis*. I recommend that you pull up the full source code for each file as I describe how it works.

### Designing the SQL Database

I started my web app with a Python script called *app.py*. You can find the full source code for this file at *https://github.com/micahflee/hacks-leaks -and-revelations/blob/main/chapter-14/discord-analysis/app.py*. First, my code imported the appropriate Flask and SQLAlchemy modules, created a new Flask app object called app, and created a new Flask-SQLAlchemy object called db:

```
from flask import Flask, render_template, request, escape, flash, redirect
from flask_sqlalchemy import SQLAlchemy

app = Flask(__name__)
app.config["SQLALCHEMY_DATABASE_URI"] = "sqlite:///database.sqlite3"
app.config["DEBUG"] = True

db = SQLAlchemy(app)
```

I started by importing several items from the flask module, like Flask and render_template, that I knew I'd need later in the program. In the next line, I also imported SQLAlchemy from the flask_sqlalchemy module.

Using the newly imported Flask, I then created a Flask object called app. Every Flask web app includes such an object (and usually by that name) to define exactly how the app will work. I modified the app.config dict to set some configuration settings, telling it that I wanted to use a SQLite3 database stored in the file *database.sqlite3*, and I wanted to turn debug mode on, which is useful while you're actively developing a web app. Finally, I created the SQLAlchemy object called db, passing in app.

For the next bit of code, I'll introduce you to a new Python concept that I didn't explicitly cover in Part III but that you've technically been using all along: classes. In Python, a *class* is a template for creating new objects that can store data (using variables called *attributes*) and perform actions (using functions called *methods*). For example, strings are technically classes. When you run the code s = "example", the variable s is an instance of the string class, the data it stores is the string example, and it has a bunch of methods you can call on it, such as s.upper(), which returns an uppercase version of the string. When you write SQLAlchemy code, you define a class for each database table. This way, you can write code that works with Python objects without needing to write the SQL queries yourself.

I started writing code to define the SQL tables that would store Discord data for servers, users, channels, and messages. For example, the following code defines the Server class, which represents the SQL table to store data about servers:

```
class Server(db.Model):
    id = db.Column(db.Integer, autoincrement=True, primary_key=True)
    name = db.Column(db.String(128), unique=True, nullable=False)

    channels = db.relationship("Channel", back_populates="server")
    messages = db.relationship("Message", back_populates="server")

    def __init__(self, name):
        self.name = name
```

Using SQLAlchemy requires that you define your own classes. You can think of this Server class as a description of a new type of Python object that represents a row in the server SQL table. Because I defined it as Server(db .Model), this class inherited all of the functionality of the db.Model class, which is part of SQLAlchemy. Inside the class definition, I defined the table's columns: id (an auto-incrementing number) and name (a string). Next, I defined this table's relationships to other tables, in this case relating servers to channels and messages—both the Channel table and the Message table have a server_id column.

Finally, I defined the __init__() method. When you define a class, you must call the first argument of every method self to represent this Python object itself. You can optionally include other arguments, too. The __init__() method is a type of method called a *constructor*, which runs as soon as you create the object. This constructor sets the value of the object's name attribute (which you access within the class as self.name) to the value of name, which is a variable passed into the __init__() method as an argument.

For example, to add a row to the Server table in the SQL database for the Vibrant Diversity Discord server, I could run the code in Listing 14-7. (My Discord Analysis app doesn't actually use this code—it loads the servers from the JSON data—but I'm including this example to help you understand how to use SQLAlchemy classes to interact with databases without needing to write SQL queries.)

```
server = Server("Vibrant Diversity")
db.session.add(server)
db.session.commit()
```

*Listing 14-7: Using SQLAlchemy to insert data into a SQL database*

The first line of code creates a `Server` object by running `Server("Vibrant Diversity")`. This would run the constructor method, passing in the string `Vibrant Diversity` as `name`. The constructor would then set the value of its `name` attribute to the name that was passed in. When the constructor finishes running, the code would save this newly created Python object in the `server` variable. The next two lines of code use the SQLAlchemy object `db` to run the INSERT query in the SQL database and insert this row. The `db.session.add()` method collects a list of SQL queries, and the `db.session.commit()` method runs those SQL queries on the database. In SQL, sometimes it's more efficient to run several queries and then commit them all at once rather than one at a time.

In other words, the code in Listing 14-7 is basically the same as running the SQL query `INSERT INTO server SET name='Vibrant Diversity';`, except this way all you need to do is interact with Python objects, not write any SQL yourself. After creating the server object, I could then access that object's ID attribute with `server.id` or the object's name attribute with `server.name`.

In addition to the `Server` table I just described, I also created the following tables, which you can view in detail in the *app.py* file at *https://github .com/micahflee/hacks-leaks-and-revelations/blob/main/chapter-14/discord-analysis/ app.py*:

**User**  A Discord user. I included the columns `id`, `discord_id`, and `name`. The `id` column is an auto-incrementing number, and `discord_id` is the original ID that Discord itself used. This is useful for identifying the same user across servers.

**Channel**  A channel in a Discord server. The columns are `id`, `discord_id`, `name`, and `server_id`. The `server_id` column forms a relationship with the `Server` table, since each server has a set of channels. Every Discord server JSON file contains a list of channels. Adding this relationship means that the SQL database I was designing would match the data structure in the JSON files.

**Message**  A Discord message. The columns are `id`, `discord_id`, `timestamp`, `message`, `attachments_json`, `user_id`, `channel_id`, and `server_id`. The `attachments _json` column contains extra data from messages with attachments, like when someone posts an image to Discord. The `user_id`, `channel_id`, and `server_id` columns form relationships with the `User`, `Channel`, and `Server` tables. These also would match the structure found in the JSON files.

Figure 14-2 shows the relationship between these four tables. The `Channel` table includes a `server_id` column, so it's related to the `Server` table.

The `Message` table includes columns for `channel_id`, `server_id`, and `user_id`, so it's related to the `Channel`, `Server`, and `User` tables.

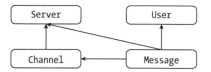

Figure 14-2: Relationships between the SQL tables in the Discord Analysis app

My goal for this web app would be to build an interface that allows me to explore the data stored in these SQL tables. I wanted to be able to search all of the messages at once, including from multiple servers, to see which users posted in multiple servers and to be able to generate links to individual messages that I could store in my notes. Before building the web interface, though, I needed to load the database with data from the JSON files.

## Importing Chat Logs into the SQL Database

I wrote a separate script, *admin.py*, that I used to import data into the SQL database. This script took a command as its first argument. If I passed in create-db, it would use SQLAlchemy to create the SQL tables that I had defined in *app.py*. When I passed in import-json, followed by the filename of a JSON file, the code would import Discord data from that JSON file into the SQL database. I also eventually added the user-stats command, which displayed how many messages each user in the whole database posted, and on which servers.

This *admin,py* file is too long to include in this chapter in its entirety, but as with *app.py*, you can find a copy of the complete code in the book's GitHub repo at *https://github.com/micahflee/hacks-leaks-and-revelations/blob/main/chapter-14/discord-analysis/admin.py*.

In this section, I'll explain how I built the import-json command (specifically, the import_json() function, which is what gets called when you run import-json), the most interesting part of the script. This is the code that opens up the JSON files containing Discord server leaks, loops through all the data, and then inserts it into the SQL database. As with the *discord-json -search.py* script, I relied on my previous manual analysis of the Discord JSON files to write this code. Basically, this is the part that requires an understanding of the structure of the original data.

The import_json() function is too long to display it all here, so instead I'll display snippets that explain the general idea of how it works. The function takes the filename for a JSON file containing Discord leaks as an argument. It opens this file, loads it into a variable called data, and then uses the information in data to add servers, users, channels, and messages to the SQL database. I'll show the code that adds users, channels, and messages soon, but first, Listing 14-8 shows the code that adds servers.

```
print("Adding servers: ", end="", flush=True)
for item in data["meta"]["servers"]:
    name = item["name"]

    try:
        server = Server(name)
        db.session.add(server)
        db.session.commit()
        print("+", end="", flush=True)
    except sqlalchemy.exc.IntegrityError:
        db.session.rollback()
        print(".", end="", flush=True)
print("")
```

*Listing 14-8: Code from* admin.py *to add servers to the database*

This code looped through all of the servers it found in data["meta"]
["servers"], adding a row to the database for each server that it found.
For example, in Listing 14-1, I used jq to view this list of servers for
*VibrantDiversity.json* and found that it contained only a single server.
Listing 14-8 uses Python code to find that same list of servers from the
same part of the target leaked JSON file.

For each server it found, the code stored the server's name in the name
variable, then tried to add that server to the database. This code used Python
exception handling, which you learned about in Chapter 7. In the try block,
the code created a new Server object (this represents a row in the Server table
in SQLAlchemy), added that row to the database using db.session.add(server),
and finally committed the database changes with db.session.commit(), just
like in the SQLAlchemy code in Listing 14-7. After the server was successfully
inserted into the database, the program displayed a plus sign (+) and moved
on to the next loop.

When I defined the Server table in *app.py*, I specified that the name column should be unique, meaning that there could be no two rows with the
same name column. If SQLAlchemy threw the sqlalchemy.exc.IntegrityError
exception while the script was trying to add the row to the database, that
meant a server with that name already existed in the database, and the
except block should run instead. If this happened, then the code rolled back
the change that it was about to make and displayed a dot (.) instead of a
plus sign.

Why did I worry about catching these exceptions to begin with instead
of just adding rows to the database? As with the programming exercises
that you completed in previous chapters, I didn't write the whole script
perfectly the first time and then run it. Instead, I wrote small bits of code at
a time and ran them to make sure my script was working so far. This exception handling allowed me to rerun an import on the same JSON file over
and over while starting where I left off. If my script showed a plus sign, I
knew it had added a new row to the database. If it showed a dot, that meant
the row already existed and the script moved on.

You might also notice that the familiar print() function calls look odd in Listing 14-8: my code passed in the end="" and flush=True keyword arguments. By default, print() displays the string the user passes in as an argument, then adds a newline character (\n) to the end. The end argument replaces that newline with something else (in this case, an empty string). In other words, this is how I could print a string without moving on to the next line. The flush=True argument makes sure that the output gets displayed to the screen immediately; without it, the output would still get displayed, but not right after the function call. This allowed me to watch the progress of an import.

After adding servers, the script added users, as shown in Listing 14-9.

```
print("Adding users: ", end="", flush=True)
for user_discord_id in data["meta"]["users"]:
    name = data["meta"]["users"][user_discord_id]["name"]

    try:
        user = User(user_discord_id, name)
        db.session.add(user)
        db.session.commit()
        print("+", end="", flush=True)
    except sqlalchemy.exc.IntegrityError:
        db.session.rollback()
        print(".", end="", flush=True)
print("")
```

*Listing 14-9: Code from admin.py to add users to the database*

This code is very similar to Listing 14-8, but instead of looping through the list data["meta"]["servers"], it looped through the dictionary data["meta"]["users"]. Listing 14-3 shows this JSON object of users from *VibrantDiversity .json*. As described in Chapter 8, when you loop through a dictionary, you're actually looping through the dictionary's keys. In this case, the script stored each key in the user_discord_id variable. Armed with the user's Discord ID, it then looked up that user's name in the metadata.

In the try block, the script then created a new User object, this time with both the user's Discord ID and name, and tried adding it to the database. When I defined the User table in *app.py*, I specified that user_discord_id should be unique in order to prevent duplicate users. Like Listing 14-8, the code displayed a plus sign when adding the user to the database and a dot if it hit an error. This error-handling code would be important when I started importing multiple servers: if a Discord user was already in the database because they were a member of a previous server, the code wouldn't create a duplicate user for them.

After adding servers and users, the script then added channels, using the code in Listing 14-10.

```
print("Adding channels: ", end="", flush=True)
for channel_discord_id in data["meta"]["channels"]:
    name = data["meta"]["channels"][channel_discord_id]["name"]
```

```
        server_id = data["meta"]["channels"][channel_discord_id]["server"]
❶   server = Server.query.filter_by(
            name=data["meta"]["servers"][server_id]["name"]
        ).first()

        try:
            channel = Channel(server, channel_discord_id, name)
            db.session.add(channel)
            db.session.commit()
            print("+", end="", flush=True)
        except sqlalchemy.exc.IntegrityError:
            db.session.rollback()
            print(".", end="", flush=True)
    print("")
```

*Listing 14-10: Code from* admin.py *to add channels to the database*

This code is also similar to Listings 14-8 and 14-9. This time however, it looped through the keys of the data["meta"]["channels"] dictionary, storing each key as channel_discord_id.

Listing 14-2 showed this JSON object of channels from *VibrantDiversity .json*, which you can revisit to remind yourself what this dictionary looks like. For each channel, the code in Listing 14-8 stored the name of the channel in name and that channel's server index in server_id. It then queried the SQL database itself to get the server row in Listing 14-10 ❶, which should have been added earlier by the code in Listing 14-9, and stored this value in server. The SQL query that the Server.query.filter_by() function call ran was similar to SELECT * FROM servers WHERE name='*name*';, where *name* is the server name.

In the try block, the code then created a new Channel object, this time telling it the server, the channel's Discord ID, and the channel name. As with the previous listings, it tried adding this channel to the database, displaying a plus sign on success and a dot if the channel already existed.

Finally, after adding servers, users, and channels, the code added all of the messages, as shown in Listing 14-11.

```
for channel_discord_id in data["data"]:
    # Get the channel
    channel = Channel.query.filter_by(discord_id=channel_discord_id).one() ❶

    # Loop through each message in this channel
    print(f"Adding messages from {channel.server.name}, #{channel.name}: ", end="", flush=True)
    for message_discord_id in data["data"][channel_discord_id]:
        try:
            timestamp = data["data"][channel_discord_id][message_discord_id]["t"]
            message = data["data"][channel_discord_id][message_discord_id]["m"]

            user_index = data["data"][channel_discord_id][message_discord_id]["u"]
            user_discord_id = data["meta"]["userindex"][user_index]
            user = User.query.filter_by(discord_id=user_discord_id).first() ❷
```

```
        if "a" in data["data"][channel_discord_id][message_discord_id]:
            attachments_json = json.dumps(
                data["data"][channel_discord_id][message_discord_id]["a"]
            )
        else:
            attachments_json = None

        message = Message(
            channel.server,
            message_discord_id,
            timestamp,
            message,
            user,
            channel,
            attachments_json,
        )
        db.session.add(message)
        db.session.commit()
        print("+", end="", flush=True)
    except sqlalchemy.exc.IntegrityError:
        db.session.rollback()
        print(".", end="", flush=True)
print("")
```

*Listing 14-11: Code from* admin.py *to add messages to the database*

This time, this code looped through all of the keys of the data["data"]
dictionary. As you learned in Listing 14-5, this dictionary's keys are the
Discord IDs of channels. My code stored each ID in the variable channel
_discord_id. I then used SQLAlchemy to query the database to load this
actual channel row ❶ (the SQL query that this command ran was similar
to SELECT * FROM channel WHERE channel_discord_id=*channel_discord_id*, where
*channel_discord_id* is the channel ID). After learning what channel it was
dealing with, the code then looped through all of that channel's messages to add them to the database, storing each message's Discord ID as
message_discord_id.

The rest of the code in Listing 14-11 is also similar to Listings 14-8
through 14-10. In the try block, for each message, the code stored the timestamp and message in the timestamp and message variables. It then looked
up the user Discord ID from the metadata and queried the SQL database
for the User object ❷, and, if the message included an attachment, it also
created a string called attachments_json. Finally, it created a Message object
and inserted this message into the database. As before, the code displayed
a plus sign if it successfully inserted a message or a dot if that message was
already in the database.

Since exception handling ensured *admin.py* wouldn't import duplicate
rows, I could use this script to import newer versions of JSON files from
the same Discord server. For example, if Unicorn Riot's infiltrator used
Discord History Tracker to save another offline copy of everything in Vibrant
Diversity a month later, and I imported that new JSON file, it would import
only the new messages.

Once this code was written, I used it to import all of the JSON Discord files that I had received from Unicorn Riot. To import data from the Vibrant Diversity channel, I would run this command:

```
python3 admin.py import-json ~/datasets/Discord-JSON-Scrapes/VibrantDiversity.json
```

And here is the output:

```
Adding servers: +
Adding users: +++++++++++++++++++++++++++++++++++++++++++++++++++++++++++++++++++++++++++++++++++++
++++++++++++++++++++++++++++++++++++++++++++++++++++++++++++++++++++++++++++++++++++++++++++++++++
--snip--
Adding channels: +++++++++
Adding messages from Vibrant Diversity, #rules: +++++++++++++++++
Adding messages from Vibrant Diversity, #general: +++++++++++++++++++++++++++++++++++++++++++++++
++++++++++++++++++++++++++++++++++++++++++++++++++++++++++++++++++++++++++++++++++++++++++++++++++
--snip--
Adding messages from Vibrant Diversity, #recruiting: +++++++++++++++++++++++++++++++++++++++++++
+++++++++
Import complete
```

Each plus sign in this output represents a different row of data inserted into the database. The *VibrantDiversity.json* file added 1 server, 530 users, 9 channels, and a total of 255,349 messages, importing a message at a time.

I then used *admin.py* to import the rest of the Discord JSON files I had, including chat logs from Anticom, 4th Reich, Ethnoserver, and other leaked servers. For example, next I imported one of the smaller servers called Pony Power, which I'll discuss further later in this chapter, like so:

```
python3 admin.py import-json ~/datasets/Discord-JSON-Scrapes/PonyPowerComplete-Sept5at155PM.txt
```

And here is the output from that command (in this case, I'd already imported the Vibrant Diversity data, and these two Discord channels had some overlapping users, so my script skipped importing some of the users):

```
Importing: /Users/micah/datasets/Discord-JSON-Scrapes/PonyPowerComplete-Sept5at155PM.txt
Adding servers: +
Adding users: .++++..+++++.+++++..++++.++.+++++++++++..+.+......
Adding channels: ++++
Adding messages from Pony Power, #general-chat: ++++++++++++++++++++++++++++++++++++++++++++++++
++++++++++++++++++++++++++++++++++++++++++++++++++++++++++++++++++++++++++++++++++++++++++++++++++
++++++++++++++++++++++++++++++++++++++++++++++++++++++++++++++++++++++++++++++++++++++++++++++++++
++++++++++++++++++++++++++++++++++++++++++++++++++++++++++++++++
--snip--
```

This JSON file included 50 users. The code skipped 17 of them (displaying dots instead of plus signs) because they were already in the database from Vibrant Diversity, and it added 33 new users.

My database was now full of neo-Nazi chat logs, preparing me to build a web interface to explore them. When you're building a web app to investigate data, you need some data to explore to make sure your app is actually working as intended. If I hadn't imported the actual data first, I would have had to make up and import some test data so I'd have something to troubleshoot with while building the web app. But I decided to import the real data first because I knew I'd need to write that code eventually anyway.

### Building the Web Interface

When you build web apps, it's often useful to split your web pages into reusable components, like headers, footers, and sidebars. Individual pages may have their own reusable components, too. For example, the page that lists chat messages might repeat the same message component for each message on the page. You define these components in *templates*, HTML files that can contain variables and logic, like if statements or for loops. You can render a template (convert it into HTML) by passing the template file along with variables into a *templating engine*, or code that converts a template into HTML.

Flask comes with a popular templating engine called Jinja. To build the web interface to explore the chat logs I'd just imported, I started by creating the layout template in Jinja. In short, I wrote the HTML code that would make up the layout of all of the pages in my web app, but also included Python variables and loops. Listing 14-12 shows the code for *layout .html*, my layout template.

```
<!doctype html>
<html>

<head>
  <title>Discord Analysis</title>
  <link rel=stylesheet type=text/css href="{{ url_for('static', filename='style.css') }}"> ❶
</head>

<body>
  <div class="wrapper">
    <div class="sidebar">
      {% for server in servers %} ❷
      <div class="server">
        <p><strong>{{ server.name }}</strong></p>
        <ul>
          {% for c in server.channels %} ❸
          <li{% if channel %}{% if c.id==channel.id %} class="active" {% endif %}{% endif %}><a
              href="{{ c.permalink() }}">#{{ c.name }}</a> <span class="message-count">[{{
              "{0:,}".format(c.message_count() | int) }}]</span></li>
          {% endfor %}
        </ul>
      </div>
      {% endfor %}
```

```
        <p><a href="/users">Users</a></p>
    </div>

    <div class="content">
      <div class="search">
        <form method="get" action="/search">
          <input type="text" name="q" class="q" placeholder="Search query" {% if q %}
            value="{{q}}" {% endif %} /> ❹
          <select name="s">
            <option value="">[all servers]</option>
            {% for server in servers %} ❺
            <option value="{{ server.id }}" {% if server.id==s %} selected="selected" {% endif
              %}>
              {{ server.name }}
            </option>
            {% endfor %}
          </select>
          <input type="submit" value="Search" />
        </form>
      </div>

      <div class="messages">
       {% for message in get_flashed_messages() %} ❻
       <div class=flash>{{ message }}</div>
       {% endfor %}
      </div>

      {% block content %}{% endblock %} ❼
    </div>
  </div>
</body>

</html>
```

*Listing 14-12: The* layout.html *layout template*

The code in Listing 14-12 looks like HTML at a glance, but if you look closely you'll see that it's actually a Jinja template. For example, look at the code that adds the *CSS (Cascading Style Sheets)* file—which defines the page's style—to the page ❶. The HTML syntax for adding a stylesheet is

```
<link rel=stylesheet type=text/css href="style.css">
```

where *style.css* is the path or URL of a CSS file. Instead of an actual filename, the code in Listing 14-12 uses this:

```
{{ url_for('static', filename='style.css') }}
```

In a Jinja template, putting a Python expression between {{ and }} means Python will evaluate this expression when the template is rendered. In this case, Listing 14-12 rendered that line as <link rel=stylesheet type=text/css href="/static/style.css"> because the url_for() function, which is part of Flask, returned the /static/style.css string.

The template in Listing 14-12 also included some for loops. In Jinja, you start a for loop with the code {% for *item* in *list* %} and end it with {% endfor %}. In the left sidebar of the layout, the template listed all of the Discord servers in the databases ❷, looping through the items in the servers list one at a time. (For this template to render properly, I'd need to make sure to pass servers into the template as a variable when I render it in the Flask code.) For each server, after displaying the server name, it looped through all of the channels in that server ❸, getting the list of channels from server.channels. For each channel, the code displayed a link to view messages in that channel followed by the number of messages it contains.

The template also included a search bar at the top of the page ❹, as well as a drop-down menu with options to search a specific server or to search them all ❺. It also included a list of notification messages ❻ I could use if I wanted to display an error message—for example, if I tried loading a link to view messages in a channel that didn't exist in the database. Finally, the template displayed the content block for that particular page ❼. While all pages shared this template, the content block differed for each page.

After starting on my templates, I wrote code for a handful of *routes*, which let the web app know which page the user's web browser was trying to view. In web development, you can think of a route as a path for a web page, except it can include placeholders. For example, if the web app is hosted at *http://localhost:5000*, and the Python code defines the route /search for the search page, users can view that route with the URL *http://localhost:5000/ search*.

The home page route (/), shown in Listing 14-13, was by far the simplest one in my web app. This page displayed the message "This is a web app that will let you research the alt-right chatroom leak, published by Unicorn Riot."

```
@app.route("/")
def index():
    servers = Server.query.all()
    return render_template("index.html", servers=servers)
```

*Listing 14-13: The home page route (/)*

In Flask, each route is a function that returns the HTML for that web page. The index() function starts with the @app.route("/") decorator, which is how Flask knows that the / route should call this function. This function first runs a SQL query to get all of the servers in the database, stored in the variable servers. It then calls the render_template() function, rendering the *index.html* template, passing the servers variable into the template, and returning the HTML it receives.

Listing 14-14 shows the code for the *index.html* Jinja template that was rendered.

```
{% extends "layout.html" %}
{% block content %}
<h2>Alt-right chatroom research</h2>
<p>This is a web app that will let you research the alt-right chatroom leak,
    published by Unicorn Riot.</p>
<p>Click on channel names to browse them. Search for keywords. Viewing
    individual messages will show you the whole conversation from an hour
    before and after that message.</p>
{% endblock %}
```

*Listing 14-14: The* index.html *template*

The first line of code in this template means that Jinja should render the *layout.html* template but replace {% block content %}{% endblock %} with the content block defined here—some text that says, "Alt-right chatroom research" and a brief description of the web app. Also notice that in Listing 14-13, I passed the servers variable into the template; the *layout.html* template in Listing 14-11 used this variable to make the list of servers in the sidebar.

Figure 14-3 shows what the app's home page looked like at this point, with the home page text as defined in *index.html* and with the servers on the left and the search bar at the top as defined in *layout.html*.

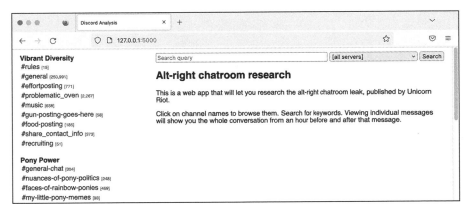

*Figure 14-3: The home page of my Discord Analysis web app*

Let's look at one more route that does a bit more than the / route, the /search route, which will help explain how one of the web app's core features—searching the chat logs—works. Here's the Python code:

```
@app.route("/search")
def search():
    q = request.args.get("q")
    s = request.args.get("s", 0)
    if s == "":
        s = 0
    page, per_page = get_pagination_args()
```

```
server = Server.query.filter_by(id=s).first()

messages = Message.query
if server:
    messages = messages.filter_by(server=server)
pagination = (
    messages.filter(Message.message.like(f"%{q}%"))
    .order_by(Message.timestamp)
    .paginate(page=page, per_page=per_page)
)

if server:
    description = f"Search {server.name}: {q}"
else:
    description = f"Search: {q}"

servers = Server.query.all()
pagination_link = f"/search?q={q}&s={s}"
return render_template(
    "results.html",
    q=q,
    s=int(s),
    servers=servers,
    pagination=pagination,
    pagination_link=pagination_link,
    description=description,
)
```

The search() function starts with the decorator @app.route("/search"), so
Flask knows that the /search route should call this function. At the beginning of the function, I defined the q, s, page, and per_page variables as the
values from the URL's query string. For example, if the URL ends in
*/search?q=berkeley*, then this code would set the value of q to the berkeley.

I got this query string information from the Flask variable request.args,
which is a dictionary containing all of the values after the ? in the URL.
The code got the value of the q key in this dictionary by evaluating request
.args.get("q"), but request.args["q"] would work just the same. When using
the .get() method on dictionaries, you can choose default values, as I did
in the following line. The expression request.args.get("s", 0) looks through
request.args for the key s and returns it if it finds it. If the expression doesn't
find s, it returns 0.

On the search page, q is the search query and s is the ID of the server
to search (if s is 0, this means I want to search all servers). The page and
per_page variables are used for *pagination*, which determines how an app
displays a limited number of results per page. The page variable is the page
number, and per_page is the number of results per page.

Since three of the routes in my app used pagination (/search, /channel,
and /user), I wrote the code to find the page and per_page query strings in
the function get_pagination_args(), which allowed me to just call that function instead of repeating the same code in multiple places.

I then queried the SQL database for the server with the ID stored in s, saving the result as server. The server variable is used to optionally search a single Discord server, rather than all of them. If the SQL database doesn't have any servers with that ID, then server is set to None, which means the app should search all servers. I then started building the SQL query to search for all of the messages, storing the results in the variable messages. If this search was limited to a specific server (that is, if there's a value for s), the code modified messages to filter just by messages from that server. Finally, I used the SQLAlchemy pagination feature to run the SQL query, making sure to select the correct page of results, storing the search results in the variable pagination. Part of the SQLAlchemy query included Message.message .like(f"%{q}%") to ultimately run a SQL query that used SQL's LIKE operator, which did a case-insensitive search for any messages containing the string q, as described in Chapter 12.

In the following if statement, my code defined the description variable as a description of the search, showing either just the search query or both it and the name of the server being searched. It then loaded all of the servers with servers = Server.query.all(), which the *layout.html* layout template needs to render the sidebar. Finally, the code rendered the *results.html* Jinja template, passing in all of the appropriate variables, resulting in the search results page.

In addition to the home page route (/) and the search route (/search), I created these other routes for my web app:

**/view/*message_id*** The hyperlink to a specific Discord message

**/channel/*channel_id*** The hyperlink to a specific channel in a Discord server

**/users** A page that listed all Discord users in the database, along with how many messages each has posted

**/users/*user_id*** A page that listed the messages that each Discord user has posted, spanned across all servers and channels that they posted in

As you can see in Figure 14-3, the Discord servers that I imported while developing the app are all listed in the left sidebar, along with each server's channels. To start my research, I could search for keywords (using the /search route), or I could click a channel name on the left and read its chat logs (using the /channel/*channel_id* route).

You can view the code for all of these routes in *app.py* at *https://github .com/micahflee/hacks-leaks-and-revelations/blob/main/chapter-14/discord-analysis/ app.py*.

Now that you know how the Discord Analysis web app works, let's look at how I went about using it to analyze the Discord leaks.

## Using Discord Analysis to Find Revelations

After I had built enough of the Discord Analysis web app that I could start using it for actual research, I started by reading a cross section of all of the Discord leaks I had imported and taking notes on what might make good articles—all the while fixing bugs as I discovered them, and adding features as I felt I needed them. I went one Discord server at a time, trying to understand the gist of what was discussed in each channel. I searched for terms like *WikiLeaks* to see what the fascists were saying about it, since it had recently played a role in Trump's 2016 election victory. I stumbled upon various conversations about digital security advice and which encrypted messaging apps to trust, all of it mixed up with numerous conspiracy theories, racist diatribes, and selfies of people holding guns.

Here's how the process of using Discord Analysis on my computer actually worked. When I wanted to run my web app to test it during development or to start researching neo-Nazi chats, I'd run `python3 app.py`. It showed this output, which is the typical output you see every time you start a Flask web app:

```
 * Serving Flask app 'app'
 * Debug mode: on
WARNING: This is a development server. Do not use it in a production
deployment. Use a production WSGI server instead.
 * Running on http://127.0.0.1:5000
Press CTRL+C to quit
 * Restarting with stat
 * Debugger is active!
 * Debugger PIN: 654-228-939
```

The output said that the Flask web server started and was running at the URL *http://127.0.0.1:5000*. The web server continued to run until I was ready to quit it by pressing CTRL-C. I loaded that URL in my web browser to view the web app. As I made web requests, my terminal output showed me web service logs. For example, when I loaded the home page, my app produced these logs:

```
127.0.0.1 - - [14/Jan/2023 11:58:30] "GET / HTTP/1.1" 200 -
127.0.0.1 - - [14/Jan/2023 11:58:30] "GET /static/style.css HTTP/1.1" 200 -
127.0.0.1 - - [14/Jan/2023 11:58:30] "GET /favicon.ico HTTP/1.1" 404 -
```

The left column is the IP address (`127.0.0.1`) of the web browser that loaded each route; in this case, I loaded routes from my own computer. It also shows the timestamp the route was loaded, which route was loaded, and other information. The first route that I loaded was the home page (you can tell because the first log line says `GET /`), and it responded with the HTTP code `200`, which means it loaded successfully. Immediately after that, my browser loaded the CSS stylesheet at `/static/style.css`, which successfully loaded too, and tried to load the favicon (the icon in the corner of a web browser tab) at `/favicon.ico`. However, the server replied with the HTTP code `404`, "File not found," because I hadn't bothered creating a favicon for my app.

At the top of each page in the web app was a search bar, next to which was the drop-down menu that let me choose to search all servers or just one. For example, I tried searching all Discord servers from which I had imported data for the string berkeley. Back in my terminal, I could see that my browser had loaded the /search?q=berkeley&s= route:

```
127.0.0.1 - - [14/Jan/2023 11:58:57] "GET /search?q=berkeley&s= HTTP/1.1" 200 -
127.0.0.1 - - [14/Jan/2023 11:58:57] "GET /static/style.css HTTP/1.1" 304 -
```

The search page loaded the CSS stylesheet at /static/style.css as well, but this time it returned with the HTTP code 304, which means that the stylesheet hadn't been modified since the last time my browser made that request.

Figure 14-4 shows the Discord Analysis web app showing these search results. You can see that the page has the URL *http://127.0.0.1:5000/search?q=berkeley&s=* and lists search results from all servers for the string berkeley.

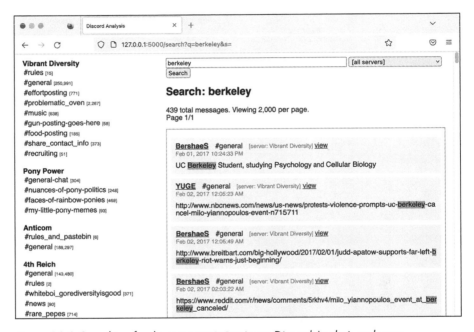

*Figure 14-4: Searching for the string* berkeley *in my Discord Analysis web app*

My search found 417 messages that contained the string berkeley, along with information on who posted each message, in what channel, in what server, at what time, and the content of the message, with the search term itself highlighted. If I clicked on the user's name, which linked to the /users/*user_id* route, I'd see all of the posts from that user, including those on multiple Discord servers.

Each message also had a view link, which led to the /view/*message_id* route and pulled up a page displaying that individual message. This allowed me to store links to individual messages in my notes. When I clicked on a view link I'd saved, the web app would show me not only that message but also the 20 messages before and after it, so I could easily see the rest of the conversation.

The app also allowed me to explore the leaked chats by manually reading through each channel. I could select individual channels by clicking the links in the left sidebar. For example, Figure 14-5 shows the #general channel in the Pony Power server. In this case, the URL was *http://127.0.0 .1:5000/channel/10*, meaning the *channel_id* in the /channel/*channel_id* route was 10. The ID field in the Channel table auto-increments, so the first row starts at 1, then 2, then 3, and so on. I imported the Vibrant Diversity JSON file first, which created channels with IDs 1 through 9, then imported the Pony Power JSON file, which created channels with IDs 10 through 13.

Figure 14-5: Viewing chat logs for the #general-chat channel in the Pony Power server in my Discord Analysis web app

With this case study as inspiration, I hope that you'll feel confident building similar custom apps for your future investigations when you get your hands on large structured datasets like these.

After spending a few days splitting my time between writing code and reading some of the worst stuff on the internet, I ultimately decided to write about Pony Power, a server set up for the sole purpose of harassing and doxing people.

## The Pony Power Discord Server

Pony Power was one of the smaller servers, with only 50 users and just over 1,000 messages posted over the course of just 10 days. More than any other server, it was full of PII for perceived members of antifa. I decided to focus my reporting on this server because this harassment campaign was clearly newsworthy, and because the server was small enough that I could read through all of the messages and write about the highlights. As a single reporter, it would have taken me considerably longer to do the same for larger servers, like Vibrant Diversity.

In the Pony Power chat logs, I found private data from over 50 people from 14 states across the country, from California to Florida. The information often included users' photographs, social media profiles, home addresses, phone numbers, email addresses, dates of birth, driver's license numbers, vehicle information, places of employment, and in one instance, a Social Security number. As I read through the Pony Power chat logs, from the beginning to the end, I built up a spreadsheet listing each person who was doxed to help me keep track of them, as well as Discord Analysis links to the messages where the doxing happened. The server's #faces-of -rainbow-ponies channel contained nearly all of the PII.

The Pony Power fascists weren't very selective about their targets. Anyone they considered to be a member of antifa or an antifa sympathizer was fair game, as were journalists they disagreed with, professors from liberal universities, or anyone who spoke out against racism.

Eight times in 2017, fascists traveled to Berkeley to hold protests. They came prepared with racist and antisemitic signs and armed with weapons for street fighting. One of these protests, a Say No to Marxism rally, was scheduled for late August. In response, antifascists began preparing a counterprotest. "So who is going to be there to stand up against Antifa? This is a good chance to dox them so we can have an idea who they are," one of the Pony Power members posted in the chat. "We should go onto their [Facebook] page if they have an active one and dox all the ones who plan on being there and who liked the post."

Another Pony Power user posted a link to a website for "white people striving to be allies in the fight for Black Liberation" and said, "These white allies need doxing." Another wanted to dox members of the Democratic Socialists of America and the Southern Poverty Law Center. Some members of the group disagreed about the strategy of doxing everyone they didn't like, though. "Fuck these random ass people to be honest," another user posted. "We need to dox journalists and leadership of activist groups." A person going by the name *Klaus Albricht* suggested, "It's time we start mapping out the liberal teachers of universities."

*Albricht* decided to dox a 22-year-old college student because her Facebook cover photo showed her wearing a shirt reading "Punch more Nazis," a reference to Richard Spencer, a white supremacist best known for the viral video in which he is punched in the face while being interviewed. *Albricht* outlined a plan to trick her into clicking a malicious link so he could learn her IP address. He also said that he would dox people who liked her shirt. Less than 20 minutes later, he posted her home address, what she was studying at college, and links to all her social media accounts.

While writing my story, I reached out to the woman who was doxed. She told me, "I never clicked the link because it seemed hella sketch." She also said that she hadn't gone out to protest fascists and that she was annoyed that they had doxed her just because she hurt their feelings. She was "terrified" that they had her address because "it's not just myself who's at risk, but now also my parents who live here as well."

In the 10 days' worth of Pony Power chat logs I had at my disposal, I also found the fascists doxing Emily Gorcenski, an antifascist data scientist from Charlottesville who had witnessed Fields's car plow into protesters. She's a trans woman, and the fascists posted her deadname (the name she went by before she transitioned) and her home address. She has since moved to Germany.

Fascists also doxed 10 alleged members of an antifa group from Gainesville, Florida. A user who went by the name *adolphus (not hitler)* posted, "I lost my job because of these [homophobic slur]s," later posting again that he lost his job because he attended the Unite the Right rally in Charlottesville, so "I've got some scores to settle with my local antifa." I searched the internet for terms like *Gainesville Charlottesville fired* and quickly found news articles about a Gainesville man who was fired from his job after marching in Charlottesville with neo-Nazis. He was a member of the pro-slavery hate group League of the South, and he had gotten arrested in Charlottesville for carrying a concealed handgun. I tracked down a court document related to his arrest and found one that included his phone number. Because I decided to name him in the article, I called him to give him a chance to provide his side of the story, per the journalistic practices described in Chapter 1. To keep my actual phone number private from him and the League of the South, I used a new virtual phone number I had created just for this purpose (today, I have a public phone number that I use solely for communicating with sources like this). I left messages, but he never responded.

---

### MENTAL HEALTH AND EXTREMISM RESEARCH

While building Discord Analysis and developing a story based on the chat logs from my Unicorn Riot contact, I spent several hours a day for two weeks reading racist, antisemitic, misogynistic, and outright genocidal rants by neo-Nazis speaking to one another online. Among these, one message in particular stuck out to me. It was written by a man, probably in his 50s, well past midnight, and it was a rant about the Jews who he believed were secretly controlling the media and the banks. It was clear to me that he was expressing deeply held beliefs rather than just trying to post something edgy, like a lot of the younger fascists seemed to be doing. While writing this chapter, I searched my Discord Analysis app for the term *jew* to see if I could find that specific message, but it came back with over 11,000 results, all of them full of hate. I decided it wasn't worth tracking it down after all.

I knew about antisemitism, of course. I'd experienced antisemitic microaggressions myself. But reading through these neo-Nazi chat logs was the first time that I realized how many people—including thousands of Americans, many of whom lived in my city—really wished that we were all dead.

After reading through a massive amount of this content, I had many ideas for articles I wanted to write, but I ended up writing only a single one, about the Pony Power server. After publishing the first article, I didn't want to spend more time reading these chats. I found it much better for my mental health to instead focus on writing code to improve my Discord search tool so that others could do the research. As I describe in the following section, this code eventually became a collaboration with Unicorn Riot called DiscordLeaks.

Reading through chat logs like this is an experience that no one should have to go through. But unfortunately, it's necessary for extremism researchers. If you're doing this sort of work, make sure to prioritize your own mental health. Take breaks and find people to talk to about the terrible things you're seeing so you don't keep it all inside. However you go about it, it's important to have a plan for making this work sustainable, because it will definitely affect you.

Pony Power members also went after Michael Novick, at the time a 70-year-old retired teacher from Los Angeles who had been an antifascist activist for over 50 years. In the late 1980s, Novick helped found a group called Anti-Racist Action, and he's been dealing with threats from neo-Nazis ever since. Because Novick's name appeared on antiracist websites, Pony Power users decided that he must be an antifa leader. "Michael is behind what we know as the power structure," *Albricht* posted. The Pony Power users then hit what they believed to be a gold mine: they discovered a video of Novick speaking at the 2011 Los Angeles Housing & Hunger Crisis Conference in which he said, "I'm of Jewish descent." "HE ADMITS HE IS JEWISH! I KNEW IT!" *Albricht* exclaimed. "We have our link. Antifa is a Jewish organization!" He added, "Now let's tear these [antisemitic slur]s apart!" and began inventing an antifa organization chart that placed Novick on top. "This man we know for a fact is the leader of Antifa. [. . .] All other branches report to him."

Novick told me it's no secret that he's Jewish. "My father came to the US in the early '30s as a teenager from Poland, and most of his family (many aunts, uncles, and cousins) were wiped out by the Nazis either in Bialystok during a ghetto rebellion or in the camps," he said. He also told me that there's no antifa "command structure" or "organization chart." He added, "Some antifa are Jewish. Hardly surprising, given the level of antisemitism displayed by the fascists and neo-Nazis."

According to a story by Unicorn Riot reporter Chris Schiano, the Pony Power server was started by Dan Kleve. At the time, Kleve was a biochemistry major at the University of Nebraska–Lincoln and a member of the neo-Nazi group Vanguard America. After Klein was outed as one of the fascists who marched in Charlottesville, people began calling the head of his department to demand that he be expelled. Schiano wrote that Kleve created the Pony Power server, in apparent retaliation against those demanding his expulsion, "to seek revenge by maliciously publishing the personal information of alleged antifascists and encouraging others to harass them and bring them harm."

You can read my full reporting on the Pony Power Discord chat logs at *https://theintercept.com/2017/09/06/how-right-wing-extremists-stalk-dox-and-harass-their-enemies/*.

## The Launch of DiscordLeaks

After publishing my Pony Power article, I was sure that there were many more revelations spread throughout the hundreds of thousands of messages in the leaked chat logs, but I decided I needed a break from Nazis. I wanted to make it possible for others to analyze the rest of the Discord servers, though, and I knew from my own experience with these datasets that there were technical challenges to analyzing them, which is why I developed Discord Analysis to begin with. I spoke with the journalists from Unicorn Riot and showed them the Discord Analysis web app I had used to write my article. We decided that Unicorn Riot would run a public version of this app for researchers, journalists, and members of the public to use. This is how DiscordLeaks was born.

DiscordLeaks (*https://discordleaks.unicornriot.ninja*) is a searchable public database designed to make it easy for anyone to access the massive corpus of fascist chat logs from hundreds of Discord servers infiltrated by antifascists. I and a small team of anonymous developers worked in our spare time to add new features to the app and handle the scaling issues that come with hosting a public website that gets lots of traffic. We kept the modified source code for DiscordLeaks private, but it's based on the Discord Analysis source code that I just described. By late 2017, DiscordLeaks was live, and by early 2018 it was full of chat logs from several Discord servers uploaded by Unicorn Riot journalists, including the one used to organize Unite the Right. The only redactions to the chat logs on DiscordLeaks are the PII for victims of doxing and harassment by far-right extremists; the rest of the data is fully public.

Over the years, Unicorn Riot has obtained a steady stream of leaked Discord chat logs from fascist groups and continued to index them into DiscordLeaks. I eventually stopped contributing to the project myself. In the time I've been away, it's matured: the infrastructure is now running in Docker containers, and the speed of search has greatly improved thanks to the addition of an Elasticsearch database (both technologies were discussed in Chapter 5). Today, DiscordLeaks contains millions of messages from nearly 300 Discord servers used by the far right, available for the public to research. It also contains chat logs from RocketChat servers, which I discuss in the next section.

## The Aftermath

By 2019, I had stopped writing code for DiscordLeaks myself, but I still kept in touch with the developers and promoted the website. I was proud of my role in developing this important tool for extremism research, but at the time I still had no idea how much positive impact it would ultimately have.

In this section I'll discuss two major developments in the DiscordLeaks project since I wrote the initial code back in 2017. In 2021, survivors of the Charlottesville terrorist attack won a $25 million settlement against the organizers of Unite the Right in a lawsuit made possible, in part, by evidence published on DiscordLeaks. DiscordLeaks continues to be a vital tool for extremism researchers: in 2022, DiscordLeaks' anonymous developers updated it to include another major leak of neo-Nazi chat logs, this time from the group Patriot Front.

## The Lawsuit Against Unite the Right

In 1871, in response to the wave of racist terrorism against Black people that swept the South after the end of the Civil War, the US Congress passed the Ku Klux Klan Act. This law allows victims of racist violence to sue the perpetrators in civil court. If the victims can prove there was a conspiracy to deprive them of their civil rights, they can force the racists to pay monetary damages. This is exactly what nine survivors from Charlottesville did.

The plaintiffs in these cases were all Charlottesville residents, some of whom were severely injured that day—one suffered a fractured skull, another a broken leg and ankle. They filed the Sines v. Kessler lawsuit in October 2017 against 14 individuals and 10 organizations, with the goal of bankrupting the American fascist movement. The individual defendants included Jason Kessler, the primary organizer of Unite the Right; James Alex Fields Jr., the neo-Nazi terrorist serving a prison sentence for Heather Heyer's murder; Richard Spencer; and leaders of the fascist groups that organized Unite the Right. Defendants also included fascist groups themselves like Vanguard America, Traditionalist Worker Party, various branches of the Ku Klux Klan, and the National Socialist Movement.

The Charlottesville survivors' lawsuit was organized and funded by a legal nonprofit called Integrity First for America (IFA). The mission of the organization, founded in response to the violence of Unite the Right, was "defending democratic norms and ensuring equal rights for every American." Using over 5TB of evidence in the form of phone records, text messages, videos from Unite the Right, email messages, social media posts, and private messages and chat logs, the plaintiffs successfully made their case. IFA made all of the evidence used in the lawsuit available to the public at *https://www.integrityfirstforamerica.org/exhibits*.

On its blog, IFA explained that while its lawyers did eventually get copies of the neo-Nazi chat logs directly from Discord as part of the lawsuit's discovery process, DiscordLeaks provided "an immense amount" of detail before the lawsuit was filed. In the chat logs published by Unicorn Riot, Unite the Right attendees discussed whether they could hit protesters with cars and then claim self-defense, which is what happened. This evidence "provided crucial early information that made the speed and breadth of the initial complaint possible."

In November 2021, the court found the fascist organizers guilty and ordered them to pay over $25 million in damages. In late 2022, IFA wound down its operations.

## The Patriot Front Chat Logs

In the aftermath of the violent Unite the Right protests in Charlottesville, one of the neo-Nazi groups in attendance, Vanguard America, broke apart due to infighting. Out of the ashes of Vanguard America, a new fascist group called Patriot Front was born. Patriot Front, based out of Texas, is known for requiring members to do weekly "activism" involving vandalizing property with racist messages and posting Patriot Front propaganda, like stickers, all over the place. According to the Anti-Defamation League, Patriot Front was responsible for 82 percent of all reported incidents in 2021 involving the distribution of racist, antisemitic, and other hateful propaganda in the US.

In January 2022, someone hacked Patriot Front and leaked 400GB of data to Unicorn Riot, including thousands of messages posted to the group's internal RocketChat server, an open source chat platform that anyone can host themselves. Unicorn Riot collaborated with DDoSecrets to publish the 400GB Patriot Front dataset, which you can find at *https://ddosecrets.com/wiki/Patriot_Front*. In response to this leak, the DiscordLeaks developers also updated the app to include support for RocketChat, and they imported over 12,000 new messages into it from two Patriot Front chat servers. You can find Patriot Front's chat logs at *https://discordleaks.unicornriot.ninja/rocket-chat/*.

Figure 14-6 shows a still from a video in the Patriot Front dataset of members reading their manifesto and chanting "Life, liberty, victory!" The video includes a few seconds at the end where one of the neo-Nazis, apparently thinking the recording was over, yells, "Seig fucking Heil!"

*Figure 14-6: Patriot Front members, from a video in the hacked dataset*

Unfortunately, the American fascist movement has steadily grown since the election of Donald Trump in 2016. But there's a wealth of public datasets about this movement, just waiting for researchers like you to dig in and expose it.

## Summary

In this chapter, you've learned how antifascists infiltrated the Discord servers used by the American fascist movement, including organizers of the deadly Unite the Right rally in 2017, and leaked millions of chat logs to Unicorn Riot in JSON format. You saw how I went about analyzing these JSON files to understand their structure, how the custom Flask and SQLAlchemy web app I built worked under the hood, and how the app ultimately became DiscordLeaks. I also described my own investigation into the Pony Power server that fascists used to dox their enemies. Finally, you read about the amazing results from the Sines v. Kessler lawsuit and the continued success of DiscordLeaks tools.

# AFTERWORD

Since I started writing this book a year and a half ago, the feeling that I'm drowning in datasets has only increased. In a single recent week, I received 18GB of data from a police intelligence firm, another 100GB of data from a mass transit agency's police department, and a copy of the Transportation Security Agency's No Fly List. This is a fairly typical week, and, as usual, I haven't had a chance to look at any of them yet.

I'm so happy that you've finished reading this book, because now you can use your newfound skills to help investigate this never-ending flood of datasets. There aren't nearly enough of us with these skills, so I'm excited that you've joined the ranks. I hope you'll use your skills to discover and publish secret revelations and make a positive impact on the world while you're at it.

This book is crammed with technical information, but it's far from a comprehensive guide to investigating leaked and hacked datasets. I merely scratched the surface on a wide swath of technologies that come into play, like using the command line, programming in Python, using Docker containers, working with SQL databases, and analyzing structured data. There are countless books dedicated to each of these topics. But while there's a lot left to learn, you should now have a solid foundation to build on.

The best way to gain confidence in these skills, and to learn more, is to jump in headfirst and just start using them. Go to the DDoSecrets website, see what the collective has published recently, and subscribe to its newsletter so you'll get email alerts when new datasets are released. If you find a dataset that looks interesting and is available for anyone to download, launch your BitTorrent client, download it, and see if you can make sense of it. If you find a dataset released under limited distribution, meaning that DDoSecrets will give it only to journalists and researchers (like you!), request access. As long as you plan on publishing any revelations you find, you shouldn't have a problem gaining access.

Depending on the dataset you're looking at, you might hit technical hurdles that aren't covered in this book and that you don't know how to solve. I often come across data that I don't recognize and don't know how to proceed with. Most of the time, I end up searching the internet to figure out my next steps. Sometimes I even learn how to use new technologies that I have no prior experience with, like new types of databases or software, so I can import and explore the data. As your skills grow, you'll be able to do the same using online documentation and, most importantly, trial and error. Don't be afraid to experiment.

As you're exploring new datasets, automate as much of your work as possible by writing simple Python scripts like the ones sprinkled throughout this book. Regularly writing code is, by far, the best way to get better at programming. Also publish your interesting findings, even if they're minor. If you don't work for a newsroom, start a blog and publish your work there. The more investigations you publish, the more likely it is that potential sources will notice you, start up secure communications with you, and send you datasets to analyze. Be precise in your reporting and, as much as possible, show your work. Investigating leaked and hacked datasets is cool, and people will love to read about the details that you've discovered, how you discovered them, and how you verified that they're true.

Good luck! Get in touch at *micah@micahflee.com* to let me know if you find any revelations.

# SOLUTIONS TO COMMON WSL PROBLEMS

It's hard for me to imagine doing the kind of data analysis work I do without Linux. However, many Linux tools that I rely on every day simply don't exist in the Windows ecosystem. Using just Windows, you can't make your datasets searchable using Aleph, for example, or quickly spin up popular SQL servers to import leaked databases. Windows Subsystem for Linux (WSL) allows you to do these tasks and considerably more, including running command line tools, in Windows without needing to set up your own Linux VM.

WSL generally works well, but you may encounter a few issues, particularly related to disk performance, when you attempt to crunch data stored on Windows-formatted disks from your Linux terminal. Some tasks may take your computer hours or days to finish when they should take just minutes. This appendix teaches Windows users more about the quirks of the Linux filesystem, as well as various possible solutions to the disk performance problem. It's optional for Windows users, but if you do run into a situation where programs are taking considerably longer to run than I describe, this appendix should help you diagnose the problem and come up with a solution.

I recommend waiting to read this appendix until after you finish Chapter 3, where you'll install WSL, and Chapter 4, where you'll learn the command line code required to implement the performance solutions described here. You might need to reference this appendix in Chapter 5, while you're bind-mounting in Docker or indexing datasets in Aleph; in Chapter 11, while you're using Linux tools to extract over a million files; and in Chapter 12, while you're importing 20GB of data into a SQL database running in Docker.

## Understanding WSL's Linux Filesystem

Before solving any problems that you might encounter with WSL, you'll need to understand how and where WSL stores your Linux files. In this section, you'll learn how the WSL Linux filesystem works in Windows, how to access Linux files in Windows, and, conversely, how to access Windows files in Linux. I also outline some of the simpler problems you might encounter and how to solve them.

Your WSL Linux filesystem contains much more than just the data you store there. It includes a complete copy of the Ubuntu operating system, and when you install new programs using apt, it installs those into the Linux filesystem, too. Just as in a real Ubuntu system, / is the root folder, and it contains all of the usual default folders for Ubuntu systems. In your Ubuntu terminal, list the folder names in the root filesystem by running the **ls /** command. This should give you the following output:

```
bin dev home lib lib64 lost+found mnt proc run snap sys usr
boot etc init lib32 libx32 media opt root sbin srv tmp var
```

This output lists all of the folders inside the root folder in your Ubuntu system. Your home folder is in */home*. For example, since my Ubuntu username is *micah*, my Ubuntu home folder is */home/micah*. If you're using Windows 11 or newer, you should be able to browse your Linux files directly from File Explorer. When you're browsing your Linux files, you see *all* of the Linux files, not just the data in your home folder. If you're running a new enough version of Windows, change to your home folder (**cd ~**) and then run the command **explorer.exe .** to open your current working folder in Linux in Windows File Explorer.

**NOTE**     *If you ever need to run a Windows program in Linux (such as* explorer.exe*), run Linux programs in Windows, or otherwise do more advanced tasks in WSL, check out Microsoft's detailed documentation at* https://learn.microsoft.com/en-us/windows/wsl/filesystems.

For example, Figure A-1 shows a list of Linux files viewed in the Windows File Explorer app.

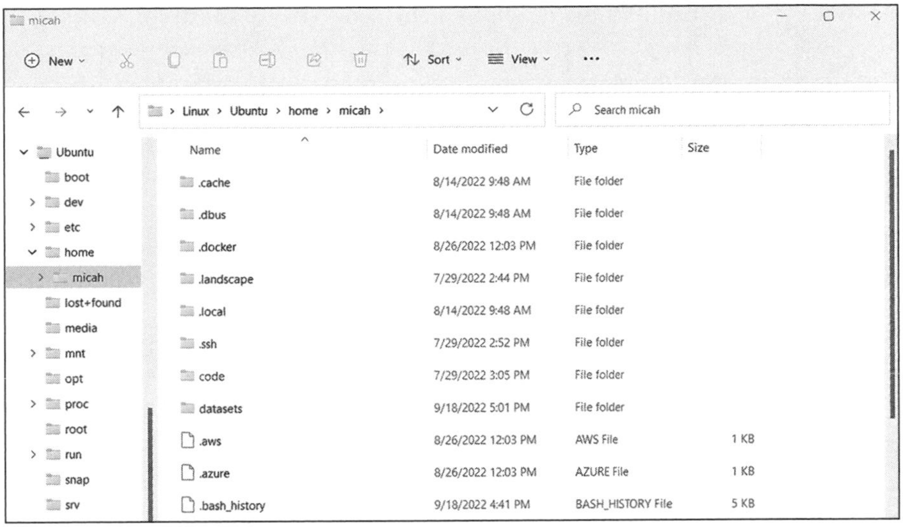

Figure A-1: Browsing Linux files in File Explorer in Windows

It's also helpful to understand the different behaviors of Windows and Linux filesystems. The Windows filesystem format is NTFS, and the most popular Linux filesystem format is ext4. Each Linux file has separate permissions for reading, writing, and executing, but files on NTFS systems don't have this metadata.

If you're accessing a Windows filesystem within Linux (when you access */mnt/c* in WSL, for example), Linux treats every file as having read, write, and execute permissions, and you can't change these permissions by default. This often isn't a problem, but it does mean that if you copy files from Linux to Windows, you'll lose their original permissions. If you want to be able to use file permissions, you'll need to work with files on a proper Linux filesystem instead.

Under the hood, the WSL Linux filesystem is stored in a single file in the *C:* drive in your user's home folder. On my Windows 11 computer, the filename is *C:\Users\micah\AppData\Local\Packages\CanonicalGroupLimited .UbuntuonWindows_79rhkp1fndgsc\LocalState\ext4.vhdx*. The path on your computer will be slightly different, but the file containing your Linux filesystem will still be called *ext4.vhdx*. The more data you store in your Linux filesystem, the bigger the *ext4.vhdx* file gets.

For example, suppose you want to save your datasets directly to your Linux filesystem in the folder *~/datasets*, rather than to a USB disk. Downloading the BlueLeaks dataset to that folder will cause your *ext4.vhdx* file to grow hundreds of gigabytes larger. Because your whole WSL Linux filesystem is stored on your *C:* drive, this means you only have as much disk space available in Linux as you have free space on that drive. In addition to the limits of free space on your *C:* drive, by default, your WSL Linux filesystem can only take up a maximum of 256GB.

If you want to store more data than this, you'll need to take additional steps to expand the size of your Linux filesystem. Find detailed instructions for doing this at *https://learn.microsoft.com/en-us/windows/wsl/vhd-size.*

Finally, you might come across a situation where you open an Ubuntu terminal, try to access a Windows-formatted USB disk in */mnt,* and find that it's just not there. This is because you need to have mounted your Windows USB disk (plugged it in and, if it's encrypted, entered your BitLocker password) *before* opening the Ubuntu shell. If you can't access a USB disk from Ubuntu at a path like */mnt/d* (assuming your USB disk is mounted to the *D:* drive), you'll need to restart WSL.

To do so, open PowerShell and run `wsl --shutdown`. This will close all open Ubuntu terminals and stop any running Docker containers. Afterward, open an Ubuntu terminal again, and you should be able to access that USB disk.

With the basics of WSL out of the way, let's discuss the primary problem you might encounter: disk performance.

## The Disk Performance Problem

Using Windows files in WSL, like the disks mounted in */mnt,* has major performance issues. Reading from and writing to disks takes considerably longer when you're working with files on a Windows disk than when you're working with them on WSL's Linux filesystem, like those in */home.* Some disk-intensive tasks, like extracting a compressed file that contains a million small files, might take several hours on a Windows disk, when the same task could be completed in seconds on a Linux disk. These performance issues can severely cut into your ability to get anything done.

For this reason, Microsoft recommends that you store data in the same operating system filesystem as the tools you plan to use. Using Linux tools like `find`, `grep`, and `unzip` (see Chapter 4) or making your data searchable using Aleph (see Chapter 5) will work best if you store your datasets in the Linux filesystem. Meanwhile, analyzing datasets with Windows software, such as 7-Zip, will work best if those datasets are stored in the Windows filesystem.

By far the simplest solution to the performance issue is to store all of your datasets in your Linux filesystem and use Linux tools to work with them. However, datasets are often too large to fit in the *C:* drive. For example, BlueLeaks alone takes up over half the disk space I have available on the laptop I'm using right now. This gives you no choice but to store the datasets on a USB disk like the *datasets* disk that you encrypted in Chapter 1. If you don't have enough space on your *C:* drive to work with all of the data that you'd like to, you'll need to implement one of the solutions I discuss in the following section.

You can sometimes work around disk performance problems by simply using native Windows programs rather than Linux programs to do your most disk-intensive tasks. Throughout this book, I suggest using native Windows tools when appropriate. For example, the Linux programs unzip and tar are used to extract compressed files. Extracting files saved on a Windows disk using these tools can be extremely slow if you're working from WSL. Instead, you can just use a Windows archive program like 7-Zip, as you did in Chapter 4 to unzip BlueLeaks. Since extracting compressed files with 7-Zip doesn't involve WSL at all, there's no disk performance problem.

Likewise, when you're running Python scripts, you can use the Windows version of Python (downloadable from *https://www.python.org*) rather than the Ubuntu version. This allows your Python scripts to crunch data from your Windows-formatted USB disk, bypassing the WSL performance problem, which is why Chapter 7 advises you to use PowerShell instead of WSL.

This technique can only take you so far, though. There aren't always native Windows alternatives. For instance, you can't run Docker containers, which are required for running software like Aleph, without WSL. For those cases, you're better off storing your data in a Linux filesystem using one of the following solutions.

## Solving the Disk Performance Problem

This section covers two potential solutions to the WSL disk performance problem: storing only datasets you're actively working with in your WSL Linux partition, or storing your entire WSL Linux partition on a USB disk with more disk space than your *C:* drive has available. I recommend the first, simpler option if you just want to be able to easily work through this book. The second option is a better long-term solution if you plan to routinely work with large datasets using Linux tools in Windows in the future.

### Storing Only Active Datasets in Linux

If you don't have enough free space for all your datasets on your *C:* drive, you can store just those you need for your current work in your Linux filesystem, keeping the rest on your USB disk. For example, you could copy the folders that you're actively working with into your Ubuntu home folder (that is, in *~/datasets*) and keep them there while you're conducting a specific investigation. When you no longer need to work with these files, copy them back to your external Windows disk and delete them from your home folder to clear up space.

### Storing Your Linux Filesystem on a USB Disk

Another option is to move your whole Ubuntu installation—that is, the *ext4 .vhdx* file that contains your Linux filesystem—to a USB disk with lots of free space. This way, if you store all your datasets in your Ubuntu home folder (in *~/datasets*), the data will physically be stored on your USB disk instead of on your internal *C:* drive.

With this solution, you won't be able to open an Ubuntu terminal unless your USB disk is plugged in and mounted, which is less convenient. If you try opening an Ubuntu terminal while your USB disk isn't mounted, you'll get the error message The system cannot find the path specified. However, I recommend using this method if you plan to investigate your own datasets in the future. Here's how to implement it.

Open a PowerShell terminal and create a new folder on your external USB disk to store your Linux filesystem by running the following command:

```
New-Item -Path D:\WSL -ItemType 'directory'
```

In PowerShell, the New-Item command creates a new file or folder. In this case, it's creating a new folder at *D:\WSL*. If you'd like to store your *ext4.vhdx* file somewhere else, you can change the path when you run this command.

WSL lets you install multiple Linux distributions (that is, versions of Linux) at the same time. In order to move one of them to your USB disk, you'll need to know its name. It's probably called Ubuntu, but you can check by running the wsl --list command:

```
PS C:\Users\micah> wsl --list
Windows Subsystem for Linux Distributions:
Ubuntu (Default)
docker-desktop-data
docker-desktop
```

This output lists each WSL distribution that you have installed. In my case, I have Ubuntu (my default distribution), as well as docker-desktop-data and docker-desktop, which are both used by Docker Desktop. If you've worked through Chapter 5 and installed Docker Desktop yourself, you should have these WSL distributions too.

The following steps show you how to move a WSL distribution from the *C:* drive to a USB disk. These instructions focus on the Ubuntu distribution, but if any other WSL distributions are taking up too much space on *C:* as well, you could follow the same steps to move them to a USB disk, making sure to change the distribution name when you run the commands. I don't recommend moving the Docker distributions, though, as this might cause issues with Docker Desktop working correctly.

Once you've confirmed the name of the distribution you'd like to move to your disk, export a copy of it with the following command, replacing *Ubuntu* with the appropriate name:

```
wsl --export Ubuntu D:\WSL\backup.tar
```

This should save a copy of all of the data from your chosen distribution into the file *D:\WSL\backup.tar*. Once this finishes, unregister the Ubuntu distribution on your *C:* drive from WSL by running this command:

```
wsl --unregister Ubuntu
```

This will remove the distribution from your computer and delete the Linux filesystem file *ext4.vhdx*. That's okay, because you just made a backup.

Next, import your backup, this time telling WSL that you want your data for this distribution to be in *D:\WSL*:

```
wsl --import Ubuntu D:\WSL D:\WSL\backup.tar
```

This command creates a new WSL distribution, in this case called Ubuntu. Now make that distribution into your default WSL distribution by running the following command:

```
wsl --set-default Ubuntu
```

When you later open a WSL terminal, it should now open a shell in the default distribution you just chose.

At this point, you've moved your Ubuntu filesystem from the *C:* drive to the *D:* drive (or whatever path you changed it to when you ran your own commands). The original *ext4.vhdx* file stored on *C:* should no longer exist, and you should have a new one in *D:\WSL\ext4.vhdx*.

Now that you've restored the temporary backup file, *D:\WSL\backup.tar*, you can delete it by running the following command in your PowerShell terminal:

```
Remove-Item -Path D:\WSL\backup.tar
```

Open a new Ubuntu terminal. It should work, with one problem: you'll automatically be logged in as the root user, while before you would automatically log in as an unprivileged user. To fix this, you'll create a file called */etc/wsl.conf*, using the nano text editor described in Chapter 4.

Run the following command to open nano:

```
nano /etc/wsl.conf
```

Enter the following two lines into the text editor file to set your default user, changing *micah* to whatever your username was before you moved *ext4 .vhdx* to a USB disk:

```
[user]
default=micah
```

Press CTRL-O, followed by ENTER, to save the file, and then press CTRL-X to exit. Back in your PowerShell terminal, shut down WSL by running this command:

```
wsl --shutdown
```

When you open a new Ubuntu terminal, you should now be logged in as your normal unprivileged user, rather than the root user.

Running your Linux filesystem off of a USB disk should now work, but your Linux filesystem is still limited to the default 256GB of data, even if your USB disk is bigger. The final step is to expand the size of your Linux filesystem so that it can take up as much space as you have available on your USB disk.

In PowerShell, shut down WSL by running:

```
wsl --shutdown
```

Next, open a Command Prompt shell as an administrator. (Since you need to open it as an administrator, it's simplest to just open Command Prompt directly instead of opening a Command Prompt tab in Windows Terminal.) Click **Start**, search for **command prompt**, right-click **Command Prompt**, and click **Run as Administrator**. In your administrator Command Prompt, open the Windows CLI program DiskPart by running the following:

```
diskpart
```

This program helps you manage your computer's drives and partitions. When you open it, it should drop you into an interactive shell similar to the Python shell. In DiskPart, you must first select the disk that you'd like to resize, in this case the *ext4.vhdx* file. Run this command, substituting the correct path to *ext4.vhdx* on your machine:

```
DISKPART> select vdisk file="D:\WSL\ext4.vhdx"

DiskPart successfully selected the virtual disk file.
```

You can then check the current size of your Linux filesystem by running this command:

```
DISKPART> detail vdisk

Device type ID: 0 (Unknown)
Vendor ID: {00000000-0000-0000-0000-000000000000} (Unknown)
State: Added
Virtual size:  256 GB
Physical size: 7664 MB
Filename: D:\WSL\ext4.vhdx
Is Child: No
Parent Filename:
Associated disk#: Not found.
```

The output of detail vdisk shows you information about the virtual disk that you're inspecting, including the total maximum size of your Linux filesystem in the Virtual size field, along with the actual disk space the Linux filesystem is currently using in the Physical size field.

Next, you'll resize your virtual disk to be larger than 256GB. First you need to determine how big you want it to be. If your USB disk is empty except for this *ext4.vhdx* file, then it's reasonable to select the size of the entire USB disk. You can find the total size of your USB disk by right-clicking your disk in File Explorer and clicking **Properties**. In the General tab, you'll see information about disk space usage, including the total capacity of the disk. You should avoid making your virtual disk larger than the total size of your USB disk; if you do, you might run out of disk space in your USB disk without WSL realizing it, leading to unpredictable Linux problems.

Once you determine how big you want your Linux partition to be, make sure you know that number in megabytes. For example, if you want its maximum size to be 1TB, then that would be 1,048,576MB. Check the "File Size Units and Conversions" box in Chapter 4 for information on how to calculate this. Now run the following command to resize it, replacing *1048576* with your chosen maximum size in megabytes:

```
DISKPART> expand vdisk maximum=1048576

  100 percent completed

DiskPart successfully expanded the virtual disk file.
```

Run **detail vdisk** again to confirm that the Virtual size field now shows the new maximum size you just set, then exit DiskPart by running the **exit** command:

```
DISKPART> exit

Leaving DiskPart...
```

Close the administrator Command Prompt.

You've now expanded the virtual disk size in *ext4.vhdx*, but you still need to expand the actual Linux partition on this disk. To do that, you need to determine the path to the virtual disk itself.

First, open an Ubuntu terminal and run the following command:

```
sudo mount -t devtmpfs none /dev
```

This command checks to be sure that */dev* is mounted in WSL. This is a special Linux folder containing files that each represent a piece of hardware attached to your computer, including hard drives. When I run this command, I get the following output:

```
[sudo] password for micah:
mount: /dev: none already mounted on /dev.
```

Since that command uses sudo, you'll first need to type your password to proceed. If you see the warning message mount: /dev: none already mounted on /dev you can safely ignore it; this means that */dev* was already mounted.

Run the following command:

```
mount | grep ext4
```

This command runs `mount`, which outputs all of the filesystems that are mounted in Linux, then pipes that output to grep to filter that down to just the ext4 filesystems. The output should show you the path to the virtual hard drive. For example, my output tells me the path to my hard drive is */dev/sdc*:

```
/dev/sdc on / type ext4 (rw,relatime,discard,errors=remount-ro,data=ordered)
```

Finally, resize your Linux partition to take up as much space as it can by running the following command, making sure to use the correct path to your virtual hard drive from the previous command:

```
sudo resize2fs /dev/sdc
```

When I run this, I get the following output:

```
resize2fs 1.45.5 (07-Jan-2020)
Filesystem at /dev/sdc is mounted on /; on-line resizing required
old_desc_blocks = 32, new_desc_blocks = 128
The filesystem on /dev/sdc is now 268435456 (4k) blocks long.
```

If all went well, you should see a message confirming that the partition has been resized and is now as large as the full virtual disk. You're done! You've expanded your Linux filesystem so that you can fit many more datasets on it.

## Next Steps

In my opinion, Microsoft made Windows a considerably more useful operating system by building WSL into it, particularly when you need to analyze hacked and leaked datasets. If you're going to use WSL on a regular basis, I recommend that you read through the official documentation at *https://learn.microsoft.com/en-us/windows/wsl/*. Those docs cover topics beyond the scope of this appendix, such as using WSL with VS Code, installing SQL database software directly in WSL instead of using it in Docker, running graphical Linux apps directly in Windows, and more.

In addition to using WSL, you may want to familiarize yourself with Linux in general by working through this book, trying out various Linux distributions by running them in VMs on your computer (see Chapter 1), and playing with Linux servers in the cloud (see Chapter 4).

# B

## SCRAPING THE WEB

Sometimes, in order to research important data publicly available online, you'll need to download a local copy. When websites don't provide this data in structured downloadable formats like spreadsheets, JSON files, or databases, you can make your own copy using *web scraping* (or *screen scraping*): writing code that loads web pages for you and extracts their contents. These might include social media posts, court documents, or any other online data. You can use web scraping to download either full datasets or the same web page again and again on a regular basis to see if its content changes over time.

For example, consider the Parler dataset discussed in Chapter 11. Before Parler was kicked offline by its hosting provider for refusing to moderate content that encourages and incites violence, the archivist @donk_enby wrote code to scrape all 32TB of videos—over a million of them—to distribute to researchers and journalists. This appendix teaches you how to do something similar, if the occasion arises.

I'll discuss legal considerations around web scraping and give a brief overview of HTTP, the protocol that web browsers use to communicate with websites. Finally, I describe three different techniques that allow you to scrape different types of websites. Complete Chapters 7, 8, 9, and 11 before following along, since you'll need the basic knowledge of Python programming, CSVs, HTML, and JSON covered there.

## Legal Considerations

Web scraping isn't a crime, but its legality is still murky. In general, using computer systems with permission (like visiting a public website) is perfectly fine, but accessing them without authorization (like logging in to someone else's account) is illegal hacking.

In the US, unauthorized access is a violation of the extremely outdated hacking law known as the Computer Fraud and Abuse Act of 1986, or CFAA. Web scraping shouldn't fall under unauthorized access because it entails writing code simply to load public web pages that everyone can already access, rather than loading those pages the normal way (using a web browser). The problem is that scraping may violate a website's terms of service, and there's no legal consensus on whether this could constitute a violation of the CFAA—courts have ruled both ways.

Despite this, web scraping is an extremely common practice. Search engines like Google are essentially massive web scraping operations, as are archive sites like the Internet Archive's Wayback Machine at *https://web .archive.org*. Companies often use web scraping to keep track of airline ticket prices, job listings, and other public data. It's also a critical tool for investigative reporting.

**NOTE** *The CFAA was originally passed, at least in part, in response to the 1983 film* WarGames. *In the film, a teenage hacker, played by Matthew Broderick, breaks into a military supercomputer and almost starts World War III by mistake. At the time, there weren't any laws against hacking computers. The wildly popular film scared Congress into passing such laws.*

The Markup, a nonprofit newsroom that investigates the tech industry, summed up the case for web scraping in an article that includes several examples of investigative journalism that relied on it. For example, the newsroom Reveal scraped content from extremist groups on Facebook, as well as law enforcement groups, and found significant overlap in membership. Reuters also scraped social media and message boards and uncovered an underground market for adopted kids; that investigation led to a kidnapping conviction. You can read the full article at *https://themarkup.org/news/2020/12/03/why-web-scraping-is-vital-to-democracy*.

Before you can start writing code to scrape the web yourself, you'll need to understand what HTTP requests are.

## HTTP Requests

When you load a web page, your web browser makes an *HTTP request*. You can think of this as the browser sending a message to the website's server, saying, "I'd like to download the content for the page at this URL so I can look at it on my computer," to which the server replies with an *HTTP response* that contains the content, typically HTML code. Your browser parses this HTML to figure out what else it needs to download to show you the full web page: images, fonts, Cascading Style Sheets (CSS) files that define how the web page looks, and JavaScript files that tell the website how to act. The browser makes another HTTP request for each of these resources, getting the content for them all. Websites also tend to make lots of HTTP requests while you're using them, such as to check for updates and display them on the page in real time.

HTTP requests and responses have *headers*, or metadata about the request or response. You might need to send specific headers for your scraping to work properly, depending on the website you're trying to scrape. You might also need your code to keep track of *cookies*, which are required for any site with a login option. There are many types of requests you can incorporate into your web scraping code, such as *POST* requests, which are used to submit forms. However, the code in this appendix will make only *GET* requests, the simplest and most common type of request, which download the content from a URL.

Many sites don't like web scrapers for a variety of reasons, including the fact that if a script is hammering a site with HTTP requests, this increases the site's bandwidth costs and could even cause it to crash. Sometimes sites will add roadblocks, such as limiting the number of requests you can make in a short amount of time or requiring that the user (or bot) fill out a CAPTCHA, in an effort to hinder or prevent scraping.

**NOTE** *Some time around 2002, when I was in high school, my friends and I decided to make a song lyrics website. Similar sites existed, but they were incomplete. I thought it would be simple to scrape the lyrics from those other sites and make a single site that had* all *of the lyrics. I wrote a script to scrape thousands of lyrics from one particular site, but my script crashed while it was running. I realized it was because the source website had gone down. A few days later, the site came back online with a message: the owner was overjoyed to learn how much traffic the site was getting, but to keep up with it, they had to raise money to keep the site online. I felt bad about it, and we never ended up launching that lyrics site.*

## Scraping Techniques

This section describes three different techniques for web scraping, each introducing a different Python module. You'll use a Python package called HTTPX to make HTTP requests, then use another called Beautiful Soup to help you select the data that you care about from a soup of messy HTML code. Finally, you'll use a package called Selenium to write code that launches a web browser and controls what it does.

Web scraping requires a lot of trial and error as well as a thorough understanding of the layout of the website that you're scraping data from. This appendix gives you just a few examples, not a comprehensive overview, but they should give you a head start on writing your own web scraping scripts in the future.

### Loading Pages with HTTPX

HTTPX is a third-party Python package that lets you make your own HTTP requests with Python. In this section, you'll learn how to use it to scrape the most recent posts from any given user on the far-right social media site Gab, which you read about in Chapters 1, 12, and 13.

Install the httpx module with pip by running `python3 -m pip install httpx`. After importing httpx into your code, you should be able to load a web page by running the `httpx.get()` function and passing in a URL. This function returns a request object, and you can access the request's content with `.content` for binary data or `.text` for text data. For example, Listing B-1 shows Python code to make an HTTP request to *https://example.com* and view its content.

```
>>> import httpx
>>> r = httpx.get("https://example.com")
>>> print(r.text)
<!doctype html>
<html>
<head>
    <title>Example Domain</title>
--snip--
</head>

<body>
<div>
    <h1>Example Domain</h1>
    <p>This domain is for use in illustrative examples in documents. You may use this
    domain in literature without prior coordination or asking for permission.</p>
    <p><a href="https://www.iana.org/domains/example">More information...</a></p>
</div>
</body>
</html>
```

Listing B-1: Scraping the HTML from https://example.com

First, this code imports the `httpx` module. It then calls the `httpx.get()` function, passing in a URL as an argument, and saves the response in the variable r. Finally, it displays the `r.text` variable, which is all of the HTML code that makes up *https://example.com.* (If you're loading a binary file, like an image, then you can get the binary data in the `r.content` variable.) This simple `httpx.get()` function is often all you need to scrape entire databases of information from the web. The script I'll show you in this section that scrapes posts from Gab relies on this function.

Since web scraping means writing code that loads URLs, your first step should be to determine which URLs you need to load. The easiest way to do this is to use the built-in developer tools in your web browser. You can open them in most browsers by pressing the F12 key. In both Firefox and Chrome, you can see the HTTP requests your browser is making, and what the responses look like, in the Network tab of the developer tools. For example, if you open your browser's developer tools and load the profile page of a Gab user, you can see what HTTP requests it makes to gather that user's most recent posts. Once you have that information, you can write a script that makes the same HTTP requests for you.

**NOTE**    *The developer tools built in to Firefox, Chrome, and other browsers are a great way to learn what data your web browser is sending back and forth on the websites you're visiting, to see exactly how web pages are laid out, and more. For more about Firefox's developer tools, see* https://firefox-source-docs.mozilla.org/devtools-user/ index.html; *for Chrome, see* https://developer.chrome.com/docs/devtools.

For example, the Gab page for Marjorie Taylor Greene, the US congressperson who's also a Christian nationalist and QAnon conspiracy theorist, is located at *https://gab.com/RealMarjorieGreene.* In a web browser, load that URL and then open the developer tools. Refresh the page to get all of the HTTP requests to show up in the Network tab.

In the Network tab, you should see several HTTP requests listed on the left half of the developer tools panel. When you click a request, the right half of the panel displays information about it. The right half has its own tabs that you can switch through to see details like the request's headers, cookies, and the body of the request and its response.

When I loaded this page and looked through my browser's HTTP requests and their responses, I decided I was most interested in the following URLs:

*https://gab.com/api/v1/account_by_username/RealMarjorieGreene*   The response to this request includes a JSON object containing information about Greene's Gab profile, including her Gab account ID, 3155503.

*https://gab.com/api/v1/accounts/3155503/statuses?sort_by=newest*   The response to this request includes a JSON array of Greene's most recent Gab posts. Her account ID is in the URL itself.

The first URL let me look up the Gab ID of any account, and the second URL let me look up the recent posts from an account, based on its Gab ID. Figure B-1 shows Firefox's developer tools in action while loading this page.

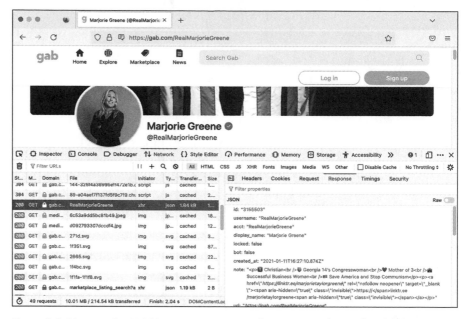

*Figure B-1: Viewing the JSON response to a specific request in the Firefox developer tools Network tab*

As you can see, this response is in JSON format. I wanted to write a script that, given a Gab username, would download the latest posts from that user. In order to write it, I had to spend some time looking at the JSON in these responses to understand how it was structured and what information I was interested in. For example, since I wanted to start with a Gab username, my script would first need to load the URL *https://gab.com/api/v1/account_by_username/<username>*, replacing *<username>* with my target username. It would then need to parse the JSON it receives to extract this Gab user's ID. Then, using that ID, it would need to load the URL *https://gab.com/api/v1/accounts/<id>/statuses?sort_by=newest*, replacing *<id>* with the Gab ID of the target account. Finally, it would need to parse that JSON response to display the latest Gab posts.

Based on this research, I wrote the following script to scrape the latest posts from any target Gab account. Here's the code for this web scraping script, *httpx-example.py*:

```python
import httpx
import click

@click.command()
@click.argument("gab_username") ❶
def main(gab_username):
    """Download a user's posts from Gab"""

    # Get information about the user
    r = httpx.get(f"https://gab.com/api/v1/account_by_username/{gab_username}") ❷
    user_info = r.json()
```

```
    if "error" in user_info:
        print(user_info["error"])
        return

    # Display some user info
    click.echo(f"Display name: {user_info['display_name']}")
    click.echo(f"{user_info['followers_count']:,} followers, {user_info['following_count']:,}
following, {user_info['statuses_count']:,} posts") ❸
    print()

    # Get this user's posts
    r = httpx.get(f"https://gab.com/api/v1/accounts/{user_info['id']}/statuses") ❹
    posts = r.json()
    for post in posts:
        if post["reblog"]:
            print(f"repost @{post['reblog']['account']['username']}:
{post['reblog']['created_at']}: {post['reblog']['content']}")
        else:
            print(f"{post['created_at']}: {post['content']}")

if __name__ == "__main__":
    main()
```

This script first imports the httpx module, since it will need that module
to make HTTP requests. Like many Python scripts throughout this book, it
uses the click module to accept CLI arguments. In this case, it accepts an
argument called gab_username, the username of the target Gab user ❶.

When the main() function runs, it downloads information about the target user by calling the httpx.get() function and passing in the URL *https://
gab.com/api/v1/account_by_username/<gab_username>*, replacing *<gab_username>*
with the value of the CLI argument and storing the result in the variable
r ❷. As my browser's developer tools made clear, the response should be a
JSON object, so the script next calls r.json() on it to make HTTPX convert
it into a dictionary called user_info. It then checks to see if user_info has an
error key; if so, it displays the error message and quits early. If you try loading that URL with an invalid username, you'll see the error message in the
error key: the string Record not found.

Once the script has successfully retrieved information about a Gab user,
it displays some of that information—the display name, number of followers, number of follows, and number of posts—in the terminal ❸. The script
then uses HTTPX to make another HTTP request, this time to load the
user's posts. Note that this URL includes user_info['id'], which is the ID of
the user discovered from the previous HTTP request ❹. As before, it calls
r.json() to convert the JSON into a Python object, this time a list called
posts. In the following for loop, the script loops through the list of posts,
displaying them one at a time.

You can find a complete copy of this code in the book's GitHub repo at
*https://github.com/micahflee/hacks-leaks-and-revelations/blob/main/appendix-b/
httpx-example.py*.

At the time of writing, I could use this script to download the recent posts of any Gab user by including their username as an argument. For example, here's what it looked like when I ran this script on the account of Andrew Torba, Gab's founder and owner and the author of the book *Christian Nationalism*, whose Gab username is a:

```
micah@trapdoor appendix-b % python3 httpx-example.py a
Display name: Andrew Torba
3,803,381 followers, 2,662 following, 67,317 posts

2022-12-07T04:56:56.989Z: Is it really so crazy to think that I care nothing
at all about a particular historical atrocity that happened on another
continent 80 years ago when there is a genocide of babies happening right
here, right now, today?
repost @ScipioAmericanus: 2022-12-07T04:50:37.560Z: Jews literally believe
that they can reject God because they're justified according to the flesh and
their own laws. Wicked stuff.
--snip--
```

The output shows Torba's display name, statistics about his account, and several of his latest posts to Gab. As you can see, they're on the fascist side. Torba has 3.8 million followers, because every Gab user automatically follows him when they create an account.

**NOTE**   *While 3.8 million followers sounds like a lot, most of those accounts aren't active. In 2021, I analyzed hacked Gab data and discovered that of the roughly 4 million accounts, only 1.5 million of them had posted any content at all, only 400,000 had posted more than 10 times, and only 100,000 of those had posted anything recently. You can read my analysis at* https://theintercept.com/2021/03/15/gab-hack -donald-trump-parler-extremists/.

Try running *httpx-example.py* on any Gab account you'd like. Unless Gab's website has changed, this should download the recent posts from that user. However, it's possible that by the time you run this script, the site may have changed so that the script doesn't work anymore. This is the unfortunate nature of web scraping. Every script you write that scrapes the web relies on websites acting one specific way; if they don't, your script might break. It's often a simple matter to update a script so it works again, though. To do so, you'd need to use your browser's developer tools to figure out how the website changed, and then update your script to match its new URLs and behavior— basically, repeat what you just did. In the worst case, if the website has changed a lot, you may need to rewrite your scraping script from scratch.

Using Python logic and HTTPX, you can also modify the script to get *all* of the posts for a given account, rather than just the recent ones. You could write a script that finds a target Gab user and downloads the list of accounts they follow. Or you can take a target Gab post and download a list of accounts that liked it. You'd just need to learn exactly which HTTP requests to make to get the information you're interested in, and then have Python make those requests for you. Some of these tasks would be more complicated than others—for example, to get the data you're looking for, you may need to create a Gab account and have your scraper make requests while you're logged in. The more web scraping scripts like these you write, the better at it you'll get.

To learn more about using the HTTPX package, check out its documentation at *https://www.python-httpx.org*.

## Parsing HTML with Beautiful Soup

Scraping Gab was simple because the responses to the HTTP requests were in JSON format, but pulling specific information out of the HTML in a web page is more challenging. The easiest way to parse HTML in Python is to use a package aptly called Beautiful Soup (BS4 for short). Install the bs4 module by running **python3 -m pip install bs4**.

For example, here's some code that uses the httpx module to download the HTML from *https://example.com*, like you did in the last section:

```
>>> import httpx
>>> from bs4 import BeautifulSoup
>>> r = httpx.get("https://example.com")
```

This code imports the httpx module, then imports Beautiful Soup from the bs4 module. Next, it uses httpx.get() to make an HTTP request to *https://example.com* and stores the result in r, allowing you to access the HTML string itself using the r.text variable. As you saw in Listing B-1, this HTTP response is in HTML format and includes the page's title inside the <title> tag, as well as two paragraphs of text within <p> tags inside the <body> tag.

Using BS4, you can parse this HTML to select specific pieces of content—in this case, the page title and the content of the first paragraph:

```
>>> soup = BeautifulSoup(r.text, "html.parser")
>>> print(soup.title.text)
Example Domain
>>> paragraph = soup.find("p")
>>> print(paragraph.text)
This domain is for use in illustrative examples in documents. You may use this
    domain in literature without prior coordination or asking for permission.
>>> for link in soup.find_all("a"):
...     print(link.get("href"))
...
https://www.iana.org/domains/example
```

This code parses the HTML string (r.text) using BS4, storing the resulting BeautifulSoup object in the soup variable defined in the first line of code. This allows you to use soup to extract whatever information you're interested in from the HTML. The code then displays the page title by printing the value of soup.title.text.

Next, the script searches for the first paragraph on the HTML page and displays its text by printing the value of paragraph.text. Finally, it finds all of the links on the page (which are <a> tags), loops through them in a for loop, and prints the URL for each link (the URL is defined in the href attribute of <a> tags). The *https://example.com* web page has only one link, so the code displays just that.

For practice, next we'll explore a script that scrapes content from Hacker News (*https://news.ycombinator.com*), a news aggregator site about tech startups and computer science. Hacker News is similar to Reddit in that anyone can post links, and users then upvote and downvote those links, with the most popular ones rising to the top. Its web design is simple and has remained the same for many years, making it a good choice for web scraping practice.

Your practice script will download the title and URL from the first five pages of popular links. The front page of Hacker News displays the 30 most popular recent posts. If you scroll to the bottom and click More, you'll see the second page of results, showing the next 30 most popular recent posts, at the *https://news.ycombinator.com/?p=2* URL. Likewise, the third page of results has the URL *https://news.ycombinator.com/?p=3*, and so on.

Figure B-2 shows a Firefox window with Hacker News loaded and the developer tools open. This time, I've switched to the Inspector tab, which allows you to inspect how the HTML of the page is laid out. The Inspector tab shows all of the HTML tags that make up the page, and when you mouse over an individual tag, your browser highlights the corresponding design element on the web page. In this example, I moused over an <a> tag, and the browser highlighted that element.

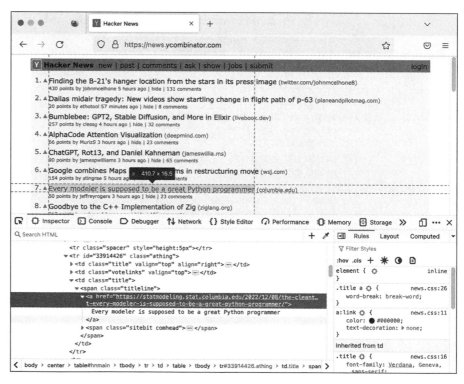

*Figure B-2: Using Firefox's developer tools to inspect the HTML that makes up a Hacker News post*

The developer tools show that all posts in the Hacker News site are laid out in an HTML table. In HTML, tables are defined within <table> tags. Each row is a <tr> tag, and each cell within it has a <td> tag. Here's the HTML code from a typical Hacker News post:

```
<tr class="athing" id="34466985">
  <td class="title" valign="top" align="right"><span class="rank">4.</span></td>
  <td class="votelinks" valign="top">
    <center>
      <a id="up_34466985" href="vote?id=34466985&amp;how=up&amp;goto=news">
      <div class="votearrow" title="upvote"></div></a>
    </center>
  </td>
  <td class="title">
    <span class="titleline">
      <a href="https://people.ece.cornell.edu/land/courses/ece4760/RP2040/C_SDK_DMA_machine/DMA
_machine_rp2040.html">
        Direct Memory Access computing machine RP2040
      </a>
      <span class="sitebit comhead"> (<a href="from?site=cornell.edu">
        <span class="sitestr">cornell.edu</span></a>)
      </span>
    </span>
  </td>
</tr>
```

The rows with class="athing", or the value of the attribute class set to athing, contain links that users have posted. Inside each athing row, there are three cells (that is, three <td> tags). The last of these cells contains the actual link, the <a> tag.

The following script, *bs4-example.py*, scrapes the titles and URLs of the first five pages of the most popular posts recently posted on Hacker News, saving them in a CSV spreadsheet and also displaying them to the terminal:

```python
import csv
import time
import httpx
from bs4 import BeautifulSoup

def main():
    with open("output.csv", "w") as f:
        writer = csv.DictWriter(f, fieldnames=["Title", "URL"])
        writer.writeheader()

        for page_number in range(1, 6):
            print(f"LOADING PAGE {page_number}")
            r = httpx.get(f"https://news.ycombinator.com/?p={page_number}")
            print("")

            soup = BeautifulSoup(r.text, "html.parser")
            for table_row in soup.find_all("tr", class_="athing"):
                table_cells = table_row.find_all("td")
                last_cell = table_cells[-1]
```

```
                          link = last_cell.find("a")
                          link_url = link.get("href")

                          print(link.text)
                          print(link_url)
                          print("")

                          writer.writerow({"Title": link.text, "URL": link_url})

                    time.sleep(1)
        if __name__ == "__main__":
            main()
```

First, the script imports the csv, time, httpx, and bs4 modules. In the main() function, it opens a new CSV for writing called *output.csv*, creates a csv.DictWriter() object, and uses that object to write the CSV headers (Title and URL, in this case), as you learned in Chapter 9.

The following for loop loops through the results of range(1, 6), saving each item as page. The range() function is useful for looping through a list of numbers; in this case, it starts with 1, then 2, and so on until it hits 6 and then stops, meaning it returns the numbers 1 through 5. The code displays the page number that it's about to load, then makes the HTTP request to load that page using httpx.get(), creating a different URL for the current page on each loop. After making each HTTP request that gets a page of results, the code parses all of the HTML from that page using BS4, storing it as soup.

Now things get slightly trickier. As noted earlier, all of the HTML table rows that have the class athing contain links that users posted. The script gets a list of all of these rows by calling soup.find_all("tr", class_="athing"). The find_all() method searches the BS4 object soup for all instances of the HTML tag <tr> and returns a list of matches. In this case, the code also includes class_="athing", which tells BS4 to include only tags that have the class attribute set to athing. The for loop loops through them, saving each item in the table_row variable.

Now that the code is looping through each table row that contains a link posted by a user, it goes on to find that link tag. There are several links in each table row, so it figures out which one is the link a user posted. First, it calls table_row.find_all("td") to get a list of all of the table cells inside table_row, storing that list in table_cells. As noted earlier, the last cell contains the link that we care about. Therefore, the code pulls out just the last cell in this list, storing it in the variable last_cell (the -1 index is the last item in a list). The code searches just last_cell for the link it contains (the <a> tag), and uses print() to display the link's title and URL. Finally, it calls writer.writerow() to also save this row into the CSV.

The code does this once for each of the page's 30 rows. It then waits one second, using time.sleep(1), and moves on to the next page, until it has extracted all the links from the first five pages. When the script is finished running, it creates a file called *output.csv* that should contain the 150 most recent popular links posted to Hacker News. Most of the time when you're scraping real data for an investigation, you'll save it to a CSV spreadsheet, like this script did, or to a SQL database (as discussed in Chapter 12) so that you can work with it later.

**NOTE** *The* find_all() *method in this code passes an argument called* class_ *instead of* class. *This is because* class *is a Python keyword and can't be used as a variable name. If you want to use* find_all() *to select tags using any other attribute, then the argument name will be the same as the attribute name. For example,* soup.find _all("a", href="https://example.com") *will find all link tags in* soup *that have an* href *attribute set to* https://example.com.

You can also find a copy of this code in the book's GitHub repo at *https://github.com/micahflee/hacks-leaks-and-revelations/blob/main/appendix-b/bs4 -example.py.*

Here's what it looked like when I ran this script:

```
micah@trapdoor appendix-b % python3 bs4-example.py
LOADING PAGE 1

Buy Hi-Resolution Satellite Images of Any Place on Earth
https://www.skyfi.com/pricing

The McMurdo Webcams
https://www.usap.gov/videoclipsandmaps/mcmwebcam.cfm

--snip--
LOADING PAGE 2

Thoughts on the Python Packaging Ecosystem
https://pradyunsg.me/blog/2023/01/21/thoughts-on-python-packaging/
--snip--
```

Try running it yourself now. Assuming Hacker News hasn't updated its web design, it should work fine; however, the URLs will differ because the most popular recent links on Hacker News are constantly changing.

This script scrapes only the first five pages of content on Hacker News. In theory, you could scrape *all* the content on the site since its founding in 2007. To do so, you'd have to modify the script to stop not after page 5 but when it gets to the very last page, presumably one that doesn't have any links on it. This assumes that the site will actually show you content that old and that you could make those millions of HTTP requests without it blocking your IP address. I don't know if this is true or not with Hacker News—I haven't attempted to scrape everything from this site myself.

I mentioned in the "HTTP Requests" section that some websites add roadblocks to make scraping more difficult, and this turned out to be true with Hacker News. When I first wrote this script, it didn't include the time .sleep(1) code, which waits one second between each HTTP request. I found that Hacker News limits how quickly you can make HTTP requests, and the fifth request in quick succession responded with an HTML page with the error message Sorry, we're not able to serve your requests this quickly. I solved this problem by waiting one second between HTTP requests. It's common to run into hurdles like this while you're writing scrapers, but it's also often a simple matter of modifying your script like this to get around these roadblocks.

---

**BS4 WEB SCRAPING FOR TRAVEL**

In 2014, shortly after Edward Snowden leaked his massive dataset of top-secret NSA documents to Laura Poitras and Glenn Greenwald, I scheduled a trip to Rio de Janeiro, where Greenwald lived, to help him with computer security and to look through the Snowden docs myself. (This was several years before Greenwald unfortunately became a far-right pundit who openly supports the American fascist movement.) At the time, Americans could travel to Brazil only if they had a visa, and they needed to visit a consulate in person to get one. However, the San Francisco consulate's website told me that all appointments were booked for the next two months.

To solve this problem, I wrote a simple Python script that scraped the consulate's availability calendar web page, using BS4 to loop through each cell in the calendar and see if any appointment slots were open. If it found an opening, my script would send me a text message. I then configured a VPS to run this script every 10 minutes so I'd be the first to know if someone canceled their appointment. In less than two days, I got a text, snagged an appointment, and got my visa. I flew to Rio a few days later.

---

To learn more about using the BS4 package, check out its documentation at *https://www.crummy.com/software/BeautifulSoup/bs4/doc/*.

## Automating Web Browsers with Selenium

Sometimes scraping websites is too challenging for Beautiful Soup alone. This is often the case with sites that are JavaScript-heavy, where viewing the HTML source doesn't result in much information you're interested in. This is true for sites like Facebook, YouTube, and Google Maps. It's much simpler to get information from this sort of site by using a web browser than by untangling the complicated web of HTTP requests that you'd need to make to get the same information. Some websites also put up barriers to scraping. They might add JavaScript code that ensures visitors are using real web browsers before showing them content, preventing users from just making HTTP requests using cURL (discussed in Chapter 4) or a Python package like HTTPX.

You can control a real web browser for scraping purposes by using software called Selenium. Scripts that just make HTTP requests are more efficient and run much quicker than using Selenium because they don't require running a whole web browser and downloading all of the resources of the target website. When I'm writing a scraper, I generally start by attempting to scrape the site using HTTPX, but if this technique turns out to be too complicated, I switch to Selenium.

To use the Selenium Python package, you must also install a *web driver*, software that Selenium uses to control a web browser. Selenium supports Chrome, Firefox, Safari, and Edge. The example in this section uses the Firefox driver, which is called geckodriver.

To continue, follow the instructions for your operating system, then skip to the "Testing Selenium in the Python Interpreter" section.

### Installing Selenium and geckodriver on Windows

For this task, Windows users should work with native Windows tools rather than WSL. Install the selenium Python module by opening PowerShell and running the following command:

```
python -m pip install selenium
```

Also make sure you have Firefox installed (see *https://www.mozilla.org/en-US/firefox/new/*).

To install geckodriver, go to *https://github.com/mozilla/geckodriver/releases*. You'll see several ZIP files for the latest version of geckodriver that you can download. Download the appropriate Windows version and unzip it. You should end up with a single file called *geckodriver.exe*. In File Explorer, copy this file and paste it into *C:\Windows\System32*. This will allow you to run geckodriver from PowerShell no matter what your working directory is.

### Installing Selenium and geckodriver on macOS

If you're using macOS, open a terminal. Install the selenium Python module by running the following:

```
python3 -m pip install selenium
```

Then install geckodriver by running the following:

```
brew install geckodriver
```

This should give you everything you need to use Selenium in Python.

### Installing Selenium and geckodriver on Linux

If you're using Linux, open a terminal. Install the selenium Python module by running the following:

```
python3 -m pip install selenium
```

Install geckodriver by running the following:

```
sudo apt update
sudo apt install firefox-geckodriver
```

This should give you everything you need to use Selenium in Python.

### Testing Selenium in the Python Interpreter

Now that you have Selenium and geckodriver installed, test them out in the Python interpreter by loading this book's git repo website on GitHub to get a feel for how Selenium allows you to control a web browser:

```
>>> from selenium import webdriver
>>> driver = webdriver.Firefox()
>>> driver.get("https://github.com/micahflee/hacks-leaks-and-revelations")
>>> print(driver.title)
GitHub - micahflee/hacks-leaks-and-revelations: Code that goes along with the Hacks, Leaks, and
Revelations book
>>> driver.quit()
```

This code first imports `webdriver` from the `selenium` module. It then creates a new Firefox driver by calling `webdriver.Firefox()` and saves it in the variable `driver`. When you create the Selenium driver, a new Firefox window should open on your computer, and a robot icon should appear in the address bar—this is how you know that this browser is being controlled by Selenium.

The code then instructs the browser to load the URL *https://github .com/micahflee/hacks-leaks-and-revelations*. After running the command, you should see Firefox load that GitHub page. Once the page is loaded, including all of its JavaScript or other complicated components, you can write code to control it. In this case, the code just displays the title of the page in the terminal with `print(driver.title)`. Finally, it quits Firefox.

### Automating Screenshots with Selenium

Now let's try something slightly more complicated. In this section, we'll go over a script that will take two arguments: a location name and the filename of a screenshot to save. Using Selenium, the script will load Google Maps at *https://maps.google.com*, search for the location, zoom in a little, turn on the satellite images layer, and take a screenshot of the satellite image of the location, saving it to disk.

While I'm programming web scrapers, I find it helpful to have an interactive Python interpreter open in a terminal where I can test out Selenium or BS4 commands, allowing me to see if they work in real time without having to start my script over. When I'm writing a Selenium script, I open developer tools inside the browser I'm driving to inspect all of the HTML tags, which helps me figure out which commands to run. Once I get something working, I copy the working code into the script that I'm writing in my text editor.

For example, to search for the location in Google Maps, I needed to make the Selenium browser select the search box, type the location, and press ENTER. In HTML, tags often have id attributes. By using the Firefox developer tools, I discovered that the search box in Google Maps, which is an <input> tag, includes the id="searchboxinput" attribute, meaning the search box has an id of searchboxinput. That allowed me to enter code into the Python interpreter that would select the search box, type a search query into it, and press ENTER in the browser it was controlling. I didn't always get it right on the first try, but after some trial and error, I wrote some working code. At this point, I added that code to my script.

I also used developer tools to figure out how to turn on the satellite image layer. In the bottom-left corner of Google Maps is an icon called the *minimap* that lets you toggle different layers on and off. The developer tools showed me that this icon had an id of minimap and that I could click one of the buttons in the minimap element to turn on the satellite layer; just like with the search box, I tested clicking this icon in the Python interpreter until I got it working.

The following script, *selenium-example.py,* uses Selenium to take satellite image screenshots from Google Maps for you:

```
import click
import time
from selenium import webdriver
from selenium.webdriver.common.keys import Keys
from selenium.webdriver.common.by import By

@click.command()
@click.argument("location")
@click.argument("screenshot_filename", type=click.Path(exists=False))
def main(location, screenshot_filename):
    driver = webdriver.Firefox()
    driver.implicitly_wait(10)

    driver.get("https://maps.google.com")
    search_box = driver.find_element(By.ID, "searchboxinput")
    search_box.clear()
    search_box.send_keys(location)
    search_box.send_keys(Keys.RETURN)

    body = driver.find_element(By.TAG_NAME, "body")
    body.send_keys(Keys.ADD)
    body.send_keys(Keys.ADD)

    minimap = driver.find_element(By.ID, "minimap")
    buttons = minimap.find_elements(By.TAG_NAME, "button")
    buttons[2].click()

    time.sleep(2)
    driver.save_screenshot(screenshot_filename)
    driver.quit()

if __name__ == "__main__":
    main()
```

First, the script imports the `click` and `time` modules and then several components from the `selenium` module. Specifically, it imports `webdriver`, the component required to actually launch and control a web browser. It also imports `Keys` and `By` to automate pressing ENTER after searching and to search for HTML elements by their `id` attribute.

**NOTE**    *Exactly what you need to import from `selenium` depends on what you're trying to do. Consult the Selenium for Python documentation to learn exactly what you need and when—that's how I figured it out.*

The code includes Click decorators before the `main()` function, making this a command line program that takes two arguments, `location` and `screenshot_filename`. The `location` variable is a Google Maps search query, like *Manhattan, NY* or *The Great Pyramid of Giza*, and `screenshot_filename` is the path to save the final screenshot.

When the `main()` function runs, the code starts by creating a Selenium web driver, which should open a Firefox window that the script will then control. The `driver.implicitly_wait(10)` function tells Selenium to wait up to 10 seconds for page elements to load. The code loads *https://maps.google.com* in Firefox with the `driver.get()` function, then finds the search box element on the page, storing it in the variable `search_box`. It finds the search box by running `driver.find_element(By.ID, "searchboxinput")`. Once the code has this search box object stored in `search_box`, it clears any text in the text box by calling the `clear()` method on it, and then it types the text in the `location` string by calling `send_keys(location)`. Finally, it presses ENTER to search for this location by calling `send_keys(Keys.RETURN)`. At this point, Google Maps should search for the location.

The code then zooms in by selecting the `<body>` tag, the main HTML tag that contains all other tags, then telling Firefox to press the + key twice, which is the Google Maps keyboard shortcut to zoom in.

At this point, Firefox has loaded Google Maps, searched for a location, and zoomed in on that location. The code then turns on the satellite image layer by locating the minimap in the corner of the screen. Once it finds this, it locates all of the `<button>` tags inside the minimap by calling the `find_elements(By.TAG_NAME, "button")` method, and then it clicks the third button, calling the `click()` method on the third element (which has an index of 2) on the list of buttons. This turns on the satellite images layer.

Finally, the script waits two seconds, just to make sure the satellite images have finished loading, and then saves a screenshot of the web page to `screenshot_filename`. When it's done, it quits Firefox.

You can find a complete copy of this code in the book's GitHub repo at *https://github.com/micahflee/hacks-leaks-and-revelations/blob/main/appendix-b/selenium-example.py*.

You can use *selenium-example.py* to generate Google Maps screenshots of any location you like. For example, I ran the following command:

```
python3 selenium-example.py "great pyramid of giza" giza.png
```

This opened a Firefox window that was controlled by Selenium. It loaded Google Maps, searched for *great pyramid of giza*, zoomed in, turned on the satellite images layer, and saved a screenshot of the window in the file *giza.png*. Figure B-3 shows *giza.png*, scraped from Google Maps.

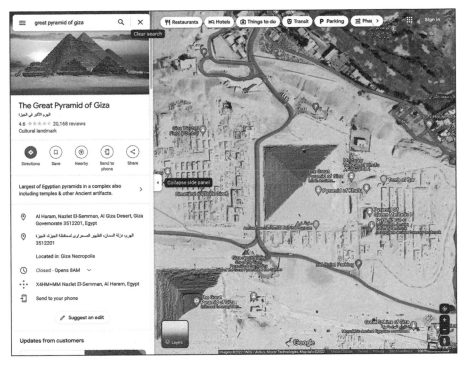

*Figure B-3: A satellite image of the Great Pyramid of Giza from Selenium*

On your own, it might also be fun to try searching for *US Capitol*; *Washington, DC*; *Kremlin, Moscow*; or *Tokyo, Japan*.

This example script used Selenium to take screenshots. You could modify it so that Selenium automatically takes a screenshot each time a public figure posts to social media, so you'll have a record of it in case they delete it. You're not limited to cataloging information in this way, though; you can also use Selenium to extract information from web pages and store them in CSV spreadsheets or any other format you'd like, just like you can with BS4.

To learn more about Selenium for Python, check out its documentation at *https://selenium-python.readthedocs.io*.

## Next Steps

In this appendix, I've gone over a few techniques for web scraping and provided some simple example scripts to show off the basics of how they work. However, in order to write code for your future web scraping projects, you'll probably need to learn more about web development than is covered in this book, depending on what site you're trying to scrape. For example, your HTTPX and BS4 scraper might need to first log in to a website and then make all of its future requests as that logged-in user in order to access the content you're after. This would require making HTTP POST requests instead of just GET requests and keeping track of cookies, neither of which I've covered here.

As a next step, I recommend getting more comfortable with the developer tools built into browsers. This will help familiarize you with the HTTP requests your browser makes and what their responses include. Spend more time browsing the layout of HTML elements, as you did in this appendix. The more you learn about web development, including more complex topics like HTTP headers and cookies, the easier it will be for you to scrape the web. If you can access information in a web browser, you can write a script that automates accessing that information.

# INDEX

MIME format, 150
modules, 200
Monster, Rob, 370
mount (Docker), 125
Mueller, Robert, 413
Multipurpose Internet Mail Extensions
        (MIME) format, 150
MySQL, 348, 351–355, 366–370

# N

nano (text editor), 108, 479
Nauru Police Force, xxvi, 153, 156–159
Navalny, Alexei, 223
NBC, xxiv
NCRIC (Northern California Regional
        Intelligence Center), 97,
        243–248, 253–260, 269–271,
        278, 282–286
nested code blocks (Python), 185
neo-Nazis, xxvii, 14, 17, 36, 223,
        370–371, 427–429, 432–436,
        443, 462–469
Netsential, 94
newline character (\n), 91, 230
*New York Times*, 34, 49, 50, 94
Northern California Regional
        Intelligence Center, 97,
        243–248, 253–260, 269–271,
        278, 282–286
Notte, Iven, 158–159
Novick, Michael, 465

# O

Oath Keepers, xxvi, 36, 113–117, 146,
        152–154, 160–161, 304, 371,
        373–374
Obama, Barack, 413
Object Relational Mapping (ORM),
        444
1Password (password manager), 19–20
OnionShare (anonymous file sharing),
        xxv, 12, 34, 42–47, 50
open source intelligence (OSINT), 6,
        10, 14, 94, 410, 422
operators, 173, 175, 182–183
        arithmetic, 173
        comparison, 182–183

in operator, 185
        logical, 182, 186–187
optical character recognition (OCR),
        29–30, 119–120, 141, 165
Organized Crime and Corruption
        Reporting Project (OCCRP),
        43, 119, 135–136, 148
Outlook (email client), 163–165
Outlook data files, 152

# P

package managers, 70–73, 208, 210
Paczkowski, John, 302
Panama Papers, 135, 148
Parallels (VM software), 32
Parler (social network), xxvii, 36,
        183, 301–309, 318–324,
        330–333, 335–344, 371,
        398, 414, 484
partitions, 25
passphrase, 20, 48
password generator, 20, 25
password manager, 18–20, 25, 41
Patel, Alpesh, 410, 422
paths, 57–58
Pence, Mike, 302
Pentagon Papers, xxiv
personal identifiable information (PII),
        7, 16, 36, 113, 154
PGP (pretty good privacy encryption
        software), 42, 47, 107
phishing, 29, 101
Pip (Package Installer for Python), 208
Pipenv (Python package manager), 210
pipe operator (|), 98
Pizzagate (conspiracy theory), 35
Podesta, John, 149
Podman, 123
Poetry (Python package manager), 210
Poitras, Laura, 14
port (networking), 129
positional argument, 193
Poulsen, Kevin, 50
PowerShell, 56, 59–60, 62, 92–93, 109,
        476, 478–480, 497
ProPublica, 50, 333
protocol, 150

whistleblowers *(continued)*
    Holly, Mary-Emma (Hazelpress), 12, 14
    Manning, Chelsea, xxiv, 14, 33, 49
    Snowden, Edward, xxiv, 9, 496
    Winner, Reality, 16, 29
WHOIS, 373–374, 380–382, 385–386
Widenius, Michael "Monty," 351–352
WikiLeaks, xxv, 7, 12–14, 34–36
WikiLeaks Twitter Group DMs, xxv, 4, 12–14
Wilson, Cam, 159
Windows Subsystem for Linux (WSL), 59–62, 473–482

Winner, Reality, 16, 29
WordPress, 120, 132–135, 350–353

# X

XML format, 334

# Y

YAML format, 132
YubiKey, 42

# Z

Zelenko, Vladimir, 408, 413
Zelenskyy, Volodymyr, 223
zsh (shell), 56, 62, 82

*Hacks, Leaks, and Revelations* is set in New Baskerville, Futura, Dogma, and TheSansMono Condensed.

Never before has the world relied so heavily on the Internet to stay connected and informed. That makes the Electronic Frontier Foundation's mission—to ensure that technology supports freedom, justice, and innovation for all people—more urgent than ever.

For over 30 years, EFF has fought for tech users through activism, in the courts, and by developing software to overcome obstacles to your privacy, security, and free expression. This dedication empowers all of us through darkness. With your help we can navigate toward a brighter digital future.